Lecture Notes in Computer Science 2788

Edited by G. Goos, J. Hartmanis, and J. van Leeuwen

Springer
Berlin
Heidelberg
New York
Hong Kong
London
Milan
Paris
Tokyo

Stuart Anderson   Massimo Felici
Bev Littlewood (Eds.)

Computer Safety, Reliability, and Security

22nd International Conference, SAFECOMP 2003
Edinburgh, UK, September 23-26, 2003
Proceedings

 Springer

Series Editors

Gerhard Goos, Karlsruhe University, Germany
Juris Hartmanis, Cornell University, NY, USA
Jan van Leeuwen, Utrecht University, The Netherlands

Volume Editors

Stuart Anderson
Massimo Felici
The University of Edinburgh
LFCS, School of Informatics
Mayfield Road, Edinburgh EH9 3JZ, UK
E-mail:
soa@inf.ed.ac.uk
massimo.felici@ed.ac.uk

Bev Littlewood
City University
Centre for Software Reliability
London EC1V 0HB, UK
E-mail: b.littlewood@csr.city.ac.uk

Cataloging-in-Publication Data applied for

A catalog record for this book is available from the Library of Congress.

Bibliographic information published by Die Deutsche Bibliothek
Die Deutsche Bibliothek lists this publication in the Deutsche Nationalbibliografie;
detailed bibliographic data is available in the Internet at <http://dnb.ddb.de>.

CR Subject Classification (1998): D.1-4, E.4, C.3, F.3, K.6.5

ISSN 0302-9743
ISBN 978-540-20126-7 Springer-Verlag Berlin Heidelberg New York

Springer-Verlag Berlin Heidelberg New York
a member of BertelsmannSpringer Science+Business Media GmbH

http://www.springer.de

© Springer-Verlag Berlin Heidelberg 2003

Typesetting: Camera-ready by author, data conversion by PTP-Berlin GmbH
Printed on acid-free paper   SPIN: 10931813   06/3142   5 4 3 2 1 0

Preface

Edinburgh, the Scottish capital, hosted SAFECOMP 2003. Since its establishment, SAFECOMP, the series of conferences on Computer Safety, Reliability and Security, has contributed to the progress of the state of the art in dependable applications of computer systems. SAFECOMP provides ample opportunity to exchange insights and experiences in emerging methods across the borders of different disciplines. SAFECOMP year after year registers new multidisciplinary trends on dependability of computer-based systems.

The cross-fertilization between different scientific communities and industry supports the achievement of long-term results contributing to the integration of multidisciplinary experiences in order to improve the design and deployment of dependable computer-based systems. Over the years the participation of industry in SAFECOMP has grown steadily. This emphasizes the importance of technology transfer between academia and industry. SAFECOMP 2003 further sustains the healthy interchange of research results and practical experiences.

The SAFECOMP 2003 program consisted of 30 papers selected from 96 submissions from all over the world. SAFECOMP 2003 acknowledges the invited keynote talks enhancing the technical and scientific merit of the conference.

We would like to thank the international program committee, the external reviewers, the keynote speakers, and the authors for their work in support of SAFECOMP 2003. We would also like to thank the conference staff at the National e-Science Centre for their valuable collaboration in organizing and hosting SAFECOMP 2003. We really enjoyed the entire work, and we hope you appreciated the care that we put into organizing an enjoyable and fruitful event. Finally, we would like to extend to you the invitation to attend and to contribute to SAFECOMP 2004 in Germany – www.safecomp.org –.

July 2003

Bev Littlewood
Stuart Anderson
Massimo Felici

General Chair

Bev Littlewood, UK

Program Co-chairs

Stuart Anderson, UK
Massimo Felici, UK

EWICS TC7 Chair

Udo Voges, DE

International Program Committee

Stuart Anderson, UK
Antonia Bertolino, IT
Helmut Bezecny, DE
Robin Bloomfield, UK
Sandro Bologna, IT
Andrea Bondavalli, IT
Helmut Breitwieser, DE
Matjaz Colnaric, SI
Peter Daniel, UK
Bas de Mol, NL
Hans R. Fankhauser, SE
Massimo Felici, UK
Robert Garnier, FR
Robert Genser, AT
Chris Goring, UK
Janusz Gorski, PL
Erwin Großpietsch, DE
Wolfgang Halang, DE
Michael Harrison, UK
Maritta Heisel, DE
Eric Hollnagel, SE
Chris Johnson, UK
Mohamed Kaâniche, FR
Karama Kanoun, FR

Floor Koornneef, NL
Jenny Li, US
Vic Maggioli, US
Patrizia Marti, IT
Odd Nordland, NO
Alberto Pasquini, IT
Gerd Rabe, DE
Felix Redmill, UK
Antonio Rizzo, IT
Hubert Roth, DE
Francesca Saglietti, DE
Abd El Kader Sahraoui, FR
Ricardo Sanz, ES
Erwin Schoitsch, AT
Jos Trienekens, NL
Meine van der Meulen, NL
Udo Voges, DE
Marc Wilikens, IT
Rune Winther, NO
Stefan Wittmann, DE
Eric Wong, US
Janus Zalewski, US
Zdzislaw Zurakowski, PL

External Reviewers

Gordon Baxter, UK
Guiem Bernat, UK
Denis Besnard, UK
Alessandra Cavarra, UK
Tadeusz Cichocki, PL
Andrea M. Coccoli, IT
Silvano Chiaradonna, IT
Yves Crouzet, FR
Hamid Demmou, FR
Felicita Di Giandomenico, IT
Giovanni Dipoppa, IT
Sudipto Ghosh, US
Fabrizio Grandoni, IT
Wolfgang Grieskamp, US
Peter Gudmunson, FR
Frank Guldenmund, NL
Tahar Jarboui, FR
Marc-Olivier Killijian, FR
Leïla Kloul, UK
Narayan Krishna, FR
Dennis Kuegler, DE

Juliana Kuester Filipe, UK
Jeff Lei, US
Eda Marchetti, IT
Raffaela Mirandola, IT
Mourad Oussalah, UK
Mario Paludetto, FR
Andrea Polini, IT
Peter Popov, UK
Stefano Porcarelli, IT
Simone Pozzi, IT
Yu Qi, US
Thomas Santen, DE
Shamus P. Smith, UK
Carsten Sühl, DE
Mark-Alexander Sujan, UK
Enrico Tronci, IT
Thierry Val, FR
Giordano Vicoli, IT
Domen Verber, SI
Andrzej Wardzinski, PL
Xianhua Xu, US

Scientific Sponsor

in collaboration with the **Scientific Co-sponsors**
AICA – Working Group on Dependability in
Computer Systems

BCS- British Computer Society

DIRC – Interdisciplinary Research Collaboration in
Dependability of Computer-Based Systems

EACE – European Association of Cognitive
Ergonomics

ENCRESS – European Network of Clubs for
Reliability and Safety of Software

GI – Gesellschaft für Informatik

IEE

IFAC – International Federation of Automatic
Control

IFIP – WG10.4 on Dependable Computing and Fault
Tolerance

IFIP – WG13.5 on Human Error, Safety and System
Development

ISA-EUNET

OCG – Austrian Computer Society

SCSC – Safety-Critical Systems Club

SRMC – Software Reliability & Metrics Club

SAFECOMP 2003 Organization

SAFECOMP 2003 Management Tool

List of Contributors

George Angelis
Department of Information and
Communications Systems
Engineering, University of the Aegean
Samos, 83200, Greece

Michael Armbruster
University of Stuttgart, Institute for
Airborne Systems, Pfaffenwaldring 27
70569 Stuttgart
Germany

Michael Bachmayer
Bachmayer GmbH
Wernstorferstr. 46
84036 Landshut
Germany

Claudio Balducelli
ENEA C.R. Casaccia
Via Anguillarese, 301
S. Maria di Galeria - 00060 - Rome
Italy

A. K. Bhattacharjee
Reactor Control Division
Bhabha Atomic Research Centre
Mumbai 400 085
India

Robin Bloomfield
CSR, City University and Adelard
Drysdale Building, 10 Northampton
Square, London EC1V 0HB
United Kingdom

Peter Bishop
CSR, City University and Adelard
Drysdale Building, 10 Northampton
Square, London EC1V 0HB
United Kingdom

Stefano Bistarelli
Dipartimento di Scienze, Università
"G. D'Annunzio" di Chieti-Pescara,
and Istituto di Informatica e
Telematica, CNR, Pisa, Italy

Sandro Bologna
ENEA C.R. Casaccia
Via Anguillarese, 301
S. Maria di Galeria - 00060 - Rome
Italy

Marco Bozzano
ITC-IRST
Via Sommarive 18
38050 Trento, Italy

Serge Büchli
DaimlerChrysler AG
HPC E104
70546 Stuttgart
Germany

Ester Ciancamerla
ENEA C.R. Casaccia
Via Anguillarese, 301
S. Maria di Galeria - 00060 - Rome
Italy

Karen Clarke
Computing Department
Lancaster University
Lancaster LA1 4YR
United Kingdom

Tim Clement
Adelard
Drysdale Building, 10 Northampton
Square, London EC1V 0HB
United Kingdom

Guy Dewsbury
Computing Department
Lancaster University
Lancaster LA1 4YR
United Kingdom

S. D. Dhodapkar
Reactor Control Division
Bhabha Atomic Research Centre
Mumbai 400 085
India

Giovanni Dipoppa
ENEA C.R. Casaccia
Via Anguillarese, 301
S. Maria di Galeria - 00060 - Rome
Italy

Kevin Driscoll
Honeywell International
3660 Technology Drive
Minneapolis, MN 55418
USA

Alastair Faulkner
CSE International Ltd.
Glanford House, Bellwin Drive
Flixborough DN15 8SN
United Kingdom

Jay Flanz
Northeast Proton Therapy Center
Massachusetts General Hospital
Boston, MA
USA

Simon N. Foley
Department of Computer Science
University College
Ireland

Stephen Gilmore
Laboratory for Foundations of
Computer Science, The University of
Edinburgh, Edinburgh EH9 3JZ
Scotland, United Kingdom

Joe Gorman
SINTEF Telecom and Informatics
Trondheim
Norway

J. Górski
Technical University of Gdańsk
Narutowicza 11/12
80-952 Gdańsk
Poland

Stefanos Gritzalis
Department of Information and
Communications Systems
Engineering, University of the Aegean
Samos, 83200, Greece

Johannes Grünbauer
Department of Computer Science
Munich University of Technology
Boltzmannstr. 3, 85748 Garching
Germany

Sofia Guerra
Adelard
Drysdale Building, 10 Northampton
Square, London EC1V 0HB
United Kingdom

Brendan Hall
Honeywell International
3660 Technology Drive
Minneapolis, MN 55418
USA

Michael D. Harrison
Department of Computer Science
University of York
York YO10 5DD
United Kingdom

John P. Hayes
Advanced Computer Architecture
Lab., University of Michigan
Ann Arbor, Michigan
USA

Constance Heitmeyer
Naval Research Laboratory
(Code 5546)
Washington, DC 20375
USA

Atte Helminen
VTT Industrial Systems
P.O. Box 1301
02044 VTT
Finland

Helia Hollmann
Secaron AG
Ludwigstraße 55
85399 Hallbergmoos
Germany

A. Iqbal
Reactor Control Division
Bhabha Atomic Research Centre
Mumbai 400 085
India

Daniel Jackson
Laboratory for Computer Science
Massachusetts Institute of
Technology, Cambridge, MA
USA

A. Jarzêbowicz
Project IST-DRIVE

Hongxia Jin
IBM Almaden Research Center
San Jose, CA, 95120
USA

Chris Johnson
Dept. of Computing Science
University of Glasgow
Glasgow, G12 9QQ
United Kingdom

Claire Jones
Adelard
Drysdale Building, 10 Northampton
Square, London EC1V 0HB
United Kingdom

Jan Jürjens
Department of Computer Science
Munich University of Technology
Boltzmannstr. 3, 85748 Garching
Germany

Mohamed Kaâniche
LAAS, CNRS
7, Av. du Colonel Roche
31077 Toulouse
France

Nagarajan Kandasamy
Institute for Software Integrated
Systems, Vanderbilt University
Nashville, Tennessee
USA

Karama Kanoun
LAAS, CNRS
7, Av. du Colonel Roche
31077 Toulouse
France

Tim Kelly
Department of Computer Science
University of York
York YO10 5DD
United Kingdom

Uwe Kiencke
University of Karlsruhe, Institute of
Industrial Information Technology
IIIT, Hertzstraße 16 - Geb. 06.35
76187 Karlsruhe, Germany

Leïla Kloul
Laboratory for Foundations of
Computer Science, The University of
Edinburgh, Edinburgh EH9 3JZ
Scotland, United Kingdom

John C. Knight
Department of Computer Science
University of Virginia, 151 Engineer's
Way, P.O. Box 400740
Charlottesville, VA 22904-4740, USA

Zeshan Kurd
Department of Computer Science
University of York
York YO10 5DD
United Kingdom

Håvard Kvålen
SINTEF Telecom and Informatics
Trondheim
Norway

Costas Lambrinoudakis
Department of Information and
Communications Systems
Engineering, University of the Aegean
Samos, 83200, Greece

R. Leszczyna
Project IST-DRIVE

Didier Leyman
Ion Beam Applications
Louvain-La-Neuve
Belgium

María José Manzano
Departamento de Electrónica
Universidad de Alcalá, Campus
Universitario, s/n, 28805 Alcalá de
Henares, Madrid, Spain

Pedro Martín
Departamento de Electrónica
Universidad de Alcalá, Campus
Universitario, s/n, 28805 Alcalá de
Henares, Madrid, Spain

Magnos Martinello
LAAS, CNRS
7, Av. du Colonel Roche
31077 Toulouse
France

P.A.J. Mason
School of Computing Science
University of Newcastle upon Tyne
United Kingdom

Gerald M. Masson
Computer Science Department
Johns Hopkins University
Baltimore, MD 21218
USA

César Mataix
Departamento de Electrónica
Universidad de Alcalá, Campus
Universitario, s/n, 28805 Alcalá de
Henares, Madrid, Spain

J. Miler
Project IST-DRIVE

Michele Minichino
ENEA C.R. Casaccia
Via Anguillarese, 301
S. Maria di Galeria - 00060 - Rome
Italy

Brian T. Murray
The Delphi Corporation
Brighton, Michigan
USA

M. Olszewski
Project IST-DRIVE

Alberto Pasquini
Deep Blue s.r.l.
Via Basento 52/D
00198 Rome
Italy

Javier Pozo
Departamento de Electrónica
Universidad de Alcalá, Campus
Universitario, s/n, 28805 Alcalá de
Henares, Madrid, Spain

Simone Pozzi
Deep Blue s.r.l.
Via Basento 52/D
00198 Rome
Italy

Urho Pulkkinen
VTT Industrial Systems
P.O. Box 1301
02044 VTT
Finland

Andrew Rae
Information Technology and
Electrical Engineering, University of
Queensland, St Lucia, QLD
Australia

Prasad Ramanan
Laboratory for Computer Science
Massachusetts Institute of
Technology, Cambridge, MA
USA

S. Ramesh
Centre for Formal Design and
Verification of Software
Indian Institute of Technology
Mumbai 400 075, India

S. Riddle
School of Computing Science
University of Newcastle upon Tyne
United Kingdom

Francisco Javier Rodríguez
Departamento de Electrónica
Universidad de Alcalá, Campus
Universitario, s/n, 28805 Alcalá de
Henares, Madrid, Spain

Oliver Rooks
University of Karlsruhe, Institute of
Industrial Information Technology
IIIT, Hertzstraße 16 - Geb. 06.35
76187 Karlsruhe, Germany

Mark Rouncefield
Computing Department
Lancaster University
Lancaster LA1 4YR
United Kingdom

A. Saeed
Advantage Business Group
The Barbican
Farnham, Surrey
United Kingdom

Stefano Serro
TECSIT Telecontrollo e Sistemi
Rome
Italy

Håkan Sivencrona
Chalmers University of Technology
Department of Computer Engineering
412 96 Göteborg
Sweden

Shamus P. Smith
Department of Computer Science
University of York
York YO10 5DD
United Kingdom

Ian Sommerville
Computing Department
Lancaster University
Lancaster LA1 4YR
United Kingdom

Gernot Spiegelberg
DaimlerChrysler AG
HPC E104
70546 Stuttgart
Germany

Neil Storey
University of Warwick
Coventry, CV4 7AL
United Kingdom

Elisabeth A. Strunk
Department of Computer Science
University of Virginia, 151 Engineer's
Way, P.O. Box 400740
Charlottesville, VA 22904-4740, USA

Gregory F. Sullivan
Computer Science Department
Johns Hopkins University
Baltimore, MD 21218
USA

Armin Sulzmann
DaimlerChrysler AG
HPC E104
70546 Stuttgart
Germany

Martyn Thomas
Oxford University
Computing Laboratory
United Kingdom

Heidemarie Tondok
EADS Military Aircraft
FCS Safety
81663 Munich
Germany

Sean R. Travis
Department of Computer Science
University of Virginia, 151 Engineer's
Way, P.O. Box 400740
Charlottesville, VA 22904-4740, USA

Enrico Tronci
Dip. di Informatica
Università di Roma "La Sapienza"
Roma, Italy

Giordano Vicoli
ENEA C.R. Casaccia
Via Anguillarese, 301
S. Maria di Galeria - 00060 - Rome
Italy

Adolfo Villafiorita
ITC-IRST
Via Sommarive 18
38050 Trento, Italy

Ståle Walderhaug
SINTEF Telecom and Informatics
Trondheim
Norway

Kimberly S. Wasson
Department of Computer Science
University of Virginia, 151 Engineer's
Way, P.O. Box 400740
Charlottesville, VA 22904-4740, USA

Wolfgang Weber
EADS Military Aircraft
FCS Safety
81663 Munich
Germany

Guido Wimmel
Department of Computer Science
Munich University of Technology
Boltzmannstr. 3, 85748 Garching
Germany

David Wright
CSR, City University
Northampton Square
London EC1V 0HB
United Kingdom

Phil Zumsteg
Honeywell International
3660 Technology Drive
Minneapolis, MN 55418
USA

Table of Contents

Keynote Talk

Issues in Safety Assurance 1
  M. Thomas

Formal Methods

Elicitation and Validation of Graphical Dependability Models 8
  D. Wright

Visual Modeling and Verification of Distributed Reactive Systems 22
  A. Iqbal, A.K. Bhattacharjee, S.D. Dhodapkar, S. Ramesh

Automatic Timeliness Verification of a Public Mobile Network 35
  E. Ciancamerla, M. Minichino, S. Serro, E. Tronci

Improving System Reliability via Model Checking:
The FSAP/NuSMV-SA Safety Analysis Platform 49
  M. Bozzano, A. Villafiorita

Design for Dependability

Integrity Static Analysis of COTS/SOUP 63
  P. Bishop, R. Bloomfield, T. Clement, S. Guerra, C. Jones

Safety Lifecycle for Developing Safety Critical Artificial
Neural Networks 77
  Z. Kurd, T. Kelly

Quantitative Reliability Estimation of a Computer-Based Motor
Protection Relay Using Bayesian Networks 92
  A. Helminen, U. Pulkkinen

A Dependability Model for Domestic Systems 103
  G. Dewsbury, I. Sommerville, K. Clarke, M. Rouncefield

Security and Formal Methods

Modelling and Verification of Layered Security Protocols:
A Bank Application 116
  J. Grünbauer, H. Hollmann, J. Jürjens, G. Wimmel

A Constraint Framework for the Qualitative Analysis of
Dependability Goals: Integrity 130
    S. Bistarelli, S.N. Foley

Software Tamper Resistance Using Program Certificates 144
    H. Jin, G.F. Sullivan, G.M. Masson

Keynote Talk

Developing High Assurance Systems: On the Role of Software Tools 159
    C. Heitmeyer

Dependability and Performance Analysis

Web Service Availability – Impact of Error Recovery 165
    M. Martinello, M. Kaâniche, K. Kanoun

A Unified Tool for Performance Modelling and Prediction 179
    S. Gilmore, L. Kloul

Dependability of Medical Systems

An Approach to Trust Case Development 193
    J. Górski, A. Jarzêbowicz, R. Leszczyna, J. Miler,
    M. Olszewski

Reliable Data Replication in a Wireless Medical Emergency Network 207
    J. Gorman, S. Walderhaug, H. Kvålen

Critical Feature Analysis of a Radiotherapy Machine 221
    A. Rae, D. Jackson, P. Ramanan, J. Flanz, D. Leyman

Fault Tolerance

Byzantine Fault Tolerance, from Theory to Reality 235
    K. Driscoll, B. Hall, H. Sivencrona, P. Zumsteg

Redundancy Management for Drive-by-Wire Computer Systems 249
    O. Rooks, M. Armbruster, S. Büchli, A. Sulzmann, G. Spiegelberg,
    U. Kiencke

Fault-Tolerant Communication System to Improve Safety in
Railway Environments 263
    C. Mataix, P. Martín, F.J. Rodríguez, M.J. Manzano, J. Pozo

Dependable Communication Synthesis for Distributed
Embedded Systems 275
    N. Kandasamy, J.P. Hayes, B.T. Murray

Tools for Dependable Design

Enhancing Software Safety by Fault Trees: Experiences from an
Application to Flight Critical SW 289
   W. Weber, H. Tondok, M. Bachmayer

On the Role of Traceability for Standards Compliance:
Tracking Requirements to Code 303
   P.A.J. Mason, A. Saeed, S. Riddle

Tools Supporting the Communication of Critical Domain Knowledge
in High-Consequence Systems Development 317
   K.S. Wasson, J.C. Knight, E.A. Strunk, S.R. Travis

Dependability of Critical Infrastructures

Security Policy Configuration Issues in Grid Computing Environments ... 331
   G. Angelis, S. Gritzalis, C. Lambrinoudakis

Dependability and Survivability of Large Complex
Critical Infrastructures 342
   S. Bologna, C. Balducelli, G. Dipoppa, G. Vicoli

Hazard and Safety Analysis

Safety Assessment of Experimental Air Traffic Management Procedures .. 354
   A. Pasquini, S. Pozzi

The Application of Causal Analysis Techniques for
Computer-Related Mishaps 368
   C. Johnson

Reuse in Hazard Analysis: Identification and Support 382
   S.P. Smith, M.D. Harrison

Design for Dependability

The Characteristics of Data in Data-Intensive Safety-Related Systems ... 396
   N. Storey, A. Faulkner

Using IEC 61508 to Guide the Investigation of Computer-Related
Incidents and Accidents.. 410
   C. Johnson

Author Index

Author Index 425

Issues in Safety Assurance

Martyn Thomas

Visiting Professor in Software Engineering, Oxford University Computing Laboratory
martyn@thomas-associates.co.uk

Abstract. The greatest problem facing the developer of a software based safety-related system is the challenge of showing that the system will provide the required service and will not cause or allow an accident to occur. It is very difficult to provide such evidence before the system is put to use, yet that is exactly what is required by society and regulators, and rightly so. Conventional wisdom recommends that systems are classified into safety integrity levels (SILs) based on some combination of the allowable rate or probability of unsafe failure and the probable consequences of such a failure; then, depending on the SIL, development methods are chosen that will (it is hoped) deliver the necessary system quality and the evidence on which to base a confident assessment that the system is, indeed, safe enough. Such conventional wisdom is founded on a number of unstated axioms, but computing is a young discipline and progress has thrown doubt on these assumptions. It is time for a new approach to safety assurance.

1   Safety: The Very Idea

Computer-based safety related systems exist in a wide range of sizes, but they are all complex. The hardware will comprise sensors, actuators and one or more processors perhaps with associated chipsets. The size of the software may range from some kilobytes up to many megabytes of program logic, possibly with a similar volume of data. A "typical" system will perhaps contain a few million transistors in the hardware and one or two hundred kilobytes of program and data, but the observations below apply *mutatis mutandis* to all software based safety related systems (abbreviated to *safety systems* in what follows).

Safety systems may cause or allow accidents only through the physical systems they are designed to control or protect. When a boiler overheats and explodes, or a reaction receives too much reagent and vents toxic gases, or an aircraft is misidentified on a radar display and destroyed by "friendly fire", one of the contributing factors leading to the accident may have been the undesired behaviour of a computer-based safety system. The same behaviour in a different environment might be neutral or beneficial. Thus safety systems have *requirements* that determine what is considered safe behaviour in the specific environment for which they have been developed (and which are often implicit and only fully recognised with hindsight); these requirements are captured in tangible form as *specifications*.

S. Anderson et al. (Eds.): SAFECOMP 2003, LNCS 2788, pp. 1–7, 2003.

Safety systems may fail for various reasons:
1. the specifications may not adequately capture the requirements, at least as these requirements are recognised with hindsight following the failure;
2. the hardware may contain a design error which, under some input conditions, causes the system to fail;
3. the software may contain a design error which, under some input conditions, causes the system to fail;
4. the hardware may contain a component which fails after a period of normal usage (for example: as a result of thermal stress);
5. the hardware may be subject to unintended external physical interference (for example: physical shock, ionising radiation, electromagnetic interference);
6. the hardware may be subject to deliberate external physical interference (for example: vandalism);
7. the fixed data may contain accidental or deliberate errors (for example: a physical constant may be entered using the wrong units);
8. the variable data may contain accidental errors (for example: a pilot error may lead to a rate of descent being entered into a flight management system instead of an angle of descent);
9. the variable data may contain deliberate errors (for example: a radio signal giving a train movement authority may be spoofed);
… and there may be other reasons that I have not listed.

For safety assurance purposes, we are interested in knowing the probability that the safety system will fail to maintain the safety of the system it controls or protects, irrespective of the reason for such failure. Some engineers may argue that one or more of the reasons listed above are outside the scope of their work: it is a critical decision where to draw the line that limits the scope of a safety system and the responsibilities of its engineers. In my opinion, it is important to draw such boundaries widely (and risk multiple engineers worrying about the same issues) rather than narrowly (and risk that there are possible causes of failure that no-one considers their responsibility). I therefore propose that a safety system should be defined as *responsible for all possible failures of the physical system it controls or protects, other than those explicitly excluded by the specifications.* This definition would increase the attention given to deciding exactly where the boundary should be drawn, rather than leaving some aspects implicit. (For example, what type and degree of physical damage to an aircraft should a fly-by-wire system be designed to accommodate?)

Some engineers may even claim that a safety system has not failed if it behaves according to its specification. Such an argument contradicts established definitions of failure[1].

---

[1] "A system **failure** occurs when the delivered service deviates from fulfilling the system **function**, the latter being what the system *is aimed at..*" [J.C. Laprie. "Dependable Computing: Concepts, Limits, Challenges," in *25th IEEE International Symposium on Fault-Tolerant Computing - Special Issue,* pp. 42-54, Pasadena, California, USA, IEEE, 1995]. 'The phrase "what the system is aimed at" is a means of avoiding reference to a system "specification" - since it is not unusual for a system's lack of dependability to be due to inadequacies in its documented specification.' [B Randell, *Facing up to Faults,* Turing Lecture, 2000].

The probability of some of the failures listed above can be estimated with useful accuracy (for example: the in service failure rates of standard hardware components can be estimated through knowledge of the components and the hardware design); others cannot, and must be designed out as far as possible (#9 for example). The only way to estimate the probability of system failure from any cause, is to measure the actual failure rate under truly representative operating conditions (including, where appropriate, deliberate attack). Such testing can deliver failure probabilities but these are rarely useful because of the difficulty of predicting and recreating the operating conditions accurately enough and because of the cost and time of carrying out the tests. In practice, we may be able to show that the system is *unusable* quite quickly, but it will rarely be practical to gather statistical evidence that it is safe enough unless the target probability of unsafe failure is higher than around 10^{-4} per hour, and even this requires heroic amounts of evidence—around a year of realistic testing with no faults found.

Despite the inherent difficulties in safety assurance, customers and regulators continue to require that safety systems achieve probabilities of unsafe failure of 10^{-8} per hour and lower, and international standards such as IEC 61508 allow such claims[2]. There is no possibility of useful evidence that such low probabilities have been achieved, at least not until the system has been in actual service for many years without failure or modification, yet safety cases are regularly written to show that such systems are safe enough to be put into service—and the safety cases are regularly accepted as providing adequate evidence.

2 Safety Integrity Levels

IEC 61508 gives the following correspondence between target probability of failure and safety integrity levels:

Safety integrity level	Low demand mode of operation (Average probability of failure to perform its design function on demand)
4	$\geq 10^{-5}$ to $< 10^{-4}$
3	$\geq 10^{-4}$ to $< 10^{-3}$
2	$\geq 10^{-3}$ to $< 10^{-2}$
1	$\geq 10^{-2}$ to $< 10^{-1}$

Safety integrity level	High demand or continuous mode of operation (Probability of a dangerous failure per hour)
4	$\geq 10^{-9}$ to $< 10^{-8}$
3	$\geq 10^{-8}$ to $< 10^{-7}$
2	$\geq 10^{-7}$ to $< 10^{-6}$
1	$\geq 10^{-6}$ to $< 10^{-5}$

[2] IEC 61508-1 1999 Functional safety of electrical/electronic/ programmable electronic safety-related systems

The difference between these modes of operation is explained by the standard as follows:

mode of operation

way in which a safety-related system is intended to be used, with respect to the frequency of demands made upon it, which may be either:

low demand mode – where the frequency of demands for operation made on a safety-related system is no greater than one per year and no greater than twice the proof test frequency; or

high demand or continuous mode – where the frequency of demands for operation made on a safety-related system is greater than one per year or greater than twice the proof check frequency.

proof test

periodic test performed to detect failures in a safety-related system so that, if necessary, the system can be restored to an "as new" condition or as close as practical to this condition.

For safety systems containing software, low demand mode should be ignored because proof testing would require exhaustive testing and is infeasible. The lowest safety integrity level, SIL 1, applies to target failure probabilities between 10^{-5} per hour and 10^{-6} per hour; as we have seen, this is already beyond practical verification.

IEC 61508 explains and illustrates the difficulties of providing adequate evidence for very low probabilities of failure, but it has to work with current approaches taken by industry and regulators.

The standard uses SILs as the basis for recommending a very large set of software development methods, with most methods being more strongly recommended at higher SILs than at lower SILs. It is implicit that (a) using these methods leads to a lower probability of failure in the resulting software; (b) using these methods costs more than developing the same software without them would cost, so their use cannot be highly recommended at lower SILs. Let us examine each of these assumptions in turn.

2.1   Do Methods Highly Recommended for Higher SILs Lead to Fewer Faults?

There is very little experimental software engineering research, but a recent paper [1] reported the results from static analysis of a wide range of avionics software developed to different SILs (actually Level A and Level B code according to RTCA DO-178b [2]) and in a variety of languages (C, Lucol, Ada and SPARK). Static analysis found significant code anomalies in all the software (ranging from one anomaly in every 6-60 SLOC in C, to one anomaly in 250 SLOC in SPARK), but "no discernible difference" between software developed to DO-178b level A (which requires extensive Modified Condition/Decision Coverage testing) and software developed to level B (which does not). In terms of the residual anomalies found by static analysis (1% of which were assessed as having safety implications) the extra testing had yielded no benefits.

The authors of [1] also conclude that their results mean that the programming language "C and its associated forms should be avoided" although McDermid [3] reports that his analysis of data in Shooman [4] suggests that "the programming language seems to have little bearing on the failure rate".

2.2   Does Stronger Software Engineering Cost More?

The great pioneer of software engineering, Edsger Dijkstra, observed in 1972 that the greatest cost in software development flowed from the work of removing errors and that the only way to achieve much higher reliability would be to avoid introducing the errors in the first place—which would eliminate much of this cost. This observation has proved to be true, and companies that use strong software engineering methods report far lower error rates combined with reduced development costs. Readers interested in following up these reports are recommended to start with the papers on line at http://www.sparkada.com/industrial.

2.3   SIL Based Software Safety: Conclusions

SILs are based on the assumption that there is a set of techniques that will substantially reduce the risk that a system will fail unsafely , but that these techniques are so expensive that they can only be justified for the most safety critical functions. Both halves of this assumption lack evidence and such evidence as exists suggests that a different approach is required. This is not a new conclusion: McDermid [3] said the same thing in 2001 and his proposals for "evidence-based approaches to demonstrating software safety" are very interesting.

3   Safety: A Pragmatic Approach

It seems to me that the development and assurance of software-based safety systems is an engineering task that merits a pragmatic engineering approach. My own experience suggests that the following changes would be beneficial.
1. Current systems are often required to show evidence for probabilities of failure so low that no scientific evidence is possible. This is damaging to our whole engineering approach, for several reasons:
   - statistical evidence from testing is devalued, because such evidence will necessarily be insufficient;
   - engineers have to make numerically based claims where no such claims can be justified;
   - many current systems fail far more often than their safety case claims, but these failures rarely lead to accidents because there are mitigating factors; this suggests that the targets are set too low, devaluing the targets themselves;
   I believe that we need to reassess the target failure probabilities used in many industries.
2. There is plenty of evidence that trying to formalise the specifications for a system (for example, using the Z notation) uncovers and resolves very many ambiguities, contradictions and omissions in the stated requirements. Such work pays for itself by reducing the cost of later stages of development. I believe that *every* safety system should have a formal specification.
3. There is growing evidence that the level of defects in delivered software can be hugely reduced by using a well defined programming language and static

analysis toolset such as SPARK, and that this costs little or nothing extra in development time and effort. I believe that *every* safety system should use such tools as far as practical, and that investment should be made to increase the power and scope of such tools.

4. Many of the tools and methods recommended by IEC 61508 part 3 are simply good software engineering practice for any system, safety related or not. I believe that the software industry needs to define a core set of methods and tools that is considered the baseline for professional competence, to force up standards across industry.

5. The notion of SILs should be abandoned as serving no useful purpose.

6. The starting point for every safety case should be that the *only acceptable evidence* that a system meets a safety requirement should be an independently reviewed proof or statistically valid evidence from testing. Any compromise from this position should be explicitly identified and justified as being the best evidence that can be provided *reasonably practicably*. If an accident occurs, this justification will be subject to challenge in court.

7. If early operational experience shows a level of error that undermines the arguments in the safety case, the system should be withdrawn from service, not patched up, even if no safety related incidents have occurred.

8. When software is modified ("maintained"), the whole system should have its safety analysis repeated *except* to the extent that it can be proved that this is unnecessary. (Good architectural partitioning and a formal specification will massively reduce the cost of this re-verification). I believe software maintenance must be a serious vulnerability with many systems currently in use, where there is no formal specification against which a rigorous analysis can be carried out to show the potential impact of changes and the extent of revalidation that is necessary.

9. COTS components should have to conform to the above principles. Where their use is justified primarily on cost grounds, but they lack the development history or statistical evidence that would justify claims of adequate safety, the organisation that selected the COTS component should be strictly liable for any in service failures attributed to the its use.

10. All safety systems should be warranted free of safety defects by their developers.

11. Any system where the safety of the public is at risk should have its development and operational history kept in escrow, so that accidents and incidents can be investigated independently of the developers and so that academic research can be carried out to improve software and systems engineering.

These proposals may appear extreme to some people but I believe they are simply good engineering practice. In the UK, most of these proposals appear to be necessary to meet the ALARP principle of the Health and Safety at Work Acts.

References

1 Air Vehicle Software Static Code Analysis Lessons Learnt, Andy German and Gavin Mooney, in "Aspects of Safety Management" - Proceedings of theNinth Safety-Critical Systems Symposium, Bristol, UK 2001. Edited by Felix Redmill and Tom Anderson. Springer-Verlag. ISBN 1-85233-411-8

2 RTCA DO 178B Software Considerations in airborne systems and equipment certification, RTCA Inc, 1992.
3 Software Safety: Where's the Evidence?, John A McDermid, Proc. 6th Australian Workshop on Industrial Experience with Safety Critical Systems and Software, Brisbane, 2001.
4 Avionics Software Problem Occurrence Rates, M.L.Shooman, IEEE Computer Society Press 1996.

Elicitation and Validation of Graphical Dependability Models

David Wright

CSR, City University, Northampton Square, London EC1V 0HB, UK
d.r.wright@city.ac.uk

Abstract. We discuss elicitation and validation of *graphical dependency models* of *dependability assessment* of complex, computer-based systems. Graphical (in)dependency models are network-graph representations of the assumed *conditional dependences* (statistical associations) of multivariate probability distributions. These powerfully 'visual', yet mathematically formal, representations have been studied theoretically, and applied in varied contexts, mainly during the last 15 years. Here, we explore the application of recent *Markov equivalence* theory, of such graphical models, to elicitation and validation of dependability assessment expertise. We propose to represent experts' statements by the class of *all* Markov non-equivalent graphical models consistent with those statements. For *any one* of these models, we can produce alternative, but formally Markov equivalent, graphical representations. Comparing different graphical models highlights subsets of their underlying assumptions.

1 Introduction

We apply recent multivariate (MV) probability theory, and in particular graphical representation of conditional independencies (CIs), to complex software systems' dependability assessment. The dependability assurance task features:-

- a need to quantify an inevitable uncertainty in predicting system failure
- a desire to document this uncertainty quantification process in a manner which is as formal and explicit as we can manage, without hindering or 'cramping' the process, or biasing its accuracy
- the insufficiency, when considered alone, for this purpose, of empirical reliability data from operational testing of the system S in question[1]
- the consequent desire to properly include in the assessment other, disparate sources of evidence, besides such historical failure data
- the likely use of expert judgment in this process of identifying, defining, measuring, and combining disparate evidence, which judgement will partly consist in the application of informal models – models which are, to some extent, subjective in nature, and perhaps not widely accepted, or in some cases may not yet be even well articulated.

---

[1] Historical failure-rate-vs-execution-time data, of the assessed system S, can be analysed with software reliability growth models [1, Ch. 3,4], [2, §4.1]. There is generally a ceiling [3,4] to the reliability levels which can be predicted from this data alone.

S. Anderson et al. (Eds.): SAFECOMP 2003, LNCS 2788, pp. 8–21, 2003.

The expert judgment employed in the dependability assessment task may comprise both assertions as to *which* sources of evidence must be examined, and views about how such evidence should be *combined* to produce a final assessment. We suppose the dependability assessment problem to be sufficiently difficult[2] that there may well be no established consensus about either these two questions or even the formal *definition*, and means of measurement or elicitation, of some proposed evidence. For example, consider the problem of modeling 'independently' developed, redundant versions, $\mathcal{A}$ and $\mathcal{B}$, of an item of software: Does the notion of 'developer competence', in such a context, refer exclusively to the competence of a development team in achieving a (likely) high reliability of the particular software version which that team is assigned to develop; or should the scope of this term extend to include the ability of that team to adhere to a requirement for *diversity* of failure behaviour (i.e. low failure correlation between their own software version and another redundant version developed by a different team)? How would these two competencies be assessed or measured differently? Where there appears to be a level of agreement about such matters, there may still be disagreement about the relative weight that should attach to different kinds of evidence. For example it seems likely that there will be differing views over the relative significance of logical arguments used in verification, vs. testing data of various types, vs. analysis of the quality of the process of requirements elicitation and of design, vs. assessment of the relevant competence and experience of key personnel or development teams [5,6]. There is likely to be a degree of informality and subjectivity in the way that dependability assessment experts use information of this kind.

In this paper we focus on *probabilistic* modeling of these uncertainties – more specifically on the notion of a *multivariate probability model*, which needs to express both the individual strengths of the different items of evidence, and the *probabilistic dependencies* between them. A MV probability model is a mathematical entity. Its development or elicitation, as a formal representation of a systems dependability problem, will be a difficult process, proceeding in a number of stages. We are interested in whether *graphical* representations of CI assumptions may be used in early, exploratory stages of model elicitation, communication, checking, and perhaps disputation, modification, or rejection.

In §2 below we review some theoretical background, and our particular application, introducing a motivating example to which we later return in §4. §3 describes our use of *Markov equivalence* theory to examine modeling alternatives systematically. §5 contains conclusions and proposals for future work.

2   Background Theory and Application

In this paper we apply the graphical notations devised to represent the CI relations associated with MV probability models. In particular, we are interested in their potential role in sharpening discussion and enriching the interplay between:

---

[2] whether because of the uniqueness or complexity of the system, inherent difficulty of the task it must perform, or stringency of its dependability requirement [2, §1.2].

- individual experts' *subjective*, and perhaps to an extent *private*, reasoning about the importance of evidence, and the role of that evidence within the process of assessment. This might involve informal versions of concepts such as the extent of 'dependence' between evidence items. Such models and modes of reasoning may be somewhat vague and verbal in nature.
- *formal* probabilistic models; or rather collections of formal properties, and conditions, required of any candidate such model, before it may be accepted as a plausible representation of the dependability assessment task.

2.1   7-Variable Bi-modular Redundancy Example

For this example, which we shall later return to in §4.1, we imagine two developers of two 'independent' system versions $\mathcal{A}$ and $\mathcal{B}$, both designed to execute the same task. The dependability of the composite, bi-modular, fault tolerant system $\mathcal{S}$ is then affected not only by the individual dependabilities of the two versions $\mathcal{A}$ and $\mathcal{B}$, but additionally by the *achieved diversity between their failure behaviours*. We introduce a single variable termed *diversity potential*, encapsulating an expert view of the potential for achieving failure-behaviour diversity in system $\mathcal{S}$. As in [7, §2], we use integers $1, \ldots, n$ as model variable names:–

1. *Intrinsic Problem Difficulty.* This refers to the difficulty of achieving a dependable solution to the application task.
2. *'Diversity Potential'.* Conceived here as an amalgamation[3] of factors such as 'intrinsic problem amenability to diverse solutions', 'developer diversity', and 'development method diversity', etc. So 1. and 2. are the *potentials* for achieving version dependability, and version failure diversity, respectively; whereas 5. and 7. below respectively represent their *actual achievement*.
3,4. Respective *competence* of developers of versions $\mathcal{A}$ and $\mathcal{B}$.
5,6. Respective *achieved failure probability* (per demand) of versions $\mathcal{A}$ and $\mathcal{B}$.
7. *Achieved $\mathcal{A}$–$\mathcal{B}$ failure correlatedness* measure (mathematically, e.g., correlation coefficient of boolean failure indicator variables for $\mathcal{A}$ and $\mathcal{B}$).

Clearly there will be causal and probabilistic associations between these 7 variables. Aspects of these associations may be amenable to representation through the formulation of some hypothesized system of consistent CI assumptions required of any candidate 7-variate probability model. These CIs may be open to question or dispute, in part because important questions of detail are left imprecise in our initial, tentative definition of the variables. We suggest that one approach to the clarification of such issues is to consider *sets* of alternative graphical CI models. Our aim here would be the systematic comparison of alternatives, using the graphical language as a communication and a reasoning tool. Both graphs as objects in themselves and their *CI meanings* are formal mathematical entities. Their manipulation can be assisted by automated tools. Later, we discuss means of exploiting this formality to address the problem of model formulation, communication, and comparison. Before we can explore this issue further, we first briefly outline relevant theory, terminology, and notation.

---

[3] for the sake of simplicity in this initial illustrative example of the ideas used here

2.2   Theory of Graphical Models of Probabilistic CI

[7, §1.2] contains a survey of the last 15 years' theoretical development of *graphical* means of representing the systems of *conditional independencies* (CIs) that are associated with MV probability models. The included material reflects our primary interest, for the purposes of our dependability assessment application, in *chain graph* (CG) models, and the determination of *Markov equivalence* between CG models. Our survey omits some areas of theory fundamental to other uses of graphical probabilistic models, such as producing architectures for efficiently mechanised inference with numerical[4] probabilities, e.g. in tools such as Hugin, & XBAIES [10,11]. We are largely concerned instead with the *very earliest phases* of probabilistic model production: Stated in terms of our graphical representations, we do not, for many dependability assessment applications, regard the *network topology construction* as unproblematic. In fact, in this paper we focus on using graphical models as a reasoning and communicating tool for formulating CIs. (Pearl [9] speaks of the notation as a 'calculator' for CI assumptions.) Note that no unique, standard usage exists for some terms we use. The different texts we cite often use inconsistent definitions. See [7, §1.2.3] for the precise definitions of terms as used *in this paper*.

Several authors have written at length on how and why graphical notation is useful [9,12,13,11]. Our brief, summary explanation is that:–

- Humans are not *naturally* good at thinking correctly about CI [14] (neither by using algebra, or probability calculus, nor by mere unassisted intuition).
- They have considerably greater natural skill with *visual depictions* of the formal mathematical abstraction known as a 'graph' (or 'network') [9, §3.1.1].
- The property of *separation* of two disjoint subsets A, B of the vertices of a mathematical graph object Γ by a third subset S—in the sense that all "legitimate routes" between A and B along edges of the graph are blocked by vertices of S—conforms to logical properties that, by chance, function, albeit imperfectly, as approximations, or metaphors, for the logical rules obeyed by systems of CI relations [15,9] in MV probability theory.

Probabilistic Definitions of CI. The probabilistic CI assumption is a ubiquitous device for constructing and reasoning with MV probability models. Expressed algebraically "A is conditionally independent of B, given S":

$$A \perp\!\!\!\perp B | S \qquad \text{means} \qquad p(A, B, S) = p(A|S)p(B|S)p(S). \tag{1}$$

A, B, S, here represent *sets* of model *random variables*[5]. Thus, each CI assumption asserts that joint (or "joint conditional") probability distributions will *factorize* – in precisely stated ways – into products of other *conditional* joint distributions, *each involving fewer variables*[6]. CI assumptions achieve a reduction

---

[4] Usually, but see [8] for an extension to an algebraic approach.

[5] – not "events". A typical *event*, would be that the configuration of values realised by some collection of the variables of these sets satisfies a specified property.

[6] *Conditional* independence means distinct factors may contain common variables.

in dimensionality of representations of MV probability distributions. The CI relation (1) is said to hold only if the same factorization of the distribution function $p(A, B, S)$ is valid for *all configurations* of states of all of the variables $A \cup B \cup S$ involved. We will use N to denote the full set of model variable names, of which A, B, and S must be (usually pairwise disjoint) subsets, $A, B, S \subseteq N$. *Unconditional independence* (synonymous with *independence*) is the special case corresponding to an empty set $S = \emptyset$ of "conditioned on" variables.

The term *conditional dependence* denotes simply the absence of a specified CI factorization. A *CI relation*[7] is synonymously referred to by a variety of terms including *(in)dependency relation*, *(in)dependency model*, and *Markov model*.

The idea captured by the ternary relation $A \perp\!\!\!\perp B | S$ can be expressed less formally by the statement: '*Observation of S renders*[8] *A irrelevant to B*', [9]. A probabilistic uncertainty model implies an $A \leftrightarrow B$-symmetry of this statement. Care is required with its interpretation: The term "observation" denotes *complete* observation, in the sense that the values of all variables in S should be made *exactly* known before a person interested (solely) in the values of B will lose interest in information about variables A [7, §1.2.1], [9,13,11,16,17,18,19].

The usual method of application of the probability theory surveyed here is ultimately to derive posterior distributions of random variables of *practical importance* (goal variables), following observation of different variables which are *directly measurable* (or amenable to direct subjective assessment through a process of human observation). The set N may also include other essential model-structural variables in neither of these categories ('mediating variables').

Calculus of Conditional Independence. The theoretical study of how a probabilistic CI model may be precisely represented by a graph is based on a comparison of the two sets of formal inference rules obeyed by: (i) probabilistic CI relations; and (ii) various notions of graphical separation. Attempts have been made to formalise the rules (i) in a notation that neatly abstracts so as to remove explicit reference to the probability distribution function, $p(N)$, and associated marginal and conditional distributions, in terms of which CI is originally defined. Two systems of derivation rules for the CI relation were named *Semi-Graphoids* and *Graphoids* by [9]. See also [15]. §1.2.2 of [7] defines the terminology we use for these systems and for related derivation rules that may be applicable to probabilistic CI and/or graph separation relations. Much of the terminology we use is taken from [9]. A sample from among the most important results of recent literature, including an important limitation that has been discovered, is:

- Every probabilistic CI relation is a *semi-graphoid*.
- If induced by a *strictly* positive joint distribution it is a *graphoid*.
- There *is no* complete characterisation of probabilistic CI relations in terms of a finite set of rules of the form exemplified by the semi-graphoid rules [20].

---

[7] an exhaustive enumeration of precisely for which triples $\langle A, B, S \rangle$ equation (1) holds
[8] or perhaps in some cases more accurately '*would render, were such observation to be expected to occur or to be in principle possible*' – both of which it *often is not* for some of the CI relations employed during the construction of useful CI models.

Graph Separation as a Model for Probabilistic CI. Informally, we are interested in notions of separation $A \perp\!\!\!\perp B \mid S \ [\Gamma]$ of two disjoint vertex sets A, B of a graph Γ by a third disjoint 'separator' vertex set S, primarily because these provide a way of 'drawing a picture' of a system of consistent CIs. In this paper, we focus on the widely used *'global', or 'LWF', separation* for CGs, also referred to by terms such as *'moralization criterion'*. See [7, §1.2.5, p19], [13,11], [21, p349], or [22, §2.4] for the definition, required in order understand our use of *Markov equivalence* in §4. Irrespective of how a separation relation is defined topologically on a graph Γ, we need to be clear about exactly what Γ states, as a CI model of some MV probability distribution(s) p for the model variables which Γ's vertices represent. We adopt Pearl's terminology [9], distinguishing:

$$\text{I-map:} \qquad A \perp\!\!\!\perp B \mid S \ [\Gamma] \implies A \perp\!\!\!\perp B \mid S \ [p] \qquad (2)$$

$$\text{Perfect map:} \qquad A \perp\!\!\!\perp B \mid S \ [\Gamma] \iff A \perp\!\!\!\perp B \mid S \ [p] \qquad (3)$$

$$\text{D-map:} \qquad A \perp\!\!\!\perp B \mid S \ [\Gamma] \impliedby A \perp\!\!\!\perp B \mid S \ [p] \qquad (4)$$

of which the first meaning is most common, and may be taken as our default. The "$[p]$" suffix distinguishes *probabilistic CI* from *graphical* vertex separation.

Equivalence of Graphs, Markov Equivalence Classes, and their Canonical Representatives. One cannot exclude the possibility that two or more different CGs, used to model CI, might mean the same thing *formally* – in the above sense. This is known as *Markov equivalence* of the two graphs. Recent work looking systematically at this *equivalence relation between graphs* has produced findings useful for dependability assessment model validation. Specifically, they offer opportunities both to sound out the depth of an expert elicitee's appreciation of the formal meaning of any graphical model considered, and to educate and clarify understanding in this area during the model elicitation exercise. One can investigate the extent to which any two or more graphs which we know to be Markov equivalent, also *appear* to be equivalent, or at least consistent, to an expert whose beliefs they purport to represent. Further questions arise as to an expert's ability to assign local conditional probability tables consistently to equivalent graphs. Of course, the very fact that formal reasoning and machine computation with probabilities is routinely used in diverse applications, illustrates the limitations of unassisted human intuitive probabilistic reasoning. Therefore the task of validation of expert beliefs in the absence of extensive statistical data is a non-trivial one: It is not a matter of simply requiring that a human expert should be able to accurately replicate the conclusions of formal probabilistic reasoning, whether it be numerical, or in terms of derived rules such as the semi-graphoid rules of [7, §1.2.2]: We know that people probably cannot do this. Nevertheless, we propose that recent theoretical advances concerning superficially different-appearing graphical models, whose formal meaning is in fact identical, can be exploited to produce multiple views of an underlying formal probability model, whose correctness[9] we wish to test.

---

[9] perhaps initially, only as a representation of what an expert 'truly believes'.

In [7, §1.2.6] we identify key discoveries concerning Markov equivalence, including those on which we rely later in §4 of the present paper, in which we enumerate some Markov *inequivalent*, but similar, CG models. In particular:

- Two CGs are Markov equivalent if, and only if, they have the same *skeleton* and the same *complex arrows* (as these two terms are defined in [7, §1.2.3]).
- Given any class of Markov equivalent CGs, there is precisely one *largest chain graph* (LCG) among its members – [7, §1.2.3], [23] and especially [22].

2.3   Limitations of the Graphical Approach

Despite the combined advantages of their easy *visual accessibility*, and *mathematical formality* (and consequent amenability to precise, and perhaps tool-assisted analysis and criticism), graphical Markov models have some limitations affecting their application to formalising or communicating expert judgment. We argue only that they have a potential role to play in addressing this problem, and in particular the special difficulties relating to model validation. For further elaboration of some important limitations and caveats, see [7, §1.3] in which we: (i) mention, with references, certain 'untidynesses' concerning the faithfulness of the formal *correspondence* between graphical separation and CI being used here; and (ii) discuss some alternative interpretations of the graphical notation which should not be overlooked: We have indicated that very precise meanings of the graphical notation exist. Nevertheless, nothing should be taken for granted about how the various participants to a real elicitation process may interpret the CG notation. If elicited from domain experts, the meaning of the graph topology may be only vaguely or partially known by one or more of the participants.

3   Identifying Graphical Models by a Process of Elimination, from an Initially Exhaustive List

In the following sections, we focus on the *specifically CI* meaning of CG models. Markov equivalence theory of graphical models has been used to identify and list Markov *in*equivalent graphical models [22]. For our dependability assessment application we wish to take a particularly skeptical view of the earliest stages of graphical model development, motivated by the special problems we have outlined that apply in this domain, such as the scarcity of historical data from previous cases, and questions relating to shared and precisely stated model variable identification and definition, etc. We suggest, therefore, that there may be some value in attempting to work systematically towards a graphical model through a procedure of methodically eliminating those graphs which violate some 'condition' we believe a model should satisfy. The recent work on identification of Markov equivalence classes of graphical models; the efficient means of representing each class by a single, canonical member; and the very precise and formal nature of the graph, as a mathematical object which has been thoroughly studied over many years, are all factors favourable to this manner of proceeding. This approach might ultimately be assisted by automated tools for selecting, computing with, and displaying graphs.

Given that the canonical LCGs can now be defined simply in terms of recognizable topological features [22], it begins to appear possible to try out such an approach. That is, we can imagine that a procedure of:

creating a set of consistent CI assumptions by 'thinking up' a single graph structure which can be sketched on a blank sheet of paper

might begin to be replaced, or complemented for validation purposes, by:

beginning with an exhaustive list of Markov inequivalent graphical models, and then successively 'sifting' through this list, eliminating models which fail to satisfy some set of identifiable, desired properties, which we can perhaps argue[10] that any plausible dependency model ought to satisfy, until we are left ultimately with a number of surviving candidate graphs which is small enough to allow careful, individual consideration.

This approach assists validation of the CG models that result against a risk – otherwise present – that graphical models directly elicited from a domain expert might *inadvertently* contain CI properties that result only from the domain expert's lack of experience with the graphical language for expressing CI. In what follows we will use the term '*condition*' to describe the composite, $\mathcal{C}$, of all of the specified properties that we shall require a candidate graphical dependency model to satisfy in order that it may be considered plausible. We would argue that this new 'model elimination' approach appears to offer advantages:

- We could automatically audit those parts of this procedure which were machine automated. We could then, if later asked, supply a set of precise reasons for the exclusion from consideration of *any* particular CG model.
- We could perhaps gain insight into the strength of each extension to our *condition* $\mathcal{C}$ by simply counting the number of LCG graphs that it rules out.
- Examination of the precise CI differences between the small number of alternative, surviving graphs might have the dual advantages of: (i) drawing attention to initially overlooked modeling issues; and (ii) providing relevant, educational examples of the graphical CI notation by the focus on interesting CI differences between surviving graphs.

3.1   Some Combinatorial Considerations

If we are initially prepared to consider *all possible* model representations within some class, requiring explicit justification for the exclusion of any one from the range of models considered plausible, then we must contemplate an exhaustive enumeration of these models: How many are there, and how should the complete set be represented, and structured? In [7, §2.1] we make some initial observations concerning the likely scale of the combinatorial explosion associated with the the enumeration of all different probabilistic CI models, or graphical models of these, as a function of the number $n=|N|$ of model variables. We raise several unan-

---

[10] at least in the earlier iterations of such a process

swered questions about numbers (both exact and asymptotic) of LCG graphs, of semi-graphoids, and of probabilistic CI relations. In [7, §2.3] we have used the topological characterization of LCGs given in [22] to produce an iterative algorithm for constructing *all unlabelled* LCGs with n vertices, which we executed for cases up to $n=7$ to produce an extension [7, Table 1, p29] of the figures for total LCG numbers provided in [22]. We have, further, developed in [7, §2.2] an algorithm for identifying the set of *all* LCG models which comply with a given *condition* $\mathcal{C}$, making efficient use of symmetry considerations so as to be able to work directly from a full list only of distinct *unlabelled* LCGs. For our method to work, our condition $\mathcal{C}$ on LCG graphical models must take the form of a logical conjunction comprised of three parts: a set of graphical separations, all of which the graph must satisfy ($\perp\!\!\!\perp$); a set of graphical separations, all of which the graph must *not* satisfy ($\top$); and a symmetry (automorphism group) property of the graph. Formally we write $(\mathcal{C}, \Gamma) = true$ when the labelled CG Γ satisfies the condition $\mathcal{C}$ where

$$(\mathcal{C}, \Gamma) = \left(\bigwedge_i A_i \perp\!\!\!\perp B_i \mid S_i \ [\Gamma] \right) \wedge \left(\bigwedge_j (A'_j \top B'_j \mid S'_j) \ [\Gamma] \right) \wedge \left(H \le \mathrm{Aut}(\Gamma) \right) \quad (5)$$

4   Illustrative Example of Proposed Approach

The example contained below serves to illustrate the kind of explorations of graphical model topologies possible using the approach outlined above. For this kind of dependability expert knowledge elicitation exercise concerning a particular system, we would not expect the graphical model identification process to be completed quickly. It ideally requires an extended, tool-assisted interaction between assessment experts. However our brief example, based on use of our initial tool prototypes, does relate to genuine attempts to reason about the dependability of a certain class of real system architectures. The peculiar visual simplicity of graphical representations of CI demands to be used to its fullest extent, which ultimately calls for more sophisticated tools for 'browsing' alternative graphical models, in ways that make the logical relationships between the different models readily apparent. As a minimum requirement for this kind of elicitation, we envisage automated tools which would assist the task of producing easily comprehended plots, and perhaps also browsing fairly large families of $\mathcal{C}$-complying plotted graphs, structured by e.g. the "subgraph-", or (see Fig. 1 below) the "is-a-weaker-CI-model-than-" partial ordering relations between CGs. Our small example, provides a flavour of the kinds of insight that would be gained – concerning both detailed consequences of a condition $\mathcal{C}$ (equation (5) on p16), and also highlighting the issues that $\mathcal{C}$ leaves unresolved – from using tools facilitating experimental adjustment to some of the individual components of the composite condition $\mathcal{C}$. Experiments in varying $\mathcal{C}$ might be prompted by for example genuine uncertainty about the probabilistic associations existing in reality; or by thoughts concerning the effects on the appropriate dependency model of small nuances of change in precise model variable definitions employed.

4.1   7-Variable Bi-modular Redundancy Example (Continued)

We resume discussion of the illustrative example proposed in §2.1 whose brief model variable definitions motivate the experimental series of C's defined in Table 1 on p18. These cumulatively defined conditions C are progressively strengthened by successively appending a series of conditional independency; conditional 'non-independency'; and symmetry assumptions, or constraints. Concerning the order in which additional components are incorporated into a series of tentative C's, perhaps the least controversial assumptions should be inserted first, and then more dubious assumptions successively added (and perhaps sometimes retracted) later. Thus, in Table 1, each row of the left hand column is intended as an 'increment' to the condition C. I.e., the number entered in the right-hand column indicates how many unlabelled LCGs have one or more labelled version that satisfies *all* of the constraints listed in the left-hand column of that row *and all rows above that row*. We employ shorthands "$A' \perp\!\!\!\perp B' \mid Q*$", and "$A' \perp\!\!\!\perp B' \mid * \backslash Q$" for certain lists of (non)separations, where the separator set S' is substituted by: *all sets disjoint from both A' and B', and containing Q* in the former case; and *all sets disjoint from all three sets A', B', and Q* in latter. Notice that, after the first three rows of the table, the left-hand column is a constraint that is meaningful only for *labelled* chain graphs. In order to be included in the count in the right-hand column, an unlabelled, connected LCG must admit at least one labeling which *satisfies all of these conditions (of that row and rows above) simultaneously*. For example, the count 12,301 is of only those unlabelled, connected LCGs possessing at least one labeling which is simultaneously *both* (34)(56)-symmetric *and* for which the three graphical separations $5 \perp\!\!\!\perp 1 \mid 3$, $5 \perp\!\!\!\perp 3 \mid 1$, $7 \perp\!\!\!\perp 2 \mid 13456$ all do not hold. The total number of complying *labelled* LCGs at each row of the table is not shown because of space constraints. We calculated these, observing a general trend that, in the upper rows of the table, the number of complying labelled LCGs is substantially greater than the number of unlabelled graphs, but, as the condition C becomes stricter, and particularly once some CIs are required, the majority of those unlabelled graphs that are not excluded by C, possess only one labeling which brings them into compliance with C. By the time we reach the bottom row, the 6 complying unlabelled LCGs each possess only one labelled version which fulfills all the requirements of C.

The reader may well disagree with aspects of our conditions C in Table 1, or may wonder why certain CI or non-CI constraints have been omitted. We believe that the fact that a critic is able to point their finger at precise alleged deficiencies of such a kind provides potential for sharpening the discussion of examples like this. Perusing the different actual LCGs remaining in the lower levels of the table (rather than just counting them) highlights logical differences between them, tending to prompt questions about whether a particular CI statement should be believed. This provides an alternative perspective on difficult issues of variable definition, particularly with generic, and often somewhat ill-defined, natural language terms like "competence", and "difficulty": Terms which we feel

---

[11] and in the absence of knowledge concerning the other 4 model variables

[12] Caution: Requiring an explicit separation may exclude some (non-perfect) I-maps.

[13] See the *weak union* semi-graphoid rule [7, §1.2.2].

Table 1. No. Complying Unlabelled LCGs as Function of Strengthening Condition $\mathcal{C}$

Cumulatively Applied Conditions	Comment	No. of Unlabelled LCGs
unrestricted	All unlabelled, 7-vertex LCGs.	179,058
connected	See footnote 57 on p29 of [7]	175,198
symmetry of some kind	Aut(Γ) $\neq \langle e \rangle$, i.e. there is at least one non-trivial automorphism of the LCG.	49,430
Group$\langle(34)(56)\rangle$	The double transposition (34)(56) is a member of Aut(Γ), for at least one labelled version Γ of the LCG.	12,845
5⫫1 | 3, 5⫫3 | 1, 7⫫2 | 13456	Given a fixed developer *competence*[11], achieved version *dependability* is inversely associated with *problem difficulty*. Similarly, with *competence* and *difficulty* interchanged (and the word 'inversely' omitted). *Diversity potential* affects version *failure correlation* in the (probably hypothetical – see footnote 8 on p12) situation that the values of all other model variables were fully known to the assessor.	12,301
5⫫1 | 3∗, 5⫫3 | 1∗, 7⫫2 | ∗, 5⫫6 | ∗\1	Strengthening of the three non-CI requirements on row above: The associations would be unbroken by being informed of values of other combinations of variables. Also assessor ignorance of problem difficulty creates an association between the performances of the two developers, irrespective of which other combinations of variables the assessor might be informed of.	8,869
3⫫6 | 124	This is the first explicit separation property[12] that the LCG is required to possess.	1,460
7⫫134 | 256	A further explicit requirement for a graphical separation.[12]	258
7⫫13456 | 2	This strengthens the CI required on the previous line.[13]	122
1⫫3 | 5	If the assessor knew only the performance, he or she would hold *difficulty* to be positively associated with *competence*.	115
3⫫4 | 1, 3⫫4 | 12	Two more explicitly required graphical separations relating the likely competencies of the two developers who have been assigned to system $\mathcal{S}$.[12]	6

require often quite extensive and painstaking clarification within the context of any particular system. An example is the question, posed on p9, about the scope of the term 'developer competence'. Our discussion on this issue was originally prompted by examining the CI differences between distinct $\mathcal{C}$-complying LCGs, such as those in Fig. 1: What should be the assumptions concerning the various kinds of conditional statistical association between our two distinguished interpretations of 'competence' (and indeed between these and their two associated kinds of achievement: version dependability; and low (or negative) multiple version failure correlation)? Such questions seem to be linked inextricably to nuances of precise variable definition. Given any two LCG models, they may be compared by plotting them and presenting the plots to a user; or, it is an easy matter to automatically calculate and present algebraically the CI differences between them. One simple way of doing this is to produce the differences in the two sets of *elementary* separation statements (see the opening paragraphs of [7, §2.1]) which characterize the separation relations of each graph. In fact there is an obvious partial order defined on labelled LCGs determined by the relation "is-a-stronger-model-than"[14]. We have produced a few Hasse diagrams [24, Ch. 12] of this order, laboriously by hand, to test their value as an aid to understanding.

---

[14] –reversed if the *d-map*, rather than the usual *I-map* interpretation is used, p13

Fig. 1 contains a small example in which the 6 labelled LCGs complying with the strongest condition $\mathcal{C}$ (the bottom row) in Table 1 are so represented. The large grey arrows between graphs depict the direction of strengthening of model assumptions (CI assumptions: That is, the head of each grey arrow points towards a graph for which the set of global Markov separations strictly *contains* the corresponding set for the graph at the tail end of the same arrow.) It would not be too difficult to develop a tool which would allow a 'space' of many more LCGs than 6 to be browsed through a 'roving' display window, with the poset structure associated with this partial order reflected in the layout of the graphs displayed as a Hasse diagram. Functions such as the ability to click on links between adjacent LCGs and be shown the logical differences between them might then be implemented. A pop-up window could display the additional *elementary separation* statements that are acquired as the model is modified by traversing along one of the grey arrows, from tail to head. For example, the upper right grey arrow in Fig. 1 corresponds to the addition of the 24 *elementary separations*[15]

$$1 \perp\!\!\!\perp 2 \mid * \backslash \{56\}, \ 1 \perp\!\!\!\perp 7 \mid * \backslash \{256\}, \ 2 \perp\!\!\!\perp 3 \mid * \backslash \{156\}, \ 2 \perp\!\!\!\perp 4 \mid * \backslash \{156\}, \ 3 \perp\!\!\!\perp 7 \mid * \backslash \{1256\}, \ 4 \perp\!\!\!\perp 7 \mid * \backslash \{1256\}.$$

The theory required for producing alternative, Markov equivalent representations of any *single* one of these graphs is easily implemented, being contained in a few simple algorithms based on theoretical elaborations of the dashed list on p14. (See e.g. [23,22,25,26] and the other relevant references cited in [7].)

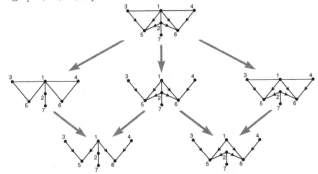

Fig. 1. Hasse Diagram of Poset Structure of 6 Labelled LCGs from bottom of Table 1

5   Conclusions and Proposals for Further Work

The approach to model elicitation and validation suggested here, based on application of the recent advances in the understanding of *Markov equivalence* of graphical representations of probabilistic CI models, requires further exploratory trial with real dependability assessment expertise before the extent of its potential merits will be properly understood. We have made a start in this direction, using prototype tools, and a small number of example problems.

The limits on dimensionality for which an automated exhaustive search approach such as we have illustrated can prove computationally tractable need

---

[15] expressed using the same shorthand explained on p17

further investigation. Are there subtler ways of using the theory, so that only *all* LCGs satisfying a set of constraints in which there is real confidence can be constructed and presented to the user; instead of the current two stage approach – that we have used up to $n=7$ – of firstly constructing a data-base of all unlabelled LCGs, and then selecting from its labelings according to a specified condition C?

There is much theory on the computation of alternative, Markov *equivalent* representations of a given CG. See e.g. the class of DAG representatives based on the *essential graph* of [26]. We have found that presenting an abundance of different-appearing but formally equivalent graphical "views" on a single tentative CI model offers potential to validate and deepen a human subject's appreciation of the exact CI-meaning of a graph. We will present examples of this approach applied to particular dependability assessment problems in future.

Acknowledgments. I would like to thank Profs. Littlewood & Strigini for many discussions and suggestions. We used tools [27,28,29], and funding from EPSRC grant GR/N06359/01.

References

1. Lyu, M.R., ed.: Handbook of Software Reliability Engineering. IEEE Computer Society Press (1996) with enclosed CD containing software failure data sets.
2. Littlewood, B., Strigini, L.: Software reliability and dependability: a roadmap. In Finkelstein, A., ed.: The Future of Software Engineering. *State of the Art Rep.* given at 22nd Int. Conf. on Softw. Engin, Limerick, ACM Press (2000) 177–88 www.csr.city.ac.uk/people/lorenzo.strigini/ls.papers/ ICSE2000SWreliabRoadmap/.
3. Butler, R.W., Finelli, G.B.: The infeasibility of quantifying the reliability of life-critical real-time software. IEEE Trans. on Software Engineering **19** (1993) 3–12
4. Littlewood, B., Strigini, L.: Validation of ultra-high dependability for software-based systems. Commun. Assoc. Computing Machinery **36** (1993) 69–80
5. Fenton, N.E., Littlewood, B., Neil, M., Strigini, L., Sutcliffe, A., Wright, D.: Assessing dependability of safety critical systems using diverse evidence. IEE Proceedings on Software Engineering **145** (1998) 35–9
6. Fenton, N., Littlewood, B., Neil, M., Strigini, L., Wright, D., Courtois, P.J.: Bayesian belief network model for the safety assessment of nuclear computer-based systems. City University (1998) 2nd Year Proj. Deliverable of ESPRIT DeVa project 20072, http://www.newcastle.research.ec.org/deva/papers/5B.ps.
7. Wright, D.R.: Elicitation & validation of graphical dependability models. City Univer. (2003) ROPA Proj. Rep.: www.csr.city.ac.uk/people/david.wright/ropa/.
8. Littlewood, B., Strigini, L., Wright, D., Courtois, P.J.: Examination of Bayesian belief network for safety assessment of nuclear computer-based systems. CSR, City University. (1998) 3rd Year Project Deliverable of ESPRIT DeVa project 20072. T.R. No. 70, http://www.newcastle.research.ec.org/deva/trs/index.html.
9. Pearl, J.: Probabilistic Reasoning in Intelligent Syst.: Networks of Plaus. Inference. Math. & Its Applics. Morgan Kauf., San Mateo, Calif. (1988) Rev. 2nd print. 1991.

10. Andersen, S.K., Olesen, K.G., Jensen, F.V., Jensen, F.: Hugin—a shell for building Bayesian belief universes for expert systems. In: Proceedings of the Eleventh International Joint Conference on Artificial Intelligence, Detroit (1989) 1080–84

11. Cowell, R.G., Dawid, A.P., Lauritzen, S.L., Spiegelhalter, D.J.: Probabilistic Networks and Exp. Syst. Stat. for Engin. & Inf. Sci. Springer-Verl., New York (1999)

12. Real-world applics. of Bayesian networks. Comm. ACM, Spec. Iss. **38** (1995) 24–57

13. Lauritzen, S.L.: Graphical Models. Oxfd. Stat. Sci. Ser. Clarend. Pr., Oxfd. (1996)

14. Dawid, A.: Some misleading arguments involving conditional independence. Journal Royal Statistical Society, Series B **41** (1979) 249–52

15. Dawid, A.P.: Conditional independence in statistical theory. Journal Royal Statistical Society, Series B **41** (1979) 1–31 with discussion.

16. Shafer, G.: Probabilistic Expert Systems. CBMS-NSF Regional Conf. Ser. in Applied Math. Society for Industrial & Applied Mathematics, Philadelphia (1996)

17. Dawid, A.P.: Conditional independence for statistical operations. Annals of Statistics **8** (1980) 598–617

18. Studený, M.: On mathematical description of probabilistic conditional independence structures (2001) Dr. of Science Thesis, Institute of Information Theory and Automation, Academy of Sciences of the Czech Republic, Prague.

19. Wermuth, N., Lauritzen, S.L.: On substantive research hypotheses, conditional independence graphs and graphical chain models. Journal Royal Statistical Society, Series B **52** (1990) 21–72 with discussion.

20. Studený, M.: Conditional independence relations have no finite complete characterisation. In: Trans. 11th Prague Conference on Information Theory, Statistical Decision Functions and Random Processes, Kluwer (1992) 377–96

21. Lauritzen, S.L., Richardson, T.S.: Chain graph models and their causal interpretation. Journal Royal Statistical Society, Series B **64** (2002) 321–61 with discussion.

22. Volf, M., Studený, M.: A graphical characteristn. of the largest chain graphs. Int. J. Approx. Reas. **20** (1999) 209–36 ftp://ftp.utia.cas.cz/pub/staff/studeny/volstu.ps.

23. Frydenberg, M.: The chain graph Markov property. Scandinavian Journal of Statistics **17** (1990) 333–53

24. Cameron, P.J.: Combinatorics: Topics, Techniques, Algorithms. CUP (1994)

25. Andersson, S.A., Madigan, D., Perlman, M.D.: On the Markov equivalence of chain graphs, undirected graphs, and acyclic digraphs. Scand. J. Stat. **24** (1997) 81–102

26. Andersson, S.A., Madigan, D., Perlman, M.D.: A characterization of Markov equivalence classes for acyclic digraphs. Annals of Statistics **25** (1997) 505–41

27. Maple ver. V.5. http://www.maplesoft.com/ (& packages *Perm*, *Linalg*, *Networks*).

28. McKay, B.D.: nauty user's guide (ver. 1.5), Tech. report TR-CS-90-02. Australian National University, Comp. Sci. Dept. (1990) http://cs.anu.edu.au/~bdm/nauty/.

29. Soicher, L.H.: GRAPE: a system for computing with graphs and groups. In Finkelstein, L., Kantor, W.M., eds.: Groups and Computation. Vol. 11 of DIMACS Ser. in Discrete Math. & Theor. Comp. Sci., Amer. Math. Soc. (1993) 287–291 : http://www-groups.dcs.st-and.ac.uk/~gap/Share/grape.html. GRAPE is a package developed for the system: GAP—Groups, Algorithms, & Programming, Ver. 4.2 (http://www.gap-system.org/).

Visual Modeling and Verification of Distributed Reactive Systems

A. Iqbal[1]*, A.K. Bhattacharjee[1], S.D. Dhodapkar[1]**, and S. Ramesh[2]

[1] Reactor Control Division, Bhabha Atomic Research Centre, Mumbai 400 085, India
{asif,anup,sdd}@magnum.barc.ernet.in
[2] Centre for Formal Design and Verification of Software, Indian Institute of
Technology, Mumbai 400 075, India
ramesh@cse.iitb.ac.in

Abstract. In this paper, we describe the design and implementation of
a tool that has been developed for the specification and verification of
distributed reactive systems. A distributed reactive system is composed
of a collection of autonomous reactive nodes which communicate over
buffered and/or unbuffered channels . Statecharts are industry accepted
formal notation to model reactive systems but lack features to model
communication. We have extended *Statecharts* [1], with primitives for
handling communication through buffered and unbuffered channels. The
extended notation is called Communicating Statecharts(CS). We have
implemented a translator to translate CS into Promela, the input modeling language for the *Spin* model checker [2]. This allows us to verify
temporal properties of the system using *Spin* model checker. As an illustrative example, we have modeled the well known *Leader Election
Protocol* used in distributed systems using CS notation. The model was
translated into Promela using the CSPROM tool and we have used the
translated model in Promela to show the correctness of the algorithm
by verifying its known properties. The verification was carried out using
the Spin model checker. The contribution of the paper is in extending the powerful visual formalism of Statecharts with features required
to model distributed systems and interfacing it with a well established
model checking tool Spin for formal verification of the model.

1 Introduction

A distributed reactive system is a class of reactive system that is composed of a
collection of autonomous reactive nodes which communicate over *communication
channels*. These nodes could be on different physical machines which exchange
data through communication links. Altogether these nodes collectively and co-
operatively achieve the overall functionality of the system. Many of the modern
control systems fall into this class.

---

* Present Address: IE Division, Honeywell Corporation, India
** Corresponding Author: sdd@magnum.barc.ernet.in, Fax 91 22 25505050

S. Anderson et al. (Eds.): SAFECOMP 2003, LNCS 2788, pp. 22–34, 2003.

The design of reactive systems is known to be complex as compared to transformational systems. Statecharts[1,3] which are an extension of finite state machines are used in the industry for modeling the behaviour of a reactive system. Visual formalisms like Statecharts are appealing to practicing software designers. Arguing the formal correctness however, is quite complex particularly when the number of states are large and hence, they need verification support.

Our earlier work [8,9,10] is based on the paradigm of using visual modeling (Statecharts) at the front end and formal model (in Esterel [4]) at the back end for formal verification. This requires the design engineers to only handle intuitively well understood visual notation such as Statecharts for model building and relieves them of the burden of learning a modeling language for formal verification task.

The Statecharts in their present form do not support modeling of distributed reactive systems. The communication mechanism in Statecharts is based on shared variables and does not support communication through channels. In this paper, we have extended Statecharts by introducing new states for handling communication through buffered channel or unbuffered channels. The extended notation is called *Communicating Statecharts (CS)* which is conceptually inspired by *Communicating Reactive Processes* [5,6] . The primitives can model synchronous as well as asynchronous communication. Each node in CS is modeled as a statechart with additional communicating states showing the communication through channels. The operational semantics of CS as defined in this paper preserves the *Step* semantics of Statecharts[3].

Unlike in our earlier work [8,9,10], where we had described translation of Statecharts into Esterel [4] for verification, in this paper we describe translation of CS into Promela, the input modeling language of Spin model Checker [7]. This is because Esterel does not have constructs to model communication through channels, which is required for CS. The translator CSPROM, described in this paper, at present supports only asynchronous mode of communication, but can be extended to synchronous mode. Using the CS to Promela translation tool (CSPROM), one can translate a CS specification into Promela and later use Spin model checking tool to verify the temporal properties of the system.

As an illustrative example, we have modeled the well known *Leader Election Protocol* [7] used in distributed systems using CS notation. The model was translated into Promela using the CSPROM tool and we have used the translated model in Promela to show the correctness of the algorithm by verifying the known properties of the algorithm. The verification was carried out using the Spin model checker.

Mikk. et. al. [11,12] had reported translating Statecharts based on *Extended Hierarchical Automata* to Promela and model checking using Spin. Their approach is limited to the standard notation of Statecharts without communication and does not allow modeling of communication in distributed systems.

The paper is organized as follows: The syntax and semantics of the communication primitives included in Statecharts are described in section 2 followed by the overview of the translation scheme in section 3. The implementation of the scheme is discussed in section 4 and the application of the tool in verifying the 3-leader election protocol is discussed in section 5.

2   Communicating Statecharts

A distributed reactive system is modeled in CS as a network of independent reactive programs or nodes, N_i, each node having its own reactive interface with separate input/output signals and its own notion of instants. Each node N_i in CS is modeled as a statechart with new communicating states showing the communication through channels. The nodes can communicate with each other using rendezvous states or buffered channels. The mechanism of rendezvous states uses unbuffered channel and the communicating state is called *Synchronous Communicating State*. On the other hand communicating state using buffered channel is called *Asynchronous Communicating State*. They are described in detail below.

2.1   Synchronous Communication State

A synchronous communication state or a rendezvous state indicates communication with the matched rendezvous state in other node via an unbuffered channel. The channel is specified as the label in rendezvous state. Figure 1 shows the representation of these states in a 2 node system in CS.

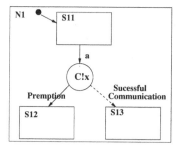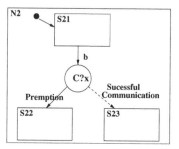

Fig. 1. Rendezvous sender and receiver states

The syntax for labeling rendezvous state is C !|? <mtype#> x   where "C" is the name of the channel through which the communication is done,"x" is the message being sent or the variable in which message is being sent, "?" implies that this is the receiver end of the channel C, "!" implies that this is the sender end of the channel C. The optional *mtype#* is the message type for the message "x". The sender does not send a message unless the receiver is ready to receive the message. There can be two types of exits from a rendezvous state. The transition labeled *Successful communication* is the exit from rendezvous state when communication succeeds and it is represented by a dashed edge. The transition labeled *Preemption* is the preemptive exit from rendezvous state when the reactive computation results in a state transition, before the actual communication completes. The rendezvous state is a special state and cannot be refined like a normal state in Statecharts. In the fig.1, N1 and N2 are two nodes of a distributed system, each represented by a statechart. The actual communication takes place between the nodes when both are at the state labeled as C!x and C?x. The intuitive executional semantics of a rendezvous state is as follows:

- If the sender enters the rendezvous state, it waits until receiver enters the matching rendezvous state and vice versa. Both the sender and receiver exit this state after successful communication.
- While waiting for synchronization preemptive exit can take place on sender or receiver which can be due to a time_out event.

In contrast to a normal Statechart state, a rendezvous state does not have history and static reactions.

2.2   Asynchronous Communication State

Here the communication is via a buffered channel specified as the label of asynchronous communication state. Every channel has a message queue associated with it and messages are stored and retrieved in FIFO fashion. The sender doesn't have to wait for receiver to receive but puts the message in the message queue and continues with its computation. The sender is blocked only when the message queue is full. On the other hand the receiver picks up the message from the message queue and continues with its computation. The receiver gets blocked only when the message queue is empty. Asynchronous communication state is drawn as a shaded circle as shown in figure 2. Here the two nodes while in states S12 and S21 check at each instant for the event a and b in conjunction with the implicit guards as shown in the fig.2. Asynchronous communicating state has only one type of exit i.e., after performing successful communication.

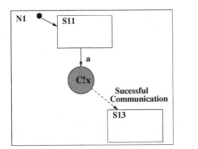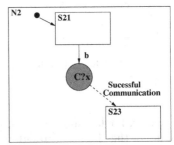

Fig. 2. Asynchronous communication sender and receiver states

Its intuitive executional semantics is explained below.

- Sender checks whether message queue is full before entering the communication state. If it is not full, it puts the message at the end of message queue and takes the non-preemptive transition in the next reaction. If the queue is full sender waits until the message can be put on the queue. The wait is always outside this state, essentially in the source state of incoming transition.

- Receiver checks whether message queue is empty before entering the communication state. If it is not empty, it reads the message from the message queue in FIFO fashion and takes the non-preemptive transition in the next reaction. If the message queue is empty, receiver waits until the message can be read from the queue. The wait is always outside this state, essentially in the source state of incoming transition.
- The waits on the message queue is defined as implicit guards on the incoming transition to this state. Thus for the asynchronous communicating states shown in figure 2 the guard on the sender side is *Not(C_full)* and on the receiver side the guard is *Not(C_empty)*.
- There is an upper bound on message queue length.

The asynchronous communication state does not have history and static reactions and cannot be refined further.

2.3   Modeling in CS: An Example of a Simple Plant Controller

The model in figure 3 depicts a simple bottling plant with two independent units namely filling bottles and stamping the bottles. Each unit is controlled by a separate controller. The filling unit controller needs to communicate with the stamping unit controller for synchronizing the stamping operation of a filled bottle. We have used synchronous communicating states to model the *lock step* operation of the system.

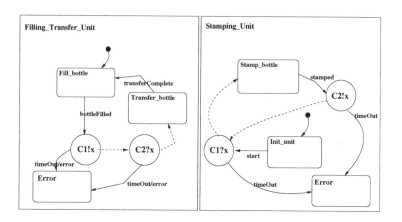

Fig. 3. A Simple Bottling Plant

Both the nodes have been drawn with a very high degree of abstraction. The example shows the outer structure and how controller can communicate. In the *Filling_Transfer_Unit* the starting state is *Fill_bottle*. After the bottle is filled indicated by the event *bottleFilled* the present state moves to communicating state *C1!x* which initiates communication with the *Stamping_Unit* and waits for synchronization. When *Filling_Unit* is in state *C1!x*, it can be preempted by a *timeOut* event *error* which moves the unit to an *Error* state for operator intervention. When the communication is successful, it waits for synchronization from the *Stamping _unit* at the *C2?x* and after successful stamping the *moveBottle* event is generated and the *Fill_bottle* node moves to *Transfer_bottle* state. From this state it makes transition to initial state on *transferComplete* event.

In *Stamping_Unit* the initial state is *Init_unit*. When it receives event *start*, it moves to communicating state *C1?x* and waits for communication indicating that the bottle is filled and ready to be stamped. If the synchronization is successful, it moves to the state *Stamp_bottle* where actual stamping of the bottle takes place and communicates the fact in the state *C2!x*. On successful completion of communication it goes back to *C1?x* state and waits for the next bottle. In case of *timeOut*, while waiting for synchronization the unit moves to *Error* state.

3   Translation Scheme

Each node of CS is mapped as a process `proctype` in Promela. Thus if there are "n" nodes in a CS model there will be "n" instances of Promela `proctypes`. Each process in Promela representing the node in CS is logically composed of two modules namely *Environment* (this is also the main process) and *Reactive Kernel*. The *Environment* invokes the *Reactive Kernel*. The job of the *Environment* is to set the input signals and call the *Reactive Kernel* module to react on these signals as shown below.

Table 1. Environment Module

```
Environment()
begin
      every step do
            set input signals
            set internal signals and outputs generated in the last step
            call reactive kernel
      end
end
```

Here the `step` is part of the operational semantics of Statecharts [3] and is associated with any event (external input events or internal events). The *reactive kernel* reacts to the signals by taking all possible transitions which are enabled from the set of active states. All state changes and output signals generated are returned to the *environment*. All reactions of the *reactive kernel* are atomic and take zero time (in reality take a bounded and a priori known amount of time, which is negligible compared to the frequency of reactions). This is the synchrony hypothesis and is the basis of all reactive models. *Reactive Kernel* waits for the *environment* to trigger the reaction. Depending upon the current state and the external input signals the *reactive kernel* reacts by taking all possible transitions.

Internal signals may be emitted or set during the reaction and those add to the set of input signals in the next reaction. Output signals generated will be active only in the next reaction.

4   The CSPROM Tool

We have implemented the scheme discussed above in a translator named CSPROM(Communicating Statecharts to Promela) that translates CS models to functionally equivalent Promela code. The translated code can be formally verified against the requirement using SPIN.

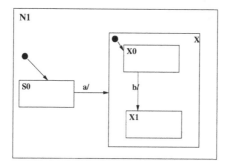

Fig. 4. A simple example to illustrate translation

As explained in section 3, every node of the CS is mapped to a process in Promela with two components, the main *Environment* process and the *reactive-kernel* as a procedure. Let us consider a single node of CS shown in Figure 4 and study its translation. Here S0 is the initial state of the system and X is a hierarchical state with two states X1 and X2. Signal a and b are two input signals. The *environment* code for this is shown below.

The *environment* first sets the initial state and then non-deterministically chooses the status of input signals and after that it makes an atomic call to *reactive_kernel* called N1_kernel.

The *kernel* first initializes the temporary state variables and initiates a do loop. Every state that has an outgoing transition has a block of code associated with it. In this example states S0 and X1 have the corresponding block of codes. If state S0 or X1 is enabled, the transition_condition is checked and if that is true state variables are set for the new configuration. The loop terminates when all the enabled transitions are taken and the next set of active states are assigned in hierarchical order.

The parts of CSPROM tool is shown schematically in the fig. 5. The tool contains two major modules, namely parser and code-generator. The parser takes the textual description of CS model, checks the syntactic correctness and builds the data structures for the code-generator module. The code generator module

Table 2. Environment Module for the example shown in figure 4

```
/*  This is the Promela code modeling the environment
    SO_N1, X_N1, X1_N1, X2_N2 are the
    state variables, representing the states
    a_N1, b_N1 represent the boolean events
    in the context of the system N1
*/
active proctype N1_Env()
{
    SO_N1 = true;
    do
    ::  if
        :: a_N1 = 0
        :: a_N1 = 1
        fi;
        if
        :: b_N1 = 0
        :: b_N1 = 1
        fi;
        atomic
        {
            N1_kernel();
        }
    od
}
```

iterates through the intermediate data structures representing the syntax tree and emits the Promela code per node basis.

Figure 6 shows the use of CSPROM tool in formal verification process. The CS model is created from the informal system/software description. As in any model building process this is the most complicated and time consuming step. Once the CS model is built, it can be translated into the Promela model using our CSPROM translator. This becomes the input to the Spin model checker. The system requirements are captured and formalized as formal specification during the model building step. These formal specifications are put either as state assertions in the obtained Promela code or as temporal properties directly given in the Spin model checker.

In the next section we illustrate the use of the tool in modeling and verification of the *Leader Election Algorithm* in a 3 node system.

5   Model of 3-Node Leader Election Ring

As an illustrative example we consider the well known algorithm for leader election in a unidirectional ring [2]. In this algorithm, each node sends a message

Table 3. Reactive Kernel code for example in figure 4

```
/* This is the Promela code modeling the kernel
inline N1_kernel()
{
    t_X_N1 = X_N1;
    t_S0_N1 = S0_N1;
    t_X1_N1 = X1_N1;
    t_X2_N1 = X2_N1;
    reaction_not_completed = true;
    do
    ::  (reaction_not_completed == true) →
        reaction_not_completed = false;
        if
        ::  (S0_N1 == true) →
            if
            ::  (a_N1 == true) →
                t_S0_N1 = false;
                S0_N1 = false;
                t_X_N1 = true;
                t_X1_N1 = true;
                reaction_not_completed = true;
            ::  else → skip
            fi
        ::  else → skip
        fi;
        if
        ::  (X1_N1 == true) →
            if
            ::  (b_N1 == true) →
                t_X1_N1 = false;
                X1_N1 = false;
                t_X2_N1 = true;
                reaction_not_completed = true;
            ::  else → skip
            fi
        ::  else → skip
        fi
    ::  else → break
    od;
    S0_N1 = t_S0_N1;
    X_N1 = t_X_N1;
    if
    ::  (X_N1 == true) →
        X1_N1 = t_X1_N1;
        X2_N1 = t_X2_N1
    ::  else →
        X1_N1 = false;
        X2_N1 = false
    fi
}
```

with its *id*, to its right neighbour, and then waits for the message from its left neighbour. When it receives such a message, it checks the *id*, in this message. If the *id*, is greater than its own *id*, it forwards the message to the right; otherwise it swallows the message and does not forward it. If a node receives a message with its own *id*, it declares itself the leader by sending a termination message to its right neighbour and exits the algorithm as the leader. A node that receives a termination message forwards it to the right, and exits as non-leader.

Assuming there are three nodes in the ring. Each node has two channels, input and output, messages are read from input channel and written to output

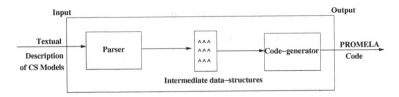

Fig. 5. The schematic of CSPROM tool

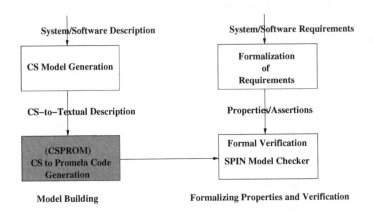

Fig. 6. The use of CSPROM in formal verification

channel. The input channel of a node is shared as the output channel of left neighbour and output channel is shared as an input channel of right neighbour. In this algorithm, all processes will participate in the election. We consider a 3 node ring and fig. 7 gives the abstract view of the connectivity of the three nodes in a ring. A typical model of a node in CS is shown in fig. 8. The nodes are identified by the node_id value.

Here the state *Leader* indicates that when that particular node is in that state, it has become the leader. Similarly the state *Lost* indicates that the particular node has lost the election.

5.1 Verification for Correctness

We illustrate the verification process below by verifying two properties related to *Safety* and *Liveness* of the algorithm.

1. *Safety Property*

   The primary goal of the algorithm is that it must guarantee that at any point of time there is only one leader. The predicate $\forall i \in \{1, 2, 3\}.L\_N_i$ is true for the node which is the leader. Hence the proposition onlyonewinner $=$

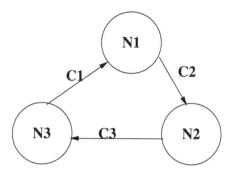

Fig. 7. Leader Election Protocol: Nodes and channels connectivity

$((\neg L\_N1 \wedge \neg L\_N2 \wedge L\_N3)$ ∨
$(\neg L\_N1 \wedge L\_N2 \wedge \neg L\_N3)$ ∨ $(L\_N1 \wedge \neg L\_N2 \wedge \neg L\_N3)$ ∨
$(\neg L\_N1 \wedge \neg L\_N2 \wedge \neg L\_N3))$ is true when there is only one leader. The
variable L_N_i is set to true when the node $i \in \{1, 2, 3\}$ reaches the *Leader*
state. The fourth term in this formula takes care of the states when there is
no leader i.e during intermediate states of execution of the algorithm. As a
safety property this should be true over all states i.e $[]onlyonewinner$ must
be satisfied by the model. By running Spin model checker, it is found that
the model satisfies this property.
In case the model does not satisfy the property, Spin produces a counter
example which can be traced in the Promela model by the guided simulator
of the Spin user interface. The output also contains information about the
state space of the model.

2. *Liveness Property*

The algorithm starts in a state where there is no leader and as the algorithm
terminates eventually a leader is selected. This property is stated in terms
of internal state variables as
$[](noofwinner = 0) \longrightarrow <> (noofwinner = 1))$
This property is also satisfied by the model. The variable noofwinner is a
global state variable keeping a count of how many states have become the
leader. It is seen that both of these properties provide the same information
regarding the algorithm but are specified differently.

6   Conclusion and Future Work

The leader election algorithm could be verified against the above mentioned
properties very easily. The model constructed using CS is easier to understand
as the specification of the system than the Promela code. But the following
points are worth mentioning

- It is required to know some of the internal state variables to encode the
  temporal properties in LTL. We need to provide a framework in which it

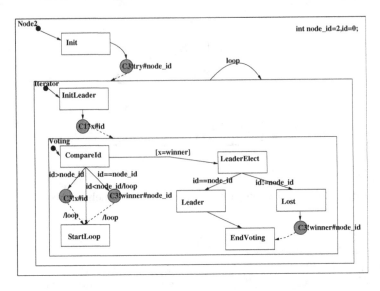

Fig. 8. A typical node modeled in CS

should be possible to express these properties at the level of abstraction of CS.

- Presently any counterexample generated by Spin during model checking for a property on the translated code has to be manually traced back to the CS model. It would be better, if the property it self can be specified as an observer in the CS notation and any counterexample generated by Spin model checker could be simulated in the CS model.
- The translated code is large as compared to hand-written Promela code. For 3-node leader election algorithm it has around 900 lines of Promela code as compared to 100 lines of hand-written Promela code. However the translated code is highly structured and it is a direct map of pictorial CS model.

Currently the translator needs the description of the CS model in a textual format which is a modified form of the syntax given in [13]. We are planning to extend the PERTS tool to integrate it with the CSPROM translator. This will enable the user to model the system in CS notation, simulate the model, and later translate it to Promela specification for model checking with Spin.We are also extending the translator to handle synchronous communication.

Acknowledgment. Authors wish to thank the Board of Research in Nuclear Sciences (BRNS) for actively supporting this work. Thanks are also due to anonymous referees for their comments which helped in making the paper more readable.

References

1. Harel D. *Statecharts: A Visual Formalism for Complex Systems*, D. Harel, Science of Computer Programming, 8, 1987
2. Holzmann G.J., *The Model Checker Spin*, G.J. Holzmann, IEEE Trans. on Software Engineering, 23(5), May 1997
3. Harel D. and Naamad A. *The* STATEMATE *semantics of Statecharts*, D. Harel, ACM Trans. on Software Engineering and Methodology, 5(4), Oct. 1996.
4. Berry G. and Gonthier G.: *The Esterel synchronous programming languages: Design, semantics, implementation.* Science of Computer Programming, 19(2):87–152, 1992
5. Ramesh S.:*Communicating Reactive State Machines: Design, Model & Implementation*, IFAC Workshop on Distributed Computer Control Systems, Pergamon Press, Sept. 1998
6. Berry G., Ramesh S., Shyamasundar R.K. :*Communicating Reactive Processes*, 20th ACM Symposium on Principles of Programming Languages, 1993
7. Holzmann G.J. *The Design and Validation of Computer Protocols*, G.J. Holzmann, Prentice Hall, 1991
8. Bhattacharjee A.K., Dhodapkar S.D., Seshia S., Shyamasundar R.K. *A Graphical Environment for Specification and Verification of Reactive System*, Lecture Notes in Computer Science, Vol 1698, Springer, 1999
9. Bhattacharjee A.K., Dhodapkar S.D., Seshia S., Shyamasundar R.K. *PERTS: an environment for specification and verification of reactive systems* , Reliability Engineering & Systems Safety Journal, 71(2001), Elsevier, UK, 2001
10. Seshia S., Shyamasundar R.K., Bhattacharjee A.K., Dhodapkar S.D. *A Translation of Statecharts to Esterel* Lecture Notes in Computer Science, Vol 1698, Springer, 1999
11. Mikk E., Lakhnech, Siegel M. *Hierarchical Automata as a model for Statecharts*, Lecture Notes in Computer Science, Vol 1345, Springer, 1997.
12. Mikk E., Lakhnech, Siegel M., Holzmann G.J. *Implementing Statecharts in Promela/SPIN*, Proc. of the 2nd IEEE Workshop on Industrial Strength Formal Specification Techniques, IEEE Computer Society,Technical Report 1999.
13. Bhattacharjee A.K., Dhodapkar S.D., Seshia S., Shyamasundar R.K. *STATEST: A Tool to Translate Statecharts to Esterel.* BARC Technical Report. BARC/1998/E/014, 1998

Automatic Timeliness Verification of a Public Mobile Network

Ester Ciancamerla[1], Michele Minichino[1], Stefano Serro[2], and Enrico Tronci[3]

[1] ENEA CR Casaccia, Roma, Italy
{ciancamerlae, minichino}@casaccia.enea.it
[2] TECSIT Telecontrollo e Sistemi, Roma, Italy
stefanoserro@inwind.it
[3] Dip. di Informatica, Università di Roma "La Sapienza", Roma, Italy -
tronci@dsi.uniroma1.it

Abstract. This paper deals with the automatic verification of the timeliness of Public Mobile Network (PMN), consisting of *Mobile Node*s (MNs) and *Base Stations* (BSs). We use the Murphi Model Checker to verify that the waiting access time of each MN, under different PMN configurations and loads, and different inter arrival times of MNs in a BS cell, is always below a preassigned threshold. Our experimental results show that Model Checking can be successfully used to generate worst case scenarios and nicely complements probabilistic methods and simulation which are typically used for performance evaluation.

1   Introduction

This work is in the frame of the evaluation activity of the EU Project SAFETUNNEL [1]. The Project aims at reducing the number of incident inside mono tube alpine road tunnels by preventive safety actions which essentially consist of vehicle prognostics, before tunnel entrance, and vehicle telecontrol, inside the tunnel, to keep safety speed and safety distances among vehicles. Such safety actions are foreseen to be performed by a digital control system, based on a PMN. The system basically consists of a Tunnel Control Centre (TCC) interconnected to on board vehicle subsystems by a PMN. For implementing preventive safety actions it is essential that each vehicle, approaching the tunnel, can get communication with the TCC in real time. Time violations in detecting dangerous tunnel conditions and/or in taking the corrective actions could lead both the control system and the tunnel under control to unsafe situations. The time response of the system, which relies on a PMN, also depends upon the time response of the PMN.

Alternative design solutions for PMN, which include the use of GSM mobile network (circuit-switched connections/reserved bandwidth) and GPRS data connection (packed switched connections /shared, unreserved bandwidth), are currently under consideration in SAFETUNNEL Project. In this paper we consider a PMN architecture at a *Cell Level*, which implements a circuit switched connection. The architecture consists of *Mobile Node*s (MNs) and *Base Stations* (BSs), where a

S. Anderson et al. (Eds.): SAFECOMP 2003, LNCS 2788, pp. 35–48, 2003.

BS is viewed as a router connecting the wireless cellular network to the wired part of the network. We investigate the use of the Murphi Model Checker to verify that the maximum waiting access time of any MN, evaluated on many network configurations, network loads and inter arrival times of MNs, is always below a given threshold. The *waiting access time* is intended as the interval of time between the instant in which a MN asks for a communication channel to a BS, and the instant in which the MN gets such a communication channel. In SAFETUNNEL context, MNs represent vehicles (e.g. trucks).

Here we are dealing with a protocol like system. From [2] it is known that for such systems *explicit* model checking can outperform *implicit* (i.e. OBDD based model checking [3, 4, 5]). This is why we decided to use an explicit Model Checker, Murphi [4,6] for our analysis.

As usual when using model checking, *state explosion* is the main obstruction to be overcome. To delay state explosion, rather then using standard Murphi [6], we used Cached Murphi [7,8] which, w.r.t. standard Murphi, saves about 40% of RAM possibly with a time overhead. Note also that, given the size of our system, tools using dense time timed automata (e.g. as HyTech, [9]) cannot be used because of state explosion.

Performances are typically evaluated by solving stochastic models in terms of average measures and distributions. Stochastic modeling can be performed by using Markov Chains, Petri Nets or other modeling concepts [10,11,12] and can hardly generate worst case scenarios. This is instead exactly what model checking can do: generate a worst case scenario and compute performances for such worst case scenario. Note, on the other hand, that model checking is not suited for an average case analysis.

The paper is organized as follows. Section 2 describes the PMN at cell level. Section 3 deals with the modeling assumptions of the PMN. Section 4 describes the Murphi model for our PMN. Section 5 shows our experimental results and Section 6 presents some discussions and conclusions.

2   Public Mobile Network

The architecture of the PMN under consideration is at cell level and consists of *Mobile Nodes* (MNs) and *Base Stations* (BS) interconnected by a circuit-switched connections/reserved bandwidth, such as the GSM connection. A BS is viewed as a router connecting the wireless cellular network to the wired part of the network.

A MN enters the BS range of action and requests a connection to the PMN. If the BS has the necessary resource, that is a communication channel, it starts the procedure to assign such a channel to the MN. Once connected, the MN communicates through the BS until the MN doesn't leave the BS cell or the BS signal power falls below a certain threshold. A BS may, or may not, be able to provide the connection to a MN, within real time constraints, depending upon the PMN configuration and parameters. Such constraints have also to be satisfied when a MN is accessing a new BS, coming from an old BS (handoff procedure management). If the new BS doesn't promptly provide the requested connection, an unsafe timing condition could occur.

The communication between MNs and a BS is based on the RSVP protocol [13], which allows resources reservation in advance, namely before a MN effectively uses them (passive reservation).

A MN can be connected only to one BS at once. To establish a connection, the MN requests the resource to the BS, through an active reservation. When the use of the resource is authorized by the BS, the active reservation becomes an active communication. Even if a MN is in an active communication with a BS, the RSVP protocol allows the MN to request resources in advance to a new BS for a future communication. Before interrupting the connection with the current BS, the MN, during its movement, can request to an adjacent BS to turn the passive reservation into an active one (figure 1).

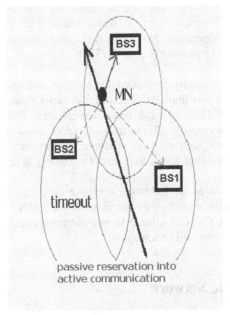

Fig. 1. Turning passive reservations into an active communication

The new BS, having already reserved the necessary resources for the MN during the passive reservation, will finalize the switching. Once the MN receives the acknowledge message, it initiates the connection with the new BS, interrupting the communication with the old BS. This mechanism allows the MN movement in the PMN range, without causing communication quality deterioration.

A BS broadcasts a *beacon signal* to contact a MN crossing the BS cell. The signal carries BS information, such as its IP address. The rate of beacon signal is correlated to the current load and the available resources of the BS. A MN can receive different beacon signals from different BSs. The MN recognizes which is the BS to request the active reservation, on the basis of the BS current load, expressed by the rate of its beacon signal.

Figure 2 shows the timing sequence of the Local Handoff Protocol messages, which carry out the handoff procedure. The initial message is the *Beacon* signal, which is broadcasted by a BS. Once such a signal is received by a MN, the MN Control Layer starts the handoff procedure with the BS. The MN sends an *Announce* message to the BS to request the PMN connection. The *Announce* message contains information on the type of service required to the BS (i.e. real-time or best-effort), the IP address of the old BS.

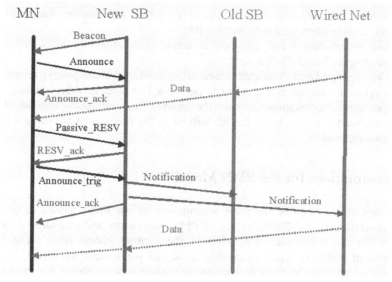

Fig. 2. Timing sequence of Local Handoff Protocol

The BS confirms the reception of the *Announce* message by an *Announce_ack* message. The MN sends a passive reservation request by a *Passive_RESV* message, in which the required resources are listed. The BS acknowledges these messages by sending a *RESV_ack* message, including the timeout reservation value.

At this point the MN can decide whether to confirm the passive reservation by sending back the *Passive_RESV* message within the timeout, or to request the use of the resource, by sending an announce message marked as triggered, *Announce_trig*, to ask for the switching of the passive reservation into an active one. After receiving the triggered message, the BS turns the passive reservation into an active one, creates a routing table entry for the new MN, transmits a *Notify* message to the old BS and sends a signal to the higher hierarchical network level to notify the current correspondence between MN and the new BS. After receiving the *Notify* message, the old BS removes the MN from the routing table entry.

If the request of real-time communication arrives from a MN that has to start up a new connection to the network, once received the *Announce_ack* message from the BS, the MN can decide whether to require an active reservation (*Announce_trig* message) or to require a passive reservation (*Passive_RESV* message). No passive reservation is allowed in case of a best-effort request of service.

The BS bandwidth determines the maximum number of MNs that a BS is able to serve, at the same time. Real-time and best-effort services are provided by the BS. Real-time service has higher priority than the best-effort service. In real-time service, higher priority is assigned to the requests originated by a MN, already connected to the PMN and moving from the current BS to a new BS   (continuity of service), respect to the requests of an initial PMN connection.

To accommodate both real time and best effort services, The BS bandwidth is divided in three classes:

- *Continuous reservation band*, assigned to active and passive reservations of MNs, already connected with another BS;
- *Initial reservation band*, assigned to active reservations of MNs, which are requesting an initial PMN access;
- *No reservation band*, dedicated to best-effort service, without passive reservation.

A reservation timeout management is performed at administrative domain level. The more busy the continuous band the shorter the reservation timeout. If the continuous band is not so busy, the BS will be in the position of affording a longer reservation timeout.

3   Assumptions for the PMN Model

In this section we describe the main assumptions of our PMN model, in terms of initial conditions of the PMN, values of PMN parameters and undesired events to consider for the automatic verification of the *waiting access time*.   The initial conditions of PMN, in terms of configuration and parameters are varied, by non-deterministic choices, in order to generate the worst case scenarios for the waiting access time of each MN. The *waiting access time* is the interval of time between the instant of time in which MN asks to BS for a communication channel and the instant of time in which MN gets such communication channel.

Preassigning a threshold value for the waiting access time, the automatic verification of the PMN timeliness consists in verifying that for all MN the waiting time is below such a threshold for all network configurations and parameters.

The PMN parameters and their initial values are:

- Number of channels reserved to the initial communication: *10 channels*;
- Number of channels reserved to the continuous communication: *40 channels*;
- MN arrival time in BS cell: *1 MN every 5 sec*;
- Range of beacon signal transmission rate: *1- 10 signals x sec*, by steps of *1 sec*;
- Values of   timeout reservation time: *8/15 sec*, depending on the current number of available channels of continuous band;
- Duration of active communication: 15 secs.

Just real-time service is considered, distinguishing between initial communication and continuous communication. A MN can transmit the access request to the BS, after the reception of the beacon signal from BS. Both the beacon signal rate and the reservation timeout are defined according to the available channels. The higher the number of available channels the higher the beacon signal rate and the duration of the timeout. Continuous communication implies a passive reservation of the communication channel which has a maximum duration. Once the communication between

MN and BS starts, it lasts a fixed time. MNs arrive into the BS cell with a fixed timing.

To perform the automatic verification of the PMN timeliness, the following *non deterministic choices* have been implemented into the model:

−   *A deviation of the fixed timing of arrival of MNs* (+1, +0 or-1 secs)

−   *The request of service that a MN makes to the BS* (active communication or passive reservation)

−   *Turning a passive reservation into an active communication.*

The *undesired events* taken into account to generate the worst case scenarios for the waiting access time of any MN are:

−   *Failed initial communication request*: MN does not obtain the communication channel in the initial band, and the maximum waiting time expires;

−   *Unsuccessful passive reservation request*: MN doesn't succeed in getting a channel in the continuous band within the maximum waiting time;

−   *Out of range*: the waiting time has expired before the node has made its request of service (active communication or passive reservation); this last case can occur when a MN waits too much time before receiving the beacon signal from BS.

4   Murphi Model of PMN

Murphi Model Checker [6,7] is a tool to perform formal verifications of systems modeled as Finite-State concurrent Machines (FSM). The system is defined by using a Pascal like programming language. Essentially a Murphi program consists of: *Constant declarations, Type declarations, Variable declarations, Function definitions, Transition Rules, Start State definition, Invariants.*

Figure 3 and 4 show some Constant and Type Declarations.

```
                        Const
            num_channels_init : 10;
            num_channels_cont : 40;
```

Fig. 3. Constant declarations

```
                        type
              arrival_deviation: -1..1;
         type_service :enum{com_init,com_cont};
      trasf_pass_res : enum{release,trasf_active};
```

Fig. 4. Type declarations

In figure 3, the model is initialized with 50 communication channels of which 40 are reserved to continuous communication and 10 are reserved to initial communication. In figure 4, a deviation of *+1, 0 or -1 secs* from the fixed timing of arrival of MN is used; the request of service (*type_service*) that a MN asks to the BS is established as initial or continuous communication; a passive reservation can turn into an active communication or release the channel (*trasf_pass_res*).

The Base Station and the Mobile Nodes are the main elements of the PMN model and their implementation will be described in detail in the following sections 4.1 and 4.2. The communication between MN and BS is implemented by the *Communication* function, as sketched in figure 5. The *Communication* function receives messages from a MN, according to its state, as current PMN parameters and gives back the appropriate answering messages coming from BS.

```
type_messagge_node: enum{nm_null, nm_announce,
nm_announce_trig_init, nm_announce_trig_cont,
nm_rsvp_resv};
type_messagge_BS: enum {sb_null, ack, ack_trig, conf_resv,
no_ack};
function communication
    (messagge_node: type_messagge_node;
     init_band: type_init_band;
     cont_band: type_cont_band): type_messagge_BS;
  begin
    switch messagge_node
     case nm_announce : return(ack);
     case nm_announce_trig_init :
                         if init_band >0
                             then return(ack_trig);
                             else return(no_ack);
                         endif;
     case nm_rsvp_resv : if cont_band >0
                             then return(conf_resv);
                             else return(no_ack);
                         endif;
     case nm_announce_trig_cont : return(ack_trig);
     else return(sb_null);
    endswitch;
  end;
```

Fig. 5. Communication Function

Another main function is the *Timeout* function which implements the management of timeout reservation time, figure 6. When a MN obtains a passive reservation, such a function verifies the available number of channels reserved to the continuous band and sends the timeout value to MN.

```
Function timeout
        (cont_band: type_cont_band) :service_time;
    begin
        -- max tempo di timeout 15 secondi
        -- min 8
      if (cont_band <=num_channels_cont)&
         (cont_band>= num_channels_cont/2)
         then return(15);
         else return(8);
      endif;
    end;
```

Fig. 6. Timeout function

The PMN model evolution is granted by transition rules (Figure 7). The rule *startstate* defines the initial state of the PMN from which the evolution of the model starts. We set BS with the whole available resource and all MN in the *absent* state.

The rule *next_state* triggers transitions among model states;it calls the procedure *next_state* that allows to:
1.   Insert a new MN at MN inter arrival time;
2.   Update the *beacon* variable;
3.   Analyze each MN which is in a state different from *absent* and call the procedure *state_evolution*, which updates the state of each MN.
4.   Update both *clock_ds* and *arrival_time* variables.

The rule *next_state* is preceded by 3 rulesets: *arrival_deviation*, *request_trasf, service*. A ruleset allows a rule implementation for each value of the variable which is defined in the ruleset. In our model one ruleset has been used to implement each non-deterministic choice.

The use of the rulesets allows, during the verification phase, to take into consideration the model's evolution in all its possible combinations of nondeteministic choices.

```
Ruleset arrival_deviation:time_arrival_deviation do
ruleset request_trasf: trasf_pass_res do
ruleset service: type_service do
  rule "next_state"
        true
        ==>
        next_state (S,N,clock_ds,
                    arrival_time,arrival_deviation,
                    request_trasf,service);
        end;
end;
end;
end;
```

Fig. 7. Transition rules

The properties to be preserved in the model are described in terms of invariants (figure 8), i.e. properties that must hold on any reachable state. In our PMN model we have the following invariants:
−   No MN has to reach the state   *Com_init_failed*;
−   No MN has to reach the state of   *Pass_res_failed*;
−   No MN has to reach the *Out_of_range* state;

```
invariant
    controllo_out_of_range (N)=false;
invariant
access_init_failed(N)=false;
invariant
    passive_reservation_failed(N)=false;
```

Fig. 8. Invariants

Such controls are accomplished by three functions, which receive the values of the parameters of each MN, and verify if there is an MN which is in an undesired state.

Once the model is written in the Murphi language, it is compiled by the Murphi compiler that produces the program for verification (verifier). The execution of the verifier allows an exhaustive analysis of the state space of the model under analysis in order to verify system properties, such as error assertions, invariants and deadlocks.

The analysis of the state space can be performed by using an algorithm of breadth-first search procedure, or by a depth-first search. There is the possibility to reduce the number of bit used to represent the state space with reduction techniques (symmetry, multiset, hash compaction).

Each transition of the PMN model occurs in a unit of time (step). We assume that a step time lasts 0.1 seconds and that transmission and the processing of messages between a BS and MNs takes a negligible amount of time. The beacon signal transmission rate is given in deciseconds. The permanence of a MN into a BS range is given in seconds and tens of second. In a step time, MN can send a message to BS and receive an answer.

4.1   Model of the Base Station

The current status of a BS have been described by the number of channels reserved to the initial communication (*type_init_band*), the number of channels reserved to the continuos communication (*type_cont_band*) and the current value of the beacon signal transmission rate (*type_beacon*).

A record has been used to model a BS. Figure 9 shows the type declaration as well as the declaration of the variable *BS*   (*BS: type_station;*). The fields of the record *init_band* and *cont_band* represent the number of channels of a BS reserved to initial and continuous communication. Note that in our model we only need one variable of type BS since our modelling is BS centric.

```
type_station: record
                 init_band: type_init_band;
                 cont_band: type_cont_band;
                 beacon: type_beacon;
              end;
BS: type_station;
```

Fig. 9. Base Station declarations

When an MN obtains a channel, the record field   *init_band*   is lowered by one, while, if an MN finishes a communication, it is increased by one. The same mechanism is applied for the record field   *cont_band.*

The record field *beacon*   represents the beacon signal transmission rate of BS. It assumes values included between *0* and *10*. A beacon value of *0* represents the action of the transmission of the beacon signal from BS to MN; only in this case a MN, that is looking for the station, is able to pass in the state announce. In the following transition the beacon is set to some value (greater than 0). The beacon value is then decreased of one unit at each transition, until it reaches to the value 0. The choice of the value to assign to beacon when it reaches the value 0, is performed by a function that considers the current available resource (initial band + continuous band) of BS. Varying such a value, the rate of dispatching of the beacon signal ranges from Fmin (1 per second) to Fmax (10 per second).

4.2   Model of the Mobile Nodes

Each MN entering the range of BS is characterized by its own state. Figure 10 describes the evolution of MN states according to the local handoff protocol reported in section 2.

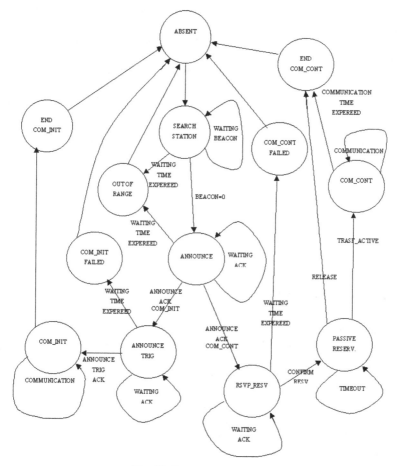

Fig. 10. Evolution of MN states

Each MN state is defined as following:
- *absent*: MN is not in the range of BS,
- *station_research*: MN is waiting for the beacon;
- *announce:* MN has sent an announce message to BS and it is waiting for the announce_ack;
- *announce_trig*: MN has asked for an active communication and it is waiting for BS acknowledge;
- *rsvp_resv*: MN has asked for a passive reservation and it is waiting for BS acknowledge;
- *init_communication*: MN is in active communication, in the initial band;

- *cont_communication*: MN is in active communication, in the continuous band;
- *passive_reservation*: MN is in passive reservation;
- *out_of_range*: the threshold waiting time has expired while MN was in announce or station_research state;
- *end_communication*:   MN has concluded an active communication;
- *com_init_failed*:   the threshold waiting time has expired while MN was in announce_trig state;
- *pass_res_failed*:   the threshold waiting time has expired while MN was in the *rsvp_resv* state.

A MN is modeled by a record as shown in figure 11. The record field *state* gives indication of the current MN state among the ones reported in figure 10. The record field   *max_time* is a counter needed to count how many seconds have elapsed since the occurrence of some specific event.

```
type_node: record
           state: node_state;
           max_time: permanence_time;
           end;
```

Fig. 11. MN declaration

5   Experimental Results

The timeliness verification of our PMN consisted in formally verifying that the waiting access time of each MN is always below a preassigned threshold. Such verification has been performed for different PMN configurations and parameters, starting from an *initial PMN configuration* and parameter values. Murphi found no errors in the *initial PMN configuration*. This means that no reachable state violates the properties to be preserved along the model evolution (invariants).

Table 1 gives some information on running Cached Murphi (with hash compaction enabled) on our Murphi model for the *initial PMN configuration* on a SUN machine.

MN initial connection and MN continuous connection to PMN have been investigated.

Table 2 reports some numerical results, for MN initial connection, obtained by varying the inter arrival time of MN in the BS cell from *5 ± 1 [sec]* to *3 ± 1 [sec]*, through non deterministic choices, and progressively decreasing of one unit the number of channels of the initial band from *10* to *5*. Particularly, fixed the threshold for *waiting access time to 1 sec,* the property under investigation (*waiting access time < 1 sec*) resulted *true* for each MN, for a number of channels of the initial band from *10* to *8*, both for arrival time of *5 ±1 [sec]* and *3 ±1 [sec]*.

As far as concerns MN continuous communication to PMN, the main parameters which affect the *waiting access time* are the *arrival time* of the incoming MNs, the number of *channels of the continuous band* and the value of *timeout*.

Table 1. Murphi performances on a SUN machine

Bytes	Reach	Rules	Diam	Mem (MB)	Time (sec)
16	11,143,131	33,429,393	258	157	20153.16

Bytes: *the number of bytes needed to represent each state value;*
Reach: *the number of reachable states;*
Rules: *the number of rules fired during verification;*
Diam: *the diameter of our model transition graph;*
Mem, Time: *the RAM memory and the amount of time to carry out verification.*

Table 2. MN waiting access time in the initial band

Arrival time (secs)	N. Channels Initial band	MN waiting access Time (secs)
5	10	< 1
3	10	< 1
3	9	< 1
3	8	< 1
3	7	> 10
3	6	> 20
3	5	> 28

Figure 12 shows some numerical results of verification for continuous connection, when the arrival time of the incoming MNs in the BS cell is *1 node every 2 ± 1 [sec]*. The number of channels of the continuous band ranges from *18 to 30*. The *timeout* is changed according to the Base Station workload, as implemented by the *Timeout* function. At any request of passive reservation the available channels of the continuous band are computed and one of two different values t_1 and t_2, (with $t_1 > t_2$) are dinamically assigned to the *timeout*. If the number of available channels is greater than an half of the total number of the channels the value t_1 is assigned to the *timeout*. Otherwise the value t_2 is assigned to the *timeout*. In particular the following sets of values of t_1 and t_2 in seconds, have been used: $t_1 = 15$ *and* $t_2 = 8; t_1 = 10$ *and* $t_2 = 5$; $t_1 = 8$ *and* $t_2 = 4$; $t_1 = 5$ *and* $t_2 = 3$.

The results, shown in figure 2, mean that, for a fixed network configuration, at least a case occurs in which a Mobile Node waits the *waiting access time* before obtaining the channel from BS.

6 Discussion and Conclusions

In this paper we investigate how model checking can be used for the automatic verification of the waiting access time of Mobile Nodes (MN) to a Public Mobile Network (PMN), based on a circuit switching connection. The PMN belongs to a real time control system for a critical infrastructure, the Frejus road tunnel. For such a system, time violations in detecting dangerous process conditions and /or in taking corrective control actions could lead both the process under control, the tunnel infrastructure, and the control system to unsafe situations. The presence of a even public PMN, as a part of the system, poses problems of dependability analysis on the frontier of the modeling efforts. That is at least due to a) the novelty and complexity of PMN b) the topology of the network, that dinamically changes for the presence of MNs c) the presence of security aspects that could weaken safety and timeliness properties of the system. Moreover it has to be considered that the current modeling methods are inadequate to deal with the complexity of PMN based real time systems, both in terms of the modeling power of the current tools and the analytical tractability of the resulting models, against the modeling power and the analytical tractability necessary to deal with such systems.

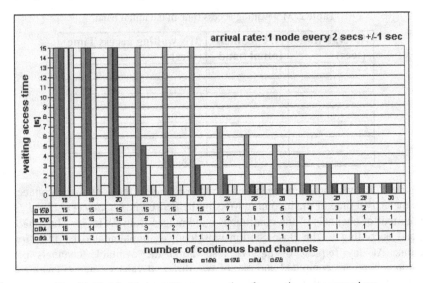

Fig. 12. Mobile Node waiting access time for continuous connections

Currently modeling and analysis for safety and dependability is actually dominated by two main lines: the functional analysis, whose goal is to ascertain for reachability properties and a stochastic analysis, whose aim is to provide performance and probability measures.

The paper follows the line of reachability analysis. Using the Murphi verifier we generated a finite representation of the PMN (the model of the PMN) and validated its timeliness, considered as a safety critical property, by exhaustively exploring all possible behaviors of the model.

Of course the *formalization* activity (i.e. going from the informal protocol specifications to the formal Murphi model) cannot be formally proved correct. What can be done is, as usual, to use simulation and verification of known properties to validate the formal model. We did this to make sure our Murphi model is indeed a model of our PMN. Our goal here was to check timeliness properties. This guided us in the choice of the invariants to be verified.

Model checkers allow an exhaustive state space exploration in a highly automated way. Exhaustive state space exploration, in turn, allows detection of seldom occurring property violations. In this sense model checking nicely complements stochatic modeling and simulation, which aim at performance evaluation, in term average measures and distributions and can hardly generate worst case scenarious. This is instead exactly what model checking can do: generate a worst case scenario and compute performances for such worst case scenario. Note, on the other hand, that model checking is not suited for an average case analysis.

Acknowledgements. This research was partially supported by EU Project SAFE-TUNNEL and MIUR Project MEFISTO.

References

[1]   SAFETUNNEL Project (IST – 2000 – 28099), http://www.crfproject-eu.org/)

[2]   D. L. Dill, A. J. Drexler, A. J. Hu, C. H. Yang, *Protocol Verification as a Hardware Design Tool*, In IEEE International Conference on Computer Aided Design, 1992

[3]   R. Bryant, *Graph-Based algorithms for Boolean function manipulation*, IEEE Trans. On Computers, C-35 (8), Aug. 1986

[4]   A. J. Hu, G. York, D. L. Dill, *New techniques for efficient verification with implicitily conjoined BDDs*. In 31st IEEE Design Automation Conference, 1994.

[5]   J. R. Burch, E. M. Clarke, K. L. McMillan, D. L. Dill, L. J. Hwang, *Symbolic Model Checking: 1020 states and beyond*. Information and Computation, (98), 1992

[6]   url: http://sprout.stanford.edu/~dill/murphi.html

[7]   url : http://www.dsi.uniroma1.it/~tronci/cached.murphi.html

[8]   E. Tronci, G. D. Penna, B. Intrigila, M. Venturini-Zilli, *Exploiting Transition Locality in Automatic Verification*, CHARME, LNCS Springer, Sept. 2001.

[9]   url: http://www.eecs.berkeley.edu/~tah/HyTech

[10] A. Bobbio, E. Ciancamerla, G.Franceschinis, R. Gaeta , M. Minichino, L. Portinale - *Methods of increasing modelling power for safety analysis, applied to a turbine digital control system* - SAFECOMP2002, Catania, Italy, September 2002

[11] A. Bobbio, L. Portinale, M. Minichino, E. Ciancamerla - *Improving the Analysis of Dependable Systems by Mapping Fault Trees into Bayesian Networks* - Reliability Engineering and System Safety Journal – 71/3- pp 249–260 - 2001

[12] M. Ajmone Marsan, M.Gribaudo, M.Meo, M. Sereno - *On Petri Net based modelling paradigms for the performance analysis of wireless internet accesses* -Petri Net and Performance Model - PNPM'01 - Aachen - Sept 2001

[13] J.Sokol and J.Widmer -*USAIA Ubiquitous Services Access Internet Architecture* -TR -01-003 International Computer Science Institute, Berkeley 2001

Improving System Reliability via Model Checking: The FSAP/NuSMV-SA Safety Analysis Platform*

Marco Bozzano and Adolfo Villafiorita

ITC-IRST, Via Sommarive 18,
38050 Trento, Italy
ph.: +39 0461 314481, fax: +39 0461 314 591
{bozzano,adolfo}@irst.itc.it
http://sra.itc.it/people/{bozzano,adolfo}

Abstract. Safety critical systems are becoming more complex, both in the type of functionality they provide and in the way they are demanded to interact with their environment. Such growing complexity requires an adequate increase in the capability of safety engineers to assess system safety, including analyzing the bahaviour of a system in degraded situations. Formal verification techniques, like symbolic model checking, have the potential of dealing with such a complexity and are more often being used during system design. In this paper we present the FSAP/NuSMV-SA platform, based on the NuSMV2 model checker, that implements known and novel techniques to help safety engineers perform safety analysis. The main functionalities of FSAP/NuSMV-SA include: failure mode definition based on a library of failure modes, fault injection, automatic fault tree construction for monotonic and non-monotonic systems, failure ordering analysis. The goal is to provide an environment that can be used both by design engineers to formally verify a system and by safety engineers to automate certain phases of safety assessment. The platform is being developed within the ESACS project (Enhanced Safety Analysis for Complex Systems), an European-Union-sponsored project in the avionics sector, whose goal is to define a methodology to improve the safety analysis practice for complex systems development.

1 Introduction

Controllers for safety critical systems are typically required to operate effectively not only in nominal conditions – i.e., when all the (sub)components of the system work as expected – but also in degraded situations – that is, when some of the (sub)components of the system are not working properly. This requirement is common in various safety critical sectors like, e.g., aeronautics, in which degraded operational conditions are stated as a set of *safety requirements*, available in

---

* This work has been and is being developed within ESACS, an European- sponsored project, contract no. G4RD-CT-2000-00361.

S. Anderson et al. (Eds.): SAFECOMP 2003, LNCS 2788, pp. 49–62, 2003.

the System Requirements Specification. Therefore, the standard development process is paired by a new set of activities (safety analysis), whose goal is to identify all possible hazards, together with their relevant causes, and to certify that the system behaves as expected in all the operational conditions.

Safety critical systems are becoming more complex, both in the type of functionality they provide and in the way they are demanded to interact with their environment. Such growing complexity requires an adequate increase in the capability of safety engineers to assess system safety. Current informal methodologies, like manual fault tree analysis (FTA) and failure mode and effect analysis (FMEA) [34], that rely on the ability of the safety engineer to understand and to foresee the system behaviour, are not ideal when dealing with highly complex systems. Emerging techniques like formal methods [35] are increasingly being used for the development of critical systems (see, e.g., [12,9,8,21]). Formal methods allow a more thorough verification of the system's correctness with respect to the requirements, by using *automated* and hopefully *exhaustive* verification procedures. In particular, model checking [13] is increasingly being used for several real-world safety-critical industrial applications. However, the use of formal methods for safety analysis purposes is still at an early stage. Moreover, even when formal methods are applied, the information linking the design and the safety assessment phases is often carried out informally. The link between design and safety analysis may be seen as an "over the wall process" [18].

In this paper we present the FSAP/NuSMV-SA platform, which is being developed at ITC-IRST. FSAP/NuSMV-SA is based on two main components: FSAP (Formal Safety Analysis Platform), that provides a graphical front-end to the user, and NuSMV-SA, based on the NuSMV2 [10] model checker, that provides an engine to perform safety assessment. The main functionality of FSAP/NuSMV-SA include: support for model construction (e.g., failure mode definition based on a library of predefined failure modes), automatic fault injection, support for safety requirements definition (in the form of temporal logic formulas), automatic fault tree construction for both monotonic and non monotonic systems, user-guided or random simulation, counterexample trace generation, and failure ordering analysis. FSAP/NuSMV-SA provides an environment that can be used both by design engineers to formally verify a system and by safety engineers to automate certain phases of safety assessment.

The major benefits provided by the FSAP/NuSMV-SA platform are a tight integration between the design and the safety analysis teams, and a (partial) automation of the activities related to both verification and safety assessment. The basic functions provided by the platform can be combined in different ways, in order to comply with any given development methodology one has in mind. It is possible to support an incremental approach, based on iterative releases of a given system model at different levels of detail (e.g., model refinement, addition of further failure modes and/or safety requirements). Furthermore, it is possible to have iterations in the execution of the different phases (design and safety assessment), e.g., it is possible to let the model refinement process be driven by the safety assessment phase outcome (e.g., disclosure of system flaws requires fixing the physical system and/or correcting the formal model). Therefore, in order to support the flow of information which is likely to be required between design and safety engineers, the FSAP/NuSMV-SA platform implements the concept of *repository* for safety analysis task results. The repository contains information about which safety analysis tasks (e.g., verification of temporal properties, fault tree generations) have been performed for which model, keeping trace of which properties do hold for a particular model and which do not, and marking tasks as being up-to-date or not. The repository thus provides traceability capabilities and makes reuse and evolution of safety cases easier.

The FSAP/NuSMV-SA platform has been and is being developed within the ESACS project [6] (Enhanced Safety Assessment for Complex Systems, see http://www.esacs.org), an European-Union-sponsored project in the area of safety analysis, involving several research institutions and leading companies in the fields of avionics and aerospace. The methodology developed within the ESACS project is supported by state-of-the-art and commercial tools for system modeling and traditional safety analysis. The tools, collectively referred with the name of ESACS platform, have been extended to support the methodology and to automate certain phases of safety analysis. Both the methodology and the ESACS platform are being trialed on a set of industrial case studies. The ESACS platform comes in different configurations, tailored to the needs of the industrial partners participating in the project.

The rest of the paper is structured as follows. In Section 2 we give an overview of the safety analysis process, we discuss its connection with model checking and the safety analysis capabilities integrated into FSAP/NuSMV-SA. In Section 3 we give an overview of the FSAP/NuSMV-SA platform. In Section 4 we discuss some related work, and, finally, in Section 5 we draw some conclusions.

2   Safety Analysis via Model Checking

Model checking [13] is a well-established method for formally verifying temporal properties of finite-state concurrent systems. It has been applied for the formal verification of a number of real-world safety-critical industrial systems [22,23, 10]. In particular, the engine of FSAP/NuSMV-SA is an extension of the model checking tool NuSMV2 [10], a BDD-based symbolic model-checker developed at ITC-IRST, originated from a re-engineering and re-implementation of SMV [28]. NuSMV2 is a well-structured, open, flexible and well-documented platform for model checking, and it has been designed to be robust and close to industrial standards [11]. Typically, system specifications are written as temporal logic formulas, and efficient symbolic algorithms (based on data structures like BDDs [7]) are used to traverse the model and check if the specification holds or not.

Being an extension of NuSMV2, FSAP/NuSMV-SA provides all the functionality of NuSMV2. Below, however, we will focus on the safety assessment capabilities of FSAP/NuSMV-SA. We do so by providing a typical scenario of usage of the platform on a toy example, namely a two-bit adder. The presented scenario derives from the ESACS methodology (see [6], for more details). The

```
MODULE bit(input)                 MODULE main
VAR                               VAR
  out : {0,1};                      random1 : {0,1};
ASSIGN                              random2 : {0,1};
  out := input;                     bit1    : bit(random1);
                                    bit2    : bit(random2);
MODULE adder(bit1,bit2)             adder   : adder(bit1.out,bit2.out);
VAR
  out : {0,1};
ASSIGN
  out := (bit1 + bit2) mod 2;
```

Fig. 1. A NuSMV model for a two-bit adder

example is deliberately simple for illustration purposes and should not be regarded as modeling a realistic system. Following the ESACS methodology, the use of the FSAP/NuSMV-SA platform is based on the following phases:

System Model Definition. In this phase a formal model of the system under development, called *system model*, is provided.

Requirements Definition. It is the phase in which the desired properties of the system model are specified. The properties may refer to the behaviour of the system both in nominal and in degraded situations.

Failure Mode Definition. In this phase, the failure modes of the components of the design model are identified.

Fault Injection and Model Extension. In this phase the failure modes defined in the previous phase are injected into the system model. As a result, a new model, called *extended system model*, is generated. The extended system model enriches the behaviour of the system model by taking into account all the set of degraded behaviours identified during the previous phase.

Formal Verification and Safety Assessment. It is the phase in which the system model and/or the extended system model are checked against a set of requirements. Verification strategies may include, e.g., guided or random simulation, formal verification of properties, generation of fault trees.

Note that the responsibility of the different phases described above may belong to different disciplines, e.g., design engineers or safety engineers. As discussed in the introduction, there are no strict constraints on the way in which the different functions can be invoked, and the overall process in which FSAP/NuSMV-SA is used can be shaped up so as to comply with different development methodologies.

2.1 System Model and Failure Mode Definition

System model definition provides an executable specification (at a given level of abstraction) of the model of the system under development. As an example, consider the simple example, written in the syntax of NuSMV2 [10], in Figure 1.

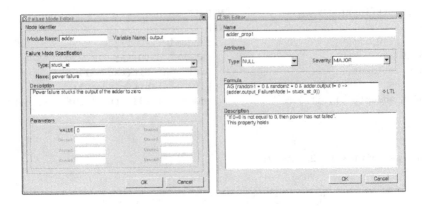

Fig. 2. Inputing of failure modes and safety requirements in FSAP

It is composed of three modules: the `bit` module, which simply copies the input bit to the output, the `adder` module, which computes the sum (module two) of two given input bits, and the `main` module, which defines the overall system as composed of an adder which takes as input two bits that may vary in a random way. In order to study the behaviour of the adder circuit in presence of degraded situations, failure mode definitions can be added to the previous specification.

In FSAP/NuSMV-SA, failure modes are defined using a graphical user interface, in which the safety engineer specifies which nodes of the system model can fail, in what ways, and according to what parameters. Figure 2 (left-hand side) shows an example of the interface currently provided by FSAP/NuSMV-SA for defining failure modes. Failure modes are retrieved from a library, called Generic Failure Mode Library (GFML, for short). The library contains the specifications of the behaviours induced by the failures and the specification of the parameters (whose values must be set by the user) that characterize the failures. The standard GFML, that is the library distributed with the platform, provides specification of failures like, e.g., *stuck-at, random output, glitch, inverted*. The library can be extended to include user-defined failure modes. In the adder case, examples of failure modes may include, e.g., the adder output being stuck at a given value (zero or one), and an input bit corruption (*inverted* failure mode).

2.2 Fault Injection and Model Extension

The failure modes defined at the previous step can be *automatically* injected by FSAP/NuSMV-SA into a system model. The result is the so-called *extended system model*, that is a model in which some of the nodes can fail according to the specification of the failure modes. As an example, consider the *inverted* failure mode for the output of the `bit` module in Figure 1. Injection of this failure mode causes the system model to be extended with a new piece of NuSMV code (instantiated from the GFML), that is automatically inserted into the extended

```
VAR    out_nominal     : {0,1};
       out_FailureMode : {no_failure, inverted};
ASSIGN out_nominal := input;
DEFINE out_inverted := ! out_nominal;
DEFINE out := case
          out_FailureMode = no_failure : out_nominal;
          out_FailureMode = inverted   : out_inverted;
       esac;
ASSIGN next(out_FailureMode) := case
          out_FailureMode = no_failure : {no_failure, inverted};
          out_FailureMode = inverted   : inverted;
       esac;
```

Fig. 3. Injecting a fault in the `bit` module

system model. The new piece of code (see Figure 3) replaces the old definition of the out variable by taking into account a possible corruption of the input bit.

2.3 Requirements Definition

System model definition, failure mode definition and model extension are just a part of the verification and safety assessment process. Formal verification is carried out by defining properties in the form of temporal specifications. For instance, the following properties may be specified for the adder example:

```
AG (random1 = 0 & random2 = 0 → adder.out = 0)
AG (random1 = 0 & random2 = 0 & adder.out != 0) →
       (bit1.out_FailureMode = inverted | bit2.out_FailureMode = inverted)
```

The first one states that the output of the adder must be zero whenever both input bits are zero (this is clearly not the case in degraded situations), whereas the second one states that whenever the sum of the zero input bits yields one it is the case that at least one of the two input bits is corrupted. Requirements defined in this way can subsequently be exhaustively verified via the underlying model checking verification engine provided by NuSMV. Properties in FSAP/NuSMV-SA are defined via a graphical user interface, in which users can enter information such as type and severity of the safety requirement. Figure 2 (right-hand side), for instance, shows how safety requirements are specified by the user. The graphical user interface does not provide, at the moment, facilities for simplifying inputing of formulas, such as patterns or visual representations.

2.4 Formal Verification and Safety Assessment

During this phase the model under development is tested against safety requirements. Using the facilities provided by the NuSMV2 engine, it is possible to perform guided or random simulation, and several kinds of formal verification analyses. In particular, below we will focus on fault tree construction and failure ordering analysis, which are more specific to the safety analysis process.

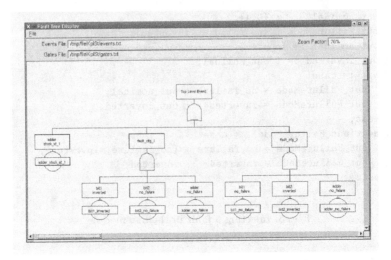

Fig. 4. A fault tree generated for the adder model

Fault Tree Construction. Fault Tree Analysis (FTA) [34,24,30] is a safety assessment strategy which is complementary with respect to exhaustive property verification. It is a deductive, top-down method to analyze system design and robustness. It usually involves specifying a *top level event* (TLE hereafter) to be analyzed (e.g., a *failure state*), and identifying all possible sets of basic events (e.g., basic *faults*) which may cause that TLE to occur. FTA allows one to identify possible system reliability or safety problems and find out root causes of equipment failures. *Fault trees* provide a convenient symbolic representation of the combination of events resulting in the occurrence of the top event. They are usually represented in a graphical way, as a parallel or sequential combination of AND/OR gates. The FSAP/NuSMV-SA platform can be used to automatically generate fault trees starting from a given model and TLE. Model checking techniques are used to extract *automatically* all collections of basic events (called *minimal cut sets*) which can trigger the TLE. The generated cut sets are minimal in the sense that only failure events that are strictly necessary for the top level event to occur are retained.

Each cut set produced by FSAP/NuSMV-SA represents a situation in which the top level event has been violated owing to the occurrence of some failures. Under the hypothesis that the system model does not violate the top level event, such failures are the cause of the violation of the top level event. Notice that the violation may be due not to a static analysis of the system but, rather, to complex interactions caused by the various failing and non-failing components of the system. Since the fault tree representation provides a static representation, NuSMV-SA associates, to each cut set, a counter-example that shows a trace, step by step, of how the top level event is violated by the failures represented in the cut set. Figure 4 shows an example of fault tree computed for the adder. It has been generated for the top level event

```
random1 = 0 & random2 = 0 & adder.out != 0
```

and it comprises three cut sets (the first one of them is a single failure, whereas the remaining two include three basic events). The fault tree states that the top level event may occur if and only if either the output of the adder is stuck at one, or one of the input bits (and *only* one) is corrupted (with the adder working properly). We note that minimality of the generated cut sets implies that, e.g., the case in which both input bits and the adder are failed is not considered (though causing the top level event as well).

Finally, we note that the fault tree in Figure 4 shows an example of *non-monotonic* fault tree analysis, i.e., basic events requiring system components *not* to fail can be part of the results of the analysis. The traditional *monotonic* analysis (i.e., where only failure events are considered) is also supported by FSAP/NuSMV-SA. The choice between the different kinds of analyses is left to the user, which may label a system model as being monotonic or non-monotonic.

Failure Ordering Analysis. A further functionality of the FSAP/NuSMV-SA platform is the so-called *event ordering analysis*. For further information on the material of this section, we refer the reader to [5], which describes the algorithm for ordering analysis, its implementation and applications in detail.

In traditional FTA, cut sets are simply flat collections (i.e, conjunctions) of events which can trigger a given TLE. However, there might be timing constraints enforcing a particular event to happen before or after another one, in order for the TLE to be triggered (i.e., the TLE would not show if the order of the two events were swapped). Ordering constraints can be due, e.g., to a causality relation or a functional dependency between events, or caused by more complex interactions involving the dynamics of a system. Whatever the reason, event ordering analysis can provide useful information which can be used by the design and safety engineers to fully understand the ultimate causes of a given system malfunction, so that adequate countermeasures can be taken.

The ordering analysis phase can be tightly integrated with fault tree analysis, as described below. Given a system model, the verification process consists of the following phases. First of all, a top level event to analyze is chosen (clearly, the analysis can be repeated for different top level events). Then, fault tree analysis is run in order to compute the *minimal cut sets* relative to the top level event. For each cut set, the event ordering analysis module of the platform generates a so-called *ordering information model* and performs ordering analysis on it. The outcome of the ordering analysis is a *precedence graph* showing the order among events (if any) which must be fulfilled in order for the top level event to occur.

3   FSAP/NuSMV-SA Platform Overview

This section briefly describes the architecture of FSAP/NuSMV-SA. The platform is based on two main components: FSAP (Formal Safety Analysis Platform) provides a graphical user interface and a manager for a repository that can be

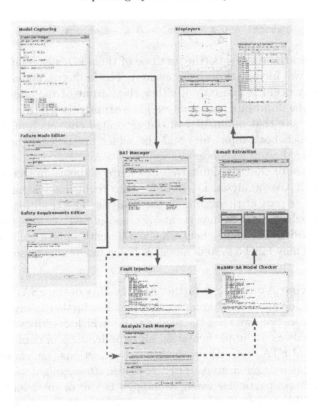

Fig. 5. The FSAP/NuSMV-SA components

used by safety engineers and design engineers to share information related to the system under development and the analysis performed; NuSMV-SA, based on the NuSMV2 model checker, provides the core algorithms for formal analysis.

FSAP is implemented in C++ as a cross-platform environment. The graphical user interface is based on the FLTK (see http://www.fltk.org) cross platform toolkit. The data produced by the platform are stored in XML format, and the parser is based on the expat library (see http://www.expat.org). As a result, FSAP/NuSMV-SA currently runs on Windows and Linux platforms (as for NuSMV, running NuSMV-SA on Windows currently requires the Cygwin environment to be installed). Figure 5 shows the components of FSAP/NuSMV-SA and the data flow (solid lines). We distinguish the following blocks:

SAT Manager. The SAT manager is the central module of the platform. It is used to store all the information relevant to verification and safety assessment. It contains references to the system model, failure modes, location of the extended system model, safety requirements, and analyses to be run. From the SAT, it is possible to call all the other components of the platform.

Model Capturing. System models are written using the NuSMV input language, that is text based. FSAP/NuSMV-SA provides users with the possibility of using their preferred text editor for editing the system model.

Failure Mode Editor & Fault Injector. These are the modules for, respectively defining failure modes and generating an extended system model.

Analysis Task Handler. This is the module to define analysis tasks. Analysis tasks are a convenient way to store the specification of the analyses to be run, they are saved in the SAT and can be retrieved across different sessions.

NuSMV-SA. This is the core, based on the NuSMV2 model checker.

Result Extraction and Displayers. All the results produced by the platform can be viewed using the result extraction and displayers. In particular, it is possible to view counterexamples in textual, structured (XML), graphical, or tabular fashion. Fault trees generated by the platform can be viewed using commercial tools (e.g. FaultTree+ v9.0 and v10.0) or using a displayer we especially developed within the project and can be exported in XML format.

4   Related Work

The FSAP/NuSMV-SA platform has been and is being developed within the ESACS project (Enhanced Safety Analysis for Complex Systems), an European-Union-sponsored project involving various research centers and industries from the avionics sector. For a more detailed description of the ESACS methodology and the project goals, we refer the reader to [6], which also discussed more realistic examples to which the methodology has been applied.

The safety analysis capabilities provided by the platform include traditional fault tree generation [34,24,30] together with formal verification capabilities typical of model checking [28,13,22,23,10]. The algorithms for cut set and prime implicant computation described in Section 2.4 are based on classical procedures for *minimization* of *boolean functions*, specifically on the implicit-search procedure described in [15,16], which is based on Binary Decision Diagrams (BDDs) [7]. This choice was quite natural, given that the NuSMV model checker makes a pervasive use of BDD data structures. The ordering analysis procedure described in Section 2.4 also makes use of these algorithms (we refer the reader to [5] for a discussion of the related literature). Explicit-search and SAT-based techniques for computation of prime implicants are described, e.g., in [26].

We also mention [25,33], which describe DIFTree (Dynamic Innovative Fault Tree), a methodology supporting (however, still at the manual level) fault tree construction and allowing for different kinds of analyses of sub-trees (e.g., Markovian or Monte Carlo simulation for dynamic ones, and BDD-based evaluation for static ones). The notation for non-logical (dynamic) gates of fault trees and the support for sample probabilistic distributions could be nice features to be integrated in our framework.

A large amount of work has been done in the area of probabilistic safety assessment (PSA) and in particular on *dynamic reliability* [31]. Dynamic reliability is concerned with extending the classical event or fault tree approaches to

PSA by taking into consideration the mutual interactions between the hardware components of a plant and the physical evolution of its process variables [27]. Examples of scenarios taken into consideration are, e.g., human intervention, expert judgment, the role of control/protection systems, the so-called failures *on demand* (i.e., failure of a component to intervene), and also the ordering of events during accident propagation. Different approaches to dynamic reliability include, e.g., state transitions or Markov models [1,29], the dynamic event tree methodology [14], and direct simulation via Monte Carlo analysis [32,27].

Concerning ordering analysis (see Section 2.4), the work which is probably closer to ours is [14], which describes dynamic event trees as a convenient means to represent the timing and order of intervention of a plant sub-systems and their eventual failures. With respect to the classification the authors propose, our approach can support *simultaneous* failures, whereas, at the moment, we are working under the hypothesis of *persistent* failures (i.e., no repair is possible).

5   Conclusions

In this paper we have presented the FSAP/NuSMV-SA safety analysis platform. The verification engine of the platform is based on the NuSMV2 model checker [10]. FSAP/NuSMV-SA can be used as a tool to assist the safety analysis process from the early phases of system design to the formal verification and safety assessment phases. The goal is to provide an environment that can be used both by design engineers to formally verify a system and by safety engineers to automate certain phases of safety assessments. To achieve these goals, FSAP/NuSMV-SA provides a set of basic functions which can be combined in arbitrary ways to realize different process development methodologies.

The functionalities provided by FSAP/NuSMV-SA integrates traditional analysis methodologies like fault tree generation, together with exhaustive property verification capabilities typical of model checking, plus model construction facilities (e.g., automatic failure injection based on a library of predefined failure modes) and traceability capabilities, which improve exchange of information and make reuse and evolution of safety cases easier. The FSAP/NuSMV-SA platform supports automatic fault tree generation, both in the case of *monotonic* systems (computation of *minimal cut sets*) and in the case of *non-monotonic* ones (computation of *prime implicants*). Furthermore, the results provided by fault tree generation can be conveniently integrated by the so-called *ordering analysis* phase, which allows one to extract ordering constraints holding between basic events in a given cut set, thus providing a deeper insight into the ultimate causes of system malfunction. As discussed in [5], timing constraints can arise very naturally in industrial systems. For a more extensive discussion about the use of model checking for safety analysis, the tool usage experience, and for a more realistic example of application of the methodology, we refer the reader to [4].

Concerning the works on dynamic reliability cited in Section 4, the most notable difference between our approach and the works mentioned there is that we present *automatic* techniques, based on model checking, for both fault tree generation and ordering analysis, whereas traditional works on dynamic reliability rely on manual analysis (e.g., Markovian analysis [29]) or simulation (e.g., Monte Carlo simulation [27], the TRETA package of [14]). Automation is clearly a point in our favour. Furthermore, we support automatic verification of arbitrary CTL properties (in particular, both safety and liveness properties).

Current work is focusing on some improvements and extensions in order to make the methodology competitive with existing approaches and usable in realistic scenarios. First of all, there are some improvements at the modeling level. The NuSMV models used so far are discrete, finite-state transition models. In order to allow for more realistic models, we are considering an extension of NuSMV with hybrid dynamics, along the lines of [19,20]. This would allow both to model more complex variable dynamics, and also a more realistic modeling of time (which, currently, is modeled by an abstract transition step). Furthermore, we need to extend our framework to deal with *probabilistic* assessment. Although not illustrated in this paper, associating probabilistic estimates to basic events and evaluating the resulting fault trees is straightforward. However, more work needs to be done in order to support more complex probabilistic dynamics (see, e.g., [17]). We also want to overcome the current limitation to permanent failures.

Concerning the FSAP/NuSMV-SA platform, we are currently working on further improving user interaction (e.g., by working on pattern-based inputing of top level events) and experimenting on SAT based techniques [3,2] for fault tree construction. The FSAP/NuSMV-SA platform is available for evaluation purposes from http://sra.itc.it/tools/FSAP (the download is currently password protected; the password can be obtained by sending an e-mail to the authors).

Acknowledgments. The work presented in this paper would have not been possible without the help of Paolo Traverso, Alessandro Cimatti, and Gabriele Zacco.

We would also like to thank the people working in the ESACS project and, in particular: Ove Åkerlund (Prover), Pierre Bieber (ONERA), Christian Bougnol (AIRBUS), E. Böde (OFFIS), Matthias Bretschneider (AIRBUS-D), Antonella Cavallo (Alenia Aeronautica), Charles Castel (ONERA), Massimo Cifaldi (SIA), Alain Griffault (LaBri, Université de Bordeaux), C. Kehren (ONERA), Benita Lawrence (AIRBUS-UK), Andreas Lüdtke (University of Oldenburg), Silvayn Metge (AIRBUS-F), Chris Papadopoulos (AIRBUS-UK), Renata Passarello (SIA), Thomas Peikenkamp (OFFIS), Per Persson (Saab), Christel Seguin (ONERA), Luigi Trotta (Alenia Aeronautica), and Laura Valacca (SIA).

References

1. T. Aldemir. Computer-assisted Markov Failure Modeling of Process Control Systems. *IEEE Transactios on Reliability*, R-36:133–144, 1987.
2. G. Audemard, P. Bertoli, A. Cimatti, A. Korniłowicz, and R. Sebastiani. A SAT Based Approach for Solving Formulas over Boolean and Linear Mathematical Propositions. In Andrei Voronkov, editor, *CADE-18: Conference on Automated Deduction*, number 2392 in LNAI, pages 195–210. Springer, 2002.

3. A. Biere, A. Cimatti, E.M. Clarke, and Y. Zhu. Symbolic Model Checking without BDDs. In R. Cleaveland, editor, *Proc. 5th International Conference on Tools and Algorithms for Construction and Analysis of Systems (TACAS'99)*, volume 1579 of *LNCS*, pages 193–207. Springer-Verlag, 1999.

4. M. Bozzano, A. Cavallo, M. Cifaldi, L. Valacca, and A. Villafiorita. Improving Safety Assessment of Complex Systems: An industrial case study. In *Proc. Formal Methods Europe (FME'03)*, 2003.

5. M. Bozzano and A. Villafiorita. Integrating Fault Tree Analysis with Event Ordering Information. In *Proc. European Safety and Reliability Conference (ESREL'03)*, 2003.

6. M. Bozzano et al. ESACS: An Integrated Methodology for Design and Safety Analysis of Complex Systems. In *Proc. European Safety and Reliability Conference (ESREL'03)*, 2003.

7. R.E. Bryant. Symbolic Boolean Manipulation with Ordered Binary Decision Diagrams. *ACM Computing Surveys*, 24(3):293–318, 1992.

8. A. Chiappini, A. Cimatti, C. Porzia, G. Rotondo, R. Sebastiani, P. Traverso, and A. Villafiorita. Formal Specification and Development of a Safety-Critical Train Management System. In M. Felici, K. Kanoun, and A. Pasquini, editors, *18th Conference on Computer Safety, Reliability and Security (SAFECOMP'99)*, volume 1698 of *LNCS*, pages 410–419. Springer-Verlag, 1999.

9. A. Cimatti. Industrial Applications of Model Checking. In F. Cassez, C. Jard, B. Rozoy, and M.D. Ryan, editors, *Modeling and Verification of Parallel Processes (MOVEP'00)*, volume 2067, pages 153–168. Springer-Verlag, 2001.

10. A. Cimatti, E.M. Clarke, E. Giunchiglia, F. Giunchiglia, M. Pistore, M. Roveri, R. Sebastiani, and A. Tacchella. NuSMV2: An OpenSource Tool for Symbolic Model Checking. In E. Brinksma and K.G. Larsen, editors, *Proc. 14th International Conference on Computer Aided Verification (CAV'02)*, LNCS, pages 359–364. Springer-Verlag, 2002.

11. A. Cimatti, E.M. Clarke, F. Giunchiglia, and M. Roveri. NuSMV: a new symbolic model checker. *International Journal on Software Tools for Technology Transfer*, 2(4):410–425, 2000.

12. A. Cimatti, P.L. Pieraccini, R. Sebastiani, P. Traverso, and A. Villafiorita. Formal Specification and Validation of a Vital Communication Protocol. In J.M. Wing, J. Woodcock, and J. Davies, editors, *World Congress on Formal Methods, (FM'99), Volume II*, volume 1709 of *LNCS*, pages 1584–1604. Springer, 1999.

13. E.M. Clarke, O. Grumberg, and D.A. Peled. *Model Checking*. MIT Press, 2000.

14. G. Cojazzi, J. M. Izquierdo, E. Meléndez, and M. S. Perea. The Reliability and Safety Assessment of Protection Systems by the Use of Dynamic Event Trees. The DYLAM-TRETA Package. In *Proc. XVIII Annual Meeting Spanish Nucl. Soc.*, 1992.

15. O. Coudert and J.C. Madre. Implicit and Incremental Computation of Primes and Essential Primes of Boolean Functions. In *Proc. 29th Design Automation Conference (DAC'98)*, pages 36–39. IEEE Computer Society Press, 1992.

16. O. Coudert and J.C. Madre. Fault Tree Analysis: 10^{20} Prime Implicants and Beyond. In *Proc. Annual Reliability and Maintainability Symposium*, 1993.

17. J. Devooght and C. Smidts. Probabilistic Dynamics; The Mathematical and Computing Problems Ahead. In T. Aldemir, N. O. Siu, A. Mosleh, P. C. Cacciabue, and B. G. Göktepe, editors, *Reliability and Safety Assessment of Dynamic Process Systems*, volume 120 of *NATO ASI Series F*, pages 85–100. Springer-Verlag, 1994.

18. P. Fenelon, J.A. McDermid, M. Nicholson, and D.J. Pumfrey. Towards Integrated Integrated Safety Analysis and Design. *Applied Computing Review*, 2(1):21–32, 1994.
19. T. A. Henzinger. The Theory of Hybrid Automata. In *Proc. 11th Annual International Symposium on Logic in Computer Science (LICS'96)*, pages 278–292. IEEE Computer Society Press, 1996.
20. T. A. Henzinger. HyTech: A Model Checker for Hybrid Systems. *Software Tools for Technology Transfer*, 1:110–122, 1997.
21. M.G. Hinchey and J.P. Bowen, editors. *Industrial Strength Formal Methods in Practice*. Formal Approaches to Computing and Information Technology. Springer-Verlag, 1999.
22. G.J. Holzmann. The Model Checker SPIN. *IEEE Transactions on Software Engineering*, 23(5):279–295, 1997.
23. K.G. Larsen, P. Pettersson, and W. Yi. UPPAAL in a Nutshell. *International Journal on Software Tools for Technology Transfer*, 1(1–2):134–152, 1997.
24. P. Liggesmeyer and M. Rothfelder. Improving System Reliability with Automatic Fault Tree Generation. In *Proc. 28th International Symposium on Fault-Tolerant Computing (FTCS'98)*, pages 90–99, Munich, Germany, 1998. IEEE Computer Society Press.
25. R. Manian, J.B. Dugan, D. Coppit, and K.J. Sullivan. Combining Various Solution Techniques for Dynamic Fault Tree Analysis of Computer Systems. In *Proc. 3rd International High-Assurance Systems Engineering Symposium (HASE'98)*, pages 21–28. IEEE Computer Society Press, 1998.
26. V.M. Manquinho, A.L. Oliveira, and J.P. Marques-Silva. Models and Algorithms for Computing Minimum-Size Prime Implicants. In *Proc. International Workshop on Boolean Problems (IWBP'98)*, 1998.
27. M. Marseguerra, E. Zio, J. Devooght, and P. E. Labeau. A concept paper on dynamic reliability via Monte Carlo simulation. *Mathematics and Computers in Simulation*, 47:371–382, 1998.
28. K.L. McMillan. *Symbolic Model Checking*. Kluwer Academic Publ., 1993.
29. I. A. Papazoglou. Markovian Reliability Analysis of Dynamic Systems. In T. Aldemir, N. O. Siu, A. Mosleh, P. C. Cacciabue, and B. G. Göktepe, editors, *Reliability and Safety Assessment of Dynamic Process Systems*, volume 120 of *NATO ASI Series F*, pages 24–43. Springer-Verlag, 1994.
30. A. Rae. Automatic Fault Tree Generation – Missile Defence System Case Study. Technical Report 00–36, Software Verification Research Centre, University of Queensland, 2000.
31. N. O. Siu. Risk Assessment for Dynamic Systems: An Overview. *Reliability Engineering ans System Safety*, 43:43–74, 1994.
32. C. Smidts and J. Devooght. Probabilistic Reactor Dynamics II. A Monte-Carlo Study of a Fast Reactor Transient. *Nuclear Science and Engineering*, 111(3):241–256, 1992.
33. K.J. Sullivan, J.B. Dugan, and D. Coppit. The Galileo Fault Tree Analysis Tool. In *Proc. 29th Annual International Symposium on Fault-Tolerant Computing (FTCS'99)*, pages 232–235. IEEE Computer Society Press, 1999.
34. W.E. Vesely, F.F. Goldberg, N.H. Roberts, and D.F. Haasl. Fault Tree Handbook. Technical Report NUREG-0492, Systems and Reliability Research Office of Nuclear Regulatory Research U.S. Nuclear Regulatory Commission, 1981.
35. J.M. Wing. A Specifier's Introduction to Formal Methods. *IEEE Computer*, 23(9):8–24, 1990.

Integrity Static Analysis of COTS/SOUP

Peter Bishop[1,2], Robin Bloomfield[1,2], Tim Clement[2], Sofia Guerra[2], and
Claire Jones[2]

CSR, City University[1]   Adelard[2]
Drysdale Building, 10 Northampton Square London EC1V 0HB, UK
{pgb,reb,tpc,aslg,ccmj}@adelard.com

Abstract. This paper describes *the integrity static analysis* approach developed
to support the justification of commercial off-the-shelf software (COTS) used in
a safety-related system. The static analysis was part of an overall software
qualification programme, which also included the work reported in our paper
presented at Safecomp 2002. Integrity static analysis focuses on unsafe
language constructs and "covert" flows, where one thread can affect the data or
control flow of another thread. The analysis addressed two main aspects: the
internal integrity of the code (especially for the more critical functions), and the
intra-component integrity, checking for covert channels. The analysis process
was supported by an aggregation of tools, combined and engineered to support
the checks done and to scale as necessary. Integrity static analysis is feasible for
industrial scale software, did not require unreasonable resources and we provide
data that illustrates its contribution to the software qualification programme.

1 Introduction

This paper describes the integrity static analysis approach that was developed to
support the justification of the use of a Commercial-Off-The-Shelf (COTS) industrial
product in a safety-related application. This paper is a continuation of the work
presented at Safecomp 2002 [1], which provides more detail to support the framework
advocated in a study we undertook for the UK HSE [2] for justifying "software of
uncertain pedigree" (SOUP). Integrity static analysis focuses on unsafe language
constructs and "covert" flows, where one thread can affect the data or control flow of
another thread. The system to be analysed was a general purpose C&I system that had
been used in control and protection applications for over 10 years and was going to be
deployed in a new safety application.

The static analysis was part of an overall software qualification programme
motivated by the need to demonstrate confidence in the safety of the system. The
primary motivation of the programme was not to find faults in the software but to
increase the confidence that it was appropriate for the new safety application. The
qualification programme involved several activities, of which static analysis was only
one. In addition to static analysis, it also included:

- Evaluation of the operating history and review of the hardware and software
  problems detected after product release and during operation.
- Evaluation of the design and lifecycle documentation.

S. Anderson et al. (Eds.): SAFECOMP 2003, LNCS 2788, pp. 63–76, 2003.

- Identification of the supporting tools used, and evaluation of their use and criticality (including compiler assessment).
- Software criticality analysis, as described in [1].
- Dynamic testing and especially stress testing.

The primary task of the static analysis was to check the structural integrity of the code and hence provide additional evidence of the software quality. This examined two main aspects:

1. The internal integrity of the code (especially for the more critical functions).
2. The intra-component integrity, checking for "covert channels" where one software component could affect another by some "back-door" method.

In [1] we described the Software Criticality Analysis (SCA) approach. The SCA identified the critical software components within the COTS software, and this information was used to prioritise the safety justification activities for the whole project. Analysis effort was concentrated where a fault would be more dangerous, i.e. the components with higher software criticality indices, as assigned by the SCA.

However, the SCA considered only overt flows in the code, via the call structure of the procedures and the way in which static variables are shared amongst them. Where many procedures share a single processor and address space, there are potentially other covert ways in which one may influence another, and evidence was needed that these covert channels were not present in practice to justify use of the SCA. This was addressed by the integrity static analysis described in this paper, and it was another objective for the approach described here.

Code description. The code comprised a real-time PLC operating system running on top of a commercial microkernel. It included device drivers for various different types of hardware, scheduling, message handling and tasking. It consisted of a large body of mixed C and assembler code totalling about 600 files, and 100k+ lines (non-comment, non-blank) of C and 20k+ lines of 68000 assembler. The C code had two components: one of about 100k lines and a second part of about 10k lines. Similarly, the assembler code had two components. However, while the two C components differ in size and style (the smaller component had been developed more recently and was more consistent in style), the two assembler components were almost identical.

The code had extensive field experience. It had been sold to users in various versions over a number of years. As expected, the code contained some very old modules that had been in use in many sites for many thousands of operating hours, and some modules which had recently been changed and which had little or no operating history. Parts of the code had been automatically translated from a different language to C. The main reason for changes had been adding new software, e.g. for new hardware, and maintenance (e.g. fixing existing bugs).

Structure of the paper. The paper is structured as follows. In Section 2 we describe the general approach taken and its rationale and the analysis process. In Section 3 we discuss the tools used, their characteristics and our evaluation of their performance. Section 4 describes the activities of the integrity static analysis, and Section 5 discusses the results of the analysis. We conclude in Section 6.

2 Integrity Static Analysis

2.1 Motivation and Objectives

The analysis approach adopted was motivated by two main factors. Firstly, the COTS system had extensive field experience, and the field data was being analysed as part of the overall qualification exercise. The field experience is likely to detect most large and obvious faults that occur during typical execution of the program. However, specific vulnerabilities of the languages used and the particular domain of application have a less frequent manifestation that could remain undetected even after many hours of field experience.

Secondly, the analyses that could be performed were constrained by feasibility, resources available and tool capabilities. For example, for a compliance analysis such as the work done with MALPAS in Sizewell B PPS [3], we would need to develop and verify a formal specification for a large body of heterogeneous C and assembler code and follow this by a proof of compliance using a tool like MALPAS. This would be very time-consuming, and some features such as the use of pointers in the COTS software make it very difficult to prove compliance. Even if a proof of compliance were achieved, analysis using MALPAS would not provide complete assurance as the analysis can only be applied to sequential, non-interruptible code. The COTS software contained many concurrent threads that could modify data in other threads and hence potentially invalidate the proof.

These resource and technical constraints led to the decision to perform an *integrity static analysis* that focuses the analysis on unsafe language constructs, and "covert" flows where one concurrent thread can affect the data or control flow of another thread. The main aspects analysed are listed in Table 1 (further details in Section 4).

Table 1. Main aspects analysed in the integrity static analysis

Unsafe Language Constructs	Covert flows
Function prototype declaration missing.	Resource sharing violations (semaphores, interrupts, etc.).
Use of "=" in conditional expressions.	Violation of program stack and register constraints (in assembler code).
No return value defined for a non-void function.	Pointer or array access outside the intended data structure.
No break between case statements.	Run-time exceptions (e.g. divide by zero).
Uninitialised variables (Possibly but not necessarily covert flows).	

The assessment of unsafe language constructs identifies potential vulnerabilities in the C code by looking for deviations from published recommendations for C programming in safety-related applications [4][5] and use of features of C identified in the ISO and ANSI standards as ill-defined or dangerous. It also includes checks for a variety of specific issues, such as the use of commonly misused constructs in C (such as "=" in conditional expressions).

Covert flow analysis examines the potential interference between different code functions. The most obvious covert mechanism in C or assembler code is the use of pointers (including their implicit use in array indexing). An incorrectly calculated pointer to a variable can give a procedure access to anywhere in the program's address space. Similarly, incorrect pointers to functions allow transfer of control to anywhere in the address space. The sharing of resources on a single processor and sharing of the stack give rise to other covert mechanisms. Static analysis was used to support an argument of the absence of these covert channels.

We observe that the existence of these covert mechanisms represents an error in the code, irrespective of its intended function, i.e. "whatever it is meant to do, it should not do this". We can thus carry out these analyses without a formal specification of the intended function, which is fortunate since this was not available. A written specification would have to be formal to support an automatic analysis, something we do not expect for legacy code, and domain experts were in short supply so code anomalies needed to be assessed where possible without the use of experts.

Where the static analysis uncovered significant faults, the code was corrected. Even within the scope of the analysis, limitations in supporting tools and manual analysis may mean that not all the faults sought will be discovered. We cannot therefore claim that the resulting code is fault free, and there is no compelling reason to repeat the analysis on the revised code provided the revisions are done carefully. However, if the static analysis detects relatively few faults, this does help to boost confidence in the code as a whole.

2.2 Analysis Process

The overall procedure used in the static analysis tasks was as follows:

- *Identification of preliminary findings.* Preliminary findings were identified as a result of tool analysis. In some cases (especially uninitialised variables), these were further processed by automatic filters that removed some of the more obvious cases where there was no real problem. These filters were designed to be conservative so any findings about which doubt remained were passed through to the next stage.
- *Provisional sentencing.* Manual inspection of the preliminary findings assigned a provisional sentence. This preliminary sentencing was based on code inspection with limited domain knowledge. Where it did not seem possible to sentence the finding without extensive domain knowledge, an open sentence was recorded together with any information that could help the sentencing.
- *Domain expert sentencing.* All the findings with a provisional sentence other than "no problem" were reported to the client. The majority was resolved and justified. A small residue of findings was accepted as genuine and sentenced for severity and technical solution.
- *Review of the final sentencing.* The analysis team reviewed the domain experts' sentencing. Clarification of the final sentence was asked for in the cases where the justification was not clear. The final decision on the solution to adopt was taken by the domain experts.

3 Tool Support

This section describes the tools used to support the analysis. The main tools are described according to their main features and use in the project, followed by a brief assessment of our experience with the tools. In addition, we name other general purpose tools used in the analysis and discuss tool evaluation issues.

3.1 PolySpace

The RTE tool from PolySpace [6] seeks to identify those points in a C program that will cause a run-time exception. These include both exceptions due to arithmetic overflow and the like, identified above as covert channels affecting control flow, and erroneous pointer and array accesses, which may result in exceptions if the address is outside physical memory. Unlike the other sources of covert flows in C tied to particular statements, run-time exceptions can arise at many points in the code and depend on the variable values at the time of program execution. This makes their analysis relatively difficult and so the use of a tool to carry out most of the work is particularly attractive.

RTE uses abstract interpretation [9] to analyse the code. It attempts to show that each potential run time exception cannot occur by establishing the possible values of the expressions involved. This requires analysis to determine the possible values of variables at each point in the code.

When the tool classifies a variable usage as not causing an exception for any value in the predicted range or as causing an exception for all possible values, the analysis is completed for that particular occurrence. However, if only some of the possible values can cause an error (marked as orange), because of the approximations, more detailed analysis of the code might sometimes show that the error could never occur. The power of the tool depends on the fraction of all possible exceptions that can be automatically labelled either red or green. PolySpace refers to this as the selectivity ratio and reported typical values on large programs in the range 85-95%.

In order to trace the flow of values through the program, PolySpace RTE requires C source for all procedures except for those in the C standard library. For the system under investigation, this meant "stubs" had to be created to represent the procedures provided by the microkernel and for assembly language routines. Tracing value flow also requires that the semantics of the code should be well defined, which implies strict adherence to the ANSI syntax. For the purpose of the analysis, the code had to be changed to be ANSI compliant, where the majority of changes involved the removal of type information from bit fields in structures.

The primary problem in using the tool was its scalability. Although PolySpace had analysed other programs of similar size, the larger component of our code defeated the analysis. This may have been a consequence of the relatively complex task structure of the system. The smaller component (10k loc) was successfully analysed, but the selectivity rate was only 50%. We also identified a number of cases where manual analysis showed the tool to be overly cautious. We understand that better results have been achieved elsewhere, and the analyser has undergone considerable development, so our experience should not be seen as indicative of what might be achieved with the current product.

3.2 CodeSurfer

CodeSurfer [7] is a Grammatech tool that analyses C programs to construct graphs showing the data and control flows through the program. The user can then explore the graphs to obtain an understanding of connections between different program parts. The analysis and exploration phases are separate, with the analysis phase producing an intermediate file containing a *system dependence graph* (SDG) that the browser program then uses to present different views of the program. Program views vary from a list of program lines where a particular variable is used, to a *slice* highlighting the program lines that can affect the value of a variable at a given point in the code (a *backward slice*) or are affected by it (a *forward slice*). CodeSurfer also provides an applications programmers' interface (API) which allows the user to write scripts that explore the program graphs and display the results in windows or write them to a file. CodeSurfer traces data flows through pointers by determining the set of variable addresses that each pointer may be assigned anywhere in the code, either directly using the & operator or indirectly by copying addresses from one pointer to another.

We originally used CodeSurfer to extract call graph information for the SCA [1]. Here CodeSurfer was used to support the analysis of variable initialisation.

CodeSurfer expects its input to be ANSI C but is less strict about full compliance than PolySpace RTE. A number of minor changes had to be made to the supplied code. The larger component of the software contained too much code for analysis as a single "project", the limit being determined by the size of the system dependence graph rather than the analysis time needed. We therefore had to divide the code into several projects, analysing them separately and combining the results in a database.

We uncovered a bug in the code flow analysis that left some of the conclusions in doubt. At the time, although Grammatech were supportive in advising us on how the tool could be used, information about potential problems was not readily available. There is now an on-line mechanism for reporting problems and suggestions, and a public list of known issues with the tool.

While CodeSurfer has some limitations, it proved to be a useful tool for static analysis. The scripting mechanism was vital for extracting information from projects, combining it to give a view of the whole system, and representing it in a form that could be used to support further analysis.

3.3 Safer C

The primary aim of the Safer C tool is to check compliance of C code with a set of almost 700 rules. These cover the dangerous constructs identified in [8], the features of C identified in the ISO and ANSI standards as ill-defined or dangerous, those MISRA C requirements and guidelines [5] that can be checked mechanically, and other potential flaws in C code that can be identified by file-by-file analysis with limited tracking of control and data flow. As well as this rule based checking, Safer C can derive some code metrics. Finally, it is possible to select a variable and display its declaration, or do data-flow analysis by highlighting its uses elsewhere in the code.

We used Safer C in the analysis of pointers and arrays, and uninitialised variables. Once it had been adopted, it made sense to make use of the information provided on the occurrence of suspicious C constructs (such as the use of "=" rather than "==" in conditional expressions), so this was added to the approach.

Our approach to pointer analysis was to use Safer C to identify all relevant pointer uses in the code and to examine each of these by hand. Array access calculations were not counted as pointer arithmetic in Safer C, but Oakwood Computing added this rule for us, and the validity of the array indexing was checked manually.

Safer C adopts the strict ANSI view that static variables are initialised when the program is loaded, so all the reported uninitialised variables are local. We covered the explicit initialisation of static variables with CodeSurfer alone. In addition, Safer C was modified by Oakwood Computing at our request to flag division by non-constant values (to confirm by code inspection that division by zero would not occur).

Safer C actually consists of a series of analysis and browsing programs that communicate via an interface that is normally controlled from the visual front end. Oakwood Computing provided documentation and guidance on this interface so that we could run the component tools on a file in batch mode from a DOS command line and extract the results from the files created. The command lines to analyse each file in our code body were generated by a `perl` script.

Safer C accepts a superset of the ANSI C language definition. However, a small number of code changes was needed to allow the tool to correctly parse and interpret the files. Because Safer C analyses each file in the source separately, we had no problems in applying it to the entire body of C code.

The tool makes no claims for the completeness of its uninitialised variable analysis, but it is not entirely clear what the limits are. When we compared the cases identified by Safer C and by our CodeSurfer analysis on real code, we found there were not many cases that Safer C had missed but CodeSurfer had found. We also ran the Safer C tool on the smaller part of the code and compared its results in detecting potentially uninitialised variables with the RTE results. The sets of possibly uninitialised variables identified by RTE and Safer C were different, but both included the few cases that were accepted as a problem and resulted in software modifications. A new version of Safer C works on a collection of files for checking global consistency (rather than only individual files, as the version used here).

3.4 Other Tools

The previous sections summarise the capabilities and uses made of the major, special purpose tools that we employed. We should not lose sight of other, less specialised tools that played a significant role in the analysis.

Assembler code made up a significant part of the code body. We needed to subject this to analysis of its pointer and stack use, but there was no special tool support available for this. Instead, we followed the strategy of mechanically marking all those lines that could cause a problem and considering each in turn to determine if it did. Assembler code is relatively simple in structure, and we used `perl` and `grep` to extract the lines of interest. This approach is less effective in C because the language is more complex (although it was used for identifying resource locking statements).

These string manipulation languages were also invaluable in translating from the different textual output forms of the various tools into tab or comma separated, columnar data files that could be read into Microsoft Access database tables. Access also filled a critical need for tool support. Many analyses involved the identification of large sets of possible problems that were then resolved by hand. This manual analysis was supported by Access. Access was also used to merge findings from different sources and in mechanical sentencing of findings. Some of the analysis was programmed using Visual Basic for Applications within Access.

3.5 Tool Evaluation Issues

Despite efforts to ensure the C analysis tools chosen would meet our requirements, we had significant difficulties in applying them to the COTS software. The most serious of these was scalability. All tools had difficulties coping with dialects of C, which were inconsistent between tools and needed code changes. All tools failed to identify some instances of anomalies they were designed to detect. A standard set of "benchmark programs" would be valuable in providing a basis for evaluation of static analysis tools prior to their use on a project. The benchmarks could cover such issues:

- limits in code size
- analysis time (and how it varies with size)
- analysis resources (memory and file storage-—and how they vary with size)
- reliability in detecting anomalies (for different types of anomaly)
- "signal to noise ratio" (how many anomalies reported with a single cause)
- likelihood of "false positives" (anomaly reported where none exists)

4 Activities of the Integrity Static Analysis

This section describes the analysis of the C and the assembler code by discussing the main activities of the integrity static analysis, their objectives and techniques.

4.1 Resource Locking

This analysis aimed at identifying all points in the code where some resource was claimed and checking that the resource was released (without excessive delay) on all possible program paths through the code. This prevents cases where a low criticality section claimed some "resource" that was never subsequently released, which could prevent a critical code section from being able to access this resource and cause a software failure. As a secondary effect, this analysis demonstrated the absence of failures due to exhaustion of resources, and some types of deadlock or livelock due to unreleased resources. The analysis process may be summarised as follows:

- Identify possible occurrences of "locking".
- For each one, search for a corresponding "unlocking" on all paths.

The domain experts identified a set of code statements as defining the locking or unlocking of a resource. We assumed that this list was complete and included all locking and unlocking statements and consequently all resource locking constructs.

In the case of C code, resource locking statements were identified using a textual search. In order to identify the corresponding unlocking statement, the neighbouring code for each "locking" code statement was examined. At this stage, we examined the branching structure of the code, as in some instances multiple unlocking is required. Further examination of the code was performed in order to validate the analysis.

In the C code, there were often many lines between disabling and enabling interrupts. This made it impossible to judge is enabling was taking place within a short space of time without domain knowledge. We provided the domain experts with a list of matched instances of interrupts disabled and enabled, ordered by the number of lines of code in the disabled section. This list could be used for further review.

For the assembler code, we began by cutting down the amount of code that needed to be reviewed by using a `perl` script. The script identified and annotated the sections of the code that contained the resource locking statements. The extraction process removed comments and irrelevant code. The remaining code displayed locking and unlocking statements, calls to subroutines, program branches and operations that affect the stack. In more complex cases there may be splits in the program flow before the resource is unlocked. In this case each flow path had to be inspected to check that the locked resource had a matching release statement. In addition any calls to routines within the locking statements needed to be checked to ensure that they did not introduce excessive delay, and that program flow always returned the calling routine.

4.2 Stack Allocation

The stack is a global resource for a task, shared by all procedures. The stack pointer is initialised and space for the stack is allocated at system start-up. It then grows and shrinks as procedures are entered and exited. If the wrong variables are addressed, a wide range of erroneous behaviours could occur. For example, if the stack of an adjacent task were overwritten, it might execute arbitrary areas of code or data in the memory with extremely unpredictable results, usually resulting in a rapid crash.

The C source code was assumed to be free of stack allocation problems as stack frames and variable references are generated by the compiler, and correct use of the stacked procedure arguments is enforced by function prototypes. The focus of the stack analysis was therefore the assembler code, although we also considered cases where C and assembler code routines interact.

The first objective of the analysis was to assess stack integrity for assembler procedures to ensure the data region accessed by the stack always remained within bounds. The second objective was to check that register integrity was preserved when C calls were made from assembler code. The C compiler guarantees that some registers' values are preserved after the call, but the remaining registers could be destroyed. The register integrity check therefore confirmed that the vulnerable registers were saved on the stack prior to a C routine call and correctly restored afterwards, or that the registers changed by the C call did not affect subsequent assembler behaviour.

In order to assess stack integrity, the assembler sources were scanned using a `perl` script to identify assembler files that contain stack manipulation instructions, i.e. those that reference the stack pointer register explicitly and implicitly. A reduced assembler program was produced (similar to that produced for the resource locking analysis) that highlighted the stack manipulation instructions. The reduced assembler was inspected to check that the stack integrity criteria were satisfied.

A similar approach was used for the register integrity analysis where assembler code calls a C routine. C routine calls were identified by a label.<procedure_name>. A simple script was used to identify the assembler files that call C routines and the code sections before and after the call. These code sections were analysed manually to check that the registers were correctly saved and restored. In cases where a C routine was called and there was no stacking of registers, the code was inspected to check if the potentially corrupted registers were relied upon after the C call. There was a difficulty in checking whether any parents in the assembler call tree were also affected. However, in some cases it could be demonstrated there were no parents (e.g. it handed control back to the microkernel).

4.3 Pointer and Array Use

In this system, all the code shares a single address space. This means that all code has access to any data structure if it generates the appropriate address. This can happen as a result of a fault in an address calculation, which results in the generation of an address beyond the data areas that the code apparently accesses. As well as pointer dereferences, this includes access to arrays determined by index calculations.

"Wild" reads will have an impact only on the procedure generating the read, and so do not affect the assessment of criticality. "Wild" writes, on the other hand, allow apparently low criticality code to affect high criticality code. Hence, when an assignment to a pointer occurs, we need to know that the procedure doing the assignment is expected to access the address to which the pointer is being assigned. This means tracing back through the calculation of the pointer value. Pointers are often initialised with the address of a variable. Subsequent pointer references are valid and so are unproblematic. The most common way to create a wild pointer is through a faulty address calculation. Manipulations to pointers also include "casting" to a pointer of a different kind. This may allow access to adjacent data storage if the resulting type is larger than the original type. Subsequent address calculations will also have a different element size that could lead to the calculation of an out of range reference even if the pointer is subsequently cast back to a correctly sized object.

The analysis of the assembler code started by the identification of the code to analyse. A `perl` script was used to parse the code into label, operator and operand fields. Once we identified the lines where calculated addresses are used for writing, we associated each with a claim that the procedure is allowed to write to the address of the instruction. We then manually propagated the claim back through the previous instructions. The propagation stops when the truth of the claim can be determined. This is typically when we have a constant address. Alternatively, we might reach a label that has no transfers of control to it from the assembler code. These labels are normally defined as external symbols that can be called from C. In principle, these need to be considered call by call to check that appropriate pointer values are being passed from the C code. In most cases, the function prototype would show that the address of a structure was being passed, and it was possible to show that the offsets from the base address being used by the assembler code lay within the structure. Provided all calls were in the scope of the function prototype (which was checked by the Safer C analysis) we could then be sure that the pointer use was safe.

The analysis of the C code was divided in two parts. The smaller part of the code (~10kloc) was supported by PolySpace RTE, and the main part by Safer C.

The PolySpace tool categorises potential sources of pointer errors in the code (and run-time errors in general) as green, orange or red, with red representing certain failure points and orange representing possible failure points. The objective of this analysis was to look in detail into the red and orange sections of code, resolve the red findings if any, and establish that the orange sections do not result in failures. The code was then examined to find a justification for the absence of error. (The process was similar for all RTE supported checks).

The analysis of the main part of the C code was supported by the Safer C tool. In addition to pointer arithmetic, the analysis also considered assignment of a structure or structure component to a pointer that might have been initially allocated to a smaller structure (widening and narrowing). In addition, we looked at all array accesses to check that the index variable was within the bounds of the array.

4.4 Uninitialised Variables

Uninitialised variables are a well-established source of software failures. Although their most direct effects are on the procedures which use them, their consequences can cross the boundaries between software of different criticalities, by causing run-time exceptions (through numeric overflow or underflow, or by generating an address that is not present in the hardware) or by direct corruption of another procedure by writing through a pointer derived using an uninitialised value.

Local variables are allocated on the stack in C and will contain whatever was previously placed in their stack frame until explicitly assigned. The C standard requires global and file static variables to be cleared by the compiler, but a null value is not necessarily appropriate and there is no guarantee that they will be re-initialised if the system is restarted, so we expect an explicit assignment to these variables too. We therefore checked that all global variables were explicitly initialised. The analysis of the smaller part of the code was supported by RTE. The main part of the code was analysed using a combination of Safer C and CodeSurfer. Both are capable of identifying uninitialised local variables, although the extent of the analysis is different in each case. Each tool led to a large number of findings, which were followed up by a range of mechanical and manual analyses to find the actual problems.

5 Analysis Results

5.1 Summary of Static Analysis Results

The integrity static analysis involved a combination of tool based and manual analysis that examined 100 000 lines of C and 20 000 lines of assembler code for typical vulnerabilities of real-time software. In this analysis, all the C code that was active (or used) in the application was analysed (around 70% of the main part and 100% of the smaller part). The unused code was justified as not interfering as a result of the SCA [1]. The analysis effort was ~3 person days/kloc.

The performance of this process is summarised in the Table 2, where "preliminary" are the findings identified by the tools, "reported" those reported to the domain experts, and "sentenced" those sentenced as other than "no problem".

Table 2. Number of finding per kilo line of code

Finding	Approx. findings per kilo line of code
Preliminary	100
Reported	10
Sentenced	1

The sentenced findings were classified as follows (in order of increasing severity):
- 70% were found to be "minor violations". These have no impact on safety or on system operation but are a violation of good practice.
- 13% were found to be "significant violations" where the code is safe in its current version (cannot cause a run-time problem), but represents a violation of good practice or a potential fault, which could be activated by maintenance.
- 17% were classified as "minor safety". All minor safety issues should be addressed through code changes in the software.

In Table 3 we compare the results of the static analysis with the other sources of evidence undertaken in the overall validation programme.

The additional analysis consisted of evaluation of lifecycle documents, evaluation of supporting tools and dynamic testing, especially stress testing. From the results, we can see that our static analysis revealed a majority of the findings (55.6% of the total findings). On the other hand, the analysis does not necessarily find the most safety-critical faults: it only found a third of the "minor safety" faults. Most of the major faults were found by field experience prior to the static analyses being undertaken.

The separate field experience analysis indicates that only a small percentage of field-detected faults are simple logic errors (i.e. detectable by static analysis of code structure). The majority of faults were due to:
- hardware/software clash (e.g. failure to modify the software for new hardware)
- timing problems (e.g. incorrect timing, incorrect time-outs, etc.)
- protocol problems (e.g. between processors interface devices, etc.)

Table 3. Findings of the overall qualification programme (percentage over total findings)

	Major safety	Minor safety	Significant violation	Minor violation	All
Integrity static analysis	0	9.5	7.1	39	55.6
Additional analysis	2.4	10	0	5.9	18.3
Field experience	14.9	11.2	0	0	26.1
Total	17.3	30.7	7.1	44.9	100

Generally speaking these analyses identified different classes of faults from those found by our static analysis, and these fault classes were the ones that resulted in significant failures. This is not surprising, as static analysis will contain a significant proportion of "lurking" problems that might not cause any failure until the code is modified. Furthermore, static analysis came after these field experience faults had been found, so they had been corrected by the time static analysis took place.

5.2 Effects of Faults on Reliability and Safety

While no fault is desirable, faults may be tolerable if there is a low probability of occurrence. Since the software has been subjected to at least 3×10^6 hours of operation, the remaining faults will tend to have a low (or zero) probability of activation. There is a theory for estimating the worst case MTTF given an estimate of residual faults (N) and operating time (T) [10]: MTTF>eT/N, where e is the exponential constant. Under the most optimistic assumptions (perfect fault reporting and correction) about 90 residual safety-related faults and 3×10^6 hours of operation would give a worst case estimate for the MTTF for the software of around 10^5 hours for dangerous failures. If the shutdown process has to operate for 100 hours with a probability of failure during that interval of 10^{-3} the MTTF should be 10^5 hours (or around 10 years). The reliability could be worse if the software had been subjected to significant upgrades and extensions, rather than simple bug fixes.

Field data was also analysed to demonstrate that all modules used in the safety-related application are stable and have accumulated sufficient operating experience without modification or bug-fixes. This gives a direct indication of time to failure for the selected modules. Both analyses give some confidence that the MTTF for the most safety-critical functions will exceed the target level of 10^5 hours.

6 Conclusion

This paper described the static analysis process used to assess the integrity of the source code of a COTS system (comprising 100k lines of C and 20k of assembler). This provided additional evidence of the software quality as a contribution to the overall validation programme for the COTS system. The analysis addressed the internal integrity of the code and intra-component integrity.

Integrity static analysis is feasible for industrial scale software and even for heterogeneous code, this type of analysis does not require unreasonable resources. However, the analysis process needs to be supported by tools to automate the analyses and to manage, classify and track the analysis findings.

The analysis made a major contribution to the safety justification of the COTS system—finding over half the faults detected in the qualification programme for the software. It also showed that most faults had little impact on safe operation—hence increasing confidence that the software was suitable for a safety related application.

All the C analysis tools had limitations, such as limits to the amount of code that could be analysed, inability to analyse some dialects of C and inability to detect some code anomalies. The use of diverse tools for the same analysis boosts confidence in the results. While it was possible to dismiss some anomalies reported by the tools automatically, a combination of automatic and manual analysis is needed to resolve most of the reported anomalies. Most of the manual analysis can be done without domain knowledge, just by intelligent code reading. However, the final resolution requires domain expertise.

We propose that static analysis has an important role to play within an approach to the assurance of COTS products. In the case where full verification of the complete system is not mandatory, static analysis can be used to justify the partitioning of the system, specialising on a small class of faults or on certain behaviours. Implementing this strategy will need to take into account the pragmatic issues of scale, complexity and tool availability highlighted in this paper. The focus of the strategy should be driven by both the capabilities of the emerging technology—the static analysis landscape is developing rapidly—and by the need to focus on classes of faults that are important in practice and that affect real-time behaviour. The selection of tools to support the analysis should be supported by common benchmarks for static analysis.

References

[1]   PG Bishop, RE Bloomfield, TP Clement, S Guerra. "*Software Criticality Analysis of COTS/SOUP*". In S.Anderson et al. (Eds.), SAFECOMP 2002, LNCS 2434, 2002.

[2]   PG Bishop, RE Bloomfield, PKD Froome. *Justifying the use of software of uncertain pedigree (SOUP) in safety-related applications*. Report No: CRR336 HSE Books 2001 ISBN 0 7176 2010 7, http://www.hse.gov.uk/research/crr_pdf/2001/crr01336.pdf.

[3]   NJ Ward. "The Rigorous Retrospective Static Analysis of the Sizewell 'B' Primary Protection System Software". In *Proceedings of the 12th International Conference on Computer Safety, Reliability and Security, Safecomp 93*. October 1993.

[4]   S Morton. "A Symptom of the Cure: Safer Language Subsets and Safe-Code Development". MISRA Guidelines Forum, October 2001.

[5]   *Guidelines for the use of the C language in vehicle based software*. MISRA, 1998.

[6]   *PolySpace Technologies*, http://www.polyspace.com/.

[7]   *CodeSurfer user guide and technical reference*. Version 1.0, Grammatech, 1999.

[8]   L Hatton, *Safer C*. McGraw Hill, 1995.

[9]   P Cousot , R Cousot. "*Abstract Interpretation: A Unified Lattice Model for Static Analysis of Programs by construction or approximation of fixpoints*". POPL77, ACM Press, 1977.

[10] PG Bishop, RE Bloomfield, "A Conservative Theory for Long-Term Reliability Growth Prediction" *IEEE Trans. Reliability*, vol. 45, No 4, Dec 1996.

Safety Lifecycle for Developing Safety Critical Artificial Neural Networks

Zeshan Kurd and Tim Kelly

Department of Computer Science
University of York, York, YO10 5DD, UK.
{zeshan.kurd, tim.kelly}@cs.york.ac.uk

Abstract. Artificial neural networks are employed in many areas of industry such as medicine and defence. There are many techniques that aim to improve the performance of neural networks for safety-critical systems. However, there is a complete absence of analytical certification methods for neural network paradigms. Consequently, their role in safety-critical applications, if any, is typically restricted to advisory systems. It is therefore desirable to enable neural networks for highly-dependable roles. Existing safety lifecycles for neural networks do not focus on suitable safety processes for analytical arguments. This paper presents a safety lifecycle for artificial neural networks. The lifecycle focuses on managing behaviour represented by neural networks and to provide acceptable forms of safety assurance. A suitable neural network model is outlined and is based upon representing knowledge in symbolic form. Requirements for safety processes similar to those used for conventional systems are also established. Although developed specifically for decision theory applications, the safety lifecycle could apply to a wide range of application domains.

1 Introduction

Typical uses of ANNs (Artificial Neural Networks) in safety-critical systems include areas such as industrial process and control, medical systems and defence. An extensive review of ANN use in safety-related applications has been provided by a U.K. HSE (Health & Safety Executive) report [1]. However, ANNs in these safety systems have been restricted to advisory roles with the continued absence of safety arguments.

There are many techniques for typical neural networks [2, 3] which aim to improve generalisation performance. However, these performance-related techniques do not provide acceptable forms of safety arguments. Any proposed ANN model must allow for trade-offs between performance and safety. Attributes or features of ANN models must satisfy safety arguments whilst ensuring that measures incorporated do not diminish the advantages associated with ANNs.

A promising approach outlined in section 2 is to utilise 'hybrid' neural networks. The term 'hybrid' in this case, refers to a neural network representing knowledge in symbolic form. This knowledge is represented by the internal structure of the ANN (within its weights, links and neurons). This has greater potential for 'transparency' or white-box style analysis. White-box analysis can potentially result in strong argu-

S. Anderson et al. (Eds.): SAFECOMP 2003, LNCS 2788, pp. 77–91, 2003.

ments about the knowledge and perhaps behaviour represented by the network. Overcoming the black-box restriction will provide strong safety arguments not only about 'what it can do' but also about 'what it cannot do'.

Developing such 'hybrid' neural networks will involve frameworks unlike conventional software development. This is primarily because of the learning characteristics of ANNs. Learning helps the network determine desired behaviour as opposed to some complete specification determined at the initial stage of development. Along with its unique development lifecycle, safety processes will need to fit around ANN development. A safety lifecycle is established in section 3 which illustrates where safety processes are performed during development. Typical processes required for the chosen ANN model may need to be adapted to deal with knowledge in symbolic forms. Although a fully defined ANN model is beyond the scope of the paper, the general concept of 'hybrid' ANNs will be considered. Certification of the ANN model can then be presented in the form of a safety case. Section 4 highlights the nature of potential safety arguments and how they resemble those associated with conventional software development. Finally, section 5 emphasises the challenge of maintaining feasibility of the ANN model by considering the performance vs. safety trade-off.

2   A Suitable ANN Model for Safety

Any potential safety case must overcome problems associated with classic neural networks i.e. multi-layered perceptrons. Some typical problems may be concerned with determining ANN structure and topology. For example, internal structure of ANNs may influence the generalisation and learning performance [4]. Another problem lies in determining training and test sets. These sets must represent the desired function using a limited number of samples. Dealing with noise during training is also problematic. Given these problems with training, it is essential to ensure that the network does not deviate from the required target function. Another issue related to the learning or training process is the 'forgetting' of previously learnt samples [5]. This can lead to poor generalisation and long training times [5]. Other problems during training may result in learning settling in local instead of a global minimum [5]. This will result in poor performance or sub-optimal solutions. Another typical problem encountered during ANN training is deciding upon appropriate stopping points for the training process (such as the total number of training samples). Although this could be aided by cross-validation [6], it relies heavily on test sets to provide an accurate representation of the desired function.

A key problem associated with typical ANNs is the inability to perform white-box style analysis over the behaviour represented by the ANN. Consequently, an overall error over some test set is often described as the generalisation performance [5]. Moreover, there is a lack of explanation mechanisms of how each ANN output is produced. This inability to analyse the internal behaviour also makes it difficult to identify and control potential 'hazards' associated with the ANN. This results in the ANN unable to provide analytic arguments for the satisfaction of safety requirements.

2.1 Requirements for Suitable ANN Model

Analytical and test arguments are needed for any proposed ANN model. To support analytical arguments, there must be means to analyse the behaviour using the internal structure (in terms of weights and neurons) of ANNs. Some common approaches to analysing the behaviour of ANNs include:

- **Pedagogical Approach**: This uses a black-box style analysis to build a behavioural description of the ANN. One particular approach is known as sensitivity analysis [7] and investigates the effects perturbing inputs have on outputs.
- **Decomposition Approach**: This is a white-box style analysis which focuses on the internal structure of the ANN to determine a behavioural description. This requires that knowledge about the problem (gathered by the ANN) is represented in a highly structured form. Typical examples for eliciting knowledge are rule extraction algorithms [8-10]. Extraction algorithms can help determine knowledge or behaviour represented by the ANN. This knowledge may be in terms of symbolic information (such as *if-then* rules).

The decomposition approach is particularly attractive for safety applications. This provides the required white-box style analysis to allow a more detailed and comprehensive view of the ANN. A particular type of ANN model that attempts to utilise this approach combines symbolic knowledge with neural learning paradigms. A common view is that symbolic approaches focus on producing discrete combinations of features (such as rules) [9]. On the other hand, the neural approach adjusts continuous, non-linear weighting of their inputs to perform learning. By combining symbolic and neural paradigms, learning can be exploited to refine or modify symbolic knowledge. Figure 1 illustrates a typical model for combining symbolic knowledge with neural (connectionist) learning.

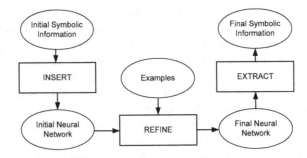

Fig. 1. Framework for combining symbolic and neural learning taken from [9]

The term 'hybrid' is associated with combining symbolic knowledge with neural learning. There are three main stages associated with the framework for 'hybrid' ANNs. The first stage involves gathering initial symbolic information. This initial information is prior knowledge known about the solution and may be in the form of rules. This initial knowledge is important since it will help neural learning achieve desired performance using less time resources [11]. The initial rule set is then 'inserted' into a neural network structure. This can be achieved through rule-to-network algorithms [9] which map parts of each rule into the internal structure of the ANN (such as weights and neurons).

Once the ANN has represented all initial symbolic information the next stage involves refinement or learning. Refinement uses training samples to modify or add new knowledge to the initial symbolic information. This is the key motivation for adopting the neural learning concept. Training data may be simulated or consist of data sampling gathered from real-world interaction. Typical algorithms used for the learning process may involve variations of back-propagation algorithms [9]. During refinement or learning, the topological structure of the ANN may require adaptation to accommodate changes in the initial rule set.

Once learning is complete, the final stage involves eliciting and evaluating symbolic knowledge from the final ANN. This process attempts to determine all changes or additions made to the initial symbolic information. There is an abundance of rule extraction algorithms [8] to elicit all symbolic knowledge stored in the network. Once the final symbolic information has been determined these rules may be evaluated and potentially used in expert systems [12]. 'Hybrid' ANNs have been demonstrated to enable quicker learning and overall better generalisation performance [9, 12] for a wide range of problems.

'Hybrid' ANNs present a useful tool for theory-refinement problems. They exploit the neural learning paradigm widely associated with machine learning in artificial intelligence. It also uses symbolic information to provide a highly structured representation of the function represented by the network. Given the nature of symbolic knowledge, possible applications are associated with decision theory domains. 'Hybrid' ANNs are well established models [8, 13] and many have been used in safety-related problems [12, 14]. Medical diagnosis [15] is one example of how 'hybrid' ANNs can be applied to real world problems. In this particular example a set of initial rules are derived through theoretical knowledge and practical experiences (this may involve representing causes of a particular disease). These rules are then translated into a neural network and *global* learning is performed. That is, the ANN can adapt its knowledge to variations of the data domain. This is performed by learning new knowledge (through input-output samples) leading to possible modification of the architecture or topology of the ANN. The learning process will produce a new set of knowledge (with the aim of improving diagnosis of a particular disease).

Along with learning, the generalisation capability can also be preserved with the 'hybrid' ANN. Conventional ANNs generalise outputs given inputs based upon the activations that occur within its architecture. Very little is known how certain outputs were produced. On the other hand, the 'hybrid' ANN has the advantage of representing some analysable form of knowledge. It is this knowledge that is the 'output' of the network which can be utilised for generalisation.

For safety-critical applications, 'hybrid' ANNs encompass the potential to overcome many problems associated with typical ANNs. Given the decomposition-style approach offered by rule extraction algorithms, techniques devised for black-box representations will not be relied upon. Analytical arguments about the solution provided by the 'hybrid' ANN may be based upon symbolic information. This enables a higher level of abstraction as opposed to dealing with low-level representation such as weights, links and neurons. For example, rather than using an overall output error (produced over some test set), the network can be analysed in terms of the rules it embodies. Consequently, this provides extra comprehensibility for analytical processes. However, analytical processes have to overcome some of the potential problems associated with symbolic information. One typical problem is associated with managing large sets of rules. When evaluating symbolic knowledge, the quantity of rules may make it hard to identify and mitigate potential 'hazards'. Work is currently on-going for a complete definition of the 'hybrid' ANN that is suitable for safety-critical applications.

2.2 Systems Development Lifecycle

There are very few existing ANN development lifecycles for safety-related applications [3, 4]. One particular lifecycle [4] is directly intended for safety-critical applications however there are several problems associated with its approach. One problem is that it relies on determining the specification and behaviour at the initial phase of development. This is not practical since the prime motivation for ANN learning is to determine its behaviour given very limited initial data. Another problem is that it emphasises control over non-functional properties. Typical examples of non-functional properties include usage of spatial or temporal resources. Instead, focus should be upon constraining functional properties such as learning or the behaviour of the ANN. Documenting each development phase (process-based arguments) are generally regarded as weak arguments for providing assurance for conventional software [16]. However, the lifecycle [4] emphasises process-based arguments such as 'Data Analysis Document' that represents all training samples used during training. Other problems associated with the lifecycle involve iterating training without clear analytical tools to determine performance or safety. The iteration also attempts to vary network topologies, input neurons and other factors. This is no clear indication of how these ANN variations will contribute to safety or performance. Instead, an appropriate ANN model should be determined which will allow time-efficient training, acceptable performance and provide suitable safety assurance.

There is another ANN development lifecycle model for safety-critical applications [3]. This lifecycle attempts to overcome several problems associated with the above model. The lifecycle acknowledges that a precise functional specification is not possible at the initial stages of development. It also emphasises that the role of data (training and test samples) requires extra tasks such as data gathering and modelling. The undefined iteration during training is also tackled.

However, the lifecycle [3] does not define a suitable ANN model for overcoming the above problems. It relies on using typical ANN models resulting in black-box analytical techniques (using network error over test sets as an indication of performance and safety). Consequently, it inherits many of the problems associated with typical ANNs. Suitable safety processes that attempt to identify and mitigate hazards are also neglected. This results in poor product-based arguments about the safety (existence of potential hazards) of the ANN.

To overcome limitations associated with current approaches, Figure 2 presents a lifecycle for developing 'hybrid' neural networks. This lifecycle ensures that the learning mechanism is preserved whilst allowing analysis and control over the network (greater potential for safety assurance).

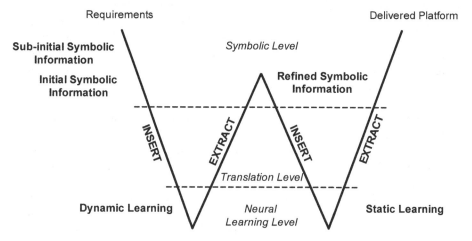

Fig. 2. Development Lifecycle for Hybrid Neural Networks

The development lifecycle is divided into three main levels starting from a symbolic representation, down to a 'hybrid' ANN. Levels in the lifecycle are as follows:

1. **Symbolic Level:** This level is associated only with symbolic information. It is separated from the neural learning paradigm and deals with analysis in terms of symbolic knowledge. Typical examples may include the gathering and processing of initial knowledge. Other uses may involve evaluating extracted knowledge gathered post-learning.
2. **Translation Level:** This is where symbolic knowledge and neural architectures are combined or separated. This is achieved though processes such as rule insertion [9] or extraction algorithms [8]. All transitions from the symbolic level to neural learning level involve rule insertion algorithms. All transitions from the neural learning level to symbolic involve rule extraction algorithms.
3. **Neural Learning Level:** This level uses neural learning to modify and refine initial symbolic knowledge. Neural learning is achieved by using specific training samples along with suitable learning algorithms [9, 12, 17].

The development of 'hybrid' ANNs initially starts by determining requirements. These requirements are a representation of the problem to be solved possibly in the form of informal descriptions. The intention of conventional software development is to have a complete set of requirements. On the other hand the initial requirements for 'hybrid' ANNs are intentionally incomplete (hence the use of learning). 'Incompleteness' of these requirements could be caused by insufficient data or a result of noise. A common factor for 'incompleteness' is if the expert doesn't have enough knowledge about the problem as would be the case in typical real-world applications. Consequently, the requirements do not represent the entire target function or solution. Requirements then need to be translated into symbolic knowledge by experts or those involved in development. A set of rules are devised and are labelled as 'sub-initial' knowledge. These rules are then converted into a form compatible for incorporation into the ANN structure [9] resulting in 'initial' symbolic knowledge. This knowledge is then 'inserted' into the ANN model using suitable rules-to-network algorithms [9]. Once 'inserted', the neural learning commences (no longer with random initial weights). Refinement and modification of the initial knowledge occurs using a two-tier learning model:

1. **Dynamic Learning:** This uses specific learning algorithms to refine the initial knowledge. It uses some training set and attempts to reduce error by adding or removing rules. This may result in architectural (topological) changes to the network [15] hence the term 'dynamic'. For example, requiring additional hidden units for adding new rules.
2. **Static Learning:** This phase is concerned with refining and modifying the set of rules represented in the network (by adjusting ANN link weights). No architectural or topological changes are allowed at this stage. Instead, the learning algorithm concentrates on changing elements of each rule (such as adding and removing antecedents). Although the ANN system states varies over time (like dynamical systems), this phase is considered 'static' since only network weights are adjusted. This learning phase can be used in critical roles and interfaced with real-time data.

Learning takes place in two distinct phases. This will be shown to be particularly advantageous in producing both analytical and test-based safety arguments. The model attempts to preserve the learning ability, which is a major contributor to its performance. The lifecycle is unlike conventional software as the ANN works towards a specification (or desired function) rather than from it. Finally, the network can be utilised in an area of expertise determined by its symbolic knowledge.

3   Using Adapted Safety Processes

Software can be regarded as safety-critical if it directly or indirectly contributes to the occurrence of a hazardous system state ("system hazard") [18]. A hazard is a situation, which is potentially dangerous to man, society or the environment [18]. When developing safety-critical software, there are a set of requirements which must be enforced. These requirements are formally defined in a safety standard such as Defence Standard 00-55 [19]. One of the main tools for determining requirements is the use of a safety case to encapsulate all safety arguments for the software. A safety case is defined in Defence Standard 00-55 [19] as:

"The software safety case shall present a well-organised and reasoned justification based on objective evidence, that the software does or will satisfy the safety aspects of the Statement of Technical Requirements and the Software Requirements specification."

Some of the main components in formulating safety requirements are hazard analysis and mitigation. Function Failure Analysis (FFA) [20] is a predictive technique to identify and refine safety requirements. It focuses upon system functions and deals with analysing effects of failures to provide a function, incorrect function outputs and determining actions to improve design. Another technique is Software Hazard and Operability Study (SHAZOP) [21] which uses 'guide words' for qualitative analysis to identify hazards not previously considered. It attempts to analyse all variations of the system based on these guide words and can uncover causes, consequences, indications and recommendations for particular identified hazards.

Arguing the satisfaction of the safety requirements is divided into two types of arguments. These two types are analytical and test-based arguments which are defined in a widely accepted Defence Standard 00-55 [19]. Arguments from testing (such as white-box or black-box) can be generated more easily than analytical arguments for typical ANNs.

There are several safety processes performed during the lifecycle of safety-critical systems e.g. ARP 4754/4761 [20]. Preliminary Hazard Identification (PHI) is the first step in the lifecycle, it forms the backbone of all following processes. It is a predictive style technique and aims to identify, manage and control all potential hazards in the proposed system. Risk Analysis and Functional Hazard Analysis (FHA) analyses the severity and probability of potential accidents for each identified hazard. FHA can be considered as confirmatory or evaluative analysis. Preliminary System Safety Assessment (PSSA) [20] ensures that the proposed design will refine and adhere to safety requirements and will help guide the design process. System Safety Analysis (SSA) demonstrates through evidence that safety requirements have been met. It uses inductive and deductive techniques to examine the completed design and implementation. Finally, the Safety Case [22] generated throughout development delivers a comprehensible and defensible argument that the system is acceptably safe to use in a given context. The intentions of these principles (safety processes) are widely accepted. The challenge is to find how these safety processes can support the ANN in safety-critical applications.

3.1 Safety Development Lifecycle

With the unique development lifecycle of 'hybrid' ANNs, it is not obvious where each safety process should be initiated. Existing safety processes need to be adapted to deal with symbolic representation. Therefore, adapted safety processes are heavily influenced by the ANN model and application domain. For example, control theory applications may result in ANNs representing control algorithms. Safety processes must then deal with this level of detail as opposed to individual weights and neurons. This is achieved by providing suitable translation algorithms [8, 9].

The aim of the lifecycle is to gather initial knowledge about the problem and to utilise a two-tier learning process. Certification must be produced post-dynamic learning and will argue how potential hazards have been identified, controlled and mitigated. The safety lifecycle also emphasises how static learning can be performed post-certification, allowing future changes to the symbolic representation. A safety lifecycle for the hybrid ANN is illustrated in Figure 3. Several safety processes have been superimposed on the development lifecycle.

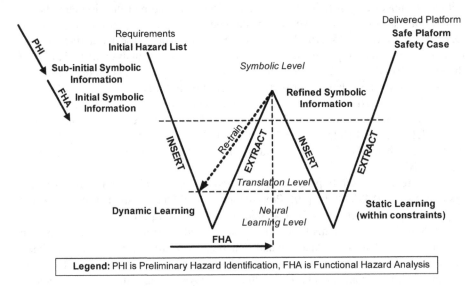

Fig. 3. Safety Lifecycle for Hybrid Neural Networks

Although detailed description of how each adapted safety process is beyond the scope of this paper, the aims and objectives for each process is highlighted. Initially, an overall description of the ANN role is determined. This process has been described in the previous section as 'requirements' and involves black-box descriptions of the role.

Preliminary Hazard Identification (PHI) deals with initial symbolic knowledge and is used to determine the initial conditions of the network. The role of this process is the initial consideration of possible system level hazards (using a black-box approach). This results in a set of rules partially fulfilling the desired function. Typical characteristics of this process must include:

1. Ability to represent knowledge in rule form.
2. Generate possible system level hazards and help understand system context.
3. Ability to remove, add, refine rules or parts of it.
4. The process must generate a set of rules suitable for translation into the ANN model.

This process may use knowledge gathered from domain experts, empirical data or any other source. It is important that PHI is performed at this stage so that any future refinements can be analysed in relation to the initial rules. This may also help relieve the workload imposed on hazard analysis which is performed at a later stage. Using the initial knowledge, PHI generates an initial set of rules partially describing the desired function.

The next phase is to perform a predictive-style technique using FHA. This is involved in the assessment of the rule set by using perturbation-style analysis. FHA presents a systematic white-box technique that may help identify rules that do not represent the desired function. The FHA approach may also help understand how symbolic knowledge could lead to potential hazards. Furthermore, FHA may also help build an understanding for the importance of certain rules. During the FHA safety process, assertions of new rules may be made to help prevent specific hazards. Identifying criticality of certain rules may result in 'targeted' training for the next phase. For example, specific training sets may be devised to focus on certain rules or areas of concern. Full details of this safety process are beyond the scope of this paper.

Once the initial conditions of the ANN have been set, safety processes must identify, control and mitigate potential hazards during learning. All other safety processes will be performed during dynamic learning and before the static learning phase.

After the dynamic learning phase has learned some training set (by reaching some error threshold), FHA is performed again. However this time, the approach of FHA is not only predictive but also evaluative. FHA is performed over the entire set of rules represented by the network. These can be elicited using rule extraction algorithms by exploiting decomposition approaches. FHA initially uses an evaluative approach by analysing the rule set and determines the existence of potential hazards. During analysis the following events may occur:

1. **Initiating further training** – Present a new training set that reflects desired direction of learning. This can be seen as guiding the design process using specific training sets. Training samples may be based upon particular areas of concern determined by critical or important rules. This iteration of re-training and re-analysing (using FHA) will contribute to the performance of the system (entire rule set). This iteration will end based upon performance results determined by FHA (by analysing the rule set).
2. **Modify rule set** – Manual assertions or modifications may be made to mitigate or control identified hazards.

It is important to remember that the function (or rule set represented by the ANN) may only partially satisfy the desired function. This is a realistic assumption since it may be infeasible to determine whether totality of the desired function has been achieved (supporting the motivation of neural learning). Certification can be provided based upon this 'partial-but-safe' approach. Although the approach so far deals with mitigating hazards associated with the rule set and improving performance, it must also control future learning.

Once sufficient performance has been gained (by the rule set) the predictive role of FHA is initiated. This attempts to utilise an exploratory safety analysis technique to identify how rules may be refined during static learning. FHA is based upon the pre-consideration of possible adaptation of rules. This may involve analysing the rule set and determining how potential hazards may be introduced if parts of rules are modified. Measures to mitigate potential hazards must then be incorporated into the network by translating rule conditions into network weights. For example, a typical condition may state that a particular antecedent of a rule may not be removed during static learning. Violating such rule conditions would result in a potentially hazardous state. Future paths of learning are therefore constrained and will provide assurance about future states of the ANN. This enables static learning to be performed without the need for further safety assurance. It is not feasible to allow dynamic learning post-certification. A prime reason for this is that predictive or evaluative analysis for identifying possible hazards is not feasible if the rule set is modified (by adding new rules) during deployment. Some of the requirements for the FHA are as follows:

1. The initial symbolic information may be incomplete or may lead to potential hazards. It is common for neural network problems to suffer from incomplete or sparse initial data. Analytical processes must also be able manage symbolic knowledge for predictive or evaluative analysis.
2. Perturbation-style analysis must attempt to discover potential hazards (in the rule set) possibly utilising a HAZOP-style [21] analysis. Furthermore, constraints must be derived for static learning (by translating conditions for rules into weights and links). This must attempt to foresee possible evolutionary states and to specify what can or can't be performed. This requires an extra amount of domain knowledge and is applicable for applications that can provide it.
3. The ability to determine whether additional rules will create new hazards or not and if they invalidate or conflict with existing rules. In other words, there must be a clear understanding about non-monotonic behaviour.

Finally, certification of the ANN will be provided using a safety case. This will be derived from the last evaluation performed by FHA and will rely on the completeness of constraints. Each safety process will be heavily involved in providing solutions or evidence for potential safety arguments. FHA will also demonstrate how all hazards in the symbolic representation have been mitigated. Safety processes associated with the 'hybrid' ANN model, exploit the translation level to achieve transparency (in terms of the rules represented by the network). This enables FHA to provide assurance that in operation (despite permitting static learning), constraints maintain safety for any future learning. Constraints over learning allow certification to be finalised before the static learning phase begins. Once certification is completed, the ANN model can then be deployed. The 'hybrid' ANN model and safety lifecycle demonstrates how safety can be assured particularly when used for theory-refinement applications. Consequently, the knowledge represented by the network can be used for highly-dependable roles in safety-critical applications.

4 Potential Safety Arguments

The safety case is a living document that is developed and maintained throughout the systems lifecycle. This contributes to safety by justifying modifications and refinements that are made during neural learning. Various attributes associated with 'hybrid' ANN development (such as the translation level), contribute to safety case arguments. Although providing a complete safety case is beyond the scope of this paper, the main goals to overcome are hazard identification and mitigation. When considering ANNs, the most problematic area is learning, since it has the ability to change itself (this can also be considered as changing its own implementation). The strategy is to exploit the two-tier learning process so that safety arguments about future refinement can be provided for smaller changes.

Preliminary Hazard Identification is the backbone for arguments related to the functional behaviour. It provides assurance that potential hazards in the initial set of rules have been identified. Since these rules will undergo changes, this process may not contribute as evidence but aid later hazard analysis processes. The ANN model facilitates this process by representing knowledge in the form of rules.

Hazard analysis will provide the strongest form of safety arguments. The arguments are mainly related to guiding training, ensuring there are no faults that could lead to potential hazards and to define all possible safe refinement. In terms of hazard identification, rule extraction algorithms will provide solutions for determining the rules represented by the network. Hazard analysis will provide assurance that all hazards have been identified (within the rule set) and measures have been taken to mitigate them. Learning algorithms and focussed training can provide assurance about the performance or the completeness of the rule set. Finally, a set of controls or constraints determined by the hazard analysis process will provide assurance for all paths during static learning. These constraints over the ANN can be determined at high-level (symbolic level) and incorporated using translation algorithms. This has the potential to provide safety assurance about the constraints in terms of meaningful representations.

It is evident for the presented lifecycle that all adapted safety processes contribute to safety argument solutions. For conventional software development it is argued that emphasis should be on product-based arguments rather than demonstrating that certain processes have been performed (and assuming that the final software or system is safe based on this fact) [16]. Conventional software safety emphasises producing evidence-based frameworks instead of blindly performing regulatory process-based approaches. This requires deriving product or process arguments that have a clear affect on mitigating or controlling hazards. The safety lifecycle presented in this paper focuses on producing product-based safety arguments. This is achieved by exploiting a suitable ANN model and utilising adapted safety processes.

5 Feasibility Issues: Performance vs. Safety Trade-Off

The aim is to maintain feasibility by providing satisfactory performance whilst generating acceptable safety assurance. Certain attributes of the model may need to be limited or constrained so that particular safety arguments are possible. Typical examples may include permissible learning during development but not whilst deployed. This may provide safety arguments about the behaviour of the network without invalidating them with future changes to implementation. But, this could lead to over-constraining the performance of ANNs. One particular type of ANN model which demonstrates poor safety assurance employs diversity [2]. This is an ensemble of ANNs where each is devised by different methods to encapsulate as much of the target function as possible. Results demonstrate improvement in generalisation performance over some test set but lack in the ability to analyse and determine the function performed by each member of the ensemble. The safety lifecycle defined in this paper attempts to generate acceptable safety arguments providing assurance comparable to that achieved with conventional software.

Some of the typical motivations for using neural networks involve dealing with problems whose complete algorithmic specification is not possible during initial stages of development (hence the use of learning). They can also deal with large input spaces and generalise outputs given novel inputs.

The hybrid ANN outlined in this paper effectively exploits learning by working towards a solution using the two-tier learning model. The model can be considered for theory refinement applications where the problem directly drives the network (through training samples) to arrive at a solution. The ANN model also presents the opportunity to not only analyse but also control the behaviour or learning of the network. The two-tier learning process may provide safety assurance but it limits learning during deployment by not allowing topological changes (adding or removing rules).

The hybrid ANN can also represent rules in a structured way allowing white-box style analysis. Consequently, rather than managing weights and neurons, analysis can take place at a higher and more comprehensible level (symbolic information). However, some of the limitations of the proposed system are that rules may have restrictions (e.g. rules must be non-recursive) [13]. Some typical problems associated with knowledge reasoning may include managing many rules and predicting consequences for changes made to rules. The knowledge or rules are also crisp so no approximate answers are presented. This however, may be a desirable property for safety-critical systems where certainty plays a crucial role for highly dependable outputs.

6 Conclusions

To justify the use of ANNs within safety critical applications will require the development of a safety case. For high-criticality applications, this safety case will require arguments of correct behaviour based both upon analysis and test. Previous approaches to justifying ANNs have focussed predominantly on (test-based) arguments of high performance.

In this paper we present the 'hybrid' ANN as a potential model and outlined a suitable development lifecycle. We then present a safety lifecycle, which emphasises the need for adapting software safety processes for the chosen ANN model. Detailed analysis of the ANN model, safety processes and potential supporting arguments are beyond the scope of this paper. We however, discussed the benefits of performing white-box style analysis over the 'hybrid ANN' and the types of potential safety arguments that can be generated. The requirements and aims of adapted safety processes were also highlighted including the necessity to constrain neural learning and other factors. The development and safety lifecycles contribute to suitable safety arguments and allow neural networks for highly dependable roles.

References

1. Lisboa, P., Industrial use of safety-related artificial neural networks. Health & Safety Executive 327, (2001).
2. Sharkey, A.J.C. and N.E. Sharkey, Combining Diverse Neural Nets, in Computer Science, University of Sheffield: Sheffield, UK (1997).
3. Nabney, I., et al., Practical Assessment of Neural Network Applications, Aston University & Lloyd's Register: UK (2000).
4. Rodvold, D.M. A Software Development Process Model for Artificial Neural Networks in Critical Applications. in Proceedings of the 1999 International Conference on Neural Networks (IJCNN'99). Washington D.C. (July 1999)
5. Principe, J.C., N.R. Euliano, and W.C. Lefebvre, Neural and Adaptive Systems: Fundamentals Through Simulations: John Wiley & Sons (2000).
6. Kearns, M., A Bound on the Error of Cross Validation Using the Approximation and Estimation Rates, with Consequences for the Training-Test Split, AT&T Bell Laboratories.
7. Kilimasaukas, C.C., Neural nets tell why. Dr Dobbs's, (April 1991) 16–24.
8. Andrews, R., J. Diederich, and A. Tickle, A survey and critique of techniques for extracting rules from trained artificial neural networks, Neurocomputing Research Centre, Queensland University of Technology (1995).
9. Shavlik, J.W., A Framework for Combining Symbolic and Neural Learning, Computer Science Department, University of Wisconsin: Madison (1992).
10. Cristea, A., P. Cristea, and T. Okamoto, Neural Network Knowledge Extraction. Série Électrotechnique et Énergétique. 42(4) (1998) 477–491.
11. Gemen, S., E. Bienenstock, and R. Doursat, Neural Networks and the Bias/Variance Dilemma. Neural Computation. 4 (1992) 1–58.
12. Taha, I. and J. Ghosh, A Hybrid Intelligent Architecture and Its Application to Water Reservoir Control, in Department of Electrical and Computer Engineering, University of Texas: Austin, TX (1995).
13. Wermter, S. and R. Sun, Hybrid Neural Systems, New York: Springer (January 2000).
14. Sordo, M., H. Buxton, and D. Watson, A Hybrid Approach to Breast Cancer Diagnosis, in School of Cognitive and Computing Sciences, University of Sussex: Falmer, Brighton (2001).
15. Osorio, F., INSS: Un Systeme Hybride Neuro-Symbolique pour l'Apprentissage Automatique Constructif, in INPG - Laboratoire, LEIBNIZ - IMAG: Grenoble - France (1998).

16. Weaver, R.A., J.A. McDermid, and T.P. Kelly. Software Safety Arguments: Towards a Systematic Categorisation of Evidence. in International System Safety Conference. Denver, CO (2002)

17. Rummelhart, D.E., G.E. Hinton, and R.J. Williams, Learning representations by back-propagating errors. Nature. 323 (1986) 533–536.

18. Leveson, N., Safeware: system safety and computers: Addison-Wesley (1995).

19. MoD, Defence Standard 00-55: Requirements for Safety Related Software in Defence Equipment, UK Ministry of Defence (1996).

20. SAE, ARP 4761 - Guidelines and Methods for Conducting the Safety Assessment Process on Civil Airborne Systems and Equipment, The Society for Automotive Engineers (1996).

21. MoD, Interim Defence Standard 00-58 Issue 1: HAZOP Studies on Systems Containing Programmable Electronics, UK Ministry of Defence (1996).

22. Kelly, T.P., Arguing Safety – A Systematic Approach to Managing Safety Cases, in Department of Computer Science, University of York: York, UK (1998).

Quantitative Reliability Estimation of a Computer-Based Motor Protection Relay Using Bayesian Networks

Atte Helminen and Urho Pulkkinen

VTT Industrial Systems, P.O.Box 1301, FIN-02044 VTT, Finland
Atte.Helminen@vtt.fi

Abstract. A quantitative reliability estimation of a computer-based motor protection relay is presented. The evidence used for the estimation consists of expert judgements on the development process and estimated operational experience of the computer-based system. The framework of Bayesian modelling and Bayesian networks was applied throughout the assessment.

A prior reliability estimation of the motor protection relay was built using the expert judgements on the product development process. The prior estimation was updated by taking into account the estimated operational experience for successive software versions. Prior estimations for possible reliability changes between different software versions were included to the assessment using the expert judgements on the version management of the motor protection relay.

The Bayesian networks seem to provide an excellent way of performing quantitative reliability estimations of computer-based systems. Bayesian networks are particularly useful when different kinds of evidence is introduced and combined in the same assessment. The assessment method described in the paper gives informative posterior probability distributions for the failure rates of different software versions. The methodology can be used as a communicative tool between different participants debating on the reliability of a system and as a follow-up of reliability trend during the life cycle of a computer-based system.

1 Introduction

Increase in the use of computer-based systems in different application areas has been rapid and nowadays computer-based systems have become an integral part of nearly every engineering application. The additional functionality provided by software has been adapted to modern instrumentation and control (I&C) systems and the computer-based I&C systems have successfully been implemented and are widely used in the energy production industry. Good experiences on the use of computer-based I&C systems in the energy production and, on the other hand, the technical and economical ageing of the current I&C systems in the existing nuclear power plants is in favour of replacing the I&C systems to corresponding computer-based I&C systems also in the nuclear industry.

S. Anderson et al. (Eds.): SAFECOMP 2003, LNCS 2788, pp. 92–102, 2003.
© Springer-Verlag Berlin Heidelberg 2003

One of the essential issues when replacing the I&C systems of nuclear power plants is the reliability of computer-based systems, and especially the question of how to assess the reliability. The reliability issue is particularly important when the system under assessment is considered as a safety-critical system such as the reactor protection system. To build sufficient confidence on the reliability of computer-based systems appropriate reliability assessment methods should be developed and applied. The assessment methods should provide useful and plausible reliability estimates, while taking the special characteristics of the reliability assessment of computer-based systems into consideration.

A problem causing extra work in the reliability assessment of computer-based safety-critical systems has at least the following characteristics. First, strict reliability goals are set for the I&C systems responsible for the safety functions of nuclear power plants and to demonstrate the achievement of these goals the systems should be well built and thoroughly tested. Second, the discontinuous behaviour of discrete logic in computer-based systems has the effect that to be sure on the functionality of the system in all occasions the system should be tested with all possible inputs. However, full testing of a system is usually not feasible because of the large number of possible inputs even for a relatively simple system and, therefore, for a more complicated computer-based system the thorough testing would require unacceptable amount of time and effort. One proposal to overcome the problem is to compensate the shortage of testing with reliability related evidence from other sources closely involved with computer-based systems.

In the paper a quantitative reliability estimation of computer-based motor protection relay is presented. The estimation and the assessment framework is based on the use of Bayesian modelling and in particular to its technical solution called Bayesian networks. Bayesian networks enable the implementation of qualitative and quantitative information flexibly together as well as updating the estimation while new information is obtained. The work is part of larger research effort to acquire, develop and test reliability assessment methods for computer-based systems. To review the work carried out in the research see reports by Helminen [1], Haapanen & Helminen [2] and Helminen & Pulkkinen [3].

The emphasis of the case study has been on the methodological analysis of the assessment approach, and the failure rate distributions in the end of the paper are given only as a demonstration of the informative results the assessment method can provide. The details related to the technical features of the case study system and to the evidence used have only been reviewed on a level necessary to test the functionality of the assessment method. The paper starts with a description of the evidence sources used for the assessment in section 2. In section 3 a general description of the assessment process is given. The case study system and the results of estimation are explained in section 4. Finally, in section 5 short conclusions of the assessment method are given.

2 Evidence Sources of Assessment

The evidence in the assessment was based on two primary sources. The first source of evidence was the expert judgements of the system developers and assessment executives. The second source was the operational experience of the computer-based system. In the assessment the development process and version management of the system was reviewed by the experts and based on their judgements a prior failure rate distribution of the first software version and prior estimates of the reliability changes between the successive software versions were concluded. In the construction of the prior failure rate distribution a specific expert judgement process was carried out. Summary of the expert judgement process and the operational experience is described in the section. More detailed presentation of the expert judgement process and the numerical values derived in the process is given in report by Helminen & Pulkkinen [3].

2.1 Prior Reliability Estimate

The prior failure rate distribution of the first software version was built using the expert judgements of the product development personnel, such as project managers, designers and programmers of the system. The prior estimation was constructed in an expert judgement process. A diagram representing the six steps of the expert judgement process is illustrated in figure 1.

In practice the expert judgement process was carried out using a collection of interviews. The purpose of the interviews was to recall the memories of the system development process. The questions of the interviews were divided to five categories based on the different development phases of a normal computer-based system. The categories were: project control and quality, requirement specification phase, design phase, implementation phase and testing phase. Before the interviews the experts received a short period of training on the assessment process and how to give probability estimations based on expert judgement overall. The training session was given to all experts simultaneously, but the interviews were carried out individually.

In the first two steps of the expert judgement process the different phases of the software development process were discussed. Based on the previous experience and the conclusions of the interviews the experts gave score values and weights for the different software development phases. The score values and weights were numerical values between zero and ten reflecting the expert's opinion on how well the production team managed in the execution of a phase and how big of importance did a certain phase have to the total reliability of the system. In the training session the numerical scale used in the assessment and the meaning of different score values were discussed from the system reliability point of view, and this way each expert was able to build an interpretation of his own about the meaning of the score values. In the third step the values given in the previous two steps were united to a total score value using an additive value function.

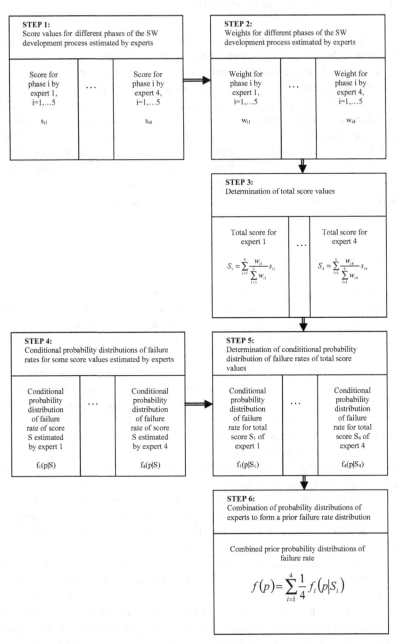

Fig. 1. Diagram presenting the six steps of the expert judgement process to estimate the prior failure probability of software

In addition to the score values and weights the experts were asked to give failure rate distributions for two or three different score values in step four. The system failure rate distributions should represent expert's opinion of score values as well as possible, since the distributions were used to calibrate the scale of score values. After the calibration it was possible to extrapolate a failure rate distribution for other score values in the scale. The conversion from the total score value to corresponding failure rate distribution was carried out in step five. In the final sixth step of the expert judgement process the reliability estimates or failure rate distributions of all experts were combined together to form the prior failure rate distribution of the first software version of the target system.

2.2 Prior Reliability Changes between Software Versions

In case there are several software versions produced during the life cycle of a computer-based system it is important to be able to use the evidence from previous software versions for the reliability estimation of the present software version. This is especially important if the operational experience for the last software version is small. However, to be consistent in the estimation the reliability changes between successive software versions need to be evaluated.

In the assessment the effects of the software modifications between successive software versions and the criticality of the modifications to the system reliability were evaluated in co-operation between the system developers and the assessment executives. The reliability changes between successive software versions were modelled so that the reliability estimate of a software version was the same as the reliability estimate of the preceding software version added with a random normal distributed change. A prior estimate on the magnitude of the random change was determined depending on the amount and criticality of changes made between software versions.

The significance of the prior reliability changes to the final results was evaluated in a sensitivity analysis. In the sensitivity analysis two different approaches of the influence of software changes were taken. In a neutral approach the prior mean value of the random change between successive software versions was assumed zero. In a conservative approach it was assumed as a prior assumption that a change in software has always a negative influence to the reliability of the system.

2.3 Estimated Operational Experience

The second main evidence source in the assessment was the operational experience estimated during the life cycle of the computer-based system. The operational experience was the approximated amount of working years and the amount and types of software defects encountered for the different software versions of the system. The software defects were classified to software faults and software inconveniences depending on the severity of a defect from the customer's point of view. The faults and inconveniences were reported either by the developer or the customers. After detection, a defect was analysed and depending on the nature of the defect it was corrected in the next software version.

In the assessment the reliability estimations were calculated for different operational experience data sets. In the first data set only the number of software faults encountered for different software versions were implemented to the estimation as fault data. In the second data set both the software faults and the software inconveniences were taken into consideration.

As well known, the reliability of a computer-based system is a factor of two properties. First of all, it is a property of the faults the system may contain. However, even though there may be faults in the software these faults are only revealed when certain inputs are introduced to the system. The probability distribution of input sequences introduced to the system varies from one operational profile to another. The reliability of a computer-based system is, therefore, a property of the system faults and the operation profile the system is functioning in. To keep the amount of work in the assessment in reasonable scales it was assumed in the model that the estimated operational experience for different software versions was obtained from a single and similar operational profile.

3   Assessment Process

The idea in the assessment process was to combine the available evidence to form an as plausible reliability estimation of the target system as possible. In the assessment the whole life cycle of the computer-based system was taken into consideration and a diagram representing the assessment process is depicted in figure 2. First, a prior estimate for the reliability of the first software version of the system was built. The prior estimate was based on the expert judgement process illustrated in figure 1. The estimate was then updated using the operational experience of the first software version. Later on, when the software was modified, the effects of the modifications to the system reliability were valuated and the estimation was updated with the operational experience of the second software version. This procedure was repeated, as many times as there were new software versions produced in the life cycle of the system.

The combination of evidence in the assessment was carried out using the framework of Bayesian modelling and in particular its technical solution called Bayesian networks. Bayesian networks have been widely applied in the reliability estimation and studies on the use of Bayesian approach in the reliability assessment of computer-based systems have been presented in the papers of previous SAFECOMP conferences for example by Littlewood et al. [4] and Gran et al. [5],[6],[7]. A detailed application of the Bayesian framework for combining expert judgements is given for example in the report by Pulkkinen & Holmberg [8]. The Bayesian modelling and calculations of the case study presented in the paper are carried out using WinBUGS program. For a closer review about WinBUGS program see Spiegelhalter et al. [9].

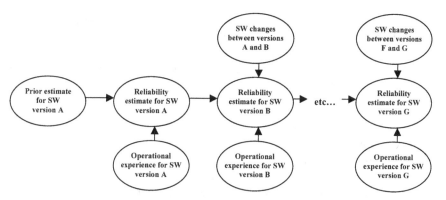

Fig. 2. Diagram representing the software (SW) reliability assessment process

4 Case Study on Reliability Estimation of a Computer-Based Motor Protection Relay

4.1 Target System

The case study system estimated was SPAM 150 C –motor protection relay produced by ABB Substation Automation. The numerical motor protection relay SPAM 150 C is an integrated design of current measuring multifunction relay for the complete protection of alternating current motors. The main area of application covers large and medium-sized three-phase motors in all types of conventional contactor or circuit-breaker controlled motor drives.

The relay continuously measures the three phase currents and the residual current of the protected object. When a fault occurs and persists long enough to exceed a set or calculated occurrence time, the relay starts and operates. Depending on the relay setting and the fault the relay either gives an alarm or launches a protection signal to protect the object. The multi-function relay module comprises seven units: a three-phase overcurrent unit, a thermal overload unit, start-up supervision unit, a phase unbalance unit, an incorrect phase sequence unit, an undercurrent unit and a non-directional earth-fault unit. For closer review of the system and the protection functions see the manual of SPAM 150 C [10].

At the time of the assessment SPAM 150 C had not been applied in safety critical functions of nuclear power plants and explicit consideration if the relay fulfils all the aspects of a safety critical system of a nuclear power plant was not carried out in the assessment. However, the motor protection relay is a computer-based application for which high reliability is required, and therefore it was an excellent case study system for the assessment.

4.2 Reliability Model

The reliability model was mainly based on the characteristics of the available evidence in the assessment. The operational experience consisted of the approximated amount of working years and the amount and types of software defects encountered for the different software versions of the computer-based system. Therefore, the appropriate conditional distribution of the number of software faults of a software version given the failure rate and the number of working years was considered as Poisson distributed as follows:

$$f(x|\lambda,T) \sim Poisson(\lambda T),$$
(1)

where x is number of software faults, λ failure rate and T estimated total working years of a software version.

The prior distribution of the first software version given by the experts was a mixture of lognormal distributions. In order to simplify the numerical computation in the assessment a log-transformed parameter of the failure rate was used, i.e. $\theta = ln(\lambda)$, where parameter θ is the log-transformed failure rate.

The failure rate of a software version in the model is constant, although unknown. However, the failure rate changes when shifting to the following software version. The change of failure rates is expressed in terms of log-transformed parameters as follows:

$$\theta_{following} = \theta_{previous} + \omega; \; \omega \sim N(\mu,\sigma^2),$$
(2)

where $\theta_{previous}$ and $\theta_{following}$ are the log-transformed failure rates of successive software versions and ω is the random normal distributed change. Parameters μ and σ^2 correspond to the prior knowledge about the failure rate change, and were determined based on the expert judgement of the assessment executives.

4.3 Results

In the life cycle of SPAM 150 C there had been seven different software versions. The software versions were labelled from A to G as shown in figure 2. Reliability estimations for the software of the motor protection relay were calculated for four different scenarios using all the evidence available at that time. The four scenarios differ by the prior assumption made on the influence of software changes and on the interpretation of the defects of the software as discussed in section 2.

The posterior failure rate distributions of different software versions of the conservative prior approach are illustrated in figure 3. The posterior failure rate distributions range from 2.5 percentile, the lower bar, to 97.5 percentile, the upper bar, and median marked as a dot somewhere in between. Corresponding graphs for the neutral prior approach are shown in figure 4.

From the graphs it can be seen how the confidence on the reliability of the motor protection relay is increased while the defects are removed and the system software is updated. For example from figure 3 it can be approximated that the median value of software version A implies that two devises out of thousand will encounter a software fault during a year of operation. For software version G the corresponding median value is four devices out of one hundred thousand. In the calculations all the devices were assumed to function in a similar operational profile.

Significant differences between the posterior failure rate distributions of the two approaches used for the influence of software changes cannot be noticed. With the conservative approach the failure rate distributions of different software versions seem to be more monotonous, i.e. the estimates for the early software versions are better than in the neutral approach and vice versa for the later software versions. However, the difference between the two approaches for the failure rate of the last and crucial software version is negligible as can be verified from the figures. Explanation to the small difference in the last software version can most probably be found from the large amount of operational experience data, and thereby the dominant role of the operational experience in the assessment.

In general, the posterior failure rate distributions of the software versions provide an informative way to follow up the evolution of reliability trend during the life cycle of the computer-based system. From the figures of the assessment it is easy to estimate whether the system has reached a maturity required by a certain application.

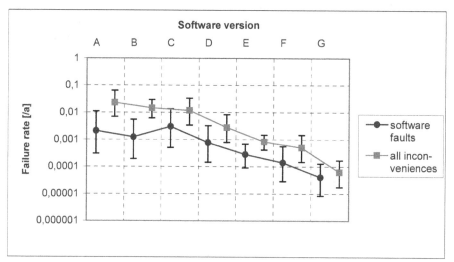

Fig. 3. Posterior 2,5–50–97,5 percentiles for failure rate distributions of different software versions of the conservative approach

5 Conclusions

The Bayesian networks seem to provide an excellent way of performing quantitative reliability estimations of computer-based systems. Bayesian networks are particularly useful when different kinds of evidence is introduced and combined in the same assessment. Especially in larger computer-based systems where the system cannot be modelled and tested presumably completely it is reasonable to take the full advantage of the operational experience and use such assessment methods as presented in the paper. However, it is important to understand that the assessment method presented utilises only a part of the reliability evidence of computer-based systems and for a better comprehension on the reliability of a system a variety of analyses like the one shown should be practised.

The assessment gives informative posterior probability distributions for the reliability of software versions of a system. At the same time, the assessment method provides means for transparent and concurrent way of reasoning one's beliefs and references about the system reliability. Carrying out sensitivity analysis for the evidence is easy and straightforward as was verified for the case study system. Probably the greatest advantage of the assessment method is, however, gained if used as a communicative tool between different participants debating on the reliability of a system. It is, therefore, justified to claim that the reliability assessment method shown here can provide strong support for the licensing process of computer-based I&C systems.

However, further research is needed for the development of the assessment. In the estimation it was assumed that all the operational experience was collected from a single and similar operational profile. In practice this is usually not the case and to improve the assessment the differences between operational profiles should be taken into consideration. The expert judgement process is another significant area of additional research. For example, the questions of the interview should be formulated so that if necessary the grounds for the answers given by an expert can be traced back to the documentation of the system.

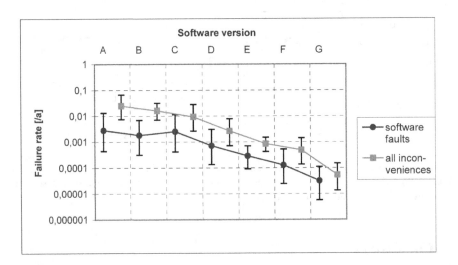

Fig. 4. Posterior 2,5–50–97,5 percentiles for failure rate distributions of different software versions of the neutral approach

Acknowledgement. The work presented in the paper was carried out in co-operation with ABB Substation Automation. The authors would like to thank the staff of ABB for their time and the expertise in the work.

References

1. Helminen A., "Reliability Estimation of Safety-Critical Software-Based Systems Using Bayesian Networks", Radiation and Nuclear Safety Authority, Helsinki, 2001, 1–23.
2. Haapanen P. and Helminen A., "Failure Mode and Effects Analysis of Software-Based Automation Systems", Radiation and Nuclear Safety Authority, Helsinki, 2002, 1–35.
3. Helminen A. and Pulkkinen P., "Reliability Assessment Using Bayesian Networks – Case Study on Quantitative Reliability Estimation of a Software-Based Motor Protection Relay", Radiation and Nuclear Safety Authority, Helsinki, 2003, 1–31.
4. Littlewood B., Popov P. and Strigini L., "Assessment of the Reliability of Fault-Tolerant Software: A Bayesian Approach", In Proceedings of 19th International Conference on Computer Safety, Reliability and Security (SAFECOMP 2000), Springer-Verlag, Berlin, 2000, 294–308.
5. Gran B. and Dahll G., "Estimating Dependability of Programmable Systems Using Bayesian Belief Nets", OECD Halden Reactor Project, HWR-627, Halden, Norway, 2000, 1–62.
6. Gran B. and Helminen A., "A Bayesian Belief Network for Reliability Assessment", OECD Halden Reactor Project, HWR-649, Halden, Norway, 2001, 1–26.
7. Gran B. and Helminen A., "The BBN Methodology: Progress report and future work", OECD Halden Reactor Project, HWR-693, Halden, Norway, 2002, 1–32.
8. Pulkkinen U. and Holmberg J., "A Method for Using Expert Judgement in PSA", Finnish Centre for Radiation and Nuclear Safety, Helsinki, 1997, 1–32.
9. Spiegelhalter D., Thomas A., Best N. and Gilks W., "BUGS 0.5 Bayesian Inference Using Gibbs Sampling Manual (version ii)", MRC Biostatistic Unit, Cambridge, 1996, 1–59.
10. "Motor Protection Relay SPAM 150 C –Product Description", ABB Substation Automation Oy, http://fisub.abb.fi/products/bghtml/spam150.htm.

A Dependability Model for Domestic Systems

Guy Dewsbury*, Ian Sommerville, Karen Clarke, and Mark Rouncefield

Computing Department, Lancaster University, Lancaster LA1 4YR, UK
{g.dewsbury,k.m.clarke,m.rouncefield}@lancaster.ac.uk
is@comp.lancs.ac.uk

Abstract. Technically-based models of dependability such as Laprie's model suggest that there are attributes that should be reflected in the design of a system. These attributes tend to be attributes of the software or hardware and the models assume that system operators can be treated in the same way as software or hardware components. While this approach may be valid for some control systems with tightly specified operational processes, we argue that it must be extended if it is to be applied to systems where there is significant discretion on the part of the user as to how they will use the system. In particular, for systems in the home, we argue that the notion of dependability should be broadened This paper suggests that through the design of assistive technology (AT) systems for older people we can demonstrate the user should be placed at the centre of the process when considering system dependability.

1   Introduction

Ever since computers and computer software were used as essential components in critical systems the dependability of computer-based systems has been a concern. The 1980's, in particular, saw a surge in research in safety-critical systems and major advances in our understanding of the dependability of computer-based systems have been made since that period. This work on dependability has been mostly concerned with the use of computer-based systems as control systems and protection systems so, inevitably, dependability research and practice has been driven by the requirements of this type of system.

Now, however, it is not only protection and control systems that are critical systems. National infrastructures and businesses depend on large scale information systems that must have a high-level of availability and reliability. Embedded systems are no longer just situated within organisations but are also fundamental to the successful operation of our cars and, increasingly, our homes. 'Failure' of these systems can have serious organisational or personal consequences so paying attention to system dependability is essential.

Home systems that incorporate computers are typically composed of assemblies of relatively low-cost, off-the-shelf devices. With a few, very expensive, exceptions these devices are stand-alone devices with hard-wired communications between them.

---

* Corresponding author: g.dewsbury@lancaster.ac.uk

S. Anderson et al. (Eds.): SAFECOMP 2003, LNCS 2788, pp. 103–115, 2003.

However, in the very near future, it is clear that connecting these devices to a home network with some centralized control system will become a reality. To some extent, standards such as ISO 9000, BS EN 29999 and BS EN 1441 [1] already allow this for assistive technology systems intended to provide support for elderly and disabled people in their home and notions of a 'home media network' have been proposed [2].

In this paper, we argue that the model of system dependability that is appropriate for control and protection systems must be extended if it is to be applicable to domestic computer-based systems. We propose an extended model that embraces the traditional model but which includes the user and the system's environment rather than positioning them outside the system boundary. That is, when a computer-based system is installed in a domestic environment, we should not just be concerned with whether or not that system is failure-free. Rather, the overall system dependability depends on whether or not it fulfils its intended purpose as far as the system users are concerned. If it does not do so, then it will not be used. This situation is equivalent to an unplanned system failure rate of 100% - hardly a dependable system.

In deriving the model proposed here, we have drawn on research that we are undertaking in dependable assistive technology design for installation in the homes of older people. The users of the assistive technologies may suffer from a range of disabilities with assistive technology used to help them overcome these disabilities and cope with everyday life in their own home. These elderly people depend on this technology to maintain a reasonable quality of life but, all too often, the technology lets them down. Sometimes, it simply fails to operate but, more often, it is not or cannot be used as intended because its design does not take into account the specific needs of the elderly users, the context where the system will be installed and the natural human desire to control rather than be controlled by technology.

In the remainder of the paper, we introduce Laprie's dependability model and examine some of the assumptions that underlie that model. We challenge the applicability of some of these assumptions for domestic systems in sections that discuss the role of the user in domestic systems and the distinctions between home and organisational environments. We then go on to introduce our view of dependability as it is applied to domestic systems, suggesting that as well as 'traditional' dependability attributes, dependable home systems must also be acceptable to their users, fit in with their daily routines and lifestyle and support user adaptation as user needs change.

2   Computer System Dependability

Dependability is defined as that property of a computer system such that reliance can justifiably be placed on the service it delivers. The service delivered by a system is its behaviour as it is perceptible by its user(s); a user is another system (human or physical) which interacts with the former. [3]

Traditionally, it is considered that computing systems are characterised by five fundamental properties: functionality, usability, performance, cost and dependability [4]. The core features of dependability models tend to assume that dependability is a technical attribute and that the dependable features are within the computer system itself. Critical systems require that the functionality of the software and hardware are free of faults, resilient to external attacks, and provide a high level of confidence. As Laprie [5] suggests (1995) dependability can be considered according to different properties that allow attributes of dependability to be defined as

> *the readiness for usage leads to availability, the continuity of service leads to reliability, the non-occurrence of catastrophic consequences on the environment leads to safety, the non-occurrence of unauthorized disclosure of information leads to confidentiality, the non-occurrence of improper alterations of information leads to integrity, the ability to undergo repairs and evolutions leads to maintainability.* [6].

These attributes and properties allow the dependability theorist to consider the distinctions between faults, errors and failures. These can be framed within the notions of 'fault prevention', 'fault tolerance', 'fault removal', and 'fault forecasting', which enable the software designer to trace and prevent undesirable problems. Laprie develops these ideas in the forms of a dependability tree which locates dependability within three categories: Attributes, Means and Impairments from which a number of attributes extend (Figure 1). The dependability tree allows the software engineer and the designer to picture how faults and problems are derived, and thus are avoided. Hence dependability can be considered to be the extent to which its operation is free of failure [7].

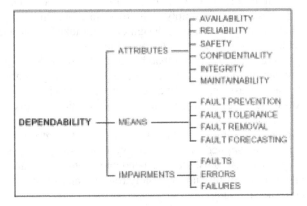

Fig. 1. Laprie's Dependability Tree [8]

The basis of Laprie's dependability model was extensive work on the safety and reliability of computer based control and protection systems. The model therefore reflects the nature of these systems and how they are used and is clearly based on a number of assumptions:

- That errors arise inevitably from faults (the hypothesised cause of an error). Faults can be failures of other systems so a failure of a development system to detect an incorrect variable initialisation is reflected as a fault in the operational system. When this initialisation is carried out, an error has arisen.

- That the system is constructed in such a way that an error (defined by Laprie as 'that part of the system state which is liable to lead to a subsequent failure') can, at least in principle, be detected by an external observer.
- That we can recognise when a system failure (defined by Laprie as a deviation from fulfilling the system function) occurs.

These assumptions are fundamental to the model of dependability that has been accepted by researchers and practitioners for a number of years. However, as we will argue later in this paper, their technical orientation means that they do not properly consider the interactions between the user and the system. Consequently, they are not wholly adequate for domestic systems. Furthermore, because of the differences between the home and organisational environment, we will also argue that, as well as the technical dependability attributes in Laprie's model, additional system attributes are central to the dependability of domestic systems.

3 The Role of the User

Most dependability theory attempts to consider humans as elements in the system that are comparable with other software or hardware elements. In his paper, Laprie recognises the importance of human operators but discusses them in terms of 'interaction faults' resulting from 'human errors'. Although the point is not made explicitly, there seems to be an assumption that the fault-error-failure model applies equally to humans as it does to technical system components.

However, if we examine the assumptions underlying the dependability model from a human perspective, it is immediately obvious that they do not hold.

- People are not automatons and they use their intelligence to discover many different ways of doing the same thing. An action that might be interpreted as a failure for one person (e.g. an air traffic controller placing aircraft on a collision course) might be part of a dependable operational process for another where the controller may have a reliable method of ensuring that they will move one of the aircraft before any danger ensues [9].
- We cannot monitor our brains to identify the erroneous state that has arisen.
- The development process for people from conception (fusing of genetic histories) through nurture to education and training is so extended and complex that identifying the 'fault' that resulted in a consequent failure is impossible.

We accept that, for some classes of highly automated system where operational processes are tightly defined and operators are highly trained then the benefits of adopting a consistent approach to all elements in the system may outweigh the disadvantages of treating the human operators in a simplistic way. However, for other classes of system where use of the system is uncontrolled any dependability model that does not consider the distinct nature of people is incomplete.

For domestic systems, the users of the system are central to the design and central to the consideration of dependability. In the home, there are no defined operational processes, enormous variation in system users and no 'quality control'. The dependability of home systems is played out daily through the routines and situated actions of the people in the home. Therefore, we contend that the requirements of dependability in the home setting are derived from different roots from traditional dependability models of software design. To achieve dependability, we must take an approach that integrates the user and environment with the technology rather than considering dependability as a property of the technology alone.

4   Domestic and Organizational Environments

Laprie's model for computer system dependability incorporates a further assumption that we have not yet discussed. This assumption is that the critical computer systems are developed and used by organisations rather than individuals. Organisations impose 'acceptable practices' upon the individual and therefore standardise and control the use of technology. As a trivial example of this, many organisations forbid their employees to install software on their own computers and insist that only allowed software be installed by system technical staff.

Products and people are covered by health and safety regulations and work practices that are designed to reduce accidents and improve productivity. Operational processes are defined and staff are trained to follow these processes. There are (at least in principle) sanctions for staff who do not 'follow the rules'. Computer-based systems may be designed and deployed to support and enforce particular processes. Because there is an 'expected' way of working, it is possible to recognise deviations from these and associated system 'failures'.

Activities and processes are consistent in organisations but not in the home where greater flexibility exists. In contrast to organisations where technologies and processes are limited, within the home people can choose whether or not to use technology, how to use it and where they wish to use it. People do not read instruction manuals, are not trained in the use of domestic technologies and the use of these technologies often depends on their previous technology experience. For example, on early video recorders the process of setting up a timed recording was difficult and error-prone. Although this has been much improved on modern machines, a large number of people simply do not use pre-recording because they consider it to be beyond their capabilities.

Another important difference between the home and organisations is in the timing of activities. In organisations, activities tend to be set in regular procedures, such that work begins at prescribed times. The organisational system has regular processes through which activities must follow. Dependable operation may rely on this timing. For example, in a hospital, a surgeon in a hospital can usually assume that appropriate pre-operative procedures have been carried out. A significant difference between the organisational system and the home system is that processes and timing standardised functions are dissimilar. Home routines are often unplanned and lacking rigid structure, although foreseen events may sometimes be planned and situated into a daily/weekly/monthly schedule.

Table 1 outlines some of the differences between technology use in organisations and the home environments; it is not to be applicable to *all* organisations or *all* homes, but a rough guide.

Table 1. Home and Organisational Differences

CRITERIA	HOME CONTEXT	ORGANISATIONAL CONTEXT
USAGE	Ad Hoc Uncontrolled	Systematically Controlled
STANDARDISATION	Legislative and Product Specific	Standardised with Organisational Environment
PROCESSES	Uncontrolled and Ad Hoc	Controlled and Systematic
OPERATORS	Untrained and Unskilled	Training Available
OPERATIONS	Unrestricted and Ad Hoc	Restricted and Systematised
ACTIONS AND ACTIVITIES	Undefined and Uncontrolled	Predefined and Limited
SAFETY	Suggested but Difficult to Enforce	Controlled through Systems

Table 1 also illustrates that the home does not provide the safeguards and assurance that many organisational environments are legally required to do. Technology in the home and organisations must pass rigorous standards laid down by law (ISO, etc) that ensure the integrity of the product for standard use in the home or workplace, but few products dictate how they should or should not be used in the domestic arena. The organisation attempts, through health and safety standards and procedures, to ensure that products are operated correctly within specific safety margins that legally safeguards them, whereas the home has no such restrictions.

The overall dependability of an organisational socio-technical system that includes a computer-based system is derived from the dependability of the computer system and how it is used. The controlled nature of the organisational environment means that usage of a computer-based system can be controlled and mandated. In the home, however, the dependability of the socio-technical system, that is, the user plus the technology, depends primarily on how (if at all) the user *chooses* to use that technology. For example, if an elderly person is offered a communication aid that they cannot fit into a pocket of their normal clothing, they may choose not to carry that aid. Therefore, the availability of the communication aid system is restricted to times when it can actually be carried by the user. The communication aid itself may be dependable but the overall *system* of helping with communication is not.

The dependability of systems extends beyond the hardware and software into the social and lived experience of the home dweller. As Lupton and Seymour [10] suggest, technology becomes part of the self-concept for the user and therefore it is essential that dependability does not just mean that a system behaves according to the expectations of its designers. Systems therefore have to be designed so that they are *acceptable* to users. We should not underestimate the difficulty of this design problem, particularly for assistive technologies.

5   Dependability Attributes for Home Systems

We have argued that techno-centric models of dependability are not appropriate for domestic computer-based systems, especially those assistive technology systems that are intended to assist elderly or disabled people. Fundamentally, techno-centric dependability models exclude the user and the user's environment from primary considerations of what dependability means. In principle at least, they can consider a system that is useless and never used to be dependable. We reject this view and believe that we should not just be concerned with dependability in use but also dependability of use. By this, we mean that it is not enough for a system to be dependable whilst it is in operation; it is also essential that we can depend on the system actually being used for its intended purpose.

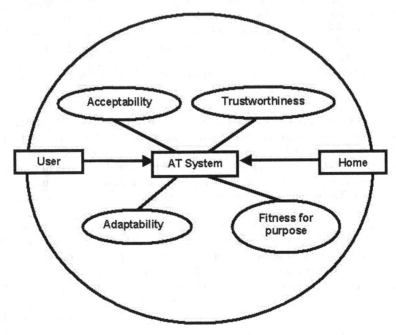

Fig. 2. Dependability Attributes of a Situated AT System

In this section, we present our initial work on the development of a dependability model for home systems. So far, we have focused on identifying and understanding the attributes of a domestic assistive technology system that contribute to its dependability. These 'dependability' attributes therefore reflect, in our view, that it is critical for practical dependability that the system is used and that its use meets real needs of the user.

For domestic systems, we need to consider the dependability of the socio-technical system as a whole where the system includes the user, the home environment and the installed assistive technology (Figure 2). To achieve system dependability, we propose that the required characteristics of the assistive technology should be considered under four headings. These are:

Trustworthiness. In order for a system to be dependable, the user must trust that the system will behave as they expect. We define this attribute to be the equivalent of 'dependability' in Laprie's model. That is, it includes the traditional dependability attributes of availability, reliability, etc. However, we will argue below that these need to be re-interpreted to some extent to take into account the characteristics of domestic systems.

Acceptability. We have argued above that a system that is not acceptable to users will simply not be used. Therefore, it is essential that system characteristics that affect its acceptability such as the system learnability and aesthetics are considered in the design process.

Fitness for purpose. Fitness for purpose is taken for granted in most of the dependability literature but, socio-technical system failures regularly arise [11] [12] because a computer-based system is not fit for the purpose for which it was designed and users of the system have had to adapt their operational processes to accommodate the system's inadequacies. When the purpose of a system is to cope with disability, users may simply not have this option and the system may simply be unused.

Adaptability. Within the home both the environment and the user's of the systems change. This is particularly true for elderly disabled people whose capabilities tend to decline as they age. Therefore, if system dependability is not to degrade, then it must be able to evolve over time, generally without interventions from the system's designers.

Of course, there are overlapping characteristics but, for the purposes of discussion, we consider them separately here. Now let us examine each of these characteristics in more detail to assess what they might mean for domestic assistive technology systems.

5.1   Trustworthiness

In the context of domestic systems, we consider the trustworthiness of a system to correspond to the technical notion of dependability as defined by Laprie. That is, the trustworthiness reflects the systems availability, reliability, safety, confidentiality, integrity and maintainability. However, the nature of home systems as assemblies of relatively cheap, off-the-shelf devices, the fact that people at home are not systematically trained in the use of a computer-based system and the nature of the home itself means that these characteristics are different in a domestic rather than organisational context.

Availability and Reliability

For assistive technologies, availability and reliability are critical attributes. An elderly or disabled person's quality of life may be dependent on their assistive technologies and failure of these systems has severe implications for them. However, assistive technology system designers are faced with a challenging problem when trying to build systems with high-levels of availability and reliability. Systems are mostly composed of off-the-shelf devices where the overall AT system designer have no control over the engineering of these devices. Typically, hardly any information may be available about device reliability so designers must trust manufacturer specifications and quality control standards which, in our experience, are often optimistic. Furthermore, occupational therapists, for example, who work with users to specify requirements are not trained to understand system dependability issues and frequently mis-specify the system reliability that is required.

Safety

Clearly safety is a very important factor in domestic systems as it is essential that these systems do not injure their users. However, given that most systems are relatively low power systems and must conform to electrical safety standards, we consider that the risks of injury associated with assistive technologies are relatively low. In fact, the home is such an inherently dangerous place, especially for elderly people, that other risks far outweigh the risks associated with assistive technologies. This does not mean, of course, that we should install unsafe systems – however, it does suggest that it is not worth incurring very high costs in activities such as detailed safety analysis.

Some systems may purport to provide people with a safer environment, but through producing false alerts, the person will cease using the device. In this case, the person might be at greater risk than before the technology was installed, as other people might still expect that they are using the technology and are therefore covered against the potential danger.

Confidentiality and Integrity

While the need for integrity goes without saying, the issue of confidentiality is much more difficult in situations where elderly people depend on monitoring technology that alerts relatives and carers when a problem arises. These elderly users often value their privacy and wish to maintain the confidentiality of their personal information. On the other hand, this may compromise the safety of the overall system as it may limit the speed and type of response in the event of a problem. The level of confidentiality in a system therefore cannot be fixed but has to be programmable and responsive to an analysis of the events being processed by the system.

Maintainability

Maintainability is the ability of a system to undergo evolution with the corollary that the system should be designed so that evolution is not likely to introduce new faults into the system. We distinguish here between maintainability as the process of making unanticipated *engineering* changes to the system and adaptability which is the process of changing a system to configure it for its environment of use. In general, we consider that the relatively low-cost of AT equipment will mean that replacement rather than maintenance is the often norm so software and hardware changes and upgrades are unlikely. Therefore, we consider maintainability under the adaptability attributes that we discuss later.

5.2   Acceptability

The notion of acceptability was initially conveyed through an advocate of Universal Design (UD). Jim Sandhu [13] considers that the basic notion of UD requires the architect and designer to consider a number of properties and attributes. Sandhu uses an ISO standard definition to extrapolate a diagrammatic representation concerning system acceptability within a Universal Design context:

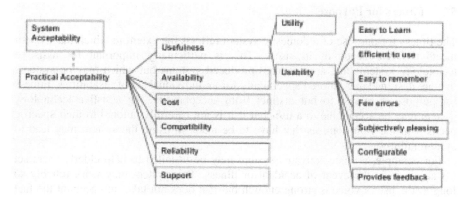

Fig. 3. Sandhu's System Acceptability Model [14]

Sandhu's diagram illustrates that for systems to meet his Universal Design criteria there are a considerable number of attributes and properties that the system and designer must address which are similar to those derived by software engineers considering dependability. The model that Sandhu proposes situates the user and the product with in the same contextual model so reflects our views on the central significance of the user when considering system dependability. Acceptability reflects the users preferences into the design as well as the users preferences for the finished product and they way it is to be used.

Our view of acceptability takes a simplified view of Sandhu's model as we consider some of his acceptability characteristics such as reliability, availability and configurability under other headings. Essentially, we consider that a system will only be acceptable if the user feels that the benefits that accrue from the system justify the costs and effort of buying, installing, learning to use and using the system. We therefore consider the principal acceptability characteristics to be:

1. **Usability** It must be possible to use the system on a regular basis without error and without having to re-learn how to benefit from the system.
2. **Learnability** It should be possible to learn to use the system relatively easily with no steep learning curve before any benefits can be gained from it.
3. **Cost** The system should also be within the budget of the person allowing for maintenance and repair costs in the future.
4. **Compatibility** The system must be compatible both physically and electronically with other systems that are installed in the home.
5. **Efficiency** The effort and time saved by using the system must significantly exceed the effort involved in making use of it.
6. **Responsiveness** The system must respond in a timely fashion to user requests and provide feedback on its operation to the user.
7. **Aesthetics** If a system is to be actively used in the home, it should be aesthetically pleasing, blending in with the décor of the existing home and the users taste.

5.3   Fitness for Purpose

The fitness for purpose of a domestic system reflects the extent to which that system meets the real needs of its users. This is particularly important for assistive technology systems that are not mass-produced systems but which may be systems that are designed and tailored specifically for an individual set of disabilities. Fitness for purpose is related to but distinct from acceptability. An assistive technology system may be acceptable to a user but if it is not carefully tailored to their specific needs then the compromises that have to be made in using the system may lead to system failures.

For example, a voice-activated system may be installed to help elderly users set off an alarm in the event of accident or illness. This system may work reliably so long as the user's voice is strong enough but if it does not take into account the fact that the elderly person's voice may be weakened in the event of an accident then it is not fit for its intended purpose.

Of course, this is not just an issue for domestic system but a more general dependability concern. For organisational systems, dealing with this concern is seen as a specification issue i.e. failure to meet real needs is equated to a specification failure. Given that the level of specification that is used for critical systems is totally impractical for domestic systems, the issue of fitness for purpose cannot be addressed in this way. Rather, the design of the system has to evolve as it is used to take into account the rhythms routines and activity patterns of the user's life and the particular characteristics of that user and their home.

5.4   Adaptability

Homes and the people living in these homes change with time [15]. Spaces are reconfigured to cope with changing demands and tastes, new people come to live in the home, children grow up and the capabilities of elderly adults typically decline as they grow older. Consequently, the requirements of users in the home for assistive technologies are constantly changing. If systems cannot be adapted *in situ* to meet new requirements they will become less and less used and, hence, less dependable.

We can identify three types of modification that may be made to domestic systems:

>*Addition of new equipment.* This can be in addition to existing equipment or can replace obsolete devices. Given the relatively low costs of domestic equipment, this will often be the most cost-effective way to modify a system.
>
>*System configuration or re-configuration by its users.* In this case, the user (or, in the case of a disabled person, possibly a relative or carer) adapts the system using built-in capabilities for adaptation. For example, if a person's eyesight degenerates, then the default font size on a screen that they regularly read may be increased.
>
>*Configuration or re-configuration of a system by its supplier.* In this case, the supplier or installer of the system may visit the home to make the system modifications. Alternatively, if the system can be connected to a network, then remote upgrades of the software may be possible. This is already commonplace for mobile phones and digital TV set-top boxes.

Of course, it is well known that dependability problems in computer systems regularly arise because of errors made during system maintenance. These occur in spite of extensive quality control and testing mechanisms that are in place. There are no such mechanisms in the home so clearly the potential for undependability after modification is significant. This fact, along with the need to support system change leads to the following adaptability attributes:

Configurability. This attribute reflects the ability of users or equipment installers to adapt the system to cope with a range of human capabilities such as variable hearing, eyesight, balance, etc.

Openness. This attribute is concerned with the system's ability to be extended with new equipment, perhaps from different manufacturers.

Visibility. This attribute reflects the extent to which the operation of the system can be made visible to users and installers of that system. This is particularly important when problems arise as it increases the chances that these problems can be diagnosed without expert assistance.

User repairability. This attribute reflects the extent to which faults in the system can be repaired by users without specialist tools or knowledge. This is important for assistive technologies as it means that problems can be fixed by either the user or a helper. Thus the system can be brought back into operation quickly and the overall availability of the system is increased.

6 Conclusion

This paper has begun to outline some distinctions between traditional dependability attributes, as exemplified by Laprie and attributes that have arisen out of designing assistive technology systems for older people. We have suggested that dependability can be reframed to account for human qualities as well as the nature of error and faults and that there is a critical distinction that should be illuminated between dependability in use and dependability of use. It is not enough to simply focus on the dependability of the technical system itself. It is essential to design the system to ensure that users will choose to use it for its intended function whilst limiting misuse. Our focus so far has been on understanding the attributes of domestic systems that contribute to its dependability and, so far, we have not considered Laprie's notions of means and impairments. We plan to address these issues in the next phase of our work.

Although the focus of our work has been domestic systems, we believe that the model we propose here potentially has a wider applicability to organisational systems where use of the system is at the discretion of the user. In particular, professionals such as doctors and senior have sufficient authority that they can choose whether or not to use organisational information systems. These systems must also therefore take into account the need to be accepted by their users.

Acknowledgements. The research described here has been funded by the EPSRC in the DIRC (http://www.dirc.org.uk/) and EQUATOR (http://www.equator.ac.uk/) projects. We would like to thank our partners in these projects and Age Concern, Barrow, MHA Care Group Penrith, and Dundee and Aberdeen Social Work departments.

References

1. Turner-Smith A, Broadhurst M, Fielden S, and Griffiths P.: IPEM policy on Rehabilitation Engineering Services, The Institute of Physics and Engineering in Medicine, (1999)
2. Bell, G. & Gemmell, J.: A Call for the Home Media Network. Comm. ACM, 45 (7), (2002) 71–75,
3. Laprie, J-C.: Dependable Computing: Concepts, Limits, Challenges FTCS-25, the 25th IEEE International Symposium on Fault-Tolerant Computing, Pasadena, California, USA, June 27–30, (1995), 42
4. Avizienis, A. Laprie J-C, Randell B.: Fundamental Concepts of Dependability, (2001)
5. Laprie, J-C.: Dependable Computing: Concepts, Limits, Challenges FTCS-25, the 25th IEEE International Symposium on Fault-Tolerant Computing, Pasadena, California, USA, June 27–30, (1995)
6. Laprie, J-C.: *op cit,* 42
7. Randell B.: Dependability - a Unifying Concept, Working Paper, University of Newcastle on Tyne
8. Laprie, J-C.: Dependable Computing: Concepts, Limits, Challenges FTCS-25, the 25th IEEE International Symposium on Fault-Tolerant Computing, Pasadena, California, USA, June 27–30, (1995), 43
9. Bentley, R., Hughes, J., Randall, D., Rodden, T., Sawyer, P., Shapiro, D. and Sommerville, I., Ethnographically-informed systems development for air traffic control, in *Proceedings of CSCW'92*, Toronto, ACM Press, 1-4 November (1992), 123–129.
10. Lupton D & Seymour W.: Technology, selfhood and physical disability, Social Science & Medicine 50 (2000) 1851–1862
11. Miller C, Haigh K, & Dewing W.: First, Cause No Harm: Issues in Building Safe, Reliable and Trustworthy Elder Care Systems, American Association for Artificial Intelligence (www.aaai.org) (2002)
12. Edwards, K & Grinter R.: At Home with Ubiquitous Computing: Seven Challenges In G. D. Abowd, B. Brumitt, S. A. N. Shafer (Eds.): Proceedings of Ubicomp 2001, LNCS 2201. Springer-Verlag Berlin Heidelberg (2001) 256–272
13. Sandhu J.: Multi-Dimensional Evaluation as a tool in Teaching Universal Design, In Christopherson, J, (Ed)) Universal Design, Hausbanken, Norway, (2002)
14. Sandhu J.: *op cit,* 111
15. Dewsbury, G. Clarke K. Hughes J. Rouncefield M, and Sommerville I.: Designing Dependable Digital Domestic Environments, Proceedings of HOIT 2003, April 6–8 2003, in Irvine, California (2003)

Modelling and Verification of Layered Security Protocols: A Bank Application

Johannes Grünbauer[1], Helia Hollmann[2], Jan Jürjens[1], and Guido Wimmel[1]

[1] Department of Computer Science, Munich University of Technology
Boltzmannstr. 3, D-85748 Garching, Germany
{gruenbau|juerjens|wimmel}@in.tum.de
[2] Secaron AG, Ludwigstrasse 55, D-85399 Hallbergmoos, Germany
hollmann@secaron.de

Abstract. Designing security-critical systems correctly is very difficult and there are many examples of weaknesses arising in practice. A particular challenge lies in the development of layered security protocols motivated by the need to combine existing or specifically designed protocols that each enforce a particular security requirement. Although appealing from a practical point of view, this approach raises the difficult question of the security properties guaranteed by the combined layered protocols, as opposed to each protocol in isolation. In this work, we apply a method for facilitating the development of trustworthy security-critical systems using the computer-aided systems engineering tool AutoFocus to the particular problem of layered security protocols. We explain our method at the example of a banking application which is currently under development by a major German bank and is about to be put to commercial use.

1 Introduction

Security aspects have become an increasingly important issue in developing distributed systems, especially in the electronic business sector. Because of the fact that failures of security mechanisms may cause very high potential damage (e.g., loss of money through fraud), the correctness of such systems is crucial.

Designing security critical systems correctly is difficult. Also, it is easy to misunderstand assumptions on the environment in which e.g. protocols are to be used and what their secure functioning may rely on. Security violations often occur at the boundaries between security mechanisms and the general system [11,1].

Therefore, the consideration of security aspects has to be integrated into general systems development [20,1] and also take into account aspects of security management [7]. Common modelling techniques used in industry, such as collaboration diagrams, state charts and message sequence charts (MSCs) have to be tailored for that purpose.

A particular challenge lies in the development of layered security protocols motivated by the need to combine existing or specifically designed protocols

S. Anderson et al. (Eds.): SAFECOMP 2003, LNCS 2788, pp. 116–129, 2003.

that each enforce a particular security requirement. Although appealing from a practical point of view, this approach raises the difficult question of the security properties guaranteed by the combined layered protocols, as opposed to each protocol in isolation.

In this work, we apply a method for facilitating the development of trustworthy security-critical systems using the computer-aided systems engineering tool AUTOFOCUS [14,15] to the particular problem of layered security protocols. Cryptographic protocols are specified with state charts. Together with a suitable attacker model, they are examined for security weaknesses using model checking.

We explain our method at the example of a banking application which is currently under development by a major German bank and is about to be put to commercial use.

We specify cryptographic protocols using state transition diagrams (STDs, similar to UML state charts). Together with the modelled adversary, this system is checked for security weaknesses automatically using the model checker SMV connected to AUTOFOCUS to verify the desired security properties of the protocol.

The approach has the benefits of combining intuitive graphical modelling, simulation and model checking in one user-friendly CASE-tool, and allows to represent possible attacks as MSCs. Since the AUTOFOCUS tool builds on the formal development method Focus [4], our approach also supports formal proofs in this framework. The intruder model used is rather flexible, e.g. the adversary can switch between acting as one or another party, intercept only certain messages or learn certain keys etc. Also, the AUTOFOCUS tool integrates several formal tools, which in [3] was identified as a major obstacle to widespread adoption of formal methods.

To put our work into context, we give some background information and related work. There has been extensive research in using formal methods to verify security protocols, following an abstract way to describe protocols in [8]. A few examples are [6,22,25]. [28] considers refinement of security-critical systems. Aspects of security engineering have been considered in [1,27,21,10]. As an example for the treatment of security in the context of general systems engineering, [17,18] presents work towards using the UML notation in security engineering. AUTOFOCUS has been used for security e.g. in [31].

This paper is structured as follows. In Section 2 we introduce the notation of AUTOFOCUS. In Section 3, we give an overview over the banking application under consideration, specify a critical part (a layered authentication protocol) and carry out a security analysis.

We end with a conclusion and indicate further planned work.

2   The Tool AUTOFOCUS

For modelling and verification of the layered protocol, we use the tool AUTO-FOCUS [14,29]. AUTOFOCUS is a CASE tool for graphically specifying distributed systems. It is based on the formal method Focus [5], and its models have a simple, formally defined semantics. AUTOFOCUS offers standard, easy-to-use description techniques for an end-user who does not necessarily need to be a formal methods expert, as well as state-of-the-art techniques for validation and verification.

Systems are specified in AUTOFOCUS using static and dynamic views, which are conceptually similar to those offered in UML-RT, a UML profile for component-based communicating systems. AUTOFOCUS has been used and adapted to model security-critical systems in a number of case studies (see e.g. [31,19]).

To specify systems, AUTOFOCUS offers the following views:

- **System Structure Diagrams (SSDs)** are similar to data flow resp. collaboration diagrams and describe the structure and the interfaces of a system. In the SSD view, a system consists of a number of communicating components, which have input and output ports (denoted as empty and filled circles) to allow for receiving and sending messages of a particular data type. The ports can be connected via channels, making it possible for the components to exchange data. SSDs can be hierarchical, i.e. a component belonging to an SSD can have a substructure that is defined by an SSD itself. Besides, the components in an SSD can be associated with local variables.
- **Data Type Definitions (DTDs)** specify the data types used in the model, with the functional language Quest [26]. In addition to basic types as integer, user-defined hierarchic data types are offered that are very similar to those used in functional programming languages such as Haskell [30].
- **State Transition Diagrams (STDs)** represent extended finite automata and are used to describe the behaviour of a component in an SSD. The automata consist of a set of states (one of which is the initial state, marked with a black dot) and a set of transitions between the states, where each transition t is annotated with

    - $\mathsf{pre}(t)$, a boolean precondition (guard) on the inputs and local variables
    - input patterns $\mathsf{inp}(t) = \mathsf{inp}_1?\mathsf{pat}_1; \mathsf{inp}_2?\mathsf{pat}_2; \ldots$, specifying that values are to be read at the ports inp_i that should match the patterns pat_i (terms in the functional language that specify values of data types and can include variables). During the execution of t, variables in the patterns are bound to the matching values. For example, the pattern $\mathsf{inp}_1?\mathsf{DataForm}(\mathsf{Form}(x))$ matches if the value $\mathsf{DataForm}(\mathsf{Form}(\mathsf{Acknowledgement}))$ is received on port inp_1 and binds x in the preconditions, output expressions and postconditions to Acknowledgement.
    - output expressions $\mathsf{outp}(t)$ of the form
      $\mathsf{out}_1!\mathsf{term}_1; \mathsf{out}_2!\mathsf{term}_2; \ldots$
    - postconditions $\mathsf{post}(t)$ of the form
      $\mathsf{lvar}_1 = \mathsf{term}_1; \mathsf{lvar}_2 = \mathsf{term}_2; \ldots$

In the concrete syntax of the STDs, the annotation is written as $\mathsf{pre}(t) : \mathsf{inp}(t) : \mathsf{outp}(t) : \mathsf{post}(t)$. Leaving out components is interpreted as **true** for preconditions, and as an empty sequence in the other cases. A transition is executable if the input patterns match the values at the input ports and the precondition is true. At each clock tick, one executable transition in each component fires, outputs the values specified by the output patterns and sets the local variables according to the postcondition. The values at the output ports can be read by the connected components in the next clock cycle.

- **Extended Event Traces (EETs)** finally make it possible to describe exemplary system runs, similar to MSCs [16].

The Quest extensions [29] to AUTOFOCUS offer various connections of AUTO-FOCUS to programming languages and formal verification tools, such as Java code generation, model checking using SMV, and bounded model checking and test case generation.

Note that although we had to select a specific tool for the case study, the general concepts we present in this paper do not depend on the use of AUTO-FOCUS. Its main prerequisites are an executable, component-based description technique and verification support.

3   The Authentication Protocol

The bank system under consideration is an Internet-based application which can be used by clients to fill out and sign digital order forms. The main security requirements of this application are that the personal data in the forms must be kept confidential, and that orders can not be submitted in the name of others.

For this purpose, when the user logs in, first an authentication protocol is run and a confidential (i.e. encrypted) connection is established. The second part of the transaction (filling out and digitally signing the order form) is carried out over this connection.

The authentication protocol is based on an SSL connection which is established at first and provides a secure connection with regard to confidentiality and server authentication. The session key generated during the SSL handshake is used to encrypt the messages of the authentication protocol on the second layer. The protocol authenticates the client by making use of a card reader and a smart card to compute digital signatures on the client's side. The need for the layered protocol arose here because the SSL client authentication feature could not be used due to technical restrictions imposed by the architecture of the bank system (the web server did not support the forwarding of client certificates).

The complete protocol run is shown in Figure 1. After the ClientHello message a randomly generated number or "number used once" (nonce) is sent by the web server. The client signs this nonce with his own private key and sends it together with his certificate back to the web server. The certificate contains the client's identity, a global identification number which references the client's data on the backend and his public key. The web server checks the signature of the nonce and compares the received nonce with the one sent before. Furthermore a plausibility check of the global ID will be done and it will be saved for later purposes. The authentication is finished after the checks have been successful. The web server sends now the global ID and an empty form to the backend system, where it is filled with the client's data and sent back to the client. The

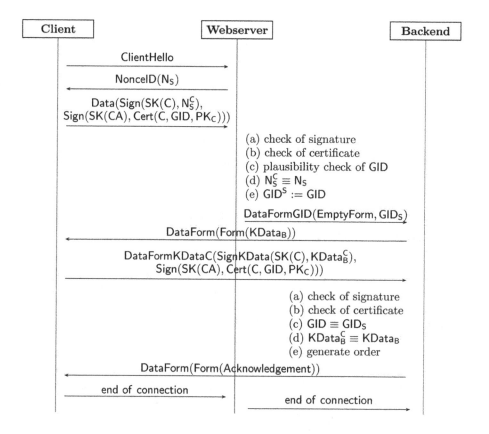

Fig. 1. Authentication Protocol

global ID is also stored on the backend. The client signs his data with his private key, thus creating an electronic signature. The backend checks the signature of the received data object and the certificate. The received global ID and the signed data object are compared with the ones stored. On success a order is generated and an acknowledgement is sent to the client. The end of connection signal can be caused by a timeout or a logout event.

3.1 Modelling

An overview of the complete modelled system can be found in the SSD in Figure 2. There are four components which are connected via channels of type TMessage, which is a user-defined data type specified in the DTDs. Is contains the message formats for the protocol, such as NonceID and DataForm. The component *Client* represents the user's system with the smart card, the card reader and a web browser. The component *Webserver* is the company's interface to the public network. Between these two components an *Intruder* is placed who tries

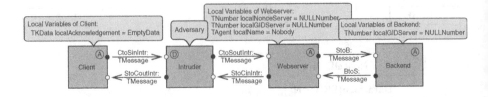

Fig. 2. SSD Main

Table 1. Local Variables of *Client*

Type	Name	Description
TKData localAcknowledgement		stores the received acknowledgement

to break the protocol run and get any client's data. Because we assume that the protocol is run over an SSL connection, either the client or the intruder can establish a connection with the web server. The fourth component is the *Backend*. It represents the host system of the bank and stores among other things the client's data. It is connected with the *Webserver* via the Intranet. Therefore we assume that no adversary is able read or manipulate data sent on these channels.

A description of the variables of the components *Client* and *Webserver* can be found in the Tables 1 and 2. For example, in `localGIDServer` of *Webserver* the global ID extracted from the client's certificate is stored. The values can be changed within the STDs which are associated to the components and describe their behaviour. In Figure 3 the STDs of the components *Client*, *Webserver* and *Backend* are shown.

The component *Intruder* is a black box view of the SSD in Figure 4(a) with the components *Overhear* and *FakeStore*. *Overhear* is the switching centre of *Intruder* and is used for forwarding the messages. If the client has established the SSL connection then the client will communicate with the web server. If the adversary starts the connection, the adversary will communicate with the web server. This behaviour is implied by the fact which component exchanged the session key with the web server within the SSL handshake. Figure 4(b) shows the STD of *Overhear*. It simulates the underlying SSL connection in the way

Table 2. Local Variables of *Webserver*

Type	Name	Description
TNumber	localNonceServer	stores the nonce sent by the web server.
TNumber	localGIDServer	stores the global ID from the client's certificate.
TAgent	localName	stores the name of the authenticated participant.

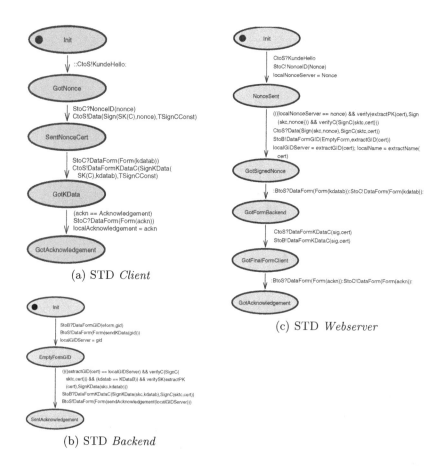

Fig. 3. State Transition Diagrams

described above and works as followed: At the start of the protocol run the internal variable `switchOv` is set to `undef`. If the client and the adversary start the protocol simultaneously, *Overhear* decides in a nondeterministic way which component is chosen for communication. Otherwise `switchOv` is set to `toClient` or to `toServer` depending on who sent the *ClientHello* message first.

3.2 Adversary

For modelling an adversary we take a *generic adversary* as a basis. A generic adversary has the following abilities or restrictions respectively.

- The adversary may know some data in advance and is assumed to know the design of the system excluding the private keys of the participants.
- The adversary can capture messages and delete them.

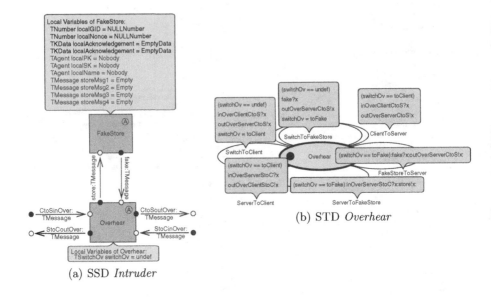

(a) SSD *Intruder*

(b) STD *Overhear*

Fig. 4. Parts of the Intruder

- The adversary can insert own messages into the protocol run. These can be arbitrary or protocol conform messages.
- The adversary cannot derive a private key from a public key. We assume the RSA encryption to be secure. In particular the adversary can only read encrypted messages with the corresponding key.
- It not possible to fake a signature. A message Sign(SK(i), x) can only be created with the private key of participant i. It can be verified with the corresponding public key.
- The adversary can split and recombine messages.

In general a generic adversary results in a model which is too complex for automatic verification. The computing time and space required by the model checker increases exponentially with the size of the model (given by its state space). Therefore we have to use a simplified adversary that is derived from the generic one in a justified way by limiting its behaviour and storage capacities. However, the modelled adversary should be strong enough so that possible attacks on the system with respect to the assumed threat scenario can be found. It is realized in the component *FakeStore* which has two purposes. Firstly, the adversary is able to authenticate as a regular client if he submits his valid certificate and can perform all operations of a normal client. Secondly, he will try to break the protocol run to get data of an arbitrary client and to perform operations such as generating fake messages.

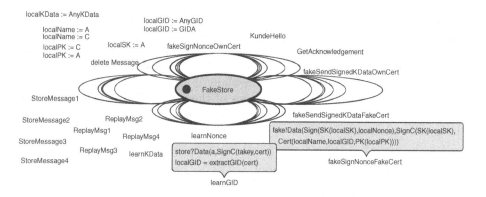

Fig. 5. STD *FakeStore*

The capabilities of the adversary are reflected by the transitions of the state transition diagram shown in Figure 5 and can be divided into several classes. The transitions *fakeSignNonceOwnCert* and *fakeSendSignedKDataOwnCert* enable the adversary to authenticate himself with his own certificate and to carry out transactions under his own identity. With the *StoreMessage* and *ReplayMsg* transitions it is possible to insert previous messages into the protocol run at a later time. The transitions with the prefix learn split the messages and extract their contents into local variables for later use. For example the transition learnGID takes the input pattern from port store and assigns the global ID from the certificate (with help from the function extractGID(cert)) to the local variable localGID. The transitions with the prefix fake use the values of the local variables to generate own messages. E.g. fakeSignNonceFakeCert sends a message with the values stored in the local variables. The unnamed transitions assign values to the local variables the adversary may know and thus is able to use. The values of the local variables are used in the faked messages the adversary sends. The manual construction of all the possible transitions can be automated and the model is then less susceptible to errors.

Justification of the Specialized Adversary. To show that the modelled adversary is adequate to the generic adversary we have to compare it to this one and make sure that he is strong enough to perform all assumed operations but is not too strong to perform operations beyond it. First of all we have to make sure that the adversary cannot read messages sent between *Client* and *Webserver* because of the SSL connection established before.

Furthermore it is neither possible for the adversary in the model to get the private key of the client nor to derive it from his public key since there is no corresponding transition. Therefore it is obviously not possible to sign data objects with anyone's private key. The adversary may know some data in advance, like the public keys of the participants and the structure of the protocol messages. With the assignment transitions in the model *FakeStore* assigns all possible values to the corresponding local variables. It is possible to delete, store and replay messages. Transitions with the prefix *learn* are used to store data in the local variables. Transitions with the prefix *fake* are taken for inserting own messages into the communication process by using the local variables. Furthermore *Fake-Store* can only sign a data object successfully if using a certificate signed itself by a certification authority. On the basis of these possibilities and restrictions with regard to the generic adversary we call the modelled adversary adequate to the generic adversary.

3.3   Verification of the Protocol

In this subsection we describe how to verify the model with regard to its security properties. For this purpose AutoFocus generates in conjunction with the Quest extensions an input file for the symbolic model checker SMV which carries out the actual model checking process. The model checking algorithm of SMV [23] is based on representing the system behaviour using Binary Decision Diagrams (BDDs). Symbolic model checking is particularly efficient for highly nondeterministic systems, such as the attacker in our model. We specify the required security properties of the system with CTL, a temporal logic defining formulas over the paths of the tree given by the possible computations of the system. In this work we use the following CTL operators: $\mathsf{AG}(e)$ means that expression e is true over all paths in the tree. $\mathsf{E}(e\ \mathsf{U}\ f)$ means that there exists at least one path in the tree where e is true until f gets true (see [9]). The security properties are translated to the SMV language as well, and during the model checking process, SMV checks if they are true with respect to the model. If SMV finds any flaw in the protocol, a message sequence chart is generated which helps to understand the way how the protocol can be attacked.

Authentication. For the authentication of the client we demand that the adversary cannot authenticate under a wrong identity. For the explanation of a correct client authentication we take a look at Figure 1. We call the authentication process correct, if the client sent the signed nonce back to the web server (step 3). That means, the client has to be in the state *SentNonceCert* and the web server in the state *GotSignedNonce*. Furthermore the web server has stored the value C in his local variable `localName` which is the identity extracted from the received certificate. The following temporal logic expression says that there does not exist any path ($\neg\mathsf{E}$) where *Webserver* is in state *GotSignedNonce* and stores the value C in his local variable `localName`, if *Client* has not been in state *SentNonceCert* before (the current control state of the Client or the Webserver is denoted with Client.@ respectively Webserver.@):

$$\neg(\mathsf{E}(\text{Client.@} \neq SentNonceCert\ \mathsf{U} \atop (\text{Webserver.@} = GotSignedNonce \wedge \text{Webserver.localName} = \text{C}))) \tag{1}$$

To verify this fact we have to add this as a property to the model and start the verification process. SMV checks the more than 700 000 reachable states in the model (out of approx. 10^{105} possible states in total) and after approximately 2 hours and 40 minutes[1] it comes to the result that the property is true under the assumptions.

Confidentiality of the Client's Data. The second property is that the adversary cannot get the client's confidential data. We have to ensure that the global ID of the client which serves as a unique identifier of the client's data is hidden from the adversary. Furthermore the adversary must not get the data served by the *Backend* and sent back signed by the client. The temporal logic expression below says that in all paths the adversary does not get the global ID, the client's data and the acknowledgement:

$$\textbf{AG}((\text{FakeStore.localGID} \neq \texttt{GID}) \wedge$$
$$(\text{FakeStore.localAcknowledgement} \neq \texttt{Acknowledgement}) \wedge \qquad (2)$$
$$(\text{FakeStore.localKData} \neq \texttt{KDataB}))$$

After a computation time of approximately 2 hours and 50 minutes the model checker concludes that the property is true under the assumptions.

3.4   Justification of the Model

The authentication protocol is based on SSL which we assume to be secure based on other works (see [24,12]). We show that there are no other attacks against the authentication protocol by the adversary.

The authentication protocol has to ensure that only authorized clients have access to their data and an adversary has no possibility to get data stored in the backend system or to carry out transactions under a false identity. The confidentiality of the protocol data sent on the second layer is ensured if the adversary cannot decrypt the data objects. Assuming that the SSL protocol is secure we can say that the protocol on the second layer is secure, too.

An unintended service (see [13]) exists, if existing messages would help the adversary to break the protocol, e.g. the adversary could get the session key of the SSL protocol on the first layer by a simple request. With the session key it would be easy for the adversary to read the confidential data sent within the authentication protocol and thus to break it.

We weaken the possibilities of the adversary on the second layer to adjust it to the security properties of SSL. This is necessary to reduce the complexity of the model. It is realized in the component *Overhear* which relies on the security properties of SSL. If a connection between *Client* and *Webserver* has been established, communication is only possible between these two components. Based on SSL the adversary has no possibility to read or modify the data sent along

---

[1] Athlon XP 1800+, 256 MB RAM, Windows XP Professional Edition. A detailed investigation on the general relationship between the size of the model (number of components, channels and data type definitions) and the corresponding complexity would go beyond the scope of this work and will be subject of future research.

the channels. Thus he is not able to send any requests to the SSL layer to get any information to break the protocol, e.g. the session key. This is also made clear in so far as both protocols own a disjoint set of messages and it is neither possible for the adversary to get the client's data nor to get secret information about the SSL connection. Thus an unintended service does not exist.

4   Conclusion and Further Work

This paper presented work regarding the formal analysis of layered security protocols using the computer-aided systems engineering tool AUTOFOCUS. An example of a banking application which is currently under development by a major German bank was modelled and analyzed for security weaknesses using model checking.

It turned out that the used approach was adequate for its purpose. By abstraction from irrelevant detail, the protocol model was kept compact enough to allow verification with the used model-checker in a few hours. The particular challenges of layered security protocols were addressed in a suitable way by informally making sure that no security weaknesses could arise from the combination of the different protocols.

Overall, the approach, which has the benefits of combining intuitive graphical modelling, simulation and model checking in one user-friendly CASE-tool, seems to be well-suited for further industry-critical applications.

Future work includes automated generation of the attacker models and giving formal arguments for their justification. We intend to apply our analysis method in further case studies to other domains and protocols, e.g. in the automotive context.

References

1. R. Anderson. *Security Engineering: A Guide to Building Dependable Distributed Systems.* Wiley, 2001.
2. S. Anderson, S. Bologna, and M. Felici, editors. *SAFECOMP 2002 – The 21st International Conference on Computer Safety, Reliabiltiy and Security,* volume 2434 of *Lecture Notes in Computer Science.* Springer-Verlag, Berlin, 2002.
3. R. Bloomfield, D. Craigen, F. Koob, M. Ullmann, and S.Wittmann. Formal methods diffusion: Past lessons and future prospects. In F. Koornneef and M. van der Meulen, editors, *Computer Safety, Reliability and Security 19th International Conference, SAFECOMP 2000,* volume 1943 of *Lecture Notes in Computer Science,* pages 211–226, Rotterdam, The Netherlands, Oct. 2000.
4. M. Broy, F. Dederich, C. Dendorfer, M. Fuchs, T. Gritzner, and R. Weber. The design of distributed systems – an introduction to FOCUS. Technical Report TUM-I9202, Technische Universität München, 1992.
5. M. Broy and K. Stolen, editors. *Specification and Development of Interactive Systems.* Springer, 2001.
6. M. Burrows, M. Abadi, and R. Needham. A logic of authentication. *Proceedings of the Royal Society of London A,* 426:233–271, 1989.

7. P. Daniel. Security of critical systems – management issues. In *Critical Systems Conference 2001*, Birmingham, 23rd–24th Oct. 2001. The Safety-Critical Systems Club and Software Reliability and Metrics Club.

8. D. Dolev and A. Yao. On the security of public key protocols. *IEEE Transactions on Information Theory*, 29(2):198–208, 1983.

9. E. Allen Emerson. Temporal and modal logic. In Jan van Leeuwen, editor, *Handbook of Theoretical Computer Science*, volume B, chapter 16, pages 995–1072. Elsevier Science Publishers, 1990.

10. R. Fredriksen, M. Kristiansen, B. Gran, K. Stolen, T. Opperud, and T. Dimitrakos. The CORAS framework for a model-based risk management process. In Anderson et al. [2], pages 94–105.

11. D. Gollmann. *Computer Security*. J. Wiley, 1999.

12. Johannes Grünbauer. Modellbasierte Sicherheitsanalyse einer Bankapplikation. Master's thesis, Technische Universität München, 2003.

13. Joshua D. Guttman. Security goals: Packet trajectories and strand spaces. *Lecture Notes in Computer Science*, 2171:197ff, 2001.

14. F. Huber, S. Molterer, A. Rausch, B. Schätz, M. Sihling, and O. Slotosch. Tool supported Specification and Simulation of Distributed Systems. In *International Symposium on Software Engineering for Parallel and Distributed Systems*, pages 155–164, 1998.

15. F. Huber, S. Molterer, B. Schätz, O. Slotosch, and A. Vilbig. Traffic Lights – An AutoFocus Case Study. In *1998 International Conference on Application of Concurrency to System Design*, pages 282–294. IEEE Computer Society, 1998.

16. ITU. ITU-TS Recommendation Z.120: Message Sequence Chart (MSC). ITU-TS, Geneva, 1996.

17. J. Jürjens. Critical Systems Development with UML. In *SAFECOMP 2002 – The 21st International Conference on Computer Safety, Reliabiltiy and Security*, Catania, Italy, Sept. 9–13 2002. EWICS TC7. Half-day tutorial.

18. J. Jürjens. *Secure Systems Development with UML*. Springer-Verlag, Berlin, 2003. To be published.

19. Jan Jürjens and Guido Wimmel. Security modelling for electronic commerce: The Common Electronic Purse Specifications. In *First IFIP conference on e-commerce, e-business, and e-government (I3E)*. Kluwer, 2001.

20. F. Koob, M. Ullmann, and S. Wittmann. The new topicality of using formal models of security policy within the security engineering process. In D. Hutter, W. Stephan, P. Traverso, and M. Ullmann, editors, *Applied Formal Methods – FM-Trends 98, International Workshop on Current Trends in Applied Formal Method*, volume 1641 of *Lecture Notes in Computer Science*, pages 302–310, Boppard, Germany, Oct. 7–9, 1998 1999. Springer-Verlag, Berlin.

21. K. Lano, D. Clark, and K. Androutsopoulos. Safety and security analysis of object-oriented models. In Anderson et al. [2].

22. G. Lowe. Breaking and fixing the Needham-Schroeder Public-Key Protocol using FDR. In Margaria and Steffen, editors, *TACAS*, volume 1055 of *Lecture Notes in Computer Science*, pages 147–166. Springer-Verlag, Berlin, 1996.

23. K. L. McMillan. *Symbolic Model Checking*. Kluwer Academic Publishers, Boston, 1993.

24. John C. Mitchell, Vitaly Shmatikov, and Ulrich Stern. Finite-state analysis of ssl 3.0. In *Seventh USENIX Security Symposium*, pages 201–216, 1998.

25. Lawrence C. Paulson. The inductive approach to verifying cryptographic protocols. *Journal of Computer Security*, 6(1–2):85–128, 1998.

26. J. Philipps and O. Slotosch. The Quest for Correct Systems: Model Checking of Diagrams and Datatypes. In *Asia Pacific Software Engineering Conference 1999*, 1999.
27. T. Rottke, D. Hatebur, M. Heisel, and M. Heiner. A problem-oriented approach to common criteria certification. In Anderson et al. [2].
28. T. Santen, A. Pfitzmann, and M. Heisel. Specification and refinement of secure it-systems. In T. Muntean M. Butler, editor, *International Workshop on Refinement of Critical Systems: Methods, Tools and Experience (RCS'2002)*, 2002.
29. O. Slotosch. Quest: Overview over the Project. In D. Hutter, W. Stephan, P Traverso, and M. Ullmann, editors, *Applied Formal Methods – FM-Trends 98*, pages 346–350. Springer LNCS 1641, 1998.
30. S. Thompson. *Haskell: The Craft of Functional Programming*. Addison-Wesley Longman, 1999.
31. Guido Wimmel and Alexander Wißpeintner. Extended Description Techniques for Security Engineering. In *Trusted Information, the New Decade Challege. 16th International Conference on Information Security (IFIP/Sec)*, 2001.

A Constraint Framework for the Qualitative Analysis of Dependability Goals: Integrity

Stefano Bistarelli[1,2]* and Simon N. Foley[3]**

[1] Dipartimento di Scienze, Università "G. D'Annunzio" di Chieti-Pescara, Italy
bista@sci.unich.it
[2] Istituto di Informatica e Telematica, CNR, Pisa, Italy
stefano.bistarelli@iit.cnr.it
[3] Department of Computer Science, University College, Ireland.
s.foley@cs.ucc.ie

Abstract. An integrity policy defines the situations when modification of information is authorized and is enforced by the security mechanisms of the system. However, in a complex application system it is possible that an integrity policy may have been incorrectly specified and, as a result, a user may be authorized to modify information that can lead to an unexpected system compromise. In this paper we propose a scalable and quantitative technique that uses constraint solving to model and analyze the effectiveness of application system integrity policies.

1 Introduction

Conventional security models such as [3, 13, 32, 27] are operational in nature in that they define *how* to achieve integrity but do not define *what* is meant by integrity. For example, the Clark-Wilson model [13] recommends that well-formed transactions, separation of duties and auditing be used to ensure integrity. However, the model does not attempt to define whether a particular security policy configuration actually achieves integrity: evaluating a system according to the Clark-Wilson model gives a confidence to the extent that good design principles have been applied. However, when we define a complex separation of duty policy, we cannot use the model to guarantee that a user of the system cannot somehow bypass the intent of the separation via some unexpected circuitous route.

In [17, 18] it is argued that to provide such guarantees it is necessary to model the behavior of both the system (with its protection mechanisms) and the *infrastructure* in which the system operates. Infrastructure is everything that serves the system requirements: software, hardware, users, and so forth. Even if a system is functionally correct, the infrastructure is likely to fail: software fails, users are dishonest, do not follow procedures, and so forth. The system and

* Partially supported by MIUR project "Constraint Based Verification of Reactive Systems" (COVER), and by the MIUR project "Network Aware Programming: Object, Languages, Implementation" (NAPOLI).
** Support received from Science Foundation Ireland under Grant 00/PI.1/C075.

S. Anderson et al. (Eds.): SAFECOMP 2003, LNCS 2788, pp. 130–143, 2003.

its security mechanisms must be designed to be resilient to these infrastructure failures. Only when a system is characterized in this way can it become possible to analyze whether a particular system configuration (including security policy) ensures integrity.

The approach in [17,18] provides a formal trace based semantics for integrity that requires detailed formal specifications to be provided for the system and its infrastructure. This requires considerable specification effort and the cost of such in-depth specification and subsequent analysis may be justified for small critical security mechanisms. However, we conjecture that such integrity analysis would not scale well to the configuration of a large and/or complex application system because it would be necessary to formally specify and reason about the potential behavior of *every* infrastructure component, user and so forth. Furthermore, [17,18] does not consider any approach to mechanizing the analysis and formal verification process.

In this paper we extend the work outlined in [6] that proposes the use of constraints as a more abstract and complementary approach to [17,18]. The approach requires less semantic detail about the operation of the system and its infrastructure. Rather than attempting to model the complete behavior of the system and infrastructure (as in [17,18]), we model only those components that are considered relevant to the security policy and configuration. This is done by modeling the system and infrastructure in terms of the *constraints* that they impose over security relevant components of the system. This results in a definition of integrity consistency that can be solved as a constraint satisfaction problem [23,22].

An advantage to expressing integrity analysis as a constraint satisfaction problem is that there exists a wide body of existing research results on solving this problem for large systems of constraints in a fully mechanized manner [11, 15,25,1,20]. Constraints have been used in many practical analysis tools, such as Concurrent Engineering and Computer Aided Verification [10,12,14]. Thus, the results in this paper provide a basis for the development of practical tools for integrity analysis of complex application system security policies.

A further advantage to using a constraint based framework is that it becomes possible to carry out a quantitative analysis of integrity using *soft constraints* [7,8,9,4,29,30,16,19,26]. A quantitative analysis provides a fine-grained measure of how secure a system is, rather the simple coarse-grained false/true provided by the conventional 'crisp' constraints.

The paper is organized as follows. Section 2 provides an introduction to constraints and the constraint satisfaction problem. Section 3 adapts the results in [17,18] and proposes a more abstract approach to modeling systems within a crisp constraint framework. Section 4 describes how soft constraints are used to carry out quantitative integrity analysis. A number of examples are used throughout the paper to illustrate the approach.

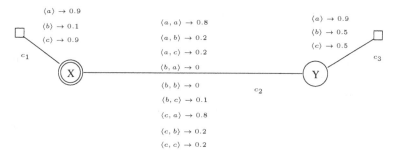

Fig. 1. A fuzzy CSP.

2   Introduction to Constraint Solving

Constraint Solving is an emerging software technology for declarative description and effective solving of large problems. The constraint programming process consists of the generation of requirements (constraints) and solution of these requirements, by specialized constraint solvers.

When the requirements of a problem are expressed as a collection of boolean predicates over variables, we obtain what is called the *crisp* (or classical) Constraint Satisfaction Problem (CSP). In this case the problem is solved by finding any assignment of the variables that satisfies all the constraints.

Sometimes, when a deeper analysis of a problem is required, *soft* constraints are used instead. Soft constraints associate a qualitative or quantitative value either to the entire constraint or to each assignment of its variables. Such values are interpreted as level of preference or importance or cost. The levels are usually ordered, reflecting the fact that some levels (constraints) are better than others. When using soft constraints it is necessary to specify, via suitable combination operators, how the level of preference of a global solution is obtained from the preferences in the constraints.

Several formalizations of the concept of *soft constraints* are currently available. In the following, we refer to the formalization based on c-semirings [7,8,9,4], which can be shown to generalize and express both crisp and soft constraints [8,5].

2.1   Semiring-Based CSPs

A semiring-based constraint assigns to each instantiation of its variables an associated value from a partially ordered set. When dealing with crisp constraints, the values are the boolean *true* and *false* representing the admissible and/or non-admissible values; when dealing with soft constraints the values are interpreted as preferences.

The framework must also handle the combination of constraints. To do this one must take into account such additional values, and thus the formalism must provide suitable operations for combination ($\times$) and comparison ($+$) of tuples of values and constraints. This is why this formalization is based on the concept of c-semiring.

Semirings. A *semiring* is a tuple $\langle A, +, \times, \mathbf{0}, \mathbf{1} \rangle$ such that: A is a set and $\mathbf{0}, \mathbf{1} \in A$; $+$ is commutative, associative and $\mathbf{0}$ is its unit element; $\times$ is associative, distributes over $+$, $\mathbf{1}$ is its unit element and $\mathbf{0}$ is its absorbing element. A c-semiring ("c" stands for "constraint-based") is a semiring $\langle A, +, \times, \mathbf{0}, \mathbf{1} \rangle$ such that $+$ is idempotent with $\mathbf{1}$ as its absorbing element and $\times$ is commutative [8,4]. In the following we will always use the word semiring as standing for c-semiring.

Let us consider the relation $\leq_S$ over A such that $a \leq_S b$ iff $a + b = b$. It is possible to prove that: $\leq_S$ is a partial order; $+$ and $\times$ are monotone on $\leq_S$; $\mathbf{0}$ is its minimum and $\mathbf{1}$ its maximum, and $\langle A, \leq_S \rangle$ is a complete lattice with lowest upper bound operator $+$. Moreover, if $\times$ is idempotent, then: $+$ distributes over $\times$, and $\langle A, \leq_S \rangle$ is a complete distributive lattice with greatest lower bound operator $\times$. The $\leq_S$ relation is what we will use to compare tuples and constraints: $a \leq_S b$ it intuitively means that b is better than a.

Constraint Problems. Given a semiring $S = \langle A, +, \times, \mathbf{0}, \mathbf{1} \rangle$ and an ordered set of variables V over a finite domain D, a *constraint* is a function which, given an assignment $\eta : V \to D$ of the variables, returns a value of the semiring.

By using this notation we define $\mathcal{C} = \eta \to A$ as the set of all possible constraints that can be built starting from S, D and V.

Consider a constraint $c \in \mathcal{C}$. We define his support as $supp(c) = \{v \in V \mid \exists \eta, d_1, d_2. c\eta[v := d_1] \neq c\eta[v := d_2]\}$, where

$$\eta[v := d]v' = \begin{cases} d & \text{if } v = v', \\ \eta v' & \text{otherwise.} \end{cases}$$

Note that $c\eta[v := d_1]$ means $c\eta'$ where η' is η modified with the association $v := d_1$ (that is the operator [ ] has precedence over application).

A *constraint satisfaction problem* is a pair $\langle C, con \rangle$ where $con \subseteq V$ and C is a set of constraints: con is the set of variables of interest for the constraint set C, which however may concern also variables not in con. Note that a classical CSP is a SCSP where the chosen c-semiring is: $S_{CSP} = \langle \{false, true\}, \vee, \wedge, false, true \rangle$.

Many other "soft" CSPs (Probabilistic, weighted, ...) can be modeled by using a suitable semiring structure ($S_{prob} = \langle [0, 1], max, \times, 0, 1 \rangle$, $S_{weight} = \langle \mathcal{R}, min, +, +\infty, 0 \rangle$, ...).

Example 1 Figure 1 shows the graph representation of a fuzzy CSP[1]. Variables X and Y, and constraints are represented respectively by nodes and by undirected (unary for c_1 and c_3 and binary for c_2) arcs, and semiring values are written to the right of the corresponding tuples. The variables of interest (that is the set con) are represented with a double circle. Here we assume that the domain D of the variables contains only elements a, b and c.

---

[1] Fuzzy CSPs can be modeled in the SCSP framework by choosing the c-semiring $S_{FCSP} = \langle [0, 1], max, min, 0, 1 \rangle$.

If semiring values represent probability/fuzziness values then, for instance, the tuple $\langle a, c \rangle \rightarrow 0.2$ in constraint c_2 can be interpreted to mean that the probability/fuzziness of X and Y having values a and c, respectively, is 0.2. $\triangle$

Combining constraints. When there is a set of soft constraints $\mathcal{C}$, the combined weight of the constraints is computed using the operator $\otimes : \mathcal{C} \times \mathcal{C} \rightarrow \mathcal{C}$ defined as $(c_1 \otimes c_2)\eta = c_1\eta \times_S c_2\eta$.

Given a constraint $c \in \mathcal{C}$ and a variable $v \in V$, the *projection* of c over $V - \{v\}$, written $c \Downarrow_{(V-\{v\})}$ is the constraint c' s.t. $c'\eta = \sum_{d \in D} c\eta[v := d]$. Informally, projecting means eliminating some variables from the support. This is done by associating to each tuple over the remaining variables a semiring element which is the sum of the elements associated by the original constraint to all the extensions of this tuple over the eliminated variables. In short, combination is performed via the multiplicative operation of the semiring, and projection via the additive one.

Solutions. The *solution* of a SCSP $P = \langle C, con \rangle$ is the constraint $Sol(P) = (\bigotimes C) \Downarrow_{con}$. That is, we combine all constraints, and then project over the variables in con. In this way we get the constraint with support (not greater than) con which is "induced" by the entire SCSP. Note that when all the variables are of interest we do not need to perform any projection.

Solutions are constraints in themselves and can be ordered by extending the $\leq_S$ order. We say that a constraint c_1 is at least as constraining as constraint c_2 if $c_1 \sqsubseteq c_2$, where for any assignment η of variables then

$$c_1 \sqsubseteq c_2 \equiv c_1\eta \leq_S c_2\eta$$

Thus, if $c_1 \sqsubseteq c_2$ holds, then constraint c_1 may be thought of as a *refinement*, or 'suitable' (more restrictive) replacement of constraint c_2.

Example 2 Consider again the solution of the fuzzy CSP of Figure 1. It associates a semiring element to every domain value of variable X. Such an element is obtained by first combining all the constraints together and then projecting the obtained constraint over X.

For instance, for the tuple $\langle a, a \rangle$ (that is, $X = Y = a$), we have to compute the minimum between 0.9 (which is the value assigned to $X = a$ in constraint c_1), 0.8 (which is the value assigned to $\langle X = a, Y = a \rangle$ in c_2) and 0.9 (which is the value for $Y = a$ in c_3). Hence, the resulting value for this tuple is 0.8. We can do the same work for tuple $\langle a, b \rangle \rightarrow 0.2$, $\langle a, c \rangle \rightarrow 0.2$, $\langle b, a \rangle \rightarrow 0$, $\langle b, b \rangle \rightarrow 0$, $\langle b, c \rangle \rightarrow 0.1$, $\langle c, a \rangle \rightarrow 0.8$, $\langle c, b \rangle \rightarrow 0.2$ and $\langle c, c \rangle \rightarrow 0.2$. The obtained tuples are then projected over variable X, obtaining the solution $\langle a \rangle \rightarrow 0.8$, $\langle b \rangle \rightarrow 0.1$ and $\langle c \rangle \rightarrow 0.8$. $\triangle$

3   Integrity Analysis with Crisp Constraints

In [17, 18] functional requirements are expressed as properties over the possible traces of actions at the interface of a system. In this section we take a more abstract approach by describing requirements in terms of constraints on variables that are invariant over the lifetime of the system.

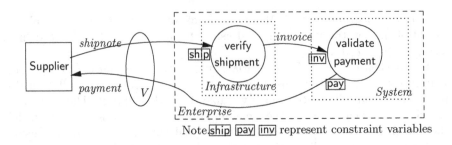

Note.[ship] [pay] [inv] represent constraint variables

Fig. 2. A simple payment enterprise

Example 3 A simple enterprise receives shipments, and generates associated payments for a supplier. Requirements Analysis identifies the actions *shipnote* and *payment*, corresponding to the arrival of a shipment (note) and its associated payment, respectively. For the purposes of integrity, the analysis has identified a requirement that the system should not pay its supplier more than the stated value of goods shipped.

Let the constraint variables ship and pay represent the total value of goods shipped to date and the total value of payments made to date, respectively. Constraint Probity describes the requirement as an invariant over variables ship and pay.

$$\text{Probity} \equiv \text{pay} \leq \text{ship}$$

Figure 2 outlines a possible implementation of this requirement. A clerk verifies shipment notes and enters invoice details (action *invoice*) to a computer system, which in turn, generates payment to the supplier. This implementation is described in terms of variables ship, pay and variable inv which represents the total value of invoices generated to date.

A clerk should not process more invoices than shipments and, therefore, the clerks behavior is represented by the following constraint.

$$\text{Clerk} \equiv \text{inv} \leq \text{ship}$$

The requirement on the invoice processing application system is

$$\text{Appl} \equiv \text{pay} \leq \text{inv}$$

and the enterprise design is specified as the constraint

$$\text{Imp1} \equiv \text{Appl} \otimes \text{Clerk}$$

obtained by combining together Appl and Clerk constraints. Intuitively, integrity is ensured in this system since Imp1 ensures the high-level requirement Probity. △

In the above example, the supplier's interface V to the system is modeled in terms of the variables ship and pay. Constraints between these variables are used to characterize our requirements for the system. We want to ensure that the implementation upholds probity through this interface, that is,

$$\text{Imp1}_{\Downarrow\{\text{ship,pay}\}} \sqsubseteq \text{Probity}$$

We are unconcerned about the possible values of the 'internal' variable inv and thus the constraint relation $\text{Imp1}_{\Downarrow\{\text{ship,pay}\}}$ describes the constraints in Imp1 that exist between variables ship and pay. By definition, the above equation defines that all of the possible solutions of $\text{Imp1}_{\Downarrow\{\text{ship,pay}\}}$ are solutions of Probity, that is, for any assignment η of variables then

$$\text{Imp1}_{\Downarrow\{\text{ship,pay}\}} \ \eta \leq_S \text{Probity} \ \eta$$

Definition 1 We say that the requirement S *locally refines* requirement R through the interface described by the set of variables V iff $S_{\Downarrow V} \sqsubseteq R_{\Downarrow V}$.   △

Example 4 Continuing Example 3, assume that the application system will behave reliably and uphold Appl. However, it is not reasonable to assume that the clerk will always act reliably as Clerk. In practice, the clerk could take on any behavior:

$$\overline{\text{Clerk}} \equiv (\text{inv} \leq \text{ship} \lor \text{inv} > \text{ship}) = true$$
$$\text{Imp2} \equiv \overline{\text{Clerk}} \otimes \text{Appl}$$

Imp2 is a more realistic representation of the actual enterprise. It more accurately reflects the reliability of its infrastructure than the previous design Imp1. However, since inv is no longer constrained it can take on any value, and therefore, pay is unconstrained and we have

$$\text{Imp2}_{\Downarrow\{\text{ship,pay}\}} \not\sqsubseteq \text{Probity}$$

that is, the implementation of the system is not sufficiently robust to be able to deal with internal failures in a safe way and uphold the original probity requirement.   △

In [21], integrity is given as one attribute of *dependability*. Dependability is characterized as a *"property of a computer system such that reliance can be justifiably placed on the service it delivers"* [21]. In [17,18] we argue that this notion of dependability may be viewed as a class of refinement whereby the nature of the reliability of the enterprise is explicitly specified.

Definition 2 (Dependability) If R gives requirements for an enterprise and S is its proposed implementation, including details about the nature of the reliability of its infrastructure, then S is as *dependably safe* as R at interface that is described by the set of variables E if and only if $S_{\Downarrow E} \sqsubseteq R_{\Downarrow E}$ △

Separation of duties [13] is a common implementation technique for achieving integrity. While fault-tolerant techniques replicate an operation, separation of duties can be thought of as a partitioning of the operation across different user domains.

Example 5 When a shipment arrives a clerk verifies the consignment at goods-inwards (entering *consign* into the system). When an invoice arrives, a different clerk enters details into the system, and if the invoice matches a consignments, a payment is generated. So long as the operations are separated then a single clerk entering a bogus consignment or invoice can be detected by the system. This is depicted in Figure 3.

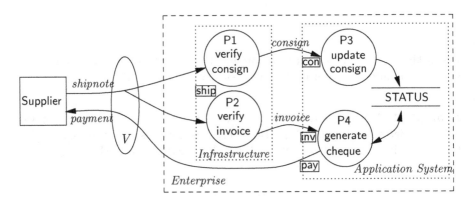

Fig. 3. Supporting separation of duties

Let variables inv and con represent the total value of invoices and consignments, respectively, received to date. Specifications Clerk1, Clerk2 and App3 define the constraints on the system variables, reflecting invariants that are expected to be upheld by the clerks and the application system.

$$\text{Clerk1} \equiv \text{con} \leq \text{ship}$$
$$\text{Clerk2} \equiv \text{inv} \leq \text{ship}$$
$$\text{App3} \equiv \text{pay} \leq min(\text{con}, \text{inv})$$

This system is as dependably safe as Probity even when a single clerk fails, that is, we have

$$(\text{Clerk1} \otimes \text{Clerk2} \otimes \text{App3})_{\Downarrow\{\text{ship,pay}\}} \sqsubseteq \text{Probity}$$
$$(\text{Clerk2} \otimes \text{App3})_{\Downarrow\{\text{ship,pay}\}} \sqsubseteq \text{Probity}$$
$$(\text{Clerk1} \otimes \text{App3})_{\Downarrow\{\text{ship,pay}\}} \sqsubseteq \text{Probity}$$

Note that the absence of a constraint means that it does not restrict variables to any values. However, the system is not resilient to the failure of both clerks nor to the failure of the application software. Removing the 'normal behavior' constraints imposed by both clerks or by the application yields the following.

$$\mathsf{App3}_{\Downarrow\{\mathsf{ship,pay}\}} \not\sqsubseteq \mathsf{Probity}$$

$$(\mathsf{Clerk1} \otimes \mathsf{Clerk2})_{\Downarrow\{\mathsf{ship,pay}\}} \not\sqsubseteq \mathsf{Probity}$$

As currently defined, our specification favors the payment-enterprise, not the supplier: payments may be very late, or not made at all, but are never bogus. If a clerk fails then payment may not be made. In reality, the infrastructure contains many additional components; audit logs to record failures and supervisors, who make judgments and rectify these inconsistencies.   △

Example 6 Another approach to dealing with unreliable systems (infrastructure) is to replicate the faulty components and make the system fault tolerant. We can make the payment enterprise fault tolerant if we replicate the clerk. We assume that every shipment is processed by $2k+1$ replicated clerks. The system votes (on the $2k+1$ invoices) to decide whether or not a consignment is valid. In this case, the abnormal behavior of the infrastructure is represented by properly constraining the behavior of at least $k+1$ clerks, and we can argue that the resulting system is as dependably safe as Probity.   △

4   Quantitative Integrity Analysis

The examples in the previous section use crisp constraints to describe system requirements and implementations. When a quantitative analysis of the system is required then it is necessary to represent these properties using soft constraints.

Example 7 Consider again the Probity requirement and suppose that we aim not only to have a correct implementation, but, if possible, to have the "best" possible implementation. To do this we consider a soft constraint between variables ship and pay that assigns to the configuration ship $= a$ and pay $= b$ the preference level represented by the integer $a - b^2$. If we are looking for the best implementation for the buyer, then we will try to maximize this level. In this way, different instances of the same system can be compared, and different implementations can be checked and analyzed.

Soft constraints also provide a basis for evaluating and comparing less resilient implementations that cannot uphold the intended requirement. For example, if an acceptable implementation Imp cannot be found to satisfy

$$\mathsf{Imp}_{\Downarrow\{\mathsf{ship,pay}\}} \sqsubseteq \mathsf{Probity}$$

---

[2] This value represent how much pay differs from ship. Our goal is to have pay=ship, but sometimes this is impossible and our goal will be to minimize the $a-b$ difference.

then one might be satisfied (in some sense) by selecting the best of the less resilient, but acceptable implementations. Given insufficiently resilient implementations Imp_1 and Imp_2 then their corresponding semiring levels provide a relative ordering that allow the selection of the 'best' of the less resilient implementations.

For example, suppose that the payment system is implemented in such a way that a payment *fully* clears the outstanding balance and that payment must be a multiple of 100. Such an implementation satisfies Probity if payments are made only when the outstanding balance is a multiple of 100. However, there a family of other implementations that round up the outstanding amount to a multiple of 100, and, while they do not uphold probity, may be acceptable in some sense. The overpayment pay-bal gives us a soft measure (defined by the semiring) of how acceptable the 'invalid' implementations might be; the 'best' implementation seeks to minimize this, that is, the solution that rounds upwards to the nearest multiple of 100.   △

Probabilistic based reasoning can also be done within the soft constraints framework. For example, consider an implementation Imp3 that ensures that the number of payments is never more than 3, regardless of the number of shipments received. This is represented as:

$$\mathsf{Imp3} \equiv \mathsf{pay} \leq 3.$$

Assume that there is a constraint on variable ship that specifies the probability of the possible number of shipments made at a certain time. If the nature of the probability distribution is such that it is generally more likely that the value of ship is greater than 3, then Imp3 is a not unreasonable implementation (despite $\mathsf{Imp3}_{\Downarrow\{\mathsf{ship},\mathsf{pay}\}} \sqsubseteq \mathsf{Probity}$ not holding).

The following example illustrates how one might consider the probability of component failure within a specification.

Example 8 Consider the assignment of probability of failure to the infrastructure components of Example 5.

For the sake of efficiency, assume that in this implementation Imp4, rather than verifying consignment values (and details), Clerk1 computes batch totals [33] by simply counting the number of consignments received to date. Let the variable contot represent this value. The invoice processing application also counts the number of invoices received to date (as invtot) and compares this against contot. If there is a discrepancy then an error is flagged and it is assumed that it is investigated and repaired.

The implementation is characterized by relationships between these variables that include:

- If contot = invtot (totals match) then the probability that the invoice is accurate is $P1$, that is, the probability that inv = ship is $P1$.
- If contot $\neq$ invtot then the probability that the invoice is accurate is $P2$, that is, the probability that inv = ship is $P2$.

- The application program could fail with an incorrect value for pay resulting in an incorrect relationship pay = inv or pay ≠ inv. Let $P3$ represent the probability of the application failing, regardless of the relationship between pay and inv.

The application Imp4 is obtained by combining all the constraints. We will easily obtain

- If contot = invtot then the probability that payment is safe (not over payment, pay ≤ ship) is $P1 \times (1 - P3)$ where $P3$ is the probability of the application failing.
- If contot ≠ invtot then the probability that payment is safe (pay ≤ ship) is $P2 \times P3$. We assume that when such a discrepancy is found then the application software can repair it and, therefore, the probability that the payment is safe in this case is also $P2 \times P3$.

The constraints between pay, ship, contot and invtot are built over the probability semiring $S_{prob} = \langle [0,1], max, \times, 0, 1 \rangle$.

When using probability in the implementation, then the specification must be defined in similar way. In this case, a correct specification must ensure that the probability that pay ≤ ship is at least $P4$.

Thus, the system specification is

$$\text{Probity}_{prob} \equiv \text{Prob} : (\text{pay} \times \text{ship}) \to \mathbb{R}$$

$$\text{Prob}(a, b) = \begin{cases} P4 & \text{if } a \leq b, \\ 1 - P4 & \text{otherwise.} \end{cases}$$

To check correctness of our implementation we have to check that

$$\text{Imp4} \Downarrow_{\{\text{pay,ship}\}} \sqsubseteq \text{Probity}_{prob}$$

$\triangle$

5   Discussion and Conclusion

The contribution of this paper is a scalable and quantitative technique for analyzing the configuration of application system integrity policies.

By modeling the system and its infrastructure only in terms of abstract constraints, we argue that it becomes more realistic (than [17]) to consider modeling large complex application systems. Constraint solving can be done for large problems and, therefore, the proposed integrity analysis (as a constraint satisfaction problem) should scale up to similarly large/complex application systems configurations.

In [28] a policy analysis technique is proposed for detecting possible conflicts between separation of duty, user role assignment and role inheritance rules. This can be thought of as providing an analysis on, what is, in effect, the constraints on user role assignments. While useful, it is limited since it does not consider any further semantic information about the system and/or infrastructure. It would be interesting to apply the integrity analysis techniques proposed in this paper to extend the results in [28] for RBAC models.

Section 4 describes how soft constraints provide a basis for a quantitative analysis of integrity. Soft constraints may be used in two ways. Firstly, they can be used to provide a measure of integrity to compare the effectiveness of different system configurations. If it is not possible to develop a resilient system configuration that fully meets the set of system requirements, then one may wish to consider the best of the less resilient, but acceptable (in some sense) configurations. For example, if it is not possible to configure a system that is resilient to all internal fraud, then an acceptable alternative might be to keep the fraud within some limit. Example 7 sketches a simplistic example of this; further research is required to develop this in general.

The second application of soft constraints to the analysis of integrity is that it allows the use of quantitative information in modeling the system and infrastructure configuration. By associating probability measures with component failures, Example 8 described the validation that a system configuration/policy achieved integrity within some degree of probability. Soft constraints provide a practical framework in which such sophisticated models can be analyzed.

In [2] soft constraints are used to represent confidentiality and authentication properties of security protocols. This approach is not unlike the strategy taken in this paper. The solution of the resulting constraint system gives a measure of the confidentiality/authentication of the system. In [2] a protocol run is compared with an "ideal" run without spies, When the solutions differ an attack to the protocol is identified. The proposed integrity analysis must consider various 'spy's, each characterizing the threats that a protection mechanism must withstand.

Sections 3 and 4 use constraints to describe invariant relationships between constraint variables over the lifetime of the system. This abstract approach means that it is possible to use verification tools to describe and automatically analyze whether system configurations achieve integrity. Developing such a environment is a topic for future research.

However, we are not limited to only this style of abstract reasoning. In [17] an unwound form of local refinement is given in terms of conditions (constraints) on states and state transitions. A system that is specified in a model-oriented manner (for example, [31]) can be characterized in terms of constraints over state variables and transitions, and therefore, this unwound version of local refinement can be used to analyze integrity of more concrete specifications within a constraint framework.

The use of soft constraints permit us to perform a quantitative analysis of system integrity (see Section 4) useful to compare two system implementation. In [24] they follow a similar strategy by approximating the notion of probabilistic non-interference with a notion of ϵ-similarity. To do this they use a concurrent constraint probabilistic language. Despite the fact that the use of constraints is common between their and our approach, they rely on the notion of path (or trace) and on the probability of each path.

References

[1] G. J. Badros, A. Borning, and P. J. Stuckey. The cassowary linear arithmetic constraint solving algorithm. *ACM Transactions on Computer Human Interaction*, 8(4):276–306, dec 2001.

[2] G. Bella and S. Bistarelli. Soft Constraints for Security Protocol Analysis: Confidentiality. In *Proc. of the 3rd International Symposium on Practical Aspects of Declarative Languages (PADL'01)*, LNCS 1990, pages 108–122. Springer-Verlag, 2001.

[3] K.J. Biba. Integrity considerations for secure computer systems. Technical Report MTR-3153 Rev 1 (ESD-TR-76-372), MITRE Corp Bedford MA, 1976.

[4] S. Bistarelli. *Soft Constraint Solving and programming: a general framework*. PhD thesis, Dipartimento di Informatica, Università di Pisa, Italy, mar 2001. TD-2/01.

[5] S. Bistarelli, H. Fargier, U. Montanari, F. Rossi, T. Schiex, and G. Verfaillie. Semiring-based CSPs and Valued CSPs: Frameworks, properties, and comparison. *CONSTRAINTS: An international journal. Kluwer*, 4(3), 1999.

[6] S. Bistarelli and S.N. Foley. Analysis of integrity policies using soft constraints. In *Proceedings of IEEE Workshop Policies for Distributed Systems and Networks*, pages 77–80, June 2003.

[7] S. Bistarelli, U. Montanari, and F. Rossi. Constraint Solving over Semirings. In *Proc. IJCAI95*, San Francisco, CA, USA, 1995. Morgan Kaufman.

[8] S. Bistarelli, U. Montanari, and F. Rossi. Semiring-based Constraint Solving and Optimization. *Journal of the ACM*, 44(2):201–236, Mar 1997.

[9] S. Bistarelli, U. Montanari, and F. Rossi. Soft concurrent constraint programming. In *Proc. ESOP, April 6–14, 2002, Grenoble, France*, LNCS. Springer-Verlag, 2002.

[10] J.A. Bowen and D. Bahler. Constraint-based software for concurrent engineering. *IEEE Computer*, 26(1):66–68, January 1993.

[11] Kirchner C. Kirchner and M.Vittek. Designing clp using computational systems. In P. Van Hentenryck and S. Saraswat, editors, *Proceedings of Principles and Practice of Constraint Programming*. MIT Press, 1995.

[12] W. Chan, R. Anderson, P. Beame, and D. Notkin. Combining constraint solving and symbolic model checking for a class of systems with non-linear constraints. In Orna Grumberg, editor, *Computer Aided Verification, 9th International Conference, CAV'97 Proceedings*, volume 1254 of *Lecture Notes in Computer Science*, pages 316–327, Haifa, Israel, June 1997. Springer-Verlag.

[13] D. D. Clark and D. R. Wilson. A comparison of commercial and military computer security models. In *Proceedings Symposium on Security and Privacy*, pages 184–194. IEEE Computer Society Press, April 1987.

[14] G. Delzanno and T. Bultan. Constraint-based verification of client-server protocols. In *Proceedings CP2001*, volume 2239 of *Lecture Notes in Computer Science*, pages 286–?? Springer-Verlag, 2001.

[15] M. Dincbas, P. Van Hentenryck, H. Simonis, A. Aggoun, T. Graf, and F. Berthier. The constraint logic programming language chip. In *Proceedings of FGCS*, pages 693–702, 1988.

[16] H. Fargier and J. Lang. Uncertainty in constraint satisfaction problems: a probabilistic approach. In *Proc. European Conference on Symbolic and Qualitative Approaches to Reasoning and Uncertainty (ECSQARU)*, volume 747 of *LNCS*, pages 97–104. Springer-Verlag, 1993.

[17] S.N. Foley. Evaluating system integrity. In *Proceedings of the ACM New Security Paradigms Workshop*, 1998.

[18] S.N. Foley. A non-functional approach to system integrity. *IEEE Journal on Selected Areas in Commications*, 2003. *forthcoming.*

[19] E.C. Freuder and R.J. Wallace. Partial constraint satisfaction. *AI Journal*, 58, 1992.

[20] T. Frühwirth. Theory and practice of constraint handling rules. *Journal of Logic Programming - Special Issue on Constraint Logic Programming*, 37(1–3):95–138, oct-dec 1998.

[21] J. Laprie. Dependability: Basic concepts and terminology.

[22] A.K. Mackworth. Constraint satisfaction. In S.C. Shapiro, editor, *Encyclopedia of AI (second edition)*, pages 285–293. John Wiley & Sons, 1992.

[23] U. Montanari. Networks of constraints: Fundamental properties and applications to picture processing. *Information Science*, 7:95–132, 1974. Also Technical Report, Carnegie Mellon University, 1971.

[24] A. Di Pierro, C. Hankin, and H. Wiklicky. On approximate non-interference. In *editor, Proceedings of WITS'02 – Workshop on Issues in the Theory of Security.* IFIP WG1.7, 2002.

[25] J.F. Puget. A c++ implementation of clp. In *Proceedings of the 2nd Singapore International Conference on Intelligent Systems*, 1994.

[26] Zs. Ruttkay. Fuzzy constraint satisfaction. In *Proc. 3rd IEEE International Conference on Fuzzy Systems*, pages 1263–1268, 1994.

[27] R Sandhu et al. Role based access control models. *IEEE Computer*, 29(2), 1996.

[28] A. Schaad and D. Moffett. The incorporation of control principles into access control policies. In *Workshop on Policies for Distributed Systems and Networks*, Bristol, UK, 2001.

[29] T. Schiex. Possibilistic constraint satisfaction problems, or "how to handle soft constraints?". In *Proc. 8th Conf. of Uncertainty in AI*, pages 269–275, 1992.

[30] T. Schiex, H. Fargier, and G. Verfaille. Valued Constraint Satisfaction Problems: Hard and Easy Problems. In *Proc. IJCAI95*, pages 631–637, San Francisco, CA, USA, 1995. Morgan Kaufmann.

[31] J. M. Spivey. *The Z Notation: A Reference Manual.* Series in Computer Science. Prentice Hall International, second edition, 1992.

[32] U. S. Department of Defense. Integrity-oriented control objectives: Proposed revisions to the trusted computer system evaluation criteria (TCSEC). Technical Report DOD 5200.28-STD, U. S. National Computer Security Center, October 1991.

[33] United States General Accounting Office, Accounting and Information Management Division. *Financial Audit Manual*, December 1996. GAO/AFMD-12.19.5A.

Software Tamper Resistance Using Program Certificates

Hongxia Jin[1], Gregory F. Sullivan[2], and Gerald M. Masson[2]

[1] IBM Almaden Research Center
San Jose, CA, 95120
jin@us.ibm.com
[2] Computer Science Department, Johns Hopkins University
Baltimore, MD 21218
{sullivan, masson}@cs.jhu.edu

Abstract. Software tamper resistence and disabling device cryptographically are investigated via run-time result checking of computations. The device needs to receive a new cryptographic key after each pre-set period of time in order to continue function. The software execution integrity is checked by the authority when deciding whether or not to give out a new key. If the modification of the software execution causes an error in the computational result, it can always be detected and the device can be disabled cryptographically by not given a new key. The detection is done via a run-time result checking using a certificate-based technique. Certificate-based techniques for run-time result verification are designed to support a secondary checker computation of a result by the authority by using the same input together with a special output, namely, the *certificate*, utilized by the primary computation in the device. We have designed the properties in the formal definition that the certificate design needs to satisfy in order to allow the result be checked in a provably "fool-proof" manner. The checker computation is done by the authority after the certificate is returned from the device. Since the checker algorithm is only known to the authority, not anybody else, it is hard for the hacker to forge the right information to be included in the certificate to fool the checker.

1 Introduction

Sophisticated modern weapons such as aircraft and tanks are increasingly filled with electronics, and often the weapons are computer-operated. In fact, I believe it is possible to design many weapons so that they do not operate if the electronics is inoperative, and the computer does not work. This is a useful property if you want to allow for the possibility of the deliberate disablement of a weapon.

Suppose that group A wants to sell/give weapons to group B, but A is concerned that the weapons might be "misused". Here is one scheme to allow A to have more control over the weapons that it sells to B - ex post facto. Imagine that weapon W has a built in a tamper proof clock. After a given period of time a special cryptographically determined number must be input into W or the

S. Anderson et al. (Eds.): SAFECOMP 2003, LNCS 2788, pp. 144–158, 2003.
© Springer-Verlag Berlin Heidelberg 2003

weapon will shut down and become unusable. Group A periodically distributes numbers to B to allow the weapons to remain operational. Numbers might be distributed by using smart cards or by transmitting them via broadcast - or by some combination of approaches. Weapons might have slots for smart cards or might listen to the electromagnetic spectrum to get the new numbers.

Note, the numbers change after each period of time and can not be predicted, i.e., they are chosen to be a cryptographically secure pseudo-random sequence. Now, if group B uses one or more weapon(s) in a way that group A disapproves of then A can disable the weapon by refusing to release the new numbers. There is some latency based on the period of time before a weapon must have a new number. But the threat of withholding new numbers should provide a substantial deterrent on the behaviors of B which are considered unacceptable by A.

Designing weapons that can be effectively disabled is probably tricky. Group A does not want B to be able to reverse engineer a weapon. Also, A does not want B to somehow patch through the electronics or bypass the electronics. Tamper-resistant packages that erase software if agitated would come in handy. Note, sophisticated target acquisition systems are heavily electronic. Even if you can fire a weapon, if you can not aim it well then its effectiveness is substantially diminished.

One can imagine variant schemes, e.g., after a weapon is used X times it must be "recharged" by inputing a new cryptographically secure number. Alternatively, a challenge-response type system could be used.

Why would a country/group buy such weapons? It might not have an alternative. Currently, only a few nations can make the most advanced weapons. In the future, each major provider country might choose to sell only weapons that can be cryptographically disabled. Indeed, there might be treaties between groups of advanced nations that specify that only such "controllable" weapons can be sold. On the other hand, there would be an incentive for some nations to sell unrestricted weapons. It is difficult to predict the reactions and counter-reactions in the domain of warfare.

The idea of disabling a device cryptographically would also be useful in non-warfare applications such as rental or leasing schemes. Imagine that company A wants to lease a car to individual B. Each time B makes a payment on time he is sent a card with the new secret crytographic numbers. If B does not make payments on time then A can disable the car by not sending the new numbers. In principle you do not even need a sophisticated crypto system for this application. You just embed a randomly chosen set of numbers in a secure package with a clock. You would want to embed one number per month for the term of the lease which might be 3-5 years. The secure package demands a new number from the driver once a month. If the number is not proffered then the car refuses to start.

Note that in the above scenarios discussed, it is relatively easy to know if group B or individual B is behaving properly, such as the weapon is not used when it should not be, or B is making the payment on time. Unfortunately, it is not always easy to detect if B is behaving properly. Adversaries do malicious things and do not want to be detected. Therefore, an integrity detection mechanism is strongly needed in order to make it possible to disable a device cryptographically. In this paper, we will talk about a detection mechanism based on run time result checking. The misbehavior it targets on detection is any type of the modification of the execution that would cause the computational result to be modified.

2   Certificate-Based Approach

Our approach to run-time result verification is based on the use of program *certificates*. The essence of the certificate-based approach, as illustrated in Figure 1, can be described as follows: we have developed methods for modifying an original program so that, with essentially negligible overhead, this modified (primary) program takes an input and not only produces a computational result, but also generates what is referred to as a *certificate*, which can be viewed at this point in our discussion as a characterization of the computational process. A secondary certifying program then takes the same input plus the certificate and either produces the same result if it is correct or otherwise indicates an error has occurred in the computation. Certificates are designed to allow the correctness of the primary program's computational result to be completely and efficiently certified in a provably "fool-proof" manner.

Fig. 1. Certificate-based approach.

Note that that we must be careful in defining this method or else its error detection capability might be reduced by the introduction of data dependency between the two executions. For example, suppose the primary program execution contains an error which causes an incorrect output and an incorrect certificate to be generated. It appears possible that the execution of the certifier program might use the incorrect certificate to generate an incorrect output which matches the incorrect output produced by the primary program. The certifier must guard against an incorrect certificate "fooling" it into producing an incorrect output. The definitions we give below explicitly exclude the possibility of being fooled. In fact, if a certificate is correctly *designed* to form a certificate-based solution to a problem, the primary and certifier programs must satisfy the two properties in the definition. As shown in the definition, the second property explicitly demand that the certifier execution either generates a correct output or detects an error in the certificate-based checking, even when the primary program leaves behind an incorrect certificate during an execution.

2.1   Formal Definition of a Run-Time Result Checking Certificate

Here we present a description of the certificate-based approach. The definition below describes the modification of a program so that it generates additional information which we call a certificate. Refer to the previous section for the definition of problem **P**.

Definition 1. *Let* $\mathbf{P} : \mathbf{D} \to \mathbf{S}$ *be a problem. A solution to this problem using a certificate consists of algorithms implementing two functions* F_1 *and* F_2 *with the following domains and ranges* $F_1 : \mathbf{D} \to \mathbf{S} \times \mathbf{C}$ *and* $F_2 : \mathbf{D} \times \mathbf{C} \to \mathbf{S} \cup \{error\}$. **C** *is the set of certificates. The symbol error is chosen such that* $error \notin \mathbf{S}$ *and* $error \notin \mathbf{C}$ *and* $error \notin \mathbf{S} \times \mathbf{C}$. *The functions must satisfy the following two properties:*

(1) for all $d \in \mathbf{D}$ *there exists* $s \in \mathbf{S}$ *and there exists* $t \in \mathbf{C}$ *such that*
    $F_1(d) = (s, t)$ *and* $F_2(d, t) = s$ *and* $(d, s) \in \mathbf{P}$
(2) for all $d \in \mathbf{D}$ *and for all* $t \in \mathbf{C}$
    either $(F_2(d, t) = s$ *and* $(d, s) \in \mathbf{P})$ *or* $F_2(d, t) = error$.

The informal interpretation of the following theorem is very similar to the one given for the two-version programming theorem. The first part of the theorem concerns the situation when F_2 is computed correctly, yet F_1 is computed incorrectly as F_1'. In this case, the comparison test allows a correct answer to be determined, or it allows the detection of an error. The second part of the theorem concerns the situation when F_1 is computed correctly, yet F_2 is computed incorrectly as F_2'. Once again, the comparison test allows the determination of a correct answer or the detection of an error.

Theorem 1. *Let* F_1 *and* F_2 *satisfy the definition of a certificate-based.*

Let F_1' *be an arbitrary function with domain* **D** *and range* $\mathbf{S} \times \mathbf{C}$.
    For all $d \in \mathbf{D}$
        let $F_1'(d) = (s', t')$ *and* $F_2(d, t') = s''$
            if $s' = s''$ *then* $(d, s') \in \mathbf{P}$ i.e., answer is correct
            if $s' \neq s''$ *then* $F_1'(d) \neq F_1(d)$ i.e., error is detected

Let F_2' *be an arbitrary function with domain* **D** *and range* $\mathbf{S} \cup \{error\}$.
    For all $d \in \mathbf{D}$
        let $F_1(d) = (s, t)$ *and* $F_2'(d, t) = s'$
            if $s = s'$ *then* $(d, s') \in \mathbf{P}$ i.e., answer is correct
            if $s \neq s'$ *then* $F_2'(d, t) \neq F_2(d, t)$ i.e., error is detected

The theorem above is somewhat surprising, because it shows that the certificate-based method and two-version programming have similar error detection properties. This is despite the fact that additional data, the certificate, is being generated and used to enable faster and simpler computation.

The certificate-based approach was deliberately defined to have desirable error-detection properties. We do not claim that the approach is a panacea. but we do believe that it always merits substantive consideration.

We also note that the theorems above do not capture all possible different types of error behavior. For example, a hardware or software fault might cause a program to enter an 'infinite loop' in which case no output would be generated. A fault might cause all available computing resources to be consumed, e.g., all free memory might be allocated. The output might be too large, e.g., a very large string might be generated. These problems are not precisely modeled by the variant primed functions used in the theorems above. But note, these behaviors are relevant to each of the error detection schemes we discuss: two-version programming, certificate-based, program checkers, and others. Clearly, there must be alternative error detection facilities such as watchdog timers for 'infinite loops', and resource utilization monitors. In addition, if a function value lying outside its proper range or domain is encountered then an error detection flag should be raised and execution should enter an error handling routine. These auxiliary detection mechanisms are needed for each of the approaches mentioned. Our work concentrates on the types of errors which we feel are prevalent, and which are the most difficult to detect and remove, i.e., the ones that result in variant functions.

Finally we note that, the theorems above do not explicitly treat the situation where errors occur during both executions. It is possible that the errors might cause the outputs of the two executions to differ, in which case the comparison test would still be able to detect the presence of errors. This desirable detection property is present in both two-version programming and certificate-based approaches. One can construct a probabilistic model to help explore this issue, but that is beyond the scope of this discussion. The second execution typically uses a different and simpler program than the first execution, and it can often be executed more quickly. Thus, the probability of error detection can be high even when errors are present in both executions.

2.2   Example of a Certificate-Based Solution for a Sorting Program

It might be beneficial at this point to give a brief example of the certificate-based technique for run-time result verification of a sorting program. We will do so for the case of a sorting program. It should be understood that this example is provided for the purposes of illustration of the essence of the concept. Therefore, the discussion has been kept at a relatively high level, and its simplicity should not mislead the reader. More details on sorting certification can be found in [1]. Also, the model of the certificate described here would be slightly different for other applications.

For convenience, we assume that the sorting certifier program is given the original input vector of items to be sorted, the output of the primary sorting program, and a certificate. The certifier must verify if the output is indeed correct. The first step performed by the certifier program is to test whether the output is monotonically increasing. Note, that this test is not sufficient to prove the correctness of the output. The certifier must also check that the output vector is a permutation of the input vector. To do this, the certifier utilizes the certificate. Assuming that the primary program operated in an error free manner, the certificate C is the permutation of indices that when applied to the input vector produces the output vector. More precisely, let I be the input vector, O the output vector, and C the certificate. The certifier program computes a vector P, such that $P[i] = I[C[i]]$. The certifier program compares P to O. If they are the same, the certifier answers that the output is correct; otherwise, the certifier program answers that the output is incorrect. It should be clear that the certifier program is easily implemented to run in linear time, provided that array accesses are assumed to take only constant time.

As an example, let I, O, and C be as follows:

$$I = [12.3, 7.2, 17.4, 16.1, 5.2]$$

$$O = [5.2, 7.2, 12.3, 15.1, 17.4]$$

$$C = [5, 2, 1, 4, 3]$$

Then the vector P constructed would be

$$P = [5.2, 7.2, 12.3, 16.1, 17.4]$$

Thus the check that $O = P$ would fail. Also notice that there is no vector C would allow the test $O = P$ to succeed in this case. It is beyond the scope of the discussion here that the sorting certificate described above adheres to the definition and theorem of Section 2.1. Nevertheless, the example does convey some sense of the concept.

3   Comparison with Other Approaches

The certificate-based approach to run-time result verification, whether implemented in hardware or software or some combination thereof, has resemblances with other techniques. In each case, however, there are significant and fundamental distinctions.

3.1   N-Version Programming

As indicated above, the certificate-based approach might be viewed as a form of N-version programming using design diversity [3,4,5]. But the fact that the certificate-based approach requires that the secondary algorithm or system use not only the input to the primary algorithm or system but also the certificate generated and provided by the execution/operation of the primary algorithm/system distinguishes it from the standard notion of design diversity. For example, the fundamental software design diversity technique known as N-version programming [3,4,5] specifies that N different implementations of an algorithm be independently executed with subsequent comparison of the resulting N outputs. There is no relationship among the executions of the different versions of the algorithms other than they all use the same input; each algorithm is executed independently without any information about the execution of the other algorithms. In marked contrast, the certificate-based approach requires that the primary system generate a trail of information while executing its algorithm that is critical to the secondary system's execution of its algorithm. In effect, N-version programming can be thought of relative to the certificate approach as the employment of a *null certificate*.

3.2   Program Checkers

Blum and Kannan [7,8] have defined what they call a *program checker*. This important and valuable work has been followed by a burst of activity in this general area [9,10,17,18]. Each of these publications, however, describes work which differs significantly from the work we present. A program checker is an algorithm which checks the output of another algorithm for correctness and thus it shares similarities with the acceptance test in a recovery block. An early example of a program checker is the algorithm developed by Tarjan [14] which takes as input a graph and a supposed minimum spanning tree and indicates whether or not the tree actually is a minimum spanning tree.

The Blum-Kannan program checking method differs from the certificate method in two important ways. First, the checker is designed to work for a problem and not a specific algorithm. That is, the checker design is based on the input/output specification of a problem and no assumptions are made about the method being used to solve the problem. Because of this the algorithm which is being checked is treated as a black box. It can not be altered nor can its internal status be examined and exploited. In the certificate-based approach the algorithm being checked is not treated as a black box. Instead, the algorithm can be modified to generate additional information (i.e., the certificate) which is considered to be useful in the checking process. By exploiting this capability it is sometimes possible to design certificate solutions which allow faster checking than Blum-Kannan program checkers. Of course, these faster solutions are more specialized than the Blum-Kannan checkers which are guaranteed to work for any algorithm which solves the original problem. We believe that the added speed often outweighs the disadvantage of specialization.

The second, important difference concerns the number of times that the program which is being checked is executed. In the Blum-Kannan approach the program may be invoked a polynomial number of times. In the certificate-based approach the program is run only once. Thus, the overall time complexity of the checking process can be significantly larger for Blum-Kannan checkers. A third less important difference stems from the fact that Blum-Kannan checkers are defined in a more general probabilistic context. certificates are currently defined only for deterministic programs and checkers. However, it is clearly possible to define them in the more general probabilistic context.

Other exciting work has been done to extend the ideas of Blum-Kannan [9,13] to give methods which allow the conversion of some programs into new programs which are self-testing and self-correcting. However, these methods are also based on treating programs as black boxes and thus have limitations similar to Blum-Kannan program checkers. Two papers which do not use a black box approach are [11] and [12]. The first paper [11] concerns checking the correctness of memories and data structures. The results described in that paper differ from our work in the validation of abstract data types in one central way. The checkers that they design are tightly constrained in memory usage. Typically, they use only $O(\log(n))$ storage to check data structures of size $O(n)$. Our results do not place space constraints on the algorithm used to validate the data structure. Without a space constraint we are able to validate abstract data types such as priority queues which are more complex than the data structures that they check, i.e., stacks and queues. Also, we are able to achieve a speed up in the checking process. For example, processing a sequence of n priority queue operations takes $O(n \log(n))$ time using standard data structures, however, we are able to validate the sequence with $O(n)$ amortized time complexity. In [11] the checking process for stacks and queues is not faster than the original computation and sometimes can be slower.

The second paper [12], presents methods which appear to allow remarkably fast checking, i.e., in polylogarithmic time. The approach has some similarities to the methods we present. Both methods modify original algorithms to yield new algorithms which output additional information. We refer to this additional information as a *certificate* and they refer to this information as a "witness". In our case we are interested in modified algorithms which have the same asymptotic time complexity as the original algorithm. Indeed, the modified algorithm should be slowed down by at most a factor of two. In [12] the modified algorithm is slowed down by more than any fixed multiplicative factor. Specifically, if the original algorithm has a time complexity of $O(T)$ then the modified algorithm has a time complexity of $O(T^{1+\epsilon})$. Note, in practice the ϵ cannot be too small because its inverse appears in the exponent of the checker time complexity. Another difference between our methods is the fact that their method requires that the input and output be encoded using an error-correcting code. The encoding process takes $O(N^{1+\epsilon})$ time for strings of length N. However, many of the checkers we have developed take only linear time so the cost of simply preparing to use their method appears to be too great in some cases. It is also necessary to decode the output after the check.

3.3   Other Alternative Techniques

Other run-time result verification and error monitoring techniques have been studied that might be thought of as bearing some resemblance to the certificate-based approach. Extensive summaries and descriptions of these techniques can be found in the literature [15,16]. Examination of these techniques reveals, however, that in each case there are fundamental distinctions from the certificate-based approach. In summary, we believe that the certificate-based approach stands alone in its employment of secondary algorithms/systems for the computation of an output for comparison that because of the availability of the certificate not only proceeds in a more efficient manner than that of the primary but also can indicate whether the execution of the primary algorithm was correct.

4 Recent Work

4.1 Run-Time Result Checking of Computationally Intensive Problems

Computationally intensive problems provide one of the greatest inducements for developing techniques for certifying run-time results. Such computations are more likely to suffer from difficulties during execution because they require extensive runtime and/or powerful hardware. Sometimes the software used to perform these computations contains intricate and error-prone 'optimizations' and 'tricks'[24][26]. Also, sometimes these computations are distributed across many machines - a process that permits a variety of additional troubles.

Problems which require vast 'searches' are one of the major types of computationally intensive problems. We have been conducting a preliminary investigation of search-type problems which are amenable to 'branch-and-bound' strategies. This powerful strategy is widely used; for example, it is possible to solve the classic Traveling Salesman problem using a branch-and-bound strategy [23] [24] [25] It is also possible to solve the Single and Multiple Knapsack problems using this strategy [26]

We believe that it is possible to use the certificate-based method to efficiently assure the correctness of many computations which are solved using a branch-and-bound strategy. Here we can only sketch some of the ideas we hope to pursue along these lines.

Consider a typical branch-and-bound search which is trying to find a combinatorial object which minimizes some objective function. The overall search can usually be represented by a tree or by a directed-acyclic graph (DAG). During the course of the search many lower-bound computations are performed. In common cases, one lower-bound computation is executed per node explored. The results from these computations are used to determine if the search from a given node can be halted. These computations can use up significant amounts of time. For example, computing a lower bound may require: a maximum-flow computation, a min-cost flow computation, an assignment computation, a linear program, or some other more intensive computation.

To design a certificate for intensive branch-and-bound computations, we are able to productively build on our previous work. We know how to design certificates for computations such as maximum-flow, min-cost flow, assignment and linear programs. These certificates can be used as part of a global certificate for the entire problem. We can sketch what such a global certificate looks like. Recall, that when the certificate-based method is used, there is a primary computation (called simply the "primary" in the following) and a second certifier computation ("secondary"). The primary generates a certificate and a supposed answer, and the certifier uses this information to certify the correctness of the supposed answer. For a branch-and-bound computation, the certificate generated by the primary consists of a tree or DAG which represents the search conducted during the execution of the primary. The tree or DAG is 'annotated' with important information about the bounding computations performed by the primary. The certifier must traverse the tree or DAG and use the annotations to determine if the primary computation manifested any errors and to certify whether the answer determined by the primary is correct.

Three goals are pursued when the certificate-based method is applied. First, the primary should not be substantially slower than the original computation which does not generate a certificate. Second, the certifier computation should be substantially faster than the primary; and third, the certifier should be simpler than the primary (hence providing diversity). Our preliminary work indicates that very often these goals can be achieved.

We have designed certificates in which the certifier computation is between ten and one-hundred times faster than the primary computation and the primary computation is at most 5 percent slower than the original computation.

Timing data was collected on both the certificates-based solutions and the original solutions using a Sun SPARCstation ELC. All the timing measurements are in seconds.

The *Basic Algorithm* gives the execution time of the original algorithm for producing the output without generating the certificates. The *Primary Execution* column gives the execution time of the algorithm for producing the solution with the additional overhead of generating the certificates. The *Certifier Execution* column gives the execution time of the algorithm in exactly checking the solution using the certificates. The *Speedup* column gives the ratio of the execution times of the original algorithm and the certifier execution for checking the solution. The *Overhead Percentage* is the ratio of the overhead for generating certificates versus the original algorithm execution time.

Table I summarizes our results when applied to the TSP problem algorithm [25]. Each entry in the input cost matrix for TSP problem was randomly generated from a uniform distribution [1,1000].

Table 1. Experimental results for TSP problem

Problem Size	Basic Algorithm	Primary Exec (Generates Certificates)	Certifier Exec (Uses Certificates)	Speedup	Overhead Percentage
20	0.72	0.73	0.04	18.00	1.39%
30	7.77	7.87	0.30	25.90	1.29%
40	105.61	105.87	3.51	30.09	0.246%
50	1636.36	1645.62	41.16	39.76	0.565%
60	3321.00	3328.44	73.55	45.15	0.224%

In the following we will attempt to present some of the overall reasons why these goals can often be achieved and why this approach is promising.

- Although the certifier must traverse the tree or DAG generated by the primary, it does not have to perform the computations necessary to determine the original structure of the tree or DAG. The difficulty of determining this structure is well illustrated by the algorithm which solves the Multiple Knapsack problem given in [26]. This algorithm computes the solution of a Single Knapsack problem at each search node to determine what its child nodes should be. Recall, the Single Knapsack problem itself is NP-hard. Thus, determining the structure of the search tree is rather expensive compared to simply traversing the tree.
- The knowledge of the supposed answer together with the annotations often allow the certifier computation to prune the tree or DAG more tightly. Often the certifier does not have to traverse the entire tree or DAG to assure the correctness of the supposed answer.
- The annotations often allow the computational work associated with individual nodes in the tree to be reduced during the certifier computation. Much of the work at nodes is associated with computing bounds. In some cases, the annotations allow the certifier to completely omit a computation, because it is known to be superfluous. In other cases, when a bound computation must be performed, the annotations can provide a certificate for the bounding computation which allow it to be performed more quickly and in a simpler fashion.
- The code implementing the certifier is often considerably simpler than the code for the original problem or the code for the primary. One reason this occurs is because the code necessary to determine the original structure of the search tree or DAG is not needed in the certifier. The certifier only needs to traverse the tree or DAG. Another reason the certifier code can be simpler stems from the bounding computations. The certifier can use information in the annotations to simplify its task of selectively checking the bounding computations. Since the certifier code is often simpler and different than the original or primary code one can assert that this is highly desirable from a design diversity standpoint.

4.2   Run-Time Result Checking of Distributed Problems

Computationally intensive problems will increasingly be distributed across multiple machines which are attached to a network, especially as the notion of "meta-computing" emerges to utilize the Internet more efficiently. Valuable tools have been developed to aid the distribution of computations such as PVM [19], Linda [20], and MPI [21]. Also, distribution of a computation across a geographically distributed network of machines is easier now because of the ubiquity of underlying protocols such as UDP, TCP/IP, HTTP, and FTP. Further, the point-and-click interface common to the World Wide Web facilitates the coordination of large numbers of participants. This provides a major motivation for developing techniques for certifying the correctness of answers generated by the cooperative work of many machines.

We have developed a technique called "Distributed Applet-based Certifiable Processing" (DACP) which distributes computationally intensive problems across a network and then certifies the correctness of the final answer efficiently by means of the certificate-based method. In our DACP approach, we envision a master machine partitioning a computationally intensive problem into sub-problems, distributing the computational workload associated with these sub-problems to other machines (clients) across a network, gathering sub-answers and the associated certificates, and then, by using this data, performing a certification of the correctness of the answer to the problem. Each participating client machine would be expected to perform the required work associated with the sub-problem and return a certificate and a supposed sub-answer back to the master machine.

Search-type computations for computationally intensive problems can often be distributed across multiple machines in an efficient manner. A deliberately simplified methodology is the following. One process would manage/coordinate the overall computation. First, a partial search from the root would be executed to obtain a collection of subproblems that could be handed out to other machines across the network. The subproblems would correspond to the roots of subtrees that must be explored. (Note, more elaborate methods with multiple coordinators and multiple tasks and dynamic balancing are possible, but here we present only a simple instantiation of the idea.) When a subproblem is executed the result would be an annotated subtree which would be returned to the main coordinator. The main coordinator would use a certifier computation to determine the correctness of the annotated subtree and would assemble the subtrees to make sure that the overall computation is correct.

We have been encouraged by some preliminary experimental results exploring the DACP concept using Java applets and a branch-and-bound approach to the solution of the well-known Traveling Salesman Problem as a test case. Although admittedly preliminary in nature, our experiments are nevertheless indicating that the total time required for DACP can be significantly less than that needed to perform the entire computation on a single machine, even when taking into account the network communication overhead. Hence, we believe that efficiencies associated with the certificate-based approach to run-time result checking are critical to the viability of economically sustainable distributed computation systems.

4.3   Approximate Run-Time Result Checking

When certifying the correctness of a result there are situations in which it is acceptable to determine that the answer is guaranteed to be approximately correct. Indeed, if it is substantially computationally 'cheaper' to show approximate correctness instead of exact correctness then it may be more 'cost-effective' to only certify approximate correctness. The situation we are considering arises when a primary computation is supposed to compute a value exactly, and then a certifier computation wishes to certify the answer. But the certifier also wishes not to expend extensive computational resources. There are several possible variants of this question depending on the precise formalization. We propose to investigate this general area.

Suppose that the accuracy demanded by the certifier is not known in advance. Is it possible to design a certificate-based solution that will allow the certifier to choose an accuracy after the certificate has been generated and still use the trail to aid its computation? We have been able to design certificate-based solutions which do allow the accuracy desired to be chosen after the fact[2]. One class of certificates that we have examined is based on the annotated search trees that we have discussed above. It turns out that these trees are ideal for allowing approximate certification. When performing an approximate certification the traversal of the tree from the root can sometimes be dramatically circumscribed [2].

5 Conclusion

We have introduced a run-time result verification technique based on program certificates. We have given its formal definition and discussed its error coverage as well as comparisons with other known run-time result verification techniques. Certificate-based run-time result verification has been successfully applied to a range of computational problems. A possible objection to the use of certificate is that considerable effort may be required to determine the information that should be put into a certificate and to design a correct certificate to satisfy the two properties in the formal definition. This is partly because this is a relatively new technique, and there is not a large body of literature that a developer can consult for solutions. However, this is a problem that is shared by other techniques that attempt to exploit design diversity. A developer using N-version programming may have to devote considerable effort to designing alternate algorithms for a problem. Even when there are well known alternate algorithms, they may not run as quickly, so effort may have to be spent in optimizing the algorithms for acceptable performance. Similarly, the use of recovery block technique requires that effort be spent developing acceptance tests as well as developing alternate versions. Of course, when the acceptance test are not required to be complete checks, then the effort may be less than that needed to develop a certificate.

In the future, it is desirable to develop a general theory and associated methodologies for certificate design, as well as to determine a general methodology for achieving software diversity and variability using certificates. It is also of our interest to investigate the automated support of the certificate design and generating process.

We also have shown the basic idea when this approach is used to do integrity check and disable device cryptograghically. The point is to keep the checker algorithm secret and make it hard for the hacker to mimic the right information that should be included in the certitificate, so that we can prevent the checker from being fooled. We want to further explore the approach as a potentially promising approach to achive software tamper resistence.

References

1. Bright, J., Sullivan, G.F., and Masson, G.M. "A Formally Verified Sorting Certifier," *IEEE Trans. Computers*, Vol. 46, 1997.
2. Jin, H., Sullivan, G.F.,and Masson, G.M.; Approximate correctness checking of computational results; *IEEE Transaction on Reliability, pp 338–350.*
3. Chen, L., and Avizienis A., "N-version programming: a fault tolerant approach to reliability of software operation," *Digest of the 1978 Fault Tolerant Computing Symposium*, pp. 3–9, IEEE Computer Society Press, 1978.
4. Avizienis, A., and Kelly, J., "Fault tolerance by design diversity: concepts and experiments," *Computer*, vol. 17, pp. 67–80, Aug., 1984.
5. Avizienis, A., "The N-version approach to fault tolerant software," *IEEE Trans. on Software Engineering*, vol. 11, pp. 1491–1501, Dec., 1985.
6. Anderson, T., and Lee, P., *Fault tolerance: principles and practices*, Prentice-Hall, Englewood Cliffs, NJ, 1981.
7. Blum, M., and Kannan, S., "Designing programs that check their work", *Proceedings of the 1989 ACM Symposium on Theory of Computing*, pp. 86–97, ACM Press, 1989.
8. Blum, M., and Kannan, S., "Designing Programs that Check Their Work", Journal of ACM, vol. 42, no. 1, pp. 269–291, 1995.
   Proceedings of the 1989 ACM Symposium on Theory of Computing, pp. 86–97, ACM Press, 1989.
9. Manuel Blum, Michael Luby, Ronitt Rubinfeld, "Self-Testing/Correcting with Applications to Numerical Problems," *Proc. 22 ACM Symp. of Theory of Computing*, pp. 73–83, 1990.
10. Andrew Chi-Chih Yao, "Coherent Functions and Program Checkers," *Proc. 22 ACM Symp. of Theory of Computing*, pp. 84–94, 1990.
11. Manuel Blum, Will Evans, Peter Gemmell, Sampath Kannan, Moni Naor, "Checking the Correctness of Memories," *Proc. 32nd IEEE Symp. on Foundations of Computer Science*, 1991, pp. 90–99.
12. Laszlo Babai, Lance Fortnow, Leonid A. Levin, Mario Szegedy, "Checking Computations in Polylogarithmic Time, " *Proc. 23 ACM Symp. of Theory of Computing*, pp. 21–31.
13. Peter Gemmell, Richard Lipton, Ronnitt Rubinfeld, Madhu Sudan, Avi Wigderson, "Self-Testing/Correcting for Polynomials and for Approximate Functions," *Proc. 23 ACM Symp. of Theory of Computing*, pp. 32–42.
14. Tarjan, R. E., "Applications of path compression on balanced trees", *J. ACM*, pp. 690–715, Oct., 1979.
15. Siewiorek, D., and Swarz, R., *The theory and practice of reliable design*, Digital Press, Bedford, MA, 1982.
16. Johnson, B., *Design and analysis of fault tolerant digital systems* Addison-Wesley, Reading, MA, 1989.
17. Blum, M., and Wasserman, H., "Reflections on the pentium bug," *IEEE Trans. Computers*, Vol. 45, 385–394–847, 1996.
18. Blum, M., and Wasserman, H., "Program result checking: a theory of testing meets a test of theory," *Proceedings of 35th Foundations of Computer Science Conference* pp. 382–392, 1994.
19. Geist, A., Beguelin, A., Dongarra, J., Jiang, W., Manchek, R., Sunderam, V., "PVM – parallel virtual machine: a users' guide and tutorial for networked parallel computing," M.I.T. Press, 1994.

20. Carriero, N., and Gelernter, D., "How to write parallel program: a first course," M.I.T. Press, 1992.
21. Gropp, W., Lusk, E., Skjellum, A., "Using MPI: portable parallel programming with the message passing interface," M.I.T. Press, 1994.
22. Miller, M., and Drexler, K., (1988), "Markets and Computation: Agoric Open Systems," in B.A. Huberman (ed.), The Ecology of Computation (Amsterdam: North-Holland), 133–205.
23. Lawler, E. L., Lenstra, J. K., Rinnooy Kan, A. H. G., Shmoys, D. B., "The Traveling Salesman Problem", John Wiley and Sons Ltd., 1985.
24. Carpaneto, G., DellAmico, M., Toth, P., "Exact Solution of Large-Scale Asymmetric Traveling Salesman Problems" ACM Transactions on Mathematical Software, Vol 21, No. 4, pp 394–409, Dec. 1995.
25. Syslo, Maciej M., Deo, Narsingh, Kowalik, J. S., "Discrete Optimization Algorithms : with Pascal Programs", Englewood Cliffs, NJ : Prentice-Hall, 1983.
26. Martello, S., Toth, P., Algorithm 632: "A Program for the 0–1 Multiple Knapsack Problem", ACM Transactions on Mathematical Software, Vol 11, No. 2, pp 135–140, June 1985.

Developing High Assurance Systems: On the Role of Software Tools

Constance Heitmeyer

Naval Research Laboratory (Code 5546), Washington, DC 20375
heitmeyer@itd.nrl.navy.mil
http://chacs.nrl.navy.mil/personnel/heitmeyer.html

Abstract. Recently, researchers have developed a number of powerful, formally based software tools, such as model checkers and theorem provers. To date, these tools have largely been used to analyze hardware designs. In the future, they should have significant value for analyzing the requirements and designs of software systems, especially *high assurance software systems*, where compelling evidence is needed that the system satisfies critical properties, such as safety and security properties. This paper briefly describes the different roles that formally based software tools can play in debugging, verifying, and testing software systems and software system artifacts. It also describes one important activity in software development not involving tools that is often neglected and that merits greater care and attention.

1 Introduction

During the past several years, our research group at the Naval Research Laboratory (NRL) has applied the SCR (Software Cost Reduction) formal method and tools [1,2,3,4] to a number of safety-critical and secure systems. Our focus has been on *high assurance software systems*—systems such as flight control systems and control systems for nuclear power plants, where compelling evidence is required that the system satisfies critical properties, e.g., security and safety properties. Two systems that we are currently investigating are a secure system called CD (Communications Device) and a safety-critical software component called the FPE (Fault Protection Engine). CD is a member of a family of software-based devices that will provide simultaneous cryptographic processing on several different logical channels for a Navy radio receiver. Because data on two different channels may have different security classifications, it is critically important that CD enforce *data separation*—i.e., ensure that data on one channel cannot influence, nor be influenced by, data on a different channel. Currently, NRL is developing a plan for specifying and verifying that the CD design, which uses a separation kernel [5], enforces data separation.

The FPE is a complex, safety-critical software component in use on current NASA spacecraft and planned for use in future spacecraft. The function of the FPE is to monitor the health of the spacecraft's software and hardware and to coordinate and track responses to detected faults [6]. Because the FPE's

S. Anderson et al. (Eds.): SAFECOMP 2003, LNCS 2788, pp. 159–164, 2003.

function is crucial to the successful operation of the spacecraft, NASA needs high assurance that the FPE is implemented correctly. To that end, NRL has developed a formal specification of the most complex part of the FPE and is also developing a suite of test cases, derived from the FPE specification, for evaluating the FPE software.

Below is a description of several kinds of tools useful in developing these and other high assurance systems and a list of ways in which such tools need improvement. Finally, an important aspect of high assurance software development is discussed that does not involve tools. Despite its importance, this aspect have been largely neglected by both researchers and software developers.

2   The Role of Tools

Tools can play an important role in obtaining a high level of confidence that a software system satisfies critical properties. Described below are five different roles that tools can play in improving the quality of software systems and software artifacts.

2.1   Demonstrate Well-Formedness

A *well-formed* specification is a specification that is syntactically and type correct, has no circular dependencies, and is complete (no missing behavior) and consistent (no ambiguity about the required behavior). Tools, such as NRL's consistency checker [2], can automatically find well-formedness errors. For example, [2] and [7] describe how a consistency checker found missing cases and ambiguity in the specifications of both an avionics system and a flight guidance system. In both cases, the consistency checker detected serious errors that were overlooked in human inspections.

2.2   Discover Property Violations

In many cases, using a tool, such as a model checker, to analyze a system specification for some critical property uncovers a violation of the property. Given diagnostic information, such as a counterexample returned by the model checker, the user may find that the specification is wrong and needs correction. Alternatively, he may discover missing assumptions or find that the property, not the specification, is incorrect. In all of these cases, the result of analysis is extremely valuable. See [3] for a description of how model checking was used to detect a violation of a safety property in a software-based weapons control system. Recently, some researchers (see, e.g., [8]) have begun using model checking to detect property violations in software, rather than in software specifications.

2.3   Verify Critical Properties

Either a theorem prover or a model checker may be able to verify that a software artifact, such as a requirements specification or a design specification, satisfies a critical property. For example, [9] describes the use of a theorem prover to verify that an early specification of CD satisfies a set of security properties.

2.4 Validate a Specification

A tool, such as a simulator, can be used to determine whether a formal specification captures the intended behavior. By running scenarios through a simulator, the user can check that the system specification does not omit required behavior nor misspecify the required behavior. In developing the FPE specification, simulation was extremely valuable in debugging the specification, in obtaining feedback about the specification from domain experts, and in demonstrating the behavior captured by the specification to the NASA sponsors.

2.5 Construct Test Cases

Using a formal specification, a tool can be used to generate a suite of test cases satisfying a given coverage criterion, e.g., branch coverage (see, e.g., [10]). These test cases can then be used to check that the software code satisfies the specification. In the FPE project as well as other projects that involve high assurance software systems, automated test case generation is of high interest for two reasons: 1) it is much cheaper than constructing and executing the test cases manually, and 2) it constructs a set of test cases that "cover" the specification. Note that the parts of the code that are exercised by the suite of test cases may be marked. Then, the unmarked code must be analyzed. This code may be either redundant code, unreachable code, *or* malicious code.

3 Needed Tool Improvements

Although tools can be enormously useful in debugging and in producing evidence of the correctness of software and software artifacts, tool improvements are urgently needed. These improvements, some previously recommended in [11], are described below.

3.1 Automated Abstraction

Before practical software specifications can be model checked efficiently, the *state explosion* problem must be addressed—i.e., the size of the state space to be analyzed must be reduced. An effective way to reduce state explosion is to apply abstraction. For example, model checking the large specification of the weapons control system [3] did not succeed until two kinds of abstraction were applied. Unfortunately, the most common approach is to develop the abstraction in ad hoc ways—the correspondence between the abstraction and the original specification is based on informal, intuitive arguments. Needed are mathematically sound abstractions that can be constructed automatically. Recent progress in automatically constructing sound abstractions has been reported in [12,3].

3.2 Understandable Feedback

When formal analysis exposes an error, the user should be provided with easy-to-understand feedback useful in correcting the error. Techniques for achieving this in consistency checking already exist (see, e.g., [13]). Although counterexamples produced by model checkers often provide useful diagnostic information, they are sometimes hard to understand. One promising approach, already common in hardware design, uses a simulator to demonstrate and validate a counterexample.

3.3 Automatically Generated Invariants

Tools, such as the tool described in [14], are needed that can automatically construct invariants from a specification. Known invariants have many uses in software development. They can be used as auxiliary lemmas in proving theorems about the software specification. For example, some of the security properties to be proven about the early CD specification [9] could not be proved without auxiliary invariants. These invariants were automatically generated using the algorithms described in [14,15]. Invariants can also be used in validating a requirements specification—domain experts can use automatically generated invariants to determine whether the specification correctly captures the required system behavior.

3.4 More "Usable" Mechanical Theorem Provers

Although mechanical theorem provers have been used by researchers to verify various algorithms and protocols, they are rarely used in practical software development. For provers to be used more widely, a number of barriers need to be overcome. First, the specification languages provided by the provers must be more natural. Second, the reasoning steps supported by a prover should be closer to the steps produced in a hand proof; current provers support reasoning steps that are at too low and detailed a level. One partial solution to this problem is to build a prover front-end designed to support specification and proofs for a special class of mathematical models. An example of such a front-end is TAME, a "natural" user interface to PVS that is designed to specify and prove properties about automata models [16]. Although using a mechanical provers will still require mathematical maturity and theorem proving skills, making the prover more "natural" and convenient to use should encourage more widespread usage.

4 What Else Is Needed?

While researchers (and many software developers) usually expend significant effort using tools, they often exert much less effort and pay much less attention to the system specification. As a result, many current specifications are difficult to understand and to change and are also poorly organized. Urgently needed are higher quality specifications of requirements and of designs. Such specifications are critically important because they serve as a medium for precise communication between the customers, the developers, the verification team, and other stakeholders.

One way to improve the quality of specifications is to choose a "good" specification language. This language must be "natural"; to the extent feasible, a language syntax and semantics familiar to the software practitioner should be supported. The language must also have an explicitly defined formal semantics, and it should scale. Specifications in this language should be automatically translated into the language of a model checker or even a mechanical theorem prover.

Our group and others (see, e.g., [7]) have had moderate success with a tabular notation for representing the required system behavior. Underlying this notation is a formal state-machine semantics [2]. Others, such as Heimdahl and Leveson [17], have proposed a hybrid notation, inspired by Statecharts [18], that combines tables and graphics; this notation also has a state-machine semantics.

Specifications based on tables are easy to understand and easy for software practitioners to produce. In addition, tables provide a precise, unambiguous basis for communication among practitioners. They also provide a natural organization which permits independent construction, review, modification, and analysis of smaller parts of a large specification. Finally, tabular notations scale. Evidence of the scalability of tabular specifications has been shown by Lockheed engineers, who used a tabular notation to specify the complete requirements of the C-130J Flight Program, a program containing over 250K lines of Ada code [19]. In addition to tables, other user-friendly notations should be explored. For example, some researchers are developing tools that analyze message sequence charts, a notation commonly used in communication protocols (see, e.g., [20]).

Even if a good specification language is chosen, a high quality specification still requires great care and skill on the part of the specifier. Building a good specification is analogous to designing a good proof. As emphasized above, such a specification should be easy to understand. It should also, for the most part, be free of redundancy, although some planned redundancy is acceptable (e.g., a list of critical system properties). Moreover, the specification should be carefully organized both for ease of understanding and for ease of change. Finally, a good specification should be a reference document, so that information in the specification is easy to find.

5   Conclusion

Tools can be enormously useful in building high assurance software systems. They can find errors that people miss, help validate a specification, provide mechanized support for verification, reduce the time and effort required to construct (and execute) a set of test cases, and provide more confidence in the results of testing by constructing a suite of test cases based on some coverage criterion. Thus, a set of powerful tools can liberate people to do the hard intellectual work required to produce high quality, high assurance software systems. Part of this intellectual effort should be channeled into the production of easy-to-understand, well organized specifications.

References

1. Heitmeyer, C.: Software Cost Reduction. In Marciniak, J.J., ed.: Encyclopedia of Software Engineering. Second edn. John Wiley & Sons, Inc., New York, NY (2002)

2. Heitmeyer, C.L., Jeffords, R.D., Labaw, B.G.: Automated consistency checking of requirements specifications. ACM Transactions on Software Engineering and Methodology **5** (1996) 231–261

3. Heitmeyer, C., Kirby, J., Labaw, B., Archer, M., Bharadwaj, R.: Using abstraction and model checking to detect safety violations in requirements specifications. IEEE Trans. on Softw. Eng. **24** (1998)

4. Heitmeyer, C., Kirby, Jr., J., Labaw, B., Bharadwaj, R.: SCR*: A toolset for specifying and analyzing software requirements. In: Proc. Computer-Aided Verification, 10th Annual Conf. (CAV'98), Vancouver, Canada (1998)

5. Rushby, J.: Design and verification of secure systems. In: Proceedings, 8th Symposium on Operating Systems Principles, Pacific Grove, CA (1981)

6. Feather, M.S., Fickas, S., Razermera-Marny, N.A.: Model-checking for validation of a Fault Protection System. In: Proc. 9th International Symposium on High Assurance Systems Engineering (HASE 2001), IEEE Computer Society (2001)

7. Miller, S.: Specifying the mode logic of a flight guidance system in CoRE and SCR. In: Proc. 2nd ACM Workshop on Formal Methods in Software Practice (FMSP'98). (1998)

8. Brat, G., Havelund, K., Park, S., Visser, W.: Model checking programs. In: Proc. IEEE Intern. Conf. on Automated Software Eng. (ASE). (2000)

9. Kirby, Jr., J., Archer, M., Heitmeyer, C.: SCR: A practical approach to building a high assurance COMSEC system. In: Proc., 15th Annual Computer Security Applications Conf. (ACSAC '99), IEEE Computer Society Press (1999)

10. Gargantini, A., Heitmeyer, C.: Automatic generation of tests from requirements specifications. In: Proc. ACM 7th Eur. Software Eng. Conf./7th ACM SIGSOFT Symp. on Foundations of Software Eng. (ESEC/FSE99), Toulouse, FR (1999)

11. Heitmeyer, C.: On the need for *practical* formal methods. In: Proc. Formal Techniques in Real-Time and Fault-Tolerant Systems (FTRTFT '98), Lyngby, Denmark (1998)

12. Bensalem, S., Lakhnech, Y., Owre, S.: Computing abstractions of infinite state systems compositionally and automatically. In: Proceedings, 10th International Conf. on Computer-Aided Verification, Vancouver, BC, Canada (1998)

13. Heitmeyer, C., Kirby, Jr., J., Labaw, B.: Tools for formal specification, verification, and validation of requirements. In: Proc. 12th Annual Conf. on Computer Assurance (COMPASS '97), Gaithersburg, MD (1997)

14. Jeffords, R., Heitmeyer, C.: Automatic generation of state invariants from requirements specifications. In: Proc. Sixth ACM SIGSOFT Symp. on Foundations of Software Engineering. (1998)

15. Jeffords, R.D., Heitmeyer, C.L.: An algorithm for strengthening state invariants generated from requirements specifications. In: Proc. of the Fifth IEEE International Symposium on Requirements Engineering. (2001)

16. Archer, M.: TAME: Using PVS strategies for special-purpose theorem proving. Annals of Mathematics and Artificial Intelligence **29** (2001)

17. Heimdahl, M.P.E., Leveson, N.: Completeness and consistency in hierarchical state-based requirements. IEEE Trans. on Software Engineering **22** (1996) 363–377

18. Harel, D.: Statecharts: A visual formalism for complex systems. Science of Computer Programming **8** (1987) 231–274

19. Faulk, S.R., Brackett, J., Ward, P., Kirby, Jr., J.: The CoRE method for real-time requirements. IEEE Software **9** (1992) 22–33

20. Peled, D.: A toolset for message sequence charts. In: Proceedings, 10th International Conf. on Computer-Aided Verification, Vancouver, BC, Canada (1998)

Web Service Availability – Impact of Error Recovery

Magnos Martinello*, Mohamed Kaâniche, and Karama Kanoun

LAAS,CNRS
7, Av. du Colonel Roche 31077 Toulouse - France
{magnos,kaaniche,kanoun}@laas.fr

Abstract. Growing usage and diversity of applications on the Internet make the issue of assessing the web service availability increasingly important. The Internet is often used for transaction based applications such as online banking, stock trading, shopping, where the service interruption or outages are unacceptable. Therefore, it is important for the developers of such applications to analyze during the design phase how hardware, software and performance related failures affect the quality of service delivered to the users. This paper presents analytical models in order to study the availability of web services implemented on web clusters. In particular, a composite performance and availability modeling approach is considered where various causes of service unavailability and two different recovery strategies are taken into account. For illustration purposes, sensitivity analysis results are presented to show the impact on the web service availability of various assumptions concerning the architecture, the servers load, as well as the failure and recovery processes.

1 Introduction

The past few years have seen an explosive growth in the size of the Internet and an extensive development of web sites delivering a large array of personal, professional, and business services for different categories of users. Many popular web sites, such as CNN, Yahoo, eBay, receive millions of requests per day providing services to a diverse spectrum of clients. For such web sites, the designers must cope with many challenging problems. Indeed, they have to satisfy the high expectations of the customers with respect to the timeliness and the availability of the delivered services. In addition, a web site must be able: i) to support thousands of simultaneous client requests, and ii) to scale to rapidly growing user population.

Several solutions have been proposed to address the above challenges. In practice, the most popular approaches are mainly based on Web cluster architectures [7,5,3,15]. Such architectures are composed of multiple web server nodes and one

---

* M. Martinello has a fellowship from CAPES-Brazil. This work was partially supported by the European Community (Project IST-1999-11825-DSoS)

S. Anderson et al. (Eds.): SAFECOMP 2003, LNCS 2788, pp. 165–178, 2003.

or several frontend dispatchers for redirecting client requests to the servers. One of the main problems faced by the designers is to find an adequate sizing of the architecture to ensure high availability and performance for the delivered services. Modeling techniques are well suited to address this problem and to find the right tradeoffs for achieving availability while providing acceptable levels of performance.

During the last few years, the performance evaluation of distributed web cluster architectures has been an active area of research. Particular attention has been devoted to the analysis of response time and throughput considering different algorithms for load distribution among the servers [16,6]. Although many efforts have been dedicated to analyzing web hosts availability using measurement based techniques [7,8,9], less emphasis was put on the modeling and analysis of the web service availability taking into account the impact of server node failures and performance degradations. A conceptual framework for modeling the user perceived dependability of Internet based applications was presented in [2], and illustrated in [1] using a web-based travel agency. However, simple assumptions were considered to analyze the impact of failures and performance degradations on the web service availability.

In this paper, we focus on the development of analytical models to study the web service availability considering distributed web cluster architectures. We provide closed form expressions for the web service availability taking into account various causes of unavailability and request loss scenarios. In particular, detailed analyses are carried out to study the impact of the error detection and recovery latency time on the web server availability, considering two different error recovery assumptions (referred to a client transparent and non client transparent error recovery). For illustration purposes, sensitivity analysis results are presented to show, for both error recovery assumptions, the impact on the web service availability of various parameters concerning the size of the cluster, the server failure and recovery rates, the error detection and latency times, as well as the request arrival and service times.

The paper is structured into five sections. Section 2 presents the architecture and the modeling assumptions considered in this study. Section 3 presents the modeling approach with the closed form expressions for the service availability measure. Section 4 presents examples of sensitivity analysis results. Finally, section 5 concludes the paper.

2   Basic Architecture and Assumptions

Web systems with multiple nodes are leading architectures for building popular web sites that have to guarantee scalable services and support ever increasing request load [15,3]. A detailed review and classification of various types of locally or geographically distributed web architectures with discussions on performance related issues is reported in [3].

In this paper, we focus on locally distributed web systems, known as Web clusters. We consider a clustered architecture composed of multiple Web servers

with a load manager node that spreads the incoming queries among the servers
(Fig. (1)). Several load distribution algorithms have been proposed in the literature [3]. For this study, we assume that the arriving traffic is dispatched among
the servers according to a round-robin strategy. It is also assumed that each
Web server has an associated buffer with a limited capacity. Thus, the requests
sent to the server when the buffer is full are rejected. In addition, the load manager node runs a monitoring process, based e.g., on heartbeat messages in order
to detect server failures. The objective is to early detect the failed servers and
disconnect them from the cluster.

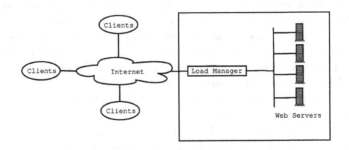

Fig. 1. Basic Web clustered architecture

In order to evaluate the Web service availability, we focus our attention on
the server side point of view, that is under the direct control of the web designer.
We do not include in our analysis the service unavailability caused by failures in
the path from the client to the server, and the failure of the load manager. We
leave this issue to further work.

The web service availability is defined as the probability in steady state that
the web requests submitted to the cluster are successfully processed. In other
words, they are not rejected due to server failures or overloads. We distinguish
two main causes of failure:

- Hardware and software failures that affect the computer hosts running the
  web servers;
- Performance-related failures that occur when the incoming requests are not
  serviced due to the limited capacity of the server buffers;

Failures of servers have a direct impact on the performance capabilities of
the web cluster. Indeed, when servers fail and are disconnected from the cluster,
the remaining healthy servers have to handle all the original traffic, including
the queries previously serviced by the failed nodes. This leads to the increase of
the workload in each of the remaining servers, with a potential degradation of
the corresponding quality of service. For example, the failure of two servers in a
five node cluster implies a 66% increase in the load that has to be processed by
each of the three remaining servers. Clearly, an accurate estimation of the web

service availability should take into account the performance degradation of the web cluster.

Moreover, detailed assumptions need to be stated to describe the consequences of web server failures on ongoing requests as well as on the input traffic directed to the failed server during detection and recovery latency time. *Detection and recovery latency* is the time between the occurrence of a server failure and the time taken by the load manager to detect the failure and remove the failed server from the list of alive servers in the cluster.

In this paper, two different assumptions are studied corresponding to two types of recovery techniques in clustered web server designs, namely: Non Client Transparent (NCT), and Client-Transparent (CT).

– NCT recovery: all requests in progress as well as the input requests directed by the load manager to the failed node before the failure is detected are lost;
– CT recovery: all requests in progress and the input requests directed by the load manager to the failed node during failover latency time are not lost; they are redirected to the non failed nodes.

The NCT recovery assumption mainly corresponds to traditional web cluster solutions. These solutions do not provide transparent handling of requests whose processing was in progress when the failure occurred [17]. A standard web browser client has no way of determining whether or not the request was processed and has therefore to reissue the request. Other problems that might be caused by web server failures are discussed in [17]. To address these problems, Web cluster solutions providing CT recovery have been proposed, e.g., in [17, 10]. These solutions enable web requests to be smoothly migrated and recovered on another working server in the presence of server failure, in a user transparent way. These capabilities are necessary for a variety of critical e-business services that are increasingly in use. It is thus important to analyze the web availability achieved for each type of these web cluster designs.

The modeling approach presented in Section 3 illustrates how the service availability can be evaluated and the results given in Section 4 illustrate different types of sensitivity analysis and design tradeoffs that can be used by the web site designers for optimal tuning of performance and availability.

3   Modeling Web Service Availability

The evaluation of the web service availability is carried out adopting a composite performance and availability (generally referred to as performability [14]) modeling approach, taking into account the assumptions discussed in Section 2. The main idea consists in combining the results obtained from two models: a pure availability model and a pure performance model.

The availability model describes the system states resulting from the occurrence of failure and repair events in the system, and evaluates probabilistic measures associated to these states. The performance model describes the request arrival and service processes evaluating performance related measures conditioned on states of the availability model. This approach is based on the assumption that the system reaches a steady state with respect to the performance related events, between successive occurrences of failure/repair events. This is a reasonable assumption because the time-scales of the failure/repair events are orders of magnitude higher than the time-scales of request arrivals and service.

In the following, we consider a web cluster system composed of N server nodes and a load manager dispatching the requests among the servers in a round-robin way, and running a daemon process to detect the failure of the servers connected to the cluster.

3.1   Availability Model

Let us assume that the times to failure of the server nodes are exponentially distributed with rate γ, and that failures detection occurs with rate γ_d. After detection, the cluster is reconfigured by disconnecting the failed node. The latter is reintegrated into the cluster after recovery. The recovery times are assumed to be exponentially distributed with rate τ.

Figure (2) shows the availability model describing the behavior of the cluster governed by server failures, detections and recovery processes. In state 0 all server nodes are failed. In states $k = 1, ..., N$, the system has k servers available for processing the input traffic. However, requests could be rejected in these states due to overload conditions. The failure of a server node in state k, leads the cluster to state D_k with a transition rate $k\gamma$. In states D_k, although the server has failed, this failure is not yet perceived by the load manager. Accordingly, client requests could still be directed by the load manager to the failed node during the failover latency time. Upon detection, the system moves to state $k - 1$ indicating that the number of operational servers has been reduced by one and the recovery of the failed server is initiated. In this model, it is assumed that no other failure can occur when the system is in state D_k. This assumption is acceptable because the failover latency times are generally very small compared to the times to failure.

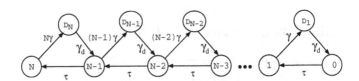

Fig. 2. Availability model of the Web cluster

We have to solve this model to obtain the steady-state probabilities for states k and D_k, denoted as π_k and π_{D_k}, respectively. Processing is straightforward and the analytical expressions are given by equations 1-4.

$$\pi_N = \left[\sum_{f=0}^{N} \frac{N!}{(N-f)!} \left(\frac{\gamma}{\tau}\right)^f + \sum_{f=0}^{N-1} \left(\frac{\gamma}{\tau}\right)^f \frac{\gamma(N-f)N!}{\gamma_d(N-f)!} \right]^{-1} \tag{1}$$

$$\pi_k = \frac{N!}{k!} \left(\frac{\gamma}{\tau}\right)^{N-k} \pi_N \ , \ k = 1, ..., N \tag{2}$$

$$\pi_{D_k} = \frac{N!}{k!} \frac{\gamma k}{\gamma_d} \left(\frac{\gamma}{\tau}\right)^{N-k} \pi_N \ , \ k = 1, ..., N \tag{3}$$

$$\pi_0 = N! \left(\frac{\gamma}{\tau}\right)^N \pi_N \tag{4}$$

3.2 Performance Model

As illustrated in Figure (3), we assume that the traffic arriving to the Web cluster is modeled as a Poisson process with rate λ req/s (requests per second) and is independent from the failure process. Assuming that there are k servers available in the cluster with the input traffic being distributed among the servers, then this system has k independent Poisson arrival processes each one with rate $\lambda' = \frac{\lambda}{k}$. Also, each Web server supports a maximum number of b requests and has a service rate of μ req/s. The requests arriving at the server when the buffer is full are rejected.

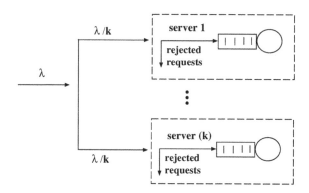

Fig. 3. A Web cluster with k servers available and load balancing

The performance behavior of each server can be modeled by an M/M/1/b queueing system[1]. Let us denote by p_i the steady state probability of having i requests in this queue which can be calculated as follows (see e.g., [12]):

$$p_i = \begin{cases} \rho^i \frac{1-\rho}{1-\rho^{b+1}} & , \text{ if } \lambda' \neq \mu \text{ and } 0 \leq i \leq b \\ \frac{1}{b+1} & , \text{ if } \lambda' = \mu \text{ and } 0 \leq i \leq b \end{cases} \tag{5}$$

where $\rho = \frac{\lambda'}{\mu}$.

---

[1] Since there are no more than b requests in the queueing system, this system is stable for all values of arrival rate λ' and service rate μ (see [13])

Note that the probability that a request is lost due to the buffer being full is given by p_b.

3.3   Composite Availability – Performance Model

Let us denote by UA the web service unavailability defined as the probability in steady state that a web request received by the cluster is not processed successfully. This means that the request is lost: i) upon arriving to the cluster, due to overload conditions,or ii) while it is being processed or waiting for service, due to the failure of the server handling the request.

In order to evaluate UA, we need to evaluate the request loss probability in states k and D_k of the availability model and during the transition between these states (see Fig.2).

Let us denote by:

- $L(k)$: the request loss probability in state k;
- $F(k)$: the request loss probability caused by a transition from state k to state D_k, due to a server failure;
- $L(D_k)$: the request loss probability in state D_k;

Hence, the web service unavailability measure UA can be computed as follows:

$$UA = \sum_{k=1}^{N} \pi_k \{L(k) + F(k)\} + \sum_{k=1}^{N} \pi_{D_k} \{L(D_k)\} + \pi_0 \qquad (6)$$

Recall that π_{D_k}, π_k, and π_0 are the steady state probabilities evaluated from the availability model, given by equations (1) to (4).

In the following, we give the analytical expressions of $L(k)$, $L(D_k)$ and $F(k)$, respectively, considering both recovery assumptions discussed in Section 2, (i.e., NCT and CT).

L(k): Given that k servers are available in the cluster, the probability that a request is rejected is given by:

$$L(k) = [1 - (1 - p_b)^k] \qquad (7)$$

Note that p_b is the probability that a request is lost due to a buffer being full. It is obtained from equation 5 with a request arrival rate to each server given by $\lambda' = \frac{\lambda}{k}$.

F(k): The probability of request loss caused by a transition from state k to state D_k corresponds to the probability that the request is lost due to a server failure while it is being processed or when it is in the buffer. This loss scenario occurs only for the NCT recovery assumption (see Section 2). For the CT assumption, $F(k)$ is zero.

Considering the NCT assumption, $F(k)$ can be obtained by evaluating the probability that the time spent by the web request in the cluster is lower than the time to failure of the server node to which the web request was directed.

Let us denote by T_i the random variable corresponding to the time spent by a request in the cluster, assuming that when it arrives at the server to which it is redirected, there are already i requests in the server. Then, the probability density function of T_i is obtained by the convolution of $i + 1$ independent exponential random variables, each with rate μ. Hence, the probability density function of T_i is a gamma function given by:

$$f(t) = \frac{\mu^{i+1} t^i e^{-\mu t}}{i!} \qquad (8)$$

Based on the availability model, the times to failure in states k, denoted by the random variable T_k, are exponentially distributed:

$$P[T_k < t] = 1 - e^{-k\gamma t} \qquad (9)$$

The probability that the failure occurs while the requests are being processed, is then calculated by conditioning on the random variable representing the total time spent in the system (with its density given by equation 8). This probability can be computed as follows:

$$\begin{aligned}
P[T_k < T_i] &= \int_0^\infty P[T_k < T_i | T_i = t] f(t) dt \\
&= \int_0^\infty (1 - e^{-k\gamma t}) f(t) dt \\
&= \int_0^\infty \frac{(\mu)^{i+1} t^i e^{-\mu t}}{i!} dt - \int_0^\infty \frac{(\mu)^{i+1} t^i e^{-(\mu + k\gamma)t}}{i!} dt \\
&= \frac{[\mu + k\gamma]^{i+1} - \mu^{i+1}}{[\mu + k\gamma]^{i+1}}
\end{aligned} \qquad (10)$$

The probability in states k of a request loss while it is being processed, due to server failure is given by:

$$F(k) = \sum_{i=0}^{b} \{ \frac{[\mu + k\gamma]^{i+1} - \mu^{i+1}}{[\mu + k\gamma]^{i+1}} \} p_i \qquad (11)$$

where p_i is given by equation 5.

$L(D_k)$: The computation of request loss probability when the cluster is in state D_k of the availability model, differs depending on the recovery assumption considered. For both assumptions, we need to evaluate the loss probability caused by the failed server and the loss probability caused by the $k-1$ operational servers in the cluster due to their limited buffer capacity.

Considering the NCT recovery assumption, all requests that arrive at the failed node before the failure is detected by the load manager are lost. In state D_k, we need to take into account two competing processes: the request arrival process with associated rate $\lambda' = \frac{\lambda}{k}$, and the failure detection process with associated rate γ_d. The probability that an arrival occurs before the detection of the failure is given by $\frac{\lambda'}{\lambda'+\gamma_d}$. Therefore, the loss probability in state D_k due to the failed server is given by $(\frac{\lambda'}{\lambda'+\gamma_d})^{\lambda'/\gamma_d}$, where λ'/γ_d is the average number of arrivals in state D_k before the failed server is perceived by the load manager.

The loss probability in state D_k caused by the $k-1$ operational servers due to their limited buffer is given by $[1 - (1 - g(\gamma_d))^{k-1}]$ where $g(\gamma_d)$ is the loss probability for one operational server, before a transition of the cluster to state $k-1$ occurs. Note that $g(\gamma_d)$ can be evaluated using the approach proposed in [4].

When the cluster enters state D_k, assume that i requests are in the queue of the server. An arriving request will be rejected by the server in state D_k if the buffer is full. The corresponding loss probability is equal to the probability that $b - i$ arrivals occur before the system exits from state D_k (i.e, transition γ_d takes place). This conditional probability is given by $(\frac{\lambda'}{\lambda'+\gamma_d})^{b-i}$. Thus $g(\gamma_d) = \sum_{i=0}^{b}(\frac{\lambda'}{\lambda'+\gamma_d})^{b-i}p_i$. Simple manipulation yields the following closed form expression:

$$g(\gamma_d) = \left[\frac{1-\rho}{1-\rho^{b+1}}\right]\left[\frac{\lambda'}{\lambda'+\gamma_d}\right]^b\left[\frac{1-[\frac{\lambda'+\gamma_d}{\mu}]^{b+1}}{1-[\frac{\lambda'+\gamma_d}{\mu}]}\right] \tag{12}$$

Finally, summing the loss probability caused by the failed server and the loss probability caused by the $k-1$ operational servers in the cluster due to their limited buffer capacity, leads to $L(D_k)$ given by:

$$L(D_k) = (\frac{\lambda'}{\lambda' + \gamma_d})^{\lambda'/\gamma_d} + [1 - (1 - g(\gamma_d))^{k-1}] \tag{13}$$

Now, suppose that the web service architecture supports the CT assumption. That is, the system can guarantee the service for all user submitted requests against any loss even when a server node fails. Therefore, the failed node behaves as an operational node during the detection and recovery latency time. The only loss scenario occurs when the server buffer is full. Thus, the loss probability $L(D_k)$ can be easily derived following the approach described for the NCT assumption yielding:

$$L(D_k) = [1 - (1 - g(\gamma_d))^k] \tag{14}$$

To summarize, the web service unavailability measure UA is computed by equation 6 using:

- Equations 7, 11 and 13, when considering the NCT recovery assumption;
- Equations 7 and 14, when considering the CT recovery assumption.

4   Sensitivity Analysis Results

This section provides numerical examples to illustrate the use of the approach for performance and availability tradeoffs during the design. The parameters used in the model may be obtained via direct observations and measurements or based on results published in the literature on similar systems. In particular, the server failure and recovery rates may be estimated for example through the analysis of the logs maintained by the operating systems. The request arrival and service rates can be estimated from traditional traffic and performance measurements. Moreover, specific experiments based on fault injection could be carried out to obtain accurate estimates of the detection and recovery latency times.

In this section, we assume the following parameters. According to [11], we assume that request arrivals to the Web service cluster follow an exponential distribution, where the mean interval time is set to 0.05 seconds ($\lambda = 20$ req/s). Also, the mean time to service of each server is set to 0.2 seconds ($\mu = 5$ req/s). In order to evaluate the impact of failures on web service availability, different values of failure rates are used ($1/\gamma = MTTF = 10$ days, 4 days, 2.7 hours. The mean time to detect a server failure MTTD (the mean sejourn time in states D_k) is set to 20 seconds ($\gamma_d = 0.05$), the mean time to recover a failed server (MTTR=$1/\tau$) is set to 200 seconds and the buffer size is $b = 20$.

In the following, we analyze the impact on the web service unavailability UA of: i) the server mean time to failure, ii) the detection and recovery mean latency time, and iii) the mean service time of the servers, considering NCT and CT recovery assumptions, respectively.

Figure 4 shows the unavailability UA as a function of the number of servers, considering three different values for the MTTF: 10 days, 4 days and 2.7 hours).

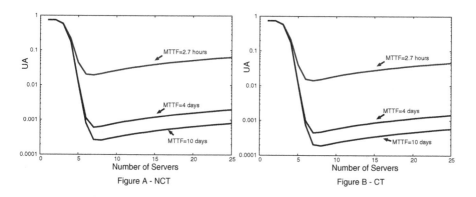

Fig. 4. UA as a function of the number of servers N for various MTTF values

Similar trends are observed when considering the NCT and CT assumptions. However, higher unavailability figures are obtained with the NCT recovery assumption. The difference is about 40 percent when the number of servers is higher than 7. For example, for $N = 20$ and $MTTF = 4$ days the unavailability is 14 hours per year with NCT whereas it is 10 hours per year with CT.

For both assumptions, increasing the number of web servers N in the cluster from 1 to 7 leads to a significant availability improvement. However, the trend is reversed for $N > 7$. This is explained by the fact that the probability for the system to be in states D_k increases, implying a higher contribution of the probability of loss due to these states (i.e., $L(D_k)$ in equation 6).

In order to analyze the impact of the mean time spent in states D_k, figure 5 plots UA as a function of the number of servers, considering two different values for the MTTD: 20 and 2 seconds, and two different values for the mean time to failure (MTTF=10 days, 4 days).

Clearly, UA decreases when the mean time to detect a failure (MTTD) increases, as expected. In fact, the probability of requests being lost while the failure is not detected will be reduced by decreasing the time to detection (for example by increasing the frequency of the heartbeat messages). Such difference is observed only when the number of servers is higher than a given value of N. These results are consistent with those presented in Figure 4.

Moreover, it can be seen that UA is more sensitive to the variation of MTTD compared to the MTTF. Also, there is a notable difference between the unavailability obtained when considering the CT recovery assumption compared to the NCT assumption. This is clearly illustrated by the curves corresponding to MTTF = 10 days, and MTTD=2 seconds. This is explained by the fact that, when the number of servers is high, the loss probability due to buffers being full is very low. In this case, when considering the NCT assumption, the main cause of unavailability is related to the loss of the requests that were in the buffer of the failed server, and those that are directed to this server before the failure is detected. Such loss scenario does not occur when considering the CT assumption.

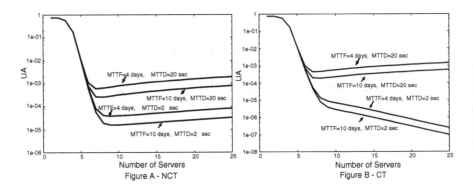

Fig. 5. Impact of detection rates on UA

Figure 6 shows the impact on UA of the service rates combined with the detection rates. Here, the MTTF is set to 10 days. Then, we evaluate UA for two different values of service rate ($\mu = 5$ req/s) and ($\mu = 10$ req/s) with the same request arrival rate ($\lambda = 20$ req/s).

According to the figure, we can observe that for both NCT and CT assumptions, the service rate plays a significant role until a certain value of N. Increasing the number of servers over this threshold value does not lead to an improvement of the availability, even with higher service rates. For instance, considering the curves in Fig. 6-A corresponding to $MTTD = 20$ with different service rates, we note that the lowest unavailability is obtained with 4 servers and a service rate of 10 req/sec. The unavailability is much higher for an architecture with 4 servers and a service rate of 5 req/s ($UA = 10^{-1}$). The fact that UA is not affected by service rate increase when the number of servers is higher than a certain value is due to the size of the buffers and the service rates which are sufficient to handle the flow of arrivals without rejecting requests.

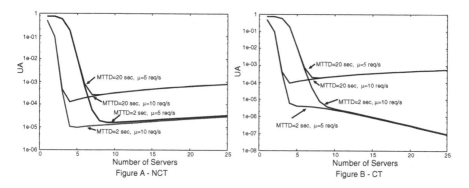

Fig. 6. Impact of service and detection rates on UA

The results presented on figures 4, 5 and 6 can be used for dimensioning the web architecture and for tuning the parameters characterizing the error detection and recovery mechanisms. In this section, we have shown the impact of two error recovery assumptions (CT and NCT) on the web service availability, by analyzing the sensitivity of the results to the variation of the failure rate of the servers, the detection and recovery latency times and the service rates. The results provide useful guidelines for the design of web based systems, since they show that the influence of the above parameters and assumptions depends on the number of servers in the web cluster. When this number is lower than a given threshold, the results suggest that the service rate has the highest influence on availability. In this case, the availability achieved based on the CT and the NCT recovery assumption is of the same order of magnitude. For web cluster systems employing a higher number of servers (in this study more than 7), a significant difference between the availability achieved by the CT and the NCT recovery assumption, is observed. The lower the detection and recovery latency time, the higher the impact of the error recovery assumption on the availability.

5   Conclusion

The evaluation of quantitative measures characterizing the Web service availability is widely recognized as highly important to faithfully reflect the impact of failures as well as performance degradation. Many research efforts have been devoted to the analysis of the causes of unavailability for web based applications. These studies are based on direct observation and monitoring of web sites. However, there is still a need for analytical modeling and examples illustrating how to use the modeling results to support the design of such systems.

This work is aimed at contributing to fill this gap by presenting an analytical model that can be used for analyzing the web service availability. In particular, we provided closed form expressions for clusters availability taking into account various causes of unavailability, including server failures, performance degradations due to server overload, and considering two different recovery strategies. Sensitivity analysis results are presented to show the impact on availability of the server failure rates, the error detection with recovery latency times, and the service rates.

The obtained results provide useful guidelines for the design of web based systems, since they can be used for dimensioning the web architecture as well as they allow to determine the right tradeoffs for achieving availability supporting acceptable levels of performance.

From the models, we have found that when the number of web servers in the cluster is lower than a given threshold (in this study lower than 7), the capacity of processing (service rate plus buffer size) has the highest influence on service availability. In this case, the availability achieved based on the CT and the NCT recovery assumption is of the same order of magnitude.

Also, the results suggest that for web cluster systems employing a higher number of servers (in this study more than 7), a significant difference is observed between the availability achieved by the CT and the NCT recovery assumption. For instance, for a web cluster composed by $N = 25$ servers with the parameters assumed in this study, the web service availability obtained is 0.999 and 0.9999999 for NCT and CT technique, respectively. This substantial difference could be greater if the error detection and recovery latency time is very low. However, the two recovery techniques considered are extreme cases. Indeed even in the CT technique some requests may be lost due to imperfect coverage. Considering a coverage factor lower than 100% (not all the requests are transfered correctly to the non-failed servers without any lost) as in this paper, will reduce the difference between the two considered techniques. It would be interesting to pursue our work considering such a coverage factor.

Future work will focus on extending our model, including in particular performance degradation failures that might occur when the response time exceeds an acceptable threshold. Also, we intend to collect real performance and availability data to validate the model based on an operational case study.

References

1. M. Kaâniche, K.Kanoun and M.Martinello: "User-Perceived Availability of a Web Based Travel Agency". To appear in International Conference on Dependable Systems and Networks (DSN) – Performance and Dependability Symposium PDS, 23–25 june (2003), San Francisco-CA, USA.
2. M. Kaâniche, K.Kanoun and M.Rabah: "A Framework for modeling the Availability of e-Business Systems". International Conference on Computer Communications and Networks, (2001), Scothdale-AZ, USA, pp. 40–45.
3. V. Cardellini, E. Casalicchio, M. Colajanni and P. S. Yu: "The state of the art in Locally Distributed Web-Server System". ACM Computing Surveys (2002), No.2, V.34, pp. 363–371.
4. S. Garg, Y. Huang, C.M.R. Kintala, K.S. Trivedi and S. Yajnik: "Performance and Reliability Evaluation of Passive Replication Schemes in Application Level Fault Tolerance". Proceedings of 29th IEEE International Symposium on Fault Tolerant Computing (FTCS-29) (1999), Madison, USA, pp. 322–329.
5. T. Schroeder, S. Goddard and B. Ramamurthy: "Scalable Web Server Clustering Technologies". IEEE Network (2000), pp. 38–45.
6. V. Cardellini, E. Casalicchio and M. Colajanni: "Mechanisms for quality of service in Web cluster". Computer Networks (2001), pp. 761–771.
7. D. Oppenheimer and D. A. Patterson: "Architecture and Dependability of Large-Scale Internet Services". IEEE Internet Computing (2002), pp. 41–49.
8. D. Long, A. Muir and R. Golding: "A Longitudinal Survey of Internet Host Reliability". Proceedings of IEEE Symposium on Reliable Distributed Systems SRDS (1995), pp. 2–9.
9. M. Kalyanakrishnan, R. K. Iyer and J. U. Patel : "Reliability of Internet Hosts: a Case Study from the End User's Perspective". Computer Networks (1999), No. 31, pp. 47–57.
10. M. Y. Luo and C. S. Yang: "Enabling fault resilience for web services". Computer Communications (2002), No.25, pp. 198–209.
11. W. Willinger and V. Paxson: "Where Mathematics meets the Internet". Notices of the American Mathematical Society (1998), No.8, v.45, pp. 961–970.
12. A. O. Allen: "Probability, Statistics and Queueing Theory". Academic Press, NY, (1978).
13. G. Bolch, S. Greiner, H. de Meer and K. S. Trivedi: "Queuing Networks and Markov Chains". John Wiley and Sons, Inc (1998).
14. J. F. Meyer: "Closed-Form Solutions of Performability". IEEE Transactions on Computing (1982), No.31, v.7, pp. 648–657.
15. E.A. Brewer: "Lessons from Giant-Scale Service". IEEE Internet Computing (2001), pp. 46–55.
16. H. Bryhni, E. Klovning and O. Kure: "A Comparison of Load Balancing Techniques for Scalable Web Servers". IEEE Network (2000), pp. 58–64.
17. N. Aghdaie and Y. Tamir: "Client-Transparent Fault-Tolerant Web Service". Proceedings of the IEEE International Performance, Computing, and Communications Conference (2001), pp. 209–216.

A Unified Tool for Performance Modelling and Prediction

Stephen Gilmore and Leïla Kloul*

Laboratory for Foundations of Computer Science, The University of Edinburgh,
Edinburgh, Scotland, EH9 3JZ

Abstract. We describe a novel performability modelling approach which facilitates the efficient solution of performance models extracted from high-level descriptions of systems. The notation which we use for our high-level designs is the UML graphical modelling language. The technology which provides the efficient representation capability for the underlying performance model is the MTBDD-based PRISM probabilistic model checker. The UML models are compiled through an intermediate language, the stochastic process algebra PEPA, before translation into MTBDDs for solution. We illustrate our approach on a real-world analysis problem from the domain of mobile telephony.

1 Introduction

Distributed, mobile and global computing environments provide robust development challenges to practising software system developers. Working with rapidly-changing implementation technology means that developers often must spend some of their development time finding and correcting errors in the software libraries and APIs which they use. Fortifying this difficulty is the arduous terrain of dynamic distributed systems where the difficulty of replaying a communication sequence which led to a system fault confounds the process of detecting and correcting implementation errors.

In this setting, application developers rarely wish to expend the investment of time which would be needed to build and analyse a performance model of the system which they are developing. The concepts and the modelling languages of performance analysis are relatively unfamiliar to software developers and when already faced with a generous range of other difficulties in the development process, early predictive performance analysis can easily be overlooked.

However, this is an imprudent practice. If performance design flaws are found early in the development process then they can be corrected at a relatively low cost. In contrast, if they are found after the development process is long underway then they may be very expensive or even unrealistic to repair. If they are then subsequently ignored, such problems will lead to unreliability of the high-end consumer electronic devices which are increasingly used in safety-critical contexts throughout society.

---

* On leave from PRiSM, Université de Versailles, 45, av. des Etats-Unis, 78000 Versailles, France

S. Anderson et al. (Eds.): SAFECOMP 2003, LNCS 2788, pp. 179–192, 2003.
© Springer-Verlag Berlin Heidelberg 2003

To combat these difficulties, a performance modelling methodology which is designed for effective development of such global, mobile or high-end distributed systems should provide at least the following two features: a convenient high-level modelling notation for expressing performance models; and efficient solution methods for realistic models of complex systems. Unfortunately these two requirements are often at variance. In order to access state-of-the-art solution methods one usually additionally needs to master sophisticated representation and analysis methods which sometimes are inconvenient or troublesome to use. Conversely, high-level modelling platforms devote much of their efforts to providing reliable graphical editors and supporting document and IDE infrastructure and this can come at the expense of equipping them with complementary analysis tools.

We provide a structured performance engineering platform for this problem domain by connecting a *specification environment* (SENV) and a *verification environment* (VENV) so that each may communicate with the other. The SENV and VENV are connected by a bridge which consists of two categories of software tools. These are:

– *extractors* which translate designs from the SENV into inputs for the VENV, omitting any aspects of the design which are not relevant for the verification task at hand; and
– *reflectors* which convert the results from the analysis performed by the VENV back into a form which can be processed and displayed by the SENV.

A series of extractors can be chained together to provide a path from one specification formalism to another. Similarly, reflectors can be chained together in order that the results of one analysis process may be presented back in the format of another. A process of *extractor/reflector chaining* is used here to connect a specification environment to multiple verification environments. We use the ArgoUML design environment [1] as our SENV and the PEPA Workbench [2] and the PRISM probabilistic symbolic model checker [3] both play the role of VENVs. ArgoUML provides the Unified Modelling Language (UML) [4] as its modelling language. The PEPA Workbench and PRISM both support the PEPA stochastic process algebra [5]. PRISM additionally supports a state-based language based on the Reactive Modules formalism of Alur and Henzinger [6].

Structure of this paper: In the next section we describe some of the background to this work, providing a summary of UML, PEPA and PRISM modelling. In Section 3 we describe the software architecture of the system, as an integrated set of components. We give details of the implementation, providing an explanation of how the components work together and calling attention to cases where some care has been needed. In Section 4 we present our case study, showing the approach applied to a realistic example. In Section 5 we survey related work. Conclusions are presented in Section 6.

2   Background

The Unified Modelling Language (UML) is an effective diagrammatic notation used to capture high-level designs of systems, especially object-oriented software systems. A UML *model* is represented by a collection of diagrams describing parts of the system from different points of view; there are seven main diagram types. For example, there will typically be a *static structure diagram* (or *class diagram*) describing the classes and interfaces in the system and their static relationships (inheritance, dependency, etc.). State diagrams, a variant of Harel state charts, can be used to record dynamic behaviour. Interaction diagrams, such as sequence diagrams, are used to illustrate the way objects of different classes interact in a particular scenario. As usual we expect that the UML modeller will make a number of diagrams of different kinds. Our analysis is based on state and collaboration diagrams.

We have introduced performance information in the state diagrams such that each transition in these diagrams is labelled with a pair '*a* / rate(*r*)' where *a* is the action type executed and *r* is an exponentially distributed rate associated with this action. We often simplify the representation of the transition labels in order to save space writing this as '*a* / *r*'. A customer arrival causes a change in the state of a queue so this would be one example of an action type which we might use. Concretely, *arrive*/rate(λ) and *serve*/rate(μ) would be suitable arc adornments for a state diagram for a queue (abbreviated to *arrive*/λ and *serve*/μ).

In Performance Evaluation Process Algebra (PEPA) [5], a system is viewed as a set of *components* which carry out *activities* either individually or in cooperation with other components. Activities which are private to the component in which they occur are represented by the distinguished action type, τ. Each activity is characterized by an *action type* and a duration which is exponentially distributed. This is written as a pair such as (α, r) where α is the action type and r is the *activity rate*. This parameter may be any positive real number, or may be unspecified. We use the distinguished symbol $\top$ to indicate that the rate is not specified by this component. This component is said to be *passive* with respect to this action type and the rate of the shared activity is defined by another component.

PEPA provides a set of combinators which allow expressions to be built which define the behaviour of components via the activities that they engage in. These combinators are presented below.

Prefix $(\alpha, r).P$: Prefix is the basic mechanism by which the behaviours of components are constructed. This combinator implies that after the component has carried out activity (α, r), it behaves as component P.

Choice $P_1 + P_2$: This combinator represents a competition between components. The system may behave either as component P_1 or as P_2. All current activities of the two components are enabled. The first activity to complete distinguishes one of these components and the other is then discarded.

Cooperation $P_1 \bowtie_L P_2$: This describes the synchronization of components P_1 and P_2 over the activities in the cooperation set L. The components may proceed independently with activities whose types do not belong to this set. A particular case of the cooperation is when $L = \emptyset$. In this case, components proceed with all activities independently. The notation $P_1 \parallel P_2$ is used as a shorthand for $P_1 \bowtie_\emptyset P_2$. In a cooperation, the rate of a shared activity is defined as the rate of the slowest component.

Hiding: P/L This component behaves like P except that any activities of types within the set L are *hidden*, i.e. such an activity exhibits the unknown type τ and the activity can be regarded as an internal delay by the component. Such an activity cannot be carried out in cooperation with any other component: the original action type of a hidden activity is no longer externally accessible, to an observer or to another component; the duration is unaffected.

Constant: $A \stackrel{def}{=} P$ Constants are components whose meaning is given by a defining equation: $A \stackrel{def}{=} P$ gives the constant A the behaviour of the component P. This is how we assign names to components (behaviours). An explicit recursion operator is not provided but components of infinite behaviour may be readily described using sets of mutually recursive defining equations.

The transition system underlying the PEPA model gives the continuous time Markov process represented by the model. The generation of this process is based on the derivation graph of the model in which syntactic terms form the nodes, and arcs represent the possible transitions between them. This derivation graph describes the possible behaviour of any PEPA component and provides a useful way to reason about a model. The use of the derivation graph is analogous to the use of the reachability graph in stochastic extensions of Petri nets such as GSPN [5].

Specifications are constructed in PRISM by defining a collection of reactive modules which synchronise on shared activities. The state of each module is determined by a set of local variables. The models which we work with here are all obtained by compiling an input PEPA model. All of these have associated constants which enumerate the states of the module and use a single local variable to record the current state. We developed the PEPA-to-PRISM compiler to allow us to analyse our PEPA models with PRISM. Our compiler has been incorporated into the latest release of PRISM (version 1.3) [7].

The behaviour of a reactive module is encoded by a list of guarded transitions which name the activity performed and specify assignments to the local variables which are to be carried out if the activity is performed. The PRISM model-checker accepts descriptions of discrete-time Markov chains (DTMCs), continuous-time Markov chains (CTMCs) and Markov decision processes (MDPs).

CSL model-checking of CTMCs allows the user to check performability properties which combine probabilities, behaviour and time, such as "the probability that a hand off call will be dropped within 100 time units is less than 0.1."

We use PRISM to solve PEPA models for their stationary probability distribution. The first step of this process is generating the full state space of the system. This is compactly stored by PRISM as a multi-terminal binary decision diagram (MTBDD). The CUDD package [8] is used as a library, providing MTBDD data structures and algorithms to PRISM.

3   The Software Architecture

Ours is a component-based software architecture in which we link substantial software tools with lightweight connectors called extractors and reflectors. This promotes significant code re-use and allows for clean interfaces between systems using formal description languages such as PEPA and PRISM's reactive modules.

A performance modeller using our tool will design a system using a UML modelling environment such as ArgoUML. UML software tools produce XML-based model interchange files called XMI files. The XMI file of the model is used by the PEPA Workbench to extract a PEPA model. The resulting PEPA file is then submitted to the model checker PRISM. PRISM produces a steady state probability vector. This is then reflected by the PRISM reflector as a PEPA steady state probability vector. Using some information in the XMI file produced initially by the UML tool, the PEPA workbench reflects these results as an XMI document.

Finally the modeller can then visualize the performance measures obtained since this last reflector of the chaining process consists in adding these new information into the user UML model.

The start of our UML performance model analysis process is an .xmi or .zargo file obtained from ArgoUML or a similar UML tool. The PEPA Workbench contains as components the PEPA Extractor and the PEPA Reflector which convert between UML models and other kinds. The PEPA Extractor is first used to process the file containing the UML model and extracts a PEPA model from this. This PEPA model is then compiled using the PEPA-to-PRISM compiler and solved by PRISM. The PRISM Reflector assumes that the PEPA Extractor and compiler have already been run. The former has extracted a .pepa file from an .xmi or .zargo file. The latter has extracted a .sm file from the .pepa file and has written a log file (.log) mapping PEPA local state identifiers onto the numeric constants used in the reactive modules notation. The output from the PRISM tool onto the standard output stream has been captured and saved in a .pres (PRISM results) file. The PRISM Extractor reads the .log file and the .pres file and writes an .xml file in the same format as the PEPA Workbench. PEPA Workbench results files can be read by the PEPA Reflector. We use the PEPA Reflector next to merge the results with the orginial input UML model to produce a modified .xmi or .zargo file which includes the results of the performance analysis. This file can be loaded into the ArgoUML tool to present the results back to the UML performance modeller.

Our extractor and reflector software tools are implemented in the programming languages Java and Standard ML [9]. The Java components handle the processing of the zipped archives (in .zargo format) of UML models produced by the ArgoUML tool and the parsing of the XMI documents containing the UML models (in .xmi format). The DOM parser from the Java 1.4 javax.xml package is used to parse the XMI files. Much of the more complex processing is implemented in the Standard ML language.

We now present a case study which demonstrates the use of these tools.

4   Case Study: Hierarchical Cellular Network

The hierarchical cellular network consists of two tiers of cells, a level of macrocells overlying a level of microcells. In this study, we consider the Manhattan model [10] where the reuse pattern is based on a five squared microcell cluster, a central cell surrounded by four peripheral cells (Fig.1). This model takes its name from the city of Manhattan which consists of square-blocks, representing buildings, with streets in between them.

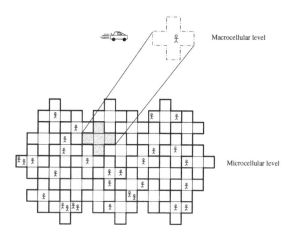

Fig. 1. Reuse pattern of Manhattan model

As in this model each microcell has four neighbouring cells, we consider a microcell cluster model composed of a central microcell surrounded by four peripheral cells. We consider a FCA scheme (Fixed Channel Allocation [11]), where S channels are distributed among the different cells. Let c_j, $j = 1 \ldots 5$ be the capacity of microcell j and c_0 the capacity of the macrocell.

Considering a homogeneous system in statistical equilibrium, any cluster of microcells overlaid by a macrocell has statistically the same behaviour as any other cluster of microcells overlayed by a macrocell. We use this observation to decouple a cluster from the rest of the system. That is, we can analyze the overall system by focusing on a given cluster under the condition that the neighbouring clusters exhibit their typical random behaviour independently.

We consider two types of customers inside the cluster, the new calls and the handover requests (ongoing calls). External arrivals to the cluster consist of the handover requests coming from other clusters and the new calls initiated in that cluster. We assume that the handover requests coming from other clusters may occur only in the macrocell or the peripheral microcells. We consider that these arrivals may never occur in the central microcell.

In this study, new calls can be assigned only to the microcell level. Moreover, we consider a hierarchical cellular network using an overflow strategy but without reversible capability, except for the external arrivals to the macrocell. A request, either a new call or a handover request, initiated at the microcell level is served in its originating microcell if a channel is available. Otherwise, according to the overflow strategy, the request is overflowed to the upper level and is satisfied if a channel is free at this level. In the case where all channels are busy at both levels, the request is dropped (in the case of a handover) or blocked (in the case of a new call).

This system is studied under the usual Markovian assumptions. New call and handover request arrivals follow a Poisson process. We assume that the average new call arrival rates and the handover arrival rates are the same for all cells in the network. The session duration which represents the duration of a communication is modelled by a service time which is exponentially distributed with parameter μ. The amount of time that a user remains within a coverage cell of a given base station, called *dwell-time*, is assumed to be exponentially distributed with parameter α.

In the next section we present the UML model corresponding to this system.

4.1   The UML Model

In the model, the external arrival process is represented by the event *in* by the cells. The arrival rate is assumed to be λ_1 in the macrocell, λ_2 in the peripheral microcells and λ_3 in the central microcell.

Because of the different types of cells (macrocell, peripheral microcell, central microcell) and the topology of the network, we make a distinction between handover requests generated by the cluster itself (Fig. 2). This distinction is based

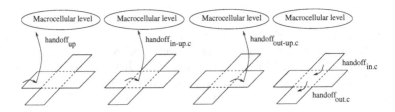

Fig. 2. The handoff requests graph

on the cell type this request originated from and the cell type satisfying this request, which means the cell where the ongoing call has to be transferred to. Thus, the arrival process of these customers is represented by the event *handoff* indexed by the type of handover request as follows:

- $handoff_{down}$ represents the transfer of a call from the macrocell to a microcell. This call is a handover request coming from outside the cluster to the macrocell and because all its channels are busy, it has to be transferred to a microcell,
- $handoff_{up}$ represents the transfer of a call from a microcell to the macrocell. This call may be either a new call or a handover request coming from outside the cluster to the microcell and because all channels in the microcell are busy, it has to be transferred to the macrocell. The rate associated with this event is the external arrival rate to the microcell,
- $handoff_{in.c}$ is the event which triggers the transfer of an ongoing call from one of the peripheral microcells to the central microcell,

- in contrast, $handoff_{out.c}$ represents the transfer of an ongoing call from the central microcell to one of the four peripheral microcells,
- $handoff_{in-up.c}$ represents the case where an ongoing call coming from a peripheral microcell and entering the central microcell, is then transferred to the macro cell because all channels of the central microcell are busy,
- $handoff_{out-up.c}$ models the arrival of an ongoing call from the central microcell to a peripheral microcell and because all channels of this cell are busy, the handover call is overflowed to the macro cell.

As the process behind the four last *handoff* events is the same, the corresponding rate is also the same and it is denoted by α (representing the mean dwell-time in a microcell). In all cells, the service process is represented by event *service*. As the service rate in each cell is assumed to be μ, when there are i, $1 \leq i \leq c_k$, customers in a cell, the event *service* is of rate $i\mu$.

In the following, we present the state diagrams of the different components of our network and the collaboration diagram showing the interactions between these components.

The State Diagrams. We denote by *macro* the macrocell overlying the cluster of microcells. *microc* and *microj*, denote the central microcell and a peripheral microcell respectively. For the sake of readability of the different state diagrams, we limit the total number of channels to $S = 18$ and these channels are fairly shared by the different cells: $c_j = 3$, $j = 0 \ldots 5$.

The state diagram of *macro* is described in Fig. 3 where $macro_i$, $i = 0 \ldots 3$, is the state where i channels are busy.

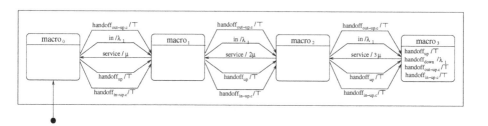

Fig. 3. The State diagram of *macro*

A transition from state $macro_i$ to state $macro_{i+1}$ denotes the arrival of either a call from outside the cluster (*in*) or a call from one of the microcells with $handoff_{up}$, $handoff_{in-up.c}$ or $handoff_{out-up.c}$. A natural termination of a call is represented by a transition from state $macro_i$ to state $macro_{i-1}$ with *service*.

When all channels are busy (state $macro_3$), if a handover call arrives from the microcells, the call is dropped and thus lost. Similarly, if a external handover call arrives when all channels are busy, the call is blocked and lost.

The state diagram of *microj* is described in Fig. 4 where $microj_k$, $k = 0 \ldots 3$, is the state where k channels are busy.

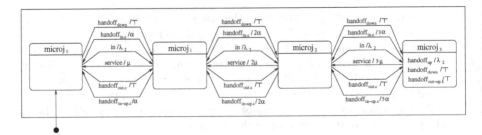

Fig. 4. The State diagram of a peripheral microcell $microj$

A transition from state $microj_k$ to state $microj_{k+1}$ denotes the arrival of either a new call (in), an ongoing call from the central microcell ($handoff_{out.c}$) or from the macrocell ($handoff_{down}$). The departure of a call from a peripheral microcell to the central microcell ($handoff_{in.c}$) or to the macrocell via the central ($handoff_{in-up.c}$) is depicted in the diagram by a transition from $microj_k$ to state $microj_{k-1}$. A similar transition with $service$ models a natural termination of a call.

As for the $macro$, all arrivals when all channels of a peripheral cell are full (state $microj_3$) are lost.

The state diagram of the central microcell $microc$ is described in Fig. 5 where $microc_i$, $i = 0 \dots 3$, is the state where i channels are busy.

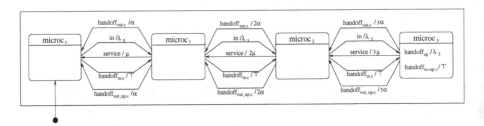

Fig. 5. The State diagram of the central microcell $microc$

In this diagram, a transition from state $microc_i$ to state $microc_{i+1}$ denotes the arrival of either a new call (in) or an ongoing call from a peripheral microcell ($handoff_{in.c}$). A call leaving the central microcell for a peripheral microcell ($handoff_{out.c}$) or for the macrocell via a peripheral one ($handoff_{out-up.c}$) is depicted by a transition from $microc_i$ to state $microc_{i-1}$.

The Collaboration Diagram. In the network, the peripheral microcells will behave independently, but will synchronize with the central microcell when there are handoff requests from one to another. Similarly both peripheral and central microcells have to synchronize. These interactions of the different components of the network are recorded in the collaboration diagram.

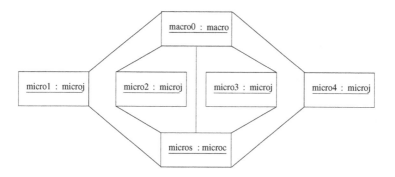

Fig. 6. The Collaboration Diagram

4.2   Processing the Model

Solving this model requires using our extractor and reflector tools and the
PRISM model checker. We solve the model for $c_j = 8$, $j = 0..5$. This implies
that there are 48 channels shared between 6 cells. The CTMC corresponding to
this model has more than a quarter of a million states (actually 262,144 states)
and the longest part of the process is generating and solving this CTMC with
PRISM. We used PRISM v1.3 for this with its Hybrid solution engine and its
Jacobi solver. The total storage for matrix and solution vectors built for the
model required 6208Kb of memory and the solver found the solution after 466
iterations. This took 45.31 seconds on a 1.6GHz Pentium IV with 256Mb of memory. The fact that this runtime is so short means that these tools can be used
by a software developer with no more significant impact on development time
than that spent on the edit-compile-run cycle in software development. We think
that this is an encouraging indicator for this method of software performance
analysis.

A screenshot showing the reflected results in the UML model can be seen in
Fig. 7. On each diagram state, we now have the name of the state and, between
the brackets, a performance measure related to this state. In this example we
have the steady-state residence probability, expressed as a percentage, for each
state.

4.3   Analysis and Model-Checking

The PRISM model checker supports the analysis of probabilistic and stochastic
systems by allowing a modeller to check a logical property against a model.
Several logics and several types of model are supported. The appropriate logic
for continuous-time Markov chains is CSL [12] and PRISM supports this type
of analysis of our models.

The syntax of CSL is:

$$\phi ::= true \mid false \mid a \mid \phi \wedge \phi \mid \phi \vee \phi \mid \neg\phi \mid \mathcal{P}_{\bowtie p}[\psi] \mid \mathcal{S}_{\bowtie p}[\phi]$$
$$\psi ::= X\,\phi \mid \phi\,U^I\,\phi \mid \phi\,U\,\phi$$

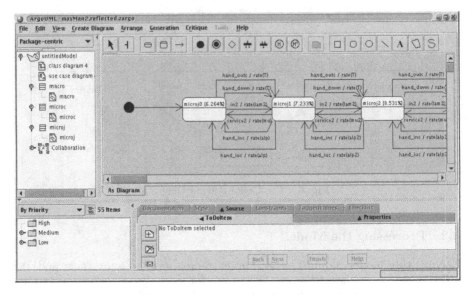

Fig. 7. The UML model with performance information added viewed in ArgoUML

where a is an atomic proposition, $\bowtie \in \{<, \leq, >, \geq\}$ is a relational parameter, $p \in [0, 1]$ is a probability, and I is an interval of $\mathbb{R}$.

Paths of interest through the states of the model are characterised by the *path formulae* specified by $\mathcal{P}$. Path formulae either refer to the next state (using the X operator), or record that one proposition is always satisfied until another is achieved (the until-formulae use the U-operator).

Performance information is encoded into the CSL formulae via the time-bounded until operator (U^I) and the steady-state operator, $\mathcal{S}$.

By expressing properties of interest using path formulae we can check *interval-of-time* performability measures over our system. By expressing properties of interest with the steady-state operator we can determine *long-run* measures over the system.

5   Related Work

Work which is similar in spirit to our own approach is that of Petriu and Shen [13] where a layered queueing network model is automatically extracted from an input UML model with performance annotations in the format specified by a special-purpose UML profile [14]. We do not follow the same UML profile because it is not supported by our modelling tool. Additionally, the performance evaluation technology which we deploy (process algebras and BDD-based solution) is quite different from layered queueing networks.

Another performance engineering method which is similar to ours is that of López-Grao, Merseguer and Campos [15] where UML diagrams are mapped into GSPNs which can be solved by GreatSPN. We use different UML diagram types from these authors and, again, a different performance evaluation technology. Stochastic Petri nets and stochastic process algebras have different, but complementary, modelling strengths [16].

One feature of our work which is distinctive from both of the above is the role of a *reflector* in the system to present the results of the performance evaluation back to the UML modeller in terms of their input model. We consider this to be a strength of our approach. We do not only compile a UML model into a performance model, we also present the results back to the modeller in the UML idiom.

6 Conclusions

We have described a component-based method of linking a collection of software tools to facilitate automated processing of UML performance models. The connectors in this method are the extractors and reflectors which we have developed. We have applied the tools to the analysis of a realistic model of a hierarchical cellular telephone network.

This approach to modelling allows the modeller to access a powerful and efficient solution technology without having to master the details of unfamiliar modelling languages such as process algebras and reactive modules. Our experience of using the PEPA and PRISM tools has been uniformly good.

One of the decisions which we have had to take in this work was the choice of UML diagrams and metaphors to employ. In part our choice in this was restricted by the degree of support offered by the UML modelling tool which we used (ArgoUML). However, the outcome of this was that it directed us to use familiar and well-understood parts of the UML modelling notation. One of our motivations for this work is reducing the potential for error in early stages of the performance modelling process and we consider that this outcome is supported by this influence to use the well-understood parts of UML.

We hope that we have gone some way to providing automated support for computing simple performance measures and to circumventing an unnecessary notational hurdle if this was acting as an impediment to the understanding and uptake of modern performance analysis technology.

The dependability and safety of computer-based systems is a complex issue with many opposing and sometimes conflicting aspects. In this paper we have focused on quantitative aspects of system dependability taking the view that it is sometimes the case that quantitative analysis takes second place to qualitative analysis of systems. Well-engineered, safe systems need to deliver reliable services in a timely fashion with good availability. For this reason, we view quantitative analysis techniques as being as important as qualitative ones.

We have recently developed an extension of the PEPA stochastic process algebra where PEPA components are used as coloured tokens in a stochastic Petri net. The resulting formalism is called PEPA nets [17]. Our future work is to integrate the PEPA nets formalism with our extractor and reflector tools. Given an extended UML tool which supports the forthcoming UML 2.0 design we would be able to map the extended UML 2.0 activity diagrams onto PEPA nets for analysis purposes. The activity diagrams in UML 2.0 are given a semantics which is based on Petri nets and queueing theory and are intended for analyses such as ours. An algorithm translating PEPA nets models into the PEPA formalism has already been developed and implemented [18]. Using this it would be possible to take extended activity diagrams through to analysis by PRISM using the method followed in this paper.

Acknowledgements. The authors are supported by the DEGAS (Design Environments for Global ApplicationS) project IST-2001-32072 funded by the FET Proactive Initiative on Global Computing. The authors thank Gethin Norman and David Parker of the University of Birmingham for the implementation of the PEPA process algebra combinators in the PRISM model checker. Jane Hillston and David Parker provided helpful comments on an earlier draft of this paper.

References

1. Tigris.org project. ArgoUML: A modelling tool for design using UML. Web page and documentation at http://argouml.tigris.org/, 2002.
2. S. Gilmore and J. Hillston. The PEPA Workbench: A Tool to Support a Process Algebra-based Approach to Performance Modelling. In *Proceedings of the Seventh International Conference on Modelling Techniques and Tools for Computer Performance Evaluation*, number 794 in Lecture Notes in Computer Science, pages 353–368, Vienna, May 1994. Springer-Verlag.
3. M. Kwiatkowska, G. Norman, and D. Parker. PRISM: Probabilistic symbolic model checker. In T. Field, P. Harrison, J. Bradley, and U. Harder, editors, *Proc. 12th International Conference on Modelling Techniques and Tools for Computer Performance Evaluation (TOOLS'02)*, volume 2324 of *LNCS*, pages 200–204. Springer, 2002. http://www.cs.bham.ac.uk/~dxp/prism/.
4. Object Management Group. Unified Modeling Language, v1.4, March 2001. OMG document number: formal/2001-09-67.
5. J. Hillston. *A Compositional Approach to Performance Modelling*. Cambridge University Press, 1996.
6. R. Alur and T.A. Henzinger. Reactive modules. *Formal Methods in System Design: An International Journal*, 15(1):7–48, July 1999.
7. D. Parker. *PRISM 1.3 User's Guide*. University of Birmingham, February 2003. http://www.cs.bham.ac.uk/~dxp/prism.
8. F. Somenzi. *CUDD: CU Decision Diagram Package*. Department of Electrical and Computer Engineering, University of Colorado at Boulder, February 2001.
9. Robin Milner, Mads Tofte, Robert Harper, and David MacQueen. *The Definition of Standard ML: Revised 1997*. The MIT Press, 1997.
10. M.D. Kulavaratharasah and A.H. Aghvami. Teletraffic performance evaluation of microcellular personal communication networks (PCN's) with prioritized handoff procedures. *IEEE Transactions on Vehicular Technology*, 48(1):137–152, January 1999.
11. I. Katzela and M. Naghshineh. Channel assignment schemes for cellular mobile telecommunication systems: A comprehensive survey. *Proceedings of the IEEE*, 82(9):1398–1430, 1994.
12. A. Aziz, K. Sanwal, V. Singhal, and R. Brayton. Verifying continuous time Markov chains. In *Computer-Aided Verification*, volume 1102 of *LNCS*, pages 169–276. Springer-Verlag, 1996.

13. D.C. Petriu and H. Shen. Applying the UML performance profile: Graph grammar-based derivation of LQN models from UML specifications. In A.J. Field and P.G. Harrison, editors, *Proceedings of the 12th International Conference on Modelling Tools and Techniques for Computer and Communication System Performance Evaluation*, number 2324 in Lecture Notes in Computer Science, pages 159–177, London, UK, April 2002. Springer-Verlag.

14. B. Selic, A. Moore, M. Woodside, B. Watson, M. Bjorkander, M. Gerhardt, and D. Petriu. Response to the OMG RFP for Schedulability, Performance, and Time, revised, June 2001. OMG document number: ad/2001-06-14.

15. J.P. López-Grao, J. Merseguer, and J. Campos. From UML activity diagrams to stochastic Petri nets: Application to software performance analysis. In *Proceedings of the Seventeenth International Symposium on Computer and Information Sciences*, pages 405–409, Orlando, Florida, October 2002. CRC Press.

16. S. Donatelli, J. Hillston, and M. Ribaudo. A comparison of Performance Evaluation Process Algebra and Generalized Stochastic Petri Nets. In *Proc. 6th International Workshop on Petri Nets and Performance Models*, Durham, North Carolina, 1995.

17. S. Gilmore, J. Hillston, L. Kloul, and M. Ribaudo. PEPA nets: A structured performance modelling formalism. *Performance Evaluation*, 2003. Special issue of selected papers from the Proceedings of the 12th International Conference on Modelling Tools and Techniques for Computer and Communication System Performance Evaluation. To appear.

18. S. Gilmore, J. Hillston, L. Kloul, and M. Ribaudo. Performance modelling with PEPA nets and PRISM. In *Proceedings of the Second PASTA workshop*, pages 23–39, Edinburgh, Scotland, June 2003.

An Approach to Trust Case Development

J. Górski[1], A. Jarzêbowicz[2], R. Leszczyna[2], J. Miler[2], and M. Olszewski[2]

[1]Technical University of Gdańsk, Narutowicza 11/12, 80-952 Gdańsk, Poland
[2]Project IST-DRIVE

Abstract. In the paper we present an approach to the architectural trust case development for DRIVE, the IT infrastructure supporting the processes of drugs distribution and application. The objectives of DRIVE included safer and cheaper drugs distribution and application. A *trust case* represents an argument supporting the trustworthiness of the system. It is decomposed into *claims* that postulate some trust related properties. Claims differ concerning their abstraction level and scope. To express a claim we need a language and a conceptual model. We used UML to represent *claim models* and related *context models* of the trust case. To specify claims we introduced *Claim Definition Language* – CDL. The paper gives a deeper description of the above concepts and illustrates how they were applied in practice.

1 Introduction

As we are becoming more and more dependent on software (both, in the individual and in the group dimensions) there is an increasing need for *software trustworthiness* understood as a guarantee that the trust that the system will meet the most critical expectations (e.g. safety and/or security) is well justified and based on evidence rather than on beliefs. This evidence can include analytical results showing that the system objectives, scope and requirements are adequately identified and understood, probabilistic failure profiles of systems and components, design decisions of which impact on safety and security is known and well understood, results of additional analyses, proofs of conformity with accepted and recommended standards and guidelines etc.

The concept of a *trust case* refers to the need of providing a complete and explicit argument justifying trust in the computer system being used in a given application context. As the trust case encompasses both, safety and security guarantees, it could be (conceptually) split into two parts: the safety case and the security case.

Safety case is a documented body of evidence that provides a convincing and valid argument that a system is adequately safe for a given application in a given environment. It is recommended that safety case is being developed in parallel with the design. The standard [1] stresses that "the Safety Case should be initiated at the earliest possible stage in the Safety Program so that hazards are identified and dealt with while the opportunities for their exclusion exist". The structure of safety cases has been examined by some EU sponsored projects, e.g. [2].

Much work has been done on security evaluation of products and systems. Two emerging standards seem to be especially influential: [6] for security management and [5], [4] for security evaluation of products and systems. A security case is the counterpart of the safety case and collects the evidence justifying the trust in that the system is sufficiently secure.

S. Anderson et al. (Eds.): SAFECOMP 2003, LNCS 2788, pp. 193–206, 2003.

Safety and security are two different (although not disjoint) system qualities. If both matter in a given situation (as it is true for medical applications) they can sometimes be in conflict. As an example take a patient related data that should have its access controlled and restricted due to the privacy considerations (a security related requirement) and simultaneously should have high availability with relaxed access control in emergency situations (a safety related requirement). In such applications the trust case should cover both, safety and security viewpoints and in addition it should consider possible conflicts and their resolutions.

The IST-DRIVE project, performed within the 5th FP, focused at medical care, undoubtedly a trust related domain. In DRIVE both safety and security mattered and consequently both aspects had to be adequately covered. We used a more neutral concept of trust in order to start with a single target and then to specialize it into security and safety targets.

In the subsequent sections we present the trust case conceptual structure that we adopted in our approach, the language used to specify the trust case structure and contents and then the experiences from applying those concepts to analyze the trustworthiness of a complex IT infrastructure developed by DRIVE. In conclusions we summarize our contribution (as compared to other approaches) and present plans for future research.

2 Project DRIVE – Objectives and Scope

The objective of the 5th Framework R&D project DRIVE - DRug In Virtual Enterprise (IST-1999-12040) was to create a safer and smarter hospital environment by means of innovative and trustworthy IT solutions. The project involved eight partners from Italy, Sweden, Spain, France and Poland representing hospitals, research institutions, software companies, pharmaceutical companies and hospital equipment manufacturers. The strategic objective of DRIVE was to improve the quality of patient care and patient safety by reducing the drug administration errors while simultaneously reducing the supply chain costs. The project resulted in an integrated IT solution (hereafter called *DRIVE solution*) supporting the drug distribution, administration and application processes, starting from pharmaceutical companies through warehouses and pharmacies down to a patient in a hospital. A pilot version of the DRIVE infrastructure was installed and is in operation in Milan, Italy.

DRIVE solution focuses on three key areas of healthcare optimization:

- Clinical process: representing the drug related processes within a hospital directly or indirectly aimed at the improvement of patient's health state, from the admission until discharge.
- Supply chain: representing the flows of the pharmaceutical products and related information, from the manufacturer to the point of use (patient's bedside).
- Trust: representing the stakeholder requirements for the protection of critical assets: personal clinical records, hospital professional accountability, enterprise value chain and privacy within the entire business model.

The structure of the clinical and supply chain processes is shown in Fig. 1.

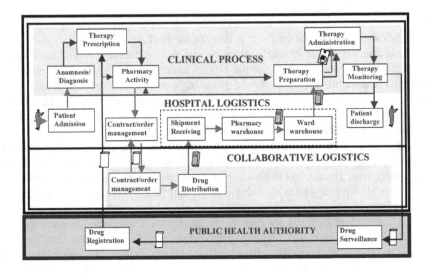

Fig. 1. The scope of DRIVE Solution (Note: the part marked as "Public Health Authority" is not covered by DRIVE)

All identification data is captured in a 2D coded wristband worn by a patient from admission to discharge. DRIVE solution supports the physician during the anamnesis, diagnosis and therapy prescription phases. It also supports nurses in the preparing and administrating therapies, providing for avoiding human errors that often occur during these phases.

The hospital logistics part of DRIVE solution supports the head nurses in maintaining the proper stock of pharmaceutical products in ward cabinets. A new 2D label, specially studied for DRIVE, encodes all the information needed for tracing the drug flows (product code, expiration date, lot number, serial number).

The collaborative logistics part of the DRIVE solution provides for sharing of logistics information between hospitals and pharmaceutical companies through a web based infrastructure. It provides for automated exchange of price lists, orders, order confirmations, advanced shipping notes and invoices.

A number of design decisions were related to trust, e.g. drug and wristband labels to uniquely identify drugs and patients, smart cards and PIN codes to identify and authenticate healthcare professionals, digital signatures to protect integrity of important assets and to provide for non-repudiation, role-based access control etc. The need of providing the *trust case*, an integrated overall argument explicitly stating the trust objectives and linking them with the supporting evidence was recognized later in the project course. It resulted in extending the project scope by adding an additional work package devoted to the trust case development.

3 Trust Case Conceptual Structure

A trust case is developed by making an explicit set of claims about the system and then collecting and producing supporting evidence and developing a structured argument that the evidence justifies the claims. A conceptual UML model describing the trust case elements and showing their relationships is shown in Fig. 2 (the arrows show the direction of reading the association names). The conceptual model of our trust case is based on the results of SHIP [2].

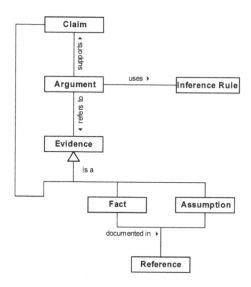

Fig. 2. The conceptual model of a trust case

The evidence used to support an argument can be of the following type:
- Facts, e.g. demonstrating adherence to established principles, documented design decisions, results of performed analyses.
- Assumptions, which are used by the argument and do not require explicit justification (nevertheless, they can be later converted into claims and supported by further argumentation).
- Sub-claims, that are developed further down by giving arguments that support them).

Facts and assumptions are linked to references (documents, reports, data, models, etc.) maintained together with the trust case.

The inference rules used in arguments are of three basic types: *quantitative* (e.g. justifying the failure probability postulated by a claim from the probabilities given by the supporting evidence), *logic* (establishing the validity of a claim from the logical assertions given by the supporting evidence) and *qualitative* (establishing the validity of a claim by referring to the common acceptance of good practices that were adhered to as demonstrated by the evidence supporting the claim). The qualitative argumentation can in particular refer to accepted standards, guidelines or so called "engineering judgement". The nature of software faults differs from the nature of hardware faults in that software is not subjected to physical degradation through aging, vibration, humidity, dust etc. Software faults are design faults (caused by humans) and their statistical properties are very hard to quantify. Therefore, for software intensive systems, the role of the logical and qualitative arguments is increased at the expense of the probabilistic arguments.

Trust case develops down into a tree-like structure (or multi tree, in case we have multiple trust targets) of arbitrary depth and is completed when all the leaves represent (well documented) facts and assumptions.

4 Modeling Claims

To define claims we need a language. A natural language (e.g. English) is the first choice, but due to its obvious limitations (the lack of precision and possible ambiguities), the natural language expressions can sometimes be misinterpreted. Another problem is that while specifying claims in a natural language it is difficult to control the scope and it is easy to mix the levels of abstraction a given claim refers to that adversely affects the soundness of the supporting argumentation.

To overcome those difficulties we decided to control the language associated with a claim by introducing what we call the Claim Definition Language – CDL. CDL introduces the following means that help the analyst to be more precise and unambiguous while building a trust case:

- A graphical language that provides constructs to represent claims, arguments, facts and assumptions and a labeling scheme that helps with their unambiguous identification. The identifier indicates the position of a given construct within the overall trust case. Each claim is associated with its *claim model* presenting a given claim, its supporting argument and all the evidence the argument refers to in a direct way.
- A graphical language that provides for representing, for each claim, its associated *context model* showing all the (physical and logical) objects that are referred to in the claim together with their relationships. To provide for avoiding possible ambiguities we also made some steps towards formalization of the meaning of the relationships occurring in context models.

The constructs used to define claim models are shown in Fig. 3.

Fig. 3. Elements of the claim model

All the elements of the claim model are defined as UML stereotypes. This helped us in using a UML-conscious graphical tool ([9], in our case) to maintain the trust case. An example of a claim model is shown in Fig. 4.

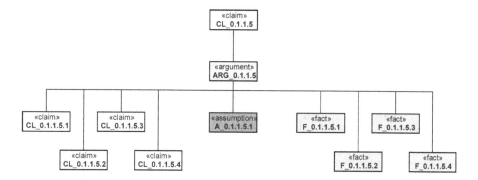

Fig. 4. Example claim model

Different shadows are used to distinguish elements of different types (claims, facts, assumptions, arguments). Each model element has its unique identifier that consists of its type identifier ('CL' for claim, 'ARG' for argument, 'A' for assumption, 'F' for fact) and a numeric identifier. The numeric identifier represents the element's position within the whole trust case. The example given in Fig. 4 represents the model of the claim CL_0.1.1.5. Such higher-level claim is called a *super-claim* and the claims that are referred to in the associated argument are called *sub-claims*. The argument has the same number as the claim it supports. The identifying numbers of sub-claims, assumptions and facts supporting the super-claim are constructed in such a way that they use the super-claim's numeric identifier as the prefix extended by the ordering number of this element (from left to right) separated by a dot. For instance, CL_0.1.1.5.3 is the third sub-claim of super-claim CL_0.1.1.5 and F_0.1.1.5.2 is the second fact supporting CL_0.1.1.5.

In general, claims are structured in two dimensions: vertically (refined claims used by the arguments justifying the higher level claims) and horizontally (complementary claims that together are used in the same argument justifying a higher level claim).

5   Modeling Claim Contexts

We defined a graphical language that provides means to grasp and represent the context within which a given claim model is being interpreted. The model is expressed in terms of UML. Object orientation and UML are becoming de-facto standard in software development. One of the advantages is that they constitute conceptual and linguistic means that can be applied at the system as well as at the software levels, providing for bridging the gap between the two views. The recent attempts to extend UML to business processes (e.g. [7]) provide for covering both, the artifact being developed (the computer system and its software) and the target environment within which it is being used. Such uniform framework can be applied not only to model the system and its target environment but also to model other important processes the trust depends on, like the development process, maintenance, installation etc. Our claim context models adhere to the common UML style and therefore can be applied to represent a broad range of business processes that can be expressed in UML. This puts the analytical task of trust case development within a uniform modeling framework.

In addition to the standard modeling means offered by UML we introduced a set of class stereotypes to represent typical objects that occurred while building our claim context models. They were especially useful while we were working with the higher level claims that were not supported by the models already developed during the system construction. Those extensions are shown in Fig. 5.

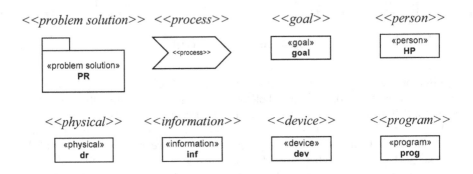

Fig. 5. Stereotypes used in claim context models

An example claim context model (borrowed from [8]) is given in Fig. 6. The context model has been derived from the documentation resulting from the DRIVE development process and shows the relations between patients, drugs, their physical identifiers and the corresponding logical entities. The model presents the object classes and their relationships that together provide the conceptual and linguistic context used while expressing the following claim:

CL_0.1.1.6
Drug Labels of the Drugs **applied** *to Patient are* **consistent** *with the Prescription Data in the* **corresponding** *Patient Record* **identified** *by the Patient's Wristband Label.*

Note that the context model in Fig. 6 includes all the objects referred to in the corresponding claim. The words given in bold in the claim definition distinguish those relationships between the objects of the claim context model the claim refers to. If those relationships are not present in the claim context model, they have to be interpreted in terms of the relationships given explicitly.

Although the objects referred to in the claim are precisely specified in the corresponding claim context model, the relationships the claim refers to can lead to ambiguous interpretations, e.g. the meaning of: "Drug *applied* to a Patient". This problem can be mitigated by formalizing the language.

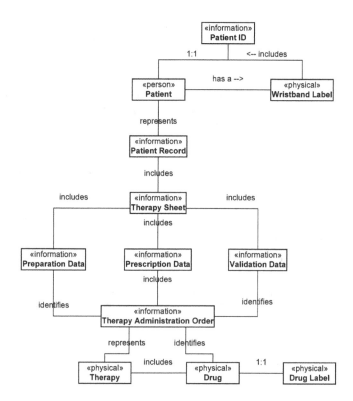

Fig. 6. Example of a claim context model

6 Formalizing the Language

Claims, arguments, assumptions and facts are specified in a natural language referring to the elements introduced by the associated claim context model. However, such natural language specifications can sometimes give rise to ambiguous interpretations. To provide for unambiguous interpretation of claims we made steps towards formalizing the meaning of the basic operations that can be performed on objects and the relationships among the objects represented in a claim context model. Then we followed a convention that to resolve possible misinterpretations, for each claim, its natural language specification is supplemented by the corresponding specification given in the formalized language. Such a formalized specification of claim CL_0.1.1.6 is given below:

> If
>> d:**Drug**<*physical*> is <u>applied</u> to p:**Patient**<*person*>
>> then exist dl:**Drug Label**<*physical&information*>, tao:**Therapy Administration Order**<*information*>, pd:**Prescription Data**<*information*>, ts:**Therapy Sheet**<*information*>, pr:**Patient Record**<*information*>, pwl:**Patient Wristband Label**<*physical&information*>, pr:**Patient Record**<*information*> such that

d(<u>1:1</u>)dl and pwl(<u>1:1</u>)p and tao(<u>includes</u>)pd(<u>includes</u>)ts(<u>includes</u>)pr and
pr(<u>represents</u>)p and tao(<u>identifies</u>)dl and pwl(<u>uniquely identifies</u>)pr

This specification imposes restrictions on each object set being an incarnation of the context model shown in Fig. 6. It explicitly refers to objects of the classes given in the corresponding context model, specifies their stereotypes (in brackets and italics) and refers to the terms (underlined in the above text) that are explicitly defined in the *CDL Dictionary*.

Below we recall from the CDL Dictionary the definitions of those terms that occur in the above formalized specification of CL_0.1.1.6 (the symbol "==" stands for "is defined as").

Resource1 is <u>applied</u> to **Resource2** == **Resource1** is <u>consumed</u> and its **State** is used to <u>update</u> **State** of **Resource2**

Resource1 <u>identifies</u> **Resource2** == **Identity** of **Resource2** can be derived from **Attributes** of **Resource1**

Resource1 <u>uniquely identifies</u> **Resource2** == **Resource1** <u>identifies</u> **Resource2** and if exists **Resource3** such that Class(**Resource2**) = Class(**Resource3**) then **Resource3** = **Resource2**

<u>consume</u>== to **<u>read</u>** the *Resource* **State** and to **<u>delete</u>** the *Resource*

<u>update</u>== to **<u>read</u>** and **<u>write</u>** the *Resource* **State**

7   Trust Case Targets for DRIVE

The trust case for DRIVE was developed in a top-down manner. We started with the top level claim CL_0 that postulates that the DRIVE Solution is trustworthy as shown in Fig. 7.

CL_0
The DRIVE solution is trustworthy in its intended context

«claim»
CL_0

Fig. 7. Top level claim model (the model for the whole Trust Case)

CL_0 was then decomposed into more specific trust targets which resulted in the claim model shown in Fig. 8.

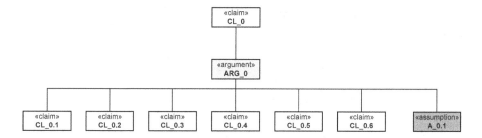

Fig. 8. Claim model for CL_0

The associated claim context model is shown in Fig. 9.

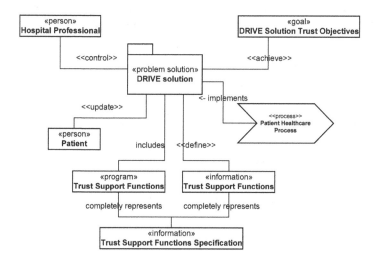

Fig. 9. Refined context model

The context introduces the following entities:

- *Hospital Professional* – Hospital Professional involved in DRIVE Solution,
- *Patient* – Patient subjected to the drug application resulting from DRIVE Solution,
- *Patient Healthcare Process* – a process implementing DRIVE Solution,
- *DRIVE Solution Trust Objectives* - a set of objectives of DRIVE Solution concerning safety and security as perceived by DRIVE Solution stakeholders,
- *Trust Support Functions* – set of DRIVE Solution functions to support safety and security of stakeholders,
- *Trust Support Functions Specification* – functional and design specification of Trust Support Functions.

The argument associated with CL_0 has the form:

ARG_0
Based on the A_0.1 if the claims CL_0.1 to CL_0.5 are justified and in addition are contradiction-free (CL_0.6), CL_0 is justified as well.

and is based on the following assumption:

A_0.1
The analysis of trust objectives in DRIVE is complete and correct.

Note: This assumption reflects the fact that the trust objectives for DRIVE solution were predefined by the DRIVE project and no further analyses were performed to identify their completeness and validity (and consequently there was no further evidence available). Nevertheless, A_0.1 reflects this explicitly in the trust case and could be later converted into a claim, provided the additional evidence were produced e.g. by performing further analyses.

The claim model includes the following claims:

CL_0.1
DRIVE solution maintains Patient safety.

CL_0.2
DRIVE solution maintains privacy of Hospital Professional.

CL_0.3
DRIVE solution maintains Patient privacy.

CL_0.4
DRIVE solution ensures that all actions related to Patient health are accountable.

CL_0.5
Trust support functions used in DRIVE are reliable.

CL_0.6
The claims CL_0.1 – CL_0.5 are mutually consistent.

Note: This last claim recognizes the need for additional argumentation that the remaining claims do not contradict each other. An example of such conflict could be if the provisions for ensuring patient privacy compromise his/her safety, e.g. by restricting access to patient health data in case of emergencies.

8 Architectural Trust Case for DRIVE

The trust targets were then further decomposed in the search for the supporting evidence. As the decomposition process progressed, we arrived at more specific claims referring to the architectural components, such as particular workstations with associated services and particular functionalities representing business logic rules. Some of the lowest level claims postulated a reliable implementation of a component of the architecture. Those claims were finally closed by converting them into assumptions (we did not have access to any evidence supporting them).

There were two main sources of the evidence referred to in the trust case: the DRIVE design documentation and the information derived from the DRIVE design team by means of interviews. Some additional evidence was obtained by applying UML-HAZOP analytical method [10] to selected design documents of DRIVE [11]. The results of those analyses were then included in the trust case as additional facts. We were also able to discover a number of (sometimes hidden) assumptions that had been made during the design process bringing them explicitly to the trust case.

All claims of the trust case are specified in a natural language and supplemented with their formalized specification. This proved to be very useful while reading and reviewing the trust case as the natural language specifications suffer the obvious limitations concerning their unambiguous interpretation.

The trust case graphical structure including claim models and claim context models is maintained in the tool, Microsoft Visio [9].

The data summarized in Table 1 gives the overview of the present DRIVE trust case size (the number of arguments differs from the number of claims because due to time limitations not all trust case targets were addressed in a complete way).

Table 1. Statistics of Trust Case for DRIVE

Trust case element's name	Number of elements used
Claim	97
Argument	92
Fact	234
Assumption	121

The relatively large number of assumptions present in the trust case reflects that in many cases we could not find enough facts supporting claims and instead had to make assumptions.

9 Conclusions

The paper presented an approach used while developing a trust case for a complex IT infrastructure supporting drug distribution and application processes. The primary decision in our approach was that we have chosen UML as the basic modeling framework for the trust case itself and for both, the subject domain and the solution domain under consideration. The concept of *claim context model* provided for controlling the scope and the language associated with a claim and made the trust case easy to communicate. UML with its mechanism of stereotypes proved to be a flexible and powerful tool to capture the contexts, especially those related to the higher level claims where the model had to cover a considerably broad scope, including people and physical objects as well as the pharmaceutical rules and knowledge. Those higher-level models did not exist before and their development was a part of our work on the trust case. The models were very useful in controlling the scope and providing the terminology for corresponding claims. What is even more important, they were very helpful in identifying (sometimes hidden) assumptions that conditioned the validity of some higher level claims. As an example take:

A_0.1.1.1
Hospital Professionals are fully qualified and their intentions are consistent with Pharmaceutical Knowledge and Patient's health state.

Without this assumption we could not argue that the DRIVE infrastructure supports patient's safety as the intentionally wrong drug prescription generally could not be prevented. To express this assumption, however, we needed to refer to the concept of Pharmaceutical Knowledge that was introduced in the corresponding context model.

We observed that when the trust case developed down into more specific claims we could use in the related context models the models that were already developed during the design process. This way the analytical work smoothly incorporated the results of the analyses already performed during system design.

Another important contribution of our approach was a step towards formalization of our claim definition language (CDL). Having all the trust case elements specified formally (in addition to the natural language specifications) was very useful during communication within the team (different parts of the trust case were developed in parallel and then the results were merged during the *composition meetings*) and was confirmed during an independent review of the whole trust case.

Having UML as the underlying framework, using claim context models and formalizing the Claim Definition Language are, in our opinion, the main contributions of our approach while comparing with the work of others [12,13,14].

Another aspect where our work differs from what was already presented in the literature is the scope of the analytical work. In our work we concentrated on the notion of *trust* which covered both safety and security (privacy, accountability) aspects. The resulting trust case brings into the surface all the facts and assumptions that support the argumentation for the trustworthiness of the analyzed target. It forms a sort of a map that shows strong and weak points of this argumentation. In our future work we consider using different colors to distinguish the arguments of different strength to provide for easier analysis.

Our work was restricted in two aspects. Firstly, we concentrated our attention only on the DRIVE architecture and its usage context without taking into account other aspects that can adversely affect trustworthiness, like development process, maintenance, installation etc. The reason was that DRIVE was a R&D project with main focus on system architecture and design and did not generate enough evidence to cover the other aspects. Consequently, our trust case is conditional and based on the assumptions that the trustworthiness of DRIVE solution is not compromised by those additional aspects. The second restriction was that the work on the trust case started late in the project, after the product was already in the implementation phase. Due to this fact, our work was a sort of *a posteriori* analysis without much influence on the system design process.

We have also performed some additional analyses aiming at producing more evidence for our trust case. This was done with the help of the UML-HAZOP method [10] and a related tool [11].

Visio 2002 [9] proved to be a useful tool for maintaining the trust case performing some simple consistency checks. The configuration management related to our trust case comprised of: claim models and claim context models maintained in the tool [9], and CDL specification, claim, argument, assumption and fact specifications and the references (derived from the DRIVE documentation) maintained in files.

We consider our approach promising and plan to continue this work in both, research and experimentation. Some of the issues to be addressed include: broadening the scope of the trust case, investigating possible feedback from the trust case to the development process, addressing internal consistency of the trust case in case of potentially conflicting trust targets, getting deeper insight of the differences in the strength of the arguments, depending on the "weight" of the supporting evidence and the nature of the argument itself. We also want to investigate the possibility of better tool support and possible merging of our approach with the already existing frameworks for safety cases, e.g. those embedded in [15].

References

[1] Defence Standard 00-56, http://wheelie.tees.ac.uk/hazop/html/56.htm
[2] EU EUREKA SHIP (Safety of Hazardous Industrial Processes) Project
     http://www.csr.city.ac.uk/csr_city/projects/ship/ship.html
[3] Safety Case Assessment Criteria http://www.hse.gov.uk/railway/criteria/
[4] Common Methodology for Information Technology Security Evaluation, version 1.0, 1999
[5] Common Criteria for Information Technology Security Evaluation version 2.1, 1999 (Parts 1,2,3)
[6] ISO/IEC Information Security Management, 2000
[7] Eriksson, H.-E., Penker, M.: Business Modeling with UML, J. Wiley, 2000
[8] DRIVE D11.1-3 –Trust Case for DRIVE, D11.1-3, version 1.1, January 2003
[9] Microsoft Visio 2002 Professional, 2002
[10] Górski J., Jarzębowicz A.: Detecting defects in object-oriented diagrams using UML-HAZOP, Found. of Comp. and Decision Sciences, vol. 27, no. 4, 2002
[11] DRIVE D11.4 – UML-HAZOP, D11.4, version 1.1, January 2003
[12] Wilson, S. P., Kelly T. P., McDermid J. A.: Safety Case Development: Current Practice, Future Prospects
[13] Adelard Safety Case Development Manual, Adelard, 1998
[14] Kelly, T.: Arguing Safety A Systematic Approach to Managing Safety Cases (1998). PhD Thesis, University of York, UK, YCST 99/05, 1998, available at http://www.cs.york.ac.uk/ftpdir/reports/YCST-99-05.ps.gz
[15] ASCE (Adelard Safety Case Editor) homepage http://www.adelard.com/software/asce

Reliable Data Replication in a Wireless Medical Emergency Network

Joe Gorman, Ståle Walderhaug, and Håvard Kvålen

SINTEF Telecom and Informatics
Trondheim, Norway
Phone: +47 73 59 70 85
joe.gorman@sintef.no

Abstract. Medical teams dealing with major accidents have an acute need to gather and share information about casualties. The paper describes how hand-held computers linked together in a wireless network can address this problem, discussing in particular how to achieve the high degree of reliability that is an essential pre-requisite for practical use in an emergency situation. The main focus is on the problem of how to achieve reliable data replication between nodes in a network that is established in a hurry, where radio links are likely to suffer intermittent failures and where the network topology can grow, shrink and change dynamically. The paper argues that off-the-shelf commercial database solutions are not suitable, and describes the design and operation of a novel approach we have implemented in a prototype.

1 Introduction

Medical teams dealing with medical emergencies have an acute need to gather and share information about the overall situation at the scene of an accident, and about the status of individual patients. The "medical team" consists of more than just the staff providing immediate help at the scene of the accident; it also refers to coordination staff at the scene, ambulance staff travelling to and from the scene, ambulance dispatchers in central control rooms, and staff at local hospitals preparing for the arrival of casualties.

Today, information about individual patients is usually recorded on paper forms accompanying the patients, and all exchange of important information amongst team members is done using ad hoc voice communication by radio. This may lead to misunderstandings, distractions, poor information flow, and difficulty in forming an overall picture of the situation. When a patient is handed over from one team member to another, the new team member typically receives only limited information about the patient. Hospital staff often get no information at all about patients before they actually arrive at the hospital. The combination of all of these problems means that treatment of patients is less effective than it might be.

SINTEF Telecom and Informatics has initiated a project, FieldCare, which addresses these problems by providing a technological system to help all members of the medical team to communicate and share information effectively in

S. Anderson et al. (Eds.): SAFECOMP 2003, LNCS 2788, pp. 207–220, 2003.

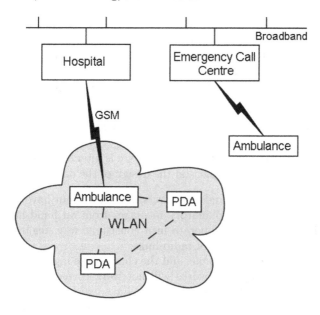

Fig. 1. The FieldCare Network.

a crisis situation. It is based on the use of small hand-held computers at the scene of the accident, connected together in a wireless network linking them to portable PCs in ambulances and fixed PCs at hospitals and control centres. Wireless communications at the scene are handled using short-range networks (e.g. WLAN), while connections to vehicles and other locations are achieved using long-range radio links such as GSM/GPRS or Tetra. This is illustrated in Figure 1.

The core functionality of FieldCare is to enable data-capture at the point of origin and to replicate the information to all team members at all sites in a robust way. The basic philosophy is to "replicate everything to everyone". This is appropriate as patient treatment are often handed over – in a quite unpredictable way – from one team member to another, and the person taking over responsibility requires access, at short notice, to all information about the patient. Rapid sharing of information over the wireless network also allows co-ordinators to maintain an up-to-date overview of what is happening, and allows hospital staff to make appropriate preparations well in advance of the arrival of patients.

The technical challenges of implementing such a system are considerable, and reliability is vital as medical teams will be using the system as a basis for life-or-death decisions. These issues are described in sections 2 to 4. The main focus of the paper is on the design of a data replication strategy which addresses the requirements of this application. As far as the authors are aware, no related work has been published addressing this specific problem. Section 5 describes some alternative approaches that were considered, using existing technologies, and explains why these proved unsuitable. Section 6 describes a novel approach which provides a robust solution that ensures data replication to all units even if some units and radio links should fail. The paper also discusses, in section 7, the related issue of consistency of time stamps on all nodes. Sections 8 and 9 summarise what has been implemented, and overall conclusions.

2   Characteristics of the Network Operating Environment

The operating environment for which FieldCare is intended has some key characteristics that have a major impact on the design of the data replication strategy:

- The situation is *chaotic* and very stressful; users do not have time to hesitate trying to understand explanatory messages from on hand-held computers. Thus, the software must operate in a consistent way, regardless of factors such as temporary failures of radio links.
- Some users will be very *mobile*, and the chances are high that they will move into zones where radio networks will not work correctly. Thus, the system must be designed on the basis that radio links *will* fail, perhaps rather often.
- The network will be very *dynamic*: team members will join/leave at very short notice, and the connection topology between nodes will vary as they move around. Individual users may be forced to re-start their units after temporary failures (such as battery loss), and will then expect to re-join the network and have all data restored automatically.
- Medical staff will view the computer units as "pack and go" devices (like the radios they use today), which might require re-charging of batteries – but very little else in the way of maintenance. They are likely to resist the notion that the devices should be subject to regular operational support (software updates, configuration etc.), and access to staff qualified to carry out such support will in any case be limited. Thus, the system must be simple, and require very little maintenance.

3   Reliability Requirements for Data Replication

The basic functionality to be implemented by the system is data replication between all the hand-held and other computers in the network. We will refer to these collectively as "nodes". The goal is that all data, about all patients, should be stored on all nodes. Thus, data entered on any one FieldCare node must be replicated to all nodes, including those with which it has a direct or indirect radio link, and other nodes that are added to the network afterwards (perhaps a long time afterwards).

In achieving this basic functionality, the system must fulfil the following reliability requirements:

1. It must be able to cope with the following situations:
   a) Individual nodes may become inoperative (due to software failure, hardware failure or deliberate de-activation), remain so for a short or long period, then be re-activated from scratch at a later stage.

b) Communication links between nodes may fail (for short periods, or long
   periods, or permanently).
c) Network topology (i.e. which nodes are in contact with which others)
   may change at any time.
d) "Network Partitioning" may occur i.e. communication failures may occur which result in the total set of nodes being split into 2 or more
   "partitions". Within each partition nodes can communicate with each
   other, but there is no communication between partitions. Each partition
   behaves like a communication "island". This situation may persist for
   quite some time, during which system operation must proceed normally.
   When the partitions are eventually re-united, full data replication must
   then take place between the partitions.
2. All nodes must have the same "status" for data replication. There should
   be no concept of a central server or similar which would constitute a single
   point of failure.
3. If the same information reaches a node by more than one route, it should be
   stored in the local copy of the database only once.
4. The volume of data communication between nodes should be minimised, to
   avoid the danger of "flooding" the network.

4   Acceptable Assumptions

The requirements listed are not easy to fulfil. Fortunately, there are some simplifying assumptions that can be made, which do not compromise the functionality
of the system, but which do ease its design and implementation:

1. The lifetime of the database will be relatively short – typically no more
   than a few hours (the duration of the accident). The total amount of data
   entered by each user will not be great. Thus, the total volume of data in the
   database will be limited. It will be feasible to store the entire database in
   main memory, on each node; secondary storage need not be used.
2. The database will have a very simple data model. It will be sufficient to have
   just one main database table, consisting of "patient observation" records,
   containing information such as patient identification number, time stamp,
   name of team member making observation, and details of the medical observation itself.
3. Only INSERT operations are allowed on the database; DELETE and MOD-
   IFY are not allowed. This is because it is a system requirement that a full log
   be maintained, so that medical staff can if necessary view the entire history
   associated with a particular patient. This considerably simplifies implementation, because it means that the order in which database transactions are
   applied on each local copy of the database does not affect the validity of the
   data.[1]

---

[1] Although the order of *application* of INSERT operations is not important, the order
in which patient observations were carried out in the real world is *very* important, so
that users can conclude which value is most current. This sorting is achieved using
time stamps, which form part of the content of all records. See section 7.

4. Full database transaction consistency is not desirable, as this would mean that transactions could not be committed (and, thus, that the data would be unavailable) until updates had been carried out on *all* nodes. It is acceptable that there are temporary inconsistencies between the local copies of the database on each node while data is being replicated.

5 Reliable Data Replication: Alternative Approaches Considered

5.1 Off-the-Shelf Database Solutions for Hand-Held Computers: Survey

Before designing our own data replication strategy, we conducted a brief evaluation of some established mobile database systems to see if any were suitable for our application. In addition, we studied data object storage technologies designed for small devices. Each technology was evaluated against our predefined system compatibility requirements:

- The database must run on a PDA compatible operating system: Windows Pocket PC [1], Linux for PDA [2] or SavaJe OS [3].
- The data in the database must be accessible from the Java [4] Application Programming Interface (API), as implementation in Java was considered most suitable for small devices.
- The database and replication mechanism must be easy to deploy and configure; the effort required to install and configure a device must be low.
- The database must be robust. Data must not be lost in case of failure; the database must restart and recover all data.

Other requirements such as data security and licensing costs were not considered in detail for the prototype, but would of course be a major issue for a commercial product.

All of the technologies we evaluated fulfilled the first two requirements (Operating System and Java compatibility). Details of the products we looked at are summarised below.

Microsoft SQL Server 2000 CE Edition. Microsoft SQL Server 2000 CE Edition [5] runs on a PDA with Windows for PDA installed. It offers two types of data replication: a merge replication and a message-based Internet replication mechanism. The first enables autonomous data updates on the portable device and the server. The data on the device and server can later be synchronised when a connection is re-established. The second performs synchronisation by establishing an HTTP connection to SQL Server through Microsoft Internet Information Server (IIS). Key properties of this product are summarised in Table 1.

Table 1. Properties of MS SQL Server CE Edition.

Installation requirements	Requires a separate installation on the devices. Has support for embedded devices, which means that it can be built in as a part of the operating system image loaded into the ROM of the device.
Configuration requirements	To set up a replication between a client and a server, it is necessary to create a publication, configure and create a snapshot on the server before one can set up a subscription on the client. The client must know the server's name to create a subscription.
Robustness	Fault tolerance is good – but is very dependent on careful attention to detail during configuration.

Sybase iAnywhere Studio UltraLite. The Sybase UltraLite technology [6] provides an ultra-small database that resides locally on mobile devices and can synchronize data with most central consolidated database management systems. The solution from Sybase is similar to the one from Microsoft, and shares the same advantages and drawbacks.

The JavaSpaces Service. A part of Sun's Jini implementation, JavaSpaces is a Jini Service [7] that stores objects in a "global" space. It can be used as a shared data structure that many distributed applications can access and process. It can be used to synchronise actions between applications. However, clients "lease" space in the object space, which means that objects will be deleted unless the client maintains the lease. Key properties of this product are summarised in Table 2.

Table 2. Properties of the JavaSpaces service.

Installation requirements	Easy: done along with Java libraries.
Configuration requirements	Configuration can be programmed and tailored to the application.
Robustness	Not fault-tolerant. If one node fails, data is lost.

5.2   Off-the-Shelf Database Solutions for Hand-Held Computers: Assessment

The Microsoft and Sybase solutions are traditional relational databases that offer standard transaction and merge replication mechanisms. As such, these products are satisfactory, but they provide static solutions that require extensive configuration and initialisation, making them unsuitable for the FieldCare prototype. The JavaSpaces technology is easy to configure and has high performance. It differs from a common DBMS by storing data in main memory. But is not fault-tolerant, and is therefore also unsuitable for the prototype.

In addition, all solutions surveyed suffer from the following deficiencies with respect to requirements:

- The solutions are all based on the use of a "server" node, which communicates with its "client" nodes to replicate data. This goes against one of our fundamental requirements, as such server nodes represent a "single point of failure": if the server should fail, then so too will the system as a whole.
- Using these products requires that the software be installed and correctly configured on all nodes. The installation and configuration tasks needed to achieve the replication functionality required are complex, and even a minor configuration error on one device can cause data replication to operate incorrectly. Given the characteristics of the network operating environment as described in section 2, the complexity of this installation and configuration task is likely to cause major problems for the people responsible for maintenance of the units. A likely consequence is that installation and configuration errors will lead to incorrect operation of the system.
- If a new device is purchased, configuration changes may be needed on all other devices. As above, the practicalities of handling this situation are so great that it is probable that the job will be done incorrectly, or not at all.
- These solutions provide full database functionality, including DELETE and MODIFY operations and full transaction consistency. None of these is required for the FieldCare system, but their implementation consumes system resources (memory and processing power) which – on small hand-helds – are often rather limited. These full database solutions therefore represent severe "overkill", compared to the very basic database functionality required.
- Most off-the-shelf solutions are expensive, both for purchase and for software maintenance. This can be a problem, particularly given the fact that multiple units must be paid for.

Based on this, we conclude that none of the off-the-shelf solutions are suitable for use in the FieldCare system.

5.3 "Brute Force" Method: Database Merge

Having concluded that off-the-shelf solutions did not fit our needs, we decided to implement a simple solution in the initial prototype of the system.

The "brute force" strategy was to transmit the whole database to all neighbouring nodes each time any change occurred in the local copy of the database (either as a result of a user-initiated action, or as a result of a new database being received from another node). On receipt of a database from a remote node, the database carried out a merge operation, so that new transactions would be added to the local database, but duplicate transactions were stored only once.

This approach had the advantage of being simple to understand and implement, and was therefore very reliable. Worries about excessive network traffic (sending the entire database) proved unfounded, because database sizes were small, and because the prototype was limited to a WLAN network, where network capacity is high.

This approach was useful in quickly providing a reliable solution which allowed us to demonstrate the viability of the overall system. Obvious scalability problems prohibit its use in a real system.

5.4 Propagation of Database Update Messages

Having rejected the "brute force" method, we began to investigate other possibilities. Our initial attempt was to use "database update" messages between nodes – instructions transmitted over the network containing details of individual transactions. The basic idea was as follows:

- Each time a user on one node generates new data interactively, the node should:
  1. Update its own local copy of the database.
  2. Send a "database update" message to each of its neighbours.
  3. Await an ACK from each node to which the database update message has been sent, re-sending as necessary until an ACK is received.
- Each time a node receives a "database update" message, it should:
  1. Update its own local copy of the database.
  2. Send an ACK to the node which sent the message.
  3. Propagate the message to each of its immediate neighbours, except the one which sent the message in the first place, and any others known to have received the message previously.

There were some details of this approach which would have required some attention in the implementation. One of these was how to avoid messages being sent endlessly in loops between nodes; another was the issue of how many ACK/re-send cycles should be attempted before giving up. We could envisage solutions to these problems[2], but abandoned the approach because of a fundamental flaw, concerning what happens when a new node is added to the network. Any database update propagations currently under way would automatically include the new node – but the results of previous propagations would not be included. Thus, new nodes joining the network would have data replicated to them for recent transactions where update messages were still circulating in the network, but would not receive data that had been successfully replicated earlier. Full data replication would not be achieved in all cases.

We were therefore forced to design another approach. This is described in the next section, and is the one implemented in the current prototype.

---

[2] We have later learned that peer-to-peer networking protocols address these issues, and provide other functionality that we have implemented in the prototype. The JXTA [8] project is particularly relevant, defining a set of protocols for ad hoc, pervasive peer-to-peer computing. The protocols establish a virtual network overlay on top of Internet and non-IP protocols that allows peers to interact directly and independently of their network location. It has its own addressing mechanisms that are used by a number of services. Message relaying, searching, establishing peergroups, and service advertisements are provided through Java-based JXTA libraries.

6   Reliable Data Replication: Proposed Approach

6.1   Basic Idea

- All nodes have a pre-defined, factory-set unique identification number.
- All database transactions are identified by a transaction identifier, which is unique throughout the network. The identifier is generated on the node at which the transaction originates, using the node's unique identification number and a locally generated sequence number.
- Each node keeps track of the identity of its immediate "neighbours" (i.e. nodes with which it has direct contact).
- Each node maintains a transaction table which shows, for each of its current neighbours, which transactions they have received.
- Nodes contact each other occasionally and carry out a "Transactions Available" protocol, to determine whether any new transactions should be transmitted.
- A node transmits "database update" messages (containing instructions for updating the local copy of the database) to a neighbour when:
  - A new transaction has been generated locally (because it is then certain that the transaction will not yet be present in the neighbour's copy of the database).
  - If a "Transactions Available" protocol has shown that some transactions are missing from the neighbour's copy of the database.
- There is no wait-for-ACK/re-send associated with transmission of database update messages. Instead, "I've got it" messages are used to update the transaction table. Re-sends, if necessary, will be triggered during the next "Transactions Available" protocol.
- By ensuring that all *pairs* are synchronised with each other, we ensure that all nodes are (eventually) synchronised, by changes being propagated from node to node.

6.2   The Transaction Table

Each node maintains its own Transaction Table. It is unique to the node, and should not be considered part of the database itself.

The table contains one row for each transaction that has been entered in the local copy of the database, and one column for each of the following:

- The unique transaction identifier.
- The sequence number (1st transaction entered has sequence number 1, next has 2 etc.)
- One column for each neighbour node, with a boolean value indicating whether that node has the transaction in its local copy of the database.

The "neighbour" columns are added and initialised when a new node communication pair is established; both nodes add a column for each other, and set all entries to "false"[3]. When communication pairs are first established, nodes should send each other a "Pleased to meet you" message; it is this which triggers column creation and initialisation.

6.3   Transactions Available Protocol

The purpose of the protocol is for a node to update its transaction table to reflect recent changes in its neighbours, and to trigger transmission of database update messages when needed. The protocol is initiated when:

- New node communication pairs are established (as discussed above). It is carried out immediately after column creation and initialisation. Note that two instances proceed in parallel: one in each direction between the two nodes.
- Periodically, to check for changes. This will also take place in both directions, but not necessarily at the same time.

The protocol proceeds as follows (between nodes A and B):

1. Node A notes its highest sequence number; call this n. The protocol is limited to transactions with sequence number between 1 and n. New transactions may be entered during execution of the protocol, and added with sequence numbers greater than n; these will be taken into account the next time the protocol is executed.
2. For each transaction in A's table which is recorded as having been absent on node B, A sends a "transaction offer" message to B. Each such message includes the identity of the sender (i.e. node A) and the transaction number of the transaction which A believes is missing from B.
3. When B receives a "transaction offer" message it checks it own transaction table to see whether it has the transaction or not. Depending on the result, it replies either with an "I've got it" message or with a "Please send" message. Both of these message types include the same fields as the "transaction offer" message, but with the value of the "sender" field changed to B.

The above description covers the main sequence of events between nodes. It remains to describe how the different types of messages are handled:

- When a node receives an "I've got it" message, it uses the data contained in it to update the column of the transaction table corresponding to the sender node.

---

[3] It may happen that a node, A, which was previously in contact with another node, B, crashes and is later re-started. When A contacts B again, it behaves as if it were a completely new node. In that case B will already have a column for A, containing the status before the crash. There is then no need for B to create a new column for A, but it is essential that all entries are set to "false", as A will have lost all its data due to the re-start.

- When a node receives a "Please send" message it sends a "Database update" command to the sender. This specifies the identity of the sender, the transaction number, and details of the database operation itself (the table name, the new data values).
- When a node receives a "Database update" command, it:
  1. Updates its own copy of the database accordingly.
  2. Adds the transaction to its transaction table (setting the column for the sender of the message to "true").
  3. Sends an "I've got it" message to the sender, so that it can update its transaction table[4].

7   Reliable Common Time Stamp Mechanism

7.1   The Problem

Each record entered in the database must have a "time stamp" added automatically, indicating the exact time at which the entry was made. This is useful in providing a formal log of the accident, which can be used for investigations or other analyses after the accident. A reliable time stamp mechanism is also needed so that team members can view the order in which observations of the same value occurred in real time. For instance: if the patient's evacuation priority has been judged as "can wait", "urgent" and "immediate" at different points in time, it is vital to be able to know which of these judgements was made most recently. Sorting by time can also be useful to view trends in key indicators, such as blood pressure, pulse etc.

The time stamp value for any particular observation must be added to the database on the node on which the observation is made. This must necessarily be done using the system clock on that device. However, we cannot be sure that all devices in the network have the same notion of time, because:

- We cannot depend on organisational procedures being in place whereby staff make sure that the system clocks on all devices are set to exactly the same time.
- The clocks used on such devices "drift" over time, often at different rates on different devices.
- It should be possible to use the system with users from different emergency organisations, even spanning national borders. In such cases, the clocks belonging to different organisations could well be set to the time in different time zones.

---

[4] This message acts as an "ACK" that the database update message has been received. If the original database update message was lost, this "I've got it" message would not be sent, and the next Transactions Available protocol would trigger a re-send. If the "I've got it" message got lost, the only damage would be that the "Database update" message would be re-sent needlessly.

7.2   Off-the-Shelf Clock Synchronisation

The de facto standard for clock synchronisation in IP networks is the Network Time Protocol (NTP) [9]. The NTP protocol specifies how a client can synchronise its clock against one or more NTP servers with high precision. The NTP server either synchronises its clock against another server, or against some external reference. GPS devices are often used as the external reference.

There are several reasons why using such protocols is not suitable to our purpose:

- In the peer-to-peer network structure used in FieldCare, with all nodes having equal status, there is no clear hierarchy which could be used to determine which node should take precedence over which others in determining which clock is most "correct".
- The problem of network partitioning poses insurmountable problems. Suppose that nodes A and B are able to communicate with each other, as are nodes C and D – but that there is no communication between these two partitions. A and B would then synchronise their clocks to one value, as would C and D – but these values would not necessarily be the same. Data entered in both these partitions would then have time stamp values based on two different views of "time" – exactly what we are trying to avoid. When, at some later stage, communication was finally established between the two partitions, all data previously entered would be synchronised to all nodes – but based on two different views of time.

7.3   Proposed Approach: Time Zone Conversion

The approach we propose is to give up on even attempting clock synchronisation, and instead:

- Prohibit changes in date/time settings during the accident.
- Regard each device as existing in its own unique time zone. Thus, two devices whose date/time settings are just a few minutes apart (due to clock drift, or whatever) should be treated in the same way as two devices from different operators in different countries where it is natural that clocks are set to different time zones.
- In each copy of the database, each entry should have two time stamp fields: the time in "local time" on the device where the entry was originally made, and the time converted to "local time" on the device where the copy is stored. The former is used for completeness in the log; the latter is used to determine the real-world order of events.
- Conversion to local time is achieved as part of the protocol for transmitting "database update" messages between nodes. When a node *transmits* such a message, it includes a field indicating the value of its system clock at the moment of transmission. When a node *receives* such a message, it immediately compares this value with its own system clock, and can therefore calculate the time zone difference between the nodes. This information is then used to update all the time stamp values in the message. As data transmission

is not instantaneous, some minor discrepancies (measured in fractions of a second) will be introduced by this process, but these are not significant for the intended use.

8   Implementation Status and Future Work

We have implemented a prototype using the data replication strategy here described. It uses WLAN for communication – links with GSM and broadband connections have not yet been implemented. The system has been tested using a network consisting of 4 nodes (2 PDAs, one tablet PC and one laptop). Testing consisted of rapid, parallel entry of data values on all nodes, with frequent removal/re-insertion of WLAN cards to simulate radio failure. Users were able to continue operating the system without problem during these radio "failures", and all data were successfully replicated to all nodes when radio links were restored.

The network infrastructure implementation does not currently allow for dynamic changes in network topology, so this aspect has not been tested.

The strategy for ensuring a common view of time on all devices has not yet been implemented. However, practical experience when testing the data replication system clearly demonstrated the importance of a clock synchronisation mechanism. A typical scenario was that a user on node A entered a value of "2" for "Patient Priority", but was very surprised to see that the user interface responded by displaying the value "1" instead. This happened because another user, on node B, had entered the value "1" some minutes before, but clock discrepancies made the system believe that this data was more recent – causing it to be given priority and presented in the user interface.

Further work should focus on:

- Implementation of the proposed method for ensuring a common view of time.
- Testing of scalability issues, regarding number of nodes and data volumes.
- Implementation of network facilities for dynamic changes in network topology, and testing of data replication when this happens.
- Extending the approach to be able to cope with a more sophisticated type of replication where nodes can "filter" the data they require (i.e. no longer replicate everything to every node). Concerns about privacy could make this a requirement in some circumstances. This would involve development of a more complex concept of which nodes are "neighbours" for replication purposes. Some nodes, for some types of transactions, would have the role of simply passing on messages to other nodes, without replicating the data locally.
- Provision of technologies addressing security concerns.

9   Conclusions

We have described an approach to data replication in an ad hoc, unreliable, wireless network, and implemented it in a demonstration prototype.

The application environment for which it is designed:

- Is highly demanding in terms of the importance of reliability.
- Is subject to major constraints in terms of organisational and technical infrastructure.
- Has some compensating characteristics which allow some simplifications to be made.

The success of the proposed approach arises from the fact that we have identified and exploited the compensating characteristics, while still addressing the strict reliability requirements.

We have shown that off-the-shelf products for implementation of distributed databases on hand-held computers are not suitable for meeting the reliability requirements of this type of application.

The whole focus of our work has been on the specific requirements of the emergency medical application. It is reasonable to assume that other types of applications for which a wireless network of mobile computers is a natural solution may share some, if not all, of the requirements and acceptable assumptions of the medical application. It does not seem likely that other types of application would have stricter requirements. It is therefore interesting to speculate about whether the data replication strategy here described may be suitable for a much wider class of mobile applications.

References

1. Microsoft Windows for PDAs:
   http://www.microsoft.com/windows/embedded/ce.net/
2. Linux for Hewlett-Packard iPaq: http://familiar.handhelds.org/
3. SavaJe OS: http://www.savaje.com/
4. Java http://www.sun.com/java/
5. Microsoft SQL Server 2000 CE Edition: http://www.microsoft.com/sql/ce/
6. Sybase iAnywhere Studio:
   http://www.ianywhere.com/datasheets/sqlany_ultralite.html
7. The Jini Network Technology:
   http://wwws.sun.com/software/jini/specs/jini1.1html/js-title.html
8. Project JXTA: http://www.jxta.org
9. David L. Mills: Network Time Protocol (Version 3) – Specification, Implementation and Analysis. RFC 1305. http://www.ietf.org/rfc/rfc1305.txt

Critical Feature Analysis
of a Radiotherapy Machine

Andrew Rae[1], Daniel Jackson[2], Prasad Ramanan[2], Jay Flanz[3], Didier Leyman[4]

[1]Information Technology and Electrical Engineering
University of Queensland, St Lucia, QLD Australia
arae@itee.uq.edu.au

[2]Laboratory for Computer Science
Massachusetts Institute of Technology, Cambridge, MA
dnj@mit.edu

[3]Northeast Proton Therapy Center
Massachusetts General Hospital, Boston, MA
flanz@hadron.mgh.harvard.edu

[4]Ion Beam Applications
Louvain-La-Neuve, Belgium
leyman@iba.be

Abstract. The software implementation of the emergency shutdown feature in a major radiotherapy system was analyzed, using a directed form of code review based on module dependences. Dependences between modules are labelled by particular assumptions; this allows one to trace through the code, and identify those fragments responsible for critical features. An 'assumption tree' is constructed in parallel, showing the assumptions which each module makes about others. The root of the assumption tree is the critical feature of interest, and its leaves represent assumptions which, if not valid, might cause the critical feature to fail. The analysis revealed some unexpected assumptions that motivated improvements to the code.

1 Introduction

A key difficulty in the analysis of large software systems is the isolation and evaluation of critical source code. Ideally, safety critical requirements would be implemented by safety critical modules, neatly isolated from the non-critical code. In practice, the safety of a system is tightly bound to its correct operation, and a single safety feature requires the cooperation of many modules.

This paper reports on our experiences analyzing the source code of a radiotherapy machine. We concentrated on a single feature of the software—the emergency stop function. As expected, we found that reasoning about this function required us to make assumptions about the behaviour of other parts of the system. Inspecting the tree of assumptions produced by our analysis exposed some conditions under which the software might not behave as intended.

S. Anderson et al. (Eds.): SAFECOMP 2003, LNCS 2788, pp. 221–234, 2003.

Our analysis strategy is simple to understand and easy to apply. It is based on a new model of dependences, in which dependences between modules are qualified by specifications. A module A is said to S-use another module B if A relies on B to provide a service described by the specification S. Making specifications explicit in this way, and associating them with dependence arcs rather than modules, is a small elaboration of standard module dependency diagrams. It has major practical ramifications, however, since it allows us to trace dependences in a more fine-grained manner, to identify the code responsible for particular features of the system.

Our paper describes the context of the system (Section 2); an overview of the analysis approach (Section 3), and its application to the case study (Section 4); an evaluation of the results of the analysis (Section 5); and a comparison to related work (Section 6).

2   Context of the Therapy Control System

The Northeast Proton Therapy Center (NPTC) is a new radiation therapy facility associated with the Massachusetts General Hospital in Boston. It is one of only two hospital-based facilities in the United States to offer treatment with protons (rather than electrons or X-rays). Proton beams require much more elaborate and expensive equipment to produce, but can be more tightly conformed, and cause less damage to surrounding tissue. They are thus more suitable for treatments in sensitive areas such as the eye, and for the treatment of tumors in the brains of children, for which collateral damage has more serious long-term consequences. The center occupies a new building adjacent to the hospital, and began treating patients in the fall of 2001.

The Software Design Group in the MIT Lab for Computer Science began a collaboration in April 2002 with NPTC and Ion Beam Applications, the developers of the system, to investigate better methods for the development of safety critical software. The NPTC system would be used as a challenging example of a modern and complex medical device for the purposes of research; in turn, the results of the research would be used where appropriate to improve the safety and reliability of the system.

The NPTC installation has at its core a cyclotron that generates a beam of protons. The beam is multiplexed amongst several treatment rooms, each with its own gantry and nozzle for positioning the beam. Technicians in a master control room supervise the cyclotron and direct the beam to the allocated treatment room. Each treatment room is paired with a treatment control room, in which clinicians enter and execute treatment prescriptions. The patient is placed on a couch which is electromechanically positioned by staff within the treatment room. The beam delivery nozzle is also positioned, and its aim verified by staff using X-rays and lights attached to the emitter. The staff then leave the room, and the treatment is initiated and controlled from the treatment control room. Treatment consists of irradiating a specific location on the patient using a beam of protons with a defined lateral and longitudinal distribution.

The machine is considered safety critical primarily due to the potential for overdose—that is, treating the patient with radiation of excessive strength or duration.

The International Atomic Energy Agency lists 80 separate accidents involving radiation therapy in the United States over the past fifty years [14]. Software was implicated in the failures of the infamous Therac-25 machine [9], and more recently in similar accidents in Panama [2].

The NPTC system was developed in the context of a sophisticated safety program. Unlike the Therac-25, the NPTC system makes extensive use of hardware interlocks, including a hardware relay system and a redundant PLC-based system which handles safety critical functions, both of which run in parallel with the software control system. Video cameras inside the control room allow the technicians to view internal mechanisms, including a beam stop that can be inserted to isolate the treatment room from the cyclotron. The software itself is instrumented with abundant runtime checks, including a software 'heartbeat monitor' to ensure continued operation of critical processes. A detailed system-level risk analysis was performed. The software implementation was heavily tested, and manually reviewed against rigorous coding standards.

2.1   Therapy Control System

The software of the system, called the *Therapy Control System* (TCS), is written primarily in C, and is installed on commodity workstations running Unix, a commercial messaging system (Talarian's SmartSockets), a centralized Oracle database, and Motif X-windows. Low-level control is implemented in assembler on a VME crate running VXWorks. About 250,000 lines of C code is organized into a few hundred modules.

The TCS handles the storage and retrieval of patient data; entry and editing of prescriptions; scheduling of treatments and maintenance; patient positioning; and beam delivery. In concert with the hardware and PLC safety systems, it is designed to help manage three main hazards: a physical collision between moving parts of the system and a patient or staff member; accidental irradiation of a patient or staff member; and inaccurate radiation of a patient (including overdoses and underdoses). In its most critical features, such as the emergency stop feature analyzed here, the software is backed up by redundant hardware.

NPTC's acquisition strategy follows an evolutionary model. The goal is to have in place a safe working system, and then to expand the functionality and enable the addition of new modes of treatment. The analysis in this paper is based on Version 1 of the software, which has been in use since 2001. Version 2 is currently undergoing planning and design.

2.2   System Architecture

A view of the system architecture is shown in Figure 1. The *Human/Computer Interface Layer* consists of a graphical user interface, implemented as a collection of definition files, listeners, etc. The *Application Layer* is the core of the system, and contains most of the code. It is divided somewhat arbitrarily into four modules: *System Management*, which controls user sessions, operational modes, and event reporting; *Beam Management*, which handles allocation and operation of the proton beam; *Treatment Management*, which handles the patient treatment sequence

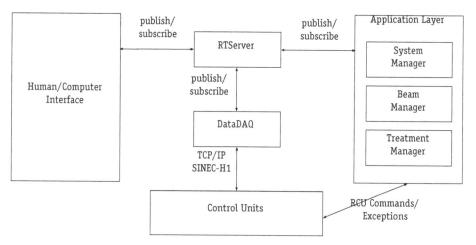

Fig. 1. *Architecture of Therapy Control System*

from prescription to irradiation; and *Database Management,* which provides functions to allow the other modules to access the TCS database. The *Control Unit Layer* contains the drivers for the physical devices; these are implemented in a table-driven fashion as low level state machines.

From a communications perspective, the core of the system is a commercial messaging system (Talarian's *SmartSockets* [17]). The control units communicate with application-level processes using various protocols, including RPC, TCP/IP and SINEC-H1, depending on the type of hardware involved and the nature of the message. The other modules communicate through the server using a publish/subscribe mechanism that it provides: modules subscribe by registering callback procedures against particular events, and when an event occurs, the server calls all registered procedures.

3   Dependence Analysis

Our approach is based on a simple dependence model, which we outline here, but which is described more fully elsewhere [6,7]. The analysis involves a traversal through the dependence graph of the code, which generates, as a byproduct, a tree of assumptions. Examination of the tree may reveal flaws in the system, in which critical features are found to depend on unwarranted assumptions.

3.1   The Dependence Graph

The dependence structure is represented as a graph. An example is shown in Figure 2. Modules are represented as nodes. The module name is shown as the upper-most label inside the node; the other annotations are explained below. An edge labelled S from module A to module B says that A has a dependence on B mediated by the specification S. In other words, to fulfill its specification, A relies on B, but only to the extent that it satisfies S.

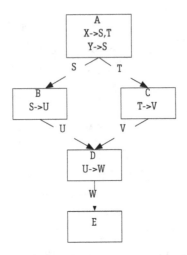

Fig. 2. *Sample dependency diagram*

A *module* is just a syntactic unit of executable code; in a C program, for example, it might correspond to a file. Source code units that are not executable—such as header files in C and interfaces in Java—are not regarded as modules.

A *specification* is, more generally, a description of an assumption that a module may make about its environment that is discharged by another module. In the simplest case, it corresponds to a distinct service, associated with some subset of the procedures or methods of a module. But it may also correspond to assumptions that are not typically viewed as specifications, such as that some procedure within the module is called with a certain frequency, or that a global variable of the module is set in a certain way. A specification does not necessarily call for actions to occur; it may say that certain actions do *not* occur. We shall talk of the provision of services rather than the discharging of assumptions, since the words flow more easily, but the reader should bear in mind that the more general notion is always implied.

A module may use any number of other modules. One module may use another module under multiple specifications; it may use several other modules under the same specification (if, for example, the service it requires is discharged at different times by different modules); and a module may itself be used under multiple specifications by different modules.

In general, then, a module offers many specifications (its exports), and makes use of other modules via many specifications (its imports). A given export will usually not require all the imports. To express this, we can record internal dependences for a module between its imported and exported specifications, writing

A: X -> S, T

for example, to say that module A's provision of X relies on A's use of modules that provide both S and T. On the other hand, we may have that

A: Y -> S

so that A's provision of Y relies on A's use of a module that provides S. In the diagram, these internal dependences are shown inside the relevant nodes.

The internal dependences of a module make a more fine-grained dependence analysis possible. In this case, we can see that in providing the service Y the module A does not actually rely on the module C. And likewise, since the internal dependences of module D show that it provides V directly, without further demands on other modules, we can see that module C depends only on module D and not module E, even though there is path in the graph from C to E.

3.2   The Assumption Tree

Given a dependence graph, and particular service offered by a particular module, we can construct a tree showing all the services that contribute directly and indirectly to this service. These services represent the assumptions underlying the correct working of the system in providing this service.

At the root lies the critical feature; at the leaves are assumptions that cannot be decomposed further and must be evaluated on their own merits: they are either assumptions about the operational environment, or assumptions that are discharged locally, in their entirety, by modules. Note that the modules whose assumptions appear as leaves need not themselves be leaves in the dependence graph: a module may discharge some assumptions directly, but delegate other assumptions to further modules.

Suppose the service of interest is X at module A. We label the root of the tree A: X. Using the internal dependences of A, as described above, we find the services on which X depends. Here, these services are S and T. Now from the dependence graph we determine that these are provide by modules B and C respectively, say. This gives us two new nodes of the tree, which we label B:S and C:T.

This process is continued until the leaves of the tree represent modules that provide the required services with no further dependences. For the diagram of Figure 2, we obtain:

1	A:X	
1.1	B:S	
1.1.1		D:U
1.1.1.1		E:W
1.2	C:T	
1.2.1		D:V

A module may depend on an assumption about the environment; by modelling the environment as a module of sorts, we ensure that the tree never has any dangling edges. A node labelled ENV:Z thus indicates that the environment discharges the assumption Z.

For constructing the assumption tree, regarding dependences as mediated by specifications is crucial. The successful provision of a service by some module often relies on other modules meeting only very partial specifications. Analysis of the emergency stop function, for example, reveals many cases in which a module relies on a procedure call to another module, but does not demand that it meet its full specification. Instead, it depends only on the procedure call terminating, or not returning an error value. In contrast, an analysis of full correctness would require that a called procedure satisfy its full specification (which could therefore be left implicit), resulting in a much larger assumption tree.

3.3 Analysis of the Assumption Tree

The value of a dependence analysis lies not just in identifying and classifying assumptions, but in assessing whether those assumptions are reasonable. In evaluating assumptions for critical functions, the following criteria are applied:

· critical functions should not depend on the performance of non-critical functions;

· critical functions should be contained within limited and well-defined sections of the software;

· fail-safe functions should only be conditional if performing the function may be more dangerous than not performing the function; and

· where critical functions depend on reused or COTS modules, the fitness of those modules should be evaluated with respect to the critical functions.

4   Applying the Analysis: Emergency Stop

Our case study investigates one particular function of the Therapy Control Software, namely the *Emergency Stop* function. When a button, known as the *Crash Button*, is pressed in one of the control rooms, the system should insert a set of 'beam stops'. These block the beam from entering any of the treatment rooms. The system should also freeze motion of the equipment. Whilst hardware interlocks provide an alternate path for the Emergency Stop function, the control software is required to provide a redundant mechanism for the function.

Figures 3 and 4 show part of the dependence diagram and assumption tree for the emergency stop feature of the Therapy Control System. The full expansion of the tree of Figure 4 is shown in the appendix. The critical feature at the root node is 'Emergency Stop Works'. For emergency stop to work, it is assumed that the RTServer, the beam manager and the PCU will all behave in certain ways. These translate into services which must be provided by these modules. These modules in turn make assumptions about other modules which appear lower in the assumption tree.

4.1 Generating the Assumption Tree

The starting point for the analysis of the Emergency Stop function was to identify the boundary between the software function and its external environment.

Selecting the boundary of an analysis such as this is necessarily somewhat arbitrary. The boundary determines which modules are included in the dependence diagrams. All assumptions relating to mdules included within the boundary should appear in the assumption tree.

When the Crash Button is pressed, a signal is sent from the Control Unit (CU) to

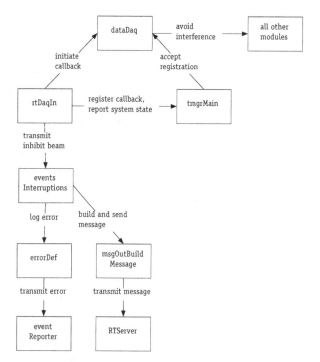

Fig. 3. *Dependency diagram for part of Therapy Control System*

2   **Entire program: Emergency Stop Works**

2.1   **rtDaqIn: Transmit INIHIBIT_BEAM.** If RTServer receives a TMGR_GLOBAL_CRASH_ PRESSED message, the Beam Manager will receive an INHIBIT_BEAM message.

2.1.1   **tmgrMain: Register Callback.** The Treatment Manager registers the rtDaqInputcallback procedure with rtdaq.

2.1.1.1   **rtDaqIn: Accept Registration.** rtdaq registers the rtDaqInputcallback.

2.1.2   **tmgrMain: Report System State.** tmgrMain reports the system state as anything but INITIALISATION.

2.1.3   **rtdaq: Initiate Callback.** rtdaq calls rtDaqInputcallback when a TMGR_GLOBAL_ CRASH_PRESSED message is received.

2.1.3.1   **Entire Program: Avoid Interference.** No other module removes or changes the rtDaqInputcallback registration.

2.1.4   **eventsInterruptions: Transmit INHIBIT_BEAM.** If eventsInterruptions is called by rtDaqIn, eventsInterruptions transmits an INHIBIT_BEAM message.

2.1.4.1   **errorDef: Log Error.** If errorDef is called to log an error, it returns a value of TRUE.

2.1.4.1.1   **eventreporter: Transmit ERROR.** If eventReporter is called to transmit an error message, the message is transmitted, stored and displayed to the HCI correctly.

2.1.4.2   **msgOutBuildMessage: Build And Send Message.** If msgOutBuildMessage is requested to build and send an INHIBIT_BEAM message, it does so correctly.

2.1.4.2.1   **RTServer: Transmit Message.** SmartSockets transmits messages correctly.

Fig. 4. *Assumption tree for part of Therapy Control System*

the dataDaq module (see Figure 1). The dataDaq module responds to the signal by transmitting a message labelled TMGR_GLOBAL_CRASH_PRESSED via the RTServer. The correct response to this message is for a set of commands to be sent to the control units stopping movement of the equipment and inserting the beam stops. For the purpose of the analysis, the function begins after a crash button message is received by dataDaq, and ends when commands are sent to the control units.

Our starting point for analysis is the module rtDaqIn, part of the RTServer of Figure 1. For rtDaqIn to be notified when a TMGR_GLOBAL_CRASH_PRESSED message to be generated, it depends on trmgrmain (the Treatment Manager) to initialise a callback, and dataDaq to notify the callback at the appropriate time. In turn, trmgrmain relies on dataDaq to register the callback. The dataDaq module relies on all other modules, since in order to guarantee that it will provide the service expected of it by rtDaqIn, it depends on all other modules not to delete or alter the callback registered by trmgrmain.

To proceed further, rtDaqIn relies on trmgrmain to report the system state. If this is INITIALISATION, the Emergency Stop function is disabled.

Once the callback has been called, rtDaqIn depends on eventsInterruptions to actually send the message to the Beam Manager. The first action eventsInterruptions takes is to log an error message. In order to complete the message send, it is not directly necessary for the logging to be done. However, since eventsInterruptions will not proceed until logging is complete, it depends on a procedure errorDef to terminate with a value of TRUE. To achieve this, errorDef depends on eventsReporter to correctly log the error message.

The eventsInterruptions module relies on msgOutBuildMessage to send the INHIBIT_BEAM message to the Beam Manager. The msgOutBuildMessage module in turn relies on the *SmartSocket* services provided by RTServer.

5   Evaluation

Software safety analysis does not take place in a vacuum, but rather as an integral part of a system safety program which includes both software and hardware. The designers of the Proton Therapy System included an elaborate hardware backup, implemented using PLC technology. The emergency stop function is handled directly by the hardware, so any flaws in the software revealed by our analysis are likely to have no impact on the behaviour of the system. Nevertheless, the developers of the system take a prudent attitude, and are concerned to preserve the redundancy in order to maximize safety.

Through our analysis, four issues were revealed in the implementation of the Emergency Stop function, discussed in the following sections. These were presented to the developers. The first highlights the need for further analysis; the remaining three were determined to be previously unidentified issues requiring rectification. None of the issues found turned out to be artifacts of the documentation or the analysis.

5.1   Implementation of Callbacks and Message Queueing

The first observation made was that there were numerous dependences on the off-the-shelf RTworks modules. In most cases, such as in assumption 2.1.3, registration and activation of a callback procedure, these dependences reflected standard, well-tested use of the COTS modules.

However, as noted in assumption 2.1.3.1, RTworks does not prevent other modules from altering callback registrations, resulting in an open-ended dependency. The RTServer, as used in the Proton Therapy System, also does not provide a mechanism for prioritising messages. Thus, assumption 2.1.4.2, that eventsInterruptions transmits the INHIBIT_BEAM message, cannot be verified without identifying all other messages that might be queued for transmission, and demonstrating that they will not cause failure or excessive delays.

This problem can be classified as a result of violation of encapsulation for the third-party software. The dependency argument identifies and documents the behaviour expected from the RTworks modules. By comparing this with the actual behaviour of the modules, shortcomings can be noticed and addressed.

5.2   Logging before Acting

Correct operation of the Emergency Stop function is dependent on correct logging of an error message (assumption 3.3.3 in the appendix). This violates the principle that critical functions should not be dependent on non-critical functions.

Whilst the functional requirements for Emergency Stop and logging have been correctly identified, priority and precedence has not been assigned to the requirements. As a result, in some parts of the code an action is performed and then logged, whilst in other parts of the code an action is logged and then performed. There are some instances where this is quite appropriate—for example, in order to avoid overdose, it seems reasonable to avoid radiating the patient unless the radiation can be logged. For Emergency Stop, however, it is more important to stop the system than to record the reason why it was stopped.

Even if both functions were equally important, there is a more immediate temporal requirement to stop the system.

5.3   Unnecessary Checks

Analysis of the Beam Manager also revealed some interesting dependences. Most notably, a series of tests must be passed before the beam can be inhibited. These are described in assumptions 3.3.4 through 3.3.5.1 in the appendix. These checks violate the principle that fail-safe functions should only be conditional if performing the function is more dangerous than not performing the function.

It seems unlikely that the developers of the system were unaware of this principle. More likely, it was not articulated explicitly, and was thus not one of the criteria applied in code review. During normal operation, it is good defensive programming to check the consistency of data at regular intervals. These same checks should not, however, be applied to Emergency Stop. The fact that the crash button has been pressed implies that something has gone wrong, and that something may well result in, or be the result of, incorrect software behaviour. Emergency procedures should not depend on the system behaving normally.

5.4   The Special Case of the Extra Treatment Room

Assumption 3.3.4 (in the appendix) is potentially a serious design error that prevents Emergency Stop from operating if the beam is assigned to any treatment room other than Room 1 or Room 2. When we discussed this error with the software engineers responsible for the system, it became evident that the error had arisen through evolution of the code during development. The original code was only designed to handle two treatment rooms. This code was insufficiently generic, and so extension of the code resulted in the other treatment rooms being treated as special cases, through the ExtraTreatmentRoom modules. Creation of this special case required many subtle changes in the software, not all of which were made consistently.

6   Related Work

Our assumption tree has something in common with a fault tree. Unlike a fault tree, however, its nodes represent the successful provision of a service or function, rather than a failure. In a conventional fault tree analysis, the structure of the fault tree is not easily obtained from the system. Our assumption tree, in contrast, is directly extracted from the dependence diagram.

The assumption tree has no *and/or* structure, since a node of the tree represents all possible behaviours associated with a given assumption, rather than a behaviour in a particular state. This dramatically reduces the size of the tree; more direct applications of fault tree analysis to code which account for control-flow structure (such as [8]) seem unlikely to scale.

Software Failure Modes and Effects Analysis (SFMEA), as applied by Lutz [10], involves considering what can go wrong with each module, and the effects that this will have on each of the dependent modules. It can be viewed as the inverse of fault tree analysis, working bottom-up rather than top-down. Hazard and Operability Studies (HAZOP) [1] obtains similar results by listing the connections between modules, and classifying them with key-phrases such as 'too fast', 'too large', and 'incorrect order'. In this way it systematically explores the effects which each module can have on other modules. Each of these techniques can be considered to ask the question 'What might go wrong?', whereas our technique asks 'What must go right?'.

The idea of module dependences goes back to Parnas's seminal work [13]. Our dependence diagram differs crucially in the labelling of edges, and in the internal dependences that link a module's incoming and outgoing dependences, thus making it possible to trace the dependence's associated with a particular subfunction. Most work on slicing [18] has been at the statement level (see, eg, [4]), although there have been efforts to apply slicing at the procedure [5] and component [15] levels. Wong discusses the phenomenon of the 'long thin slice' of source code related to any given hazard [19].

With appropriate tool support, the extraction of the tree could be made largely automatic. A static analysis that can account for aliasing and procedures-as-values is required; a type based analyzer such as Lackwit [12] may suffice, in combination with a means of lifting statement-level results to the module level (such as the reflexion model tool [11]).

Since no tools were ideally suited to our analysis, we used a simple syntactic analyzer [16] to generate cross references, and then processed the results with a combination of scripts and manual editing. How easy such an analysis is to do depends heavily on how well lexical features of the code (such as the names of identifiers) capture semantic properties. In some cases, for example, two different constants were used for the same message type; this makes it very hard to locate code that reads of writes messages of that type. This confirms Griswold's argument for the importance of 'transparency' in lexical structure [3].

7   Conclusion

The analysis we have presented is simple but effective. It can be conducted without extensive knowledge of the code, since the analysis itself highlights those parts of the code that are relevant. It is feasible without tool support, although tool support would make it less burdensome, and would make mistakes less likely. Even on a well-tested system, it exposed interesting issues. An analysis of this form should perhaps be included in standard code reviews for safety critical code.

Acknowledgments.
This research was performed when the first author was a post-doctoral fellow in the Software Design Group at MIT. It was funded by grant 0086154 from the ITR program of the National Science Foundation, and by the High Dependability Computing Program from NASA Ames, cooperative agreement NCC-2-1298.

References

1. P. Fenelon and B. Hebbron. Applying HAZOP to software engineering models. *Risk Management And Critical Protective Systems: Proceedings of SARSS*. Altrincham, England. The Safety And Reliability Society. Oct. 1994. pp. 11–116.
2. Food and Drug Admininstration. *FDA Statement on Radiation Overexposures in Panama*. Available at http://www.fda.gov/cdrh/ocd/panamaradexp.html.
3. William G. Griswold. *Coping With Software Change Using Information Transparency*. Technical Report CS98-585, Department of Computer Science and Engineering, University of California, San Diego, April 1998 (revised August 1998).
4. S. Horwitz, T. Reps and D. Binkley. Interprocedural slicing using dependence graphs. *ACM Transactions on Programming Languages and Systems*. Volume 12. 1990. pp. 26–60.
5. Daniel Jackson and Eugene J. Rollins. A New Model of Program Dependences for Reverse Engineering. *Proc. SIGSOFT Conf. on Foundations of Software Engineering*, New Orleans, December 1994.
6. Daniel Jackson. Module dependences in software design. *Monterey Workshop on Radical Innovations of Software and Systems Engineering in the Future*, Venice, Italy, October 2002.

7. Daniel Jackson. *Dependences and decoupling*. Lecture notes, 6170: Laboratory in Software Engineering. Dept. of Electrical Engineering and Computer Science, MIT, Sept. 2002, Available at: http://6170.lcs.mit.edu/www-archive/Old-2002-Fall/lectures/lecture-09.pdf.
8. Nancy G. Leveson, Stephen S. Cha, and Timothy J. Shimeall. Safety Verification of Ada Programs Using Software Fault Trees. *IEEE Software*. Vol. 8, No. 4. July/August 1991, pp. 48–59.
9. Nancy G. Leveson and C. Turner. An investigation of the therac-25 accidents. *IEEE Computer*. Vol. 7, No. 26, 1993, pp. 18–41.
10. Robyn R. Lutz and Robert M. Woodhouse. *Experience Report: Contributions of SFMEA to Requirements Analysis*. pp. 44-51. Available at http://citeseer.nj.nec.com/article/lutz96experience.html.
11. Gail C. Murphy, David Notkin, and Kevin Sullivan. Software Reflexion Models: Bridging the Gap Between Source and High-Level Models. *Proceedings of the Third ACM SIGSOFT Symposium on the Foundations of Software Engineering*, 1995, pp. 18–28.
12. Robert O'Callahan and Daniel Jackson. Lackwit: A program understanding tool based on type inference. *Proceedings of the 1997 International Conference on Software Engineering (ICSE'96)*, Boston, MA, May 1997.
13. David Parnas. Designing Software for Ease of Extension and Contraction. *IEEE Transactions on Software Engineering*, Vol. SE-5, No 2, 1979.
14. Robert C. Ricks, Mary Ellen Berger, Elizabeth C. Holloway and Ronald E. Goans. *REACTS Radiation Accident Registry: Update of Accidents in the United States*. International Radiation Protection Association, 2000.
15. Judith A. Stafford and Debra J. Richardson and Alexander L. Wolf. Architecture-Level Dependence Analysis for Software Systems. *International Journal of Software Engineering and Knowledge Engineering*. Volume 11, No. 4, 2001. pp. 431–451.
16. Red Hat, Inc. *The Source Navigator IDE*. Available at: http://sourcenav.sourceforge.net.
17. Talarian, Inc. *SmartSockets*. http://www.talarian.com/rtworks.html.
18. Mark Weiser. Program Slicing. *IEEE Transactions on Software Engineering*. Vol. SE-10, No. 4, 1984, pp. 352-357.
19. Ken Wong. Looking at Code With Your Safety Goggles On. *Reliable Software Technologies: 1998 Ada-Europe International Conference on Reliable Software Technologies*. Lars Asplund, ed. Uppsala, Sweden,1998. Lecture Notes in Computer Science, Vol. 1411. Springer, 1998.

Appendix: Assumption Tree

3   Entire program: Emergency Stop Works

3.1   rtDaqIn: Transmit INIHIBIT_BEAM. If RTServer receives a TMGR_GLOBAL_CRASH_PRESSED message, the Beam Manager will receive an INHIBIT_BEAM message.

3.1.1   tmgrMain: Register Callback. The Treatment Manager registers the rtDaqInputcallback procedure with rtdaq.

3.1.1.1   rtDaqIn: Accept Registration. rtdaq registers the rtDaqInputcallback.

3.1.2   tmgrMain: Report System State. tmgrMain reports the system state as anything but INITIALISATION.

3.1.3   rtdaq: Initiate Callback. rtdaq calls rtDaqInputcallback when a TMGR_GLOBAL_CRASH_PRESSED message is received.

3.1.3.1   Entire Program: Avoid Interference. No other module removes or changes the rtDaqInputcallback registration.

3.1.4   eventsInterruptions: Transmit INHIBIT_BEAM. If eventsInterruptions is called by rtDaqIn, eventsInterruptions transmits an INHIBIT_BEAM message.

3.1.4.1   errorDef: Log Error. If errorDef is called to log an error, it returns a value of TRUE.

3.1.4.1.1   eventreporter: Transmit ERROR. If eventReporter is called to transmit an error message, the message is transmitted, stored and displayed to the HCI correctly.

3.1.4.2   msgOutBuildMessage: Build And Send Message. If msgOutBuildMessage is requested to build and send an INHIBIT_BEAM message, it does so correctly.

3.1.4.2.1   RTServer: Transmit Message. SmartSockets transmits messages correctly.

3.2   rtDaqin: Transmit pcuCrashStop. If RTServer receives a TMGR_GLOBAL_CRASH_PRESSED message, the PCU will receive a pcuCrashStop call.

3.2.1   eventsInterruptions: Transmit pcuCrashStop. If the eventsSafetyEvent procedure of eventsInterruptions is called, eventsInterruptions calls pcuCrashStop of the PCU.

3.3   beamMgr: Insert Beam Stops. If beamMgr receives an INHIBIT_BEAM message, the beam stops are inserted.

3.3.1   rtdaq: Accept Registration. rtdaq registers the beamConnMsgBeamActionCb.

3.3.2   rtdaq: Initiate Callback. rtdaq calls beamConnMsgBeamActionCb when an INHIBIT_BEAM message is received.

3.3.3   beamMgrErrorLib: Log Error. beamMgrErrorLib terminates and returns.

3.3.3.1   eventReporter: Transmit ERROR. If eventReporter is called to transmit an error message, eventReporter terminates and returns.

3.3.4   extraRoom: Report Beam Allocation. extraRoom reports that the beam is allocated to room 1 or room 2.

3.3.5   beamMgrTools: Report Beam Allocation. beamMgrTools reports that the beam is allocated to the room referred to by the INHIBIT_BEAM message.

3.3.5.1   Entire Program: Avoid Interference. No module changes the beam allocation between when the INHIBIT_BEAM message is constructed and when the allocation is checked by beamMgrTools.

3.3.6   beamControl: Insert Beam Stops. beamControl inserts the beam stops.

3.3.6.1   bsIoLib: Insert Beam Stops. bsIoLib inserts the beam stops.

3.3.6.1.1   ecubctu: Return. ecubctu does not generate an exception.

3.3.6.1.2   vxWorks: Transmit STOP. vxWorks transmits to the beam stop hardware.

3.4   PCU: Immobilise Gantry. If the PCU receives a pcuCrashStop call, the commands to immobilise the gantry will be issued.

3.4.1   pcuStateMgr: Immobilise All Movement. If pcuCrashStop is called, pcuStateMgr halts all gantry movement.

3.4.1.1   jogLib: Stop Jog Movement. If jogStop is called, jogLib stops jog movement.

3.4.1.2   pathLib: Stop Path Movement. If pathStop is called, pathLib stops path movement.

3.4.1.3   axisLib: Stop All Axes. If axisAllStop is called, axisLib stops movement on all axes.

3.4.1.3.1   macLib: Stop Mac Movement. If macStop is called, macLib stops mac movement.

3.4.1.3.2   steuLib: Stop STEU Movement. If steuStop is called, steuLib stops gantry movement.

3.4.1.3.3   sreuLib: Stop SREU Movement. If sreuStop is called, sreuLib stops snout movement.

Byzantine Fault Tolerance, from Theory to Reality

Kevin Driscoll[1], Brendan Hall[1], Håkan Sivencrona[2], and Phil Zumsteg[1]

[1]Honeywell International
3660 Technology Drive, Minneapolis, MN 55418
{brendan.hall,kevin.driscoll,phil.j.zumsteg}@Honeywell.com
[2]Chalmers University of Technology
Department of Computer Engineering, SE-412 96 Göteborg, Sweden
sivis@computer.org

Abstract. Since its introduction nearly 20 years ago, the Byzantine Generals Problem has been the subject of many papers having the scrutiny of the fault tolerance community. Numerous Byzantine tolerant algorithms and architectures have been proposed. However, this problem is not yet sufficiently understood by those who design, build, and maintain systems with high dependability requirements. Today, there are still many misconceptions relating to Byzantine failure, what makes a system vulnerable, and indeed the very nature and reality of Byzantine faults. This paper revisits the Byzantine problem from a practitioner's perspective. It has the intention to provide the reader with a working appreciation of the Byzantine failure from a practical as well as a theoretical perspective. A discussion of typical failure properties and the difficulties in preventing the associated failure propagation is presented. These are illustrated with real Byzantine failure observations. Finally, various architectural solutions to the Byzantine problem are presented.

1 What You Thought Could Never Happen

In English, the phrase "one in a million" is popularly used to describe the highly improbable. The ratio itself is difficult to comprehend. The easiest way to give it reason is to equate it to real-world expectations. For example, the probability of winning the U.K. National Lottery is around one in fourteen million; the probability of getting struck by lightning in the U.S. is around one in six hundred thousand [1]. It is not safe to rely on intuition for reasoning about unfathomably small probabilities (for example, the 1-in-1,000,000,000 maximum failure probability for critical aerospace systems[1]). It is problematic in two ways: (1) real-world parallels are beyond typical human experience and comprehension; (2) faults that are not recognized, such as Byzantine faults, are incorrectly assumed to occur with zero or very low probability. The lack of recognition causes additional issues in that it allows the manifestation of such faults to pass unnoticed or be otherwise misclassified, reinforcing the misconception of low probability of occurrence.

---

[1] Usually written as a failure rate of 10^{-9}/hr

S. Anderson et al. (Eds.): SAFECOMP 2003, LNCS 2788, pp. 235–248, 2003.

The lack of recognition leads to repeating the "Legionnaire's Disease" phenomenon. After its "discovery" in 1976, a search of medical records found that the disease had seldom occurred for many decades. The lack of shared knowledge and the disease's rarity made each occurrence appear to be unique. Only after 1976 was it realized that all these "unique" occurrences had a common cause. Similarly, an observation of a Byzantine failure will not be recognized as being an instance of a known class of failure by those who are not intimately familiar with Byzantine failures.

The intent of this paper is to redress this situation. Drawing from the authors' experiences with Byzantine failures in real-world systems, this paper shows that Byzantine problems are real, have nasty properties, and are likely to increase in frequency with emerging technology trends. Some of the myths with respect to the containment of Byzantine faults are dispelled and suitable mitigation strategies and architectures are discussed.

2 The Byzantine Army Is Growing

The microprocessor revolution has seen electronic and software technologies proliferate into almost every domain of life, including an increasing responsibility in safety-critical domains. High assurance processes (e.g. DO-254 [2]) have been matured to manage the development of high integrity systems. The cost of using high assurance processes is relatively high in comparison to equivalent levels of functionality in commercial counterparts. In recent years, there has been a push to adopt commercial off-the-shelf (COTS) technology into high integrity systems. The timing of the COTS push is alarming, considering the decreasing reliability and dependability trends emerging within the COTS integrated circuit (IC) arena. With increasing clock frequencies, decreasing process geometries, and decreasing power supply voltages, studies [3] conclude that the dependability of modern ICs is decreasing. This development reverses the historical trend of increasing IC dependability. Bounding the failure behaviors of emerging COTS ICs will become increasingly more difficult. The expected lifetime of ICs is also decreasing, as modes of "silicon wear-out" (i.e. time-dependent dielectric breakdown, hot carrier aging, and electro-migration) become more significant. The anticipated working life of current ICs may be on the order of 5-10 years. Although viable in the commercial arena, this is a world away from the requirements for high integrity systems, which have traditionally had deployment lifetimes ranging over multiple decades. Strategies to mitigate the problems are in development [4]. It is safe to assume that the anticipated rate of IC failure will increase and the modes of failure will become ever more difficult to characterize.

Another significant trend is the move towards more distributed, safety-critical processing system topologies. These distributed architectures appear to be favored for the emerging automotive "by-wire" control systems [5], where a new breed of safety critical communications protocols and associated COTS are being developed [6]. Such technologies, if developed in compliance with the traditional high assurance processes, show promise to answer the cost challenges of high integrity applications. However, it is imperative that such technologies are developed with full knowledge of all possible failure modes. Distributed control systems, by their very nature, require consensus among their constituent elements. The required consensus might be low-level (e.g. in the form of mutual synchronization) or at a higher level (e.g. in the form of some coordinated system action such as controlling a braking force). Addressing Byzantine faults that can disrupt consensus is thus a crucial system requirement.

We expect Byzantine faults to be of increasing concern given the two major trends described in this section: (1) Byzantine faults are more likely to occur due to trends in device physics; (2) systems are becoming more vulnerable due to increasing emphasis on safety-critical distributed topologies. It is therefore imperative that Byzantine faults and failure mechanisms become widely understood and that the design of safety-critical systems includes mitigation strategies.

3   Parables from the Classical Byzantine Age

The initial definition of Byzantine failure was given in a landmark paper by Lamport et al [7]. They present the scenario of a group of Byzantine Generals whose divisions surround an enemy camp. After observing the enemy, the Generals must communicate amongst themselves and come to consensus on a plan of action—whether to attack or retreat. If they all attack, they win; if none attack, they live to fight another day. If only some of the generals attack, then the generals will die. The generals communicate via messages. The problem is that one or more of the generals may be traitors who send inconsistent messages to disrupt the loyal generals from reaching consensus.

The original paper discusses the problem in the context of oral messages and written signed messages that are attributed different properties. Oral messages are characterized as follows:

A1. Every message that is sent is delivered correctly (messages are not lost).
A2. The receiver of a message knows who sent it.
A3. The absence of a message can be detected.

For messages with these properties, it has been proven that consensus cannot be achieved with three generals, if one of the generals is assumed to be a traitor. A solution is presented in which each of four general exchanges information with his peers and a majority vote makes selections over all of the data exchanged. This solution is generalized to accommodate multiple traitors, concluding: to tolerate m traitorous generals, requires $3m + 1$ generals utilizing $m + 1$ rounds of information exchange.

Written, signed messages assume all of the properties (A1-A3) of the oral messages, and are further characterized by the properties below:

A4. A loyal general's signature cannot be forged.
A5. Anyone can verify the authenticity of a signature.

Assuming the signed message properties above, it is shown that consensus is possible with just three generals, using a simple majority voting function. The solution is further generalized to address multiple fault scenarios, concluding: to tolerate m traitorous generals requires $2m + 1$ loyal generals and $m + 1$ rounds of information exchange.

The initial proofs presented in the paper assume that all generals communicate directly with one another. The assumptions are later relaxed to address topologies of less connectivity. It is proven that for oral messages, consensus is possible if the generals are connected in a p regular graph, where $p > 3m - 1$. For signed (authenticated) messages, it is proven that consensus is possible if the loyal generals are connected to each other. However, this solution requires additional rounds of information exchange to mitigate the lack of direct connectivity. It is shown that the required communication equates to $(m + d - 1)$ rounds, where d is the diameter of the sub-graph of loyal generals.

Since its initial presentation, nearly two decades ago, the Byzantine Generals problem has been the subject of intense academic study, leading to the development and formal validation of numerous Byzantine-tolerant algorithms and architectures. As stated previously, industry's recognition and treatment of the problem has been far less formal and rigorous. A reason for this might be the anthropomorphic tone and presentation of the problem definition. Although the authors warned against adopting too literal an interpretation, much of the related literature that has followed the original text has reinforced the "traitorous" anthropomorphic failure model. Such treatment has resulted in the work being ignored by a large segment of the community. Practicing engineers, who intuitively know that processors have no volition and cannot "lie," quickly dismiss concepts of "traitorous generals" hiding within their digital systems.

Similarly, while the arguments of unforgeable signed messages make sense in the context of communicating generals, the validity of necessary assumptions in a digital processing environment is not supportable. In fact, the philosophical approach of utilizing cryptography to address the problem within the real world of digital electronics makes little sense. The assumptions required to support the validity of unbreakable signatures are equally applicable to simpler approaches (such as appending a simple source ID or a CRC to the end of a message). It is not possible to prove such assumptions analytically for systems with failure probability requirements near 10^{-9}/hr.

The implications of the Byzantine Generals' Problem and the associated proofs to modern systems are significant. Consider a system-level requirement to tolerate any two failures (which includes Byzantine faults). Such a system requires seven-fold $(3m + 1 = 3(2) + 1 = 7)$ redundancy. This redundancy must include all elements used in data processing and transfer, not just processors. The system also must use three rounds $(m + 1 = 2 + 1 = 3)$ of information exchange. This corresponds to a twenty-one times increase in the required data bandwidth over a simplex system (seven-fold redundancy times three rounds of information exchange each).

To more easily identify the problem, concise definitions of Byzantine fault and Byzantine failure are presented here:

Byzantine fault: a fault presenting different symptoms to different observers.
Byzantine failure: the loss of a system service due to a Byzantine fault.

Note that for a system to exhibit a Byzantine failure, there must be a system-level requirement for consensus. If there is no consensus requirement, a Byzantine fault will not result in a Byzantine failure. For example, many distributed systems will have an implied system-level consensus requirement such as a mutual clock synchronization service. Failure of this service will bring the complete system down. Asynchronous approaches do not remove the problems; any coordinated system actions will still require consensus agreement. In addition, adequately validating asynchronous systems to the required assured failure rate of 10^{-9} failures per hour is usually much more difficult than for synchronous systems.

4 Meet the Byzantine Generals (They're Real and They Like to Travel)

Byzantine problems are not mythical. On the contrary, Byzantine faults in safety-critical systems are real and occur with failure rates far more frequently than 10^{-9} faults per hour. In addition, the very nature of Byzantine faults allows them to propagate through traditional fault containment zones, thereby invalidating system architectural assumptions. To illustrate these concepts, a discussion of physical Byzantine fault properties is presented below.

A typical example of a Byzantine fault is a digital signal that is stuck at "½", e.g. a voltage that is anywhere between the voltages for a valid logical "0" (V_{IL}) and a valid logical "1" (V_{IH}). Such behavior is commonly observed with CMOS bridging faults [8] or signal path "opens" (the most common type of fault). A similar behavior can be seen in a metastable flip-flop, which oscillates rapidly between a "0" and a "1", existing in neither state long enough to exhibit a valid output voltage. Receivers downstream of these signals may interpret them as either a "0" or a "1" depending on their respective thresholds, biases, gains, and timing. These ambiguous logic levels can propagate through almost any digital circuit. This happens because "digital circuits are just analog circuits driven to extremes." For any "½" signal output from a logic circuit, one can use the inverse of that circuit's transfer function to find an input voltage which will produce that output. Schmidt triggers can help, but are not guaranteed to be effective. The high gain of modern digital circuits means that small noise riding on a ½ input signal becomes large noise on the output. Thus, ½ signals tend to be oscillatory, and their amplitude can easily exceed a Schmidt trigger's hysteresis.

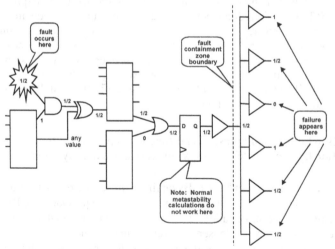

Fig. 1. Byzantine Failure Propagation

As indicated in Fig. 1, such a signal can propagate through multiple stages of logic and still remain at an ambiguous level. The differences in the resulting values at the right side of the figure are due to normal manufacturing and environment differences, which permit their threshold voltages (V_T) to be anywhere in the range of V_{IL} to V_{IH}. Propagation through an arbitrary logic stage or a flip-flop cannot be guaranteed to "clean up" the logic level. The only form of logic that will always prevent an ambiguous logic signal from propagating is "masking logic", the behavior of which removes the causality of the ambiguous logic level behavior. Examples of masking logic are an AND gate with one of its other inputs at a logic "0", and an OR gate with one of its other inputs at logic "1". In either case, the gate's output is solely determined by the masking action of the dominate signal ("0" for AND, "1" for OR). With a dominate input, other gate inputs can have no output effect (even a Byzantine input). The well-known 3-input majority logic "voter" is an illustrative composite example. If one input is ½ and the other two inputs are both 0 or both 1, then the output is 0 or 1 respectively (due to masking within the voter). When one input is ½ and the other two inputs are different values, the output can be 0, ½, or 1, depending on the specific gain and threshold voltages of the voter gates and the specific characteristics of the ½ signal. An XOR gate has no dominate input value; thus a ½ can always pass through it. A flip-flop with its data (or other input) at ½, can output ½ continuously. The commonly used metastability calculation [10] does not apply here because that equation assumes well-formed clock and data inputs that have known frequencies and uniformly distributed skews between the clock and the data.

To further illustrate the Byzantine propagation capability, one can envision a "Schrödinger's CRC" similar to the "Copenhagen" misinterpretation of "Schrödinger's Cat" [9] where the CRC is simultaneously correct for any interpretation of Byzantine data. The behavior of a ½ bit on a CCITT-8 CRC circuit is shown in Fig. 2. This figure shows 8 data bits (with one of the data bits to be transmitted stuck at ½) followed by 8 bits of CCITT-8 CRC. Because the transmitter's CRC calculation is a linear (XOR) combination of its data bits, each CRC bit affected by the ½ data bit can also be ½. The switching threshold voltages are shown for two receivers (*a* and *b*). These thresholds fall within the legal range of V_{IL} to V_{IH}. The resulting data received by *a* and *b* are different, but each copy has a correct CRC for its data. Other receivers of this signal can be divided in three camps: those that agree with *a*, those that agree with *b*, and those that see a bad CRC.

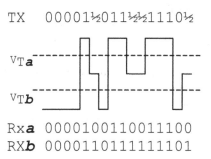

Fig. 2. A "Schrödinger's CRC"

While the failure behaviors in this example appear to be complex, they are all the natural result of a single stuck-at-½ fault somewhere in the transmitter. Thus, CRCs can provide no guarantee of protection against Byzantine fault propagation.

Although the ½ problem is easier to describe, the more common problems are in the time domain. These can be either on the micro-scale where data changing edges occur at the same time as sensing clock edges (i.e. the metastability problem) or on the macro-scale where an event occurs exactly at its deadline. For example, events in a real-time system must occur before a deadline. An event occurring exactly at its deadline can be seen as timely by some observers and late by other observers. Different observations occur because time is continuous, and no matter how tightly the receivers are synchronized to each other, the faulty signal can arrive between any arbitrary sets of deadline expirations. Tighter clock synchronization cannot solve this problem; it only can reduce the probability to some unknown level, which is useless in critical systems where proof of adequate design is needed.

Value and temporal domain affects can be combined in producing Byzantine faults. For example, as shown in Figure 3, a rise time that has become artificially lengthened can present both amplitude and time symptoms. Fig. 3 shows how a long rise time (possibly due to a weak driver, increased line capacitance, etc.) can convert a normal transition between threshold voltages into a time difference (ΔT).

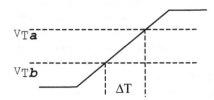

Fig. 3. Variation in Amplitude and Time

When making the required conservative estimate for the probability that a Byzantine fault effect will escape a fault containment (FC) zone[2], the failure probabilities of all the FC zone's components must be considered. For example, if all 9 components to the left of Fig. 1's FC zone boundary resided in different integrated circuits, each with a one hour exposure failure probability of 10^{-6}, the probability of a Byzantine fault escaping the containment zone could be $1 - (1 - 10^{-6})^9 = 8.9 \times 10^{-6} \cong 10^{-5}$. A system with four such fault containment zones could have a failure probability of $1 - (1 - 8.9 \times 10^{-6})^4 = 3.6 \times 10^{-5}$ from Byzantine problems alone. This failure probability is so high that it would not meet the requirements for most dependable systems. Note that typical fault containment zones have many more than 9 components. Note that we say "could" instead of "would" because the actual probabilities are not known—all that is known is the chip failure rates. Because the proportion of failures that are Byzantine rather than benign is typically not known to any degree, one must assume the worst case. Note that the certification agencies for large transport aircraft do not allow one to make an unsubstantiated guess about the relative probabilities of different failure modes for electronic components.

---

[2] A fault containment zone is a set of components within a boundary designed to stop fault effect propagation.

5 The Generals Are Attacking

The Byzantine Generals have been observed attacking systems. The authors have personal experience observing Byzantine failures. As alluded to earlier, being aware of Byzantine behavior enabled these observations. Had this not been the case, the observed behaviors may have been dismissed as an unknown or extremely rare "anomaly". It is hoped that discussion of the Byzantine observations will show that the problem is real and dispel some myths about the characteristics of these faults.

5.1 The Time Triggered Architecture

The Time Triggered Architecture (TTA) [11] is a generic time-triggered computer architecture for fault-tolerant distributed real-time systems. Developed from over 20 years of research, TTA is targeted to address the needs of the emerging automotive "by-wire" industry. A key component of this architecture is a dedicated communications controller that implements a deterministic fault tolerant communications protocol: TTP/C. Due to its low target cost and high dependability characteristics, TTP/C has recently found significant acceptance within the aerospace arena. TTP/C can be characterized as a TDMA-based serial communications protocol that guarantees synchronization and deterministic message communication. In addition to these services, TTP/C is unique in that it provides a membership service at the protocol level. The function of the membership service is to provide global consensus on message distribution and system state.

Addressing the consensus problem at the protocol level can greatly reduce system software complexity; however, placing a requirement for protocol level consensus leaves the protocol itself vulnerable to Byzantine failure. Such were the findings of the Fault Injection for Time Triggered Architecture (FIT) project [12].

As part of the FIT project, a first generation time-triggered communication controller (C1) was radiated with heavy ions. The errors caused by this experiment were not controlled; they were the result of random radioactive decay. The reported fault manifestations were bit-flips in register and RAM locations.

During the many thousands of fault injection runs, several system failures due to Byzantine faults were recorded [12]. The dominant Byzantine failure mode observed was due to marginal transmission timing. Corruptions in the time-base of the fault-injected node led it to transmit messages at periods that were slightly off specification (SOS), i.e. slightly too early or too late relative to the globally agreed upon time base. A message transmitted slightly too early was accepted only by the nodes of the system having slightly fast clocks; nodes with slightly slower clocks rejected the message. Even though such a timing failure would have been tolerated by the Byzantine tolerant clock synchronization algorithm [13], the dependency of this service on TTP/C's membership service prevented it from succeeding. After a Byzantine erroneous transmission, the membership consensus logic of TTP/C prevented nodes that had different perceptions of this transmission's validity from communicating with each other[3]. Therefore, following such a faulty transmission, the system is partitioned into two sets or cliques—one clique containing the nodes that

---

[3] In TTP/C, agreement on global state is a prerequisite for communication.

accepted the erroneous transmission, the other clique comprising the nodes that rejected the transmission.

TTP/C incorporates a mechanism to deal with these unexpected faults—as long as the errors are transient. The clique avoidance algorithm is executed on every node prior to its sending slot. Nodes that find themselves in a minority clique (i.e. unable to receive messages from the majority of active nodes) are expected to cease operation before transmitting. However, if the faulty node is in the majority clique or is programmed to re-integrate after a failure, then a permanent SOS fault can cause repeated failures. This behavior was observed during the FIT fault injections. In several fault injection tests, the faulty node did not cease transmission and the SOS fault persisted. The persistence of this fault prevented the clique avoidance mechanism from successfully recovering. In several instances, the faulty node continued to divide the membership of the remaining cliques, which resulted in eventual system failure.

In later analysis of the faulty behavior, these effects were repeated with software simulated fault injection. The original faults were traced to upsets in either the C1 controller time base registers or the micro-code instruction RAM [14]. Later generations of the TTP/C controller implementation have incorporated parity and other mechanisms to reduce the influence of random upsets (e.g. ROM based microcode execution). SOS failures in the TTA are also mitigated with a central guardian, as discussed in Section 6.3.

5.2 Multi-microprocessor Flight Control System

The Multi-Microprocessor Flight Control System (MMFCS) was developed by Honeywell Labs during the late 1970's. The system pioneered the concepts of self-checking pairs and utilized a dual self-checking pair bus distribution topology (total 4 busses) between nodes of fail-silent, self-checking processing boards. The system's self-checking pair comparisons of processors, bus transmission, and bus reception enabled the precise detection of Byzantine failures and the ability to differentiate them from other failures.

During testing of the MMFCS system prototype, Byzantine failures were observed with a mean repetition period of 50 seconds with a variance of 10 seconds. Because this was in a 20 Hz control loop, the probability of any loop experiencing a Byzantine fault was 1/1000. The root cause of these failures was isolated to the marginal behavior of the physical layer that had been pushed to the limits in the initial prototype set-up.

A common fallacy is to assume random events are uniformly distributed in time (e.g. if we have a 1 in 500 year weather event this year, it will be about another 500 years before it happens again). In reality, the precipitating conditions which cause an event may well persist, so that the probability of clustering is high. Similarly, there is a myth that Byzantine faults are so rare that they will occur in isolation. The MMFCS observations (and those from the TTA FIT above), seriously contradict that myth. In both of these cases, the fault was persistent—typical behavior of an SOS fault. Such faults form a subset of Byzantine faults that occur repeatedly (either permanent or intermittent) due to a shift in a device's characteristics such that it is on the edge of being able to provide its intended service correctly.

5.3 Quad-Redundant Control System

A further example illustrates the fact that having enough good hardware is not sufficient to achieve Byzantine fault tolerance; information exchange is required. The system outlined in Fig. 4 comprised quad redundant processing elements that act on shared data collected by remote data concentrators (DC). Each data concentrator communicated via its own dedicated bus. On first examination, the system would appear to be classical in its approach; however, there was no congruence exchange between the processing elements. The data was used from the data concentrators as is. It was initially assumed that all processing would receive the same data, as they were connected to the same source.

This system failed due to a Byzantine fault that was caused by an incorrect termination resistance on one of the DC-to-processor links. This bad termination caused reflections on one of the data concentrator buses. The processing elements located at nodes and anti-nodes of the reflected interference received different message values. In the worst manifestation, this situation resulted in a 2:2 split of the digital redundancy that forced the system offline, leaving an independent 5th back-up processing function as the only operational unit.

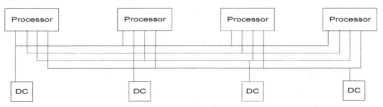

Fig. 4. A Quad Redundant Control System

The above example also illustrates the dangers of Byzantine fault propagation that may invalidate the system failure assumptions; the loss of a single termination resulted in the complete loss of the digital system redundancy. As with the previous examples, the fault that led to the SOS manifestation was hard, and the SOS condition persisted.

5.4 Potential Large Economic Impact Example

If a system is not originally designed to tolerate Byzantine faults, ensuing accidents or recalls due to their occurrence can be very expensive. The possible economic impact is illustrated in an incident where Byzantine failures threatened to ground all of one type of aircraft. This aircraft had a massively redundant system (theoretically, enough redundancy to tolerate at least two Byzantine faults). But, no amount of redundancy can succeed in the event of a Byzantine fault unless the system has been designed specifically to tolerate these faults. In this case, each Byzantine fault occurrence caused the simultaneous failures of two or three "independent" units. The calculated probability of two or three simultaneous random hardware failures in the reporting period was 5×10^{-13} and 6×10^{-23} respectively. After several of these incidents, it was clear that these were not multiple random failures, but a systematic problem. The fleet was just a few days away from being grounded, when a fix was identified that could be implemented fast enough to prevent idling a large number of expensive aircraft.

6 Byzantine Battle Plans

Effective methods for dealing with Byzantine faults can be divided into three types: full exchange (e.g. the SIFT [15], FTMP [16], and SPIDER [17] architectures), hierarchical exchange (e.g. the SAFEbus [18] architecture), and filtering (e.g. TTP star topologies [19]). The first method directly implements the exchanges described in the classical Byzantine papers. The second method uses private exchanges inside subsets of a system's nodes followed by simplified exchanges between the subsets. The third method tries to remove a Byzantine failure's asymmetry via "filtering". An example of each method is given below.

6.1 Full Exchange Example—SPIDER

The Scalable Processor-Independent Design for Electromagnetic Resilience (SPIDER) [17] implements a classical approach to Byzantine fault mitigation using full message exchange and voting. The ultra-Reliable Optical BUS (ROBUS) provides a time-division, multiple-access broadcast bus between N simplex general-purpose nodes (PE n) connected via the ROBUS. The topology is shown in Fig. 5.

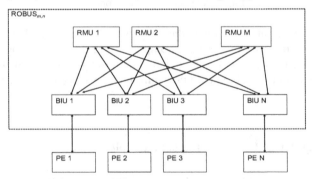

Fig. 5. SPIDER - Classical Full Exchange

The n bus interface units (BIU) and the m redundancy management units (RMU) provide the fault containment zones, which are required to fail independently. The SPIDER architecture incorporates an interactive consistency (IC) protocol that guarantees consistent message exchange. This protocol has been formally verified to provide containment of Byzantine faults. It requires each BIU to send its message to all RMUs; which in turn, forward the messages to all other BIUs. The BIUs then perform a majority vote to ascertain the message status and validity. Note that it is the "masking logic" of the voters and an assumption that RMUs do not propagate Byzantine signals that combine to provide Byzantine fault tolerance.

SPIDER leverages the IC protocol to implement other system services such as synchronization and a system-level diagnosis. Diagnosis enables re-configuration that further enhances the system fault tolerance by preventing faulty components from participating in votes.

The SPIDER project is being developed as a demonstrator for certification under the new DO-254 guidelines.

6.2 Hierarchical Exchange Example—SAFEbus®

Honeywell's SAFEbus (ARINC 659) [18] uses self-checking pair (SCP) buses and SCP BIUs to ensure that Byzantine faults are not propagated (i.e. a Byzantine input will not cause the halves of a pair to disagree). The hardware configuration is shown in Fig. 6.

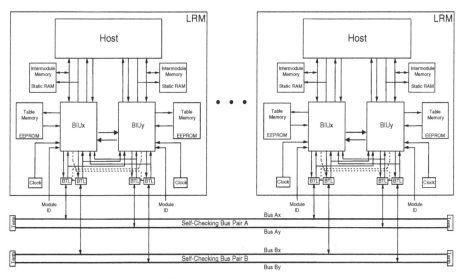

Fig. 6. Two Hosts Connected Via SAFEbus

The private exchange of "syndromes" between BIUs in a pair provides the "masking logic" that prevents Byzantine fault propagation. Each BIU produces a 4-bit syndrome vector that is the result of all 4 ways of comparing an X and a Y bus (see Fig. 6). The BIUs AND their syndromes together and use the result to select the same good input from the busses (if both BIUs agree that there is at least one good input). Consensus among multiple pairs can be achieved by sending only message reception status in a subsequent round of message exchange. SAFEbus® is the only standard bus topology that can tolerate a Byzantine fault, made possible by SAFEbus®'s full-coverage, fault-tolerant hardware.

6.3 Filtering Example—TTP Star

The TTP star topology [19] was developed in response to the FIT project findings described previously. The aims of the star topology are to provide the architecture with a truly independent guardian function and a mechanism to prevent systematic failure due to any persistent SOS node failure.

The TTA star employs centralized filtering to remove the asymmetric manifestation of a Byzantine fault. The star actively reshapes the line signals, transforming ½ signals into valid logic signals. SOS timed transmissions are truncated if they lie too far away from the guardian's notion of the expected transmission time. Thus, only well-timed transmissions (guaranteed to be temporarily valid to all receivers in the system) will propagate.

The filtering and guardian functions are replicated, one instance for each of the two channels.

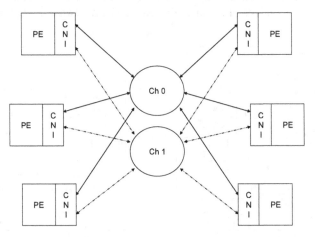

Fig. 7. TTP Star Topology

Note that because the filtering scheme has no "masking logic", it must be designed such that a proof of its Byzantine fault coverage can be constructed. This method cannot be guaranteed to work for all faults. Very careful design is needed to allow pseudo-exhaustive testing to establish a coverage factor meeting system dependability requirements.

6.4 Equivalence of Full Exchange and Filtering

It is important to note that most, if not all, of the existing solutions based on classical full-exchange techniques, have an instance of the filtering method buried inside. That is, they all assume that the 2nd round of exchange via the intermediaries is non-Byzantine and that the intermediaries have suitably filtered the data. Thus, as with the direct filtering approach, these classical solutions must also include pseudo-exhaustive testing as part of their coverage arguments to validate such assumptions. We would like to thank Wilfredo Torres for bringing this fact our attention.

7 Conclusions

Byzantine Problems are real. The probability of their occurrence is much higher than most practitioners believe. The myth that Byzantine faults are only isolated transients is contradicted by real experience. Their propensity for escaping normal fault containment zones can make each Byzantine fault a threat to whole system dependability.

Anyone designing a system with dependability requirements must thoroughly understand these failures.

References

1.   NOAA/American Red Cross: Thunderstorms and Lightning, safety brochure. (1994)
2.   RTCA Inc.: DO-254, Design Assurance Guidance for Airborne Electronic Hardware.
3.   C. Constantinescu: Impact of Deep Submicron Technology on Dependability of VLSI Circuits. In: Proc. Dependable Systems and Networks (2002)
4.   Systems Standard & Technology Council: Avionics Process Management Committee. http://www.geia.org/sstc/APM/.
5.   Kelling, N., Heck, W.: The Brake Project—Centralized Versus Distributed Redundancy for Brake-By-Wire Systems. Paper No 2002-01-0266, SAE (2002)
6.   TTTech Computertechnik AG, "Specification of the TTP/C Protocol V1.0"
7.   Lamport, L., Shostak, R., Pease, M.: The Byzantine Generals Problem. In: ACM Transactions on Programming Languages and Systems, 4(3): 382–401 (1982)
8.   Lavo, D., Larrabee, B., Chess, T.: Beyond the Byzantine Generals: Unexpected Behavior and Bridging Fault Diagnosis. In: Proc. Int. Test Conference, 611–619 (1996)
9.   Bohr, N.: The quantum postulate and the recent development of atomic theory. Nature, 121, 580–89 (1928). Reprinted in Quantum Theory and Measurement.
10. Chaney, T.: Measured Flip-Flop Responses to Marginal Triggering. In: IEEE Transactions of Computers, Vol. C-32, No. 12 (December 1983) 1207–1209.
11. Kopetz, H. Real-Time Systems. Design Principles for Distributed Embedded Applications. Kluwer Academic Publishers, Boston (1997)
12. Fault Injection for TTA. Deliverable 5.1–5.5 Combined Report IST 1999 10748.
13. Pfeifer, H., Schwier, D., von Henke, F. W.: Formal Verification for Time Triggered Clock Synchronization. In: Proc. 7th IFIP International Working Conference on Dependable Computing for Critical Applications (Jan 1999)
14. Ademaj. A, Slightly-Off-Specification Failures in the Time Triggered Architecture. In: 7th IEEE Int. Workshop on High Level Design Validation and Test (Oct, 2002)
15. Wensly, J. H., Lamport, L., Goldberg, J., Levitt, K. N., Melliar-Smith, P. M., Shostak, R. E., Weinstock, C. B.: SIFT : Design and Analysis of fault tolerant computer control for aircraft. In: Proceedings of IEEE 66(10):1240–1255 (1978)
16. Hopkins, A., Smith,   T. Lala, J.: FTMP—A Highly Reliable Fault Tolerant Multi-processor for Aircraft. In: Proceedings of IEEE 66(10):1221–1239 (1978)
17. Miner, P., Malekpour, M., Torres, W.: A Conceptual Design for a Reliable Optical Bus (ROBUS). Proc. 21st Digital Avionics Systems Conference (2002)
18. Hoyme, K., Driscoll, K.: SAFEbus. In: Proc. 11th Digital Avionics Systems Conference. (October 5–9, 1992)
19. Kopetz, H., Bauer, G., Poledna, S.: Tolerating Arbitrary Node Failure in the Time-Triggered Architecture. Doc No 2001-01-0677, SAE (2001)

Redundancy Management for Drive-by-Wire Computer Systems

Oliver Rooks[1], Michael Armbruster[2], Serge Büchli[3], Armin Sulzmann[3],
Gernot Spiegelberg[3], and Uwe Kiencke[1]

[1] University of Karlsruhe, Institute of Industrial Information Technology IIIT,
Hertzstraße 16 - Geb. 06.35, 76187 Karlsruhe, Germany
phone: +49 721 608 4518, fax: +49 721 608 4500
{Rooks, Kiencke}@iiit.etec.uni-karlsruhe.de
[2] University of Stuttgart, Institute for Airborne Systems,
Pfaffenwaldring 27, 70569 Stuttgart, Germany
Michael.Armbruster@ils.uni-stuttgart.de
[3] DaimlerChrysler AG
HPC E104, 70546 Stuttgart, Germany
{Serge.Buechli, Armin.Sulzmann, Gernot.Spiegelberg}@daimlerchrysler.com

Abstract. The integration of drive-by-wire systems into the future generations of vehicles requires a reliable and safe processing of the driver's input requests. Many approaches presented in the last years apply specialized control units as well as communication systems not available in high quantities. This results in cost-intensive systems and increasing developmental periods, which proves to be harmful in the highly competitive automotive sector. Therefore this article describes a safety relevant control system composed of commercial-off-the-shelf (COTS) components designed for automotive applications. The paper explains the hardware structure consisting of four electronic control units (ECU), connected via CAN, which constitute a duo duplex system. Furthermore a detailed description of the *redundancy management* is given, which is the software operating the redundant computer system. Safety relevant software components have to meet requirements of high software quality standards. For this reason the last part of the paper concentrates on the software development process and its supporting tool chain. The application of automated code generation for safety relevant drive-by-wire systems is discussed in detail.

1 Introduction

The integration of drive-by-wire technology into the field of vehicle construction provides the opportunity to implement innovative driver-assistance systems in order to improve the interior space of the vehicles as well as to increase the road safety [1]. In the last ten years by-wire systems associated with mechanical backup (throttle-by-wire, ABS) were developed and integrated in the large-scale production, whereas complete electrical systems are still the focus of research. These systems generate electrical commands given by the driver and transfer

S. Anderson et al. (Eds.): SAFECOMP 2003, LNCS 2788, pp. 249–262, 2003.
© Springer-Verlag Berlin Heidelberg 2003

them to computer controlled actuators. Usually no safe state exists in the case a failure occurs. For these systems it is necessary to apply fault tolerant components, whereas today's requirements ask for the compensation of one safety relevant fault [2] [3].

In the automotive field the appliance of the so-called *fail-silent strategy* seems to be appropriate. If an error occurs in an electrical or mechatronic part of the drive-by-wire system, then this component will stop its communication. Thus a conversion of different faults to a unique observable symptom takes place, which proves to be a great advantage.

Following this strategy a computer system of a drive-by-wire vehicle could be designed following the duo duplex structure (see figure 1). It consists of four ECUs, divided into two duplex channels which behave fail-silent [4]. Each ECU processes the same input data simultaneously. Two comparison units (see (1) in figure 1) observe the accordance of the outputs within the channels. In a fault free situation the first channel is active and communicates with its environment. If an error occurs inside the first duplex system the switching unit (see (2) in figure 1) activates the previous passive channel.

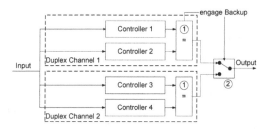

Fig. 1. Duo Duplex Structure based on [4]

In cooperation with DaimlerChrysler Powersystems the research project *Softwarebased Safety Mechanisms of a Drive-by-Wire Powertrain* has been established at the Institute of Industrial Information Technology (IIIT). It concentrates on the development of a system management for drive-by-wire computer systems. The system management is designed as a middleware between the operating system and the application layer. It provides services in the field of fault diagnosis and data fusion to the applications which are called coordination functions. Therefore it is possible to develop these functions without considering the special needs of the safety relevant environment. The redundancy management is an integral part of the system management. Its major task is the control of the redundant ECU system.

This paper concentrates on a prototype of a drive-by-wire computer system. Its architecture follows the duo duplex structure. It differs from the state-of-the-art systems by applying commercial-off-the-shelf (COTS) components available for the application in the automotive sector. Specialized computer nodes are replaced by standard ECUs, which until now were not used in drive-by-wire systems. These ECUs are supplemented by an additional hardware component cutting of the ECU's communication channels in the case an error occurs. It is called BUSPWR block as it cuts off the communication (BUS) as well as the power supply (PWR) of the attached ECU. The inner channel communication and the communication between the duo duplex system and its environment is based on the CAN bus. The development of the redundancy management follows a software engineering process adapted for automotive ECUs, which is designed to use autocode generation.

The article is structured as follows: Section 2 describes the main components of the duo duplex system. It is followed by an introduction of the redundancy management. Insights are offered into the inner channel communication and the coordination task between the duplex channels. Section 4 illustrates the behaviour of the whole system showing a communication sequence in a faulty situation. It describes the switching between the duplex channels due to an inner channel communication interception. Section 5 deals with the aspects of software development. Its main focus lies on the automatic generation of code for safety relevant software components like the redundancy management. The last section gives a summary of the article.

2   System Overview

Figure 2 shows the basic structure of the new duo duplex system. It consists of two *duplex channels* - channel 1 and channel 2. Both of them provide fail-silent behaviour. Each channel is composed of two *computer nodes*. The computer node itself contains one processing unit - the COTS ECU - and a hardware supplement - the BUSPWR block. The task of the latter is the reliable disconnection of the computer node's communication channels in the case that errors are detected. Each computer node comprises three communication ports. The first of them is used to connect the nodes of one channel with each other. The communication busses two and three establish a connection between the two duplex channels. Furthermore they deliver the input data to the duo duplex system and send their output data to the environment. Between the computer nodes of one duplex channel another connection is established: Via two digital outputs *out1* and *out2* each ECU is connected to both of the BUSPWR blocks included in its channel. To shut down the ECUs another digital link connects the BUSPWR block (*out* port) and the corresponding ECU (*in* port). By this connection the power management is assigned to deactivate the computer node.

Software diversification applied to tolerate software faults is not addressed in this paper. In contrast to the aerospace industry computer systems for automotive applications have to be developed with a lower budget in a shorter period of time. Additionally, software versions of control functions change often within the life cycle of such a computer system. Therefore the conditions for the integration of software fault tolerance are unfavourable considering that a duo duplex system would have to include four independent software versions.

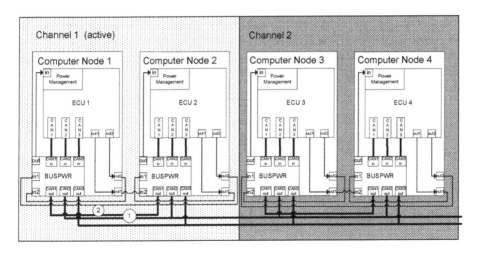

Fig. 2. Duo Duplex System Prototype

2.1   Electronic Control Unit (ECU)

As mentioned above, COTS ECUs serve as processing units. They were used for various applications under different conditions and as a consequence their behaviour is well known. Computer systems especially developed for drive-by-wire control suffer from the lack of knowledge regarding their behaviour. Thus from the dependability's point of view the approach of using COTS ECUs makes sense. Beside that, the utilisation of COTS components enables the development of cost effective drive-by-wire computer systems. Considering the cost pressure for electronic systems in the automotive sector, this is an important advantage. Moreover, the ECUs are designed for automotive environmental conditions (temperature range, vibration load). This allows to develop drive-by-wire computer systems ready for the in-car use in a short period of time. Besides the demand for sufficient computation power and an adequate number of I/O ports the ECU's microcontroller has to provide an interface for TargetLink, which is a software tool for automated code generation (see section 5).

2.2   BUSPWR Block

In comparing the processing results of the computer nodes errors within the ECUs of one channel will be detected. Ideally the faulty node is able to fail silent. But in some cases the faulty component inside the ECU could prevent the fault detection mechanisms to reveal the erroneous situation. For this reason an independent hardware component is designed to disconnect the ECU's communication reliably. This BUSPWR block prevents the computer node from sending wrong output data to the environment. In addition to the ECU the BUSPWR block is the second element of the computer nodes. Both BUSPWR blocks of the duplex channels are connected to both ECUs. Therefore if a fault is detected by one ECU it interrupts the communication of the complete channel by controlling both BUSPWR blocks. As they are not designed as a redundant element, a simple structure and its complete testability is required.

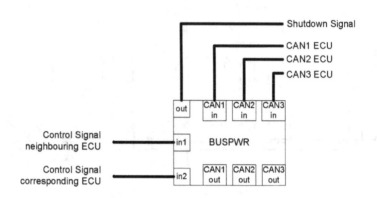

Fig. 3. Interface of the BUSPWR Block

Figure 3 shows the interfaces of the BUSPWR block. It consists of six bus connectors of which ports 1 to 3 are connected to the ECU. The remaining 3 ports establish a connection to the inner channel bus 1 as well as to the busses 2 and 3 connecting the duo duplex system with its environment. Besides the communication ports the BUSPWR block comprises 2 inputs for signals activating the interruption of the communication channels (see figure 2). These signal ports are connected to the digital outputs of both ECUs. At present the BUSPWR block will disconnect the communication if the signal level of the inputs "in1" or "in2" is ground.

2.3   Communication System

In the automotive sector there are different approaches integrating time triggered and deterministic communication processes into drive-by-wire systems [5] [6] [7]. Unfortunately right now there is no standard, which is accepted by the automotive industry or whose components are available in sufficient quantities. Hence the duo duplex prototype presented uses the Controller Area Network (CAN), which has been established as a standard of automotive communication. It is organized as a serial broadcast system, whereas the priority of message transmission depends on the importance of the message and not on the attributes of the sending node. As the CAN bus applies this priority-based algorithm the bus load has to be reduced to 10-20% for safety relevant applications. In this case the channel's communication is assumed to be approximately deterministic [8].

As the CAN bus was developed with the focus on automotive applications it offers mechanisms for fault detection in this interference-prone environment.

Each sending node detects its own transmission faults by concurrent readout of the bus (bit monitoring). The information within a CAN message is secured by cyclic redundancy checks. Via acknowledgement-bits the sending nodes detect if at least one node has received the message correctly. Error-bits sent by the receiving nodes indicate transmission faults. These detection mechanisms as well as their compensation methods are implemented in the CAN transceivers, which are part of the ECUs. Therefore the operating software of the duo duplex system only has to address the error *communication system not available*.

3   Redundancy Management

After the given system overview and the description of the different hardware parts this section concentrates on the software components operating the duo duplex system. As mentioned before, the introduced prototype does not comprise external comparison and switching units like the duo duplex system shown in figure 1. Software components inside the ECUs which compose the redundancy management replace these hardware parts. Firstly the information flow of the whole system is outlined. Secondly this section focuses on the redundancy management consisting of two processes.

3.1   Information Flow

The information flow of the prototype comprises the following steps as shown in figure 4: The duo duplex system reads its input data from the communication busses two and three. The inner channel synchronisation observes this process to guarantee consistent input data within each duplex system. The coordination functions process this information and generate output data which are transferred to the redundancy management. The corresponding main processes exchange the results of computation within the channel using the communication bus one. Afterwards every ECU compares its own result with the received one. If the similarity meets the predefined criteria then one of the computer nodes will send its result to the environment. Besides these functionalities implemented in the main processes one alive process is part of the redundancy management.

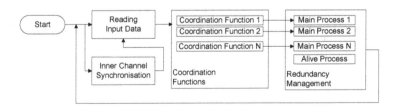

Fig. 4. Information Flow

It is obvious that a mechanism is required generating one valid output data out of four processing results. To succeed in this the computer nodes are ordered by priority represented by *controller numbers* shown in table 1. At first it is necessary to differ between an active and a passive channel. The active channel is entitled to send output data to the environment. Computation results of the passive channel do not leave the duo duplex system. Within one channel there is also a difference in the behaviour of the computer nodes. Passive nodes only generate data for inner channel comparison purposes. Therefore no information sent by passive ECUs can be found on the communication channels two and three. To guarantee this the CAN transceiver of the passive ECUs are configured read only for busses two and three. As a result, only the active computer node in the active channel (controller number 1) is allowed to send information to the environment of the drive-by-wire system. Additionally the active node of the passive channel (controller number 3) transmits an alive message via channel two and three. In case a computer node detects its malfunction the controller number is replaced by the value 5.

Table 1. Controller Numbers

Fault Free	ECU	Channel	Final Output	Failure Channel 1	Failure Channel 2
1	active	active	Yes	5	1
2	passive	active	No	5	2
3	active	passive	No	1	5
4	passive	passive	No	2	5

The redundancy management replaces the external comparison and switching units of the standard duo-duplex system. It has to meet the following requirements:

1. If an error occurs within an ECU, the corresponding duplex channel has to stop its communication and the ECUs have to be turned off.
2. If the communication within one channel or between the channel and its environment is interrupted, the ECUs of this channel have to stop their ongoing communication and the ECUs have to be turned off.
3. If channel 1 behaves silent, the remaining pair of computer nodes has to detect this situation and activate itself.
4. If an error occurs and only one channel of the duo duplex system is operating, this channel has to quit communication and to switch off itself.
5. If channel 2 behaves silent, channel 1 has to detect this situation.

These tasks are accomplished by two parallel processes. The main process within one ECUs deal with the requirements one to four as the alive process is designed to fulfill the fifth condition.

3.2   Main Process

The main process is shown in figure 5. It is implemented in each computer for every coordination function (see figure 4). Some operations are linked to a specific position of the ECU in the redundant system. In the following the main process is explained in detail. The numbers in brackets correspond to the flowchart in figure 5.

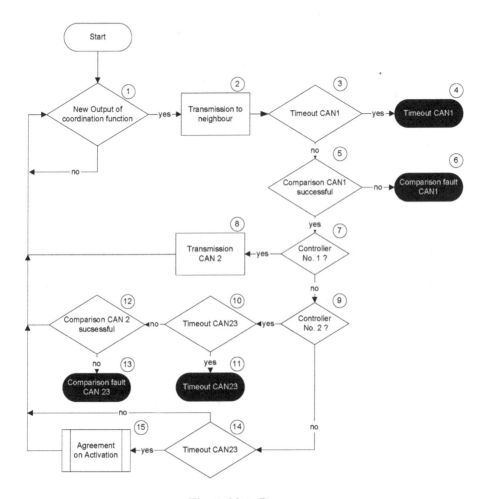

Fig. 5. Main Process

As soon as a new processing result of the control functions is available (1), it is transmitted via CAN1 to the neighbouring ECU (2). Afterwards the ECU observes CAN1 waiting for the corresponding data coming from the channel neighbour (3). After its reception both computer nodes are aware of the two channel results. If the corresponding data of the channel neighbour was not received within a predefined period of time, then a timeout occurs which is called *Timeout CAN1* (4). In case the processing result of the channel neighbour was received in time the process compares the two data items (5). If a determined comparison criterion is not met *Comparison Fault CAN1* emerges (6). The process will continue according to the controller number if the comparison has been successful:

ECU 1 (7): The ECU with the controller number 1 transmits its verified output data to the environment via the busses 2 and 3 (8). After this operation the computer node awaits new processing results of the corresponding control function (1).

ECU 2 (9): After a successful inner channel comparison this ECU observes the reception of the first ECU's final output on the CAN busses 2 and 3 (10). If the data is not received within a predefined period of time, then *Timeout CAN23* will occur (11). Otherwise the data is compared to the result of ECU1 known from the inner channel comparison (5). In the case of discrepancy the process terminates in the error state *Comparison Fault 23* (13). If the values match the process will wait for new processing results of the corresponding control function (1).

ECU 3 and 4 (9): After their inner channel comparison (5) they also wait for the final result of ECU1 on channel 2 and 3 (14). If it fails to appear, ECU3 and ECU4 vote on the failure of channel one (15). If both ECUs detect the absence of the final result channel two activates itself. Otherwise the disagreement is interpreted as an error within the passive channel. If the final data of ECU1 was received within the predefined period of time, the process in ECU3 and ECU4 will wait for new processing results of the corresponding control function (1).

In the following the reaction to the error states is introduced. Channel 1 always behaves in the same way. As soon as one of the errors is detected the ECUs assign both BUSPWR blocks to disconnect the channel's communication and to shut down the ECUs. In case of the errors *Timeout CAN1* and *Comparison Fault CAN1* the passive channel behaves like the active duplex system. But in the case of a missing final result on CAN 2 and 3 the failure of the active channel was detected. As described above the passive channel becomes active by replacing its controller numbers 3 and 4 with 1 resp. 2 (see table 1).

3.3   Alive Process

The main process meets the requirements one to four of the redundancy management. To be aware of the current situation of the duo duplex system it is necessary to identify the loss of the passive backup channel (requirement five). The alive process provides this mechanism as shown in figure 6. It is implemented on each of the ECUs but its functionality depends on the current controller number. The main goal is to send a special CAN message - the so called *alive message* - from the passive channel to the active one. As long as an error inside the passive channel is not detected, the ECU with the controller number 3 transmits

the alive message via the communication channels 2 and 3. The ECUs of the
active channel receive these messages. In the case they are not received within
a predefined period of time, the ECUs with the controller number 1 and 2 assume the failure of the passive channel. This situation has to be reported to the
environment of the duo duplex system, because the fault-tolerant properties of
the drive-by-wire computer system are lost.

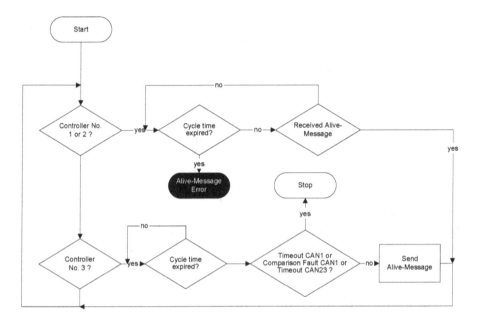

Fig. 6. Alive Message Process

4   Application

After the detailed description of the processes composing the redundancy management this section gives proof of the system's operation by showing a communication plot. The information is gathered at position 1 in figure 2. Therefore it
is possible to record the inner channel communication between computer node
one and two as well as the messages written on the bus CAN 2. Messages on
bus 3 are not logged. The plot does not include alive messages as they are not
necessary for describing the failure of channel 1. The demonstration concentrates
on one processing result representing the reference velocity of a truck. Figure 7
illustrates the progress of communication.

At first two regular communication cycles of the active channel 1 are shown.
They consist of three messages. At the point of time 45.83s ECU1 transmits
its processing result via bus 1 and waits until ECU2 responds with its output

data. This has to be done within the period of time displayed by the arrow *ECU1: Timer CAN1*. Timely, the reference velocity of ECU2 is available on CAN1 (45.84s).

Now the inner channel comparison takes place. Since both data items on CAN1 are matching ECU1 writes its output on CAN2. As this result is available in time (*ECU2: Timer CAN2*) and as the sent data item corresponds to that offered on CAN1 channel 1 stays active and the next communication cycle proceeds at 45, 91s.

As described by the main process channel 2 observes the communication on CAN2. It monitors the alive status of channel 1. As soon as the final result of channel 1 arrives on the bus *Timer Channel 2* is started waiting for the next output data of channel 1 on CAN2.

At the point of time 45.95s an error occurs inside channel 1. The communication via CAN1 is interrupted at the position 2 in figure 2. As a result the internal communication of channel 1 fails.

At 45.99s the processing result of ECU2 appears on CAN1. The corresponding data item of ECU1 is not available. The timeout of *ECU2: Timer CAN1* indicates the failure of channel 1. ECU2 activates the BUSPWR block of the computer node 1 and 2. They disconnect ECU 1 and ECU2 from all of their communication lines and initialize their shut-down. As soon as *Timer Channel 2* runs out the passive channel identifies the failure of the duplex system 1. Therefore the passive channel activates itself by changing the ECUs controller numbers 3 and 4 to 1 resp. 2. At the point of time 46.08s the first output data of channel 2 appears on CAN2.

5   Software-Engineering Aspects

Besides the functional point of view, the article outlines the software engineering aspects of the redundancy management. Its development has to meet the following requirements:

1. independency of underlying hardware associated with easy portability to different target platforms
2. decreasing periods of development by adaptation of an automotive software engineering process

To meet these requirements autocode generation was applied. The tool TargetLink from dSpace was used. It provides a development environment for the generation of C-code optimized for different microcontrollers used in the automotive industry [9]. TargetLink is integrated into the user interface of Simulink/Stateflow. It enables the development of control flow and data flow oriented functions, respectively. The function blocks of TargetLink are similar to the blocks of Simulink. Additionally, parameters for the automated code generation like data types or scaling options can be specified.

Generating C-code from a graphical function TargetLink uses so called *backends*. Their task is the optimization of the C-code for the chosen combination

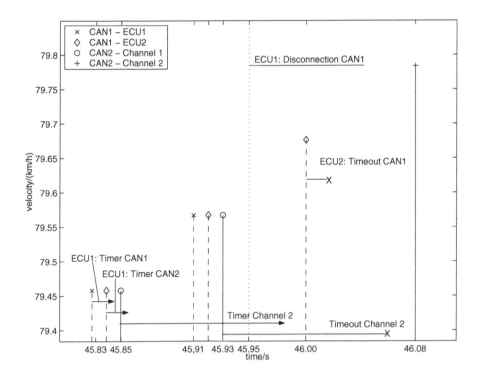

Fig. 7. Changeover Channel 1 - Channel 2

of microcontroller and compiler. By applying different backends it is possible to generate code for different microcontrollers without making major modifications to the sources. This enables the porting of the redundancy management to more powerful ECUs without loosing the effect of optimized code. Therefore one major requirement for possible target platforms is their support by a TargetLink backend.

The need for decreasing developmental cycles also affects the development of safety relevant functions like the redundancy management. It makes sense to adapt the development processes available for automotive software components [10]. This increases the software quality and simultaneously reduces the number of time-consuming in-car tests. To succeed in this, software tools support the different steps of the process [11] like TargetLink replacing the manual code generation. This step is error-prone and depends on the abilities of the programmer.

The redundancy management was developed using TargetLink models. For these models a test environment was created simulating the environment of the redundancy management (BUSPWR blocks, CAN busses, coordinations functions). As a result, the basic functionality of the redundancy management could be tested in early implementation stages (MiL - model in the loop test). The automated code generation enables the transfer of these tested simulation models to C-code, which could be tested in the same simulation environment (SiL

- software in the loop). This decreases the error ratio of the generated software components. The duration of development is reduced by the time of manual code generation. Additionally, costly and error-prone scaling operations for fixed-point ECUs are handled by the automated code generator.

During the start up of the redundancy management a fault analysis was performed, identifying the failure cause in the software components (see table 2). It has to be distinguished between errors found inside the redundancy management's TargetLink model and its handwritten C-code implementing the task management as well as the CAN bus connections. This analysis exposes the matured status of the C-code generated out of the TargetLink model in comparison to the hand-written sources. It has to be mentioned that before the start up of the system the hand written C-code could not be tested at the same extent as the TargetLink model. This is caused by its dependence on the hardware target. Therefore the information presented in table 2 shows the *trend* of quality improvement caused by automated code generation.

Table 2. Software Faults during Start-Up

Software Part	Estimated No. of Software Faults	Lines of Code	Conditions
TargetLink Code	15	3445	- Extended evaluation of software in Simulink test-environment.
Handwritten Code	31	378	- Implements only communication functions. Therefore no evaluation of software before start-up.

6   Summary

The integration of drive-by-wire systems into future generations of vehicles requires a reliable and safe processing of the driver's input requests. By now, the applied computer systems use redundant hardware structures. In this paper a duo duplex system is introduced. It differs from the state of the art implementations by utilizing commercial-off-the-shelf components. The four processing units are represented by automotive ECUs. The communication inside the system and between the system and its environment bases on CAN busses. In case that one of the computer nodes fails, its communication is disconnected by an external hardware unit - the BUSPWR block. The software component redundancy management operates the duo duplex system. It is implemented by each computer node and includes the comparison of the inner channel computation results as well as the communication between the two duplex-channels.

The last part of the article focuses on the software engineering process underlying the development of the redundancy management. Particularly the advantages of the autocode generation for safety relevant computer systems are presented. The increased testability of the software components affects the error ratio during the start up of the system in a positive way. Further on the autocode generation enables the migration to more powerful ECUs without major changes on the source code of the system.

References

1. Spiegelberg, G.: Ein Beitrag zur Erhöhung der Verkehrssicherheit und Funktionalität von Fahrzeugen unter Einbindung des Antriebstrangmoduls $MOT_{ion}X - ACT$. Dissertation. Cuvillier Verlag, Göttingen (2002)
2. Isermann, R., Schwarz, R., Stölzl, S.: Fault-tolerant drive-by-wire systems. In: IEEE Control System Magazine, Vol. 22, No. 5. (2002) 64–81
3. Reichart, G.: Safe electronic systems in vehicles. In: at - Automatisierungstechnik, Vol. 46, No. 2. (1998) 78–83
4. Hammett, R.: Design by extrapolation: an evaluation of fault tolerant avionics. In: IEEE Aerospace and Electronics Systems Magazine, Vol. 17, No. 4. (2002) 17–25
5. Kopetz, H.: Time-triggered real-time computing. IFAC World Congress, Barcelona, (2002)
6. Heinecke, H., Schedl, A., Berwanger, J., Peller, M., Nieten, V., Belschner, R., Hedenetz, B., Lohrmann, P., Bracklo, C.: Flexray - Ein Kommunikationssystem für das Automobil der Zukunft. In: Elektronik Automotive, September (2002), 36–45
7. Grießbach, R., Berwanger, J., Peller, M.: Byteflight - Neues Hochleistungs-Datenbussystem für sicherheitsrelevante Anwendungen. In: ATZ-Sonderausgabe: Automotive Electronics (2000) 60–67
8. Ellims, M., Parker, S., Zurlo, J.: Design and analysis of a robust real-time engine control network. In: IEEE Micro, Vol. 22, No. 4. (2002) 20–27
9. Kiffmeier, U., Köster, L., Meyer, M., Witte, C.: Automatic production code generation for electronic control units. In: at - Automatisierungstechnik, Vol. 47, No. 7. (1999) 295–304
10. Bortolazzi, J., Steinhauer, S., Weber, T.: Development and quality management of in-vehicle software. In: Electronic Systems for Vehicles, VDI Berichte, Vol. 1547. (2000) 355–370
11. Gehring, O., Schwarzhaupt, A., Spiegelberg, G., Rooks, O.: Software function development process for a drive-by-wire drivetrain. In: 4. VDI Mechatronik Tagung 2001 "Innovative Produktentwicklung", VDI-Berichte, Vol. 1631. (2001) 73–91

Fault-Tolerant Communication System to Improve Safety in Railway Environments

César Mataix, Pedro Martín, Francisco Javier Rodríguez, María José Manzano, and Javier Pozo

Departamento de Electrónica, Universidad de Alcalá, Campus Universitario, s/n, 28805 Alcalá de Henares, Madrid, Spain
Tel.: +34 91 885 65 50. Fax: +34 91 885 65 91
{mataix, martin, fjrs}@depeca.uah.es

Abstract. This paper presents a network that connects various safety sensors located on level crossings and in stations. These sensors are used to detect obstacles on the railway line and proximity between trains. The information is centralised in the Operations and Control Centre. The network has been designed in sections, each of which consists of a dual bus structure, with the particular feature that if one of the buses fails, the packets are routed to the other. Fault detection on the network is performed using intelligent diagnostic techniques, applying the IEEE 1232-2002 standard. By examining the result of the diagnosis, it is possible to ascertain the optimal route from each sensor to the OCC. Monitoring is performed using active network techniques. The diagnostic system sends packets containing code that is executed at each node.

1 Introduction

The Department of Electronics of the University of Alcalá, in co-operation with the state-owned rail operator RENFE (*Red Nacional de Ferrocarriles Españoles*) and the firm Logitel, is working on a research project financed by the Ministry of Science and Technology. This project, titled TELEVÍA (*Control Integral de la Circulación y Seguridad en Líneas Ferroviarias* - Integral Control of Traffic and Safety on Railway Lines), takes an integrated approach to the various problems related to automated control and safety for rail traffic on lines with low-to-medium traffic density.

Part of this project focuses on telecontrol and telemonitoring, the objective being to monitor the status of a series of systems installed in stations or their environment (axle detector, signalling, level crossing control, presence of obstacles on the track, etc.) [1]. At the present time, in most of the railway lines the intermediate stations monitors the state of the systems located near them. It doesn't exist any central system that allows to obtain a global vision of the state of the railway line. The exception is the high-speed lines. Also, the employment of telecontrol systems is scarce. By using sensors located on level crossings and in stations, it is possible to detect critical safety situations [2] that could have grave consequences, such as, for example, obstructed level crossings, people crossing the track at prohibited points, excessive train axle

S. Anderson et al. (Eds.): SAFECOMP 2003, LNCS 2788, pp. 263–274, 2003.

temperature, etc. Depending on the circumstance that needs to be detected, the sensors may be one of the following types:

- Ultrasonic sensors: based on multiple transducers and relatively high emission powers, these may be used to warn of the presence of obstacles in the monitored zones.
- Infrared sensors: by emitting structured light and using CCD sensors, these are able to detect the presence of obstacles, even in very poor light conditions.
- Machine vision sensors: intelligent analysis of images in outside environments makes it possible to ascertain whether or not the track is free of obstacles.
- Axle detection and temperature measurement sensors: installed alongside the track, these detect the presence of a train and the number of axles of the same. Moreover, these measure the temperature of all of the axles, brake discs and wheels of any train that passes over them.

Each of these has to be connected to the Operations and Control Centre (OCC), which is located at a rail terminal and is where the information is centralised. When a hazard situation is detected by a particular sensor, a warning is sent to the OCC, where appropriate measures will be taken [3].

Given that the number of sensors that may exist along a route covering hundreds of kilometres is likely to be high, the problem arises of establishing communication in a practical, safe and reliable manner [4]. This paper presents a new fault-tolerant communication system that reliably interconnects the various safety sensors and the OCC. It describes a Wide Area Network that incorporates intelligent diagnosis to detect faults using active network techniques and optimal routing of the packets to the OCC. Section 2 describes previous works on the railway environment. Section 3 describes the hardware architecture for the communication network. Section 4 presents the intelligent diagnosis system used for fault detection. Section 5 presents the results and the conclusions of the paper.

2 Background

Previous works have been written on communication networks applied to the rail environment, but these have tended to focus on monitoring the energy system and SCADA systems. Communication between the remote terminal units (RTU) and the control centre is established in [5] via a dual fibre optic ring and duplicated servers, the aim being to increase availability and reliability, but the work does not incorporate any elements to diagnose the status of the communications network. The RTUs are connected to front-ends, which perform the communication protocol adaptation and historical data storage tasks. Among the future works suggested, it highlights the possibility of including intelligent diagnosis, as well as improvements to facilitate maintenance. In [6], a monitoring system for a level crossing is designed. Access to the variables measured is facilitated either via an HTTP server incorporated in the remote system or via a local terminal located on the level crossing itself. The remote system is equipped with Telnet and FTP servers, which makes it possible to carry out maintenance operations, enabling, for example, the software version to be upgraded.

Some of the drawbacks are that data analysis is performed off-line by an operator and the system is not provided with redundancy of any kind. In [7], a remote system able to detect the presence of rocks on the track using acoustic and infrared sensors is designed. The data capture and processing tasks, which require shorter processing times, are programmed in C++, whilst visualisation of the results is achieved via an applet that is downloaded to the client's browser from an incorporated HTTP server. An additional telephone line is included to monitor the status of the same. In [8], trends in railway energy management using distributed systems based on independent dual bus LANs and TCP/IP are presented. These operate in client-server mode to provide a high-availability rapid response in real time, as well as reducing network traffic. The possibility of checking the proper operation of the communications system is not included in this paper either. In [9], the monitoring network for the CERN energy system is described. It is designed around a hybrid architecture that combines a centralised system (SCADA) and a distributed one to facilitate maintainability, extendibility, modularity and configurability. In [10], a communications system is designed for automatic traffic control (ATC). This is a distributed system connected using sections of two independent fibre optic rings. The need to add a reliable fault detection system that activates back-up equipment is commented on.

3 Network Architecture

The communication network has been designed on a modular structure divided into sections (each section existing between two gateways), thereby facilitating maintenance and implementation. Fig. 1 shows one of the sections that make up the network.

In addition, the network is organised into three hierarchical levels - sensor level, intermediate level and control level.

The *sensor level* is composed of the various sensors, the safety node (SN) and a LonWorks double fieldbus that interconnects them, covering a distance of many kilometres. When the sensors detect a hazard situation, they generate an alarm packet that is sent to the safety node. The format of the packet depends on the type of sensor that has generated it, but it generally contains the sensor's unique identifier, the date and time and the alarm identification code. This, at the same time, stores the event in an historical file and transmits the packet to the intermediate level over a TCP/IP network. The machine vision sensors are able to provide, on demand, the sequence of images prior and subsequent to the moment at which the alarm was produced, which will be visualised in the OCC.

The *intermediate level* consists of the intermediate modules (IM), the gateways (G) and the dual communication bus. Each section can cover distances of up to 80 km. The intermediate modules are located in the stations along the route and in the electric power substations. The safety nodes connected to bus *ghg i* send the alarm packets to the intermediate module connected to its own bus. In the case of the nodes connected to bus *gg i*, the packets are sent to the nearest gateway, which will resend the packet via bus *ghg i*. In the case that the intermediate module of the section is not available, the packets are sent, via the gateways, to the nearest adjacent intermediate module, and if this is also unavailable, to the next one until an operative intermediate module is found. A particular characteristic of the proposed architecture is that the two buses are not independent, as is usually the case, making it possible to route the packets to one or the other in the gateways, depending on the level of congestion or availability. This, along with the feature of being able to send alarm packets to any intermediate module, increases the reliability of the system and guarantees its operation, even in degraded mode.

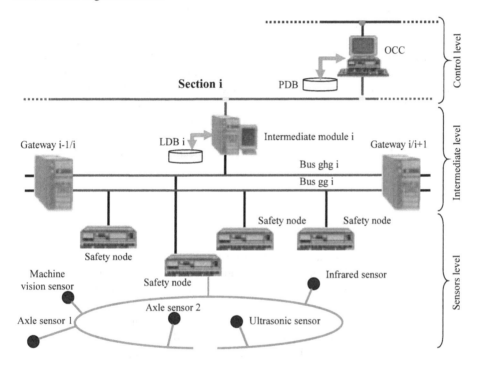

Fig. 1. Network Architecture

Packet routing in the gateways is based on the data supplied by the intelligent diagnostic system. By periodically sending monitoring packets, it is possible to ascertain the operational status of each intermediate module and gateway, as well as the delay of each of the possible routes to the nearest intermediate module. Analysis of this information will determine the routing tables to send to each gateway, thereby achieving faster response times.

Although the intermediate modules are not assigned the control task, which is reserved for the OCC, it would be possible to place the system in a standby state from them if none of the OCCs were available. For this purpose, they are equipped with a screen that shows the status of their section and they store all of the alarm information in their local database (LDB).

The *control level* is composed of the OCCs, a bus for communications between the various intermediate modules and the OCCs, and a high-speed bus that enables database replication in real time. The route contains two OCCs, although only one of them will be in operational mode (able to perform actions), whilst the other will be in monitoring mode and will not be able to perform any actions. These concentrate the alarm warnings generated by all of the sensors along the route. Using acoustic and visual signals, these will display any possible alarms detected to the operator. The high-speed networks will be used to make periodic replicas of the OCCs databases (PDB), so that at any moment either of them will be able to take control of the network, if the situation so requires.

To facilitate network configuration and maintenance, each of the buses on the route has been assigned an IP address on a different network and the nodes connected to the same will have an address on this same network. Configuration of the nodes connected to the buses is performed automatically by multicast. Multicast packets are sent periodically over each bus. The nodes respond and identify themselves, and in this way the network configuration is known at all times.

As it is a distributed system, with a local time in each of the digital systems, the problem of clock synchronisation arises. This is dealt with by using an NTP server located on the control level [11].

4 Intelligent Fault Detection

The critical safety network designed, made up of the sensors, the communication system and the Operations and Control Centres, enables safety in a rail environment to be enhanced, but the possible operational faults that may be produced in the same, such as bus failure, out-of-order nodes or intermediate modules, etc., also need to be taken into account. It is thus vital to establish a fault detection system that is able to ascertain whether a certain element is out-of-order and, if so, take appropriate measures to ensure that it affects the operation of the communication system as little as possible.

As it is a distributed system covering hundreds of kilometres, it seems obvious that bus and digital systems monitoring should be performed using the network infrastructure and the TCP/IP protocol. By sending probe packets to each digital system and receiving the response, it will be possible to ascertain if these are operational. Moreover, if some packets do not reach their destination, it will be possible to deduce the existence of a fault in one of the sections of the bus.

In a preliminary implementation of the communication system, the network probe was implemented as a static task in each of the safety nodes, gateways and intermediate modules. The results of the probe were sent to the OCC, where they were displayed on screen, but it was still necessary for the operator to analyse them. It was then observed that it would be useful to add a result analysis system that would back up the operator's decision-making process. Thus, an intelligent diagnostic system has been included for this purpose.

Intelligent diagnostic systems enable the problem to be identified by analysing the symptoms observed, acting in a way similar to a human expert. The decision element (reasoner) can be based on any of the artificial intelligence techniques, such as neural networks, expert systems, induced learning systems, decision trees, etc. Said system was implemented in compliance with the AI-STATE standard that makes the decision system independent of the test system, and at the same time uses standard data and knowledge models.

4.1 The AI-STATE Standard

In November 2002, the definitive version of the IEEE 1232-2002 standard was published, titled AI-STATE (Artificial Intelligence and Service Tie to All Test Environments) [12], with the aim of providing a reference for the development of artificial intelligence applications in diagnostic systems. This standard unifies and extends a series that was started in 1995 with the release of the first standard, IEEE 1232-1995 [13], which defines the architecture. This was continued with the IEEE 1232.1-1997 standard [14], which defined the data and knowledge models, and IEEE 1232.2-1998 standard [15], which defined the software services for the diagnostic system.

AI-STATE defines a methodology to develop interoperable diagnostic systems, based on open architecture, that can easily include decision systems based on various artificial intelligence techniques and that generate reusable software. The architecture of a diagnostic system compatible with the standard is shown in Fig. 2.

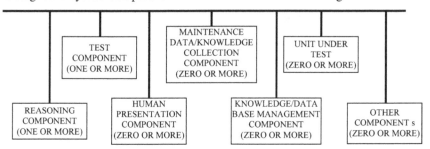

Fig. 2. AI-STATE Architecture

An AI-STATE application may be made up of any combination of these components, but at least one decision system and one test system must always exist, the other components being optional [16][17]. The reasoner will include the test sequence generators, the maintenance data analysers, the intelligent interfaces and the test programs. Each of the components may be found in different computers connected over a network, or all of them may be executed on the same computer.

The standard defines four types of model for use in diagnostic systems - common element model, fault tree model, diagnostic inference model, enhanced diagnostic inference model and dynamic context model. All of these are defined using the EXPRESS language [18]. The common element model (CEM) defines the basic information entities. The other three models represent data and knowledge specific to the application, taking as a basis the entities defined in the CEM. The last of these makes it possible to perform model management and operate the reasoner during the diagnostic process.

4.2 Application of the Diagnostic Standard on the Network Architecture

Fault detection in the communication system designed is performed using an intelligent diagnostic system conform with the AI-STATE standard. An additional computer has been connected on the control level of the network that implements the architecture shown in Fig. 3.

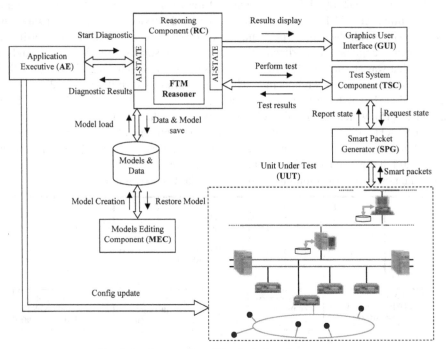

Fig. 3. Implementation of the fault detection system

The *Application Executive* (AE) sends a diagnostic execution request at 5-second intervals to the *Reasoning Component* (RC), invoking the services of the standard that have been implemented . This loads the network model from the database and sends the test vector to use to the *Test System Component* (TSC). This vector contains the list of elements and buses that should be probed, identifying them by their IP address. Testing of each of the elements of the communication system is performed by executing a test task that checks the execution status of the operation tasks and returns the result of the test to the TSC. In order to increase the maintainability of the system, the code of the test task is sent over the network every time that it is executed, employing active network techniques [19][20][21]. This enables the functionality of the test to be modified remotely, depending on the network model loaded or on the configuration. The test packets are routed through the gateways, in the same

way as the alarm, image and configuration packets. Based on the test vector, the
Smart Packet Generator (SPG) sends three active packets over each of the sections of
the network - the first to the safety nodes, the second to the two gateways and the
third to the intermediate module-. Each packet contains the IP addresses of the nodes
in which the task test should be executed. The result of execution of this task is returned to the SPG. The information returned will vary depending on the element in
which it has been executed. Thus, for example, the result of a gateway test is composed of the execution status of the operation task, the integrity of the four connected
buses, the current routing table and the time that the bus probe packets have taken to
traverse them.

The results of the test are returned to the RC, where they are evaluated using a
fault tree model, ascertaining the status of each element, as well as identifying possible faults in the communication buses. The result of the diagnosis is returned to the
AE and is displayed in the *Graphics User Interface* (GUI). The AE determines the
optimal route from each node to the intermediate module for the alarm packets, this
being the fastest route to an intermediate module. Based on the optimal routes, the
new routing tables are calculated for each gateway and these are sent to the same.
Therefore, although there may be a fault in one of the buses, it will still be possible to
route the alarm packets to the intermediate module, avoiding the faulty bus. At the
same time, the network status information is sent to the OCCs, where network monitoring is performed by the operator.

5 Results Obtained

Initially, a prototype of the network was implemented in the laboratory without intelligent diagnosis. The safety nodes, intermediate modules and gateways were implemented in VxWorks 5.4 on a Pentium IV. The test task code was stored statically in
each element. These tasks, as well as the operation tasks, were programmed in C. A
test network was designed in a laboratory using an ethernet for the data network and
setting up a section made up of two gateways, two safety nodes, two intermediate
modules and an OCC (Fig. 4).

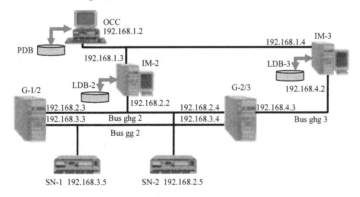

Fig. 4. Communication system employed in the trials

As no sensors were available, their operation was simulated from the safety node itself, which enabled operation in various scenarios to be tested.

One of the drawbacks presented by the initial development was that the status of the buses was not known *a priori* and, therefore, it was not known when the packets were not reaching the OCC. In this case, a certain amount of time was allowed for the packet acknowledgement to be received and, if this did not occur, the packet was sent via a different route, with the subsequent delay in the alarm's arrival.

In order to test the response of the communications network, several response time measurement tests were performed. Some of the results may be observed in Table 1.

Table 1. Delay measurements taken in the initial tests

ORIGIN	DESTINATION	TYPE	DELAY
SN-2	IM-2	Alarm packet	170 ms
SN-2	IM-2	Historical packet 10Kb	1300 ms
SN-2	IM-2	Image packet 64 Kb	1900 ms
SN-2	IM-2	Alarm packet	340 ms
SN-2	IM-3	Historical packet 10Kb	2600 ms
SN-2	IM-3	Image packet 64 Kb	3800 ms
SN-1	G-2/3	Alarm packet	170 ms
SN-1	G-2/3	Historical packet 10Kb	1300 ms
SN-1	G-2/3	Image packet 64 Kb	1900 ms
SN-1	G-2/3	Integrity packets	170 ms
G-2/3	IM-2	Alarm packet	170 ms
G-2/3	IM-2	Historical packet 10Kb	1300 ms
G-2/3	IM-2	Image packet 64 Kb	1900 ms
G-2/3	IM-2	Integrity packets 10 Kb	1300 ms
IM-3	G-2/3	Integrity packets	170 ms

The safety nodes send three types of operation packets - alarm, historical and image-. The alarm packets originate from one of the connected sensors and have a size of 256 bytes. The historical packets contain the list of alarms that have been produced in the sensors connected to this node, whilst the image packets are sent by the machine vision sensors and contain an image of the scene in JPEG format. In order to check the status of each element, integrity packets were sent, which enabled the operational status of each of them to be checked. The integrity information for each section was stored in the gateways, from where it could be queried by the intermediate modules.

The OCC was composed of a PC running the Microsoft Windows™ 2000 server operating system and an application written in Java. The application supplies the operator with three types of information:

– Alarm history: containing a list of the alarms produced, indicating the date, time, sensor generating the alarm, etc. The alarms originating from a machine vision sensor will also display the image sequence (Fig. 5).

- Integrity table: showing the status of the network and representing the information supplied by the diagnostic system. The operator will be able to observe whether any faults exist and to take appropriate measures.
- Routing table: enabling the routing tables for the gateways to be observed. Their function is designed to facilitate maintenance.

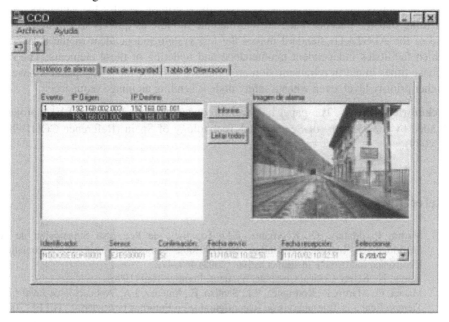

Fig. 5. OCC application window. Alarm history showing the information originating from a obstacle detection sensor in a station

The fault detection system implemented in this preliminary version (based on the integrity packets) was basic. In order to increase the reliability of the system, intelligent diagnosis was added, applying the AI-STATE standard. It was necessary to replace the operating system with Linux, as the execution environments for active networks, required for the test tasks, are implemented on this operating system. By coding the operation tasks on the new operating system, similar response times to those shown in Table 1 were obtained. Currently, fine-tuning of the prototype of the diagnostic system is underway, and implementation of the services necessary for the models employed in the reasoner is being concluded. Once concluded, the safety case wil will be made.

6 Conclusions

This paper proposes a fault-tolerant communication system for a network of safety sensors on railway lines. The architecture, which has been divided into sections and structured into three hierarchical levels, along with automatic configuration of the elements, facilitates extension and maintenance. The dual bus structure that links the safety nodes and intermediate modules, along with the gateways, enables correct operation to continue, even though faults may exist in the network, thereby increasing system availability and reliability. The intelligent diagnostic system, in addition to detecting faults, makes it possible to update the routing tables for the gateways, thus ensuring that the packets reach an intermediate module as quickly as possible. The use of the AI-STATE standard makes the test system independent of the reasoner, which facilitates independent maintenance and updating of these elements. The response times in alarm retransmission are bounded because the safety packets have a higher priority level, even when a safety node is sending an image sequence.

Acknowledgements. The paper has been produced as part of the TELEVÍA project funded by the Ministry of Science and Technology of Spain (Reference COO1999-AX049).

References

1   Martín, P., Mataix, C., Rodríguez, F.J.: Topología de Red para Supervisión de la Seguridad en Líneas Ferroviarias. SAAEI'2002 Seminario Anual de Automática Electrónica Industrial e Instrumentación. (2002) 469–472

2   Storey, N.: Safety-Critical Computer Systems. Prentice-Hall (1996)

3   Mataix, C., Martín, P., Rodríguez, F.J., Santiso, E., Jiménez, J.A.: Aplicación de Java™ en Tiempo Real a la Telesupervisión Reconfigurable en Entornos Ferroviarios. TELEC'2002 (2002)

4   Birman, K. P.: Building Secure and Reliable Network Applications. Department of Computer Science. Cornell University (1995)

5   Brunton, J., Digby, G., Doherty, A.: Network Management System Architectures for a Railway Environment. IEE Colloqium on Network Management System Architecture. 1996.

6   Zhou, F.B., Duta, M.D., Henry, M.P.: Remote Condition Monitoring for Railway Point Machine. Proceedings of the 2002 ASME/IEEE Joint Rail Conference. Washington DC. (2002)

7   Myers, L.F., Lovette, M., Kilgus, C.C., Giannini, J.A., Swanson, D.C.: A Java-Based Information System for Wayside Sensing and Control. Proceedings of the 1998 ASME/IEEE Joint Rail Road Conference. (1998)

8   Dy-Liacco, T.E.: Modern Control Centers and Computer Networking. IEEE Computer Application in Power, n° 10. (1994) 17–22

9   Roldan, M.C.S.-C., Alonso-Betanzos, A., Arias-Rodriguez, J.E.: Developing an electrical distribution monitoring system. IEEE Computer Applications in Power, Vol: 10 Issue: 1. (1997) 36–41

10   Matsumoto, M., Kitamura, S., Sato, M.: High assurance technologies for autonomous decentralized train control system. High Assurance Systems Engineering, Sixth IEEE International Symposium on (2001) 220–227

11   Mills, D.L.: Network Time Protocol (Version 3): Specification, Implementation and Analysis. Network Working Group Report RFC-1305. University of Delaware. (1992)

12 IEEE Std 1232–1995: IEEE Standard for Artificial Intelligence Exchange and Service Tie to All Test Environments (AI-STATE): Overview and Architecture, Piscataway, NJ: IEEE Standard Press (1995)

13 IEEE Std 1232.1–1997: IEEE Trail-Use Standard for Artificial Intelligence Exchange and Service Tie to All Test Environments (AI-STATE): Data and Knowledge Specification, Piscataway, NJ: IEEE Standard Press (1997)

14 IEEE Std 1232.2–1998: IEEE Trial-Use Standard for Artificial Intelligence Exchange and Service Tie to All Test Environments (AI-STATE): Service Specification, Piscataway, NJ: IEEE Standard Press (1998)

15 IEEE Std 1232–2002: IEEE Standard for Artificial Intelligence Exchange and Service Tie to All Test Environments (AI-STATE), Piscataway, NJ: IEEE Standard Press (2002)

16 Sheppard, J., Kaufman, M.: AI-ESTATE-the next generation. AUTOTESTCON '99. IEEE Systems Readiness Technology Conference. (1999) 11–18

17 Sheppard, J., Kaufman, M.: IEEE test and diagnostics standards. Digital Avionics Systems Conferences, 2000. Proceedings. DASC. The 19th , Volume: 2 (2000) 6B1/1 - 6B1/8

18 ISO 10303-11: Industrial Automatic Systems – Product Data Representation and Exchange Part 11: EXPRESS Language Reference Manual. (1992)

19 Tennenhouse, D.L., Wetherall, D.J.: Towards an Active Network Architecture. Proceedings of the DARPA Active Networks Conference and Exposition (DANCE'02) (2002) 2–15

20 Calvert, K.L., Bhattacharjee, S., Zegura, E., Sterbenz, J.: Directions in Active Networks. IEEE Communications Magazine , Vol 36 Issue 10, (1998) 72–78

21 Branden, R., Lindell, B., Berson, S. Faber, T.: The ASP EE: An Active Network Execution Environment. Proceedings of the DARPA Active Networks Conference and Exposition (DANCE'02) (2002) 238–254

Dependable Communication Synthesis for Distributed Embedded Systems[*]

Nagarajan Kandasamy[1], John P. Hayes[2], and Brian T. Murray[3]

[1]Institute for Software Integrated Systems, Vanderbilt University, Nashville, Tennessee, U.S.A
[2]Advanced Computer Architecture Lab., University of Michigan, Ann Arbor, Michigan, U.S.A
[3]The Delphi Corporation, Brighton, Michigan, U.S.A

Abstract. Embedded control applications such as drive-by-wire in cars require dependable interaction between various sensors, processors, and actuators. This paper addresses the design of low-cost communication networks guaranteeing to meet both the performance and fault-tolerance requirements of such distributed applications. We develop a fault-tolerant allocation and scheduling method which maps messages on to a minimum-cost multiple-bus system to ensure predictable inter-processor communication. The proposed method targets time-division multiple access (TDMA) communication protocols, and is applicable to protocols such as FlexRay and TTP which have recently emerged as networking standards for embedded systems such as automobile controllers. Finally, we present a case study involving some advanced automotive control applications to show that our approach uses the available network bandwidth efficiently to achieve jitter-free message transmission.

1 Introduction

Embedded computer systems are being increasingly used in cost-sensitive consumer products such as automobiles to replace safety-critical mechanical and hydraulic systems [2]. Drive-by-wire is one example where traditional hydraulic steering and braking are replaced by a networked microprocessor-controlled electro-mechanical system [1]. Sensors measure the steering-wheel angle and brake-pedal position, and processors calculate the desired road-wheel and braking parameters which are then applied via electro-mechanical actuators at the wheels. Other computerized vehicle-control applications including adaptive cruise control, collision avoidance, and autonomous driving are also being developed. These applications will be realized as real-time distributed systems requiring dependable interaction between sensors, processors, and actuators. This paper addresses the design of low-cost communication networks to meet both the performance and fault-tolerance requirements of such applications.

Related work in communication synthesis for distributed embedded systems belongs in two broad categories–those that assume a fixed network topology and schedule messages to meet deadlines [3] [4] [5], and those that synthesize a topology satisfying message deadlines [6] [8]. Ortega and Boriello [3] assume a fixed network topology using the controller area network (CAN) protocol and schedule messages by assigning appropriate priorities to help meet their deadlines. Abdelzaher and Shin [4] present an

*This research was supported by a contract from The Delphi Corporation.

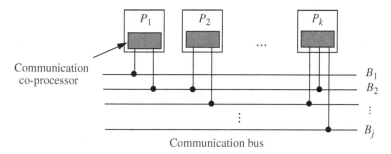

Fig. 1. An example multiple-bus system where each processor connects to a subset of the communication buses

off-line algorithm which schedules both tasks and messages in combined fashion to minimize the overall schedule length. Rhodes and Wolf [7] assign priorities to processors and schedule messages on a single communication bus using fixed priority, or round-robin arbitration for network access. A network topology satisfying message deadlines can also be constructed from application requirements. Given task graphs corresponding to embedded applications, Yen and Wolf [6] estimate the communication delay for inter-processor messages and schedule them on the minimum number of buses, while [8] generates point-to-point communication links.

Unlike [3] [4] [5] which assume a given topology, the approach proposed in this paper synthesizes the network topology from application requirements. Moreover, while synthesis methods such as [6] assume an underlying CAN communication protocol and arbitrate bus access using message (processor) priorities, we target TDMA communication protocols where processors are allotted transmission slots according to a static, periodic, and global communication schedule [9]. Recently, TDMA protocols such as TTP [10] and FlexRay [11] have emerged as possible networking standards for an important class of embedded systems–automobiles.

Rather than generate arbitrary networks, we restrict the topology space to multiple-bus systems. Figure 1 shows an example where each processor P_i connects to a subset of the communication buses. A co-processor handles message communication without interfering with task execution on P_i. A multiple-bus topology allows fault-tolerant message allocation. Also, since communication protocols for the embedded systems of interest are typically implemented over low-cost physical media, individual buses have limited bandwidth; multiple buses may be needed to accommodate the message load.

Given a set of distributed applications represented by task graphs $\{G_i\}$, our approach constructs a low-cost communication network that satisfies the performance and fault-tolerance requirements of each G_i. Messages are allocated and scheduled on the minimum number of buses $\{B_i\}$ where each B_i has a specified bandwidth. We now summarize the major features of our approach:

- It assumes a multi-rate system where each graph G_i may have a different execution period $period(G_i)$.
- It targets a generic TDMA communication protocol.

Procedure FT-DESIGN($\{G_i\}$, $\{P_i\}$) /* $\{G_i\}$:= Task graphs, $\{P_i\}$:= Processors */
    for (each G_i)
        Distribute G_i's deadline to obtain the scheduling range $[r_i, d_i]$ for each task T_i;
    for (each k-FT message m_i) **begin**   /* Obtain the initial network topology */
        Determine m_i's transmission delay $tdelay(m_i)$;
        Allocate each copy of m_i to a separate bus B_j;
    end;
    for (each task T_i) **begin**   /* Determine task schedulability */
        w_i := Worst-case response time of T_i on its allocated processor P_i;
        if ($w_i + tdelay(m_i) > d_i - r_i$) **return** $\varnothing$; /* Solution is infeasible */
    end;
    s := **CLUSTER** ($\{m_i\}$);   /* Reduce topology cost via message clustering */
    Allocate each cluster C_i in s to a separate bus B_j;
    return $\{B_j\}$;   /* Return the set of communication buses */

Fig. 2. The overall approach to fault-tolerant communication network synthesis

- It supports fault-tolerant message communication by establishing redundant transmission paths between processors.

Finally, using some representative automotive control applications, we show that the proposed method guarantees jitter-free and predictable message transmission.

The rest of this paper is organized as follows. Section 2 presents an overview of the proposed approach, while Section 3 discusses some preliminaries. The message allocation method is developed in Section 4, and Section 5 presents the case study. We briefly discuss some related issues and conclude the paper in Section 6.

2 Design Overview

As the primary objective, we construct a network topology meeting the fault-tolerance and performance goals of the embedded applications. The secondary objective is to minimize hardware cost in terms of communication buses. An iterative method is developed where a feasible network topology satisfying performance goals is first obtained. Its cost is then reduced via a series of steps which minimize the number of buses by appropriately grouping (clustering) messages while preserving the feasibility of the original solution. Since clustering is an NP-complete problem [12], we use heuristics to obtain a feasible solution.

Figure 2 shows the main steps of the proposed heuristic approach. For a given allocation of tasks to processors, FT-DESIGN accepts a set of task graphs $\{G_i\}$ and processors $\{P_i\}$ as inputs, and returns as output, a low-cost network topology comprising identical buses $\{B_i\}$. Redundant routes are provided for messages with specific fault-tolerance requirements; for a *k-fault-tolerant* (*k*-FT) message m_i, k replicas or copies are allocated to separate buses. The network is designed assuming a generic TDMA protocol, and can accommodate specific cases such as TTP and FlexRay after some modification.

We assume that each task graph G_i must meet its deadline by the end of its period $period(G_i)$. First, the graph deadline is distributed over its tasks to generate a scheduling range $[r_i, d_i]$ for each task T_i where r_i and d_i denote its release time and deadline, respectively. The initial network topology is obtained by simply allocating each message m_i to a separate bus. Without bus contention, m_i's transmission delay is given by the message size and bus bandwidth. The overall solution is feasible if all tasks complete before their respective deadlines. Section 3 discusses these initial steps in greater detail.

The number of communication buses in the initial solution is then minimized via an iterative message clustering procedure which groups multiple messages on bus B_i. A message m_i is grouped with an existing cluster $C_j = \{m_i\}$ if the resulting communication schedule satisfies the following requirements: (1) No two replicas of a k-FT message are allocated to C_j. (2) All messages belonging to C_j continue to meet their deadlines. (3) The duration (length) of the communication schedule corresponding to C_j does not exceed a designer-specified threshold; if a dedicated co-processor handles message communication as in Fig. 1, the schedule must be compact enough to fit within the available memory. (4) The schedule provides jitter-free message transmission, where *jitter* is the uncertainty in the time intervals between successive transmissions of a message m_i. The proposed clustering approach also uses bus bandwidth efficiently by sharing or re-using transmission slots between multiple messages whenever possible. Each message cluster is allocated to a separate bus in the final topology. Section 4 describes this procedure in greater detail.

3 Preliminaries

This section shows how to obtain the initial solution where tasks are assigned deadlines and scheduled on processors, and messages allocated to separate communication buses.

Deadline Assignment. Initially, only entry and exit tasks having no predecessors and successors, respectively, have their release times and deadlines fixed. To schedule an intermediate task T_i in the task graph, however, its scheduling range $[r_i, d_i]$ must first be obtained. This is termed the *deadline assignment problem* where the deadline D_i of the task graph G_i must be distributed over each intermediate task such that all tasks are feasibly scheduled on their respective processors. Deadline distribution is NP-complete and various heuristics have been proposed to solve it. We use the approach of Natale and Stankovic [14] which maximizes the slack added to each task in graph G_i while still satisfying its deadline D_i. Their heuristic is simple, and for general task graphs, its performance compares favourably with other heuristics [13].

We now describe the deadline distribution algorithm. Entry and exit tasks in the graph are first assigned release times and deadlines. A path $path_i$ through G_i comprises one or more tasks $\{T_i\}$; the slack available for distribution to these tasks is $slack_i = D_i - \sum c_i$ where D_i is the deadline of $path_i$ and c_i the execution time of a task T_i along this path. The distribution heuristic in [14] maximizes the minimum slack added to each T_i along $path_i$ by dividing $slack_i$ equally among tasks. During each iteration through G_i, $path_i$ minimizing $slack_i / n$, where n denotes the number of tasks along $path_i$, is chosen and the corresponding slack added to each task along that path. The deadlines (release times) of the predecessors (successors) of tasks belonging to $path_i$

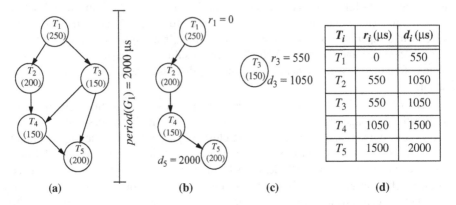

Fig. 3. (a) Example task graph; (b) and (c) paths selected for deadline distribution, and (d) the resulting scheduling ranges for each task

are updated. Tasks along $path_i$ are then removed from the original graph, and the above process is repeated until all tasks are assigned release times and deadlines.

We use the graph in Fig. 3(a) to illustrate the above procedure. First, the release time of entry task T_1 and the deadline of exit task T_5 are set to $r_1 = 0$ µs and $d_5 = 2000$ µs, respectively. Next, we select the path $T_1T_2T_4T_5$ shown in Fig. 3(b); the total execution time of tasks along this path is 800 µs, and as per the heuristic, a slack of $(2000 - 800)/4 = 300$ µs is distributed to each task. Once their release times and deadlines are fixed, these tasks are removed from the graph. Figure 3(c) shows the remaining path comprising only task T_3–it has its release time and deadline fixed by T_1 and T_4, respectively. Figure 3(d) shows the resulting scheduling range for each task.

Task Scheduling. Once the scheduling ranges of tasks in the graph are fixed, each T_i may now be considered independent with release time r_i and deadline d_i, and scheduled as such. To tackle multi-rate systems, we use *fixed-priority scheduling* where tasks are first assigned priorities according to their periods [15], and at any time instant, the processor executes the highest-priority ready task. Again, the schedule is feasible if all tasks finish before their deadlines; Feasibility analysis of schedules using simple closed-form processor-utilization-based tests has been extensively studied under fixed-priority scheduling [15]. However, in addition to feasibility, we also require a precise estimate of task T_i's response time w_i, given by the time interval between T_i's release and finish times; the response time is used in the next stage of our algorithm to determine the message delays to be satisfied by the network.

For multi-rate task graphs, the schedules on individual processors are simulated for a duration equal to the least common multiple (LCM) of the graph periods [16]. Since this duration evaluates all possible interactions between tasks belonging to the different graph iterations, the worst-case response time for each task T_i is obtained. Figure 4(a) shows a simple multi-rate system comprising two task graphs with periods 2000 µs and 3000 µs; Figs. 4(b) and 4(c) show the task allocation and scheduling ranges, respectively. Figure 4(d) shows the corresponding schedule for 6000 µs–the LCM of the graph periods. Task response times within this time interval are shown in Fig. 4(e). Multiple

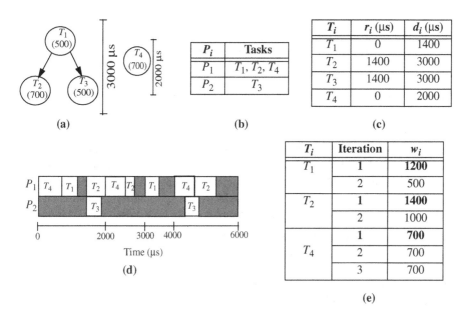

Fig. 4. (a) An example multi-rate system, (b) task-to-processor allocation, (c) task scheduling ranges, (d) task schedule for the duration of the least common multiple of the task periods, and (e) the response times of different task iterations over the simulated time interval

iterations of a task are evaluated to obtain its worst-case response time. For example, in Fig. 4(e), the first iteration of tasks T_1, T_2, and T_4 (in bold) has the maximum response time among the iterations within the given time duration. The task scheduling on processors is successful if, for each task T_i, $w_i \leq d_i - r_i$. However, for the overall solution to be feasible, all messages must also meet their deadlines.

Initial Network Topology. A k-FT message m_i sent by task T_i has deadline $delay(m_i) = d_i - r_i - w_i$ where w_i denotes T_i's worst-case response time. Initially, the network topology allocates a separate communication bus for each message copy. Therefore, in this topology, m_i experiences no network contention and its transmission delay is $size(m_i) \times B_j^{speed}$ where $size(m_i)$ and B_j^{speed} denote the message size in bits and bus bandwidth in Kb/s, respectively. The solution is feasible if, for each m_i, $delay(m_i)$ is greater than the corresponding transmission delay.

4 Fault-Tolerant Message Clustering

We now develop a message clustering approach to reduce the cost of the initial network topology obtained in Section 3. Multiple messages are grouped on a single bus while preserving the feasibility of the original solution. The fault-tolerance requirement of each k-FT message is also satisfied.

First, we briefly review message transmission in a generic TDMA communication protocol. As an example, we choose the FlexRay protocol currently under development by a consortium of automotive companies to provide predictable and high speed message communication for distributed control applications [11]. Figure 5 shows a a typi-

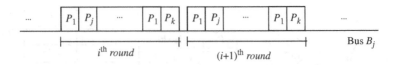

Fig. 5. A TDMA-based allocation of transmission slots to processors on communication bus B_j

cal TDMA scheme where messages are transmitted according to a static, periodic, and global communication schedule called a *TDMA round*. Each processor P_i is allotted one or more sending slots during a round comprising a fixed number of identical-sized slots–both size and number of slots per round are fixed by the system designer and determine the round duration or period. Though successive rounds are constructed identically, the messages sent by individual processors may vary during a given round.

Clustering Algorithm. We now state the fault-tolerant message clustering problem as follows. Given the communication deadline $delay(m_i)$ for each k-FT message m_i sent by processor P_j, construct TDMA rounds on the minimum number of communication buses such that during any time interval corresponding to $delay(m_i)$, P_j is allotted a sufficient number of transmission slots to transmit m_i.

We treat each m_i as a periodic message with period $period(m_i)$ equal to its deadline $delay(m_i)$ and generate message clusters $\{C_j\}$, such that the corresponding TDMA round $round(C_j)$ satisfies the constraints previously introduced in Section 2: (1) No two replicas of a k-FT message m_i are allocated to C_j. (2) the duration of $round(C_j)$ does not exceed a designer-specified threshold. (3) the slots within $round(C_j)$ provide jitter-free message transmission, i.e., the time interval between successive sending slots for a message m_i equals its period.

Each message cluster C_j is allocated to a separate communication bus in the final network topology. Our method also makes efficient use of bus bandwidth by minimizing the number of transmission slots needed to satisfy message deadlines within a TDMA round. This is achieved by reusing slots among the messages sent by a processor whenever possible. The following discussion describes the clustering procedure in greater detail. We assume an upper bound on TDMA-round duration provided by the designer in terms of the maximum number of slots n_{max} and slot duration Δ_{slot}. Typically, the choice of n_{max} depends on the memory available within the communication co-processor such as the number of transmit and receive buffers. Each transmission slot $slot(i)$ within the round has duration $\Delta_{slot} = \min_i\{size(m_i)\} \times b_j^{speed}$ μs. The message period $delay(m_i)$, originally expressed in time units, is now discretized as $\lfloor delay(m_i)/\Delta_{slot}\rfloor$ and expressed in terms of transmission-slot intervals. To simplify the notation, we use $delay(m_i)$ to denote this discrete quantity from here on.

The clustering procedure in Fig. 6 takes as input messages $\{m_i\}$ sorted in terms of increasing $period(m_i)$ and returns a set of message clusters where each C_j is allocated to a separate communication bus. Given a set of clusters $\{C_j\}$ and a k-FT message m_i, we first obtain all feasible message to cluster allocations by grouping m_i with C_j and generating $round(C_j \cup m_i)$. New clusters are created if needed to accommodate all copies of m_i. Also, if for the k-FT message m_i, n feasible message-cluster allocations are obtained, where $n > k$, then the k best solutions are chosen based on bandwidth-utiliza-

---

Procedure CLUSTER(S_{msg}) /* S_{msg} := Messages $\{m_i\}$ sorted by increasing period */
$\quad S_{clust}$:= $\varnothing$;   /* Initialize set of message clusters */
$\quad$ **while** $(S_{msg} \neq \varnothing)$ **begin**
$\qquad m_i$:= k-FT message in S_{msg} with minimum period;
$\qquad S_{cand}$:= $\varnothing$;   /* Initialize set of possible candidate clusters */
$\qquad$ **for** (each compatible cluster C_j in S_{clust}) /* Allocate k-FT message to clusters */
$\qquad\quad$ **if** (**ALLOC**(C_j, m_i) returns a feasible $round(C_j)$) S_{cand} := $S_{cand} \cup C_j$;
$\qquad n_{cand}$:= Number of clusters in set S_{cand};
$\qquad$ **if** $(n_{cand} < k)$ **begin** /* New clusters are needed to accommodate copies of m_i */
$\qquad\quad S_{clust}$:= $S_{clust} \cup S_{cand}$;
$\qquad\quad$ Allocate m_i to $(k - n_{cand})$ new clusters and add them to S_{clust};
$\qquad$ **end**;
$\qquad$ **if** $(n_{cand} \geq k)$ **begin**   /* Select the best k clusters in terms of slot reuse */
$\qquad\quad$ Sort clusters in S_{cand} in terms of decreasing slot reuse;
$\qquad\quad$ Select the first k clusters in the sorted set S_{cand} and add to S_{clust};
$\qquad\quad$ Remove m_i from the non-selected clusters;
$\qquad$ **end**;
$\qquad S_{msg}$:= $S_{msg} - m_i$;
$\quad$ **end**;

Fig. 6. The clustering algorithm generating the reduced-cost network topology

tion efficiency–the exact evaluation criterion is discussed later this chapter. The computational complexity of the clustering procedure is $O(n^3)$ where n is the number of messages; the outer **while** loop iterates through all n messages, and during each iteration, ALLOC explores all message to cluster allocations, a process of complexity $O(n^2)$.

Transmission-Slot Allocation. Given a message cluster C_j and m_i, the ALLOC procedure generates a feasible TDMA round for the new allocation $C_j \cup m_i$. Allocation of messages to multiple buses is related to *bin-packing* where fixed-size objects (messages) are packed into a bin (round) of finite size while minimizing the number of bins. The general bin-packing problem is NP-complete and heuristics are typically used to obtain a solution [17].

An important requirement during slot allocation for the messages in cluster C_j is jitter-free communication. Unpredictable delay or jitter during transmission may lead to missed message deadlines. Figure 7(a) shows multiple TDMA rounds corresponding to messages m_1 and m_2 with periods $delay(m_1) = 2$ and $delay(m_2) = 5$, respectively. Transmission slots are allocated in first-fit (FF) fashion where messages are ordered in terms of increasing period and the first available slots allocated to each m_i within the round. Though this allocation satisfies the periodicity requirements of m_1 and m_2, it results in timing jitter–the minimum and maximum distances between two successive slots for m_2 are 4 and 6 slots, respectively. Clearly, this results in a timing violation. Therefore, a minimum-distance constraint between two successive transmission slots for m_2 must also be satisfied during allocation. Fortunately, jitter-free transmission can be achieved by appropriately modifying the message periods; Fig. 7(b) shows a jitter-free slot allocation for both messages when m_2's period is modified to 4 slots.

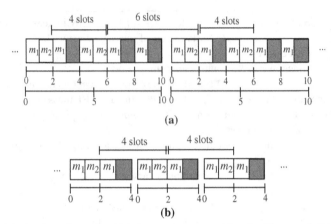

Fig. 7. (a) A clustering of multiple messages resulting in jitter, and **(b)** jitter-free slot allocation by appropriately modifying message periods

The above discussion suggests that the original message periods need modification prior to allocating slots within the TDMA round. Clearly, message periods may be modified in a variety of ways; we adopt a strategy where the periods of all messages within a cluster C_j are constrained to be harmonic multiples of each other. Two messages m_i and m_j have harmonically-related periods if $period(m_i) = 2^k \times period(m_j)$. A similar concept is used in task scheduling in multi-processors where tasks having harmonic periods are allocated to the same processor to increase utilization and minimize completion-time jitter [18] [19]. In [20], we formally prove that allocating messages with harmonically-related periods in FF fashion within C_j guarantees jitter-free transmission. It also maximizes bus utilization and results in a shorter TDMA-round duration thereby reducing the memory requirements of the communication co-processor. Let $P_{min} = \min_i\{period(m_i)\}$ denote the smallest period among cluster C_j's messages. Then, when allocating a new message m_i to C_j, we select its period to be the maximum integer $period(m_i) \leq n_{max}$ satisfying $2^k \cdot P_{min} \leq delay(m_i) < 2^{k+1} \cdot P_{min}$.

Figure 8 shows the ALLOC procedure which accepts an existing message cluster C_j and a message m_i and generates a feasible TDMA round (if possible) for the new allocation $C_j \cup m_i$. As discussed above, message m_i's period $period(m_i)$ is first transformed to relate harmonically to those in C_j and the messages are sorted in increasing period order. The duration of the new round $round(C_j \cup m_i)$ is $P_{max} = \max_i\{period(m_i)\}$. To allocate transmission slots for message m_i, ALLOC divides $round(C_j)$ into k disjoint time intervals $\{I_k\}$ where $k = P_{max}/period(m_i)$ and I_k has duration $period(m_i)$. Transmission slots are then allotted within each interval using the FF packing strategy. Jitter-free transmission of each message m_i is guaranteed if the allotted transmission slots occur in the same positions within each interval I_k. Again, the interested reader is referred to [20] where we formally prove that ALLOC generates a communication schedule guaranteeing jitter-free message transmission.

Procedure ALLOC (C_j, m_i) /* C_j := Message cluster; m_i := Message */
   S_{msg} := Set of messages $\{C_j \cup m_i\}$ sorted in increasing period order;
   Create an empty TDMA round *round*(s) with $p_{max} = \max_i\{period(m_i)\}$ slots;
   while $(S_{msg} \neq \varnothing)$ **begin**
      m_i := Message with shortest period in S_{msg};
      $k = p_{max}/period(m_i)$;   /* k := Number of intervals */
      Divide *round*(S_{msg}) into k intervals $\{I_k\}$, each of duration $period(m_i)$;
      $n := \lceil size(m_i)/\Delta_{slot}\rceil$; /* Number of slots needed to accommodate m_i */
      for (each interval I_k) **begin**
         if (n free slots are unavailable) **return** $\varnothing$; /* Allocation is infeasible */
         Allocate n slots within I_k to message m_i in first-fit (FF) fashion;
      end;
   end;
   return *round*(S_{msg}); /* Return the feasible allocation */

Fig. 8. The transmission-slot allocation procedure

Transmission-Slot Reuse. During clustering, each message m_i is treated as periodic with period $period(m_i)$. However, if the task T_i transmitting m_i does not execute at that rate, then the bus bandwidth is over-utilized. We can improve bandwidth utilization by reusing the transmission slots allotted to processor P_k among multiple messages. Let $\{m_i\}$ be the set of messages sent by the processor within the message cluster C_j. Now, assume message m_{i+1}, also transmitted by P_k, to be allotted slots within *round*(C_j). Each message m_i is allotted a number of transmission slots n_i within the time interval $period(m_{i+1})$ in *round*(C_j). If n_{reuse} denotes the number of slots available for reuse by m_{i+1} with the time interval $period(m_{i+1})$, then

$$n_{reuse} = \sum_i n_i - \sum_i \left\lceil \frac{period(m_i)}{period(T_i)}\right\rceil \times n_i$$

where $period(T_i)$ denotes the period of task T_i transmitting message m_i. Therefore, the number of transmission slots to be allotted to message m_{i+1} is $\lceil size(m_{i+1})/\Delta_{slot}\rceil - n_{reuse}$. Given clusters $\{C_j\}$ and the message m_{i+1} to be allocated to one, CLUSTER explores all possible cluster-message allocation scenarios. Slot reuse is used as the deciding factor in selecting the best allocation since the cluster allocation resulting in maximum reuse minimizes the bandwidth utilization.

5   Case Study

We now illustrate the proposed network construction method using some advanced automotive control applications as examples. These include adaptive cruise control (ACC), electric power steering (EPS), and traction control (TC), and are detailed in Figs. 9(a)-(c). The ACC application automatically maintains a safe following distance between two cars, while EPS uses an electric motor to provide necessary steering assistance to the driver. The TC application actively stabilizes the vehicle to maintain its intended path even under slippery road conditions. These applications demand timely interaction between distributed sensors, processors, and actuators, i.e., have specific end-to-end deadlines, and therefore require a dependable communication network. Fig-

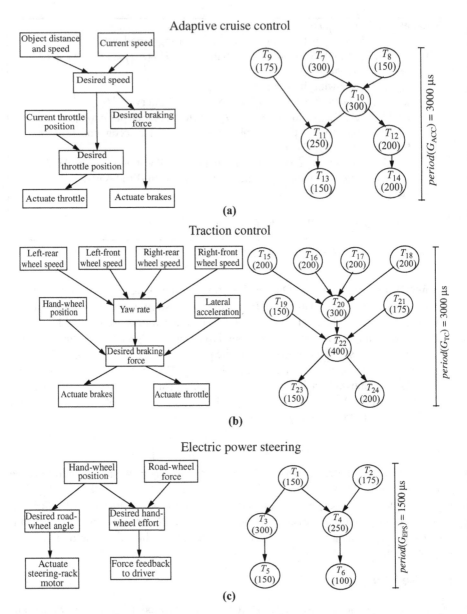

Fig. 9. The (a) adaptive cruise control, (b) traction control, and (c) electric power steering applications, and the corresponding flow-graph representations

ure 10(a) shows the physical architecture of the system where sensors and actuators are directly connected to the network and the task-to-processor allocation, while Fig. 10(b) summarizes the various message attributes affecting network topology generation. We assume 1-FT messages throughout. Columns 2 and 3 list the sending and receiving tasks for each message and the message size $size(m_i)$ in bits, respectively, while columns 4 and 5 list the communication delay $delay(m_i)$ for messages in µs, and the trans-

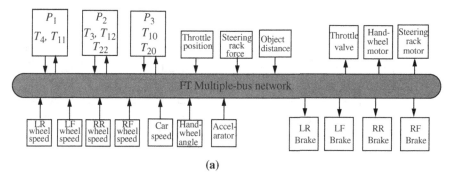

(a)

Message m_i	(Sender, receiver)	size(m_i) (bits)	delay(m_i) (μs)	delay(m_i) (slot intervals)
m_1	(T_1, T_3) (T_1, T_4)	12	300	6
m_2	(T_2, T_4)	12	275	5
m_3	(T_3, T_5)	20	300	6
m_4	(T_4, T_6)	12	350	7
m_5	(T_7, T_{10})	12	500	10
m_6	(T_8, T_{10})	12	650	6
m_7	(T_9, T_{11})	10	1425	28
m_8	(T_{10}, T_{11}) (T_{10}, T_{12})	12	500	10
m_9	(T_{11}, T_{13})	10	500	10
m_{10}	(T_{12}, T_{14})	10	500	10
m_{11}	(T_{15}, T_{20})	12	475	9
m_{12}	(T_{16}, T_{20})	12	475	9
m_{13}	(T_{17}, T_{20})	12	475	9
m_{14}	(T_{18}, T_{20})	12	475	9
m_{15}	(T_{19}, T_{22})	10	1100	22
m_{16}	(T_{20}, T_{22})	22	275	5
m_{17}	(T_{21}, T_{22})	20	1025	20
m_{18}	(T_{22}, T_{23}) (T_{22}, T_{24})	12	650	6

(b)

Fig. 10. (a) The physical architecture including task-to-processor allocation, and (b) the message attributes required for network generation

mission-slot intervals. These delay values are obtained by first assigning deadlines to tasks and then performing a schedulability analysis on their respective processors–a topic discussed previously in Section 3.

We assume a version of the FlexRay communication protocol having a bandwidth of 250 kb/s and a minimum width of 50 μs for the transmission slots in a TDMA round.

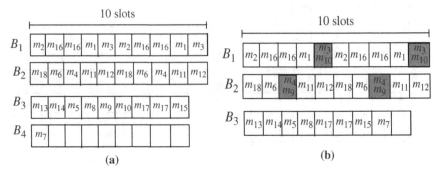

Fig. 11. Communication schedules generated by ALLOC (a) without slot reuse, and (b) with reuse where the shared transmission slots are shaded

Figure 11(a) shows the communication schedules generated on buses B_1, B_2, B_3, and B_4 without reusing transmission slots. We now show how to share transmission slots between appropriate messages and reduce the number of buses. Consider messages m_3 and m_{10} sent by tasks T_3 and T_{12}, respectively, where both tasks are allocated to processor P_2. Message m_3's period is set to its transmission deadline of 300 µs (5 slots) when constructing the TDMA round. Note, however, that the EPS application comprising task T_3 has a 1500 µs period; this also corresponds to the time interval between successive m_3 transmissions. Therefore, in Fig. 11(a), m_3's transmission needs only one of two allocated slots on bus B_1. (Task T_3, however, may request m_3's transmission anytime during a TDMA round). Message m_{10} with a period of 10 slots can use the remaining slot. Figure 11(b) shows the schedules obtained by ALLOC with slot reuse; the shared slots between messages $\{m_4, m_9\}$ and $\{m_3, m_{10}\}$, transmitted by processors P_1 and P_2, respectively, are shaded. Also, slot reuse eliminates the bus B_4 in Fig. 11(a).

When TDMA slots are shared between messages sent by a processor, as in Fig. 11(b), the communication co-processor must correctly schedule their transmission, i.e., given a slot, decide which message to transmit in it. Though this paper does not address message-scheduling logic, an earliest-deadline first approach seems appropriate.

6   Conclusion

This paper has addressed the design of low-cost TDMA communication networks for distributed embedded applications. We have developed a fault-tolerant clustering method which allocates and schedules k-FT messages on the minimum number of buses to provide jitter-free and predictable transmission. Finally, a case study involving some advanced automotive control applications was discussed and it was shown that the efficient use of communication bandwidth by sharing transmission slots among multiple messages can reduce network topology cost.

This paper does not address the design and implementation of the message scheduler on the co-processors. The message scheduler is responsible for transmitting and receiving messages in their respective slots. We also do not address the fault-tolerant allocation of tasks to processors. The message allocation scheme can be easily incorporated as a subfunction into an overall scheme that deals with both the problems. The above issues will be investigated as part of future work.

References

[1]   E. A. Bretz, "By-Wire Cars Turn the Corner," *IEEE Spectrum*, vol. 38, no. 4, pp. 68–73, April 2001.

[2]   G. Leen and D. Heffernan, "Expanding Automotive Electronic Systems," *IEEE Computer*, vol. 35, no. 1, pp. 88–93, Jan. 2002.

[3]   R. B. Ortega and G. Borriello, "Communication Synthesis for Distributed Embedded Systems," *Proc. Intl. Conf. Computer-Aided Design (ICCAD)*, pp. 437–444, 1998.

[4]   T. F. Abdelzaher and K. G. Shin, "Combined Task and Message Scheduling in Distributed Real-Time Systems," *IEEE Trans. Parallel & Distributed Syst.*, vol. 10, no. 11, pp. 1179–1191, Nov. 1999.

[5]   A. Doboli, P. Eles, Z. Peng, and P. Pop, "Scheduling with Bus Access Optimization for Distributed Embedded Systems," *IEEE Trans. VLSI Syst.*, vol. 8, no. 5, pp. 472–491, Oct. 2000.

[6]   T-Y. Yen and W. Wolf, "Communication Synthesis for Distributed Embedded Systems," *Proc. Intl. Conf. Computer-Aided Design (ICCAD)*, pp. 288–294, 1995.

[7]   D. L. Rhodes and W. Wolf, "Co-Synthesis of Heterogeneous Multiprocessor Systems using Arbitrated Communication," *Proc. Intl. Conf. Computer-Aided Design (ICCAD)*, pp. 339–342, 1999.

[8]   S. Prakash and A. C. Parker, "Synthesis of Application-Specific Multiprocessor Architectures," *Proc. ACM/IEEE Design Automation Conference*, pp. 8–13, 1991.

[9]   H. Kopetz, *Real-Time Systems: Design Principles for Distributed Embedded Applications*, Kluwer Academic Publishers, Boston, 1997.

[10] H. Kopetz, "TTP - A Time-Triggered Protocol for Fault-Tolerant Real-Time Systems," *Proc. IEEE Fault-Tolerant Computing Symp.*, pp. 524–533, 1993.

[11] J. Berwanger et al., "FlexRay - The Communication System for Advanced Automotive Control Systems," *Proc. SAE World Congress*, Paper: 2001-01-0676, 2001.

[12] W. H. Wolf, "An Architectural Co-Synthesis Algorithm for Distributed, Embedded Computing Systems," *IEEE Trans. VLSI Systems*, vol. 5, no. 2, pp. 218–229, Jun. 1997.

[13] B. Kao and H. Garcia-Molina, "Deadline Assignment in a Distributed Soft Real-Time System," *IEEE Trans. Parallel and Distributed Syst.*, vol. 8, no. 12, pp. 1268–1274, Dec. 1997.

[14] M. D. Natale and J. A. Stankovic, "Dynamic End-to-End Guarantees in Distributed Real-Time Systems," *Proc. Real-Time Systems Symp.*, pp. 216–227, 1994.

[15] C. L. Liu and J. Layland, "Scheduling Algorithms for Multiprogramming in a Hard Real-Time Environment," *J. ACM*, vol. 24, pp. 46–61, 1973.

[16] X. Hu, J. G. D'Ambrosio, B. T. Murray, and D-L. Tang, "Codesign of Architectures for Automotive Powertrain Modules," *IEEE Micro*, vol. 14, no. 4, pp. 17–25, Aug. 1994.

[17] D. S. Johnson, "Fast Algorithms for Bin Packing," *J. Computer & System Sciences*, vol. 3, no. 3, pp. 272–314, 1974.

[18] K-J. Lin and A. Herkert, "Jitter Control in Time-Triggered Systems," *Proc. Hawaii Intl. Conf. System Sciences*, pp. 451–459, 1996.

[19] C-C. Han, K-J. Lin, and C-J. Hou, "Distance-Constrained Scheduling and its Applications to Real-Time Systems," *IEEE Trans. Computers*, vol. 45, no. 7, pp. 814–826, July 1996.

[20] N. Kandasamy, *Design of Low-Cost Dependable Systems for Distributed Embedded Applications*, Ph.D. Thesis, University of Michigan, 2003.

Enhancing Software Safety by Fault Trees: Experiences from an Application to Flight Critical SW

Wolfgang Weber[1], Heidemarie Tondok[1], and Michael Bachmayer[2]

[1] EADS Military Aircraft, FCS Safety,
81663 Munich, Germany
{Wolfgang.P.Weber, Heidemarie.Tondok}@m.eads.net
[2] Bachmayer GmbH, Wernstorferstr. 46,
84036 Landshut, Germany
Michael.Bachmayer@bachmayer-gmbh.de

Abstract. The fault tree analysis is a well established method in system safety and reliability assessment. We transferred the principles of this technique to an assembler code analysis, regarding any incorrect output of the software as the undesired top-level event. Starting from the instructions providing the outputs and tracing back to all instructions contributing to these outputs a hierarchical system of references is generated that may graphically be represented as a fault tree. To cope with the large number of relations in the code, a tool suite has been developed, which automatically creates these references and checks for unfulfilled preconditions of instructions. The tool was applied to the operational software of an inertial measurement unit, which provides safety critical signals for artificial stabilization of an aircraft. The method and its implementation as a software tool is presented and the benefits, surprising results, and limitations we have experienced are discussed.

1 Introduction

Fault tree analysis is a powerful and widely used technique for the identification of potential process hazards in a system [1]. Its purpose is to find all possible combinations of causes and faults leading to an undesired event and to represent these combinations and dependencies graphically by means of a tree like structure. The fault tree is a depiction of the logical interrelationships of basic events that may lead to a particular hazardous condition.

The principles of this method have been transferred from system to software analysis by Leveson et al. [2], [3], [4], who introduced templates for the translation of Ada language elements into fault tree building blocks. In the meanwhile, Software Fault Tree Analysis (SFTA) has been used in real software projects on all development stages as requirements analysis, design and coding [5], [6]. It serves as an additional method to gain confidence about the absence of safety critical errors in the software. Tools have been developed that assist fault tree generation from design languages (UML) [7], [8], modeling languages (Matlab/Simulink) [9], or programming

S. Anderson et al. (Eds.): SAFECOMP 2003, LNCS 2788, pp. 289–302, 2003.
© Springer-Verlag Berlin Heidelberg 2003

languages (Ada) [10]. However, SFTA is still an active field of research and given the complex nature of most real life software programs, the application of the method is in no way a trivial or straightforward task.

The software development standards of the Eurofighter Typhoon aircraft require a fault tree analysis on code for any assembler software classified by the highest possible risk level (class 1). This is software for which the occurrence of any failure condition or design error would prevent the continued safe flight or landing of the aircraft. This risk classification applies to the assembler code of the inertial measurement unit (IMU), which supplies flight control computers with measured angular rates and accelerations necessary to artificially control this inherently unstable aircraft.

To cope with the 17000 assembler instructions to be analysed, a detailed procedure for application of the SFTA method was worked out and a powerful suite of tools was developed assisting the analysis by highly automated functions. After a description of the most important features of the tool, we present the results we have obtained from the analysis and improvements to be taken on the analysed code. In the next section our experiences of the technique including benefits and limitations are discussed, addressing possible extensions to other assembler implementations as well. We finish the paper with a summary and a prospect to future applications.

2   Method of Software Fault Tree Analysis for Assembler Code

Fault tree analysis is an established top down analysis method. It starts from system level and can be continued as SW fault tree analysis through SW requirements level, design level, down to code level.

The purpose of a fault tree analysis on assembler code is to identify the environmental conditions which would lead to software induced failures and to provide confidence, within the scope of this analysis method, that the assembler code is free from errors and does not generate incorrect safety critical output data. Thus, its purpose is to verify that the SW does not produce system safety failures. Apart from this, the method can be used to cover some aspects of a code walk through, as identification of control flow, detection of dead code which is not executed or is of no relevance for the functions of the SW, detection of variables which are read before a value was assigned, detection of unused input variables, or detection of not reachable program labels. Additionally, the method can be used to check for assignment of output variables of each unit, for registers affected by a subroutine, and for consistency of code with unit headers (formal comments).

The method is described in detail below. It starts with preparation work as the identification of the top-level events, the identification of outputs of the SW contributing to the top-level events, and proceeds then with the intrinsic fault tree analysis on the assembler code units. For documentation purposes a graphical description has been selected, which is also described in the following sections.

Identification of Top-Level Events for Code Level SFTA. If a preceding system fault tree analysis exists, the SW basic events (SWBEs) from the resulting basic event list may be used to determine the top-level events for the fault tree analysis on assembler code. Then the basic event description of each SWBE is used to identify the associated output or set of output parameters generated by the software. This may be a signal or a status indication. The complete code is regarded as a black box at this stage. Only external variables are considered.

If a preceding fault tree analysis is not available, each external output of the assembler code is considered as a potential contribution to a hazard, if it is not correct.

The associated output or set of output parameters, in combination with the hazardous condition, represents a "Top-Level Event" for the Code Level Fault Tree Analysis. Normally this will be an expression like "Output 'x' incorrect due to SW failure". All Top-Level Events are listed in the "List of Top-Level Events". This list builds the entry point to the fault tree analysis of the code units.

Identification of Code Unit Outputs Related to Top-Level Events. All output data of the SW specified in the HW/SW interface description are analysed for their possible contribution to the events listed in the "Top-Level Event List". SW outputs, which may cause the occurrence of a particular top-level event, are associated with this event.

The identification of all code locations providing the output data of the SW completes the link between the top-level events and the fault trees of assembler code: Each top-level event comprises all SW output data related to this event, which again span the set of code locations providing the output at the HW/SW interface. Fault trees of assembler code starting from the "output instructions" then develop the top-level events further to the code. Other units in turn providing input to the "output units" are developed into a fault tree as well. In this way a hierarchical structure of linked fault trees is generated, that reflects the calling structure of the SW.

Fault Tree Hazard Analysis of Assembler Code. For all units of the code fault trees are constructed in consecutive actions as described below.

Beginning from the last instruction of a code unit, for all instructions all conditions are identified, which can contribute to a faulty execution of this instruction.

In the next step all possible predecessors providing input to this instruction are identified. These instructions are possible candidates contributing to an error condition of the instruction under analysis. All of these predecessor instructions have to be analysed to determine if and how they contribute to the error condition of the instruction under analysis.

Manual execution of these tasks would be error-prone and very time and cost consuming. In section 3 a method is described to extract references automatically from the code, leaving only complex cases to manual work. These references to predecessors are stored in a database, which is used as basis for the automatic generation of the fault trees. The database is used to trace back the sequence of predecessor instructions and the sequence of code units. The information gathered during this trace back analysis forms one complete branch of the fault tree for one start instruction under analysis of a top-level event.

For each output under analysis the fault tree will be constructed separately. If there is more than one start instruction contributing to a top-level event the sum of all fault tree branches for the list of start instructions forms the fault tree of this top-level event.

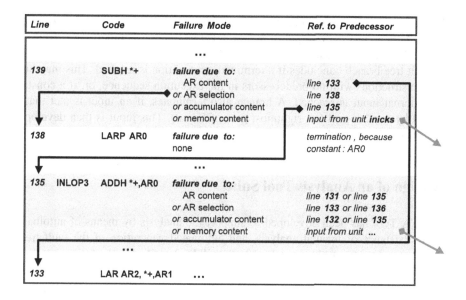

Fig. 1. Example for a trace back of the sequence of predecessor instructions

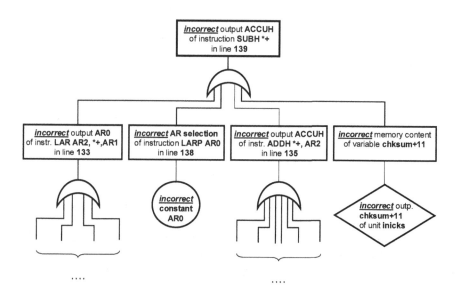

Fig. 2. Graphical representation of the code references displayed in Fig. 1

Fig. 1 gives an example for the application of the method to TMS320C25 assembler language. It shows the dependence of the top-level instruction (in line 139) from 4 preceding instructions, which provide input to the top-level instruction. The corresponding part of the fault tree is depicted in Fig. 2. The top-level instruction is OR-linked to the 4 predecessors indicating that an incorrect output of any of the predecessors results in an incorrect output of the top-level instruction. Similarly, the events of the second level are evaluated further.

A fault tree branch concludes if a termination condition is reached. This may happen for instructions with no predecessors in the execution sequence, or, if a constant or an external input is reached. A branch also terminates, if an input is met that is provided by another unit (cf. rightmost gate of Fig. 2). This input is then developed further in a fault tree of the other unit.

3   Design of an Analysis Tool Suite

The SFTA Tool has been developed to support the analysis by means of automated checks, assistance of manual analysis, and automated generation of the fault trees. The tool components are shown in Fig. 3 and will be described in the following:

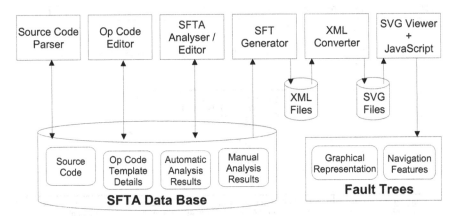

Fig. 3. FTA Tool – Functional Components

Source Code Parser. All information about the source code and the analysis results is stored in the SFTA Data Base. This is set up with the help of the Source Code Parser, which reads assembler files, data definition files, and the link map. For all assembler instructions (opcodes) and parameter specifications found in the source code, a template is generated for further editing within the Opcode Editor.

However, before the real analysis work begins, some further automatic steps for database preparation must be performed at this stage: The physical page information and absolute memory addresses are assigned to symbols, code lines executing jumps, branches and calls are identified, and the calling tree of the software is created. An interface specification is also generated (automatically) for every unit using formal comments (headers) in the source code files. This header information comprises variables and registers serving for input and output of the unit and additional information such as variables and constants used by the unit.

Opcode Editor. The usage of each opcode template identified by the Source Code Parser has to be specified within the Opcode Editor. For example, this would likely include the parameter types (variable, constant or register) and usage (input/output), any processor flags used, and any side effects such as registers modified by the instruction. This information also specifies the failure modes for each instruction template and is a prerequisite for the subsequent analysis. However, it only needs to be generated once for each set of opcodes. Also, in order to minimize the required effort, only those opcodes that are actually used in the source code under analysis are included. This means that the Opcode Editor has to be reapplied should previously unused opcodes be introduced in a source code update.

Having prepared the SFTA Database, it is ready to be loaded into the SFTA Editor/Analyser.

SFTA Editor/Analyser. Each code unit (specified by its entry label) is analysed as a complete entity on its own being linked to the rest of the code by the interface specification (initially generated from the unit's header). In case of erroneous or incomplete header information, unresolved references are displayed in the SFTA Editor and the analyst will have to correct these data. This allows the detection and correction of incorrect assumptions about the interaction of a unit with the rest of the code.

From the opcode templates and interface specifications, the automatic analysis function of the tool creates references from instructions to the predecessors, which provide input to each particular instruction. These references correspond to the trace back of failure modes as described in section 2 and displayed in Fig. 1. See Fig. 4 for a view of the source code window of the SFTA Editor/Analyser, showing references from a selected code line (shaded line) to predecessor instructions. The inputs required from the predecessors are indicated in shaded fields to the left of the corresponding instruction lines.

If input or output data is expected from or to other units then the corresponding variables or registers must be specified in the interface specification. For input data a reference to the unit header is created. Fig 5 shows the property sheet for specification of the input/output data of the unit. With these methods, registers (and under certain conditions variables) can be traced over subunit calls. If references to all the required input data of a particular instruction can be found for all possible execution paths of the program, the preconditions of the instruction are fulfilled. Otherwise, at least one open reference is displayed in the SFTA Editor source window and the reason for this has to be investigated further. If a justification for correctness can be given, the open reference can be closed manually, otherwise an error in the analysed code may have been detected.

Indirect addressing is a common way for accessing memory in assembler languages. In this case the address of a memory location is specified via an address register. Indirect addressing can be used for passing different (depending on the context of the call) variables to subunits or for indexing through memory by incrementing or decrementing the register value in loops. In contrast to direct addressing via symbol names, the analyser cannot identify the referenced variables due to lack of information about the register value. If it is necessary to trace all memory accesses, then all the possible values of an address register have to be specified by the analyst for each instruction that modifies it.

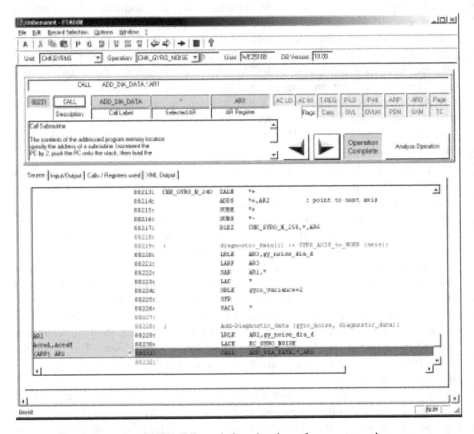

Fig. 4. Example of SFTA Editor window showing references to predecessors

The identified top-level events of the code are directly related to output signals, which, in turn, are derived from the variables and code locations that provide the output at the hardware/software interface. Therefore these code locations equate to the entry points of the fault trees and must be assigned to the top-level events by the analysts. Similarly, external inputs from the hardware also have to be specified and subsequently fulfil the role of basic events in the SFTA.

After manual analysis has been completed, a rerun of the SFTA Analyser is initiated. Any open references in a code unit are clearly displayed. If this happens that code unit must be checked, to determine whether the problem requires a correction of the unit header, or either the manual setting or justification of an unresolved reference. Otherwise it is a strong indication of an error or an inconsistency in the code.

SFT Generator. References to instructions belonging to the same code unit can adequately be inspected by means of the SFTA Editor. For inter-unit relations a graphical representation utilizing the hyper-link technology is the best way for displaying the analysis results. To this end fault trees for all output data of all code units can be extracted from the relations stored in the SFTA Data Base by the SFT Generator and written to files in XML format.

Every event in a FT corresponds to a particular failure mode of a code instruction. All events not being basic events are linked to the preconditions of the instruction, which may cause an incorrect output of this instruction. A fault tree is hyper-linked to other fault trees via the input data provided by other code units and via calls to other units. Basic events are, for example, external inputs at the hardware/software interface or constants stored in the code itself. Starting from top-level events, the outputs of the code can in principle be traced back to the inputs by means of a linked system of fault trees and gates. Since every event is linked to its predecessor events by OR gates, each basic event linked to a top-level event may cause the hazard.

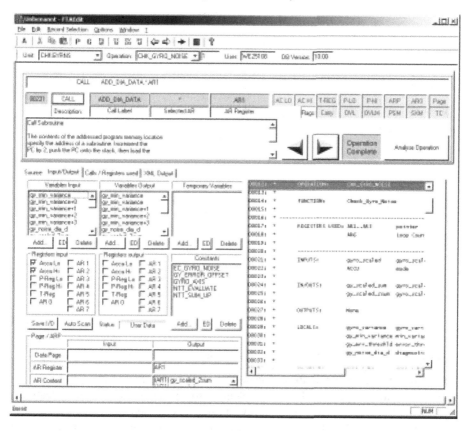

Fig. 5. Property sheet for interface specification of a unit

XML Converter. The XML files will be translated with the XML Converter into scaleable vector graphics (SVG) files, which contain the graphical information necessary to display the fault trees within an Internet browser. Each output of a code instruction is represented by a fault tree event with its corresponding gate, whereas references to preceding instructions are represented by connector lines between events and gates. In addition, the concept of graphical objects of SVG has been exploited to assign attributes to all nodes. The attributes denote the links to other nodes, which may either be located in the same or in other fault trees.

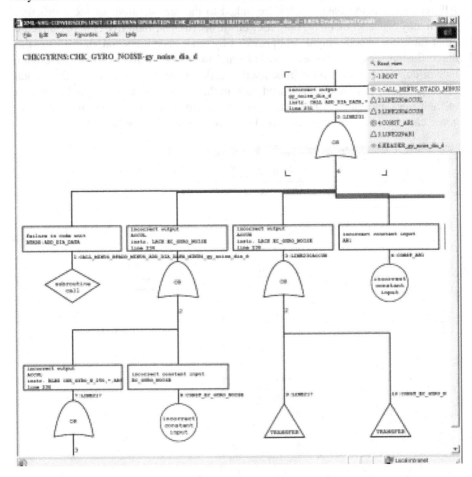

Fig. 6. Part of automatically generated fault tree developing selected instruction of Fig. 4

SVG Viewer + JavaScript Procedures. The attributes of nodes are used in combination with JavaScript procedures to implement some interactive navigation features. By clicking on a graphical object (an event with its corresponding gate), a menu is displayed showing all links to the referenced predecessor instructions. Selection of a link in the menu sets the focus to the related predecessor node. If the selected link is a hyper-link to another fault tree, the tree is loaded and displayed in the browser. This allows navigation in the whole set of fault trees of the software. Fig. 6 gives an example of an automatically generated fault tree, displayed with Microsoft Internet Explorer. The menu appearing after a mouse-click on the top node can be seen in the top right corner of the window.

The SFTA tool has passed the validation process as required by the Eurofighter project standards. Thereafter, the tool development followed a structured software development including the definition and tracing of tool functions from requirements to code level and coverage of all functions by test cases. To test the tool features TMS320C25 assembler example code was generated and the results of the SFTA analyser were verified against manual analysis results.

4 Application to Flight Critical IMU Software

The Eurofighter Typhoon aircraft is designed to be both directionally and longitudinally unstable in certain areas of the flight envelope. The inertial measurement unit (IMU) senses aircraft rates and accelerations, and calculates parameters for use in various aircraft functions. Most important, the data are processed in the control loops of the flight control computers to provide artificial stabilization of the aircraft. The IMU signals are therefore regarded as flight safety critical and are provided on a quadruplex basis. Each of the four processing lanes consists of gyro and accelerometer electronics, two processor cards (with a Motorola MC68020 microprocessor and a Texas Instruments TMS320C25 digital signal processor), and an interface card.

The main purpose of the assembler SW of the TMS320C25 is to perform sensor data management and sensor data processing. These computations provide angular rates, accelerations, and air data estimations to the flight control computers. Furthermore, the SW performs hardware monitoring and built-in testing, and implements a complex redundancy management of the 4 processing lanes.

Since the same software is running on each lane, i.e. an architecture with independent dissimilar programs in different lanes has not been applied, an error in the software could undermine the redundancy concept and could cause the top hazard of the flight control system "incorrect control of control surfaces". This results in assigning risk class 1 to the software of the IMU. The software development standards of the project require a fault tree analysis to be performed on risk class 1 assembler code as part of the safety assessment process.

Because the software running on the MC68020 processor is written in Ada, the SFTA was only carried out for the code running on the TMS320C25. Details of objectives and procedures have been outlined in section 2. According to section 2 only those code units ought to be analysed, which are directly related to the code level outputs or supply these code units with intermediate results. However, due to the nested structure of the software and having available the automatic functions of the tool, it was regarded as advantageous to cover the total code with a SFTA. This also allows the detection of logical and formal errors in all code units. The tools and manual analysis steps described in section 3 could be directly applied to the TMS320 assembler.

The code under investigation was a legacy system that has never been designed for applying such a SFTA. Furthermore, the analysis was carried out after extensive testing of the code. At that time nobody really expected a considerable improvement of the code by application of this analysis technique. However, in the run of the analysis, we encountered a number of shortfalls of the code. All these errors are either formal ones or are related to lack of fulfillment of preconditions in the program flow. Errors like wrong implementation of algorithms are not subject to this kind of analysis.

All coding errors found are related to data memory page selection and usage of auxiliary registers:

1. The addressable data memory of the TMS320C25 processor is divided into 512 data pages. Before accessing a variable by name using the direct addressing mode, it is an essential precondition that the data page register points to the memory page, where the particular variable is located in. The analysis revealed two program paths with a wrong page selected, resulting in wrong memory access or corruption of memory contents. These program paths are not executed in the normal program flow but as a reaction to a failure condition encountered by the program before.

The processor provides 8 auxiliary registers, which are either used for data memory access via addresses (indirect addressing mode) or for temporary data storage. These registers are pointed to by an auxiliary register pointer, which can take values from 0 through 7 corresponding to the auxiliary registers AR0 to AR7. An auxiliary register is selected, if the pointer is set accordingly. Many instructions use the auxiliary register pointer to operate with the content of the selected AR. Necessary preconditions for these instructions are both a valid selection of an AR and a valid content of the selected AR. Two types of coding errors have been detected within this context:

2. The AR pointer is changed unintentionally as a side effect of a subroutine call, which is executed in an exceptional situation. As a consequence, the content of a wrong AR is used or manipulated. This error was found in one program path. Two other program paths with the same finding have been detected, however without negative consequences for the program execution due to conditions based on the dynamic values of variables. To recognize this lies outside the scope of a static analysis that cannot trace the contents of variables. Nevertheless, such a kind of programming may be error-prone for later updates of the code.

3. The content of an AR has not been set in a defined manner before it is used. Since the content of the AR may be used for addressing or temporary storage purposes, the consequences are access to wrong memory locations or the assignment of an incorrect value to a variable. Two occurrences of this type of error have been found.

Although not necessary for the detection of coding errors but in order to represent the dependencies in the code in the usual form of a fault tree, more than 8000 XML and SVG files were generated, containing fault trees for all return values of all code units. All fault trees together contain a total number of nearly 2 million failure events, which are linked by OR gates. In principle, this structure reflects the signal flow from input data to output data of the software. The high number of events clearly demonstrates the necessity for automation.

Besides the detection of coding errors, further quality deficiencies have been found as a by-product. Since the SFTA Analyser requires interface specifications of all code units, which were taken from the unit headers at the beginning of the analysis, inconsistencies of unit headers with the code could be discovered. Unused input and output variables and registers declared in the header have also been revealed as well as missing declarations of variables and registers used.

In addition, the SFTA provides a way to find code instructions, which can never be executed or are meaningless for the functions of the program. Because all outputs of the software have been subject to the analysis, dead or meaningless instructions can be identified as those lines that do not occur in any fault tree of the software.

All together five coding errors and a number of formal errors have been found. Formal errors could promote coding errors in later maintenance phases. A detailed analysis of the coding errors showed that fortunately, they would not have a serious impact on safety in case of their activation. Failures due to these errors would only occur in exceptional situations, after other failures had already preceded. In those situations the failures would have prevented the software from correct execution of some mitigating actions for a short time. Eventually the situations would have been handled by hardware redundancy or a recovery strategy. This result however may have been obtained by chance and one should not rely on it for the future. Particularly, uncritical errors in the present configuration of the software can be a dormant risk, that may be activated in future upgrades.

The tracing of variables across unit interfaces is a difficult task due to extensive usage of indirect addressing and the fact, that only variables employed in different object files are listed in the linker map file. The tracing has been performed as far as possible, principal problems preventing from a rigorous treatment. For this reason, an unsatisfied precondition of an input variable of a code unit was not treated as an open reference, which must either be justified by the analyst or is regarded as a coding error. Therefore, the initialization of variables, before they are used in another unit, could not be checked systematically, explaining the fact that no error of this type has been found in the analysis. This topic will be discussed further in the next section.

5 Discussion of Experiences

At the beginning of the analysis some trials with a solely manual SFTA showed that the task would become too time consuming and error-prone. This is due to the large amount of possible program paths especially in exceptional situations like failure recovery. Therefore the idea arose to develop a tool to assist the analysts and to perform automatically as much of the analysis work as possible. This should also facilitate shorter reaction times to updates of the IMU software, better traceability of analysis results, and less analysis errors. The total effort for the analysis has been three working years, 2/3 of which has been spent on specification of the procedure and developing the SFTA tool. Since the analysis procedure and the tool are now available for application, a significant reduction of the effort is expected in case of repetition of the analysis for future updates of the code.

Despite of numerous benefits, some problems with the semi-automatic analysis have been encountered. Whereas preconditions concerning registers and data pages are treated well, preconditions concerning variables suffer from several shortfalls:

- References from input variables of units to output variables of previously called units cannot always be determined reliably. This is due to the runtime behavior of the program, because the sequence of read and write operations on variables is not always predictable. Some code units are only called during the initialisation phase of the software, others are only called if an error or an external event occurs. Hence, all possible program flows cannot be mapped to a SFT on code level, if the software is driven by a scheduler and/or interrupts may occur in an unpredictable manner.

- Memory access via addresses (indirect addressing) is the most frequent way to read and write variables. Incrementing and decrementing of addresses, e.g. in loops, often depends on the current dynamic context and cannot be analysed automatically. The information must be added from the analyst with means of the tool editor. However, the analyst encounters similar problems as the tool. At least a good understanding of the functions, data flows, and scheduling of the SW is required. Due to this and the large amount of code lines requiring address information, the task of manually providing the information is susceptible to mistakes. Investigations for additional assistance at this point are under way. For instance, the tool could clearly indicate, where information from the analyst is requested, and could provide values of address registers before entering a loop.

- If more than one variable name is mapped to the same memory location, equivalence of these variables is only recognized by the tool, if both variables are listed in the linker map file. This places restrictions on tracing of memory access through the code. A possible improvement for future versions of the tool will be the use of assembler listings to get absolute addresses of all variables appearing in the code.

The previous three items prevented tracing of the signal flow completely through the code. A possible solution of this problem is to run the software in a simulation environment and to generate a protocol of all accesses to processor registers and memory including the chronological order. From this, references may be generated from a read location to all preceding write locations of the code. All possible execution paths had to be covered by the simulation to get a complete set of dependencies with this approach.

The relative simplicity of the TMS320 assembler supports automation of the SFTA on code level, problems still remaining with indirect addressing modes. From there most CISC processors, especially newer ones like INTEL Pentium or Motorola 68xxx, cannot be processed in the same way like a simple digital signal processor. These CPUs use indirect and multiple indirect addressing modes. For practical applications it is impossible to trace variable access manually that is caused by indirect or multiple indirect addressing instructions. Better results may be expected for RISC processors that use a load-store architecture, e.g. Motorola PowerPC, because they rarely use indirect addressing modes. The ideas from this analysis may be transferred to those processors, nevertheless requiring re-implementation of most components of the tool.

6 Summary and Conclusion

We presented a general procedure in combination with a tool that adapts the SFTA technique to assembler code and demonstrated its applicability to a complex flight critical software. The SFTA has been proven to be a valuable validation technique detecting deficiencies in the data flow (e.g. through incorrect usage of registers/memory areas) especially at the interfaces between the code units and unveiling certain kinds of weak spots of the software, which could have become a safety issue with forthcoming software updates.

The large number of generated fault trees and the total number of events over all fault trees clearly show that a purely manual analysis would not have been a practical way to perform the task. A tool suite had to be developed that performs most steps automatically from analysing the code to drawing the fault trees.

Also limitations of the SFTA have been encountered, especially in tracing variable access through the code. It would be worthwhile to investigate, if measures like improvement of automatic analysis functions, a more rigorous treatment by the analysts, or a processor simulation allow to go beyond the results achieved till now. However, the scope of a static analysis method will then be left.

References

1. U. S. Nuclear Regulatory Commission: Fault Tree Handbook, NUREG-0492, Washington, D.C (1981).
2. Leveson, N., Harvey, P.: Analyzing Software Safety, IEEE Transaction on Software Engineering, Vol. 9, No. 5, pp 569–579 (1983).
3. Leveson, N., Cha, S., and Shimeall, T.: Safety Verification of Ada Programs Using Software Fault Trees, IEEE Software, Volume 8, No. 4, pp 48–59 (1991).
4. Leveson, N.: Safeware: System Safety and Computers. Addison-Wesley, Reading, MA, USA, 1995.
5. Helmer, G., Wong, J., Slagell, M., Honavar, V., Miller, Lutz, R.: A Software Fault Tree Approach to Requirements Analysis of an Intrusion Detection System. In: Proceedings of the Symposium on Requirements Engineering for Information Security, Indianapolis, IN, USA (2001), http://www.palisadesys.com/~ghelmer/background.html.
6. Bowman, W.C., Archinoff, G.H., Raina V.M., Tremaine D.R., Leveson N.G.: An application of fault tree analysis to safety critical software at Ontario Hydro. In Conference on Probabilistic Safety Assessment and Management (PSAM), Beverly Hills, April 1991
7. D'Ambrogio, A., Iazeolla, G. Mirandola, R., A.: Method for the Prediction of Software Reliability, Proc. of the 6-th IASTED Software Engineering and Applications Conference (SEA2002), 2002, Cambridge, MA (USA), http://sel.info.uniroma2.it/publications.htm.
8. Pai G., Bechta Dugan, J.: Automatic Synthesis of Dynamic Fault Trees from UML System Models, International Symposium on Software Reliability Engineering (ISSRE 2002), 2002, Annapolis, ML (USA), www.ee.virginia.edu/~gjp5j/professional/research/research.htm.
9. Papadopoulos, Y., Maruhn, M.: Model-Based Automated Synthesis of Fault Trees from Matlab-Simulink Models, The International Conference on Dependable Systems and Networks (DSN'01), 2001, Goteborg, Sweden, http://www2.dcs.hull.ac.uk/people/cssyp/.
10. Mason, R. W.: Fault Isolator Tool for Software Fault Tree Analysis, Storming Media, Washington (1995), www.stormingmedia.us/cgi-bin/99/9934/A993492-54-33t.php.

On the Role of Traceability for Standards Compliance: Tracking Requirements to Code

P.A.J. Mason[1], A. Saeed[2], and S. Riddle[1]

[1] School of Computing Science, University of Newcastle upon Tyne, United Kingdom
[2] Advantage Business Group, The Barbican, Farnham, Surrey, United Kingdom

Abstract. Traceability is the common term for mechanisms to record and navigate relationships between development and assessment artifacts. While often seen as a way of reducing systematic development errors and despite being a requirement of industry standards, lack of tool integration can make it difficult to achieve traceability in practice. This paper proposes a framework enabling traceability links to be established across tool 'boundaries'. The framework is realised by exporting data from CASE tools - concentrating here on examples used to express requirements and program code - to meta-models represented in a common format; traceability links (represented in the same format) can then be established between elements of these models. In turn, safety cases - structured using an appropriate graphical technique and with computer-based support - can make direct appeal to sets of these links as evidence of meeting traceability goals.

1 Introduction

Most safety critical systems must be certified before entering service. This normally involves submission to the appropriate regulatory authority of a safety case (a reasoned argument that the system is acceptably safe to operate), typically including claims and supporting evidence of adherence to appropriate industrial standards [e.g. 1, 2]. Such standards increasingly include objectives for traceability, mechanisms to record and navigate relationships between artifacts produced by development and assessment processes. For example, DO178b [1], an international standard covering software in airborne systems requires demonstration of traceability between *low level requirements* (design) and *source code.*

Practitioners use a range of notations to express these and other artifact types, including Real-Time Networks and SPARK for development and Fault Trees for assessment. Most have tool support, although a lack of integration leads to inconsistencies and limits traceability between their respective data sets (i.e., data populating the tools internal data structures) - see figure 1. This makes it difficult to realise (and hence demonstrate realisation of) safety objectives for standards.

The rest of this paper is organised as follows: section 2 considers the gathering of evidence of traceability for safety cases, including a framework addressing tool integration. In the context of this framework, sections 3 and 4 propose an approach to structuring program code (or more generally any language with a formal foundation)

S. Anderson et al. (Eds.): SAFECOMP 2003, LNCS 2788, pp. 303–316, 2003.

for traceability; examples illustrate application of the approach to SPARK source code and RTN-SL statements. Section 5 models links across these notations to allow traceability, while section 6 illustrates appeal to the links in demonstrating standards compliance. Section 7 offers some concluding remarks.

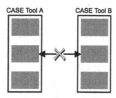

Fig. 1. Inter-tool Traceability Problem

2   Safety Case Evidence from Traceability

The traditional presentation of a safety case is as a linear document. However, the level of detail often obscures the arguments presented and so graphical notations with computer-based support have been developed to improve their structure and scrutability. These explicitly link requirements to analysis results and evidence, as well as recording rationale, assumptions and justifications. Examples include ASCAD (Adelard Safety Case Development) [3], SGS (Safety Goal Structure) [4] and GSN (Goal Structuring Notation) [5, 6].

2.1   Role of Traceability in the Safety Case

Following an approach based on [7], this paper uses Goal Structuring Notation to structure goals (claims) and related evidence in arguing compliance with industry standards - in this case DO178b. The subset of GSN elements necessary to accomplish this are: i) *goals* (denoted as rectangles) – constraints on the target system, or its development and assessment process (note goals can be decomposed into a hierarchy of sub-goals); ii) *strategies* (denoted as parallelograms) - courses of action for achieving a goal or goals; and iii) *solutions* (denoted as circles) - individual pieces of analysis or evidence, in this case sets of traceability links. A guidance note on the application of DO178b in SW01 (which forms part of CAP 670 [8] - the regulatory objective for safety in air traffic service equipment) provides direction on construction of safety cases using a goal-based approach.

Figure 2 depicts a top-level goal "*Risks are ALARP (As Low As Reasonably Practicable) and Tolerable*" (G1). Given this goal, a strategy is introduced to "*Argue that risks in deploying software are ALARP and tolerable*" (S1). In turn, this strategy is realised through goals for validation and traceability, G1.1, G1.2 and G1.3. Again these goals have strategies for their realisation, including: S2 and S3; note, we address the issue of strategies and sub-goals for discharging G1.2 (*Configuration is consistent*) in the Conclusions (section 7) as it relates to work mentioned only briefly in this paper, but reported extensively elsewhere. Finally, these strategies decompose into the following goals: for S2, GS2.1, GS2.2 and GS2.3; and for S3, GS3.1 GS3.2.

Each leaf node in the goal structure addressing traceability should be discharged by direct appeal to evidence from a traceability approach - sets of associations between artifacts. This is exemplified in the figure by goal GS3.1 which is supported by **SysToSwRqtLinks**, the set of traceability associations between System and Software requirements. However, as previously stated, these and the other artifact types are often expressed in different notations using different tools. Therefore to realise traceability between the two sets of requirements and hence argue that this and similar objectives have been met, means are required to allow creation of such associations (note we return to the featured goal structure goal in section 6).

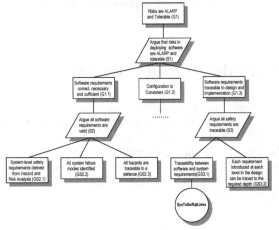

Fig. 2. Top-level Goal Structure

2.2   Supporting the Production of Traceability Evidence

MATra (*M*eta-modelling *A*pproach to *Tra*ceability) [9] is a framework addressing the above-mentioned inter-tool traceability problem by allowing links to be established across data from disjoint tools. The framework is realised by exporting information from the internal data structures of tools to a Workspace of 'notation dependent' structures or meta-models capable of receiving this data [cf. 10, 11]. By expressing these structures in a uniform format (i.e., in a common language), links (expressed in the same language as the structures) can be inserted that capture dependencies among data in CASE tools, within the Workspace. To maintain consistency, the structures are verified against a (notation independent) system model – the Product Data Synthesis (PDS) - that defines generic building blocks underlying the various notations, e.g. Module, Function, Transaction, etc. That is, such entities must exist in the PDS in order to exist in the notation dependent structures (for more information, readers are referred to [9]).

The mechanics of mappings across the CASE tool/MATra interface are described here by an (undefined) function, *tool2matra* that takes as its input, a populated CASE tool (internal) data structure (pCDS), with a corresponding un-populated notation dependent structure (uNDS) and the PDS, and returns a populated notation dependent structure (pNDS). This is expressed as follows:-

pNDS tool2matra (pCDS, uNDS, PDS)

The resulting Workspace provides an integrated environment allowing traceability to be established between otherwise disjoint data; for instance, from a use case in a Use Case Model, to a Real-Time Network activity, to a SPARK procedure specification. The concepts outlined above are summarised in figure 3.

We focus here on traceability (from low level requirements) to source code, as that is potentially the most challenging *vis à vis* information structuring and (notwithstanding [12]) receives little attention in existing literature.

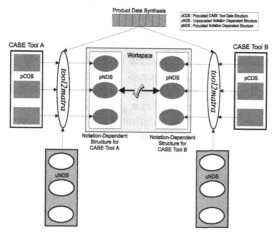

Fig. 3. Realising Inter-tool Traceability

3   Structuring Spark Code for Traceability

This section introduces a structure capturing a subset of the concrete syntax for SPARK, a language used in development of safety-critical systems. The structure (specified using UML [13]) was developed in parallel with a modelling philosophy - a set of guidelines by which the structure may be extended to include the complete SPARK syntax [14]. Here we concentrate on representation of a single construct - the procedure. The following illustrates use of procedure specification statements:-

```
procedure Read_Master_Switch(Position: out Switch);
```

Procedure specification statements comprise a procedure name, together with the types and modes of their parameters. Valid modes are in and out, indicating direction of information flow; thus in the above, Position of Read_Master_Switch is an **out** parameter as it provides the outgoing information produced by the read operation.

3.1   A Modelling Philosophy for the Structuring of String Grammars

Representation of the nominated construct takes as its starting point the concrete SPARK grammar stated in Backus Naur Form (BNF). In BNF, categories (i.e., entities) are defined in terms of other categories using productions consisting of the name being defined, followed by the ::= symbol and a defining sequence (which may include punctuation and reserved word 'tokens'); categories that cannot be further decomposed are known as terminals. Other symbols of note are [ ] square brackets enclosing optional items, { } braces enclosing optional items that may appear zero to n times and the | vertical bar separating alternatives.

Our philosophy (developed in parallel with the SPARK meta-model) provides a series of principles allowing object-based representation of language constructs stated as BNF categories, and to do so at a level of abstraction which is sufficient to identify traceability primitives. The guidelines are deliberately general allowing their application to any language with a concrete BNF syntax (see section 4)

Further MATra modelling concepts referenced are StructureElement and SystemsEngineeringEntity [9]. The former ensures a common basis for all notation dependent structures, while the latter is a generalisation of all elements of notation dependent structures that simplifies definition. A further concept is ArtifactProperty which subsumes all built-in and abstract data types. With these considerations in minds, the guidelines are as follows:-

1. Each BNF category is represented as a class (both an instance of the StructureElement meta-class and a specialisation of SystemsEngineeringEntity).

2. Categories forming the defining sequence of a category are themselves represented as classes (related to the subject class through aggregation), except where rule 3 applies.

3. Where nothing is gained traceability-wise by mirroring definition of a category in terms of other categories (and hence the corresponding class in terms of other classes) - that is, no constituent categories can be represented by classes that map to PDS elements (nor trace to elements of other notations) - it is treated as atomic and represented through specialisation of the String type (as well as an instance of StructureElement and a specialisation of SystemsEngineeringEntity).

4. All tokens (i.e., reserved words - such as from, global, inherit, etc. - together with punctuation marks - such as commas, semicolons, parentheses and ampersands) are represented as specialisations of the standard String class (and also as instances of ArtifactProperty).

5. Categories of a defining sequence that exist exactly once are modelled with a multiplicity constraint of one (1) for aggregate component classes; attributes representing tokens have an implicit multiplicity of one.

6. Optional items from a defining sequence (expressed in BNF using square brackets) are modelled as follows:-
    a) Categories are represented by applying a zero-or-one multiplicity constraint (0..1) on the component side of associations between the class representing the category being described (aggregate) and each class representing an optional defining category (component).
    b) Tokens are promoted from attributes to classes (linked to their host class using composition) to allow for expression of optionality.

7. Categories of a defining sequence that may be omitted, appear once, or be repeated several times (expressed in BNF using the braces formalism) are modelled using a zero-to-many multiplicity constraint (0..*) on the component side of associations between the class representing the category being described (aggregate) and each class representing an optional, singular or repeated defining category (component).
8. Categories decomposed into alternatives (expressed in BNF using the vertical bar separator) are modelled differently depending on what form their defining sequence takes. Readers are referred to [9] for more information.
9. The modelling of a defining sequence in which an item type appears at least once, but which may be repeated (as a comma or semicolon delimited list) - i.e., category ::= item {, item} - features a subtle variation from the BNF syntax; we represent the mandatory single item as a class (corresponding to a 'list head') and the optional repeated part (enclosed between braces in BNF) as a separate 'list-item' class containing an appropriate delimiter attribute, together with an aggregation association (multiplicity of one) to the afore-mentioned item class.

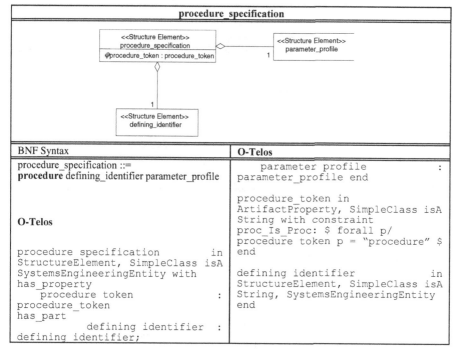

Fig. 4. procedure_specification schema

3.2 SPARK Procedure: Meta-model Definitions

In this subsection we present a series of schemas representing a partial SPARK structure capturing the procedure statement outlined above. Each constituent element is systematically expressed in terms of its BNF syntax and corresponding UML representation. To give a flavour of tool support, the UML classes are implemented in O-Telos using ConceptBase [15]. We further highlight the influence of our modelling philosophy in deriving these structures. We begin by describing the procedure_specification syntax which marks the origin for our modelling.

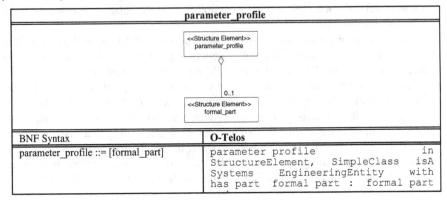

Fig. 5. parameter_profile schema

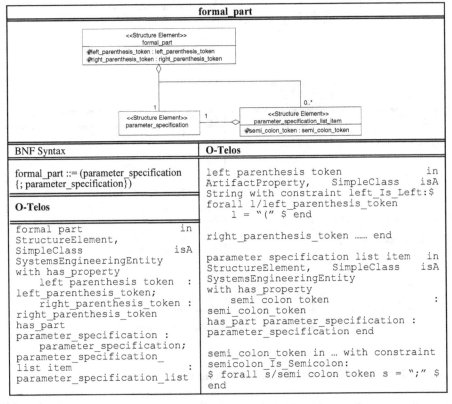

Fig. 6. formal_part schema

- **procedure_specification:** consists of the procedure_token reserved word, followed by defining_identifier and parameter_profile elements (see figure 4).
- **parameter_profile:** comprises an optional formal_part element (see figure 5).
- **formal_part:** consists of one or more parameter_specifications represented as a semicolon-delimited list between left and right parentheses (figure 6). The UML and O-Telos representations introduce an additional class (in accordance with rule 9) - parameter_specification_list_item - to represent optional parameter_specification elements following the single mandatory instance.
- **parameter_specification:** contains a defining_identifier_list, colon_token, mode and subtype_mark. In the UML model, mode and subtype_mark are treated as specialisations of String as per rule 3 (see figure 7).
- **defining_identifier_list :** Finally, the defining_identifier_list (schema not shown) consists of one or more comma-delimited defining_identifier elements. As per rule 9, the UML and O-Telos representations again employ an additional class - defining_identifier_list_item - to represent optional defining_identifier elements following the single mandatory instance.

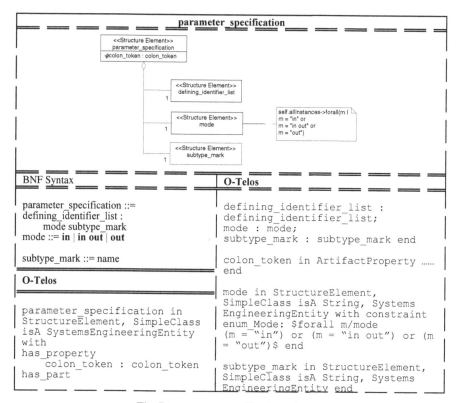

Fig. 7. parameter_specification schema

'Pitching' the model at this detailed level gives full compatibility with the source language, as well as offering fine-grained traceability (especially desirable for critical code fragments) among individual elements in the specification and implementation.

The above schemas will now be used as the basis of a worked example that instantiates the procedure statement structure elements.

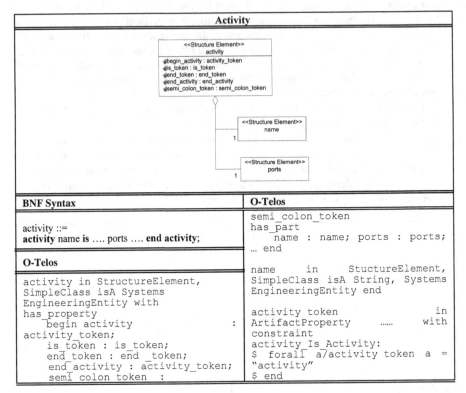

Activity	

BNF Syntax	**O-Telos**
activity ::= **activity** name **is** .... ports .... **end activity;**	semi_colon_token has_part name : name; ports : ports; ... end
O-Telos	name in StuctureElement, SimpleClass isA String, Systems EngineeringEntity end

activity in StructureElement,
SimpleClass isA Systems
EngineeringEntity with
has_property
    begin_activity
activity_token;
    is_token : is_token;
    end_token : end _token;
    end_activity : activity_token;
    semi_colon_token   :
	activity token in
	ArtifactProperty ...... with
	constraint
	activity_Is_Activity:
	$ forall a/activity token a =
	"activity"
	$ end

Fig. 8. Activity schema

3.3   SPARK Meta-model: Procedure Statement Worked Example

The code fragment for the Read_Master_Switch procedure introduced in section 3 (and repeated below) will be used as the subject of this example.

```
procedure Read_Master_Switch(Position: out Switch);
```

Instantiation of procedure_specification schema (figure 4)
read_master_switch_procedure_specification in procedure_specification,
Token with procedure_token procedureToken : "procedure"
defining_identifier definingIdentifier : "Read_Master_Switch"
parameter_profile parameterProfile :
read_master_switch_parameter_profile end

Instantiation of parameter_profile schema (figure 5)
read_master_switch_parameter_profile in parameter_profile, Token with
formal_part formalPart : read_master_switch_formal_part end

Instantiation of formal_part schema (figure 6)
read_master_switch_formal_part in formal_part, Token with
left_parenthesis_token leftParenthesisToken : "("

```
parameter_specification parameterSpecification :
    read_master_switch_parameter_specification ... end
```

Instantiation of parameter_specification **schema (figure 7)**
```
read_master_switch_parameter_specification in parameter_specification,
Token with defining_identifier_list definingIdentifierList :
    read_master_switch_defining_identifier_list
colon_token colonToken : ":"
mode parameterMode : "out"
subtype_mark subtypeMark : "Switch" end
```

Instantiation of defining_identifier_list **schema**
```
read_master_switch_defining_identifier_list in defining_identifier_list,
Token with defining_identifier definingIdentifier : "Position" end
```

Note, while the above code yields from a single line of SPARK, there is a 1:1 mapping between the underlying BNF elements and schemas for these elements.

4   Structuring (Low Level) Requirements for Traceability

According to DO178b guidelines, the low level requirements and software architecture are generated from high level requirements which strictly speaking is a design activity. As such we demonstrate representation of a (partial) low level specification expressed in the Real-Time Network Specification Language (RTN-SL) [16], a formal notation based on MASCOT [17].

Using RTN-SL as our example specification language allows us to demonstrate versatility of the modelling philosophy introduced in subsection 3.1 (and used to develop the SPARK structure in 3.2). It is also stressed that the example here is only intended to provide a flavour of an RTN-SL meta-model and is therefore restricted to (partial) representation of the activity element (figure 8).

We begin by illustrating the core syntax for activity descriptions by specifying an abbreviation of a Read_Master_Switch activity which provides the specification for the SPARK procedure in section 3.

```
activity Read_Master_Switch is ......
    ports p1 : (channel, Position, out); end ports ......
end activity;
```

Note, given further schemas describing the above ports element , it would be possible to show traceability between the RTN-SL activity and SPARK procedure at a finer granularity, e.g., through links between corresponding parameters (Position and out).

We now present the O-Telos representation of this schema for the Read_Master_Switch activity introduced above:

```
read_master_switch_activity in activity, Token with
    begin_activity beginActivity : "activity"
    name name : "Read_Master_Switch"
    is_token isToken : "is"
    ports ports : -- not shown
    end_token endToken : "end"
    end_activity endActivity : "activity"
    semi_colon_token semiColonToken : ";"
end
```

The above example, combined with the SPARK meta-model and modelling philosophy in section 3 illustrate our approach to representing (in this case formal textual) notations as meta-models capable of receiving data from CASE tools via *tool2matra*. Given a common representation format such as this, associations represented in the same format can now be added between models, and elements of the models to support traceability, as the following section demonstrates.

5 Realising Traceability from (Low Level) Requirements to Code

In MATra, traceability associations are modelled as classes (figure 9). Specifically, TraceabilityAssociation is an abstract class whose subtypes – such as ImplementedBy featured in this example - realise traceability between two SystemsEngineeringEntity subtypes. Recall from section 3.1, the latter is simply a generalisation of all elements of notation dependent structures (and also the structures themselves) and is intended to simplify definition.

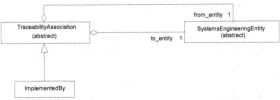

Fig. 9. Traceability Association

ImplementedBy represents relationships between requirements and their implementation. This is illustrated in figure 10 using the SPARK and RTN-SL code fragments featured in sections 3 and 4 respectively. Instances of ImplementedBy can then be used to demonstrate traceability between low-level requirements (design) and source code artifacts such as these, as section 6 demonstrates.

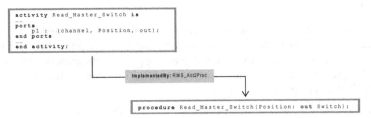

Fig. 10. Example Traceability Association: RTN-SL (Activity) to SPARK (Procedure Specification)

To realise this representation, the appropriate O-Telos base class, an implementation of ImplementedBy (from figure 9) is instantiated (see below). Its source is the read_master_switch_activity element, an instance of activity (from section 4) and its target,   the   read_master_switch_procedure_specification,   an   instance   of procedure_specification (from section 3).

```
RMS_Act2Proc in ImplementedBy, Token with
from_entity fromEntity : read_master_switch_activity
to_entity toEntity : read_master_switch_procedure_specification end
```

Note, [9] illustrates traceability across a more extensive Workspace, including structures supporting Use Case, Natural Language Editor and Fault Tree tools.

6   Demonstrating Traceability for Standards Compliance

The goal structure from section 2.1 will now be further decomposed to identify traceability goals supported by MATra with respect to the artifact types represented in sections 3 and 4 and the example traceability association from section 5.

Figure 11a decomposes the claim "Each requirement introduced at each level in the design can be traced to the required depth" via a strategy "Argue traceability from software requirements to source code is achieved" (S4); sub-goals of S4 are "Traceability between high-level requirements and low-level requirements (design)" (GS4.1) and "Traceability between low-level requirements (design) and source code" (GS4.2)., both of which make direct appeal to sets of traceability links providing evidence to corroborate these claims.

For the claim of interest - *Traceability between low level requirements and source code* - it can be seen that RMS_Act2Proc (created in Section 5) appears as an element of the set **LowLevelRqtToCodeLinks** (Low-level Requirements To Code Links).

Figure 11b further demonstrates decomposition of goal GS2.2, as suggested in section 2.1. Note, MATra includes meta-models for the HAZOPS and Software Fault Tree Analysis techniques which may be used to perform the failure analyses referred to in goals GS5.1 and GS5.2. Readers are referred to [9] for more information.

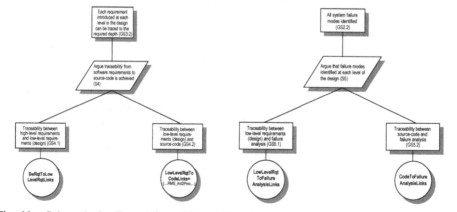

Fig. 11a. Sub-goals for Traceability Objectives (including Solution for Claim *Traceability Between Low-level Requirements (Design) and Source Code)'*

Fig. 11b. Further 'Sub-goals Discharged by Traceability

7 Conclusions

This paper has considered the role of traceability in providing evidence for a safety case demonstrating standards compliance. It was shown that much of this evidence takes the form of traceability associations between artifacts. These are typically expressed in a range of notations, most of which have tool support. However, traceability between these tools and thus the ability to produce evidence for a safety case is limited by a lack of well-defined approaches to tool integration.

A framework (MATra) was therefore proposed to enable traceability across information created and stored in different tools. The framework is achieved by exporting data from the internal models of these tools to structures (meta-models) expressed in a common modelling language. This allows traceability associations (expressed in the same language as the structures) to be established between the models and between elements of these models. A further structure - the Product Data Synthesis (PDS).- is used to maintain consistency. Note PDS may be used to provide evidence in discharging goal G1.2 from the top-level goal structure in figure 2. For more information readers are referred to [9] and [18].

The paper concentrated on a meta-model for representing program code - specifically SPARK (based on the concrete BNF syntax). The structure was developed in conjunction with guidelines for developing meta-models for BNF supported languages generally - a point subsequently emphasised using a fragment of RTN-SL. Means of realising associations between structures was also shown.

Focusing on the SPARK and RTN-SL meta-models, Goal Structuring Notation was used to demonstrate how traceability associations created within MATra can contribute to safety case claims relating to traceability for the standard DO178b. With computer-based support for GSN this task becomes almost trivial; the real difficulty lies in establishing traceability in the first place.

In terms of work presented here, the novelty of MATra lies in the following:-

♦   A framework (based on meta-modelling) that enables traceability between tools, across artifacts represented using different notations.
♦   (Partial) meta-models for the SPARK and RTN-SL notations, together with a generic modelling philosophy applicable to any BNF supported language.
♦   Means of creating associations among the meta-models, which in turn can be used in providing evidence for a safety case to discharge traceability goals.

Two further (more general) points are worth emphasising. Firstly, we note that any project artifact may be related to multiple other artifacts - for instance a design component may link to high-level requirements, source code and results of failure analysis. All these associations contribute to a safety case and are supported by MATra. For more information readers are again referred to [9] and [18].

Finally, we note that the role of traceability for a safety case can be defined as part of the project planning process, possibly through identification of relevant strategies. This means 'traceability effort' can focus on areas that will make a genuine contribution to the safety case. Moreover, the maturity of a traceability strategy can be checked against needs imposed by the safety case which, could be used as the basis of a capability audit or for process improvement. Put another way, we support the principle of agreeing the safety case format from the outset of a project [19, 20], in particular establishing the role of traceability in gathering evidence.

References

1. RTCA/DO178b – European Organisation for Civil Aviation Electronics – Software Considerations in Airborne Systems and Equipment Certification (1992)
2. SAE ARP 4754 – Certification Considerations in Airborne Systems and Equipment Certification, Society of Automotive Engineers (1996)
3. Bishop, P. & Bloomfield, R. – A Methodology for Safety Case Development, Procs. Safety-Critical Systems Symposium, UK, Feb. (1998)
4. Pearson, S., Riddle, S. & Saeed, A. - Traceability for the Development and Assessment of Safe Avionics Systems, Procs. INCOSE '98, Canada, Jul. (1998) , 445–452
5. Wilson, S.P., Kelly, T. P., & McDermid, J. A. – Safety Case Development: Current Practice, Future Prospects, Procs. 12th CSR Workshop/1st ENCRESS Conf., Belgium (1995)
6. Wilson, S., McDermid, J., Pygott, C. & Tombs, D. – Assessing Complex Computer Based Systems Using the Goal Structure Notation: Procs. ECBS, Canada, Oct. (1996), 498–505
7. Wilson, S., McDermid, J., Kirkham, P., Pygott, C. & Tombs, D. – Computer Based Support for Standards and Processes in Safety Critical Systems, Procs. SafeComp, York (1997), 197–209
8. CAP 670 – Air Traffic Services Safety Requirements, Civil Aviation Authority (1998)
9. Mason, P. – Meta-modelling Approach to Traceability, Newcastle University PhD Thesis (2002)
10. Telelogic – DOORS Ref. Manual: v5.1, 2001
11. Johnson, J. – The Latest Developments in Design Data Exchange: Towards Fully Integrated Aerospace Design Environments, Procs. Int'l Congress of Aeronautical Sciences, UK (2000)
12. Han, Jun – A Document Based Approach to Software Engineering Environments, Procs. 5th Int'l CASE Symposium, China, Oct./Nov. (1995), 128–133
13. Muller, Pierre-Alain - Instant UML, Wrox Press Ltd. (1997)
14. Barnes, J. – High Integrity Ada: The Spark Approach, Addison Wesley (1997)
15. Jarke, M., Gallersdorfer, R., Jeusfeld, M., Staudt, M. & Eherer, S.- ConceptBase: A Deductive Object Base for Meta Data, Journal of Intelligent Info. Sys., Mar. (1995), 167–192
16. Paynter, S. – Real-Time Network Specification Language, MBDA TR 20656, Nov. (2000)
17. Simpson, H. R. – The Mascot Method, Software Engineering Journal, May, (1986), 103–120
18. Mason, P., Saeed, A., Riddle, S. & Arkley, P. – Traceability: A Systems Integration Perspective, A Systems Integration Perspective, Procs. INCOSE '03, to appear (2003)
19. DS 00-55: Requirements for Safety-Related Software in Defence Equipment, MoD (1996)
20. DS 00-56 (Issue 2): Safety Management Requirements for Defence Systems, MoD (1996)

Tools Supporting the Communication of Critical Domain Knowledge in High-Consequence Systems Development

Kimberly S. Wasson, John C. Knight, Elisabeth A. Strunk, and Sean R. Travis

Department of Computer Science
University of Virginia
151 Engineer's Way, P.O. Box 400740
Charlottesville, VA 22904-4740, USA
{ksh4q|knight|strunk|srt3k}@cs.virginia.edu

Abstract. Predictably achieving requirements validity has proven extremely difficult because of the informal nature of this property, and poor communication of application domain knowledge is implicated as a main barrier to increasing this validity. In related work, we developed a methodology that exploits cognitive psychology research to improve this communication. In this work, we describe support for the methodology via a toolset that directs involved parties in the construction of artifacts defined by the methodology; these artifacts by their structure and content enable the spread of application domain knowledge among developers and throughout the lifecycle. The toolset in addition supports documentation, various forms of analysis, and integration with other lifecycle artifacts. We used these tools in collaboration with an industry partner to develop experimental documentation for recording and dissemination of domain knowledge relevant to the design of a medical device, and we here describe this experience.

1 Introduction

Erroneous or *invalid* requirements are implicated as a major source of defects in the software of high-consequence systems [14]. Achieving high-quality requirements necessitates high-integrity communication [7], but innate mechanisms of human communication are not well-suited to this goal [6, 5]. Researchers who study human communication have generated results that can be exploited for purposes of improving communication in the development of such systems. Linguistic knowledge about particular aspects of human communication can be embodied in an artifact that serves to organize and allow processing of content essential to the effective communication of critical domain knowledge [4, 6, 5]. This approach generates a large amount of natural language content that is highly structured, but difficult to manage effectively. In this work, we offer a proof of concept of tool support for acquiring, organizing and processing that material. The tools we describe automate much of the application of important results from linguistics to software engineering thereby providing the opportunity for significant improvement in the quality of documented requirements.

We begin with a brief examination of the relationship between communication and software validity. Validity refers to whether a software artifact intended for a purpose is "the right thing," that is, whether it fulfills its intended functionality under intended constraints and without unintended consequences. Validity is necessarily an

S. Anderson et al. (Eds.): SAFECOMP 2003, LNCS 2788, pp. 317–330, 2003.

informal property since it is a measure of mapping to human intent. It is thus difficult to achieve and demonstrate, since intent might change, vary among stakeholders, be incompletely considered by either developers or stakeholders, include inconsistencies that result from poor logic or ambiguity, or simply be inaccessible as a result of insufficient acquisition methods or lack of propagation of sufficiently acquired intent.

Natural language is the primary medium for the communication of intent, and herein lies much of the problem. Not only must this intent be isolated and captured in order to get the requirements right, but it must be propagated through the development process with integrity at any number of transfer points. Thus far, those developing high-consequence systems have rarely been able to get this right, and even then, not systematically or predictably. This fact is demonstrated by the numerous incidents, accidents, and other failures in high-assurance software, as well as in the schedule slippages and cost overruns that plague even non-safety-critical projects. By and large, these problems derive from communication deficiencies early in the lifecycle [7, 14].

In related work, we developed a methodology that exploits cognitive psychology research to improve this communication. In this work, we describe support for the methodology via a toolset that directs involved parties in the construction of artifacts defined by the methodology; these artifacts by their structure and content enable the spread of application domain knowledge among developers and throughout the lifecycle. The approach was brought into an industrial environment and used to develop experimental requirements and specification documentation relevant to the development of a medical device. This allowed us to demonstrate the feasibility of construction of a complex requirements artifact that is theoretically founded in a linguistic model using extensive tool support. The artifact is scalable in both representable complexity and processibility into new knowledge, and integratable with existing development processes. It provides a proof-of-concept that certain forms of breakdown that plague communication of application domain knowledge can be systematically overcome or avoided while keeping within the confines of a professional development process.

The structure of the paper is as follows: we first provide the context of related work, followed by a brief review of the approach. We then discuss the toolset and its enabled facilities. Finally, we report on our experience with industrial collaborators, which demonstrated the feasibility of construction of a theoretically-founded complex artifact and its manipulation and analysis on a realistic scale and in a realistic environment. Further, it provided insight that directed later development of the approach and tools in specific ways.

2   Related Work

A number of other researchers have investigated the application of knowledge about language to the problem of requirements validity. Goguen and Potts advocate forms of naturalistic inquiry as it is practiced in social and anthropological endeavors. Naturalistic inquiry involves a data collection process whereby an analyst observes participants in a community and pieces together a picture of their interaction through various techniques including interviewing and artifact collection [16]. The goal is generally to expose the "...meanings and tacit understandings that participants in social contexts negotiate and derive from interactions with the artifacts and other participants there" [16]. Potts proceeds in a direction that uses observations of human interaction to motivate strategies to enhance communication. For example, he proposes a structured conversation model for communicating requirements based on what he calls the *inquiry cycle*, the patterns according to which humans iteratively request and process information in constructing new understanding [17].

The idea that domain knowledge needs to be documented in a specification has been proposed by others, e.g., the *text macros* of Heninger [8] and the *designations* of Zave and Jackson [19], but without a theoretical basis. Leveson recognizes the need to capture expert intent and proposes structures in which to record it, but applies psychology only at the level of compound, high-order activities, and does not suggest methods to connect meanings to the elements in a model [12]. Even so, this approach produces complex artifacts, and the complexity is difficult to manage without automated support. She has thus enhanced the SpecTRM toolset to support the approach [13].

Berry explicitly recognizes the need for both elements: attention to the cognitive mechanisms that allow semantic generation and comprehension as well as to the relationship of semantics to the forms in a model [1]. However, both his problem characterization and solution approach can be enhanced with the rigor available in psychological and linguistic methods.

Maiden and Hare have employed an element of psycholinguistic theory to improving the efficacy of certain activities that contribute to their work in problem domains. For example, they used a card sorting technique to elicit facts about the storage organization of their subjects in order to improve the modeling of domain information in a database of reusable domain models [15].

While others have thus applied psychology and linguistics at some level and to various elements of the requirements problem, our approach differs in that it is thoroughly based on psycholinguistic theories that account for the low-level mechanics of language comprehension and production. In previous work, we examined how the ways in which humans innately use natural language result in statements of requirements that are incomplete, inconsistent, and open to misinterpretation [6, 5]. To support this finding, we exploited results from cognitive linguistics that detail the ways in which humans organize and communicate conceptual information. We extended this model to account for the breakdown that occurs in communication of information across boundaries of domain expertise, breakdown that is implicated as a major limiting factor of the quality of large and complex software systems [2].

Our goal was to develop an approach that injected more rigor into getting from the initial idea for a software element to the eventual model of its structure and function, upon which implementations would be based. We wanted to be able to do so demonstrably, predictably and repeatably. Specific findings of the linguistic analysis dictated that our approach have certain properties. The approach developed entails the introduction of an abstraction called the *domain map* that can be used to organize and document for non-experts critical application domain information. The need to manage the complexity of represented entities within our approach motivated the work that led to the toolset described in this paper.

To review, others have applied psychology and linguistics to some extent to the requirements problem. Our approach seeks to do so comprehensively and rigorously, which, because of the complexity generated, motivates automated support. This support then enables not only practical usability, but experience that advances development of the complete approach.

3   The *domain map*

We have argued previously that developers, who are non-experts in a particular domain, are unable to access the intended semantics directly from domain experts because the lexicon of the domain expert is partially incompatible with that of the developers [6, 5]. This implies the need that this information be processed into a form that is both cognitively accessible to developers and agreed with and among domain experts. The domain map is a structure designed to allow explicit and systematic access to essential domain semantics in a form that is meaningful to those who do not possess expert knowledge of the domain in question.

This need not preclude dynamic requirements, which are a reality with which we have to deal. Rather, it precludes inconsistency of the currency of the description and unavailability of a mapping of that currency into a form comprehensible to developers. A requirement might change, but the language available to describe it should not, and the description should be meaningful to all who need to use it.

The linguistic analysis indicated at least three areas in which a structured approach built around an artifact held promise to reduce miscommunication. Based on the analysis, the domain map artifact was designed to provide mechanisms to do the following:

- reduce the ease with which a non-expert may make an assumption about the meaning of a domain-specific term, by providing directed explication,

- account for the recursive nature of understanding, by grounding explications of all domain-specific terms directly or indirectly in terms that are in the common lexicon, and

- provide characterization mechanisms that alone or in collection with metrics collected from other instances of the artifact can allow visualization of trends and aid in allocation of resources.

3.1   Artifact Definition

More specifically, then, a domain map is a structure that documents the conversion of a domain specific, explicit representation of essential semantics to a form accessible to those with a common base set of representations. This entity in effect maps domain specific representations to representations built out of common terms and phrases. For these purposes, we define *common* and *domain* narrowly as follows. *Common* refers to that set of terms for which the association between a particular term and its semantics is sufficiently similar among interlocutors that relevant miscommunication is highly unlikely. In other words, a term is common if the respective storage structures and content possessed by any two people within a project are essentially the same with regard to salient linguistic elements [6, 5]. *Domain*, then, refers simply to all terms that are not *common*; if a term has domain-specific meaning, its storage structure and/or the content it contains differ for any two people from within and outside the domain, respectively.

To better serve its purpose of documenting this mapping, constraints are placed on the domain map such that the following properties are observed:

- A requirements specification for a software system includes a domain map.
- All domain specific terms that are relevant to the development of the specified software system are associated directly or indirectly with definitions consisting of exclusively common terms.
- No cycles are permitted in the use of definitions within definitions.
- The domain map and the documents to which it points are the only sources of domain-specific definitions to which developers can refer.

A domain map, then, at the highest level, is a structure that, from a set of terms drawn from a natural language requirements source, documents a partition of this set into *domain* and *common* terms and explicitly relates members of these partitions to each other, supplementing with additional *domain* and *common* terms where necessary in order to construct a completely *common* representation for every *domain* term.

Further, once a domain map is instantiated, it can provide additional value, since the artifact described can be subjected to analysis. The definition of any term or phrase in the original set describes a tree of dependency in which the root and all of the remaining non-terminal nodes are domain terms, and all of the terminal nodes are common terms (technically, it describes a directed acyclic graph since some definitions will include the same terms, but, for our purposes, conceiving of the domain map as a tree is equally valid). In particular, we would like to know about several properties of the tree, and collectively about the set of trees resulting from the original term set. A simple check to determine whether the terminal condition has been reached, i.e., whether every domain specific term can be paraphrased directly or indirectly by exclusively common terms, indicates whether the domain map is legal, i.e., whether there is a definition completely accessible to a non-expert. The depth of the tree gives some idea of the semantic complexity of a given term, and the maximum and average depths give an idea of the overall complexity of the domain lexicon, i.e., a measure of how far removed it is from everyday common language. These measures can be used to flag concepts at high risk for miscommunication, and to drive the amount of rigor applied in maximizing the validity of a model.

For further discussion of the domain map artifact, the reader is directed to [4, 6, 5].

3.2 Validation of the Artifact

As an example of the issues described, consider the following. In a small-scale study we undertook during the development of the domain map concept, developers were asked to work from an industrial natural language specification for a maritime track control system standard [9]. Among the quantities that were modeled was a ship's *bearing*, which was not defined within the specification, i.e., the original specification was, as they often are, incomplete. This left the researcher conducting the study to rely on her assumptions, based on her previous experience with things named *bearing*, which turned out to be erroneous with regard to the system context. Upon construction of a domain map, however, not only was the term associated with a common language definition that corrected the developer's misunderstanding, but dependencies in which it participated were also made apparent. The domain map showed explicitly that the correct understanding of over 37% of the 102 terms defined in this case *depended on* a correct understanding of the term *bearing*. This demonstrates just how important it is not only to fully expand definitions to common representations, but to recognize that the misunderstanding of a single term can have a tremendous impact on a developer's conception of an entire domain.

In a more rigorous test in a controlled environment, the domain map was further demonstrated to contribute positively to higher-integrity communication of domain-specific semantics. 114 subjects participated in a 2-group true-random experiment in which the control group was provided with a set of industrial natural language requirements and the experimental group was provided with the same natural language requirements complemented by a domain map. All members of both groups took a diagnostic test of domain-specific knowledge pertaining to the requirements. The experimental group performed significantly better overall, scoring higher on 7 out of 8 questions, and by more than 50% on 3 [4].

What the domain map provides is an organized and structured entity that documents essential domain knowledge. It accomplishes by design the goals set out in the earlier problem analysis. The domain map provides explicit and considered common access to the intended semantics, and it has permanence enabling it to become an element of the documentation for use later in the process by those even further removed from the domain experts. It provides as well the flexibility to be adapted to the needs and resources of the client and development organization, through selective application to the areas at highest risk for miscommunication, and by allowing applications of various levels of rigor.

While structures like the domain map that instantiate linguistically founded abstractions are conceivable and manually realizable, in practice there are severe limits on the value achievable through strictly manual means. These limits derive from size and complexity of the generated artifacts, but with automation, the representable complexity of such structures grows and further forms of processing can be performed. We next present a toolset that directs the creation of significant added value to and from such representations; this is value that is not predictably or systematically achievable without both the theoretical basis upon which the structures are founded as well as the automation of processes that the structures allow.

4   The Toolset

As illustrated in Figure 1, our goal for the toolset was to provide a support mechanism for applying the linguistic model, via the domain map, to the creation of early lifecycle artifacts such as requirements documents and specifications. Linguistically sound artifacts can be instantiated manually, but these instantiations are necessarily of limited complexity. Further, manually creating and analyzing even a relatively non-complex domain map is both time consuming and difficult. Developers must sift through all

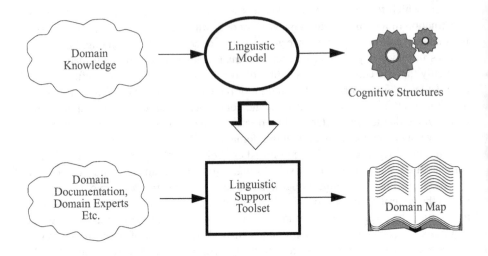

Fig. 1. Toolset goal.

material to ensure that all terms at issue have been identified, that they have each been provided with grounded and agreed-upon definitions, that all definitions are analyzed for legality, that overall organization and usability of the information is maintained, and so on. For a realistic requirements specification, this information and its organization can quickly become exhaustingly complex. Further, any manual analysis can be tedious and error-prone, and when done sufficiently rigorously to be valuable, it is likely to be prohibitively costly.

Clearly, automated support for the initial creation of the domain map and execution of the various forms of analysis that are possible is an attractive idea. More importantly, in addition to providing efficiency and reducing errors in processing, tools could allow the construction of representations that are more complex, as well as more realistically useful kinds of analysis capability than can be achieved manually. The following specific goals guided our support strategy:

- *Complexity management.*

  A key requirement for the toolset is to permit the creation of a domain map in a manner that embodies critical components of the linguistic theory as they apply to the problem. Our analysis indicated that lack of explicit attention to facts of semantic storage structure allowed breakdown in communication. The tool must provide effective control and management of the data elements representing these facts and their relationships as the structure grows in size, as well as facile alternations between related but separate views.

- *Completeness and Consistency analysis.*

  The domain map must be complete in the sense that all terms indicated to be domain-specific by the linguistic model are present and defined appropriately. "Appropriately" refers to one of three possible forms: (a) an explicit definition using only common terms, (b) an explicit definition using common and domain-

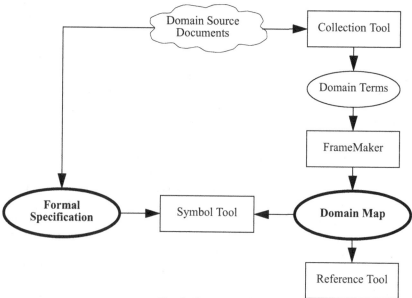

Fig. 2. Support toolset.

specific terms (themselves defined appropriately), or (c) a link to a domain-specific formalism. The tool must examine definitions for compliance with these forms. It must further examine for consistency the resulting graph structure that relates the definitions, checking for circularities and redefinitions.

- *Human Direction*

  The tool must provide direction to users in creation, refinement, and analysis of the structure. For example, upon selecting a term for definition from source materials, the tool should create the appropriate fields and guide the user in completing them. Further, it should systematically organize sets of situations where human judgment calls are necessary, such that users are more likely to resolve such situations. For example, it should collect and display location information for all instances of a term so that a user can examine instances in context for consistent usage. The tools should also provide a method of enforcing that processes are carried out, possibly in the form of requiring confirmation before proclaiming the structure to be legal according to all embedded constraints.

  To enable support for these activities, we have enhanced an existing toolset, Zeus [10], to provide facilities for systematic direction of the creation, refinement and analysis of domain maps, as well as possibilities for their integration with other lifecycle artifacts. The tools and their relationship to various entities are shown in Figure 2.

  Zeus is based on the FrameMaker desktop publishing system and the Z/EVES verification system. It provides comprehensive facilities for manipulation of both natural language and Z [10]. Its support for natural language is used in two ways. The primary use is to create and modify formal specifications that integrate formal elements written in Z with natural language that is organized to exploit linguistic theory. It can also be used to manipulate project and domain-related documents in whatever format domain experts and developers require using all of the facilities of unmodified FrameMaker.

4.1 Collection Tool

In order to support the creation of domain maps, Zeus has been extended with a facility that allows the collection of domain-specific terms and phrases. The creation of the list of domain terms and phrases is undertaken by developers and domain experts who make a number of passes through source materials. For example, a scenario we have exercised is one in which a developer makes the first pass through an original require-ments draft, indicating words and phrases he either outright does not understand, or has reason to believe might have domain-specific meaning of which he is not aware. Then a domain expert makes a pass through the same document, annotated with the developer's indications. The domain expert thus has a chance to validate the devel-oper's indications as well as add to them. This trade of active role can be iterated as necessary for the involved parties to converge on a set of terms in need of semantic accessibility from outside of the domain. Further, in the version of the tool under development, terms and phrases of interest, as well as descriptive information pertain-ing to them, can also be collected directly from structured artifacts that result from an elicitation process we have since defined.

The Zeus *Collection Tool* enables the above described passes through natural lan-guage requirements and the capturing of terms and phrases to be entered into the domain set. The mechanism is the selection (highlighting) of a term while in capture mode, followed by a keystroke, which creates a blank domain map entry for the term. The list of domain terms can be manipulated as different passes are made over the source materials, and natural language definitions, again negotiated by the involved parties, are entered for domain terms using the text manipulation facilities of FrameMaker. Thus the construction of an initial domain map abides by the necessary informality imposed by the development of ideas and their expression in natural lan-guage, but the Zeus tool guides navigation and systematic exploration of this informal space by providing the artifact structure and operations that allow explicit accounting for critical elements.

4.2 Reference Tool

Refinement and use of the domain map are supported by the *Reference Tool*. The refer-ence tool creates a graphic display of the domain map that shows all of the defined terms in alphabetical order. An example of the reference tool's display when applied to a sample specification is shown in the left portion of Figure 3. Since definitions are stated frequently using other domain terms or phrases, the reference tool displays for each domain term the set of domain terms upon which it depends. Further, it displays the definition of any term if the right mouse button is clicked over it (right portion of Figure 3), and if there are any additional domain terms in a definition, they are indi-cated with underlining.

The reference tool performs a variety of analyses on the domain map as the dis-play is built, allowing refinement from a draft to a legal form. For example, it checks for definitions that are either duplicates or empty, i.e., there is a placeholder for the definition text but no text has been entered. It detects cycles so that terms with circular

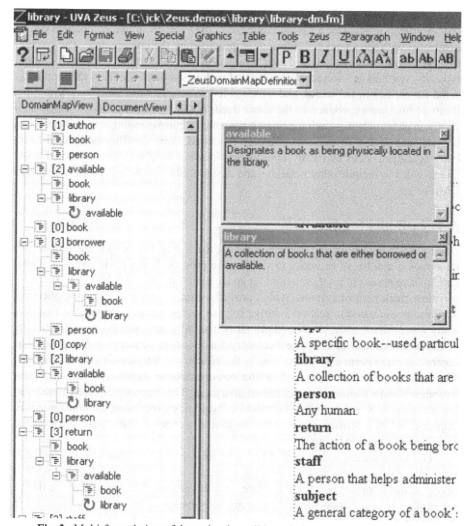

Fig. 3. Multi-framed view of dependencies, editing window, and pop-up definitions.

definitions can be refined to comply with the no-cycle rule (note examples in Figure 3 marked by circular arrows). Further, it checks the dependencies for all definitions and ensures that each is completely grounded in common terms.

Finally, the reference tool computes various metrics from the domain map, for example, the distribution of the number of levels required to ground domain terms (that is, the distribution of the depths of dependency) and the number of defined terms or phrases relative to the total word count for a requirements document. These metrics are useful in gaining a picture of the semantic complexity of individual terms and entire lexicons, allowing intuition regarding the most efficient application of resources.

4.3 Symbol Tool

If a specification includes a formal component, the symbols in that component can be associated with the contextual information provided by the domain map. The connection between formal symbols and their referents in the real world is complex [6, 5], but typically, symbols in a formalism are labeled with mnemonic identifiers that implicitly stand for entities in the world, and a user is left to interpret the identifiers within the limits of his own experience of the terms used. A third tool within Zeus, the *Symbol Tool*, can check whether each mnemonic possesses a corresponding, explicit entry in a domain map and is thereby intentionally grounded. Any identifier not linked to an entry is flagged. Zeus currently supports this function for Z specifications, and could be expanded to include other notations and design tools with formal elements, such as UML or Visio.

5 Feasibility Study

During development of the domain map approach and the supporting toolset, we undertook a number of activities to validate the progress being made. We were fortunate to have access to a set of natural language requirements describing a standard for maritime track control systems, which proved useful as an early testbed application. The results addressed in section 3 derive from this experience. However, the first case study was of small scale, performed primarily manually, and used to assess practicality of the approach and identify the necessary functionality of automated support. The controlled experiment assessed primarily the efficacy of the domain map artifact, but while prototype tools were used in the construction of experiment materials, the hypothesis under examination did not involve them. The functionality determined during the case study and prototyped for use in developing experiment materials was then implemented as a toolset, and to give the toolset a more realistic trial, we sought a more realistic environment.

This environment was provided for us by an industrial collaborator. Our collaborator allowed us access to development materials for a medical device, as well as access to development personnel familiar with the project. The purpose of the device we studied is to generate surgical planning information to be used by physicians in determining a course of therapy. We restricted our inquiry to a part of the system that calculates specific therapeutic effects. We began from the set of materials that constituted the requirements and specification for this element from which developers were expected to produce designs and implementations.

The Zeus toolset automated much of the construction and refinement of the domain map. In particular, it provided the necessary complexity management services thereby facilitating the efficient and complete development of the domain map for this application. The use of the completeness and consistency mechanisms enabled rapid checking of the form of the domain map and its essential properties. Zeus fulfills the goals stated in the previous section of complexity management, completeness and consistency analysis, and human direction. Using the toolset in an industrial context also generated ideas about how domain maps might be integrated with other lifecycle artifacts, in ways that were discussed earlier.

Notably, the case study forced out issues that were not fully apparent under the controlled circumstances of early approach and tool development. Of particular interest are the method of selection of terms for inclusion in the domain map, and the process by which definitions were constructed. The case study provided the clearest demonstration up to that time that both of these processes were underspecified and ad hoc; foundations were needed and new methods had to be added to the approach. In succeeding work, both of these activities have undergone rigorous (re)definition. In addition, a companion elicitation process, also built on linguistic principles, has been developed that supports and complements the domain map recording and propagation process. As of this writing, Zeus is undergoing enhancement to support these activities.

An issue that we would like to explore in future work is that of expert understanding stored as narrative or procedural memory versus that stored as hierarchical or ontological memory. While the domain map by its nature lends itself to the latter, we recognize that much expert or tacit knowledge is represented by the former. Linguistic theory concerning the semantics of procedural memory supports the existence of cognitive entities called *frames*, *schemas*, and *scripts* [11, 18] that could form the basis of an approach to representing procedural expert knowledge. Since these are compound entities that relate lower-level ones, such as the entities represented in a domain map, an approach to representing procedural knowledge using them could be integrated with the existing artifacts to provide a comprehensive model of the relationships that hold. Tool support would be expected to contribute to the practicality of such an approach.

Thus the experience illuminated both strengths and areas for improvement in both the approach and the tools. In particular, the tools proved to be a powerful aid to constructing and refining the domain map in an organized and efficient manner, and demonstrated that they allow an originally manual approach to scale to more realistic environments. Further, the experience gave the approach its first trial in a realistic setting, generating a number of insights that have since led to modifications in both the approach and the tools.

6   Summary

Effective communication of application domain knowledge among domain experts and software developers is crucial if the quality of requirements for high-consequence systems is to be improved. We developed a strategy to exploit systemic linguistic knowledge about particular aspects of human communication by embodying it in an artifact that can serve to organize and allow automated processing of meaning essential to the communication of critical application domain knowledge with integrity.

Earlier work addressed the cognitive and linguistic barriers to effective communication between domain experts and non-experts. Our approach exploits research in these fields to improve the communication of application domain knowledge. In this paper, we reviewed this approach and introduced tools built to support its deployment in real projects. While manual construction of our theoretically-founded artifacts is possible, there are limits to the complexity that can be represented as well as to the kinds of analysis that can be performed effectively and efficiently. The toolset was designed with the goal of automating not only what was achievable manually, but enhancing that set of functionality to handle realistic complexity in organization as well as in processing. The toolset directs involved parties in the construction of artifacts that by their structure and content enable the spread of domain knowledge among developers and throughout the lifecycle. The main artifact, a domain map, and its several views, provides documentation of domain knowledge that by design is more complete and consistent than are ad hoc or intuitive attempts at recording this information. The tools further support various forms of analysis of domain maps, providing information that directs their refinement as well as metrics that provide indications of semantic complexity. Further, the tools allow domain maps to be integrated with formal specifications as well as natural language documents that can benefit from such a reference.

We used these tools in collaboration with an industry partner to develop experimental documentation for recording and dissemination of domain knowledge relevant to the design of a medical device. The experience illuminated both strengths and areas for improvement in both the approach and the tools. In particular, the tools proved to be a powerful aid to constructing and refining the domain map in an organized and efficient manner, and demonstrated that they allow an originally manual approach to scale to realistic environments. The exercise provided a proof-of-concept that the construction of such an artifact, one that embodies systemic linguistic knowledge about miscommunication, and provides for a systematic, repeatable, and predictable process, can be realized in an industrial environment and on a useful scale.

We thus conclude that the approach, originally applied on only a small scale, is feasible for realistic projects, and that the combination of a theoretical foundation to motivate a structure and an industrial-strength support tool to direct its instantiation and analysis provides value not before achievable in reducing the incidence and severity of miscommunication. Practical construction and refinement of artifacts, as well as analysis and integration, were made tractable. The result was a set of documents that held value, demonstrated by additions, corrections, and enhancements beyond the original materials, and recognized by members of the collaborating organization. Further the experience generated insights that led to improvement of both the approach and the tools.

Acknowledgements.
It is a pleasure to thank our industrial collaborator for access to their materials and personnel. This work was funded in part by NSF under contract number CCR-0205447 and in part by NASA under contract NAG-1-2290.

References

1. Berry, D.: The Importance of Ignorance in Requirements Engineering. Journal of Systems and Software 28 (1995) 179–184
2. Curtis, B., Krasner, H., Iscoe, N.: A Field Study of the Software Design Process for Large Systems. Communications of the ACM 31(11) (1988) 1268–1287
3. Goguen, J.: Formality and Informality in Requirements Engineering. Journal of Systems and Software 28 (1995) 179–184

4. Hanks, K., Knight, J.: Improving Communication of Critical Domain Knowledge in High-Consequence Software Development: An Empirical Study. Proceedings: 21st International System Safety Conference (2003)

5. Hanks, K., Knight, J., Strunk, E.: A Linguistic Analysis of Requirements Errors and Its Application. University of Virginia Department of Computer Science Technical Report CS-2001–30 (2001)

6. Hanks, K., Knight, J., Strunk, E.: Erroneous Requirements: A Linguistic Basis for Their Occurrence and an Approach to Their Reduction. Proceedings: 26th Annual IEEE NASA Software Engineering Workshop (2001) 115–119

7. Hayhurst, K., Holloway, C.M.: Challenges in Software Aspects of Aerospace Systems. Proceedings: 26th Annual IEEE NASA Software Engineering Workshop (2001) 7–13

8. Heninger, K.: Specifying Requirements for Complex Systems: New Techniques and Their Applications. IEEE Transactions on Software Engineering SE-6(1) (1980) 2–12

9. International Electrotechnical Commission: Maritime Navigation and Radio Communication Equipment and Systems – Track Control Systems – Operational and Performance Requirements, Methods of Testing and Required Test Results. Project number: 62065/Ed. 1 (2000)

10. Knight, J., Hanks, K., Travis, S.: Tool Support for Production Use of Formal Techniques. Proceedings: International Symposium on Software Reliability Engineering (2001)

11. Langacker, R.: Concept, Image, and Symbol: The Cognitive Basis of Grammar. Mouton de Gruyter, Berlin (1990)

12. Leveson, N.: Intent Specifications: An Approach to Building Human-Centered Specifications. IEEE Transactions on Software Engineering 26 (2000) 15–35

13. Leveson, N., Reese, J., Heimdahl, M.: SpecTRM: A CAD Tool for Digital Automation. Proceedings: 17th Digital Avionics Systems Conference (1998)

14. Lutz, R.: Analyzing Software Requirements Errors in Safety-Critical, Embedded Systems. Proceedings: IEEE International Symposium on Requirements Engineering (1993) 126–133

15. Maiden, N., Hare, M.: Problem Domain Categories in Requirements Engineering. Int. J. Human-Computer Studies 49 (1998) 281–304

16. Potts, C., Newstetter, W.: Naturalistic Inquiry and Requirements Engineering: Reconciling Their Theoretical Foundations. Proceedings: IEEE International Symposium on Requirements Engineering (1997) 118–127

17. Potts, C., Takahashi, K., Anton, A. Inquiry-Based Requirements Analysis. IEEE Software 2(11) (1994) 21–32

18. Ungerer, F., Schmid, H.: An Introduction to Cognitive Linguistics. Longman, London (1996)

19. Zave, P., Jackson, M.: Four Dark Corners of Requirements Engineering. ACM Transactions on Software Engineering and Methodology 6(1) (1997) 1–30

Security Policy Configuration Issues in Grid Computing Environments

George Angelis, Stefanos Gritzalis, and Costas Lambrinoudakis

Department of Information and Communications Systems Engineering
University of the Aegean, Samos, GR-83200, Greece
{george.angelis, sgritz, clam}@aegean.gr

Abstract. A computational Grid is a hardware and software infrastructure that provides dependable, consistent, pervasive, and inexpensive access to high-end computational capabilities. The aim is to share among dynamic collections of individuals, institutions and resources in a flexible, secure, and coordinated manner. However, without an adequate understanding of the security implications of a Grid, both the owner who contributes resources to the Grid and the resource requestor can be subject to significant compromises in security. The basic prerequisite of establishing a secure Grid environment is the definition and implementation of a concrete security policy. Currently, in the existing Grid environments, security policy is often specified only by configuring access control lists associated with individual resources. It is obvious that significant work is needed in this area, which will lead to the specification of integrated security policies in this special environment where principals from multiple administrative domains co-exist. The purpose of this paper is to review a number of the security policies that have already been configured in existing Grid environments, identify the deficiencies and introduce a collection of all the issues that should be taken under consideration while building an integrated security policy in a Grid computing environment.

1 Introduction

Recently, evolutionary terms like collaboration, data sharing, interaction and distributed resources have been introduced in the world of computing, resulting in an increased focus on the interconnection of systems both within and across enterprises, whether in the form of intelligent networks, switching devices, caching services, appliance servers and storage systems. Distributed computing has matured from the notion of simple workload balancing to a ubiquitous solution that has been embraced by some of the world's leading organizations across multiple industry sectors.

One of the hottest tickets in distributed computing is Grid computing. According to [1], Grid computing is concerned with "coordinated resource sharing and problem solving in dynamic, multi-institutional virtual organizations". In other words, the Grid could be described as an infrastructure that tightly integrates computations devices, software, databases, specialized instruments, displays and people from widespread locations and under different management authorities. A Grid enforces users by allow-

S. Anderson et al. (Eds.): SAFECOMP 2003, LNCS 2788, pp. 331–341, 2003.

ing them to access heterogeneous resources, such as the above mentioned, that are distributed geographically and organisationally. It also benefits organizations by allowing them to offer unused resources on existing hardware. This is summarized in the following fact: A large number of applications are starved for computation resources, whereas an overwhelming majority of computers are often idle. This can be bridged by allowing computation-intensive applications to be executed on otherwise idle resources, no matter where the latter are located.

Along with the positive impact that the creation and deployment of Grid environments have had to the increase of computational performance, they have also introduced a new set of security concerns and issues. Since grid resources are managed by many widely dispersed organizations, often with different security requirements and possibly conflicting security policies, managing security for such an environment is not easy. The specific characteristics of Grids lead to security problems that have not been addressed by existing security technologies for distributed systems.

In this paper, we are focusing on the importance of a concrete security policy that should encompass the Grid environment. In section 2 we explain the role of a security policy within a computing environment, we try to prove its importance, and we present some issues related to security policies in the specific distributed structure of the Grid. In section 3 we review the established security policies of some existing Grid environments discussing also some major deficiencies. Section 4 introduces a complete inventory of all the special administrative, technical and structural issues that should be taken under consideration when building a security policy for Grid computing environments. After the description and analysis of each special issue, we propose how the security policy should be configured to overcome the problem or address the issue. This could be utilized as a brief but fairly complete reference guide for the security policy designers of a Grid computing environment. Finally, in section 5 we conclude the paper.

2   Security Policy in Grid Computing Environments

The Grid computing environment, combining the distributed resources and process flow concept and the heterogeneity of the components that it consists of, has introduced a lot of design issues that until now had not been considered.

Grid is a multi-user environment and the user population is dynamic. Members of many institutions collaborate and change frequently. An individual user may be associated with different local user-names, credentials, certificates and accounts at different sites. Even worse, user-names are often duplicated across name-space domains. This may cause the problem of systems not being able to easily distinguish in an unambiguous manner between two different users who have been assigned the same user-name on two different domains.

The resource pool is also large and dynamic. Since individual institutions decide when to contribute resources and when to withdraw them, the availability of these can change rapidly. A dynamic number of different resources may be combined during a single process. In other words, a computation may acquire, reserve and release many resources from many different institutions until being completed. As an example a single computation could spawn multiple processes that could be distributed to be executed in multiple remote sites, and finally each returning the results to the parent process or even to a third destination. This may result to the dynamic creation and destruction of communication channels between them as well (like TCP/IP sockets).

Interoperability of security policies is perhaps the most important but also complicated factor that impacts the design and effectiveness of a Grid computing environment. It is extremely rare to find two organizations that are identical in security policy, or in the way they carry it out. In order to participate in a Grid community you need to be able to adapt your policy so that it can be enforced by the Grid security services. As a first rule, both your security policy and the security policy of the Grid community you wish to join need to be well defined. Since there are multiple authentication and authorization mechanisms, there may be no single syntax for the specification of principals or credentials. Policy integration should incorporate the diverse mechanisms and policies that can co-exist in such a multipolicy environment. Security policies of distributed participants may have limited ability to change and adapt to their co-operators' ones. Since the security of the entire Grid depends on the security of individual institutions, a vulnerability to the security mechanism of one of them may compromise the entire environment.

3   Security Policies Review

The cornerstone of establishing a Grid computing environment is the configuration and implementation of a well-defined security policy. An overview of how the most widely-used modern metasystems address the important security issues is presented in the following paragraphs.

3.1   Globus

Globus, developed at USC, is the best known and probably the most widely-used end-to-end Grid infrastructure available today [5]. *GSI* is the component/part of the *Globus Toolkit* that configures the basic security mechanisms and consequently defines the security policy of the Globus-based Grids.

GSI mainly focuses on authentication, since this can be the base for other security services like authorization and encryption [6]. Authentication in GSI is based on proxies. A special process called a user proxy is created by the user on his local Globus host and is given permission to act on behalf of the user for authentication purposes. A temporary certificate is also created for the user proxy. To enable authentication on the resource side, a resource proxy responsible for scheduling access to a resource, maps global to local credentials/identities (e.g. Kerberos tickets). In order to implement the above, authentication is based on both TLS and SSL protocols, which provide for public key based authentication, message integrity and confidentiality, and the X.509 Certificates PKI mechanism.

GSI, evaluated in terms of authorization and security logging can be rated as inadequate, while it partially deals with the problem of preserving autonomy of local security policies.

Early in 2002, the Globus team has introduced an *Open Grid Services Architecture (OGSA)* that supports the creation, maintenance, and application of ensembles of services maintained by dynamic sets of resources and people called *virtual organizations* [7]. The OGSA approach to security (although it has been omitted from the specifications) is to treat it as an implementation issue, which should be addressed in the development of protocol bindings, hosting environments and service implementations.

3.2   Legion

Developed at University of Virginia, Legion is an architectural model for the meta-computing environment, implemented in the Mentat Programming Language (MPL), an object-safe language [8]. Resources and users within the Legion model are represented by independent, active objects, which communicate via asynchronous method invocations, supported by an underlying message passing mechanism. For the purpose of communication, every object is identified by a unique, location independent Legion Object Identifier (LOID).

Security in Legion is based on a public key infrastructure for authentication, and access control lists (ACLs) for authorization. However, it can be retargeted to other authentication mechanisms such as Kerberos. Identity, and consequently authentication in Legion are based on LOIDs. The LOID of each object contain its credential which is a X.509 certificate with an RSA public key. The concept of PKI is completed with the existence of a Certification Authority. Authorization in Legion follows the local access list model. The ACL associated with any object encodes the permissions for that object. When any method of a Legion object is invoked, the protocol stack associated with the object ensures that the security layer is invoked to check the defined permissions, before the request is forwarded to the method itself. Integrity in Legion is provided at the level of Legion messages. Public keys are used, either for encryption of the messages or just for hashing (message digest computation), depending on the needs and the risk of the communication.

Legion provides a rather high-level security model without describing architecture or special protocols. Security mechanisms in Legion are hardcoded into the security architecture, thus making incorporation of new standards difficult. Legion certificates do not have a time-out, therefore the period of time during which the certificate is vulnerable to attack is not limited. Multiple-sign-on, which consists one of the major problems in Grid computing environments, seems not to be addressed by Legion's security policy. Within each domain, it is Legion (and not the domain administrators) that dictates protection measures. This intrusive approach to isolation may be unacceptable at some sites.

3.3   WebOS & CRISIS

WebOS was developed at Berkeley as an effort to simplify the development of wide-area applications while providing efficient global resource utilization [9]. It meant to be an extension to the conventional OS, proposing distributed techniques in order to include most of a distributed OS's functionality (e.g. resources load balancing, fail-over processes, distributed file systems, etc).

CRISIS is the security subsystem of WebOS, in other words the subsystem based on which applied security policy is configured. It emphasizes a number of design principles for highly secure distributed system, such as redundancy to eliminate single points of attack, lightweight control of permissions, strict process control to make each access decision, caching credentials for performance, as well as timing-out identity certificates for security. Public keys signed by a Certificate Authority compose the basic authentication mechanism of CRISIS. The signed certificates are attached to all future messages of the specific user. In terms of authorization, CRISIS uses the security manager approach. In other words, as all programs execute in the context of a security domain, each domain runs a security manager responsible for granting or refusing access to all local resources. This is an approach that respects the most (compared to the other Grids' security policies) the Grid participants' local security policies. However, CRISIS does not support development of new policies for new security mechanisms as they are added to WebOS, and existing security policies cannot be modified.

Generally CRISIS seems to propose a more complete security policy than the previously described Grids. However, it still has some deficiencies. In terms of autonomy, CRISIS, while still allowing local control over security policy, doesn't allow local administrators to choose the security mechanism used. Like Legion, it also seems not to address multiple-sign-on problems that arise in distributed computing environments.

3.4   UNICORE

Originally developed by Fujitsu, UNICORE is a Grid environment which includes large computing centers, public offices, universities, commercial sites and individual users, and is implemented using Java language [10]. Java has its own built-in security model, but the question is in what extent UNICORE takes advantage of it in order to protect the local domains from the execution of remote jobs containing malicious code.

A key feature of the UNICORE security model is confidentiality and integrity of the transmitted data. The security model supports both job signing (using hashing techniques and message digest features) and data encryption. Not only for the secure data communication but for user authentication as well, UNICORE is based upon a Public Key Infrastructure. The PKI architecture is implemented based on a centralized model with a single Certification Authority (CA) and multiple Registration Agents (RAs). X.509 certificates are used to authenticate users, jobs, and Gateways, to sign jobs, and to grant to developers the authority for code signing. Public LDAP directory servers located in the users' local sites can be used for the storage of their certificates. However, this is optional. The PKI architecture described can also be extended to cover authorization issues in UNICORE. Finally, SSL has been proposed as a low-level network protocol for the secure implementation of PKI.

Compared with Globus, the security model of UNICORE is stronger. However, the fact that UNICORE is currently not based upon multiple CAs but rather upon a single one causes some drawbacks to the proposed policy. The existence of a common single CA, compromises in a way the concept of the decentralized logic of the Grids, since it constitutes a single point of failure, a single point of load and delay increase, so the advantage of an efficient access control gained by the single CA is counterbalanced. Other less important deficiencies of the security policy related to the lack of further authentication procedures (e.g. for participant institutes not having their own RAs) also exist.

3.5   NASA IPG

Information Power Grid (IPG) is the name of NASA's project to build a fully distributed computing and data management environment [11]. The aim is to provide the NASA scientific and engineering communities a substantial increase in their ability to solve problems that depend on use of large scale and dispersed resources.

The security policy adopted by IPG is focusing in the following Grid related security issues:

☐ Single-sign-on. This is achieved based on cryptographic credentials that are maintained in the users' desktop.

☐ End-to-end encrypted communication channels, to ensure confidentiality and integrity. This is provided by X.509 identity certificates implementing PKI, together with the Globus security services that IPG has chosen to adapt to its environment.

☐ Authorization and access control that provides for management of user rights and trusted third parties to attest to corresponding user attributes.

☐ Infrastructure security including technologies like IPSec and secure DNS to authenticate IP packet origin, secure network devices management and configuration.

IPG is currently still in an early experimental phase and its goal to establish a uniform approach to distributed management of locally controlled resources has not yet been achieved. Consequently, it is too early to have high expectations from the proposed security policy whose effort though trying to cover most of the security issues experimented in existing Grid computing environments should definitely be acknowledged.

3.6   DataGRID

The DataGRID project (http://web.datagrid.cnr.it) is a European Community supported project that has the objective to enable next generation scientific exploration which requires intensive computation and analysis of shared large-scale databases, from hundreds of Terabytes to Petabytes, across widely distributed scientific communities.

As with IPG, DataGRID has also chosen Globus for some underlying infrastructures, including the security services it provides mainly in order to address authentication. The authorization model suggests a role-based community in which the virtual organization decides the roles of its users, the rights associated with each role and the degree of delegation allowed. It also classifies information managed, and defines roles depending on this classification (e.g. only some resources are allowed to store and handle confidential data). Auditing issues are also covered in the security policy, as well as the protection of the produced logs, so that it is hard for an attacker to perform an attack, either successful or failed, and then try to obliterate and remain unobserved. Finally, confidentiality based on encryption is also addressed in the security policy with the unusual requirement of data being encrypted in storage in an encrypted format that the local administrators are not able to decrypt. This has been included, in order to accomplish confidentiality of data and in this way only the data owner can actually view the data contents. However, the concern is that anybody can load offensive or malicious data into another host's storage areas, without the domain administrators being able to detect it, which may have legal and regulatory impact to the specific domain unintentionally hosting these data.

At the moment, the lack of easily operated and secure authorization technology is the most obvious shortcoming in the security policy of the DataGRID.

4   Security Policy Configuration Issues

All organizations participating in the above described Grid environments seem to be well informed about the need for a security policy, and they do not ignore or connive at the risks that result from a poorly or deficiently configured policy. Grid computing though, is a fairly new extension of the distributed environments, and has not yet matured enough to offer the experience and the knowledge needed to face all security problems that arise. Moreover, we should not forget the fundamental and common rule in security that no matter what efforts you make you will never be 100% sure that you have a totally protected environment where nobody will be able to intrude. •t is not in the scope of this paper trying to compare the security policies currently proposed and implemented in the above described distributed systems; rather than that we have tried in the following paragraphs to collect and list all the issues and challenges that one should take under consideration when building a security policy for a Grid computing environment, in order to minimize the risk of a security breach.

4.1   Delegation

The creation of a proxy credential so that in essence an agent will act on behalf of a principle is a form of delegation, an operation of fundamental importance in Grid computing environments. The conventional approach when an entity • requests an entity B to act on behalf of A, is to grant unlimited delegation, which in fact means that entity B is unconditionally granted the ability to impersonate entity A. As has already been discussed the Grid is not a fully trusted environment due to the heterogeneity and the dynamic population of participants. Therefore the issue of delegation has to be faced with more scepticism. Authentication operations – and hence further delegated credentials – are involved at each stage, as resources determine whether to grant requests, and computations determine whether resources are trustworthy. It is obvious that delegating too many rights could lead to abuse, while delegating too few rights could prevent the task from being completed. What a security policy should do is specify the rights that may be delegated, the principals to which these rights may be delegated (including intermediaries), and care for the *protection of the delegated credentials* imposing controls like validity expiration after a time period.

4.2   Identity Mapping

Different sites participating in a Grid environment may use different local authentication solutions, such as Kerberos, Secure Shell (SSH), userid and plain password, etc. Mapping Grid identities to local userids is a way to enable a user to have a *single-sign-on* and yet do not violate or reject legacy access control mechanisms on those sites that require it. Single-sign-on means that a user should be able to authenticate once, in the initiation phase of a computation, and fork other computations that acquire, reserve and release resources, and communicate internally, without further authentication of the user, since this is impractical and generally unacceptable. In order to achieve identity mapping the user must have a local id at the sites to be accessed, and the site administrator must agree with the Grid administrator on the mapping to be used. However, this may raise several security implications, related to the rights that eventually the user will have to the local domain. A security policy should prefer to incorporate a mechanism for allowing the local administrator to specify trust relations with various Certificate Authorities, rather than trying to directly map the ids. In this case the CAs rather than the local administrators are the responsible units for the trust relationship between a user and a local domain that needs to be accessed.

4.3   Policies Interoperability

Grid security policy may provide interdomain security mechanisms, however access to local resources will typically be determined by a local security policy which is enforced by a local security mechanism. It is impractical to modify every local resource to accommodate interdomain access policy. The Grid security policy should respect and integrate with local security solutions for the achievement of an overall high-level security.

4.4   Grid Information Services

A Grid security policy should care for an information service to allow potential users to locate resources and to query them about access and availability. Access to these services for query or update should be very carefully secured, and strictly controlled, since any attacker could retrieve valuable and detailed information related to the available resources of the site. The security policy should have defined the proper processes for this access with not only authentication and authorization procedures, but with confidentiality and integrity features in the answers to the users' queries as well. LDAP protocol, which has its own password based access control, is a solution that addresses authentication and authorization. A mechanism is needed to use Grid credentials as the basis for directory service access. In case of X.509 credentials and public key infrastructure, the above mentioned needs for confidentiality and integrity could also be fulfilled.

4.5   Exportability

This is an issue mostly related to encryption features supported by a Grid security policy. It is has already been stated that export control laws regarding encryption technologies vary from country to country. As a result, it is more complicated for a Security Policy to select and encourage the usage of specific encryption algorithms in order to offer integrity and confidentiality. Luckily there are is a plethora of encryption mechanisms (PKI, symmetric/asymmetric encryption, digital signatures, message digests based on hashing techniques, etc), infrastructure and protocols (SSL, TLS, etc), as well as algorithms (RSA, DSA, DES, IDEA, Twofish, etc), that a security policy can chose of, in order to overcome the problem of exportability without downgrading the level of security offered. Of course, selection of a standard is imperative to ensure uniformity.

4.6   Resource Selection

One of the principles of the Grid computing environments is the selection and usage of resources located in multiple administrative domains. The fact that users typically have little or no knowledge of the resources contributed by other participants, poses a significant obstacle to their use. For this reason, information services mentioned above, designed to support the initial discovery and evaluation as well as the ongoing monitoring of the existence and the characteristics of resources, are a vital part of a Grid environment. The choice of the "best" suited resource among a number of these depends on physical characteristics of the resource itself, of the connectivity, of the security, of the frequency of access requests that it receives and its possibility of being released at the moment of the request, and of course of the policy that governs access to this system. The common security approach must be intended to support a wide range of these local access control policies.

4.7   Firewalls and Virtual Private Networks

Grids that span multiple administrative rights and encourage the dynamic addition of resources are not likely to benefit from the security provided by static, centrally administered commercial firewalls or VPNs. Existence of a firewall in front of an administrative domain where a required resource is located can result in prohibition of access. Grid Information services must also be informed about existence of firewalls, so that resource requestors may reject the resource protected by the firewall from the beginning. A Grid security policy however, should not oblige administrative domains to eliminate usage of their already configured firewalls, since the existence of the firewall may be an enforcement rule of the local security policy, which in that way will be disrespected and violated. Instead, a Grid security policy should look for a solution that will constitute the golden section in this issue: Some VPNs support X.509 identity certificates for authorization and might be able to use Grid ids. Such a VPN might present a way to get through firewalls and allow the standard Grid access control to work, without forcing local security policies to exclude any of their security standards.

The above can be used as a reference guide, either when intention is to establish a new Grid environment and you need to define the governing security policy, or when being security policy designer for an institution needing to participate to an already existing Grid environment, you have chosen to somehow accommodate your policy in order to adapt to the global one of the Grid. Even if not all of the proposed solutions are incorporated into the security policy under creation/review, the above constitutes a good base for discussion and consideration that could definitely lead to better awareness of the distinctiveness of the Grid computing environment.

5   Conclusions

As the Grid matures, security problems are more clearly defined, emerging technologies are standardized and solutions are proposed which eventually will be able to address in a great extent these issues. Current Grid environments are making efforts to incorporate security within their functionality and build policies which are continuously updated to address the arising security problems. The drawback is that there is not enough experience in the peculiar Grid environment which would help to perfect the existing security policies, and experience from conventional stand-alone and centrally managed environments could leave a lot of gaps. Perhaps the most obvious direction for immediate future work is in further testing and deployment of the existing systems. Many potential bottlenecks and limitations of these systems cannot be discovered except through real-world experience.

In this paper we presented a first full inventory of the most common security issues that have been experienced in the Grid computing environments, and how security policies should accommodate in order to address these. This can be used as a brief but complete reference guide for the Grid participant institutions which would like to enrich their security policy or build a new one from scratch. In addition, this inventory offers a wide discussion field regarding security issues in the Grid environment, based on the knowledge that has been acquired from security policy configurations of existing Grids as these were described earlier in this paper.

Since this is an ongoing effort, we intend to continue enhancing the Security Policy configuration process by combining the received feedback from the real-world experience, and the contribution of emerging technologies. The aim is to achieve an adequate level of experience and knowledge that will enable us to propose a security policy configuration mechanism that will automate the creation and validation of a Grid security policy, by consulting a security issues inventory like the one proposed here. This inventory could be implemented as a continuously updated knowledge and analysis database, parameterised in such a way that upgrades and improvements of the Security Policy could be automatic and completely transparent to the users and the participant institutions, and eventually all introduced security problems would be effectively addressed.

References

1. Foster, C. Kesselman, The GRID Blueprint for a New Computing Infrastructure, Morgan Kaufmann Publishers Inc, 1999.
2. Foster, C. Kesselman, G. Tsudik, S. Tuecke, A Security Architecture for Computational Grids, Proc. 5th ACM Conference on Computer and Communications, pp. 83–192, 1998.
3. M. Humphrey, M. Thompson, Security Implications of Typical Computing Usage Scenarios, Proc. 10th IEEE International Symposium on High Performance Distributed Computing, 2001.
4. N. Minsky, V. Ungureanu, Unified Support for Heterogeneous Security Policies in Distributed Systems, 7th USENIX Security Symposium, 1998.
5. Foster, C. Kesselman, The Globus Project: A Status Report, IPPS/SPDP '98 Heterogeneous Computing Workshop, 1998.
6. S. Tuecke, Grid Security Infrastructure (GSI) Roadmap, Internet Draft, 2001.
7. Foster, C. Kesselman, J. Nick, S. Tuecke, The Physiology of the Grid, An Open Grid Services Architecture for Distributed Systems Integration, Globus Project, 2002.
8. Ferrari, F. Knabe, M. Humphrey, S. Chapin, A. Grimshaw, A Flexible Security System for Metacomputing Environments, Department of Computer Science, University of Virginia, Technical Report CS-98-36, 1998.
9. E. Belani, A. Vahdat, T. Anderson, M. Dahlin, The CRISIS Wide Area Security Architecture, Proc. Of the USENIX Security Symposium, 1998.
10. T. Walter, R. Letz, T. Kentemich, H. Hoppe, P, Wieder, An Analysis of the UNICORE Security Model, Copyright Global Grid Forum, 2002.
11. W. Johnston, D. Gannon, B. Nitzberg, Grids as Production Computing Environments: The Engineering Aspects of NASA's Information Power Grid, 8th IEEE International Symposium on High Performance Distributed Computing, 1999.

Dependability and Survivability of Large Complex Critical Infrastructures

Sandro Bologna, Claudio Balducelli, Giovanni Dipoppa, and Giordano Vicoli

ENEA C.R.Casaccia
Via Anguillarese, 301
S.Maria di Galeria - 00060 - ROMA - ITALY
{bologna, balducell_c, giovanni.dipoppa,
vicoli}@casaccia.enea.it

Abstract. This paper refers to research activities related to SAFEGUARD project (IST Project Number: IST-2001-32685). The aims of the project is to examine LCCI's in terms of nature of different facets in each infrastructure: organizational, computational (cyber) and physical layers. Critical inter-dependencies among layers can thus be analyzed. Possible impact of bad events, early classified in attack scenarios with and without SAFEGUARD, will be coped with countermeasures to maintain at acceptable level system's operability. SAFEGUARD, an agent-based middleware, is conceived to operate embedded inside of the cyber-layers, the more sensitive part to malicious attacks and anomalies, and is designed to enhance dependability and survivability of a LCCI. Self-healing mechanism of SAFEGUARD agents will start with the trouble diagnosis and classification using Hybrid Intrusion Detection techniques (software instrumentation, novelty detection, etc.). Once the problem has been diagnosed, a number of techniques will be used to solve and repair the fault (i.e.: adaptive middleware technology, backup, hot standby and so on). More self-healing mechanisms will have to be combined and coordinated to with an attempt to deal with the source of the problem.

1 Introduction

The term Large Complex Critical Infrastructure (LCCI) defines a distributed network of distributed and independent processes that work collaboratively and synergistically to produce and distribute essential services. The Achilles' heel of a LCCI is in its same architecture, heterogeneous and decentralized. So, in order to find proportionate countermeasures to new and always different threats, was conceived SAFEGUARD (see Acknowledgment), the project will investigate new ways of protecting large complex critical infrastructures against hacker's attacks, but also from failures and accidents. It is currently developing a system that will be able to detect anomalies in these infrastructures, by interacting with existing applications and providing some self-healing mechanism. On the basis of requirements, SAFEGUARD design will be concentrated on new kinds of vulnerabilities, and more the interaction of SAFEGUARD with networks management will consist in the monitoring and the control of hardware and software, in a constant state of change as adjustments are

S. Anderson et al. (Eds.): SAFECOMP 2003, LNCS 2788, pp. 342–353, 2003.

made to the network. So need of mechanisms [1] arise to detect unusual conditions and automatically to try to strengthen networked systems against malicious insiders and outsiders, operator mistakes and hardware and software faults intervening where the fault is reported.

While complexity and interdependencies of the systems arise, the possibility of always new and unexpected events increase too; in such situation, being impossible to forecast all typologies of attacks and faults, learning the "normal" operating behaviour of the system is a precondition to detect "novel" working conditions indicating more or less deviations from a safer state.

Special low level agents, acting as "smart sensors" of sequences of events and data patterns, are designed to generate normal/abnormal conditions from different locations inside the distributed infrastructure. These conditions will be correlated together to confirm or disclaim the anomalies. If anomaly detection agents generate early alarm conditions in some part of the network, recovery and self- isolation strategies could be fired.

The chosen multi-agent platform realises a middleware that can be embedded inside of LCCI or deployed on the crucial nodes of the infrastructure.

2   Architecture of SAFEGUARD Platform

Final product of SAFEGUARD project will consist in an agent-based middleware [2] [3] [4], which will build up a model of the normal operation of the networked infrastructure and responds promptly to anomalies. Every agent has a well definite role inside the architecture showed in Fig.1. Problems in the network will be grouped and classified by Correlation agents, which will bring together information from Hybrid Anomaly Detecting agents and Topology agents. Wrapper agents will envelop existing security and diagnostic applications (such as intrusion detection systems, firewalls, virus checkers and so on). This evaluation of the state of the network will be passed on to Action agents for a response, which may include contacting human operators or a feedback to the anomaly detecting and wrapper agents. Negotiation agents will communicate with agents located in other large complex critical infrastructures to request services and exchange information about security alerts. Again Fig.1 does show the arrangement and interactions among these agents.

In order to scale SAFEGUARD over a system with many hundreds or thousands of nodes, the Correlation agents will be organized hierarchically to place high level Correlation agents that receive information from lower level Correlation agents, which in turn gather information from Hybrid Anomaly Detecting, Topology and Wrapper agents.

3   Agent Structure

3.1   An Example: Inside Hybrid Anomaly Detecting Agent

The primary role of SAFAGUARD is to detect anomalous behaviours by mean of agents trained to monitor the network and pass information related to non conven-

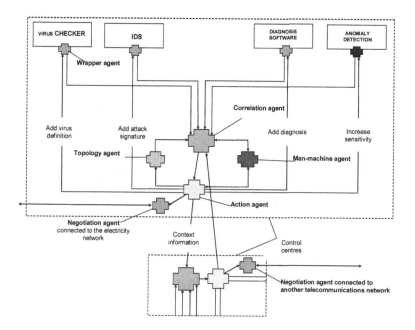

Fig. 1. SAFEGUARD Architecture

tional facts to agents for analysis and action. A number of different types of anomaly detectors will be employed in the SAFEGUARD system, all of which should have learned, in a high intensive training phase [15],[16],[17],[18], the normal behaviour of the system whilst no attacks, failures and accidents are present and then monitor the behaviour of the system for deviations from this normal model. These anomaly detectors will be capable of learning from their mistakes and adjusting to gradual changes in the system over time. A panoply of estimation methods were candidate for an effective utilization and implementation inside SAFEGUARD anomaly detection agents. In some case they may be alternative options and in some other cases options applicable at the same time to improve the system detection performance. Independently by the adopted estimation method the anomaly agent has the necessity, ahead of SAFEGUARD deployment (and some times during the course of time), to "learn" more about the normal/abnormal behaviour of the network. Depending on the estimation method adopted, the learning activity could be driven by the human expert or through on line data acquisition from the external network. The generic architecture of hybrid anomaly detecting agent in SAFEGUARD is visualized in Fig.2.

It is subdivided and specialized in three main containers (or modules):

- Information Container: the information container acquires data (courses of events) from the instrumentation installed in the lower layer containing the infrastructure controlling software. Courses are transmitted to the Intelligence container, from which, after the inference phase, information about system working state and, eventually, fault alarms are returned. State information and fault alarms are made available to the top level agents like correlation, topology and human interface agents.

- Command Container: these modules are activated by the top level agents, as the correlation and human interface agents, to select (Start/Stop) rule or case based engines. Top level agents have also the possibility to select the types of event courses to be considered during the inferential process. This functionality allows for example to the action agents to increase/decrease the sensitivity of anomaly detecting agents. The Command container has also the possibility to activate/deactivate some instrumentations.

- Intelligence Container: it contains the two above described modules, acting as Rule base engine and Case base engine. Each one has a corresponding data base containing rules and cases. Data flows coming to and from the Intelligence container are processed by the other two agent containers.

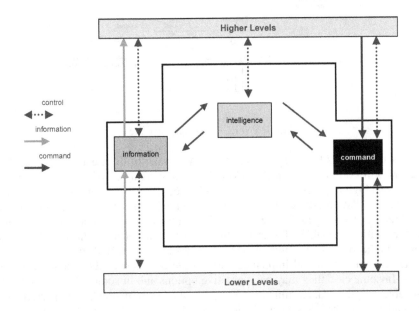

Fig. 2. Inside Hybrid Anomaly Detecting agent

Typically inside a Intelligence container of a hybrid anomaly detecting agent there could be many anomaly detection engines based on different "novelty" detection mechanisms:

- Case Based Reasoning engine [7],[8],[10],[11]
- Data Mining engine [12],[13]
- Neural Network Back Propagation engine [6],[9],[20],[21],[22]
- Other promising approaches, e.g.: N-GRAM scanning, Invariants method [16] [24]

Let it suppose that some, but not all, of these engines generates an anomaly detection alert signal. What should happen ? There are many approaches to address this problem. Examples are Majority Vote and Stacking. More in detail:

- a Majority Vote schema simply takes a vote on engines output. This assumes that all engines perform comparably well on average. A priori this may not be the case. From the voting process we can also generate alert degrees. For example: an alert signal from just one engine gives a yellow alert, two alert signals give a orange alert and three alert signals (i.e. all engines output an alert) give a red alert (e.g. a definitively confirmed alarm for intrusion).
- a Stacking schema [19] tries to learn which engines are the reliable ones using another learning algorithm, the meta-learner, to discover how best to combine the output of the base learners (engines). This is done again using standard data mining techniques.

Which supervisor is best for the purposes can only be determined experimentally. The tuning process of various tools and approaches will constitute the training of the Intelligence part of SAFEGUARD.

4   Other Agents

Other agents, which primary scope is to support the anomaly detecting agents, constitute the necessary corollary so that this multi-agent platform will work fine and effectively. They gather, coordinate, filter, communicate with the world, exchange information, and so on. The extreme differentiation and specialization of these agents make the platform more flexible and suitable to be scaled or deployed in different contexts.

4.1   Wrapper Agent

Wrapper Agents (WA) are the interface between existing standard software and sensors, our Intrusion Detection System (IDS), and the actual agent-based SAFEGUARD system. Typically these applications are: IDS, Host based IDS, firewalls, virus checkers and other diagnostic software. The task of the WA's is two fold:

- on the one hand it has to send information acquired from standard or SAFEGUARD low layer applications to the appropriate agents, e.g. Correlation Agent or Topology Agent
- it has to convey information and commands from Action Agents or MMI (Man Machine Interface) Agents to standard applications for reconfiguration or safe policy updates.

Standard applications mentioned above normally create output in form of Database tables or ASCII text streams, e.g. in XML format. For example BlackIce IDS for Windows generates output in CSV Microsoft Excel format, whereas SNORT IDS creates Database event tables. A Wrapper agent either polls this information using SQL statements or just receives Events and converts them into a format which can be read by the agents. In order to avoid information overflow in the agent world pre-filtering has to be performed in the information part of the Wrapper agent.

Another type of information for the WA is the current status of the system in terms of memory consumption, CPU load, running processes, etc. Anomalous changes of these system parameters could be symptoms of some anomalies deriving from malfunctions or intrusion detections. All functionalities of these two types of Wrapper agents are outlined in the Use Case Diagram in Fig.3.

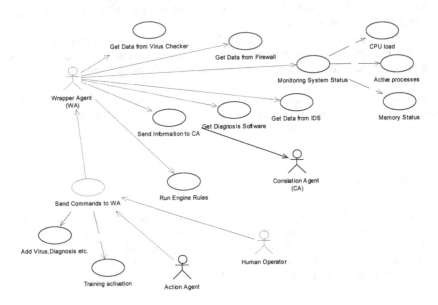

Fig. 3. The role of Wrapper agent

The Use Case Diagram shows the WA Actor that gets data from virus checker, firewall, diagnosis software. It also monitors the system status - parameters such as the CPU load, available memory and active processes. It also activates the rule engine and sends information to Correlation Agent. It receives commands from Human operator and from Action Agent about the training activation and updating of virus definition, attack signature and diagnosis.

4.2   Correlation Agent

The Correlation agents will be responsible for building and maintaining a model of what is happening in the network. They will do this by integrating information from Hybrid Anomaly Detecting agents, Topology agents and Wrapper agents and requesting more information once a problem has been detected. Ambiguous situations could be resolved by fine tuning the sensitivity of the anomaly detectors. In addition to their coordination functions, the correlation agents will look for connections in the information that they receive and use this to update applications on the system. For example, by correlating information about an anomalous process with a positive result from the virus checker they can explicitly identify the anomalous process as a virus and learn its anomaly pattern, so that it (and its variants) can be recognized more quickly in the future. This will be especially useful for polymorphic viruses. The correlation agents could also update the IDS knowledge base when Hybrid Anomaly Detecting agent discover the signature of an unknown buffer overflow attack.

4.3   Action Agent

The Action agents will observe the network model generated by the Correlation agents and decide upon an appropriate course of actions when problems arise. The actions of these agents could include (only to cite some of these):

- increasing the sensitivity of the anomaly detecting agents
- setting the action policies of other applications, for example the action which the virus checker should take upon discovering a virus or start a new or planned learning activities
- killing anomalous processes or dropping a user who is responsible for a large number of anomalies
- repairing functions that are consistently associated with system failure. This could be done through the intervention of human operators, or using genetic programming if a way could be found to automatically guide the evolution of a program.
- reconfiguring the system to work around hardware and software failures
- contacting a system's operator for help

These self-healing mechanisms will have to be carefully controlled so that they cannot be abused to create in opposite a denial of service. To help with this some form of voting could be used on important decisions. For example, if different estimation methods are applied to detect the same type of anomaly, a voting mechanism between them could improve the reliability of the final diagnosis. In addition it will enable the Action agents to combine information from agents with different information and expertise and it would reduce the chances of a compromised agent gaining complete control over the system.

5   SAFEGUARD System during Operation

The response of SAFEGUARD may be analysed for the following couple of likely attacks and failures in Power Control System [5]:

1. Fault course of events detected inside control processing (caused by data transmission failure);
2. External intrusion attack against system data sets (caused by external attack).

5.1   Description of Scenario 1

Suppose that a tele-command is initiated by the operator of a CC (Control Centre), for example the request to open a breaker of a power transmission line. The tele-command is sent to an RTU and, after the request , the CC software system waits for the TS (tele-signal) confirming that the breaker is effectively closed. Suppose that a fault inside data transmission protocol causes the loss of the TS message, traveling from RTU to CC. In this situation a time out elapses at CC level, and the breaker is considered "not closed", although power flow through the line is interrupted. The operator may become aware of some fault but he doesn't understand where is the fault's location. He doesn't know if the fault comes from the Control Centre, from a RTU or from some other dangerous event inside the physical electrical layer.

5.2   SAFEGUARD Countermeasures

In such situation, the use case of Fig. 3 4 does illustrate the response of SAFEGUARD agents activation sequence, as shown by the numbers in the figure, is the following:

1. Anomaly agents at RTU and CC levels, using the normal "event sequence" estimation method will detect events relative to the tele-command. Correlation agent is informed.
2. After a certain time, usually a handful of seconds, low level anomaly agents at RTU level inform Correlation agent that the "event sequence" of an answering TS is detected, but any TS events is detected by anomaly agent at CC level.
3. Correlation agent informs Topology and Action agents about possible loss of data messages between a RTU and a Control Centre. Topology agent memorizes a "possible fault" during the transmission between the RTU and the CC.
4. Action agent does inform the operator and improves the sensitivity of anomaly detection agents to discover if the fault, memorized by topology agent, could be persistent in the future operations

5.3   Description of Scenario 2

The scenario number 2 (an external attack towards system data sets) could be initiated by an intruder entering inside the system, at CC or at RTU level, and setting some power flow measures to wrong values. This could be done, for example, by mean of malicious code looping every second and setting to 0.0 the memorized value of power flow through a transmission line. Also in such cases SAFEGUARD system provides a similar response. The main difference of this case respect to the previous one is the use of different estimation methods (novelty detection mechanisms) by the anomaly detection agents. In this case also the Wrapper agent may have a role and may contribute to the diagnostic process detecting some anomalies inside the system parameters behaviour.

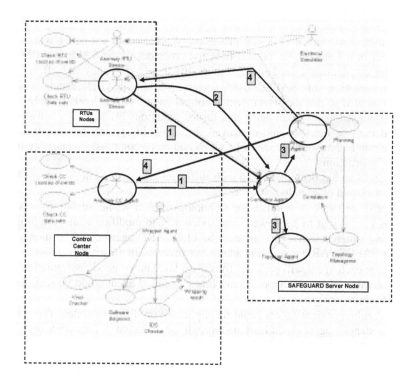

Fig. 4. Attack scenario

6   Self-Healing of SAFEGUARD Platform

As all the LCCI's components (software and hardware), in the turn SAFEGUARD agents could be susceptible to malicious attacks on their files and processes, software errors, operating system crashes and the use of enemy agents, infiltrated with a SAFEAGUARD "camouflage", to manipulate or attack others. The self-healing of the SAFEGUARD multi-agent platform will start with a diagnosis of the problem, which will be carried out in a number of ways:

- Communication between agents in different parts of the system. SAFEGUARD agents in different parts of the system will monitor each other to detect problems. An effective way in which this monitoring could be carried out is through the inhibition of failure signals. Each agent could inhibit failure signals in the other agents on its node. If the inhibiting agent fails, the inhibition signals would cease and the other agents on the node would broadcast failure signals to SAFEGUARD agents on other nodes. They could also send email messages to systems administrator. The advantage of inhibition signals is that they do not need explicit instructions to carry out an emergency action.

- Monitoring of critical files and processes. Agents could explicitly watch, in the manner of a Tripwire, the critical files and processes of the SAFEGUARD system and intercept unauthorized attempts to modify them before they take effect.
- Instrumentation of SAFEGUARD agents. SAFEGUARD agents could be instrumented so that they can detect abnormal patterns in each other's behaviour. A compromised agent or an agent that turned malicious because of a software error could then be detected and destroyed. Limit of this promising almost infallible technique is that source code of LCCI should be re-compiled by inserting the new set of instructions.

Once a problem has been diagnosed with sufficient accuracy, a number of self-healing techniques could be used to resolve it:

- Adaptive software: a middleware technology which would enable aspects of the agent's behaviour to be viewed (introspection) and modified whilst the program is running (intercession). Parts of each SAFEGUARD agent could be monitored by other SAFEGUARD agents and adapted or restarted in the event of failure.
- Backup: each agent will periodically store a last known good configuration on one or a number of its neighbouring machines. A failed agent could be restarted from this backup configuration.
- Hot standby: critical agents could be duplicated on different nodes. The activation of the standby agent could be done through the cessation of inhibition signals from the active agent.

All or part of these self-healing mechanisms will have to be combined with an attempt to deal with the source of the problem. Restarting agents that have been killed by a virus is ineffective without disinfecting the virus first. Project requirements press for a hard integration of SAFEGUARD Platform inside of a LCCI: this will make sure that the good health of SAFEGUARD itself should grant in his turn the integrity of LCCI.

7   Conclusions

SAFEGUARD agent-based architecture will increase the survivability of the management networks of large complex critical infrastructures such as electricity or telecommunications networks. This platform will defend against first of all from unknown attacks, but also from failures and accidents. In a well coordinated way, detector agent identifies that anomalies are occurred somewhere inside of LCCI, a requesting information from diagnosis and security applications starts for correlation agents and then reasoning about an appropriate self-healing response is arranged from action agents. The architecture's design has been studied such that SAFEGUARD could be installed on any platform - it could even run on the RTUs (Remote Terminal Units) in an electricity network or the routers and switches in a telecommunications network. The focus of this paper has been on the capability of SAFEGUARD to analyze a fault, to classify it as possible intrusion and to alert the whole system or the part locally interested. Scenario's attacks have been assumed in which a LCCI does operate with and without SAFEGUARD and the preliminary results of these proofs have provided the goodness of the design.

The preliminary phases of the Project were focused on the drawing and organizing agent architecture that could be suitable for several kinds of networked environment. In order to complete the design of a platform that could be deployed on different Operating Systems, Java language was chosen as foundation for executable and portable code. Problems of performance, the non excellent rate of response in operation typical of Java code does force to evaluate carefully this aspect of the project, has been studied and it doesn't represent a real problem due at the light structure of single agents and at the technology trend of Java language and its supporting libraries.

Safeguard agents will be tested and evaluated over a complete sets of attack/fault scenarios that will be automatically produced by an attack generation tools. Attack trees [23], will be used as a general model to produce different attack patterns inside the electricity testing environment. For telecommunication domain a random calls traffic generation was adopted and connected to a Call Centre emulating environment. Complete reports of the infrastructures behaviour, during the chosen sets of attack/faults scenarios, will be generated and comparisons will be done about the services availability with and without the Safeguard agent systems.

The conclusions are that a LCCI, protected by mean of SAFEGUARD system, could enhance its capacity of survivability to attacks, also when these actions deliberately carry unknown and never diagnosed features. The practical approach of SAFEGUARD in applying machine learning theories in order to learn and consequently to survey the normal behaviour of a LCCI, will make more dependable the networked systems that render essential services for the citizens.

Acknowledgement. SAFEGUARD [http://www.ist-safeguard.org], IST Project Number: IST-2001-32685, will investigate new ways of protecting large complex critical infrastructures and has been partially funded from the Project EU-IST SAFEGUARD European Commission. Partners of Project are: ENEA (Italy), AIA (Spain), QMUL (UK), SWISSCOM (Swiss), LIU (Sweden).

References

1. Anderson, D., Teresa F. Lunt, Harold Javitz, Ann Tamaru, Alfonso Valdes. 'Detecting Unusual Program Behaviour Using the Statistical Component of the Next-generation Intrusion Detection Expert System (NIDES)' SRI International technical report May 1995 SRI-CSL-95-06.
2. Balasubramaniyan, J. S., J. O. Garcia-Fernandez, D. Isacoff, E. Spafford and D. Zamboni. 'An Architecture for Intrusion Detection using Autonomous Agents', COAST Technical Report 98/ 05, June 11, 1998.
3. Neumann, Peter G. 'Practical Architectures for Survivable Systems and Networks', SRI Report, 2000.
4. Stillerman, Matthew, Carla Marceau and Maureen Stillman. 'Intrusion Detection Distributed', Communications of the ACM, Vol. 42, No. 7, July 1999.
5. Wood, Allen J. and Wollenberg, Bruce F., Power Generation, Operation and Control (Second Edition), New York: John Wiley & Sons, Inc., 1996.

6.   Thompson B.B., Marks II R.J., Choi J.J., El-Sharkawi M.A., Huang M.Y., Bunje C.,
      'Implicit Learning in Autoencoder Novelty Asssement', Proceedings of the 2002
      International Joint Conference on Neural Networks, 2002 IEEE World Congress on
      Computational Intelligence, May12-17, 2002, Honolulu, pp. 2878–2883.
7.   Aamodt A. and Plaza E. 1994. "Case Based Reasoning: Fundamental Issues,
      Methodological Variation, and System Approaches". AI Communications 7(1), 39–59.
8.   Wettschereck D. and D. W. Aha. 1995. "Weighting features". In Proceedings of the First
      International Conference on Case-Based Reasoning (Lisbon, Portugal). Springer-Verlag.
      347–358.
9.   Lowe D.G. 1995. "Similarity metric learning for a variable-kernel classifier", Neural
      Computation, 7:72–85
10.   Ricci F. and Avesani P. 1995. "Learning an asymmetric and anisotropic similarity metric
      for Case-Based Reasoning", AI Review: Special Issue on Lazy Learning, (Apr. 1995).
11.   Balducelli C. and Brusoni F. 1996. "A CBR tool to simulate diagnostic Case-Based
      operator models", In Proceedings of ESS96 European Simulation Symposium and
      Exhibition (Genoa,Italy Oct. 24–26 1996).
12.   H. Witten and E. Frank, "Data Mining", 2000, Morgan Kaufmann Publishers, San
      Francisco, CA, USA
13.   Weka Data Miner: url: http://www.cs.waikato.ac.nz/ml/weka
14.   R. C. Holte, "Very simple classification rules perform well on most data commonly used
      datasets", Machine Learning 1993, 11:63–91
15.   J. R. Quinlan, "Programs for Machine Learning", San Francisco, 1993, Morgan Kaufmann
16.   P. Langley nd S. Sage, "Induction on selective Bayesian classifiers", In Proc. of 10th
      Conference on Uncertainty in Artificial Intelligence, Seattle, WA USA, 1994 Morgan
      Kauffmann pp. 399–406
17.   D. Heckermann, D. Geiger and D.M. Chickering, "Learning Bayesian Networks: The
      combination of Knowledge and statistical data", Machine Learning 1995, 20(3):197–243
18.   D. Aha, "Tolerating noisy, irrelevant and novel attributes in instance-based learning
      algorithms", International Journal of Man-Machine Studies, 1992, 36(2):267–287
19.   D. H. Wolpert, "Stacked Generalization", Neural Networks, 1992, 5:241–259
20.   John Hertz, Anders Krogh, Richard G. Palmer, "Introduction to the theory of Neural
      Computation", Addison-Wesley Publishing Company, 1991.
21.   Carpenter, G., Grossberg, S., & Reynolds, J. (1991) "ARTMAP: Supervised Real-Time
      Learning and Classification of Nonstationary Date by a Self-Organizing Neural Network."
      Neural Networks, 4, pp. 565 Lars Liden,
      ftp://cns-ftp.bu.edu/pub/ART_GALLERY/Unix/unix_gal.tar, laliden@cns.bu.edu
22.   Donald R. Tveter, http://www.mcs.com/~drt/home.html, drt@mcs.com
23.   Schneier, B. (1999), Attack Trees: Modeling Security Threats, Dr. Dobb's Journal,
      December 1999, ISSN 1044-789X.
24.   John Bigham, David Gamez and Ning Lu1 Safeguarding SCADA Systems with Anomaly
      Detection Department of Electronic Engineering, Queen Mary, University of London,
      London, E1 4NS, UK

Safety Assessment of Experimental Air Traffic Management Procedures

Alberto Pasquini and Simone Pozzi

Deep Blue s.r.l., Via Basento 52/D
00198 Rome, Italy
{alberto, simone}@dblue.it

Abstract. This paper presents and discusses the application of safety assessment methodologies to a pre-operational project in the Air Traffic Control field. In the case analysed in the present paper a peculiar aspect was the necessity to effectively assess new operational procedures and tools. In particular we exploited an integrated methodology to evaluate computer-based applications and their interactions with the operational environment. Current ATC safety practices, methodologies, guidelines and standards were critically revised, in order to identify how they could be applied to the project under consideration. Thus specific problematic areas for the safety assessment in a pre-operational experimental project are highlighted and, on the basis of theoretical principles, some possible solutions taken into consideration. The latter are described highlighting the rationale of most relevant decisions, in order to provide guidance for generalisation or re-use.

Keywords: Safety Assessment, Air Traffic Management, Human-Computer Interaction

Air Traffic Control is an interesting example of the successful employing of safety practices and methodologies. A considerable safety record has been achieved, since actually European Air Traffic Control contributes as a major cause in approximately 2% of aircraft accidents, with only two air collisions between civil aircraft over the last 50 years (Zagreb 1976, Lake Constance 2002). However if the accident rate remains unchanged but the traffic volume increases, the total number of bad events will probably become unacceptable (combining a static accident rate and increasing traffic ICAO[1] estimated an accident per week. See also: EUROCONTROL [4], pag. 16). Hence considerable efforts are constantly put in designing and experimenting with technological or process innovation. The object is two-fold: an increase of safety in current conditions, and assurance of appropriate safety levels in future operational environments.

The present paper deals with the safety assessment of an experimental project. Safety activities were thus conducted in order to explore future operational environments. However before a meaningful description of the safety assessment process could be done, it is necessary to draw our attention to some specific characteristics of the Air Traffic Management (ATM) domain.

---

[1] International Civil Aviation Organisation: ICAO was established in 1947 to develop principles and techniques of international air navigation and to support planning and development of international flight transportation.

S. Anderson et al. (Eds.): SAFECOMP 2003, LNCS 2788, pp. 354–367, 2003.

1   The Air Traffic Management System

While describing the ATM Services it is common place to speak in terms of a system. This definition is meant to take into account two key characteristics of ATM: there is a large number of elements (human and organizational actors, but also hardware components); multiple interactions are taking place, with feedback loops and complex causal dependencies. What we deem relevant in this definition is the parallel with natural systems (as opposed to mechanical ones). A natural system is largely unpredictable (non-deterministic) and self-producing the causes of its own development. Each part has to described on its own (because of its own peculiar behaviour), but it is also necessary to refer to the interactions with other system's elements. This causes the system behaviour to be to a certain extent unpredictable and far from perfectly known. Unexpected interactions may occur and, in addition, external factors affect the system. In case of a local malfunction, failures are likely to spread very quickly to other parts of the system.

In respect to other safety critical domains, the ATM system is characterized by the key role played by human actors. As a matter of fact safety relevant decisions are taken mostly by humans, whereas computer systems are supporting tools for monitoring and data presentations. Hence controllers has a key-role in facing system complexity, because their main objective is to actively manage unpredictable situations affected by multiple elements.[2] It is important to highlight that complexity does not barely regard the environment. Indeed no clear cut separation has to be traced between the environment and the ATM system. The environment perception and the feasible actions are strongly affected by how controllers' working tools present information. In other words while defining the ATM system as a complex system, we need to consider that controllers' tools are entirely part of that system. Indeed radio communications, phone communications, radar displays and computers are system elements, that add to its complexity.

A peculiar characteristic of the ATM work (at least of the en-route ATM work, that is the focus of the case presented in this paper) is that controllers usually perform few recurring tasks. Anyway even if these tasks are well-known, their order remains largely unpredictable because of two main reasons. The former is that tasks are mainly event-driven and situation specific, thus spoiling most of the efforts to identify and predict task sequences. The latter is that the tasks' order is strongly affected by the complex strategic planning carried out by air traffic controllers. They do not simply react to local conditions, on the contrary they are constantly trying to predict traffic development in order to arrange safe traffic configurations.

These characteristics well justify the claim that ATM shall be analysed as a complex system, and that any technological innovation shall be assessed by taking into account how the system accommodates for its introduction.

---

[2] This definition reflects a shift of emphasis from *traffic control* to *traffic management* occurred in the last 10 years. Consequently it is underlined the active role of flow management and traffic structuring, rather than "simple" conflicts avoidance. The term Air Traffic Management has accordingly replaced the Air Traffic Control one.

2   Safety Assessment in ATM

Safety issues have always played a primary role in ATM and continuous efforts and resources are being put in making the system safer. The travelling public acceptance of risks is relatively low compared to other transportation systems, thus safety represents a primary concern within the ATM community. Different general approaches were adopted in the ATM history, in order to cope with the main safety problems present at that stage of development. During the pioneering years, when the aircraft technology was still being developed, a fly-and-fix model was applied. Analyses were conducted after major incidents, in order to prevent their occurrence. The main efforts were thus concentrated on reacting to bad events. Clearly this model was bound to change, as soon as the increasing rate of technological innovations and of aircraft usage made unrealistic and uneconomical to follow the accident-investigate-fix model [Levenson [8], pag. 87].

Development of "proactive models" marked the maturity of civil aviation, and the ATM domain readily adopted them. Proactive models are based on the early identification, assessment and mitigation of any credible hazards, thus assuring an inherently safe design, rather than reacting to bad events. The official date of adoption of this philosophy in ATM may be the 1979 ICAO Accident Prevention and Investigation Divisional Meeting. On that occasion the accident prevention was defined as involving an active search for hazards to be eliminated or avoided. As a guidance for proactive safety, ICAO delivered the Accident Prevention Manual (ICAO [7]). Although the manual was intended for pilots, the underlying approach was valid also for ATM and the rest of the civil aviation community.

Current safety practices are still based on proactive approaches, with some significant changes as far as the human role in the system is concerned. While the initial focus was on hardware elements, the fundamental role of humans in the system is now recognised. Theoretical contributions are adopted, that take into account human operators as part of the system design, not as following add-ons (Edwards [2]). Moreover during the last 15 years, the massive introduction of new digital technologies brought into light the necessity to adopt an user-centred point of view in the design and evaluation of the systems. The revolutionary opportunities offered by innovative technologies need to be driven by research on human cognitive skills, in order not to overwhelm the operator with meaningless information and functions. However integration between successful traditional hardware safety assessment techniques and human reliability methods is still an open problematic issue.

In the ATM domain, a state-of-the-art synthesis of Safety Management is provided by the Eurocontrol Safety Regulatory Requirements.[3] These documents are issued as guidance for the Service Providers and they identify the requirements to comply with for adequate and effective safety management. In particular the ESARR4 defines the requirements for risk assessment and mitigation when introducing changes in ATM systems. This requirement covers the human, procedural and equipment (hardware, software) elements of the ATM system, as well as its environment and operations.

---

[3] Eurocontrol is the European organisation for the safety of air navigation. It currently numbers 31 Member States. Eurocontrol has as its primary objective the development of a seamless, pan-European air traffic management (ATM) system

The objective of the ESARR4 is to ensure that the *risks associated with hazards in the ATM System are systematically and formally identified, assessed, and managed within safety levels, which as a minimum, meet those approved by the designated authority.* (EUROCONTROL [5], pag. 9). The risk assessment process may be divided in the following phases: identify all relevant hazards; identify their effects on the system (also combination of different hazards' effects); assess consequences and severity under worst case scenario (a classification of severity is provided by "ESARR4 severity scheme"); derive an appropriate risk mitigation strategy.[4]

It should be emphasised that in order to deduce the effect of a hazard and to determine its severity, the systematic assessment shall include the effects of hazards on the various elements of the ATM system, such as: air crew, Air Traffic controllers, aircraft functional capabilities, functional capabilities of the ground part of the ATM system, ability to provide safe ATM services.

Further requirements relate to the final documentation to be produced by the risk assessment process. End results (including rationales and evidences) shall be collated in order to ensure that: the arguments demonstrating the overall safety of the system are correct and complete; all safety requirements related to the implementation of a change are traceable to the intended operations/functions.

Besides identifying state-of-the-art risk assessment principles, the ESARR4 satisfies another major goal of Eurocontrol: providing a common standard for the European ATM Service Providers. The general requirement for that may be identified in the deregulation and privatisation of the airline industry. In fact a general tendency to separate the provision of Air Navigation Services and national governments is apparent in Europe, thus exposing Air Traffic Service Providers to commercial pressures. This may seriously hamper safety and the coordination between organisations based all over Europe. On the contrary ATM need to assure comparable levels of safety all over Europe. Standardisation (and coherence with national legislations) has thus become a major issue.

A major open issue is the extent to which specific objectives may constrain adherence to standards. In the case discussed in the present paper the international guidelines and standards (ESARR4, EUROCAE ED-78A/RTCA DO-264 [3], SAE ARP 4754 [14], SAE ARP 4761 [15]) had to be taken into account considering the specific needs and characteristics of the project. This inevitably lead to some significant differences. On the other hand a too strict standard hampers customisation to specific projects, making the standard useless.

Reliance on everyday operational experience is another key matter in the ATM risk assessment. It is widely recognised that human actors involved in the system daily functioning can provide fundamental feedback to system designers and safety experts. The argument is two-fold. First of all not all the occurrences can be foreseen and dealt with during the design phase. Secondly a system is likely to change significantly

---

[4] There's an obvious difference between what it is described in a standard and what is feasible in the real world. Usually the time and resources availability seriously constrains the possibility to identify all relevant hazards. Furthermore it is highly unlikely that there are enough resources to mitigate all of them. Anyway the ESARR4 risk assessment process may also be intended as a proper way to prioritize hazards.

during its life cycle, due to environmental pressures or local adjustments. As a result reliance on reporting from pilots and controllers is the major information source for an effective monitoring during the operational phase (see ESARR4 par 8.2.3)

3   Role of Computer Systems

The concepts and principles steering ATM have been slow in evolving, despite the traffic growth and the technological evolution. The result is a gap between technological possibilities and their exploitation by ATM. The increasing integration of computerised support systems have thus generated several debates and studies to clarify technologies' impact on ATM practices and procedures (Mackay [9]). Nonetheless nowadays the ATM system certainly presents high density of computer systems. Computer support systems are used for a variety of functions, that we may roughly summarise in three categories, outlined below.

As a monitor of human actions: given the high relevance of human decisions, computer systems are sometimes used to monitor the situation and alert the controller whenever a dangerous situation is detected. Computer tools in this category are known as "safety nets", and for instance they may alert the controllers when two aircraft will be conflicting in one minute (Short Term Conflict Alert). Clearly the STCA is not a managing tool, rather it is meant to bring to the controller's attention undetected dangerous situations.

As planning advisors: this category represents the focus of many current researches. The computer system is used to help controllers in managing the traffic. This may be done for instance by algorithms that predicts aircraft trajectories, or by proposing ranked solutions from existing databases. All these systems leave the final decision to the human controller, but attempt to support his/her work by taking advantage of advanced computations.

Anyway the most pervasive category of computer usage is a very basic one: that is when computer systems are utilised in the essential working tasks. This category encompasses the vast majority of current computer systems. In this case computer systems form the infrastructure of the ATM domain, enabling the most basic activities. The most striking example is probably the controller working position itself. Any information, apart from audio communications, passes through it, and it is transformed by appropriate data filtering or by customised representations that facilitate information gathering and decisions. Controllers continuously interacts with its functionalities, and many controllers' actions possess a meaning only in relation to it.

The result is a tight integration between humans and computer systems, that possesses significant consequences on the safety assessment methodology. Any method that studies separately the controllers and their tools is probably running the risk to build non-existent boundaries between them, thus failing to grasp a correct understanding of controllers' activity. A systemic approach is required, in order to consider the various parts of the system without isolating single elements. As already pointed out above (see ESARR4, par. 2), in case of hazards assessment the analysis shall include the effects of hazards on the various elements of the ATM system, such as: air crew, Air Traffic controllers, aircraft functional capabilities, functional capabilities of the ground part of the ATM system, ability to provide safe ATM services. Thus only an integrated methodology can be adequate for an effective safety assessment, addressing the various system elements in interaction.

The above conclusion may be well illustrated by a specific case, where the integration between operator and tool leads to specify different procedures according to system characteristics. While managing the airspace between Italy and Greece, controllers have to work with radar displays with a scale that is larger than usual, due to the geographical extension of the area. This kind of visualisation makes it very difficult to work with usual separation minima that appear extremely small compared to the whole area. Prescribed separation minima are thus doubled. Therefore a specific hardware configuration is recognised as requiring different procedures. The underlying rationale is that the system (made of humans, tools and procedures) has to be taken into account as a whole.

In particular it should be highlighted that, in the daily working environment, practices and procedures always appear integrated with either a tool or a human actor. It is clearly possible to isolate and write down a procedure or a practice, but it should not be overlooked that its manifestation in the working activity is always bound to a physical support (human or tool). The integration between procedure-tool (or procedure-human) has relevant practical consequences on the safety assessment process and methodology (see par. 5.4).

4   The Mediterranean Free Flight Project

As mentioned in the previous paragraph the ATM domain has long been characterised by a gap between technological possibilities and their exploitation. Currently ATM is based on ground-controlled traffic, airspace structured in fixed airways, ground controller responsibility for maintaining separation minima between aircraft, aircraft dependence on controllers' instructions and ground-based sources of information. To achieve the required targets in terms of safety, efficiency and cost-effectiveness, radical changes in the organization and methods of ATM are needed. The ideas of Free Routes and Free Flight are possible answers to these problems.

Compared to the actual fixed routes situation (i.e.: aircraft move along pre-defined and fixed trajectories), the Free Routes airspace is based on the idea of user preferred routes (see fig. 1 and 2). On entering an airspace sector, aircraft should be able to select whichever trajectory they prefer, in order to shorten the travelled distance.

The Free Flight concept refers to the capability of aircraft to self-separate. Suitably equipped aircraft will have the freedom to choose route and speed in real-time. Responsibility for separation assurance will rest with the aircraft in almost all circumstances.

The Mediterranean Free Flight project aims to investigate, simulate and assess these new ATM concepts and functions in a live ATM environment. For this purpose evaluation exercises are executed in Free Routes and Free Flight environments.

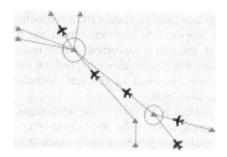
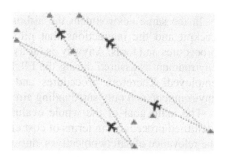

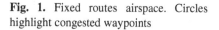

Fig. 1. Fixed routes airspace. Circles highlight congested waypoints

Fig. 2. Free routes airspace, with user-preferred routes

The MFF process starts with the definition of high level ideas of new ATM methods, then specifies procedures and requirements for their applications. The evaluation[5] and refinement of procedures is carried out through evaluation exercises conducted in different environments, namely Fast Time (or Model Based) Simulations, Real Time Simulations and Flight Trials. The MFF project is based on several iterative cycles. Evaluation exercises will be repeated different times, to ensure appropriate feedback loops. Findings from the evaluation exercises will be utilised to refine ideas, procedures and requirements, that will be evaluated again in the following iterative step.

The most interesting findings for the safety assessment process are definitely obtained through Real Time Simulations and Flight Trials. The Real Time Simulation setting is a very interesting mixture of reality and simulation: basically controllers and pilots are humans, whereas the aircraft traffic is simulated on a computer platform. Controllers interact with the usual working position and speak via an audio-LAN with other controllers and with pilots. The latter are named pseudo-pilot, because they control the simulated aircraft through a computer console. Observers are also present in the simulation room, in order to gather data on controllers' behaviour and interactions, and to evaluate human-machine interface, procedures and working methods. This environment makes it possible to set up interesting traffic patterns (also very high density ones), observing controllers' reactions in real time. Traffic patterns can be managed in two ways. First of all they can be shaped directly changing the software parameters of the computer platform running the simulated traffic. But it is also possible to involve controllers and pseudo-pilots, in order to have them perform necessary actions (see par. 5.4, tab. 1 for examples of accomplice pilots actions). Since Real Time Simulations can exploit an airspace of more than one sector, in the latter case observers can focus on just one or two sectors and arrange with remaining controllers to set up the configurations under analysis. The involvement of accomplice controllers or pseudo-pilots will be a key-characteristic for the definition of an integrated methodology for the MFF safety assessment (see par. 5.4).

---

[5] In the present paper the term *evaluation* will be used as a synonymous of the term *validation*, that usually appears in ATM technical documents. The term *validation* refers to the process through which it is ensured that an ATM concept addresses the ATM problem for which it was designed and that it achieves its stated aims. See MAEVA. A Master ATM European Validation Plan. Validation Guideline Handbook [10]

In the same environment the airborne part can also be simulated, reproducing a cockpit and the interactions that pilots are supposed to experience with the new procedures and tools. Anyway as far as the airborne part is concerned, a more realistic environment is assured during the Flight Trials, where a suitably equipped aircraft is employed. Therefore procedures and tools are evaluated in the real operational environment, and only surrounding aircraft are simulated.

The main goal of the whole evaluation process is to analyse the advantages of identified procedures in terms of cost effectiveness, safety, efficiency, capacity. Given the relevance of safety objectives, during the evaluation process a safety assessment is also completed. The safety assessment ensures that each proposed concept is evaluated in terms of its safety impact on the activity. The overall safety objective, explicitly stated in the MFF Safety Policy [12] (pag. 21), is to improve or, at least, to maintain the safety level of current procedures. In particular a safety case will gather safety data in order to ensure that the procedures developed within the MFF project are compliant with the ATM 2000+ strategy, which is: *To improve safety levels by ensuring that the number of ATM induced accidents and serious or risk bearing incidents do not increase and, where possible, decrease* (EUROCONTROL [4], pag.28). No operational benefits can justify a decrease in terms of safety.

The MFF safety assessment process was designed to make the most of ATM safety assessment best practices. Thus it is complaint with international standards and safety principles, and with the guidelines therein (see MFF Safety Plan [11] and MFF Safety Policy [12]). Anyway, as already stated before, a thoughtless standard application can't assure efficacy: the general framework had to be adapted to MFF specific objectives and resources. In the present case particular attention was paid to the difference between an operative project and the MFF pre-operative experimental status.

5   Solutions for the MFF Safety Assessment

In the previous paragraphs we identified and illustrated some major open issues to be taken into account in designing an effective safety case for a ATM project. During the MFF project some solutions that proved to be effective were considered. Thus it was possible to cope with the particular requirements of the ATM field and to the actual needs of the project.

5.1   Compliance with International Standards

The MFF safety case is designed to comply with the process and the requirements of ESARR4. According to the phases illustrated above (hazards identification, hazards evaluation, mitigation means) it was planned to develop three main steps: Operational Services and Environment Definition (corresponding to hazards identification), Operational Hazard Assessment (hazards evaluation), Allocation of Safety Objectives and Requirements (mitigation).

This process is meant to guarantee traceability of decisions from operational requirements to hazards. At the same time it is intended to make explicit any underlining assumption about the expected operational environment. The introduction of unmotivated assumptions in the risk assessment process is a widely recognised issue in the scientific literature (Clarke [1]; Slovic, Fischhoff e Lichtenstein [16]; Tversky e Kahneman [18]). In fact assumptions are often necessary to provide a frame for the evaluation process, but it should not be underestimated the powerful effect of the chosen frame on the conclusions. That means that the framing of a problem and of the possible solutions is very likely to give shape to the decisions taken. In a pre-operational project like MFF some reasonable assumptions may turn out to be inappropriate at a later stage of development. As a consequence the frame of reference for safety relevant decisions may happen to change. For that reason a clear traceability between safety decisions, hazards and operational context is mandatory. However this requirement would be of little use if proper feedback loops aren't included in the process.

Consequently the second solution adopted in the MFF deals with feedback loops.

5.2   Providing Safety Feedback

Three different safety cases are planned, for effective feedback between the safety cases and the project life cycle. Each one of them will be developed in different phases of the MFF project. As already mentioned the MFF project is based on several iterative cycles (see fig. 3), that allow to gather feedback from simulations and live trials. From one cycle to the next one, requirements and procedures are revised and specified accordingly, thus enabling a more fine-grained safety analysis at each step.

The three Safety Cases (Preliminary, Intermediate and Final) have been designed following the same time frame. Thus their level of detail will depend on the data available at the moment, according to the simulations and live trials already performed and to the development and detail level of requirements and procedures.

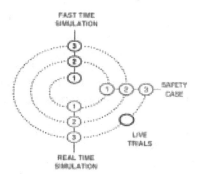

The Preliminary and the Intermediate safety cases are most of all means of communication and coordination between MFF safety experts and people involved in the different MFF activities, whereas the third and final safety case has to be effective in providing the appropriate information to future projects moving from the pre-operational status of a project like MFF to operational status (as the MFF project did in analysing safety activities of related projects).

Fig. 3. Feedback loops between safety cases and evaluation exercises.

With reference to the design of the process, feedback inputs to the other MFF activities were explicitly planned.

According to the MFF plan formal safety inputs will be provided three times (by the above mentioned Safety Cases), at different moments. As a consequence the ability to affect the development of the project is maximised, since safety insights can be assured for the whole duration of the project. Hence simulations and live trials can be designed according to safety analyses to be performed, providing new data on hazards, or testing mitigation means. A single safety case would have run the risk of identifying interesting issues too late, and it would have also faced a too large amount of information.

5.3   Coordination and Integration of Different Evaluation Exercises

The overall safety objectives of the MFF project are defined in abstract terms, that can't be related to specific measurable (or observable) issues. To assure an effective safety assessment these objectives had to be associated to more detailed and low level objectives. Actually a low level objective identifies the specific aspects of the activity to be analysed, in order to assess the high level objective. The relation between these two levels is many-to-many, that is a low level objective can be related to more than one high level objective, while a high level objective is assessed through more than one low level objective (see fig. 4).

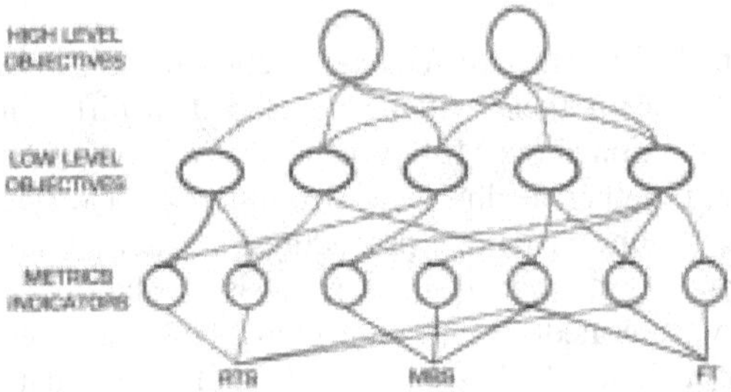

The third level depicted in the figure is represented by metrics and indicators. This level is meant to identify what can be observed or measured in the system, in order to analyse and assess low level objectives. The link between the second and the third level is not a straightforward one. Low level objectives are usually expressed in rather specific terms, but they typically refer to the overall system behaviour. On the contrary the metrics should be related to individual actions or interactions. Drawing from complex systems theory we may say that metrics constitute local elements interacting, whereas the low level objectives may be identified with emerging properties, that can only be observed at a systemic level. No need to further highlight that an emerging property can't be related by definition to the local level. The extent to which the link between these levels may be apparent and clearly connected to an appropriate system model varies depending on the matter analysed.

Fig. 4. Hierarchy of safety objectives and metrics

A detailed example may help clarify the issue. A general safety objective of the MFF project is *to assure that the system is at least as safe as current operating conditions* (see MFF Safety Policy [12], pag. 21). Some of the corresponding low level objectives may be: *determine whether the overall level of workload is changed by the introduction of new support system, determine whether the overall level of workload is changed by the introduction of new procedures, determine whether military activities impact differently in the new operational environment*, etc...

Corresponding metrics and indicators: *number and duration of radio communications, number of altitude, heading and speed changes, number and duration of phone communications with adjacent sectors or military controllers,* etc...

The process of identification of all the metrics needs to take into account the experience of many key-roles: safety experts, human factors, and most of all people involved in the organisation of the evaluation exercise, whose knowledge of the evaluation environment should not be overlooked.

The number and variety of metrics to be studied required the preparation and coordination of different evaluation exercises, because during each exercise data could be collected only on some specific qualitative or quantitative metrics. The main reason is that each exercise was carried out in a peculiar environment (i.e.: Real Time Simulations, Flight Trials or Model Based Simulations), where only some methodologies were appropriate. The coordination and integration of different evaluation exercises allowed to make the most of each one's strong points.

Coordination of many metrics is required to evaluate any low level objective, since it is highly unusual that a low-level objective can be evaluated using only one metric. In the same way each metric may be related to more than one low level objective. The integration and coordination of several metrics allows to consider the whole system, without isolating a single aspect and overestimating the relevance thereof.

Last but not the least, almost independent data sources (in this case different environments and exercises) assure a methodologically sound cross-checking of results, highlighting potential discrepancies (or consistencies).

5.4   Assessing the Tool-Procedure Integration

The MFF project relied extensively on Real Time Simulations and Flight Trials as sources of data. By definition an experimental project has to gather and produce new data, since no previous experience is available. The validity of related project findings or of generic databases is usually questionable. Indeed it has to be verified the extent to which results may be transferred from one context to another. For instance probabilistic research on human reliability has too often turned out to be highly context sensitive, thus losing nearly all of their predictive power (Reason [13], pag. 231). The MFF project exploited generic hazards database, and to maximise their validity it was performed a cross-checking with domain experts' opinions. The experts were selected among experienced controllers or among controllers involved in the Real Time Simulations. Anyway even after the experts' validation these data needed to be considered taking into account well-known cognitive biases (i.e.: novelty can make underestimate a hazard frequency, whilst an infrequent hazard can be highly overestimated if it happens to occur during the Real Time Simulations (Slovic, Fischhoff e Lichtenstein [16]).

To overcome these limitations it was planned to make extensive use of data collected during Real Time Simulations and Flight Trials. These experimental environments present many advantages, that largely compensate resources devoted to their planning and management. First of all Real Time Simulations and Flight Trials allow to evaluate the system as a whole. As mentioned above (see par. 3) the tight integration of human and computer systems in the real work settings makes unrealistic any assessment that considers each element in isolation. On the contrary during Real Time Simulation and Flight Trial human-computer interactions are placed in a realistic context, thus enabling a systemic analysis of safety issues.

In more detail, the evaluation of new tools and new procedures was an essential part of the MFF exercises, that is to study how controllers' usual working practices and tools could accommodate to the introduction of new tools and procedures. As mentioned before it can't be overlooked that ATM procedures and practices always appear as integrated with either humans or tools. The safety assessment should therefore study the properties of the integration, and not merely address the "disembodied aspect" of procedures. For this reason new procedures and tools should be studied in the operative context, where the integration can be apparent. A de-contextualised comparison of a procedure with the one it is supposed to replace is likely to keep out of the assessment essential elements. For instance it can't evaluate the interactions between the tools normally associated with the replaced procedure and the new one. On the contrary it can be easily figured out that the new tool-procedure integration may interfere with the old ones, maybe disrupting efficient and semi-automated sequence of interactions.

The major strong point of the Real Time Simulations and Flight Trials settings is that they enable to employ integrated methodologies, that combine careful analyses of each element with the study of their interactions. In these environments it is possible to gather data on each single element from a systemic point of view, that is to assess a new procedure by how a system accommodates for its introduction. One of the main means employed by MFF for this purpose was to implement some relevant scenarios in the simulation. A scenario describes an operational situation by identifying the actors involved, the operations going on, the tools and procedures being utilised. The structure provided by a scenario enables the observer to gain a deeper understanding of controllers' activity, by making their specific goals and intentions apparent. Interactions can then be analysed in this light. Scenario building is a time consuming activity, since it requires the coordination of many expertise. Each scenario needs to present relevant situations for the analyst, it shall be defined in a way that can be implemented, and it has to be realistic. Thus several iterations may be necessary between analysts, simulation programmers, and operational experts. In this respect scenarios were also an effective means of communication between people directly involved in the simulation preparation and safety experts. The latter could effectively use their work (i.e.: OHA drafts), transferring it to a consistent format that did not cause awkward translation of technical concepts. Scenarios may be developed starting from controllers' operational experience, from accident databases, but also from the specific procedures under analysis.

Furthermore safety scenarios could be implemented, thus exploiting the simulated environment to recreate critical situations. Credible hazards were placed in realistic scenarios, identified relying on operational controllers' experience. Scenarios were selected on the basis of three different criteria: their relevance for the hazard under analysis; frequency and likelihood of occurrence; criticality.

It is almost impossible to predict a scenario development, thus controllers' reactions offer very relevant insights, that could not be gathered in other experimental settings. Moreover it is worth while emphasising that the Real Time Simulation environment allows to simulate and analyse worst case situations, that are fundamental for a risk assessment process.

According to the high relevance of control systems in the ATM domain, specific computer malfunctions could also be studied. Failure of the computer systems were first assessed through reliability analyses. Then, the credible control system failures were placed as hazards in realistic scenarios. In order to simulate control system breakdowns it was often necessary to set up adequate traffic patterns, planning well ahead also the actions of controllers and pilots (see tab. 1). As stated above this methodology enables a systemic view, since the control system malfunctions could be observed in interaction with all the other involved elements, with no oversimplification or unrealistic isolation, thus satisfying the requirement for an integrated analysis of the tool-procedure integration. This methodology is compliant with the recommendation from the ESARR4 to study the combined effects of hazards, and not only their immediate consequences.

Table 1. Scenario story board and actions

Hazard: SA2	Sector: EW	
Time		Events and Microscenarios
9.48	Accomplice Pilot Action	OYJLD asks to descend to FL290 for technical reasons
9.50	If Accomplice Pilot Action	IBE3674 and OYJLD are cleared to ASAS crossing
9.50	then Possible Event	CCU501 interfere with IBE3674 and OYJLD (in ASAS)

It is worthwhile emphasizing again the importance of the rich environments provided by Real Time Simulations and Flight Trials to the analysis. Only by studying a realistic context it was possible to assess the introduction of new procedures. Indeed the MFF procedures can bring major benefits to the system, but they also entail drastic innovations that need to be studied extensively with the proper tools.

6   Conclusions

The present paper intends to present the major open issues we faced in conducting the safety assessment of an experimental project. Some relevant characteristics of the ATM domain were taken into account, reflecting on strong and weak points of current safety practices. To identify effective solutions, we tried to take advantage of a sound theoretical framework. Some proposals are thus explained at the light of abstract theoretical principles, in order to provide a broader scope to the MFF experience. If *ad hoc* (practical and local) solutions had been applied without a proper theoretical background behind, they would have probably provided a too narrow focus. As a consequence any generalisation or re-use would have been impossible, or at least highly constrained.

It should also be emphasized that the theories and methodologies proposed in the present paper are far from representing a fixed point. First of all large efforts and resources are required to conduct the integrated analysis described. Then, more and more standardisation is likely to be achieved, whereas a larger integration of computer systems will deeply affect the characteristics of the ATM domain.

Acknowledgements. The MFF project is partially funded by the EU under the *TEN-T program.*
We would like to thank all the colleagues of the MFF project and especially those of the WA7 for the fruitful collaboration on the activity. We would also like to thank the anonymous reviewers who provided several useful suggestions for improvements. The limited number of pages did not allow us to address all these very interesting comments, but they will be surely included in an extended version.

References

1. Clarke, L.: Acceptable Risk? Making Decisions in a Toxic Environment. University of California Press, Berkeley (1989)
2. Edwards, E.: Man and Machine: Systems for Safety. Proceedings of British Airlines Pilots Association Technical Symposium. London (1972) 21–36
3. EUROCAE ED-78A/RTCA DO-264: Guidelines for Approval of the Provision and Use of Air Traffic Services Supported by Data Communications
4. EUROCONTROL: ECAC Air Traffic Management Strategy for the Years 2000+ (2000)
5. EUROCONTROL: Eurocontrol Safety Regulatory Requirements (ESARR) 4. Risk Assessment and Mitigation in ATM (2001)
6. Hutchins, E.: Cognition in the Wild. The MIT Press, Cambridge (MA) (1994)
7. ICAO: Accident Prevention Manual. doc 9422-AN/923 (1984)
8. Levenson, N.G.: Safeware. System Safety and Computers. Addison Wesley Publishing Company, Reading (MA) (1995)
9. Mackay, W.: Is Paper Safer? The Role of Paper Flight Strips in Air Traffic Control. ACM Transactions on Human-Computer Interaction, Vol. 6, N. 4 (1999) 311–340
10. MAEVA. A Master ATM European Validation Plan. Validation Guideline Handbook
11. Mediterranean Free Flight Safety Plan
12. Mediterranean Free Flight Safety Policy
13. Reason, J.T.: The Human Error. Cambridge University Press, Cambridge (1990)
14. SAE ARP 4754: Certification Consideration for highly integrated or complex aircraft systems
15. SAE ARP 4761: Guidelines and Methods for conducting the Safety Assessment process on civil airborne systems and equipment
16. Slovic, P., Fischhoff, B., Lichtenstein, S.: Response Mode, Framing, and Information-Processing Effects in Risk Assessment (1982). Bell, D.E., Raiffa, H., Tversky, A. (ed.): Decision Making. Descriptive, Normative, and Prescriptive Interactions. Cambridge University Press, Cambridge (1988)
17. Stephenson, J.: System Safety 2000. A Practical Guide for Planning, Managing, and Conducting System Safety Programs. John Wiley & Sons Inc., New York (1991)
18. Tversky, A., Kahneman, D.: Judgment under Uncertainty: Heuristics and Biases. Science, N. 185 (1974) 1124–1131

The Application of Causal Analysis Techniques for Computer-Related Mishaps

Chris Johnson

Dept. of Computing Science, University of Glasgow, Glasgow, G12 9QQ
Tel.: +44 141 330 6053, Fax: +44 141 330 4913
johnson@dcs.gla.ac.uk

Abstract. Causal analysis techniques support the investigation of incidents and accidents. These include elicitation methods, such as Barrier Analysis, and event-based techniques, for example accident fault trees. Other approaches rely on flow charts, including those within the PRISMA approach and accident models, including the control theory model in STAMP. A further class of causal analysis techniques relies upon models of argumentation, such as the counterfactual approach in WBA. This paper reviews the support that different causal analysis techniques provide for the investigation of adverse events and near misses involving Electrical, Electronic or Programmable, Electronic Systems (E/E/PES). The events leading to an explosion and fires at a fluidized catalytic cracking unit are used to illustrate the application of these different techniques. This is then used to assess the degree of support that different techniques provide for the identification of latent failures at different stages in the software and systems lifecycle.

1   Introduction

The following pages introduce techniques that investigators can use to identify the root causes of incidents involving Electrical, Electronic or Programmable, Electronic Systems (E/E/PES). We refer to E/E/PES rather than 'software' or 'hardware' because this is the term adopted by the UK Health and Safety Executive when referring to the broad class of programmable systems that are exploited by the process industries. Causal analysis is a process by which investigators can identify the reasons *why* a mishap occurs. In contrast, mishap reconstruction identifies *what* happened during an accident or incident.

An E/E/PES case study will be used to illustrate the causal analysis techniques in this paper. This incident has been chosen through consultation with the UK Health and Safety Executive (HSE) and industry representatives because it typifies the adverse events that currently threaten many safety-critical industries. The following pages describe an incident involving a fluidised catalytic cracking unit, part of a UK refinery complex. The plant receives crude oil, which is then separated by fractional distillation into intermediate products, including light and heavy diesel, naptha, kerosese and other heavier components. These heavier elements are eventually fed into the fluidised catalytic cracking unit. This is a continuous process to convert

S. Anderson et al. (Eds.): SAFECOMP 2003, LNCS 2788, pp. 368–381, 2003.

'long' chain hydrocarbons into smaller hydrocarbon products used in fuels. The immediate events leading to the incident started when lightning started a fire in part of the crude distillation unit within the plant. This led to a number of knock-on effects, including power disruption, which affected elements in the fluidised catalytic cracking unit. Initially, hydrocarbon flow was lost to the deethaniser, illustrated in Figure 1. This caused the liquid in the vessel to empty into the next stage debutanizer.   The control system was programmed to prevent total liquid loss in these stages and so valve A was closed.   This starved the debutanizer of feed. The programmable system again intervened to close valve B. The liquid trapped in the debutanizer was still being heated even though both valves now isolated it. Pressure rose and the vessel vented to a flare. Shortly afterwards, the liquid level in the deethaniser was restored, the control system opened valve A and the debutanizer received further flow. Valve B should have opened at this time to allow fluid from the pressurised debutanizer into the naptha splitter. Operators in the control room received misleading signals that valve B had been successfully reopened by their control system even though this had not occurred. As a result the debutanizer filled with liquid while the naptha splitter was emptied.

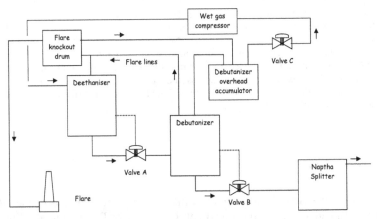

Fig. 1. High-level Overview of Components in the Fluidised Catalytic Cracking Unit

The control room displays separated crucial information that was necessary to diagnose the source of the rising pressure in the debutanizer. Rather than checking the status of valve B, the operators took action to open valve C. This allowed liquid in the full overhead accumulator to flow back into a recovery section of the plant but was insufficient to prevent the debutanizer from becoming logged with fluid entering from the deethanizer. Again, the debutanizer vented to the flare line. Opening valve C created a flow of fluid into previous 'dry' stages of the process that eventually caused a compressor trip. Large volumes of gas now had nowhere to go within the process and had to be vented to the flare stack to be burned off. At this stage, the volume of materials in the flare knockout drum was further increased by attempts to use fire hoses to drain the flooding from the dry stage directly into the flare line. However, this enabled the wet gas compressor to be restarted. This should have made matters better by increasing the flow of materials through the unit but had the unwanted effect of causing a further increase of pressure in the debutanizer. The operators responded again by opening valve C causing a further trip of the compressor. More materials were vented to an already full flare drum. Liquid was forced into a corroded discharge pipe, which broke at an elbow bend causing 20 tonnes of highly flammable hydrocarbon to be discharged. The resulting vapour cloud ignited causing damage estimated to be in excess of £50 million. This case study has been chosen to illustrate the remainder of the paper because it is typical of the way in which incidents stem from the interaction between E/E/PES-related failures, operator 'error', hardware faults and management issues. It is important to observe that both the suppliers and the operators involved in the incidents that form this case study were entirely unaware of the particular failure modes before they occurred. It is also important to emphasise that the case study cannot be characterised as software or a hardware failure. It stemmed from complex interactions between a number of system components.

2   Elicitation Methods: Barrier Analysis

Incident reporting forms are unlikely to yield sufficient information about the causes of complex incidents and accidents. Barrier analysis provides a high-level framework for thinking about the factors that should be considered when gathering additional information. It stems from work in energy production (US Department of Energy, 1992). The central idea is that incidents are caused when unwanted energy flows between a source and a target. The analysis progresses by examining the barriers that might prevent a hazard from affecting the targets. Analysts must account for the reasons why each barrier actually did or might have failed to protect the target. Table 1 illustrates the output from this stage. The control loops illustrated in Figure 1 were intended to prevent the hazards associated with vessels becoming over-pressurized. The E/E/PES intervened by increasing the discharge rate if sensors detected that the level of material in the vessel had risen above an acceptable limit. There was, however, no backup system to reduce input to the vessel. A hazardous situation could arise if the input exceeded the capacity of the automated system to increase the outflow from the vessel. In other words, the E/E/PES logic was based on the assumption that output could always be increased beyond the input to each stage of the process. The meta-level point is that Barrier analysis encourages designers to look beyond the immediate triggering events that led to the mishap, to design issues rather than individual operator action.

Table 1. Example Barrier Analysis

Barrier	Reason for failure?
Control loops link level in each vessel to discharge rate.	No control over vessel input, incorrectly assumed discharge rate always exceed input rate.
	No secondary backup control loop to monitor input and limit it if this exceeded output.
	Key sensors provided erroneous information to control system.
Control system displays linked to multiple level alarms.	Operators could not identify reason for alarms, especially valve B problem, displays were grouped according to sub-processes with no over view of system state.
	Operators were progressively overloaded with alarms. In the last eleven minutes they were expected to read and confirm 275 individual alarms, with similar high severity levels.

3   Event-Based Techniques: Timelines and Event Models

Once necessary information has been gathered about an incident, it is often used to develop some form of graphical timeline. Timelines provide arguably the simplest form of event-based analysis technique. Figure 2 provides an example for our case study. It uses a technique that was pioneered by groups within the US National Transportation Safety Board (Johnson, 2002). Events are placed on a horizontal time-line and are grouped according to the agents involved. In this case, events relating to the debutanizer and deethanizer are separated from the operator actions and so on. Such structuring mechanisms are important if analysts are not to be overwhelmed by the mass of detail that can be obtained in the aftermath of an adverse event. A number of problems affect the use of time-lines in the reconstruction and causal analysis of E/E/PES related incidents. There will often be inconsistencies and contradictory evidence for exact timings. It can also be impossible to obtain exact timings for some events. Figure 2 illustrates a point in the investigation where we know that the level alarm for the Naptha splitter occurred at some point after 08.40 but further analysis of the alarm logs is needed to determine the exact timing for this event.

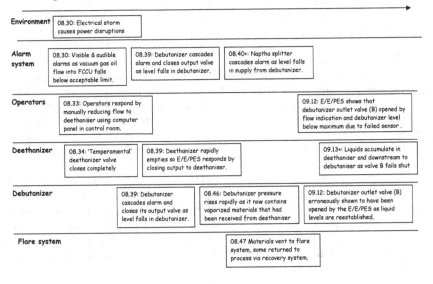

Fig. 2. High-level Timeline of the Case Study Incident

A number of attempts have been made to extend fault-tree notations from the design of safety-critical systems to support the analysis of incidents and accidents. This approach has the obvious benefit that engineers who are trained in the existing use of Fault Trees can apply their knowledge and tool support to investigate the causes of adverse events. Figure 3 shows how events that contribute to a mishap are represented as rectangles. Logic gates are used to describe relationships between these events. In this case, the tree only includes 'AND' gates. For example, the bottom right sub-tree shows that the 'Excess material was recovered from the flare system at two slow a rate' as a result of a 'Decision to disable the high capacity pump to slops' AND the 'Operators failure to recognize the need to manually set-up discharge pumps' AND the lack of any 'formal risk assessment of the modifications to the flare system'.

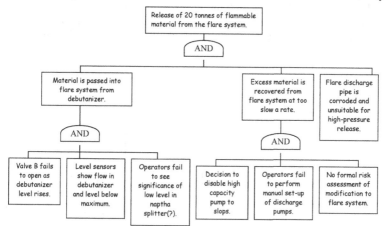

Fig. 3. Overview of an Accident Fault Tree

Figure 3 illustrates a number of important differences that distinguish the use of fault trees in accident investigation from their more conventional use to support the design of safety-critical systems. OR gates are not used. This would imply uncertainty in the reconstruction – there would be two alternative paths of events leading to the failure. Such uncertainty is, in general, avoided in incident investigation unless analysts are explicitly looking for alternative failure mechanisms that might lead to slightly different mishaps in the future. There are further differences between accident fault trees and the use of this technique for design. For example, it is unclear how to represent the events that occur in the immediate aftermath of a mishap. This is important because the response to an incident can help to determine the eventual outcome. In conventional fault-trees the analysis stops with a potential hazard. This is particularly significant in our case study. There were no plans to deal with a large fire burning for longer than twenty-four hours. This placed extreme demands on local water supplies that were needed both to fight the fire and to cool nearby vessels that might have been affected by rising temperatures.

There are several more complex techniques for plotting out the events that contribute to accidents and incidents. Figure 4 illustrates a Failure Event Tree that is similar to the output from Events and Causal Factors charting (ECF), Multilinear Events Sequencing (MES) and Sequential Timed Event Plotting (STEP) (US Department of Energy, 1992). A sequence of events leads to the mishap. These are denoted by the rectangles on the top half of the image. Outcomes are denoted by bold rectangles with dotted borders. Figure 4 also captures direct factors that influence the course of the incident but which cannot conveniently be represented by discrete events. These are denoted by rectangles with a double line border, such as 'No second back-up feedback control loop to ensure input flow reduced or shut-off when material accumulates'. Finally, Figure 4 captures a series of less direct factors that contribute to the incident. Many would argue that these factors represent the root causes of an accident or near miss. They include observations that there were 'poor maintenance procedures' and 'alarms cascade with low prioritization and requirement for explicit acknowledgement from operators'. We have extended the basic form of Failure Event Trees by shading those events that directly refer to intervention by E/E/PES related systems. This illustrates the way in which programmable devices compound operator 'error', maintenance failures and many other types of events during the course of most mishaps. They are seldom the 'only cause' of adverse events in complex, safety-critical systems.

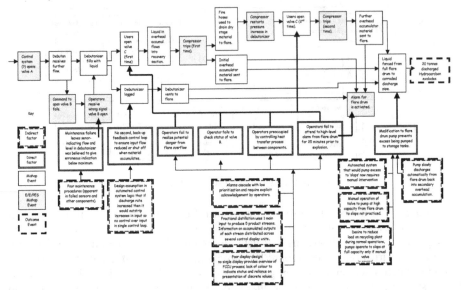

Fig. 4. A Failure Event Tree

Many event based techniques, including Failure Event Trees, exploit counter-factual arguments to distinguish root causes from less significant events. These arguments take the form 'if X did not occur then the accident/incident would have been avoided'. This form of argument is 'counterfactual' because we know that the accident or incident did take place. We are trying to imagine ways in which we might have avoided the failure. Analysts use this form of reasoning by looking at the event closest to the incident. In Figure 4, we ask would the mishap still have occurred if liquid had not been forced from the full flare drum into the corroded discharge pipe. If the answer is yes and the mishap would still have happened then this event cannot be a candidate root cause of the incident. If the answer is no and the mishap would not have occurred without this event then we can argue that it was necessary for the incident to occur so it can be considered as a root cause. The process continues for each of the mishap events shown in the diagram. In this example, it can reasonably be argued that the incident would still have occurred even if the pipe had not failed. The increasing pressure in the flare drum is likely to have led to another form of failure. The search for root causes then continues amongst the previous events. This form of reasoning might, for instance, be used to focus on the operators' decision to open valve C rather than examine the possibility that their control system was presenting misleading information about the state of valve B.

4   Flow Charts and Taxonomies: MORT and PRISMA

Management Oversight and Risk Trees (MORT) provide a flow charting approach to the identification of causal factors (W. Johnson, 1980). Figure 5 provides an abbreviated version of a MORT diagram. Investigators first consider the top levels of the tree. They must ask themselves whether the mishap was the result of an omission of some management function and whether the incident occurred from a risk that had already been recognized. LTA refers to a 'less than adequate' performance of some necessary activity. If there was an oversight problem then analysis progresses to the next level of the tree. Investigators are encouraged to consider both what happened and why it happened. The reasons why an oversight might occur include less than adequate management policy, implementation or risk assessment. Investigators work their way through the tree shown in Figure 5 until they reach a terminal node that describes the incident under consideration. These terminal nodes are not shown here. The full MORT diagram contains several hundred components.

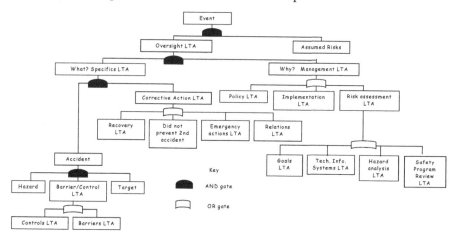

Fig. 5. Abbreviated form of a MORT diagram

The leaves of the MORT tree describe the detailed managerial causes of adverse events. For example, the analysis of the case study might begin by asking whether there was adequate oversight during development. If it was not then we can begin to analyze what happened during the incident by going down the far left branch of the tree. After having identified what occurred, analysts consider the right branches including the reasons why management might have been less than adequate. The right most sub-branch encourages analysts to determine whether this was due to incorrect goals, to problems in the technical information systems that were available to management, to inadequate hazard analysis or problems in the safety program review process. For instance, modifications to the E/E/PES controlled high-capacity flare excess pumping system could be a result of inadequate hazard analysis because the danger of operators failing to manually reconfigure the lower capacity reclamation pumps was not considered in sufficient detail.

PRISMA provides a further example of a flow chart technique that can be used to identify the causes of E/E/PES related incidents. It starts with an initial reconstruction based on an accident fault tree (van der Schaaf, 1992). The leaf or terminal nodes on the tree are then classified to identify more generic causes using a flow chart. Figure 6 illustrates a PRISMA flow chart that was developed to identify higher-level causal factors in the process industries. As can be seen, each terminal node is associated with a particular abbreviation such as TE for a technical, engineering related cause. The developers of the PRISMA approach encourage investigators to extend the classification to support their particular domain of interest. For example, medical versions include 'patient related factors' as a potential cause in healthcare incidents. In our case study, we might extend the flow chart to explicitly consider more detailed technical factors than those shown in Figure 6. For instance, we might introduce nodes to capture failures that are due to the discrepancies between the state of process components and their representation on the control system display. Similarly, the flowchart might be refined to help investigators categorise incidents in which E/E/PES embodied hazardous assumptions about process components. This would include the erroneous use of the argument that a single control loop would suffice because it would always be possible to increase sub-processes' outflow beyond their input.

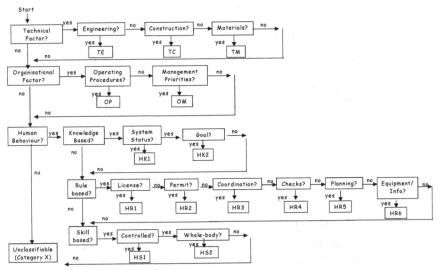

Fig. 6. PRISMA Flow Chart (van der Schaaf, 1992, 1996)

An important strength of flow-chart methods such as PRISMA is that the generic causal classification can direct investigators towards a number of general solutions. Table 2 illustrates a classification action matrix. This shows that if, for example, an incident were due to problems with management priorities then subsequent recommendations might focus more on 'bottom-up communication'. If incidents continue to recur with the same set of causal factors then safety managers might decide that the remedies advocated in Table 6 are ineffective and should be revised. In our case study, it might be advocated that modifications be made to introduce secondary control loops for the E/E/PES monitoring levels in each of the process stages. Such a detailed remedial action could only be represented in a classification/

action matrix if the associated flow chart were extended to a similar level of complexity.

Table 2. Example PRISMA Classification/Action Matrix Van Vuuren (1998)

	External Factors (O-EX)	Knowledge Transfer (OK)	Operating procedures (OP)	Manag. priorities (OM)	Culture (OC)
Inter-departmental communication	X				
Training and coaching		X			
Procedures and protocols			X		
Bottom-up communication				X	
Maximise reflexivity					X

5   Accident Models: TRIPOD and STAMP

A number of causal analysis techniques have been developed around 'accident models'; these provide templates that investigators must instantiate with the details of a particular mishap. The Tripod approach builds on the notion that most adverse events and near misses are caused by more general failure types: Hardware; Maintenance management; Design; Operating procedures; Error-enforcing conditions; Housekeeping; Incompatible goals; Communication; Organisation; Training; Defence planning. Software is a notable omission from this list and must certainly be included. Figure 7 illustrates a Tripod graphical model that can be used to show how specific instances of these general failure types combine to create an incident or accident. Elements of barrier analysis are used to show to associate a number of active failures with each of the defences that did not protect the target. These active failures can be thought of as the immediate events leading to the incident. The context in which they can occur is often created by a number of preconditions. For instance, the preconditions for the accumulation of material in the debutanizer were valve B sticking shut while the E/E/PES sensors continued to detect both a flow and a level below the maximum. These active failures and preconditions were, in turn, due to latent problems in the maintenance procedures that ensured E/E/PES functionality.

Leveson's Systems Theory Accident Modeling and Process (STAMP) exploits elements of control theory to help identify causal factors. This is motivated by the observation that mishaps occur when external disturbances are inadequately controlled. Control failures can arise from 'dysfunctional interactions' between system components. For example, if one subsystem embodies inappropriate assumptions about the performance characteristics of another process component. In this view, mishaps do not stem from events but from inappropriate or inadequate constraints on the interactions among the elements that form complex, safety-critical applications. Safety is viewed as a dynamic property of the system because the degree to which a system satisfies those constraints will continually evolve over time. Figure 8 illustrates this approach. Arrows represent communication and control flows.

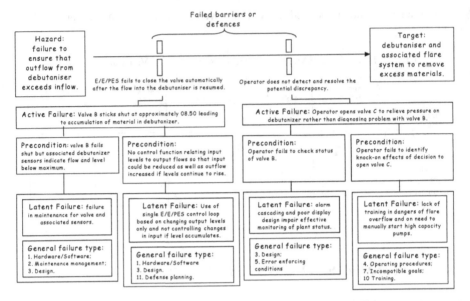

Fig. 7. Example Application of a TRIPOD General Failure Types

Rectangles are entities, including people, systems and organizations. STAMP control analysis extends from the operator, and the systems under their immediate control to also consider the relationships between project and company management, between management and regulatory agencies and between regulation and system vendors. After having conducted this extended form of control analysis, STAMP considers each of the control loops that are identified in the 'socio-technical system'. Potential mishaps stem from missing or inadequate constraints on processes or from the inadequate enforcement of a constraint that contributed to its violation. It might be argued that there were unidentified hazards in the control loops between the control system, valve B and the debutaniser. Similarly, subsequent investigation might identify flaws in the creation process that led to the operators' control system display of the state of process components.

6   Argumentation Techniques: WBA and CAE

Several techniques have been developed to help ensure that investigators form 'reasonable' causal arguments from the evidence that is embodied in timelines and other reconstructions. Ladkin and Loer's (1998) Why-Because Analysis reconstructs sequences of events leading to a mishap. It is important to stress, however, that this sequential information does not imply causation. Mathematically based proof techniques provide a method for establishing such causal arguments. Informally, we must demonstrate that we have identified sufficient causes for an 'effect' to occur. This transition from temporal sequences to more rigid causal relationships can produce insights that are not apparent in purely event-based approaches, such as timelines. The most striking feature of WBA is that it provides a set of mathematically based procedures that analysts must follow in order to replace temporal sequence with causal relationships. These procedures are necessary to ensure that we have established sufficient causes for the effect to occur. They are based on arguments of the form 'A causes B' if B is true in possible worlds that are close to those in which A is true, which can in turn be given a counterfactual semantics. Ladkin and Loer also provide a range of additional proof rules that can be used to ensure both the consistency and sufficiency of arguments about the causes of a mishap.

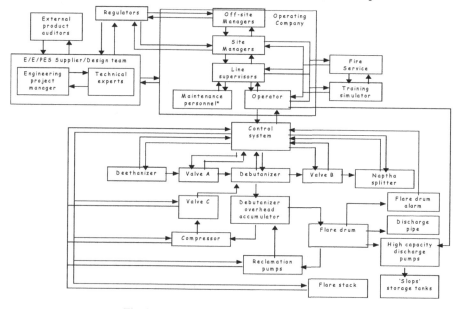

Fig. 8. Example Control Model from STAMP

Conclusion, Analysis and Evidence (CAE) diagrams help designers to map out the competing arguments for and against particular conclusions or recommendations in the aftermath of a complex incident. This approach lacks the consistency and completeness checks that are provided by the formal reasoning in the WBA technique. However, the reliance on a graphical formalism together with less strict rules on how to conduct the analysis can arguably reduce the costs and increase the flexibility of this approach. Figure 9 provides an example of a CAE diagram. Rectangles are connected to form a network that summaries arguments about an incident or accident. As the CAE name suggests, the rectangles labeled with a C are used to denote conclusions or recommendations, those labeled with an A are lines of analysis while the E rectangles denote evidence. Lines are drawn to show those lines of analysis that support particular conclusions. For example, the recommendation that the operators' safety management system be revised to explicitly store, retrieve and review incident information from other plants (C.1) is taken directly from the primary recommendation of the official report into this incident. The conclusion is supported by the observation that previous incidents were caused by a similar failure to assess the hazards of process modifications (A1.1). The evidence for this assertion is provided by the Grangemouth hydrocracker incident (E.1.1.1) and by the Flixborough explosion (E.1.1.2). It is important to note that Figure 10 also captures contradictory arguments. For instance, the dotted line in the first network denotes that the existing safety management system is not guaranteed to have acted on previous incident information even if it had been gathered more explicitly (A.1.2) given that there were other failings in the monitoring of maintenance and modification tasks (E1.2.1). As can be seen from Figure 9, CAE diagrams capture general arguments about incidents and accidents. For example, a conclusion might refer to a recommended action; it need not simply capture a causal relationship. It is also important to mention that this technique was specifically developed to enable investigators to sketch out the arguments that might appear in an incident report. This helps to ensure that any document avoids contradictory arguments.

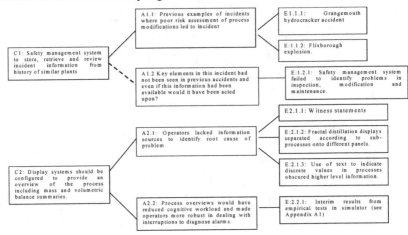

Fig. 9. Example of a CAE Diagra

7   Comparisons

Most companies and regulatory organizations lack the resources to train investigators in a range of different causal analysis techniques. It is, therefore, important to help managers focus finite resources by identifying those techniques that are best suited to analyzing the causes of computer-related incidents. Table 3, therefore, presents a subjective assessment of whether each of the previous approaches can be used to uncover problems in particular stages of the E/E/PES lifecycle or in requirements that must be satisfied across those different stages, such as staff competency. Lifecycle components and common requirements were derived from an analysis of the IEC 61508 standard. This decision was partly justified by pragmatics; this approach was recommended in consultation with the UK Health and Safety Executive. Other lifecycle models could have been used. The initial assessments in Table 4 were validated during consultations with members of the HSE, with experts on the IEC 61508 standard and by the members of several safety-critical software consultancies. We are currently extending this exercise to incorporate the opinions of safety managers across the UK process industries.

Table 3. Mapping Causal Analysis Technique to Failures in IEC61508 Lifecycle Requirements

	Elicitation and Analysis techniques		Event Based Techniques		Flowcharts and taxonomies		Accident Model		Argument. Technique
	Barrier Anal.	Time lines	Acc. Fault Trees	MORT	PRISMA	TRIPOD	STAMP	WBA	CAE
IEC 61508 Lifecycle phase									
Concept	F	U	U	F	P	F	P	U	F
Scope	F	U	U	F	P	F	P	U	F
Risk Assessment	P	P	P	F	P	P	F	U	F
Safety Requirement	F	U	U	P	P	F	F	U	F
Allocation	F	P	U	P	P	F	P	U	U
Planning of Validation, Operation & maintenance	U	P	P	F	F	U	P	P	U
Realisation	U	F	P	U	P	U	F	F	U
Installation / Commission	U	F	P	P	P	P	P	F	P
Validation	P	F	P	P	P	P	U	F	P
Operation & Maintenance	P	F	P	P	P	F	F	F	P
Modification	U	F	P	P	P	U	F	F	P
IEC 61508 Common Requirements									
Competency	P	P	P	P	P	F	P	P	P
Lifecycle	U	P	P	P	P	P	P	P	P
Verification	P	P	P	P	F	P	P	P	P
Safety management	P	P	P	P	P	P	P	P	P
Document.	P	P	P	P	P	P	P	P	P
Functional safety assessment	P	P	P	P	P	P	P	P	P

Key: (U)nsupported, (P)artially supported, (F)ully supported

MORT supports the identification of problems in the management mechanisms that protect safety-critical systems (Johnson, 1980). Table 3 therefore denotes that this causal analysis technique might support the analysis of failures in the IEC 61508 common requirements relating to competency, establishing safety management procedures etc. The subjective assessment of PRISMA in Table 3 is less a reflection of the underlying ideas than an assessment of the existing classification schemes. For example, the previous PRISMA flow chart considers engineering, construction and materials in the technical reasons for an adverse event. We could extend this to represent the requirements associated with realization phase in Table 3. The STAMP constraint checklist guides the identification of problems in risk and hazard assessment. It offers less support for identifying the meta-level validation processes that ensure that constraints between control entities are satisfied. Introducing more sophisticated hierarchical control models could do this. There is a danger that such an extension would sacrifice the tractability of the approach. WBA provides rules to establish that a causal argument is correct without predetermining what types of failures or behaviors that argument is about. This makes it difficult to classify the degree of support that this approach provides as a tool to identify the failure of IEC 61508 requirements. This flexibility is achieved at a cost in terms of the level of skill and expertise that must be acquired before the technique can be applied.

8 Conclusions

This paper has provided a brief overview of causal analysis techniques for Electrical, Electronic or Programmable, Electronic Systems (E/E/PES) related incidents. These approaches differ according to the amount of investment, in terms of training and investigators' time, that is required in order to apply them. The intention has, however, been to provide a basic road map for the approaches that might be used to analyse the causes of E/E/PES related incidents. The closing sections of this report have presented a subjective comparison of the approaches that we have introduced. We have identified whether each technique provides full, partial or no support for identifying problems in the tasks that comprise the IEC 61508 development model. Our use of the standard was partly justified by pragmatics; other models might have been used. We have partially validated the techniques by consultation with safety-critical software engineering consultancies and industry regulators. We are now engaged in a second stage involving safety managers throughout the UK process industries.

Acknowledgements. Thanks are due to Bill Black (Black Safe Consulting), Mark Bowell (UK HSE) and Peter Bishop (Adelard) for providing comments on the initial draft of this document.

References

Department of Energy, Guideline Root Cause Analysis Guidance Document, Office of Nuclear Energy, Washington DC, DOE-NE-STD-1004-92, 1992.

J.A. Doran and G.C. van der Graaf, Tripod-Beta, International Conference on Health, Safety and the Environment, Society of Petroleum Engineers, New Orleans, USA, 9–12 June, 1996.

W.G. Johnson, MORT Safety Assurance Systems, Marcel Dekker, New York, USA, 1980.

C.W. Johnson, Handbook for the Reporting of Incidents and Accidents, Springer Verlag, London, UK, 2003 in press.

P. Ladkin and K. Loer , Why-Because Analysis, RVS-Bk-98-01, Technischen Fakultät der Univ. Bielefeld, 1998.

N. Leveson, A Systems Model of Accidents.   In J.H. Wiggins and S. Thomason (eds) 20th International System Safety Conference, 476-486, International Systems Safety Society, Unionville, USA, 2002.

T.W. van der Schaaf, Near Miss Reporting in the Chemical Process Industry, PhD Thesis, Technical University of Eindhoven, Eindhoven, The Netherlands, 1992.

W. van Vuuren, Organisational Failure, PhD Thesis, Institute for Business Engineering and Technology Application, Technical University of Eindhoven, Netherlands, 2000.

Reuse in Hazard Analysis: Identification and Support

Shamus P. Smith and Michael D. Harrison

The Dependability Interdisciplinary Research Collaboration,
Department of Computer Science,
University of York, York YO10 5DD,
United Kingdom.
{Shamus.Smith, Michael.Harrison}@cs.york.ac.uk

Abstract. This paper investigates the nature of hazard analysis reuse over two case studies. Initially reuse in an existing safety argument is described. Argument structures within the hazard analysis are identified and the amount of verbatim reuse examined. A second study is concerned with how reuse changes as a result of tool support. In contrast to the first case, the defined arguments are more diverse - reuse has occurred but is less verbatim in nature. Tool supported argument adaptation has aided the customisation of the reused arguments.

1 Introduction

Descriptive dependability arguments[1] have become a standard part of the process of determining the dependability of a system. At the centre of this demonstration process is the use of techniques for systematic hazard analysis. Hazard identification, classification and mitigation techniques establish that either hazards can be avoided or that they will not affect the dependability of the system. To aid this process, descriptive arguments are commonly produced to mitigate the *perceived* severity of hazards.

In such a process there are two main requirements that need to be fulfilled, that the analysis has (1) sufficient rigour and (2) sufficient coverage. Our confidence in the rigour of a safety case, of which a hazard analysis is a component, is directly linked to the confidence we have in the hazard analysis itself. This confidence will be reinforced by objective evidence of coverage and depth of the analysis - that there are no unexpected adverse consequences within a safety-critical system. In recognition of these issues, a range of methods have been developed to support systematic hazard analysis, for example, Hazard and Operability Studies (HAZOP) [11], Failure Modes and Effect Analysis (FMEA) [6] and THEA (Technique for Human Error Assessment) [14].

Methods such as these commonly involve significant personnel effort and time commitment. Such analysis also generates large amounts of documentation, best

---

[1] We consider descriptive arguments as informal arguments in contrast to more quantitative, numeric arguments.

S. Anderson et al. (Eds.): SAFECOMP 2003, LNCS 2788, pp. 382–395, 2003.
© Springer-Verlag Berlin Heidelberg 2003

supported by appropriate tools. The tools that exist typically aim for productivity and can inadvertently promote 'ad hoc' levels of analysis reuse. Verbatim copying and pasting is common practice and there is a risk that such reuse might be used inappropriately and inconsistently [10,16]. This is particularly the case when portions of a hazard analysis are reused without examining the associated descriptive arguments. In summary current tools aim to obtain sufficient coverage but at the cost of rigour that in this situation is obviously unacceptable.

In what follows two case studies are examined. Firstly, an investigation into reuse in a hazard analysis used as part of an existing safety argument is described. Verbatim reuse[2] is used as a measure to determine the frequency of actual reuse in practice. Secondly, tool supported reuse is demonstrated and the nature of the resulting reuse examined in a hazard analysis carried out by the authors on a proposed system.

2   Reuse in Practice: DUST-EXPERT

2.1   Introduction

For understandable reasons it is rare to find complete examples of hazard analysis in the open literature. It is therefore difficult to verify reuse practices within real world cases. However informal discussions with experts in safety-critical systems seem to indicate that reuse is common within industry based hazard analysis. These views appear to be consistent with the results of the following analysis.

2.2   The Domain

DUST-EXPERT is an application that advises on the safe design and operation of manufacturing plants subject to dust explosions. Dust explosion reduction strategies are suggested by the tool which employs a user-extensible database that captures properties of dust and construction materials [5]. Because of concerns about the consequences of wrong advice a safety case argument was developed [5]. Part of this argument involves a hazard analysis utilising the HAZOP technique.

HAZOP is described as a technique of *imaginative anticipation* of hazards and operation problems [15, pg43]. It is a systematic technique that attempts to consider events in a system or process exhaustively. A full description of the method is not relevant to the argument of this paper and the reader is directed to [11]. Suffice to say that a key feature is the way that implicit descriptive arguments are defined, how these arguments can be structured and the extent of their reuse, particularly verbatim reuse. Figure 1 shows a fragment of the software HAZOP for DUST-EXPERT. Verbatim reuse can be seen at references *h 16* and *h 17*.

The HAZOP argument leg of the DUST-EXPERT safety case involves the identification and mitigation of hazards. This part of the analysis contains 334

---

[2] Verbatim reuse is reuse without modifications [9, pg7].

Hazop Ref.	Item	Guide word	Cause	Consequence/ Implication	Indication/ Protection	Question/ Recommendation	
h 14	CHANGEVALUE	No Action	Windows limitations	User types and nothing happens. *No hazard* provided user notices	Addressed by testing	r14	(a)—ensure tests are included to cover changing variables in subwindows (b)—Investigate e.g. colour change when value registered internally
h 15	CHANGEVALUE	More Action	Windows limitations	New value bound to several internal variables	Addressed by testing and possibly internal validation	r15	(a)—ensure tests are included to cover this case. (b)—Investigate redisplaying whole screen when individual value updated.
h 16	CHANGEVALUE	Less Action		As h 14			
h 17	CHANGEVALUE	As well as Action		As h 15			

Fig. 1. Fragment of software HAZOP.

individual HAZOP rows. In order to perform the analysis, descriptive arguments for the HAZOP rows were transformed into a XML[3] structure that faithfully preserves the meaning of the original analysis. An example argument corresponding to the HAZOP reference *h 15* in Figure 1 is shown in Figure 2.

For the descriptive arguments described in this paper the consequence elements are elicited from the *Consequence/Implication* column of the HAZOP and the claim elements are elicited from the *Indication/Protection* and *Question/Recommendation* columns of the HAZOP (for example see Figures 1 and 2). The structure of the arguments in this form is that the claims *support* the mitigation of the consequence. Arguments of this type are used to reduce, or mitigate, the perceived severity of hazardous consequences.

```
CONSEQUENCE_MITIGATION
REF: h15
CONSEQUENCE
----CORRUPT_SYSTEM_DATA: New value bound to several internal variables, hazard
SUPPORT
----CLAIM
------TESTING_CLAIM: Can be picked up in testing
SUPPORT
-----CLAIM
-------SYSTEM_CLAIM: Detected by internal validation
```

Fig. 2. Example descriptive argument.

---

[3] There is a vast array of texts on XML (Extensible Markup Language) including [12].

2.3   Analysis

Given this example of HAZOP in practice, it is possible to investigate verbatim reuse in the HAZOP data through propagated arguments. Arguments consist of two types: *consequence mitigation* arguments describe how an undesirable consequence can be mitigated by some claim(s) over an environment, for example a claim that appropriate test cases will show that a consequence will not happen; *no meaning* arguments arise when items in an environment cannot be considered meaningfully with HAZOP deviation keywords, for example *more action, less action* and *no action*. In this case study, there were 265 consequence mitigation arguments and 69 no meaning arguments. For this analysis only the consequence mitigation arguments have been considered relevant.

To search the XML structure several filtering algorithms were developed to identify interesting features and patterns over the arguments. Arguments in this case study are tree structures with nodes for consequences and support claims. When building the XML argument trees, the data in each node was examined to generate a general classification tag for each node. For example in Figure 2 *COR-RUPT_SYSTEM_DATA* is a general consequence tag and *TESTING_CLAIM* is a general claim tag. The tags were used in conjunction with the natural structure of the argument trees, e.g. breadth and depth, to represent a "meta" structure for comparing the arguments. The developed algorithms focused on the general tags assigned to each consequence, and the similarity of data within the arguments. In the DUST-EXPERT domain, five consequence tags were identified.

- *Input failure* consequences involved problems with the user inputting information into the system, for example "user types and nothing happens".
- *Redundancy* consequences typically involve the duplication of system features, for example "several identical help screens appear".
- *Output failures* occur when expected output from the system is not observed by the user, for example "help screen does not appear".
- *System failure* consequences occur when internal system events cause undesirable results, for example, "system spontaneously changes password or adds user".
- *Corrupt system data* consequences are when the DUST-EXPERT database or internal variables have been corrupted via some event, for example, "new values are bound to several internal variables".

These general consequence tags were used to group the consequence descriptions into common themes, thus aiding both the transformation of the arguments into a consistent XML structure and the reuse mechanism. There is no implication here that an exhaustive set of consequence tags are discovered, only that these were the tags that were encountered during the analysis.

Row one of Table 1 shows the number of arguments with each consequence tag. Two filtering results are reported here.

- The first filter identified the amount of verbatim, copy-and-paste, reuse over the arguments. The algorithm produced a list of the arguments with unique

Table 1. Reuse within consequence tags over argument data.

Consequence	Input Failure	Redundancy	Output Failure	System Failure	Corrupt System Data
1) Total arguments	65	18	105	9	68
2) Unique args (Reuse)	42 (35%)	18 (0%)	85 (19%)	8 (11%)	59 (13%)

structure, by physical depth, breadth and tag labels, and unique data. Over the 265 consequence mitigations, 212 are unique data arguments while the remaining 53 occurrences are verbatim reuse. In this example therefore 20% of the arguments have been reused in a verbatim fashion.

– A second filter was applied over the five consequence tags in order to provide a list of the unique arguments for each consequence. Row two of Table 1 shows the number of unique arguments, by data, for each consequence tag followed by the implied percentage of verbatim reuse.

The total amount of verbatim reuse in this example is 20%. This is a considerable amount of potentially unjustified or inconsistently reused analysis. Such reuse will have a direct bearing on any confidence issues in terms of the validity of the analysis. Typically confidence in the analysis is subjectively determined by the regulator's or auditor's confidence in the skill of the analyst. As hazard analysis is a lengthy process and can involve hundreds of lines it seems possible that confidence may be misplaced. Ad hoc approaches to reuse can propagate inconsistencies that can undermine the confidence in the hazard analysis itself and in any associated dependability arguments. It is therefore essential to support the process with a structured approach hereby clarifying how reuse is to be applied. The next section explores these issues and the application of tool support within the context of a second case study.

3   Supported Reuse: Mammography

3.1   Introduction

The analysis in Section 2 and informal discussions indicate that reuse within hazard analysis is common, but that ad hoc application may render an argument unsafe. Due to the systematic nature of hazard analysis techniques one solution is the integration of tool support. Tool support may give the analyst the ability to reflect efficiently on particular examples of reuse. In [16] a mechanism for systematic argument reuse was proposed. A prototype tool [17] to support this mechanism has been developed by the authors and applied to the following case study. The tool provides a platform for documenting a HAZOP style hazard analysis and enables the construction and reuse of consequence mitigation arguments. The motivation for the tool has been to enable the authors to investigate the application of reuse within a constructed case. Hence details of the tools development, evaluation and detailed use are out of the scope of this paper.

As with the study in Section 2 the reuse is applied to the arguments line-by-line with the prototype tool prompting the user with reuse candidates. A specific case is presented to illustrate and explore the approach, namely the hazard analysis of a computer-aided detection tool (CADT) for mammography.

3.2   The Domain

The UK Breast Screening Program is a national service that involves a number of screening clinics, each with two or more radiologists. Initial screening tests are by mammography, where one or more X-ray films (mammograms) are taken by a radiographer. Each mammogram is then examined for evidence of abnormality by two experienced radiologists [8]. A decision is then made on whether to recall a patient for further tests because there is suspicion of cancer [2]. Over the screening process it is desirable to achieve a low number of false positives (FPs), so that fewer women are recalled for further tests unnecessarily, and a high true positive (TP) rate, so that few cancers will be missed [8]. Unfortunately the radiologists' task is a difficult one because the small number of cancers is hidden among a large number of normal cases. Also the use of two experienced radiologists, for *double readings*, makes this process labour intensive.

A solution that is being explored is the use of computer-based image analysis techniques to enable a single radiologist to achieve performance that is equivalent or similar to that achieved by double readings [3,8]. Computer-aided detection systems can provide radiologists with a useful "second opinion" [18]. The case study in this section involves the introduction of a CADT as an aid in screening mammograms. When a CADT is used, the radiologist initially views the mammogram and records a recall decision. Then the CADT marks a digitised version of the X-ray film with "prompts" that the radiologist should examine. A final decision on a patient's recall is then taken by the human radiologist based on the original decision and the examination of the marked-up X-ray. A summary of this process can be seen in Figure 3 (from [2]).

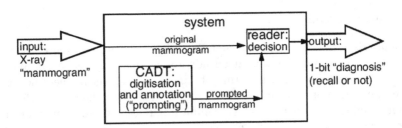

Fig. 3. Model for person using computerised aid for reading mammograms in breast screening.

A system based on the model shown in Figure 3 has been investigated to identify the undesirable consequences, for example an incorrect recall decision, that may arise. The activities and tasks that make up the diagnosis process form the basis of the analysis (see Figure 4). The argument for safe use involves a number of argument legs covering three main activities namely (i) human analysis of the X-ray, (ii) CADT analysis of the X-ray and (iii) the recall decision by the human based on a review of their original analysis and the CADT analysis.

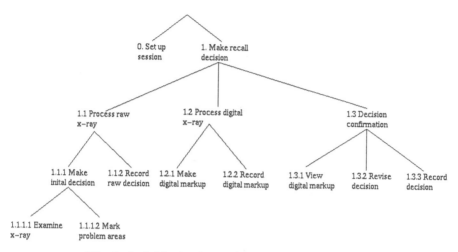

Fig. 4. Activities in the recall decision making process.

3.3   Reuse and Tool Support

When investigating the introduction of new technology the construction of a safety case is common. For this domain a safety case would consist of several elements including reliability analysis for the marking of the digital mammogram, the CADT performance and the consequences of human-error. However, for this paper one element of the safety case analysis will be considered, namely hazards and consequences in the diagnosis process as defined in the overall system model (see Figure 3).

A hazard analysis for the system was completed by a team including the authors using a line-by-line approach for reusing analysis components. The identified consequences in the current case were individually matched against consequence examples already defined in the current domain, i.e. from a library of already defined consequence arguments. This can be illustrated as follows.

Suppose there was a case in a current domain with an activity A_1 that resulted in outcome O_1 where the outcome could be mitigated by argument M_1 and verified by evidence E_1. If a new case also has a (A_1, O_1) pairing, it may be possible to mitigate the new pairing with either the (M_1, E_1) pair of mitigation claim and evidence (see Case 2 in Table 2) or an adaptation of the pairing appropriate to the current situation.

Table 2. Reuse examples.

Case 1				Case 2			
Activity	Outcome	Arg	Evidence	Activity	Outcome	Arg	Evidence
A_1	O_1	M_1	E_1	A_1	O_1	M_1?	E_1?
A_2	O_2	M_2	E_2				
A_3	O_2	M_3	E_3	A_4	O_2	M_2?M_3?	

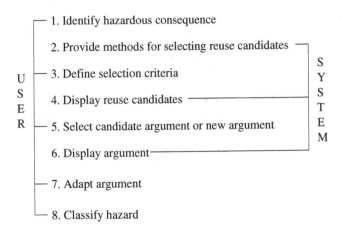

1. Identify hazardous consequence

2. Provide methods for selecting reuse candidates

3. Define selection criteria

4. Display reuse candidates

5. Select candidate argument or new argument

6. Display argument

7. Adapt argument

8. Classify hazard

USER

SYSTEM

Fig. 5. Argument reuse process for hazard mitigation and classification.

Alternatively, if multiple reuse candidates are identified, expert judgement would be required to select the most appropriate candidate. For example consider that in Table 2 activities A_2 and A_3 in Case 1 both share outcome O_2. If either of these arguments were to be reused for Case 2 activity A_4, which argument would be reused, M_2 or M_3?

The approach attempts to highlight potential candidates for reuse from the previous arguments and transfer the mitigation arguments and associated claim and evidence reasoning to the current case. However, candidate selection is only half of the approach. After selection, a reused candidate is typically adapted. Adaptation involves customising existing elements in the analysis and the addition of new argument and evidence elements. This process is context sensitive and requires expert domain knowledge.

A method to support this process has been developed [17] and includes steps for the identification of hazardous consequences, the definition of selection criteria to search for possible reusable arguments and the selection of reuse candidates or the definition of a new argument form. The new argument (either from a reuse candidate or a new argument template) must then be adapted to meet the specifics of the current analysis row. Finally a judgement on the nature of the hazard or consequence, i.e. whether it has been completely mitigated or not, is produced. An overview of the method can be seen in Figure 5 where the major tasks, both user and system, are identified.

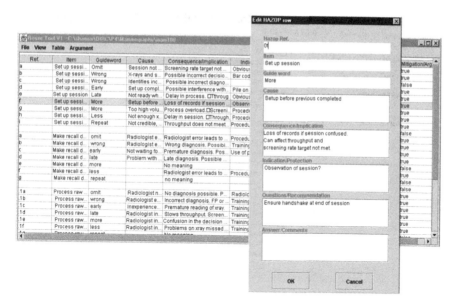

Fig. 6. Editor for collating hazard data.

A prototype tool [17] has been developed to support this process. The tool aids both the gathering of hazard documentation (see Figure 6) and the selection and adaptation of reuse candidates. The tool automates the matching process between arguments to find suitable candidates for reuse either by keywords or via consequence and/or claim tag matching. The matching process compares arguments based on a notion of structural similarity [4,13] over argument structure and data elements.

Figure 7 shows a selection of arguments presented as candidates for possible reuse after a keyword search. Multiple reuse candidates are commonly identified for each query and the final selection for reuse and the adaptation is left to the domain expert/tool user. As not all searches will provide an appropriate candidate for reuse, the tool also allows arguments to be defined as new argument forms.

Having completed one analysis the significant question is how tool support affects the natural occurrence of reuse as described in Section 2. There are a number of ways in which reuse may have been altered.

- The tool may produce a bias toward more verbatim reuse. Users may skip the argument adaptation step and leave the reused arguments in their initial form with the same argument structure and data.
- By prompting the user to select and adapt arguments from previous examples, a greater amount of artificial argument diversity may result. For instance more varied argument forms may be defined as users trivially adapt a reused argument. An example from the mammography case study can be seen in Figures 8 and 9. The Figure 8 argument has been reused in the

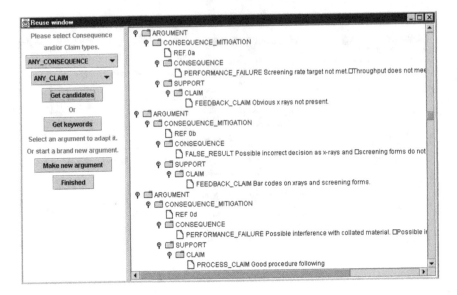

Fig. 7. Presenting argument reuse candidates.

Figure 9 argument by matching the consequence tag, in this case *OUT-PUT_FAILURE*. The consequence data in the second argument (Figure 9) has been adapted while the structure and claims of the argument itself are unchanged. Thus, although the structure remains the same, a unique, by data, argument has been defined.

– Users may try to adapt every instance of reuse to form new argument forms. This may have the advantage of customising the fit of the arguments to the current situation but may not be cost effective due in part to time considerations. Also producing large libraries of unique arguments increases the searching cost for selecting reuse candidates.

REF: 1.2.1e
OUTPUT_FAILURE: Additional markups of features. Possible FP
mitigated by
---TRAINING_CLAIM: Large training set for examples for Neural Net
mitigated by
---DIVERSITY_CLAIM: Use of diverse marking algorithms
mitigated by
---TESTING_CLAIM: Test cases meet expert option and actual outcomes
-----------**supported by**
-----------TESTING_CLAIM: Coverage by test cases

Fig. 8. Original mammography argument.

REF: 1.2.1g
OUTPUT_FAILURE: Confusion in the decision making due to multiple markups
mitigated by
---TRAINING_CLAIM: Large training set for examples for Neural Net
mitigated by
---DIVERSITY_CLAIM: Use of diverse marking algorithms
mitigated by
---TESTING_CLAIM: Test cases meet expert option and actual outcomes
------------**supported by**
------------TESTING_CLAIM: Coverage by test cases

Fig. 9. Adaptation of consequence data after reuse.

The following section presents an analysis of the application of reuse within a constructed case in comparison to the raw data case described in Section 2 and the issues noted above.

3.4   Analysis

A total of 61 consequence mitigation arguments were defined for the activities shown in Figure 4. The support tool was used to transform the arguments into a XML structure and for this domain eight consequence tags were identified: *input failure, performance failure, output failure, false result, corrupt system data, record loss, CADT failure* and *false positive*. Row one of Table 3 shows the number of each consequence tag over the arguments.

Table 3. Reuse within consequence tags.

Consequence	Input Failure	Performance Failure	Output Failure	False Result	Corrupt System Data	Record Loss	CADT Failure	False Positive
1) Total args	1	17	21	8	1	8	4	1
2) Unique args (Reuse)	1 (0%)	16 (6%)	18 (14%)	7 (13%)	1 (0%)	8 (0%)	4 (0%)	1 (0%)
3) Adapted args (Reuse)	0 (0%)	12 (71%)	14 (67%)	5 (63%)	0 (0%)	4 (50%)	2 (50%)	0 (0%)

The algorithms described in Section 2.3 were used in the mammography system analysis to identify the amount of verbatim reuse over the arguments. The first algorithm produced a list of arguments with unique structure, by physical depth, breadth and tag labels, and unique data. Over the 61 consequence mitigations there are 56 unique arguments making 5 occurrences of verbatim reuse. Thus in this case, 8% of the arguments have been reused in a verbatim fashion. The spread of these arguments can be seen in row two of Table 3.

For each new argument, the tool provides a list of candidates for reuse that have been matched either on the basis of consequence tags or keyword matching (see Figure 7). The user then adapts the new argument, on-the-fly, to one of these candidates. The reuse mechanism simplifies the adaptation process producing more unique argument forms and a smaller number of arguments with verbatim data. Although these adapted arguments are unique by data, they are still a product of the reuse mechanism. Unfortunately, they can not be identified using the algorithms applied in Section 2.3. Therefore the data and structural elements of the arguments were manually examined to determine whether any similarities between arguments were a product of the reuse process. The complete set of arguments was separated into three groups, (i) arguments produced with verbatim reuse, (ii) arguments produced via reuse and adaptation and (iii) new argument forms.

Over the 61 consequence mitigations there are 37 arguments that had been adapted via the reuse process. This results in 61% of the arguments being adapted in this case. The spread of these arguments over the consequence tags can be seen in row three of Table 3.

As with the case in Section 2 there has been a significant amount of reuse over the hazard analysis. However in this case the reuse has been coupled with argument adaptation. This process provides the benefits of allowing consistency to be maintained between reused arguments while customising the arguments to the context of the current analysis.

4   Conclusions

Descriptive arguments are a standard part of the process of determining the dependability of any system. Such arguments are typically at the core of hazard analysis techniques that contribute to the construction of safety cases. Unfortunately hazard analysis is a time consuming and labour intensive process and hence reuse of analysis components is common. Reuse of analysis also results in the reuse of the associated descriptive arguments. However, when dependability issues are concerned, inappropriate reuse can lead to misleading levels of confidence in the final analysis. This is clearly undesirable in areas such as safety-critical systems.

This paper has described the nature of reuse over two case studies. Reuse issues in a hazard analysis used in partial support of a safety case for an advisory system have been described. Argument structures within the hazard analysis were constructed and the amount of verbatim reuse examined. A reuse support tool aided the analysis of a new proposed system for providing automated support in mammography. In contrast to the first case, the defined arguments are more diverse - reuse has occurred but is less verbatim in nature. Tool support has promoted active reflection by the analyst on the arguments to be reused and has resulted in increased argument adaptation. This has the advantage of a better fit for the reused arguments to the current situation.

However, one issue of concern with tool support is that bias may be incorporated into the reuse process. For example, new forms of arguments may be ignored in preferance to arguments suggested by the tool. Currently, this issue is the responsibility of the user who applies expert judgement in the argument construction and adaptation process. We are investigating if the process supported by the tool promotes undue bias towards certain kinds of arguments and whether tool support could be configured to avoid bias.

Another issue is the cost of the reuse process. There will be costs associated with both the organisation of the raw data into argument structures and the ease of the final reuse. Also there is the overhead of identifying appropriate reuse arguments. Such issues must be balanced against any proposed benefits. However, issues of cost and benefit typically require some form of measure to allow realistic predictions to be made. We are currently investigating a notion of confidence (and confidence in the worth of an argument) as such a measure to demonstrate that argument reuse will lead to improved arguments and consequently improved confidence in the arguments.

Acknowledgements. This work was supported in part by the UK EPSRC DIRC project [7], Grant GR/N13999. The authors are grateful to Adelard [1] for providing the DUST-EXPERT safety case, and Eugenio Alberdi and Andrey Povyakalo who provided helpful feedback on a field test of the prototype tool in the mammography domain.

References

1. Adelard. Dependability and safety consultants. http://www.adelard.com [last access 6/06/03].
2. Eugenio Alberdi, Andrey Povyakalo, and Lorenzo Strigini. "Diversity modelling" of computer aided diagnosis in breast screening. DIRC workshop, November 2002, London.
   http://www.csr.city.ac.uk/people/lorenzo.strigini/ls.papers/2003_CADT/ [last access 6/06/03].
3. Caroline R. M. Boggis and Susan M. Astley. Computer-assisted mammographic imaging. *Breast Cancer Research*, 2(6):392–395, 2000.
4. Katy Börner. Structural similarity as guidance in case-based design. In Stefan Wess, Klaus-Dieter Althoff, and Michael M. Richter, editors, *Topic in Case-Based Reasoning*, volume 837 of *Lecture Notes in Artificial Intelligence*, pages 197–208. Springer-Verlag, Berlin, 1993.
5. Tim Clement, Ian Cottam, Peter Froome, and Claire Jones. The development of a commercial "shrink-wrapped application" to safety integrity level 2: The DUST-EXPERT^{TM} story. In Massimo Felici, Karama Kanoun, and Alberto Pasquini, editors, *18th International Conference on Computer Safety, Reliability, and Security (SAFECOMP 1999)*, volume 1698 of *Lecture Notes in Computer Science (LNCS)*, pages 216–225, Toulouse, France, 1999. Berlin: Springer.
6. B. S. Dhillon. Failure modes and effects analysis – bibliography. *Microelectronics and Reliability*, 32(5):719–731, 1992.
7. DIRC. Interdisciplinary research collaboration on dependability of computer-based systems. http://www.dirc.org.uk [last access 6/06/03].

8. Mark Hartswood and Rob Proctor. Computer-aided mammography: A case study of error management in a skilled decision-making task. In Chris Johnson, editor, *Proceedings of the first workshop on Human Error and Clinical Systems (HECS'99)*. University of Glasgow, April 1999. Glasgow Accident Analysis Group Technical Report G99-1.

9. Santhi Karunanithi and James M. Bieman. Measuring software reuse in object oriented systems and ada software. Technical Report CS-93-125, Department of Computer Science, Colorado State University, October 1993.

10. Tim P. Kelly. *Arguing Safety – A Systematic Approach to Managing Safety Cases*. PhD thesis, Department of Computer Science, The University of York, 1999.

11. Trevor Kletz. *Hazop and Hazan: Identifying and Assessing Process Industrial Hazards*. Institution of Chemical Engineers, third edition, 1992. ISBN 0-85295-285-6.

12. William J. Pardi. *XML in Action: Web Technology*. IT Professional. Microsoft Press, Redmond, Washington, 1999.

13. Enric Plaza. Cases as terms: A feature term approach to the structured representation of cases. In *First International Conference on Case-based Reasoning (ICCBR-95)*, pages 265–276, 1995.

14. Steven Pocock, Michael Harrison, Peter Wright, and Paul Johnson. THEA – a technique for human error assessment early in design. In Michitaka Hirose, editor, *Human-Computer Interaction: INTERACT'01*, pages 247–254. IOS Press, 2001.

15. David. J. Pumfrey. *The Principled Design of Computer System Safety Analysis*. PhD thesis, Department of Computer Science, The University of York, 2000.

16. Shamus P. Smith and Michael D. Harrison. Improving hazard classification through the reuse of descriptive arguments. In Cristina Gacek, editor, *Software Reuse: Methods, Techniques, and Tools*, volume 2319 of *Lecture Notes in Computer Science (LNCS)*, pages 255–268, Berlin Heidelberg New York, 2002. Springer.

17. Shamus P. Smith and Michael D. Harrison. Supporting reuse in hazard analysis. DIRC workshop, November 2002, London.
http://www.cs.york.ac.york/~shamus/papers/smithdirc02.pdf
[last access 6/06/03].

18. Bin Zheng, Ratan Shah, Luisa Wallance, Christiane Hakim, Marie A. Ganott, and David Gur. Computer-aided detection in mammography: An assessment of performance on current and prior images. *Academic Radiology*, 9(11):1245–1250, November 2002. AUR.

The Characteristics of Data in Data-Intensive Safety-Related Systems

Neil Storey[1] and Alastair Faulkner[2]

[1] University of Warwick, Coventry, CV4 7AL, UK
N.Storey@warwick.ac.uk
[2] CSE International Ltd., Glanford House, Bellwin Dr, Flixborough DN15 8SN, UK
agf@cse-euro.com

Abstract. An increasing number of systems now use standardised hardware and software that is customised for a particular application using data. These data-driven systems offer flexibility and speed of implementation, but are dependent on the correctness of their data to ensure safe operation.

Despite the obvious importance of the data within such systems, there is much evidence to suggest that this does not receive the same attention as other system elements. In many cases the data is developed quite separately from the remainder of the system, and may not benefit from the same level of hazard analysis, verification and validation.

This paper considers the use of data in data-driven safety-related systems and suggests that in such systems it is appropriate to consider data as a distinct and separate component with its own development lifecycle. The paper then considers the architectural design of data-driven systems and the problems of validating such systems.

1   Introduction

While all computer-based systems make use of some form of data, some applications make more extensive use of data than others. Many safety-related systems are created by assembling standardised hardware and software components and tailoring them for a particular application through the use of *configuration data*. This approach is often adopted when using pre-existing hardware and software components, such as COTS products, allowing similar components to be used in a wide range of situations [1]. Data is also used to adapt custom-designed systems to a range of similar applications – for example, to configure a control system for a particular plant. Where large quantities of data play a major role in determining the behaviour of a system we describe the arrangement as a '*data-driven system*'.

In many cases, much of the data used by a data-driven system is *static* configuration data that is used to describe the environment in which the system is to operate. For example, an Air Traffic Control (ATC) system is an example of a data-driven system that uses large amounts of static data to describe the terrain within a section of airspace, the location of airfields within it and the characteristics of the

S. Anderson et al. (Eds.): SAFECOMP 2003, LNCS 2788, pp. 396–409, 2003.

different types of aircraft. Here a standard ATC package may be tailored for use in a number of locations simply by changing the data describing its location.

While many systems make extensive use of static configuration data, most also depend heavily on *dynamic* data. For example, the ATC system mentioned above also uses large amounts of dynamic data to describe the position and movement of aircraft within its airspace.

It should be noted that the data within data-driven systems is not restricted to that used by the hardware and software elements of the system. In our ongoing example of an ATC system, data relating to aircraft movements is used not only by the automated systems but also by the air traffic controllers. Whether the data takes the form of information stored within a computer, or information written on a piece of paper (as in the case of the flight strips used in ATC) the correctness of the data will affect the safe operation of the system. Therefore, when considering data we must include not only the information stored electronically within the system, but also the information stored in other ways, such as within manuals, documents and the minds of the human operators! Many semi-automated systems rely on the flexibility of operators to deal with unusual or fault conditions. Clearly their ability to do this will be compromised if the information supplied to them is incorrect.

While we have used a single example (an ATC system) to illustrate the role of data within safety-related installations, data-driven systems are used in a wide range of situations, in applications as diverse as railway control and battlefield management. It is clear that in such applications the data plays a major role within the system, and the correctness of this data is essential to assure overall safety. Within the literature, and within the various standards and guidelines in this area, data is almost always considered as an integral part of software. These documents often give useful guidance (or requirements) for the development and testing of the *executable* aspects of software, but invariably say nothing about the development of the *data*. Unfortunately, data has very different characteristics from executable code and requires different techniques. At present, little guidance is available on appropriate development methods for data and anecdotal evidence suggests that data is often being largely ignored during system development [2].

In data-driven systems the data often represents a major part of the system and its generation and maintenance often represent a substantial part of the cost of the system. For this reason, it would seem appropriate to identify data as a distinct entity in such systems, and to consider it separately from the executable software. This would help to ensure that data is treated appropriately in such systems and would simplify the task of providing detailed guidance that is specific to data.

2   The Case for Considering Data Separately from Software

One reason that is often given for *not* considering data as a distinct entity is that it is an integral and essential part of software. All programs make use of both static data (in the form of constants) and dynamic data (as values within calculations) and the programs would not function without them. These elements are indeed integral to the software and this paper is *not* suggesting that such data should be considered separately. However, some systems make use of large quantities of data that is often developed separately from the executable software. This is particularly true when a standard package is customised for a specific application using data. While the data set for the first installation may well be developed in parallel with other aspects of the system, in subsequent installations the data is usually developed quite independently. In such cases, later versions of the data are often produced with little or no input from the original development team [3].

Another reason for considering data to be separate from the hardware and software elements of the system is that it has very different characteristics. One of these differences is that the hardware and software parts of a system generally remain the same during the life of the system (unless they are modified during maintenance or as a result of upgrading) while the data element is normally subject to considerable change. Data-driven systems invariably use status data that represents the time-varying characteristics of the application and this is clearly dynamic in nature. However, the apparently static configuration data is also subject to modification as the plant or the environment changes. Indeed, in many cases a major reason for using a data-driven approach is to allow the system to easily adapt to changes in its environment. Unfortunately, the changing nature of data causes particular problems when considering the continuing safety of a system.

Data also differs from software in other ways, such as: the way it is developed; its functional characteristics; the fault mechanisms that affect it; and the verification and validation methods that are required. The use of data may also represent an alternative and distinct implementation method.

3   Selecting Implementation Strategies

When performing the top-level or architectural design of a system, engineers will partition the required functions between system resources. Some functions may be performed using a human operator; others may use mechanical arrangements while others will use electrical or electronic circuits. In many cases a computer system will provide some of the functionality and under these circumstances it is normal to partition the requirements between the hardware and the software. However, in many cases the use of data offers a third distinct implementation and functions may be partitioned between hardware, software and data, as shown in Fig. 1.

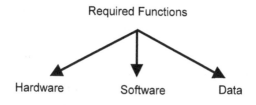

Fig. 1. Partitioning of System Functions

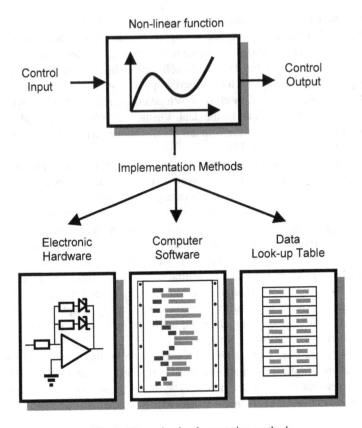

Fig. 2. Alternative implementation methods

An example of this approach is illustrated in Fig. 2, which shows part of a control system that is required to implement some form of non-linear translation of an input value. This function could be performed in a number of ways and the figure illustrates three possible approaches. The first is to use some form of non-programmable hardware, perhaps based on a non-linear curve-fitting circuit. The second and third approaches each use a computer-based technique. The former implements the non-linear function using a mathematical model that is executed within software. The latter approach stores the relationship between the input and the output within a data table. It should be noted that any computer-based approach required computer hardware in order to operate. However, where a particular function is achieved using a model implemented within a program, we would normally describe this as a *software* implementation. Similarly, when a function is achieved using a data table we can describe this as a *data* implementation even though computer hardware and computer software are required for its execution.

The reason why it is important to distinguish between software-based and data-based approaches is that these have different characteristics. When a designer assigns functions to a particular component, he or she needs to consider the characteristics of that element and how these will influence the performance and cost of the overall system. The general characteristics of hardware and software are well understood and many designers are very experienced at partitioning between these two resources. However, the characteristics of data are less well understood and there is much evidence to suggest that the implications of data use are not always considered in sufficient detail [2].

4   A Survey of Data Development Methods

In order to investigate current development methods for data-driven systems, a series of structured interviews were carried out, with representatives from a range of industries. The survey produces a great deal of useful information and demonstrated, as expected, that data is treated very differently from other system elements. Key points raised by the survey, were:

- Data is often not subjected to any systematic hazard or risk analysis.
- Data is often not assigned any specific integrity requirements.
- Data is often poorly structured, making errors more likely and harder to detect.
- Data is often not subjected to any form of verification.

Perhaps the most striking result to come from the survey was the total lack of any uniform approach to the development or maintenance of data. In many cases engineers had not considered data in any detail and had no specific strategy for dealing with the particular problems that it presents.

5   A Data Development Lifecycle

Many of the problems identified above stem from the fact that data is often ignored during the hazard and risk analyses stage of system development. If data-related hazards were identified at an early stage then the conventional methods of requirements capture and requirements traceability would ensure that these hazards were appropriately dealt with.

One way of ensuring that data is treated appropriately throughout the development process is to consider it as a separate entity having its own development lifecycle. This would not only ensure that the various stages of the process where applied to the data, but would also simplify the task of specifying requirements and giving guidance on the process of data development. International standards such as IEC 61508 [4] give detailed guidance on many aspects of the development of software and suggest a range of techniques that might be appropriate for each stage of the work. However, this standard says almost nothing about the methods or tools that would be appropriate for the production of data. The use of a separate lifecycle for the data within a system would simplify the task of giving such guidance.

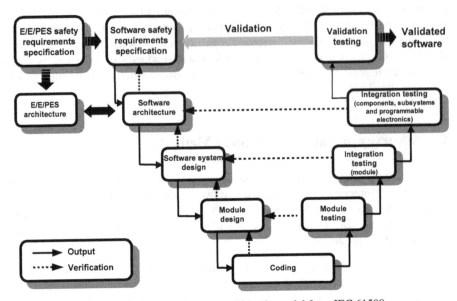

Fig. 3.   A software development lifecycle model from IEC 61508

A wide range of lifecycle models is available and engineers differ in their preferences in this area. IEC 61508 uses a generic 'V' lifecycle model to describe the development of software and this is shown in Fig. 3. The top left-hand corner of this diagram represents the system level analysis of the system and the partitioning of the system to form an appropriate architecture. Those aspects of the system that are assigned to software are then developed as described in the remainder of the diagram.

It could be argued that the model of Fig. 3 could be used directly for the production of data, or that a separate lifecycle model is unnecessary since this model already includes both executable software and data within its various elements. While this might be true, the model of Fig. 3 does nothing to emphasize the role of data within the system and does not highlight any aspects that are directly related to data. Given the identified lack of attention being given to data, it seems appropriate to take some 'affirmative action' by defining a unique lifecycle for data.

In such a model, the 'module design' associated with software development is replaced by 'data structure design' in the case of data development. This phase represents a key element in the production of data-driven systems and is required to format the data in such a way that it may be verified at a later stage. Many current systems store data in a completely unstructured way making any form of verification impossible. This phase should also consider whether any form of fault detection or fault tolerance is necessary to achieve the required data integrity requirements.

The 'coding' associated with software is replaced by the process of 'data generation or collection' required to populate the various data structures.

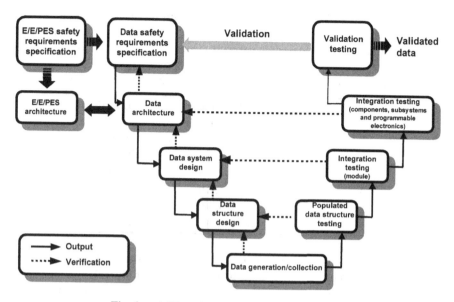

Fig. 4.   A lifecycle model for data development

A possible development lifecycle for data is shown in Fig. 4. This is based on the software model of Fig. 3 with appropriate changes to reflect the different nature of data. As with the development of all safety-related components, key elements of the model are the various verification and validation activities.

6   Verification and Validation in Data-Driven Systems

Within data-driven systems we are concerned with both the verification and validation of the data, and with the validation of the overall system.

While few standards have anything significant to say about data, one standard is specifically concerned with this topic. This is RTCA DO 200A [5], which is concerned with the processing of aeronautical data for use in air traffic control. However, this standard is concerned only with the communication and manipulation of data before it is presented to its target system. It does not look at the generation of data or the use of appropriate data structures. This standard assumes that the data supplied to the communication chain is already validated, and relies on 'end-to-end' verification of the chain to guarantee the integrity of the communication process. The actual production of aeronautical data is covered by a companion standard RTCA DO 201A [6], but this standard is primarily concerned with data requirements (in terms of such factors as accuracy, resolution and timeliness) and says very little about the selection of data structures or data validation. Thus very little published information is available on data validation and we must look elsewhere for guidance.

The difficulty of validating a system increases with the integrity requirements of that system. IEC 61508 states target failure rates for the safety functions within systems of different safety integrity levels (SILs) and these are shown in Table 1.

Table 1. Target failure rates for systems of different safety integrity levels from IEC 61508

SIL	High demand or continuous mode (Probability of a dangerous failure per hour)	Low demand mode (Probability of failure on demand)
4	$\geq 10^{-9}$ to $< 10^{-8}$	$\geq 10^{-5}$ to $< 10^{-4}$
3	$\geq 10^{-8}$ to $< 10^{-7}$	$\geq 10^{-4}$ to $< 10^{-3}$
2	$\geq 10^{-7}$ to $< 10^{-6}$	$\geq 10^{-3}$ to $< 10^{-2}$
1	$\geq 10^{-6}$ to $< 10^{-5}$	$\geq 10^{-2}$ to $< 10^{-1}$

It is generally accepted that it is not possible to demonstrate that a system meets these target failure rates by testing alone (except perhaps for low SIL systems) and so confidence must be gained from a combination of dynamic testing, static testing and evidence from the development process.

Over the years the various safety-related industries have gained considerable experience in assessing the safety of software-driven systems. A wide range of static code analysis tools are available to investigate the properties of software and standards such as IEC 61508 give detailed guidance on which development techniques are appropriate for systems of each SIL. Using these techniques, together with appropriate dynamic testing, it is possible to have reasonable confidence that: the target failure rates have been achieved; that the system has an appropriate integrity; and that the hazards associated with the safety function have been identified and dealt with.

The situation with regard to data-driven systems is very different. Logic would suggest that the target failure rates for data-driven systems should be similar to those of software-driven systems of equivalent SIL. However, few static tools are available to investigate the correctness of data, and little guidance is available on the development techniques appropriate for system systems. Given this situation it is difficult to see how a system developer can reasonably demonstrate that their data-driven system will satisfy the requirements of IEC 61508.

Another problem associated with data-driven systems relates to their dependence on changing data. When a safety-related system is modified by making changes to its *software*, it would be normal to revalidate the system to ensure that the changes have not affected its safety. This would suggest that when using a data-driven system, the system should be revalidated whenever changes are made to the *data* being used. In practice this is impractical since some elements of the data are changing continually. This would seem to suggest that the original validation of the system should prove that the system is safe for *any* combination of data. In fact this is rarely the case and the safety of the system is crucially dependent on the data used. This leaves us with the problem of how we validate this data.

We noted earlier that data-driven systems use many different forms of data. Dynamic data is often continually changing and it will never be feasible to revalidate the system each time a value alters. Safety must be achieved either by ensuring that the data is correct by validating it before applying it to the system, or by validating the data in real-time within the system. In many cases a combination of these two techniques is used. For example, an operator may be responsible for checking the data that is input to the system, and then some form of reasonability testing will be performed to check these entries. In such cases it is likely that the overall safety of the system will depend on the skill of the operator and the ability of the system to detect errors in the input data.

In many situations dynamic data is supplied to a data-driven system from another computer network. This allows the possibility that errors in this external system, or in the communication channel, will lead to incorrect or corrupted data being supplied. Again, validation must be done in real-time to ensure safety.

When using dynamic data it may be possible to validate the data in real-time to ensure that this is correct. However, a second requirement is the validation of the overall system to ensure that it is safe for any valid combination of input data. In large systems this may be extremely difficult given the vast size of the input domain.

The situation for static data is somewhat different. In many cases static data takes the form of configuration data that defines the environment in which the system will operate. Here the nature of the data dramatically changes the behaviour of the system and different data sets will define very different systems. Under these circumstances it will normally be impossible to design the system such that it is safe for any combination of configuration data, and it will be necessary to validate each distinct implementation of the system.

When a safety-related system is modified, the amount of work required to revalidate the system depends very much on its design. A well thought-out modular approach may allow a particular module to be redesigned and revalidated with some confidence that the effects of these changes on the remainder of the system will be minimal. While the complete system will need to be revalidated, it will generally not be necessary to revalidate each of the other modules. In order for this to be true the designer must achieve 'isolation' between the modules such that the operation of one module does not interfere with the operation of another.

When designing data-driven systems we should aim to partition the configuration data as a separate isolated module such that it may be changed without requiring all the other modules in the system to be revalidated. If this is done successfully this will dramatically reduce the effort needed to validate each instantiation of a data-driven application. Under these circumstances it is likely that the first instance of a new system will require a considerable amount of validation effort, but future implementations will require considerably less work. However, it is essential that full details of the design and validation of the system are available to those working on later installations to allow them to effectively validate the system [3].

It is worth noting that despite the clear advantages of a well-structured, modular approach to configuration data, the survey suggests that few companies adopt such a strategy. It also suggests that validation of data is limited or sometimes non-existent.

7   Large-Scale Systems

As data-driven systems become larger they tend to make more extensive use of data, and the identification and management of *data* integrity becomes a significant factor in the demonstration of *system* integrity. Larger systems often form part of a hierarchy of computer systems that share data. The various elements of this hierarchy will invariably use the data in different ways, and will impose different requirements on it. Where data-intensive systems are linked to distributed information systems, the same data may be used by a range of machines for very different purposes. Under these circumstances the requirements of the data (including the integrity requirements) will vary between these machines. For example, in a railway system, data that represents the current position of the trains is used by signaling control systems (where its use is safety-related) and also by passenger information systems (where it is not).

Implicit in the development or implementation of a data-driven system is a description of the data model and the data requirements. The data model, in common with other system components, should be developed to the same integrity as the overall system. Unfortunately, experience and anecdotal evidence suggests that this is not commonly the case. Development of the data model is complicated by the fact that many control systems have peer, subordinate and supervisory systems.

Fig. 5 identifies a number of layers within a system and proposes a method of categorising these layers based upon their nature and their role within the hierarchy of the system [7].

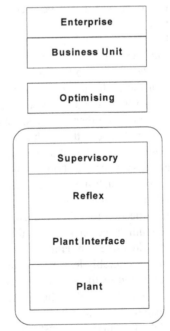

Fig. 5. A layered model for a hierarchy of systems

1. The '*plant*' layer represents single instances of elements of the plant infrastructure, the physical equipment;

2. The '*plant interface*' layer represents the interface to the plant infrastructure elements. This layer converts information from sensors (including feedback from actuators) into abstract representations such as electrical signals or data, and also produces signals to drive the various actuators;

3. The '*reflex*' layer is the lowest layer at which the measured status is interpreted and control (or protection) actions are carried out. These actions may be based upon information (which may include stored information), any demands upon the system and some set of rules. In this reflex layer the rules and information completely determine the control action. In principle all activities in the reflex layer can be automated. Where a protection system does not require the intervention of an operator these protection systems are described as reflex actions. These reflex actions are in essence rule based. Safety-critical functions often require a fast response and therefore often make use of reflex actions;

4. The '*supervisory*' layer represents a more complex level of control. This complexity may be a result of large-scale operation, integrating a number of dissimilar functions, or of interpreting complex or ambiguous data (or of some combination of these). The distinction between the reflex and supervisory layers is the judgement or knowledge that must be applied, particularly in degraded or emergency situations. Supervisory systems are characterised by the need to support the judgement of the operator doing the supervision. Predominantly the supervisory layer is downward looking, viewing the performance of the lower levels;

5. The '*optimisation*' layer represents the most sophisticated control layer. At its most developed the optimisation layer should maximise the use of resources for the delivery of the service. The optimisation layer should respect the performance and safety constraints of the underlying system. The information demands on the optimisation layer are high, requiring a full understanding of the underlying system, the planned service and contingency plans. The full understanding of the underlying system includes the performance capabilities and constraints of the various layers of the system;

6. The '*business unit*' layer represents the divisional responsibility of the delivery of service by the organisation. This layer normally plays little part in the real-time operation of the operational parts of the system, being more concerned with the medium term maintenance (including competencies) and development of the infrastructure, and the subsequent future delivery of the planned service. The business unit will become involved in the short-term operation of the system in response to a serious incident that causes substantial impact on the delivery of the service; and

7. The '*enterprise*' layer represents the corporate entity; responsible for the planning and execution of large-scale changes to the infrastructure; responding to changes in legislation; setting and maintaining standards, procedures and competency requirements.

In this work the authors propose that the supervisory layer should be the highest layer at which a safety function should be implemented. This boundary is depicted in Fig. 5 by the box surrounding the plant, plant interface, reflex and supervisory layers. The optimisation layer should take into account knowledge of current and possible future operational conditions. These operational conditions may be restrictions on the use of the plant due to planned or unplanned maintenance. Optimisation is therefore required to respect the performance and safety constraints of the system. Clearly, optimisation should only employ safe functions; that is, the optimisation of the execution of the planned service should not be capable of compromising the safety of the system.

The implementation of large-scale control systems requires a framework in which to express the role played by respective system components and provide a mechanism by which large-scale system safety may be argued. The layered model may be used to represent an organisation where several systems are used in the provision of a single function or service. This is illustrated in Fig. 6, which represents the coupling between the constituent components of an organisation.

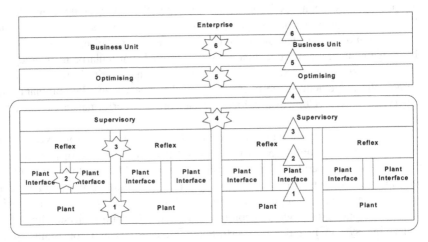

Fig. 6. An organisation employing a hierarchy of systems

The functional decomposition or partitioning of a design may be described in terms of its 'coupling'.

In this paper *coupling* is taken to be the degree of interdependence between elements of the design. A common design goal should be to minimise coupling. Low coupling, between well-designed modules, reduces the overall design complexity, creating products that lend themselves to analysis.

In a systems context, coupling is not restricted to the elements of a single design. The system will interact with its environment and quite possibly with other instantiations of the same or similar systems, or with subordinate and supervisory systems. Therefore the concept of coupling should be extended to consider vertical coupling between the system and subordinate and supervisory systems, and horizontal coupling between other instantiation of the same or similar peers systems.

Within this paper we are primarily concerned with coupling related to the exchange of data either through a shared (static) description of the infrastructure, or through dynamic data passed across the system boundary. In Fig. 6 vertical coupling is identified by the numbered triangles, and horizontal coupling is shown by the numbered stars.

A system possessing low coupling should not only possess the desirable design properties of resilience and stability, but should also have the characteristic that changes to one component should have limited effects on other components. The benefits of these properties are self evident for both good software and good systems design, and are described in many texts. However anecdotal evidence suggests that the same cannot be said of the data used by data-intensive systems. While data differs in many respects from hardware and software, it is likely that broad parallels may be drawn in terms of the desirable properties of good data design.

8   Discussion and Conclusions

Growing commercial pressures to use standardised hardware and software are leading to an increased use of data-driven systems. These are often complex in comparison with conventional computer-based systems and very often form part of a hierarchy of computers. This complexity makes data-driven systems challenging to design. There are also indications that the data at the heart of these systems is not receiving the attention it deserves. For this reason this paper suggests that data should be identified as a separate component within a data-driven system. This would highlight the importance of data to the correct operation of the system, and would simplify the process of giving guidance in this area.

An informal survey of engineers working in this area suggests that data is often largely ignored within the development process. Data is often not subjected to hazard analysis and is not assigned a specific integrity level. Perhaps for these reasons, data is often poorly structured and is not subjected to any form of verification.

Given finite economic resources, all data cannot be treated equally and other more realistic strategies are required. One such strategy would be to develop data integrity requirements that allow the targeting of development resources by a classification of risk, based upon failures due to data errors or data faults. This pragmatic approach develops the position advocated by standards such as IEC 61508 for hardware and software.

The key to successful data management lies in the use of well-designed data structures that permit and ease verification. Good design practice requires the design of components which have low coupling. Such components are usually modular, with interfaces that are resilient to changes in design. Isolation of data modules is also important since this can dramatically reduce the effort required for system validation.

References

1. McDermid, J.A.: The cost of COTS. IEE Colloquium - COTS and Safety critical systems London (1998)
2. Storey, N., Faulkner, A.: The Role of Data in Safety-Related Systems, Proc. 19th International System Safety Conference, Huntsville (2001)
3. Storey, N., Faulkner, A.: Data Management in Data-Driven Safety-Related Systems, Proc. 20th International System Safety Conference, Denver (2002)
4. IEC: 61508 Functional Safety of electrical / electronic / programmable electronic safety-related systems, International Electrotechnical Commission, Geneva (1998)
5. RTCA: DO 200A Standards for Processing Aeronautical Data, Radio Technical Commission for Aeronautics, Washington (1998)
6. RTCA: DO 201A Standards for Aeronautical Information, Radio Technical Commission for Aeronautics, Washington (2000)
7. Faulkner, A.: Safer Data: The use of data in the context of a railway control system", Proc. 10th Safety-critical Systems Symposium, pp 217–230 ISBN: 1-85233-561-0, Southampton, UK (2002)

Using IEC 61508 to Guide the Investigation of Computer-Related Incidents and Accidents

Chris Johnson

Dept. of Computing Science, University of Glasgow, Glasgow, G12 9QQ
Tel.: +44 141 330 6053, Fax: +44 141 330 4913
johnson@dcs.gla.ac.uk

Abstract. Relatively few investigation techniques have been specifically developed to identify the causal factors that contribute to mishaps involving safety-critical computer systems. The following pages, therefore, presents two complementary investigation techniques that are intended to support the analysis of Electrical, Electronic or Programmable, Electronic Systems (E/E/PES)-related mishaps. One is intended to provide a low-cost and lightweight approach that is appropriate for low consequence events. It is based around a flowchart that prompts investigators to identify potential causal factors through a series of questions about the events leading to a failure and the context in which they occurred. The second approach is more complex. It involves additional documentation and analysis. It is, therefore, more appropriate for incidents that have greater potential consequences or a higher likelihood of recurrence. This approach uses Events and Causal Factors (ECF) modelling promoted by the US Department of Energy (1992). Both approaches provide means of mapping causal factors back to the lifecycle phases and common requirements described in the IEC 61508 standard. This provides an important bridge from the products of mishap analysis to the design and operation of future systems. The UK Health and Safety Executive sponsored this work as part of an initiative to develop analysis techniques for E/E/PES related incidents. The events leading to an explosion and fires in a fractional distillation unit are used to illustrate the application of our techniques. Our techniques are likely to identify incidents that cannot easily be attributed to lifecycle phases or common requirements in IEC 61508. The link between constructive design standards and analytical investigation techniques can, therefore, yield insights into the limitations of these standards. An implicit motivation in our work is to provide the feedback mechanisms that are necessary to improve the application of standards, such as IEC 61508 and DO-178B.

1 Introduction

Very few accident analysis techniques support the investigation of adverse events involving programmable systems. There are some notable exceptions, including Leveson's (2002) STAMP and the Why-Because Analysis proposed by Ladkin and Loer (1998). Unfortunately, these techniques provide limited support for the generation of recommendations. They say little about possible intervention in the

S. Anderson et al. (Eds.): SAFECOMP 2003, LNCS 2788, pp. 410–423, 2003.

software or hardware development processes. In contrast, this paper presents two causal analysis techniques that are well integrated with development techniques for E/E/PES-related systems. In particular, we focus on methods for using the findings of incident investigations to inform the application of the IEC 61508 standard. This approach is justified by the current commercial acceptance of 61508, although both of our approaches can be integrated with other standards.

1.1   The Case Study Incident

The following pages describe an incident involving a fluidised catalytic cracking unit, part of a UK refinery complex. The plant receives crude oil, which is then separated by fractional distillation into intermediate products, including light and heavy diesel, naptha, kerosese and other heavier components. These heavier elements are eventually fed into the fluidised catalytic cracking unit. This is a continuous process to convert 'long' chain hydrocarbons into smaller hydrocarbon products used in fuels. The immediate events leading to the incident started when lightning started a fire in part of the crude distillation unit within the plant. This led to a number of knock-on effects, including power disruption, which affected elements in the fluidised catalytic cracking unit. Initially, hydrocarbon flow was lost to the deethaniser, illustrated in Figure 1. This caused the liquid in the vessel to empty into the next stage debutanizer.

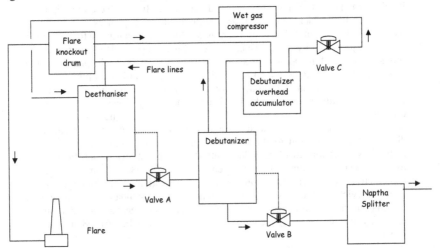

Fig. 1. High-level Overview of Components in the Fluidised Catalytic Cracking Unit

The control system was programmed to prevent total liquid loss in these stages and so valve A was closed. This starved the debutanizer of feed. The programmable system again intervened to close valve B. The liquid trapped in the debutanizer was still being heated even though both valves now isolated it. Pressure rose and the vessel vented to a flare. Shortly afterwards, the liquid level in the deethaniser was restored, the control system opened valve A and the debutanizer received further flow. Valve B should have opened at this time to allow fluid from the pressurised debutanizer into the naptha splitter. Operators in the control room received misleading signals that valve B had been successfully reopened by their control system even though this had not occurred. As a result the debutanizer filled with liquid while the naptha splitter was emptied.

The control room displays separated crucial information that was necessary to diagnose the source of the rising pressure in the debutanizer. Rather than checking the status of valve B, the operators took action to open valve C. This allowed liquid in the full overhead accumulator to flow back into a recovery section of the plant but was insufficient to prevent the debutanizer from becoming logged with fluid entering from the deethanizer. Again, the debutanizer vented to the flare line. Opening valve C created a flow of fluid into previous 'dry' stages of the process that eventually caused a compressor trip.

Large volumes of gas now had nowhere to go within the process and had to be vented to the flare stack to be burned off. At this stage, the volume of materials in the flare knockout drum was further increased by attempts to use fire hoses to drain the flooding from the dry stage directly into the flare line. However, this enabled the wet gas compressor to be restarted. This should have made matters better by increasing the flow of materials through the unit but had the unwanted effect of causing a further increase of pressure in the debutanizer. The operators responded again by opening valve C causing a further trip of the compressor. More materials were vented to an already full flare drum. Liquid was forced into a corroded discharge pipe, which broke at an elbow bend causing 20 tonnes of highly flammable hydrocarbon to be discharged. The resulting vapour cloud ignited causing damage estimated to be in excess of £50 million.

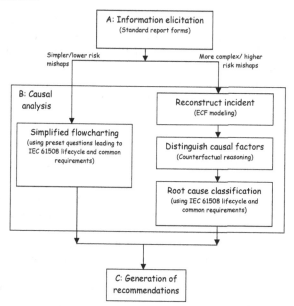

Fig. 2. Structure of the paper and an overview of the two candidate investigation schemes

This case study has been chosen to illustrate the remainder of the paper because it is typical of the way in which incidents stem from the interaction between E/E/PES-related failures, operator 'error', hardware faults and management issues. Figure 2 illustrates both the stages in our proposed analysis techniques and also the structure for the remainder of the paper. A section on information elicitation is followed by detailed discussions of our two proposed techniques. Later sections describe how recommendations can be derived from the results of a causal analysis. The closing sections of this paper identify a number of conclusions and areas for further work.

2   Elicitation

Incident reporting forms need to be specifically tailored to elicit information about E/E/PES-related failures. For example, end-users who initially observe a failure may have little reason to suspect the involvement of programmable systems. In such circumstances, reporting forms should prompt operators to consider the involvement of such systems and take appropriate actions. These can include the preservation of automated logs and data sources. Similarly, reporting forms can be revised to request details about both hardware and software version numbers. Such distinctions are not routinely made in existing forms but can be crucial when reporting adverse events back to manufacturers and regulators. The nature of the information obtained will largely be determined by their knowledge of the systems involved. For instance, someone involved in the development or integration of an E/E/PES will be able to provide additional detail and insight beyond that which might normally be expected of a system operator. Conversely, someone involved in the operation of the application can provide information about the previous operating history that might not be available to system developers. Different forms must be developed to elicit the different information available to these different groups of people. Brevity prevents a detailed discussion of form design for the elicitation of information about computer-related mishaps. This topic is discussed and sample forms are provided in Emett et al (2002). Additional requirements for the processing of system logs and other forms of automated records that must be safeguarded in the aftermath of an incident are discussed in Johnson, Le Galo and Blaize (2000).

3   Root Causes of E/E/PES Related Incidents under IEC 61508

Most computer-related incidents stem from problems in the development lifecycle. Latent causes occur in risk assessment, design, implementation, testing, maintenance etc. Other problems, such as poor project management; affect many stages of development. It is for this reason that both of the causal analysis techniques in this paper exploit the lifecycle and process requirements embedded within the IEC 61508 standard. This standard is one of several that could have been used (Johnson, 2003). The decision to adopt this standard is justified by its relatively widespread adoption for E/E/PES development within the process industries. The UK Health and Safety Executive have identified this application area as a focus for our work. Table 1 provides a high-level classification of the potential problems that affect phases of the IEC 61508 lifecycle or the common requirements that hold across several phases. These issues are enumerated in the middle column. The right column provides a reference to areas of the standard that provide additional detail about each requirement. The rows in this table will be used in the remainder of this report to provide a taxonomy or checklist of causal factors. As our analysis progresses we will attempt to identify which of these potential failures contributed to the particular causes of our case study.

Table 1. Taxonomy for Computer Related Failures Under IEC 61508 (Emmet et al 2003).

Lifecycle phase	Detailed taxonomy	IEC 61508 ref
Concept, Scope and Risk Assess.	1. Hazard identification 2. Consequence and likelihood estimation	7.2, 7.3, 7.4
Safety Req	1. specification	7.2 (2), 7.4.2.2 (2)
Allocation	2. selection of equipment 3. design and development	7.4 (2) 7.4.4/5 (2)
Planning	4. installation design 5. maintenance facilities	7.4.4.3(2), 7.4.5.2/3 (2)
Realization	6. operations facilities	7.4.5.1/3
Installation and commissioning	1. installation 2. commissioning	7.5 (2), .13.2.1/2, 7.13.2.3/4
Validation	1. function testing 2. discrepancies analysis 3. validation techniques	7.7.2.1/2/3 (2) 7.7.2.5 (2) 7.7.2.7 (2)
Operation and maintenance	1. maintenance procedures not applied 2. maintenance procedures need improvement 3. operation procedures not applied 4. operations procedures need improvement 5. permit/hand over procedures 6. test interval not sufficient 7. maintenance procedures not impact assessed 8. operation procedures not assessed 9. LTA procedures to monitor system performance 10. LTA procedures to initiate modification after systematic failures or vendor notification of faults 11. tools incorrectly selected or not applied correctly	7.7.2.1 7.6.2.2.1/2/3 (2) 7.6.2.1 7.6.2.2 7.6.2.1 7.6.2.1 7.6.2.4 (2) 7.6.2.4 (2) 7.6.2.1 (2) 7.8.2.2 (2), 7.16.2.2 7.6.2.1 (2)
Modification	1. impact analysis incorrect 2. LTA manufacturers information 3. full lifecycle not implemented 4. LTA verification and validation	7.8.2.1 (2) 7.8.2.2 (2) 7.8.2.3 (2) 7.8.2.4 (2)
IEC 61508 common requirements		
Competency	1. LTA operations competency 2. LTA maintenance competency 3. LTA modification competency	6.2.1 h 6.2.1 h 6.2.1 h
Lifecycle	1. LTA definition of operations accountabilities 2. LTA definition of maintenance accountabilities 3. LTA definition of modification accountabilities	7.1.4 7.1.4 7.1.4
Verification	1. LTA verification of operations 2. LTA verification of maintenance 3. LTA verification of modification	7.18.2, 7.9 (2) 7.18.2, 7.9 (2) 7.18.2, 7.9 (2)
Safety management	1. LTA safety culture 2. LTA safety audits 3. LTA management of suppliers	6.2.1 6.2.1 6.2.5
Documentation	1. documentation unclear or ambiguous 2. documentation incomplete 3. documentation not up to date	5.2.6 5.2.3 5.2.11
Functional safety assessment	1. LTA O & M assessment 2. modification assessment LTA 3. assessment incomplete 4. insufficient skills in assessment team	8.2 8.2 8.2.3 8.2.11/12/13/14

Key: LTA is Less Than Adequate, IEC 61508 references to Part 1 unless parentheses are used e.g. (2)

3.1   Flow Charting Scheme

Figures 3 and 4 provide an overview of our flow-charting technique[1]. Analysis begins by asking a series of high-level questions about the nature of the E/E/PES-related incident. Investigators must determine whether or not the system correctly intervened to prevent a hazard, as might be the case in a near miss incident. If the answer is yes, then the analysis progresses by moving horizontally along the arrows to identify the nature of the failure. If the system intervened to address problems created by maintenance activities then the investigator would follow the arrow in Figure 3 down to the associated table entry. By reading each cell in the column of the table indicated by the arrow, investigators can identify potential causes in the simplified stages of the IEC 61508 lifecycle. Latent failures that might have been the source of computer-related incident could also be considered by examining the items listed under all six of the common requirements in the third row from the bottom. Investigators continue along the top horizontal line repeating the classification against the cells in the table in the same manner described for maintenance related incidents. Analysis progresses by following the top-level questions down the flow chart. For some incidents, there will be failures identified by analyzing several of these different questions. A system may operate correctly to prevent a hazard although in the process there may also be further subsystem failures or operator interventions that initially fail to rectify the situation. In this case, analysts would focus on the top line in Figure 3 and the further line of analysis continued on Figure 4.

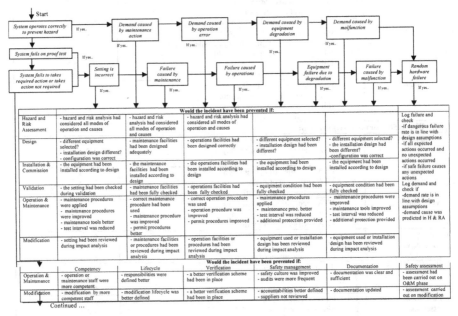

Fig. 3. High-Level Causal Flow Chart Using IEC 61508 Taxonomy [Cont. in next figure] (Emmet et al, 2003)

---

[1] Initial ideas for this technique were provided by Bill Black and are documented in Emmet et al. (2002).

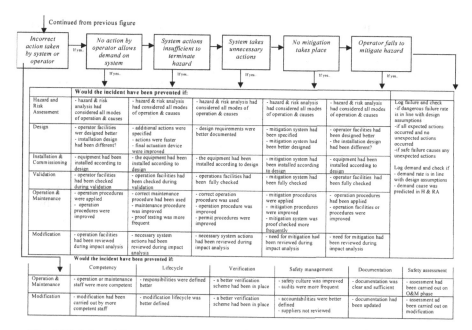

Continued from previous figure

	Incorrect action taken by system or operator	No action by operator allows demand on system	System actions insufficient to terminate hazard	System takes unnecessary actions	No mitigation takes place	Operator fails to mitigate hazard	
Would the incident have been prevented if:							
Hazard and Risk Assessment	- hazard & risk analysis had considered all modes of operation & causes	- hazard & risk analysis had considered all modes of operation & causes	- hazard & risk analysis had considered all modes of operation & causes	- hazard & risk analysis had considered all modes of operation & causes	- hazard & risk analysis had considered all modes of operation & causes	- hazard & risk analysis had considered all modes of operation & causes	Log failure and check -if dangerous failure rate is in line with design assumptions
Design	- operator facilities wer designed better - installation design had been different?	- additional actions were specified - actions were faster - final actuation device were improved	- design requirements were better documented		- mitigation system had been specified - mitigation system had been better designed	- operator facilities had been designed better - the installation design had been different?	-if all expected actions occurred and no unexpected actions occurred -if safe failure causes any unexpected actions
Installation & Commissioning	- equipment had been installed according to design	- the equipment had been installed according to design	- the equipment had been installed according to design		- mitigation system had been installed according to design	- equipment had been installed according to design	Log demand and check if - demand rate is in line with design assumptions - demand cause was predicted in H & R A
Validation	- operator facilities had been checked during validation	- operation facilities had been checked during validation	- operations facilities had been fully checked		- mitigation system had been fully checked	- operator facilities had been fully checked	
Operation & Maintenance	- operation procedures were applied - operation procedures were improved	- correct maintenance procedure had been used - maintenance procedure was improved - proof testing was more frequent	- correct operation procedure was used - operation procedure was improved - permit procedures were improved		- mitigation procedures were applied - mitigation procedures were improved - mitigation system was proof checked more frequently	- operation procedures had been applied - operation facilities or procedures were improved	
Modification	- operation facilities had been reviewed during impact analysis	- necessary system actions had been reviewed during impact analysis	- necessary system actions had been reviewed during impact analysis		- need for mitigation had been reviewed during impact analysis	- need for mitigation had been reviewed during impact analysis	

	Would the incident have been prevented if:					
	Competency	Lifecycle	Verification	Safety management	Documentation	Safety assessment
Operation & Maintenance	- operation or maintenance staff were more competent	- responsibilities were defined better	- a better verification scheme had been in place	- safety culture was improved - audits were more frequent	- documentation was clear and sufficient	- assessment had been carried out on O&M phase
Modification	- modification had been carried out by more competent staff	- modification lifecycle was better defined	- a better verification scheme had been in place	- accountabilities were better defined - suppliers not reviewed	- documentation had been updated	- assessment ad been carried out on modification

Fig. 4. High-Level Causal Flow Chart Using IEC 61508 Taxonomy (Emmet et al, 2003).

It is difficult to justify this exhaustive form of analysis for relatively minor incidents. In such cases, investigators may choose to stop once they have identified an initial selection of potential causes from the IEC 61508 flowcharts. In this case, it is important that Safety Managers consider the order of questions in Figures 3 and 4. For instance, the current format asks whether maintenance issues potentially caused an incident before it elicits information about operator failures. This ordering can bias partial analyses towards the initial causal factors. It is for this reason that we recommend a more sustained and exhaustive analysis of the flow charts. If this is not possible then safety managers should monitor the products of any causal analysis to identify the effects of any potential ordering bias.

The flowcharts illustrated in Figures 3 and 4 have been validated against a series of case study incidents. These were identified by the Health and Safety Executive as in some way 'typical' of the E/E/PES related failures that occur in the process industries. Each of the incidents that we have examined has helped to drive further refinements to the flowchart. This process is continuing as we have now begun a series of usability studies and validation exercises involving safety managers from across the process industries, including nuclear power generation and petrochemical production. These validation exercises also include participation from companies who supply and integrate E/E/PES applications. This is important because they are often called upon to identify the causes of mishaps that are reported by end-users. It is expected that further revisions will be made to the flowcharts as a result of this consultation exercise. However, Figures 3 and 4 do provide an indication of the general approach that we have adopted to support the analysis of less complex incidents and accidents.

Most incidents involve multiple causes. Our case study, amongst other things, stemmed from the operators decision to open valve C as a means of decreasing pressure in the debutanizer whilst failing to notice that the E/E/PES had failed to open valve B. Their decision was informed by erroneous information from their control system, which indicated that valve B was open and from a sensor malfunction that indicated the flow and level in the debutanizer had not reached their maximum values. These problems were compounded by poor interface design. Fractal distillation takes one primary source material and produces five product streams. Critical information about the volume of production on each of these streams was distributed across several displays. The analysis might identify several requirements or lifecycle activities that might have prevented this incident from occurring in the manner described. It is important to document the outcome of this flowchart analysis. This is done using the form illustrated in Table 2. Immediate events that are identified in incident reporting forms are related back to failures in the lifecycle stages and common requirements of IEC 61508. This allocation process is guided by the questions in Figures 3 and 4. The allocation is also supported by a justification that is intended to document any intermediate reasoning to other investigators and co-workers.

Table 2. Abridged IEC 61508 Flowchart Causal Summary for Case Study

Causal Event	IEC 61508 Classification	Route through flow chart	Rationale
Decision to open valve C.	**Validation**	Incorrect action taken by system or operator-> Operator fails to mitigate hazard -> Accident would have been avoided if operator facilities had been fully checked.	The operators intervened in the automated control system to open valve C this twice led the compressor to trip and forced excess fluid into the flare system. The poorly designed displays prevented them from diagnosing the source of the increased pressure in the debutanizer and the potential hazard from their actions in opening C. Improved display design might have occurred if they had been validated against a wider range of operational scenarios.
Failure to open valve B.	**Operation and maintenance**	System fails to take required action -> Failure caused by maintenance -> Accident would have been avoided if maintenance procedure were improved.	The computer control system was designed to automatically open valve B when flow was restored to the debutanizer. This command failed. Subsequent investigation found of 39 instrument loops 24 needed attention ranging from minor mechanical damage to major maintenance faults.

3.2   Event & Causal Factor Analysis

As can be seen, the flowchart analysis in Table 2 is relatively superficial. It provides a causal analysis that might be performed in the initial stages of an investigation. In order to look more closely at detailed design issues, additional questions would be needed in the Flowcharts of Figures 3 and 4. The resulting diagrams would sacrifice many of the benefits associated with this simple causal analysis technique. The following section, therefore, presents a more sophisticated approach.

First Stage: Information Elicitation and ECF Modelling. Figure 5 shows a simplified form of Events and Causal Factors (ECF) diagram. This modeling technique was developed by Johnson and promoted by the US Department of Energy (1992) to provide an overview of events leading to an incident. Rectangles represent events. Ovals represent the conditions that make those events more likely. The diamond shape represents the outcome of the E/E/PES related mishap.

This figure is in three parts. The top line represents the chain of events that created the immediate preconditions for the accident. The lightning strike leads to a loss of flow into the debutanizer and an E/E/PES intervened close valve B. The middle line describes a series of intermediate events in which, in particular, the E/E/PES fails to open valve B. The flow of materials into the deethanizer and debutanizer creates a build-up, which in turn, leads to materials being passed to the flare. The middle diagram includes continuation symbols marked a, b and c. These feed into the bottom row of the ECF diagram. This illustrates the events and conditions that ultimately lead to the flare drum being filled beyond its capacity so that materials are forced into a corroded discharge pipe and out into the environment. The development of a detailed ECF chart continues until all of the parties involved in an investigation agree that it provides a reasonable representation of the events that contributed to an adverse occurrence or near miss. This decision is influenced by the scope of the investigation and by pragmatics. For instance, we could extend Figure 5 to consider the circumstances that led to 'poor maintenance procedures (apparent in failed sensors and other components)'. This could only be done if incident investigators gain access to the appropriate site documentation or witness statements. It is also important to emphasise that the identification of preconditions is a skilled activity that requires both training and practice, although techniques such as Barrier and Change Analysis can be used. An important benefit of this form of analysis is that the identification of recurring patterns of preconditions can be used pro-actively to identify the potential for future mishaps. Brevity prevents a full exposition of this approach, the interested reader is directed to Johnson (2003).

Second Stage: Causal Reasoning. A further stage of analysis is required in order to distinguish potential causal factors from more contextual information. Starting at the outcome event, investigators must ask whether the incident would have occurred if that event had not taken place. If the incident would still have happened then the event cannot be considered as a casual factor. For example, the incident would arguably not have happened if material had not been forced from the full flare drum into the corroded discharge pipe. This is, therefore, a cause of the incident. Similarly, we can argue that the incident would not have happened if further overhead accumulator material had not been sent to the flare. Conversely, the high-level alarm for the flare had no impact on the course of the incident and so cannot be considered a causal factor. The incident would still have occurred even if the alarm had not sounded.

The causal factors in the ECF diagram are then used to identify potential problems in the development stages and common requirements of IEC 61508, illustrated in Table 1. One means of doing this is to identify the conditions that contributed to each causal event in the ECF chart. These conditions typically capture latent issues, including development and operation decisions that create the context for E/E/PES-related mishaps. For instance, the operator's second intervention to open valve C as a means of reducing pressure in the debutanizer was made more likely by the maintenance failure that prevented them from accurately observing the state of the debutanizer. Poor display design also contributed to their decision, as did their preoccupation with heat transfer within the plant. Heat generated as a by-product of a process was not directly dissipated but was instead used to support other processes in the plant. If either too much or too little heat was generated within the plant then these delicate dependencies that could be disturbed.

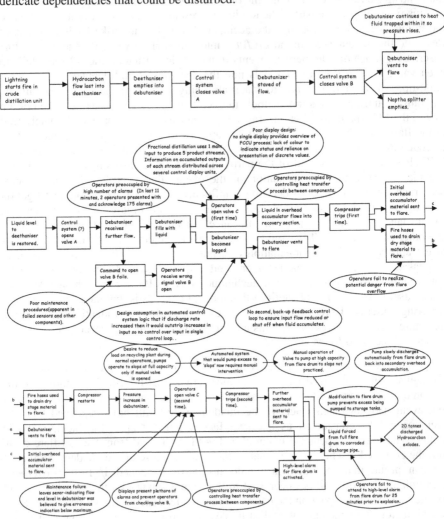

Fig. 5. ECF Diagrams Including Developer/System Integrator Information

The causal analysis of our case study illustrates an important point about adverse events involving programmable systems. As can be seen, it is difficult to extract the contribution of computer-related systems from wider failures in the maintenance, operation and safety-management systems. Operators did not intervene to address the automated flare drum alarm because they were busy trying to diagnose the causes of the pressure increase in the debutanizer. They failed to diagnose the problems with the debutanizer because they assumed that the automation had closed valve B. Their task was further exacerbated by their systems' presentation of erroneous sensor readings from the debutanizer. As mentioned, we have exploited the lifecycle and common requirements of IEC 61508 to provide a taxonomy for the causal factors involved in computer-related incidents. This decision was motivated partially by the commercial uptake of this standard and also by the organizational objectives of the UK Health and Safety Executive who sponsored this work. If another taxonomy were to be used for this purpose then it too would have to support the analysis of incidents in which the failure of programmable devices formed a component of more complex failures in operation, management and the equipment under control.

4   Generating Recommendations

The generation of recommendations uses the outcome of previous stages to identify potential recommendations. These recommendations are domain and incident dependent. It is important, however, that investigators document the actions that are intended to avoid any recurrence of an incident involving programmable systems. Each recommendation should be associated with a priority assessment, with an individual or organization responsible for implementing it and with a potential timescale for intervention. Typically, a safety manager will then respond with a written report stating whether each recommendation has been accepted or rejected (Johnson, 2003). Investigators must consider whether similar interventions have been advocated in the past. Electronic information systems can be used to assist in this task. The key point, however, is that ineffective recommendations should not continue to be issued in the face of recurrent incidents. Similarly, it is important to identify situations in which recommendations are consistently rejected or inadequately implemented. Any accepted recommendations must be disseminated to those who are responsible for acting upon them. Safety managers must also assume responsibility for checking that any necessary changes are implemented according to the agreed timescale. System documentation must be updated to reflect any subsequent modifications. Table 3 provides an example of a form that can be used to record recommendations from incidents involving programmable systems.

A key concern behind the design of Table 3 is that investigators should be accountable for their recommendations. By this we mean that co-workers, safety managers and regulators should be able to trace back particular recommendations through the previous stages of any causal analysis so that it is possible to identify the reasons why particular interventions are proposed in the aftermath of an adverse event. For example, recommendation 4 proposes a redesign of the control system displays. This is based on the observation that operations and maintenance assessments had been less than adequate prior to the incident. In particular, these assessments had failed to predict the impact that multiple alarms had upon their ability to correctly diagnose the status of valve B. If they had not been forced their observation of multiple low priority warnings then they might have been better able to recognize that their control system had failed to complete their command to open the flow from the debutanizer.

Table 3. Recommendation Summary Form (LTA – Less Than Adequate)

Causal Event	Associated Conditions	IEC 61508 Lifecycle Class.	IEC 61508 Common Requirements Violation	Recommendation	Priority	Responsible authority	Date
Liquid forced from full flare drum to corroded discharge pipe.	Modification to flare drum pump prevents excess being pumped to storage tanks.	**Modification:** 1 impact analysis incorrect	**Functional Safety Assessment:** 2. Modification assessment LTA	1. Flare system must be redesigned to provide effective removal of slops from knock-out drum at adequate rate to prevent overfilling.	High	Production engineering team manager	Accepted 15/2/2003
			Verification: 3. LTA verification of modification	2. There should be a formal controlled procedure for hazard identification following all modification proposals.	High	Plant safety manager	Accepted 15/2/2003
		Modification: 4 LTA verification and validation		3. Control and protection systems should be independent, particularly where they involve programmable systems.	High	Plant safety manager	Accepted 15/2/2003
	Operators fail to attend to high-level alarm for flare drum during 25 minutes prior to explosion.	**Operation and Maintenance:** 9. LTA procedures to monitor system performance.	**Functional Safety Assessment:** 1. LTA Operations and Maintenance assessment.	4. Display systems to be redesigned to provide clearer indication of source of flow problems. Greater prioritisation of alarms will assist in this (see rec 7).	Medium	Production engineering team manager & Plant safety manager	
Operators open valve C	Maintenance failure leaves sensor indicating that the flow and level in the debutanizer was believed to give erroneous indication below maximum.	**Operations and maintenance:** 2. maintenance procedures need improvement.	**Safety management:** 2. LTA Safety Audits	5. Safety management system to record and review incident information from other similar plants, causes of mishap already well documented.	Medium	Plant safety manager	
				6. Safety management system to include monitoring of its own performance – for instance over assessment of modifications.	High	Plant safety manager	Accepted 15/2/2003
	Display presents plethora of alarms that prevent operators from checking the status of valve B.	**Allocation.** 4. installation design.		7. Training of staff will focus on high-stress situations as well as production critical issues. (see also recommendation 4)	Medium	Plant safety manager	
	Operators preoccupied controlling heat transfers process between components.	**Overall safety requirements:** 4. installation design.					

5   Conclusions

A range of techniques has been developed to support the analysis and investigation of adverse events and near miss incidents. Very few of these techniques have been specifically designed to support the investigation of incidents involving programmable systems. This report, therefore, introduces two investigation methods for this class of adverse events. The first builds on a relatively simple flowchart. Investigators can identify and categorize the causes of a mishap by answering a series of questions. The responses that they provide guide the causal analysis to underlying problems in the design, development or operation of E/E/PES hardware and software.

The second, more complex, approach introduces several additional stages of analysis. It is appropriate for more complex incidents where the questions that guide a simpler form of analysis may not be directly applicable. These additional stages also provide intermediate documentation that is necessary when investigators must justify their conclusions to other investigators, safety managers and courts of law. In particular, this second approach relies upon a timeline reconstruction of an adverse event using a technique known as Events and Causal Factors (ECF) charting. This produces a graphical sketch of the events leading to an incident. This can then be used to distinguish contextual information from causal factors. In our proposed method, these causal factors are then analyzed to identify potential failures in the lifecycle of programmable systems using a checklist approach.

Both of our investigation techniques have been tailored to provide information that guides the future development and operation of safety-critical systems. In particular, the flowchart and checklist help investigators to map from the causes of hardware and software related incidents to the clauses of the IEC 61508 standard. IEC 61508 provides guidance on the activities that should be conducted during the concept development, hazard and risk assessment, verification, validation, operation and maintenance, and modification of safety critical computer systems. In addition there are a range of requirements that are common to all lifecycle phases. These include the need to ensure the competency of those involved in operation and maintenance. They also include requirements relating to the 'safety culture' of the organizations involved in the development of programmable systems. Our use of this standard is justified because it provides a means of feeding the insights derived from any incident investigation back into the future maintenance and development of hardware and software within safety-critical applications.

Much remains to be done. We have yet to consider the role that incident databases and the outcomes of previous investigations might play in guiding future investigations or the generation of recommendations. Our techniques are likely to identify incidents that cannot easily be attributed to lifecycle phases or common requirements in IEC 61508. The link between constructive design standards and analytical investigation techniques can, therefore, yield insights into the limitations of these standards. An implicit motivation in our work is to provide the feedback mechanisms that are necessary to improve the application of standards, such as IEC 61508 and DO-178B.

Acknowledgements. Bill Black (Black Safe), Mark Bowell (HSE), Peter Bishop (Adelard) and Michael Holloway (NASA) for provided comments on the initial draft of this document.

References

L. Emmet, P. Bishop, B. Black and V. Hamilton, Outline Scheme for E/E/PES Related Incidents, Adelard Technical Report , 2002.

Department of Energy, Root Cause Analysis, Washington DC, USA, Revised as SCIE-DOE-01-TRAC-14-95 on http://tis.eh.doe.gov/analysis/trac/14/trac14.html

International Electrotechnical Commission, IEC 61508 Functional Safety of Programmable Electronic Safety-Related Systems. Available via http://www.iec.ch/functionalsafety. 2003.

C.W. Johnson, A Handbook for the Reporting of Incidents and Accidents, Springer Verlag, London, UK, 2003 in press.

C.W. Johnson, G. Le Galo and M. Blaize, Guidelines for the Development of Occurrence Reporting Systems in European Air Traffic Control, European Organisation for Air Traffic Control (EUROCONTROL), Brussels, Belgium, 2000.

P. Ladkin and K. Loer, Why-Because Analysis: Formal Reasoning About Incidents, Bielefeld, Germany, Document RVS-Bk-98-01, Technischen Fakultat der Universitat Bielefeld, Germany, 1998.

N. Leveson, A Systems Model of Accidents. In J.H. Wiggins and S. Thomason (eds) Proceedings of the 20th International System Safety Conference, 476–486, International Systems Safety Society, Unionville, USA, 2002.

Author Index

Angelis, G. 331
Armbruster, M. 249

Bachmayer, M. 289
Balducelli, C. 342
Bhattacharjee, A.K. 22
Bishop, P. 63
Bistarelli, S. 130
Bloomfield, R. 63
Bologna, S. 342
Bozzano, M. 49
Büchli, S. 249

Ciancamerla, E. 35
Clarke, K. 103
Clement, T. 63

Dewsbury, G. 103
Dhodapkar, S.D. 22
Dipoppa, G. 342
Driscoll, K. 235

Faulkner, A. 396
Flanz, J. 221
Foley, S.N. 130

Gilmore, S. 179
Gorman, J. 207
Gritzalis, S. 331
Grünbauer, J. 116
Guerra, S. 63
Górski, J. 193

Hall, B. 235
Harrison, M.D. 382
Hayes, J.P. 275
Heitmeyer, C. 159
Helminen, A. 92
Hollmann, H. 116

Iqbal, A. 22

Jackson, D. 221
Jarzębowicz, A. 193
Jin, H. 144
Johnson, C. 368, 410

Jones, C. 63
Jürjens, J. 116

Kaâniche, M. 165
Kandasamy, N. 275
Kanoun, K. 165
Kelly, T. 77
Kiencke, U. 249
Kloul, L. 179
Knight, J.C. 317
Kurd, Z. 77
Kvålen, H. 207

Lambrinoudakis, C. 331
Leszczyna, R. 193
Leyman, D. 221

Manzano, M.J. 263
Martín, P. 263
Martinello, M. 165
Mason, P.A.J. 303
Masson, G.M. 144
Mataix, C. 263
Miler, J. 193
Minichino, M. 35
Murray, B.T. 275

Olszewski, M. 193

Pasquini, A. 354
Pozo, J. 263
Pozzi, S. 354
Pulkkinen, U. 92

Rae, A. 221
Ramanan, P. 221
Ramesh, S. 22
Riddle, S. 303
Rodríguez, F.J. 263
Rooks, O. 249
Rouncefield, M. 103

Saeed, A. 303
Serro, S. 35
Sivencrona, H. 235
Smith, S.P. 382
Sommerville, I. 103

Spiegelberg, G.   249
Storey, N.   396
Strunk, E.A.   317
Sullivan, G.F.   144
Sulzmann, A.   249

Thomas, M.   1
Tondok, H.   289
Travis, S.R.   317
Tronci, E.   35

Vicoli, G.   342
Villafiorita, A.   49

Walderhaug, S.   207
Wasson, K.S.   317
Weber, W.   289
Wimmel, G.   116
Wright, D.   8

Zumsteg, P.   235

Printed in the United States
By Bookmasters